# Borland C++ 3.1
Programming For Windows™

OTHER TITLES IN THE BORLAND BANTAM SERIES

*Borland C++ Programming for Windows*
by Paul Yao

*ObjectVision 2.0 Developer's Guide*
by Allen G. Taylor

*Paradox 3.5 Handbook, 3rd Edition*
by Douglas Cobb, Jane Richter, Jeff Yocom, and Brian Smith

*Quattro Pro 4.0 Handbook, 4th Edition*
by Mary Campbell

*Turbo Pascal for Windows 3.0 Programming*
by Tom Swan

*dBASE IV 1.5 Handbook*
by Mary Campbell

*Borland C++ 3.1 Object-Oriented Programming*
by Marco Cantu and Steve Tendon

BORLAND BANTAM

# Borland C++ 3.1 Programming For Windows™

VERSION 3.1

Paul L. Yao

BANTAM BOOKS
NEW YORK • TORONTO • LONDON • SYDNEY • AUCKLAND

Borland C++ Programming for Windows
A Bantam Book/January 1992

All rights reserved.
Copyright © 1992 by Peter Norton and Paul Yao
Cover Design © 1992 by Bantam Books

Composed by Electric Ink, Ltd.
Internal design by Nancy Sugihara

Borland® is a registered trademark of Borland International.
Windows™ is a trademark of Microsoft Corporation.

Throughout this book, tradenames and trademarks of some companies and products have been used, and no such uses are intended to convey endorsement of or other affiliations with the book.

No part of this book may be reproduced or transmitted in any form or by any means, electronic or mechanical, including photocopying, recording, or by any information storage and retrieval system, without permission in writing from the publisher.
For information address: Bantam Books.

ISBN 0-553-37209-2

Bantam Books are published by Bantam Books, Inc., a division of Bantam Doubleday Dell Publishing Group, Inc. Its trademark, consisting of the words "Bantam Books" and the portrayal of a rooster, is Registered in U.S. Patent and Trademark Office and in other countries. Marca Registrada, Bantam Books, 666 Fifth Avenue, New York, New York 10103.

PRINTED IN THE UNITED STATES OF AMERICA

0 9 8 7 6 5 4 3

# Dedication

To my mother, Mary Grace Yao.

# Foreword

One of the chief challenges in developing Windows applications is the need to master the myriad calls of the Windows Applications Program Interface (API). While we at Borland feel that our ObjectWindows library greatly simplifies the task of successfully dealing with the API, one still needs to know how Windows is put together, and how its various facets are called, in order to create well-behaved applications that fully adhere to Windows standards.

We're extremely pleased to welcome well-known Windows expert, Paul Yao, to this task, as an official Bantam/Borland author. Paul brings to this project a depth of understanding of Windows issues that few can approach, let alone rival.

This is a programmer's book, as a quick glance at the extensive code listings will demonstrate. But it's a lot more than the sum of the listings, as the concepts and mindset of Windows are also covered in detail. Borland C++ gives you the tools to master Windows; Paul gives you the skills and insights to use those tools effectively. By focusing on OWL, he shows you how quickly and efficiently you can create your own custom applications using the full range of Windows features—text, graphics, menus, dialog boxes, scroll bars, and more.

We think you'll find this book a very useful adjunct to your Windows programming efforts.

Philippe Kahn,
CEO, Borland International

# Preface

Several months after the introduction of the C version of *Peter Norton's Windows 3.0 Power Programming Techniques*, Borland International introduced the Borland C++ Compiler for Windows. While most Windows developers today use C, I predict that C++ will soon dominate the development landscape. For C developers, C++ provides a smooth migration path for adding object programming to existing systems written in C. This book was created to help developers take advantage of the Borland C++ compiler and the Borland ObjectWindows libraries (OWL), because both provide a good framework for building applications.

The fundamentals of Windows programming remain the same no matter what language you use. For this reason, much of this book is nearly identical to the C version. Significant exceptions to this statement include the following:

- Chapters 2, 3, 4, and 5 have been completely rewritten for the C++ edition. This reflects the fact that a "minimum" Windows program written in C differs quite substantially from a similar program written using OWL in C++. Among other topics, these chapters describe the fundamental organization of two basic OWL objects: the application object and the window object.
- All the sample programs are written in C++. They provide a good framework for understanding how C++ and Windows programming can be blended together.

This book was written to help experienced C++ programmers learn to program in Windows. There are a couple of resources that are invaluable when learning about a new environment. One is sample code that shows the basic techniques necessary to take advantage of the features of the environment. Another is the help of a guru who knows the ins and outs of the environment. This book provides you with both.

Here you'll find dozens of programs to demonstrate the use of different features in Windows. There are complete listings for these programs to give you the total picture of the pieces that you must work with. Someone once said that only one Windows program has ever been written and every other Windows program has been cut and pasted from the very first one. Feel free to use any of the code in your Windows development projects. (These programs are available in machine-readable form. For more details, see the inside back cover.)

To get started in programming for Windows, you're going to need the following:

- One of two Borland programming products, either: (1) Turbo C++ for Windows, version 3.1 or (2) Borland C++ and Application Frameworks, version 3.1.
- Windows version 3.0 or later

Although it's not a requirement, if you plan to run the Turbo Debugger, you'll also want the following hardware, which will give the Turbo Debugger its own output device:

- On a computer equipped with an AT-style bus, an MDA card and a monochrome monitor. A Hercules-compatible graphics card can often be used in the place of an MDA card.
- On a computer equipped with an MCA bus, you'll want to have an 8514/a adapter and a compatible display, in addition to a VGA-style monitor.

Intertwined with the discussion of Windows programming, is a description of the architecture and inner-workings of Windows. We worked closely with the Windows development teams—both past and present—to learn about the inner workings of Windows. For this version of the book, we spent time working with the developers of OWL to ensure that we fully understood the design of the OWL class library.

This book is divided into six sections. Part I provides a brief history of Windows and describes the three challenges that new programmers face: message-driven programming, creating and controlling graphical output, and learning how to use the various user-interface objects.

Part II dissects a minimum Windows program, and explores several fundamental topics in Windows programming. The purpose of this section is to help you understand the basic structure that all Windows programs share. As you'll see, an OWL Windows program is made up of at least two pieces: an application object and a window object.

Part III introduces you to Windows' Graphics Device Interface (GDI). Your programs will use GDI to create device-independent graphic output on displays, printers, and plotters. Chapter 6 describes basic concepts in graphic programming, such as drawing coordinates, GDI's device context, and clipping. From there, subsequent chapters cover the output of pixels, lines, filled areas, and text.

Part IV covers three key user-interface objects: menus, windows, and dialog boxes. This section describes the inner-workings of each type of object and all of the basics in making them operational.

Part V is dedicated to getting user input. Windows is a message driven operating environment, so it is not surprising to find that keyboard and mouse input arrive in the form of messages. Part V describes the flow of data from the physical hardware, through the system buffers and into a Windows program.

Part VI covers operating system considerations. Included are two basic areas: memory and dynamic linking. One of the big news items of Windows 3 is the improvements that have been made in memory use. To help you understand exactly what this means, the inner workings of each of Windows' operating modes are described.

# Acknowledgments

Researching and organizing the amount of information required for a book like this is impossible without the help many people. I am fortunate to be associated with a group of individuals who share an incredible commitment to the success of Windows.

I'd like to start off by thanking the development teams of Windows 1.x, 2.x, and 3. In particular, we want to thank the developers and marketers who gave their time and energies to help us understand the subtle nuances of the way Windows works: Peter Belew, John Butler, Mark Cligget, Clark Cyr, Rick Dill, Marlin Eller, Ron Gery, Bob Gunderson, Paul Klinger, Scott MacGregor, Ed Mills, Walt Moore, Gabe Newell, Chris Peters, John Pollock, Rao Remala, Lin Shaw, Charles Simonyi, Tandy Trower, Manny Vellon, David Weise, and Steve Wood.

Elsewhere at Microsoft, thanks to those who helped and supported us in the creation of this book. First, a special thank you to David Durant, who is and always will be our first Windows programming instructor. Within the Application's Development Division, thanks to Jim Cash for helping us solve the puzzle of making Windows programming comprehensible, and to Paul Klemond, a crackerjack Windows application developer who helped us solve more than a few Windows programming riddles.

At Borland International, thanks go to Eugene Wang, Nan Borreson, and Charles Dickerson for their support during this project. Thanks to Glenn Cochran for a thorough technical review of the book, and to Peter Eden and Eric Swenson for helping us understand some of the design details behind the Borland's C++ compiler and the Borland OWL Libraries.

At International Systems Design, special words of thanks to Rebecca Brocard and Jim Treacy for lending their talents to this project.

At Bantam Electronic Publishing, we'd like to thank our publisher and the vice-president of publishing, Kenzi Sugihara. Thanks also to Stephen Guty, our editor, for his long hours and painstaking efforts. And thanks are also due to Jeff Rian and Tom Szalkiewicz, who handled the production of the book itself. Kudos to Katie DuBois and the rest of the production team at Electric Ink, Ltd.

And finally, a special word of thanks to Nancy and Helen of Pogacha Restaurant, the official caterer of this book.

# Contents

*Foreword* vii
*Preface* ix
*Acknowledgments* xi

PART ONE

## An Introduction to Windows   1

1   An Introduction to Windows   3

   A History of Windows   4
   Windows NT   9
   The Windows Programming Challenges   10
      *Challenge 1: Message-Driven Programming*   10   *Challenge 2: Graphical Output*   15   *Challenge 3: User-Interface Objects*   17

PART TWO

## A Minimum Windows Program   27

2   A Minimum Windows Program   29

   The Mechanics of Compiling and Linking MIN.EXE   35

The MAKE Utility   35
Compiler Switches   37
The Resource File   39
The Linker   40
The Linker and the Module Definition File   42

## 3   Windows and OWL Programming Conventions   45

Hungarian Naming   46
OWL Naming Conventions   49
Handles   50
The OWL Include Files   50
The Windows Include File   52
   *Symbolic Constants*   52   *Data Type Definitions*   52
   *Function Prototypes*   54
An Outdated Practice: Casting   55
Messages   57

## 4   The Application Object   59

WinMain Procedure Declaration   59
The TModule Class   62
The TApplication Class   64
MIN's TMinApplication Class   69
Messages: Input Mechanism and Multitasking Time-Slice   70
The Standard Message Loop   72
The OWL Message Loop   75

## 5   OWL's Window Object Classes   77

The TWindowsObject Class   78
The TWindow Class   82
MIN's TMinWindow Class   84
Window Creation in MS-Windows   84
Window Creation   87
Window Creation and OWL   91
The Window Procedure Declaration   92
OWL Message Response Functions   93
Program Termination   96

Default Message Handling 98
A Taxonomy of Messages 99
   *Hardware Messages* 101    *Window Maintenance Messages* 104
   *User-Interface Messages* 106    *Termination Messages* 108
   *Private Messages* 109    *System Resource Notification* 110
   *Data Sharing Messages* 111    *Internal System Messages* 112

**PART THREE**

---

# Introduction to the Graphics Device Interface   113

## 6  Overview of GDI  115

An Overview of the Graphics Device Interface 115
   *GDI Capabilities* 116    *GDI Devices* 116
The Programming Interface 118
Drawing Coordinates 118
Logical Drawing Objects 120
The Device Context 121
Clipping and the Window Manager 127

## 7  Pixels and Markers  129

The BeginPaint Routine 133
GetClientRect Routine 135
SetPixel Routine 136
EndPaint Routine 138
The Windows Sandwich 138
Creating Markers 141

## 8  Drawing Lines  149

Line Drawing Primitives 150
   *MoveTo and LineTo* 150
DC Attributes 157

About Pens 158
    Pens and Device Independence 159    Creating and Using Pens 159
Drawing Modes and Lines 167

## 9 Drawing Filled Figures 171

GDI Filled Figure Routines 179
    Polygon and PolyPolygon 179    Ellipse, Chord, and Pie 181
    Rectangle and RoundRect 183
DC Attributes 185
About Brushes 186
Creating and Using Brushes 187

## 10 Drawing Text 197

Text Drawing Primitives 199
    TextOut 200    ExtTextOut 201    TabbedTextOut 210
    DrawText 211    GrayString 213
DC Attributes for Text Drawing 214
    Color 215    Text Alignment 217    Intercharacter Spacing 219
    About Fonts 221
GetTextExtent 223
GetTextMetrics 223
Creating and Using Logical Fonts 225

PART FOUR

# USER INTERFACE OBJECTS 235

## 11 Commands: Menu and Accelerator Basics 237

User-Interface Standards 238
Menu Programming Issues 241
Menu Template 243
A Sample Program: STANMENU 247
Menu Support Routines 253

Contents    xvii

*Menu Creation* 255   *Connect to a Window* 259
*Menu Destruction* 260   *Menu Modification* 262
*Query* 266   *Tracking* 270

Keyboard Accelerators  272

## 12 Enhancing Menus with Graphics  285

Owner-Draw Menu Items  285
*The WM_MEASUREITEM Message* 286   *The WM_DRAWITEM Message* 289   *A Sample Program: OWNDRAW* 291

Bitmaps in Menus  301
Creating Custom Menu Check Marks  312

## 13 Windowing  325

The Window Creation Process  326
*Window Classes* 326   *Window Class Style Bits* 331
*Creating a Window* 336   *Window Creation Style Bits* 341

Top-Level Window Considerations  351
*System Metrics* 357   *Private Profile Files* 361

Creating a Child Window  363
*STATLINE: Menu Status Information* 364

## 14 Dialog Boxes  377

Dialog Box User-Interface Standards  378
Modal Dialog Boxes  383
*Dialog Box Template* 383   *The Resource Workshop Dialog Box Editor* 385   *Creating a Modal Dialog Box* 387
*Maintaining the Dialog Box* 391   *A Simple Dialog Box: ABOUT* 393

Modeless Dialog Boxes  399
*Dialog Box Template* 399   *Creating a Modeless Dialog Box* 400
*Maintaining a Modeless Dialog Box* 402   *A Modeless Dialog Box: FIND* 404

File Open and Save As Dialog Boxes  414

PART FIVE

# Message Driven Input  421

## 15 Keyboard Input  423

How a Windows Program Receives Keyboard Input  423
  *The Keyboard*  424  *The Windows Keyboard Device Driver*  425
  *The Hardware Event Queue*  428  *The GetMessage Loop*  431
  *The Window Object*  434  *The Default Window Procedure*  435
  *Hooks*  435  *A Sample Program*  436

Character Sets and International Support  443
  *Converting Between Character Sets*  445  *Upper- and Lowercase Conversion*  446  *Sorting Character Strings*  447
  *String Tables*  448  *Entering Characters from the Numeric Keypad*  449

Multitasking Issues  449
  *Creating a Keyboard Pointer: Carets*  451

## 16 Mouse Input  467

The Uses of a Mouse  468
How a Windows Program Receives Mouse Input  470
  *The Mouse*  470  *The Mouse Device Driver*  471
  *The Hardware Event Queue*  471  *The GetMessage Loop*  472
  *The Mouse and the Window Object*  476  *The Default Window Procedure*  480

A Mouse Input Sample: CARET2  481
  *System Cursors*  492  *Hit-Testing*  495

Dragable Objects and Stretchable Rectangles  497
  *Dragging and Stretching*  510  *The Mouse Capture*  511

Creating Dynamic Cursors  512
  *The DYNACURS Program*  513  *How Cursors Work*  519
  *Creating a GDI Bitmap*  521  *Using the GDI Bitmap*  522
  *Dynamically Allocating Memory*  524

A Simpler Dynamic Cursor  527

PART SIX

# Operating System Considerations  531

## 17  Memory, Part I: System Memory Management  533

The Intel-86 Family of Processors  534
  *The Physical Address Space*  534   *Segmented Memory*  534
  *The Logical Address*  536

Real Mode Operation  537
  *The Real Mode Address Space*  539   *Real Mode and Windows*  540
  *Moveable Memory*  541   *Discardable Memory*  541
  *Fixed Memory*  542   *EMS and Real Mode Windows*  543

Standard and Enhanced Mode  545
Protected Mode  545
  *Memory Addressing in Protected Mode*  546   *Windows and Protected Mode*  549   *32-Bit Addressing*  550

Windows Virtual Memory Support  550
How Windows Selects a Segment for Discarding  552
The KERNEL's Private Memory Use  553
  *KERNEL Data Objects*  554

## 18  Memory, Part II: Application Memory Use  557

Overview of Application Memory Use  559
  *Default Data Segment*  559   *Dynamically Allocated Segments*  568
  *Resources*  570   *GDI Data Segment*  571   *USER Data Segment*  571

Global Heap Allocation  573
  *As Few as Possible*  574   *As Small as Possible*  575
  *As Discardable as Possible*  575   *Global Heap API*  576
  *Locked, Wired, Fixed, and Page Locked*  584   *A Sample Program: SEGALLOC*  587

Code Structure and Memory Use  594
  *A Sample Segmented Program*  595

Local Heap Allocation  599
  *LocalInit*  600   *LocalAlloc*  601   *LocalLock*  602
  *LocalReAlloc*  603   *LocalUnlock*  605   *LocalFree*  606

LOCALMEM: A Sample Heap Allocation Program 606
Local Heap Allocation in a Dynamically Allocated Segment 614

SUBSEG: A Combined Local/Global Heap Allocation Program 617
Custom Resources 628

## 19 Dynamic Linking 641

The Dynamic Linking Mechanism 642
Dynamic Linking and Discardable Code Segments 643
Dynamic Linking and Fixed Code Segments 647
Other Real Mode Dynamic Linking Considerations 649
    *Stack Patching* 650    *Return Thunks* 650

Dynamic Linking and Module Data Segments 651
The Instance Thunk 655
Clean Up Before You Go Home 657

# Appendices 659

Appendix A: A Taxonomy of Messages 661

Appendix B: The Default Window Procedure 675

Appendic C: Glossary 687

Appendic D: Contents of a Device Context 703

Appendix E: ANSI and OEM Character Sets 705

Appendix F: The Windows Virtual Key Codes 707

Appendix G: Setting Up the Integrated Development Environment 711

Appendix H: The MAGNIFY Program 721

Index 731

# PART ONE

# An Introduction to Windows

# 1

# An Introduction to Windows

Microsoft Windows is a graphical extension to the MS-DOS operating system. Windows extends DOS in several ways. DOS is built to support a single program at a time; Windows runs multiple programs concurrently. DOS has limited support for graphical output; Windows supports sophisticated, high-level graphics. DOS requires each program to provide its own user interface, which means that users must learn a different set of commands for every DOS program they use. A different command structure in different programs is like having a different steering mechanism and gear shift in different cars: Variety is nice, but a standard interface allows the user to operate any Windows program with a minimum of training. Windows provides a standard set of user-interface objects like windows, menus, and icons. A common set of user-interface objects means a consistent "look and feel" for all Windows programs, which help make Windows programs easy to learn and easy to use.

Windows provides a multitasking, graphical user interface, or **GUI**, that fosters the creation of interactive programs. Windows represents a relatively new type of operating environment that is optimized for interaction between human beings and computer programs. Windows programs have a different structure from programs in more traditional environments. This structure has a lot in common with programs written for other GUI systems, like the Apple Macintosh and the OS/2 Presentation Manager. Programs that run in these environments are **event driven**. That is to say, the structure and operation of these types of programs center around user-generated events (like keystrokes and mouse clicks). The architecture of such programs has more in common with operating-system software and interrupt-management routines than with traditional application software.

Traditionally, application programs have been sequence driven and not event driven. That is to say, *the program* dictates the sequence that the user must follow to accomplish the goal of the program. Event-driven programs, on the other hand, allow *the user* to dictate the steps required to complete a given task. The change from sequence-driven programming to event-driven programming requires a new way of thinking. Helping you learn this new way of thinking is what this book is all about.

# A History of Windows

All GUI systems trace their roots back to the work done at Xerox. In 1970, Xerox created the Palo Alto Research Center (PARC). Its charter was to create a new architecture for the way information is handled. Among its other accomplishments, PARC is credited with the development of laser printing, local area networks, graphical user interfaces, and object-oriented programming.

The researchers at PARC built several versions of a machine they dubbed "Alto." Over the years, several hundred of these internal research machines were built and were in widespread use. Built on the research with Alto, Xerox created a commercial GUI system: the Star 8010 workstation. Xerox introduced the Star in April 1981, four months before the IBM PC was made public. This multitasking system came equipped with a mouse and a bitmapped graphical display on which were displayed icons, windows, and proportionally spaced text. Although its high price kept it from becoming a commercial success, the Star marks an important milestone as the first commercially available GUI system.

The story is told that Steve Jobs, a co-founder of Apple Computer, was taken on a tour of Xerox PARC in 1979 or so. He was so impressed by the various Alto systems that he saw, that he returned to Apple and pushed for research in the development of a similar system. Apple introduced its first GUI system in 1983: the Apple Lisa. Apple followed the Lisa with its second GUI system, the Apple Macintosh. For its announcement, Apple bought time during the Super Bowl in January 1984 and aired a commercial that introduced the Macintosh as the computer to save the world from the nightmare of Big Brother described in George Orwell's novel *1984*. The importance of the Apple Macintosh is that it was the first commercially successful GUI system.

Microsoft started working on Windows in the spring of 1983. Eight years had passed since Microsoft's founders, Bill Gates and Paul Allen, wrote a BASIC interpreter for the world's first computer kit, the MITS Altair. And two years had passed since IBM introduced its personal computer, which came bundled with two Microsoft products: DOS and BASIC. Microsoft was just getting ready to ship version 2.0 of DOS, with its support for a hierarchical file system to support the hard disk of another new product, IBM's PC/XT computer.

At that time, there was talk at Microsoft of building a GUI system for the IBM personal computers, but no firm plans had been put in place. The primary reason was that the typical PC in those days had two floppy drives, 64K of RAM, and an 8088 CPU. For a GUI system to have acceptable performance, it was felt that more powerful hardware was needed. Hard disks would have to be available to provide fast access, and more memory would be needed to accommodate both the sophisticated code and the memory-hungry graphic data that such systems require. But something happened to spur Microsoft into GUI development.

In February 1983, VisiCorp, makers of the (then) popular spreadsheet VisiCalc, announced a GUI product for the IBM PC. Dubbed "VisiOn," it provided the motivation for Microsoft to begin working on its own GUI system. After all, if VisiOn caught on, it presented the possibility of taking software developers off the MS-DOS standard. And one thing was clear very early on at Microsoft: Software standards and compatibility would always be critical to the success of the microcomputer industry.

A team of developers that became known as the "Interactive Systems Group," or ISG, was assembled at Microsoft. Among the members of the team was a Xerox PARC alumnus, Scott MacGregor. Another Windows developer, Neil Konzen, had worked on porting Microsoft's spreadsheet, Multiplan, to the Macintosh. When the first version of Windows was introduced in November 1985, it had features that reflect the influence of Xerox PARC and the Apple Macintosh. But Windows itself was home-grown Microsoft, with features that anticipated the power of an operating system yet to be born: OS/2.

Version 1.01 of Windows started shipping in November 1985. As depicted in Figure 1.1, the first version of Windows provided automatic tiling of program windows. It was felt that the automatic arrangement of windows minimized the amount of work required of the user. This first version also supported overlapping or "popup" windows, which served primarily for the creation of dialog boxes. Windows 1 sported a "three-slice toaster," which provided access to the system menu. Some of the developers joked that this was actually a tiny vent that served to cool the screen lest it become overheated from the speed of the graphics.

The first version of Windows was built to run on a two-floppy-drive IBM PC with 256K RAM and an Intel 8088 CPU. This, incidentally, was the configuration used by ISG team members themselves during the earliest days of Windows development. Only later were tools available that developers today take for granted: hard disks and high-speed local area networks with file servers and print servers. And while this slowed development somewhat, Microsoft knew that this was the equipment that application developers would someday use to create software that would run under Windows. Developing in this environment, then, helped to stress test Windows' suitability for application development.

The next major revision of Windows was version 2, which started shipping in September 1987. Windows 2, shown in Figure 1.2, featured overlapping windows. The primary reason for the change from automatic tiling was feedback Microsoft had received from end users who did not appreciate the benefits of tiled windows, but who felt rather that tiling got in the way. The change away from automatic tiling was also part of an effort to make Windows consistent with another graphical environment that had been announced in April of that year: the OS/2 Presentation Manager.

6  *An Introduction to Windows*

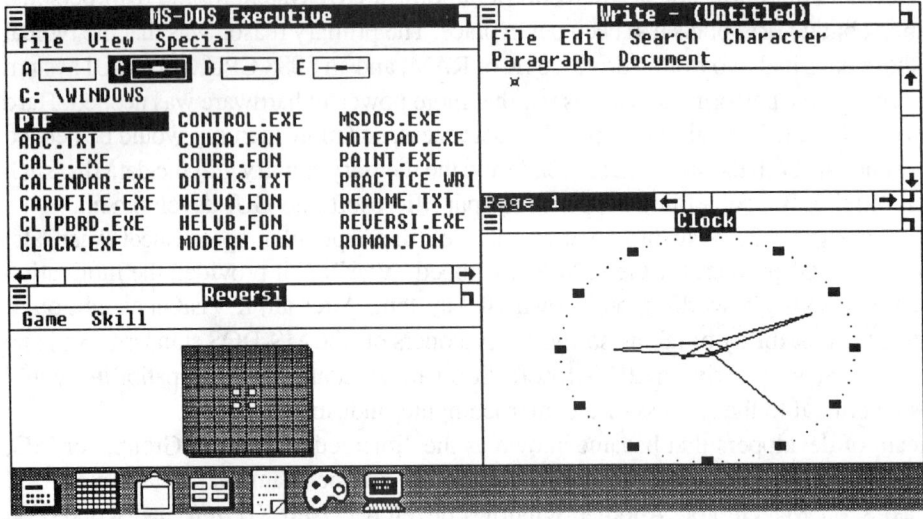

**Figure 1.1** Windows version 1.01

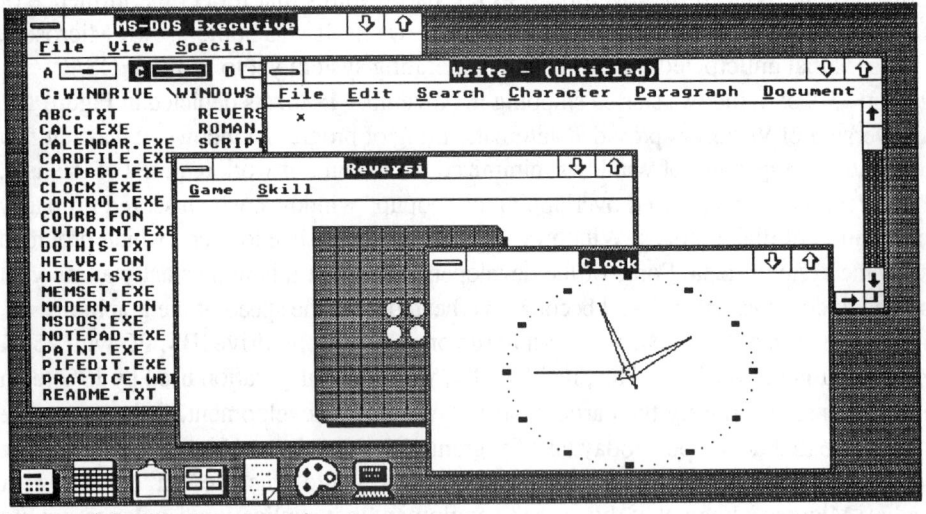

**Figure 1.2** Windows version 2

The similarity between the Windows and the OS/2 user interfaces is intended to help users move easily from one environment to the other. In fact, the user interface shared by these two environments is part of a much larger IBM strategy to create software consistency that extends from the smallest personal computer to the largest mainframe. This strategy is called **Systems Application Architecture**, or **SAA**. A primary goal of SAA is to allow a program written on one platform to be easily ported to another environment. For example, if SAA comes to complete fruition, you will someday see

OS/2 Presentation Manager programs running on IBM mainframes, minicomputers, and, of course, on personal computers. The part of SAA that addresses user-interface issues is known as **Common User Access**, or **CUA**.

Besides a new user interface, one of the key improvements introduced in Windows 2 was better use of memory in the form of support for expanded memory—memory made available according to the **Expanded Memory Specification (EMS)**. EMS describes a bank switching technique that allows additional memory to be available, although bank-switched memory is not *simultaneously* available. EMS under Windows 2 allowed more Windows programs to reside in memory at the same time, since each program was given a private EMS bank. EMS helped relieve the memory crunch that Windows 1 users had experienced, but didn't completely solve the memory shortage problem since Windows 2 only ran in Real Mode. Even on the powerful Intel 80286 and 80386 chips, for compatibility reasons, Intel gave these chips the same one-megabyte address space as its less powerful siblings, the 8088 and 8086.

With much fanfare, Microsoft announced version 3 of Windows on May 22, 1990, and started shipping shrink-wrapped packages immediately. Within six weeks, Microsoft had shipped 500,000 copies of the new version, breaking every record for the sale of any software product in a six-week period. From a sales standpoint, industry watchers worldwide have found Windows 3 to be a smashing success.

Figure 1.3 shows the new Windows 3 user interface, created to give Windows a new look for the 1990s. It features a proportional system font, to give Windows a more refined look and to make text easier to read. Three-dimensional shadowing, color icons, and redesigned applications combine to make Windows more appealing to the average user. Windows 3 also has better support for running DOS applications, which has prompted many to use it as the primary user interface for DOS-based computers.

From a programming point of view, Microsoft has provided an even richer set of capabilities in the user interface: Support for owner-draw menus, owner-draw listboxes, and owner-draw buttons gives programmers the capability to customize Windows more than ever before. Menus in the new Windows can be nested as deeply as programmers can make them, and tear-off menus give programmers the freedom to place menus anywhere they please. The MS-DOS Executive, which was so familiar to users of earlier versions, has been fired and replaced by a set of programs that manage programs and files: the **Program Manager**, the **Task List**, and the **File Manager**.

Internally, the most significant feature of Windows 3 is support for extended memory. Under Windows 3, Windows programs can access up to 16 megabytes of RAM. And when an 80386 or higher CPU is present, Windows uses the memory management features of these chips to provide virtual memory. In its 386-Enhanced mode, virtual memory up to four times the installed physical memory is available. For example, with 16 megabytes of physical memory (and enough room on the swap disk) Windows provides a 64-megabyte address space!

## 8   An Introduction to Windows

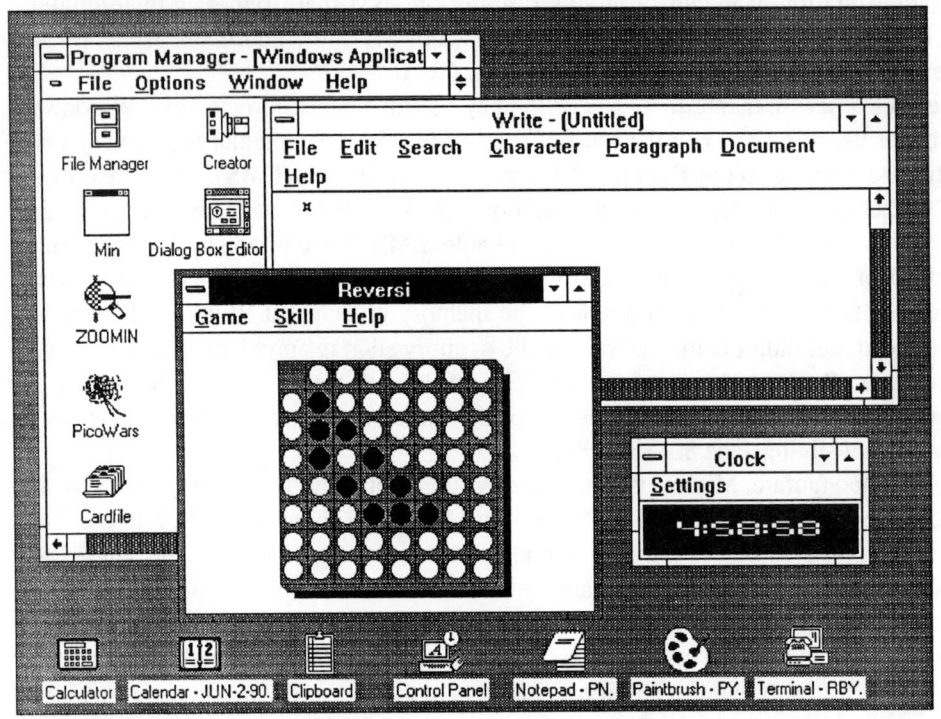

**Figure 1.3**  Windows version 3

Windows 3 also has better network support than earlier versions, making it easy to connect network file servers and print servers. It supports a device-independent bitmap format that provides a standard for sharing color bitmaps among devices; and on devices that support more than 256 colors, applications are even given access to the hardware color palette. This means that support for picture-perfect images, such as those that a multimedia system might use, is now available in Windows. Another new feature is a built-in, sophisticated help facility that you can use to provide hypertext help to the users of your programs.

As this book was going to press, Microsoft started to make public a new operating system that will ship in 1992: Windows NT (New Technology). This operating system will support quite a few different types of programs: Windows 3.x programs, MS-DOS programs, and Posix-compliant programs (Posix is a Unix-like programming interface). It will also provide a 32-bit version of Windows. Programs written to the 32-bit Windows API will have a host of new features available to them, including access to a flat address space, semaphores, threads, and a more powerful GDI. Let's consider some of the implications of this new operating system.

# Windows NT

It seems that every company that develops a GUI system has gone on to build "new and improved" versions. Xerox first built the Alto, then went on to create the Star. Apple started with its Lisa and later built the Macintosh. After Windows, Microsoft joined forces with IBM to create the OS/2 Presentation Manager.

One goal of OS/2 was to provide a migration path for existing Windows applications. While some Windows applications *did* make the move to OS/2, many did not. The reason? Although the Presentation Manager is architecturally very similar to Windows, it provides a completely new API. Every function name is different. For example, Presentation Manager has `WinCreateWindow` to replace Windows' `CreateWindow`. Parameters to similar functions are in a different order or are missing. Presentation Manager introduced a completely new set of symbolic constants. If a Windows developer was thinking of porting code to a new operating system, the work required to move to OS/2 was about the same as moving to any other GUI environment: Macintosh, X-Windows, etc.

Windows NT represents Microsoft's admission that it made a mistake with OS/2. Although there are warts on the Windows API, enough application software has been written to make them *our* warts. While the Windows 32-bit API cures some of the ills of Windows, in general, it represents an API that is based on and derived from the Windows 16-bit API of Windows 3.0. The new API was created with portability in mind, and retains the same function names, symbolic constants, and data structures as the old API.

One change that does occur between the two APIs is that every 16-bit element has been made 32 bits wide. While this may sound like a radical change, it's not. As you'll see, every Windows data type is defined using portable types. In other words, instead of using `short int` or `long int`, there are uppercase types like `HWND` and `HDC`. When you compile a program for either of the APIs, it's a simple matter to select the correct include file for the target API. The compiler then sorts out the differences between 16-bit and 32-bit values.

What does all this mean to you as a Windows programmer? As you begin using the Borland C++ compiler and the OWL libraries to create your Windows programs, you can feel confident that your software will have a long life. After all, the programs you write for Windows 3.x will be binary compatible with Windows NT—even when Windows NT is running on non-Intel processors. At present, Windows NT is being co-developed on Intel-based computers and computers built using the MIPS RISC processors.

Now that you know where Windows has come from, and have an idea about where it's going, the time has come to discuss the major obstacles that you will encounter as you learn to program in Windows. It is important to be aware of the required effort, because it is easy to look at Windows' flexible user interface and conclude (incorrectly) that the programming interface is just as easy to work with.

In fact, the challenge to Windows programmers is to understand the fundamental principles and models embodied in its architecture. Once you understand the "Windows-way" of thinking, you'll find that Windows programming is as easy to tackle as any other type of programming that you have done. Incidentally, if you have programmed with any other GUI system, such as the Apple Macintosh, the OS/2 Presentation Manager, or the various X-Windows systems, you'll find much that is familiar in Windows. Let's consider, then, the challenges that lie ahead.

## The Windows Programming Challenges

Consider the following scenario. It is Friday afternoon, and on your way out of the office you run into your boss. He has good news: The proposal that you made for the Windows development project has been approved. This means that you, and the crack team of programmers who work for you, are going to get to build your company's first Windows program. One of the first things you'll have to do is make sure that everyone on your team is up to speed on Windows. What challenges will be faced by the programmers who work for you who have no previous Windows programming experience?

Assuming that a programmer is proficient in C++, the three primary challenges are understanding message-driven programming, controlling graphical output, and using the various user-interface objects like windows, menus, dialog boxes, etc. Incidentally, if a programmer has been exposed to one or more of these areas, it makes it easier to learn Windows programming.

Before we discuss each of these areas in detail, one suggestion we'd like to make is that you become a full-time Windows user. There are subtleties in the Windows user interface that only become evident when you have spent time as an *end user*. For example, the way the keyboard and mouse work together, the ways that menus and accelerator keys operate, and the operation of the various types of dialog box controls. If you become a full-time Windows user, it will help you to become a better Windows programmer. At the very least, try to find one Windows program that you can use on a daily basis: It might be a word processing program, a drawing package, terminal emulation software, or even a game.

Let's take a look at the three challenges that every new Windows programmer faces, starting with message-driven programming.

### *Challenge 1: Message-Driven Programming*

Most programmers are used to writing code that runs in a sequential, procedure-driven manner. Such a program has a well-defined beginning, middle, and end. Consider, for example, a program that displays a series of data entry screens for the creation of some written document, which might be an airplane ticket or a company purchase order. The flowchart in Figure 1.4 depicts the strict sequence in which such a program might operate.

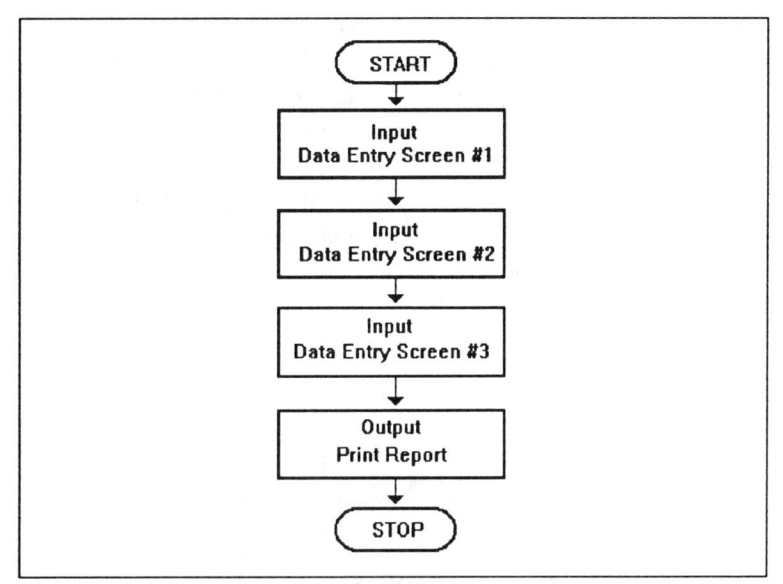

```
┌─────────────────────────────────────┐
│            ( START )                │
│               ↓                     │
│     ┌───────────────────┐           │
│     │      Input        │           │
│     │ Data Entry Screen #1 │        │
│     └───────────────────┘           │
│               ↓                     │
│     ┌───────────────────┐           │
│     │      Input        │           │
│     │ Data Entry Screen #2 │        │
│     └───────────────────┘           │
│               ↓                     │
│     ┌───────────────────┐           │
│     │      Input        │           │
│     │ Data Entry Screen #3 │        │
│     └───────────────────┘           │
│               ↓                     │
│     ┌───────────────────┐           │
│     │     Output        │           │
│     │   Print Report    │           │
│     └───────────────────┘           │
│               ↓                     │
│            ( STOP )                 │
└─────────────────────────────────────┘
```

**Figure 1.4**  A sequence-driven program

For the sake of this discussion, let's say that this flowchart represents a program used by travel agents to issue airplane tickets. The first entry screen accepts passenger information: name, address, etc. The second screen allows the input of flight information and provides fares and scheduling information. And finally, the third screen accepts payment information based on the fares in the previous screen. Each data entry screen must be correctly filled in before the travel agent can proceed to the next step, and all three screens must have correct information to issue a ticket.

At first glance, this seems like a reasonable way for such a program to proceed. After all, the job of the computer program is not only to issue tickets, but to make sure that correct passenger information has been received and that the payment provided agrees with the currently available fares. There are limitations to this approach, however, that are a direct result of this sequence-driven orientation.

For example, since the program dictates the sequence of operation, a travel agent cannot get to the second screen—for fare and flight information—without first entering complete passenger information. While a travel agency might like this feature, since it allows them to avoid giving away free information, the net result is the creation of unnecessary steps.

While the program ensures that all required information has been entered, it doesn't take into account real-world exceptions. For example, if a travel agent were to sell a group of tickets—perhaps to a family that is going on vacation—the travel agent must traverse all

12  *An Introduction to Windows*

three screens for every ticket that is issued. Once again, the program does its job of ensuring that all the necessary information has been collected, but at a cost to the travel agent in the form of the additional work required.

An event-driven program, on the other hand, allows a travel agent to enter the data in whatever order seems appropriate. Perhaps an agent would choose the same order that the sequence-driven program dictated. However, an agent would be free to perform the necessary tasks in a sequence that fit the requirements of different customers. Figure 1.5 gives a rough idea of how an event-driven approach might change the traditional, sequence-driven program that we described earlier.

And yet, this is only one aspect of the way that an event-driven program differs from a sequence-driven program. An event-driven operating system like Windows goes even further so that, for example, within the data entry screens, the travel agent would have a tremendous amount of flexibility in the order in which fields were entered.

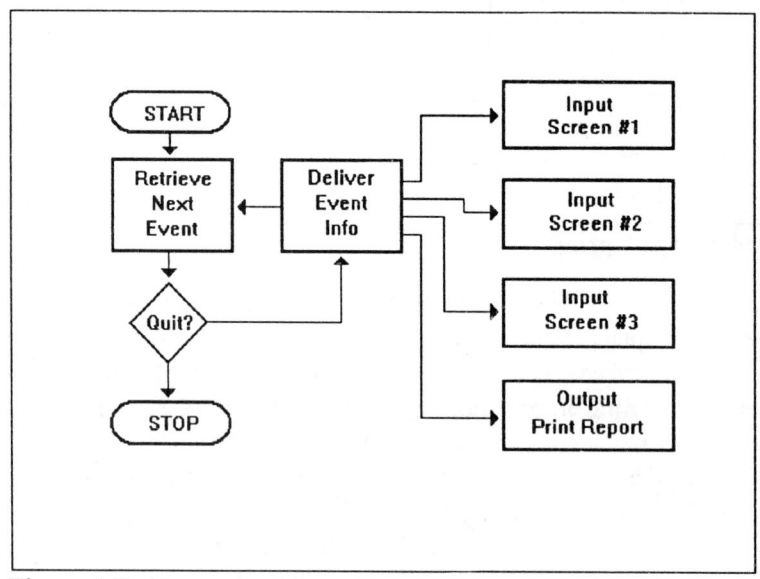

**Figure 1.5**  An event-driven program

A sequence-driven program is built on an awkwardly arranged set of **modes**. A mode is a state of a program in which user actions are interpreted in a specific way and produce a specific set of results. In a reaction against sequence-driven programs, some GUI programmers may tell you that modes are bad. Unfortunately, this is a bit of an oversimplification.

A primary problem having to do with modes occurs when the user cannot easily move from one mode to another. In our sequence-driven ticketing program, for example, each of the four steps is a mode. But since the program dictates that the user traverse the modes in a strict sequence, the user is prevented from structuring his use of the program to meet the various demands that are made.

Another problem with modes occurs in programs that rely on the user to remember the current mode. Instead, a program should provide visual clues to help the user identify the program's current mode. In Windows, there are many user-interface objects that support this. The shape of the mouse cursor, for example, can indicate when a drawing package is in rectangle drawing mode and when it is in text drawing mode. You will see that modal dialog boxes are a very common way to retrieve input from the user that is required to complete a command.

The modes in a program should be carefully designed to prevent data loss when the user accidentally fumbles into a mode. A story often told about modes involves a text editor called Bravo, which was built at Xerox PARC in the 1970s. In this editor, regular keyboard keys are used for commands. For example, the letter "i" puts the program into insert mode, "d" is used for delete mode, etc. One user wanted to place the word "edit" in a document, but forget to first enter insert mode. The editor interpreted these keystrokes as

| | |
|---|---|
| E (verything) | select everything in the document. |
| D (elete) | delete it. |
| I (nsert) | enter insert mode. |
| T | type the letter "t." |

Oops. The entire contents of the document were replaced by the letter "t." When designing the user interface of a program, you should be aware of the modes that are created, and build in the necessary safeguards to help users avoid such unpleasant surprises.

From a programming point of view, modal programs are easier to implement than modeless programs. The code that supports each mode can be written and debugged in relative isolation from the other parts of the program. And yet, Windows makes it easier to create modeless programs because all interaction with the outside world—all events—are funneled to a program in a modeless manner. All events of interest generate messages.

What is a message? It is information about some change in the user interface, such as a window getting moved, or a keyboard key being pressed. Messages notify a program that a timer has gone off. Messages are used for data-sharing operations.

From a programming point of view, a message is a 16-bit unsigned value that, for ease of reading, is assigned a symbolic constant that starts with the letters WM_ (short for "Window Message"). For example, the **WM_LBUTTONDOWN** message tells a program that the user has pushed the left mouse button. Another message, which gets sent after the left mouse button has been released, is **WM_LBUTTONUP**. Throughout this book, we'll introduce messages in the context of the different topics that are covered. But if you're impatient to see all the different types of messages in the system, you may want to skip ahead to Appendix A, which summarizes the various types of Windows messages.

14   *An Introduction to Windows*

Messages are very important to a Windows programmer. Most of the work that you will do as a Windows programmer involves deciding which messages to process and which messages to ignore. One thing to keep in mind is that messages do not appear in any predefined order. If you are used to a sequentially oriented program, things may seem disorganized and chaotic at first. It may seem that messages fly at you like bullets. To help you understand the flow of messages in the system, Borland provides you with a program called WinSight. Figure 1.6 shows WinSight listening to the messages of the Windows Program Manager.

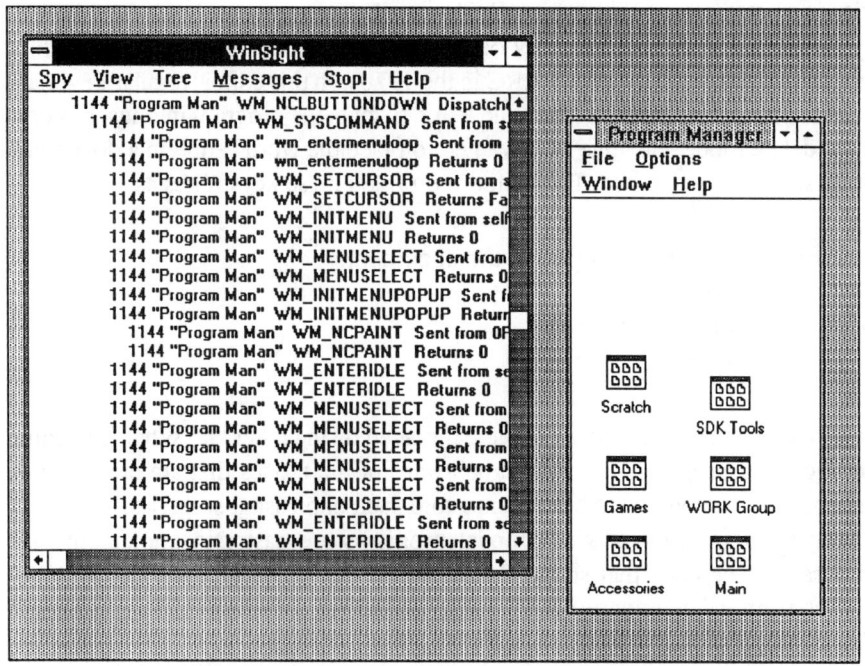

**Figure 1.6** WinSight listening to messages belonging to the Program Manager

Windows' message orientation is best suited for programs that require a high level of interaction with the user. Therefore, language compilers, which tend to have very little interaction with the user, gain little from running as Windows programs. But games and word processing programs are well suited for Windows, since both require a high level of user interaction. Spreadsheets and data entry programs are also good candidates for interactive, event-driven applications.

A message-driven operating system like Windows puts a high priority on allowing the user to intervene at any point in a process. A sequence-driven program, on the other hand, puts a high priority on dictating the sequence in which a job must be performed. In a sequence-driven program, it is all too tempting for the programmer to create arbitrary rules about the order in which steps should be taken. While it is possible to create sequence-driven programs in Windows, the extra effort it requires virtually guarantees that such restrictions will only be put in place where they are actually needed.

### Messages and Program Scheduling

Windows is a multitasking system. To a user, this means that several programs can run "at the same time." Of course, with a single CPU, programs do not run at the same time. Instead, each is scheduled and each runs one at a time. In traditional operating systems, this scheduling is done by the clock. Each program is allotted a "time-slice" during which it can run. When its time is up, one program is interrupted, and another program is allowed to run. This is called preemptive scheduling. In preemptive scheduling, programs are interrupted by the operating system.

Windows does not schedule programs preemptively. Instead, Windows has a nonpreemptive scheduling system. Windows programs are not interrupted by the operating system; instead, each program voluntarily interrupts its own operation to let other programs run.

Windows' scheduling system is built into its message delivery mechanism. When a program has finished processing a message, it asks for another message. A message-based scheduling system means that the user is the ultimate source of scheduling decisions. When the user wishes to work with a program, he focuses his attention on one of the program's windows, perhaps by clicking the mouse, or by selecting a window using the keyboard. Each of these actions causes messages to flow to a program, which gives it the "time-slices" that it needs to run.

Messages provide a program with input, but that's only half the story. The other half involves the output that a program produces. And output in Windows means just one thing: graphical output. This is the second challenge that new Windows programmers must face, and our next topic of discussion.

## *Challenge 2: Graphical Output*

All output created by Windows programs is graphical. Figure 1.7 shows a sample of some of the lines, filled figures, and text that GDI can draw. Programmers who are used to working in a character-oriented environment will find that graphical output requires a new way of thinking. As you might expect, graphical output means that geometric figures can be drawn—lines, circles, boxes, etc. In addition, text itself is treated as a graphical object. This makes it easier, for example, to freely mix text and geometric figures. Paradoxically, while graphical output systems make the output of geometric shapes easier, they also tend to make the output of text harder.

16   *An Introduction to Windows*

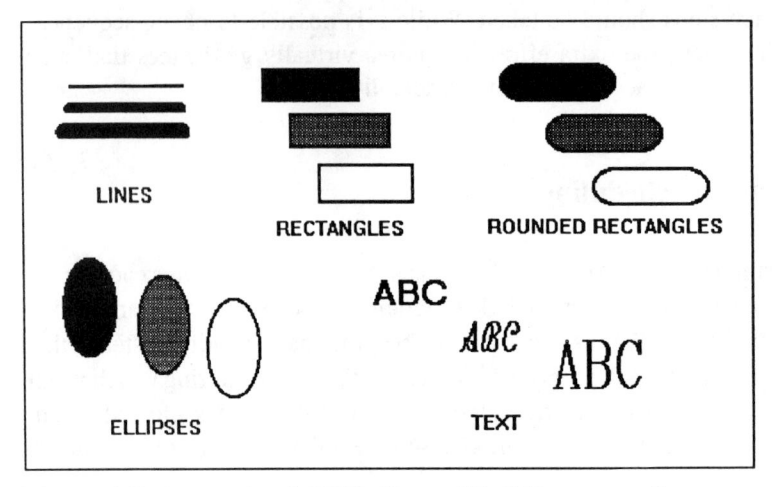

**Figure 1.7**  A sample of GDI's lines, filled figures, and text

Geometric shapes are easier because your program does not have to calculate each pixel. By simply calling the `Rectangle` routine, for example, GDI draws a filled rectangle for you. Text output is harder, because GDI's graphical orientation requires that you deal with text as a graphical object. Text is positioned using pixel coordinates rather than by character cell position.

### Device-Independent Graphics

GDI provides device-independent graphics. This means a Windows program can draw on any device using the same set of calls. For example, the `Rectangle` routine is called to draw rectangles on the display screen as well as on printers. GDI works hard so that, from the point of view of a program, all devices look similar. This includes devices that only know how to turn pixels on and off—like the CGA display card—as well as very smart devices that know how to do complex graphics, like PostScript printers. Each device has a device driver that is responsible for doing the actual drawing. For devices that require assistance, GDI provides **software simulations** that use the low-level capabilities of a device to provide high-level functionality.

GDI knows about four types of devices: the display screen, hard-copy devices (like printers and plotters), bitmaps, and metafiles. Two of these are physical devices: the display screen and hard-copy devices. The other two, bitmaps and metafiles, are pseudodevices. A pseudodevice provides a means to store a picture in RAM or on disk, as well as a standard way to share graphical images between applications.

When displaying information on the display screen, GDI provides window-oriented graphics. Window-oriented graphics means several things. Each window is treated like a separate drawing surface. When a program draws in a window, the default drawing coordinates are set up so that the origin (0,0) is in the upper-left corner of the window's client area (see Figure 1.8).

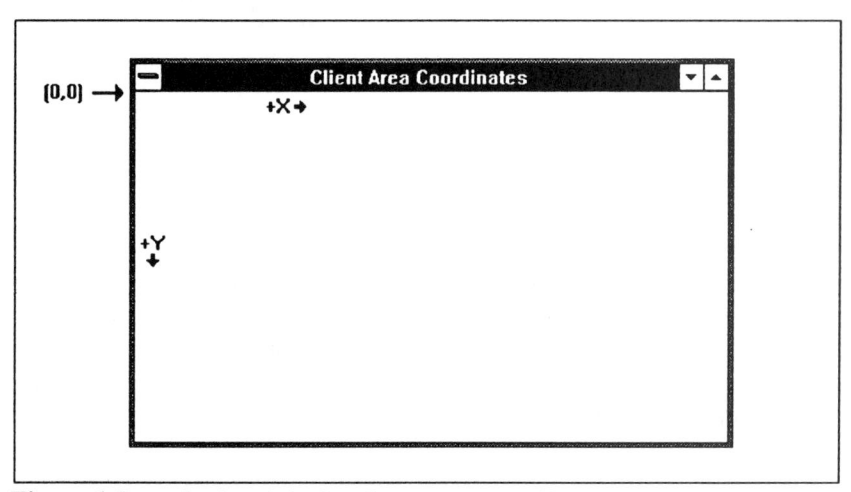

**Figure 1.8** Default origin in client-area coordinates

Window-oriented graphics also means that drawings are automatically clipped to a window. Clipping means that the drawing done for each window is limited to the window's border. Even if a window tried to draw beyond its own border, it would not be able to. A window is automatically protected from the wayward pixels that other windows might send its way. This protection mechanism works both ways, so that when you draw, you don't have to worry about accidentally overwriting another program's window.

## *Challenge 3: User-Interface Objects*

Windows has built-in support for a number of user-interface objects: windows, icons, menus, dialog boxes, etc. Built-in support means that the amount of effort required to create and maintain these objects is fairly minimal. In particular, if you were to write your own code to support these objects, it would require a vast amount of effort on your part. And the results would probably not be as flexible nor as robust as the user-interface objects that Windows provides.

Taking advantage of what these user-interface objects can provide requires you to understand how each is implemented. As we look at the different types of user-interface objects, we'll provide some insights into the design and implementation of each. In many cases, this will mean a discussion of the messages that are associated with a given user-interface object. In other cases, this means delving into the various Windows library routines that control each type of object. For now, we're going to introduce you to the user-interface objects and describe the role of each in the user interface.

Among user-interface objects, the most important is the window. Any program that wishes to interact with the user must have a window, since a window receives mouse and keyboard input and displays a program's output. All other user-interface objects, like menus, scroll bars, and cursors, play supporting roles for the leading character: the window.

## The Window

The window is the most important part of the user interface. From the perspective of a user, a window provides a view of some data object inside the computer. But it is more than that, since to a user, a window *is* an application. When the user starts to run an application, a window is expected to appear. A user closes a window to shut down an application. To decide the specific application to be worked with, a user selects the application's window. Figure 1.9 shows the standard parts of a typical program's main window.

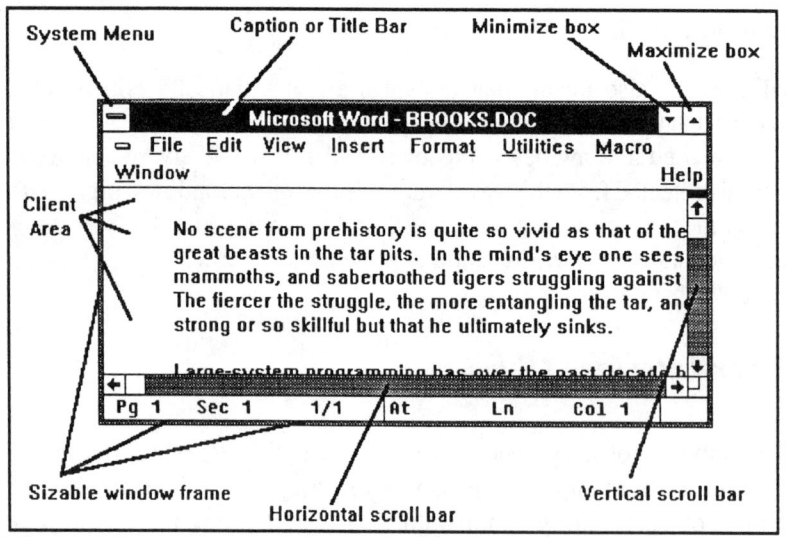

**Figure 1.9** The standard parts of a window

To programmers, a window represents several things. It serves to organize the other user-interface objects together and directs the flow of messages in the system. A window provides a display area that can be used to communicate with the user. Input is channeled to a window and thereby directed to the program. Applications also use windows to subdivide other windows. For example, dialog boxes are implemented as a collection of small windows inside a larger window.

Every window is created from a **window class**. A window class provides a template from which to create windows. Associated with every window class—and therefore with every window—is a special type of subroutine called a **window procedure**. The job of a window procedure is to process messages. In a message-oriented operating system like Windows, you can imagine that this is an important task. In fact, most of the work that you will do as a Windows programmer will involve deciding how to handle one message or another that is received in a window procedure. It receives the mouse and keyboard input that is directed to a window, which arrives in the form of messages. It receives notifications about other events of interest, such as changes in the size and location of a window. One of the first areas that we're going to explore, starting with the next few chapters, is the way that messages arrive at and are processed by window procedures.

## Icons

An icon is a symbol that serves as a reminder to the user. GUI systems are built on the principle that what is concrete and visible is more easily understood than what is abstract and invisible. Icons provide a concrete, visible symbol of a command, a program, or some data. By making such things visible, a Windows program makes them accessible. By making all of a user's choices visible, Windows programs lessen the user's dependence on memorized information.

Examples of icons include standard window ornaments: the system menu box, the minimize box, and the maximize box. As depicted in Figure 1.10, one of the most common uses of an icon is to represent a program. In the Program Manager's window, an icon reminds the user of the programs that are available to be run. On the desktop, an icon serves to remind the user of the programs that are currently running, but whose windows have been closed. Icons can also be used to represent commands. For example, Figure 1.11 shows icons displayed by the Paintbrush program to show users the set of drawing operations available in this program, as well as the available fill patterns.

## 20  An Introduction to Windows

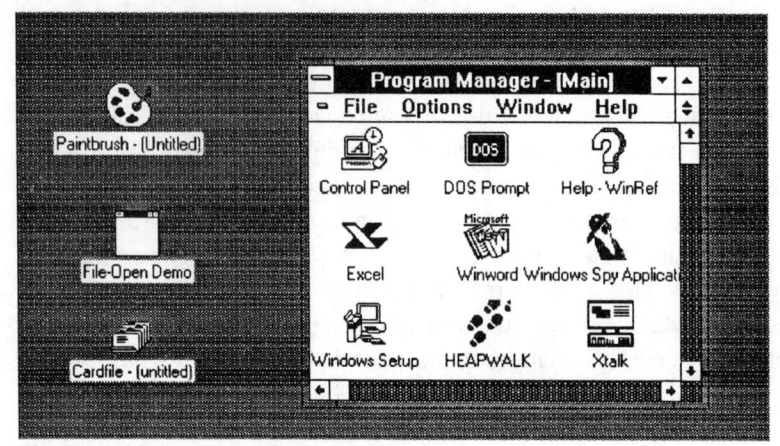

**Figure 1.10**  Icons in the Program Manager and on the desktop

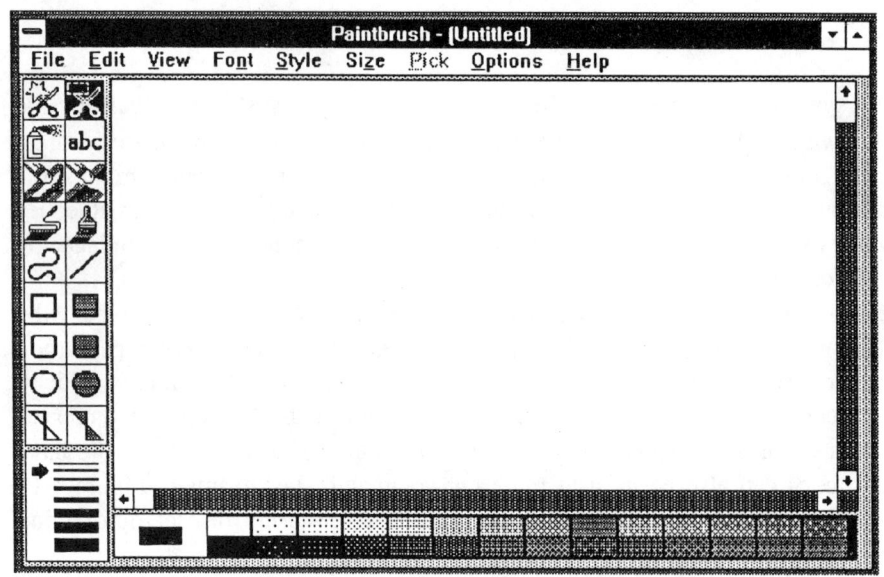

**Figure 1.11**  Icons as commands in the Paintbrush program

### Menus

A menu is a list of commands and program options. Windows has five types of menus: system menus, menu-bar menus, pull-down menus, nested menus, and tear-off menus. The system menu, shown in Figure 1.12, provides a standard set of operations that can be performed on a window. These operations are referred to as "system commands." Users

*An Introduction to Windows* 21

expect to find a system menu on the top-level window of every program they run. System commands require very little work on the part of a program, since Windows itself does everything to make system commands operational and uniform throughout the system.

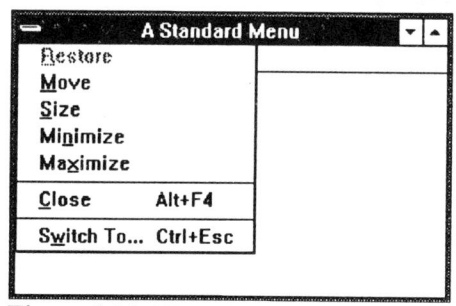

**Figure 1.12** The system menu

Figure 1.13 shows the three types of menus that are connected together: The menu-bar menu connects to the top of a window, popup menus appear when a menu-bar item is selected, and nested menus are displayed when a popup menu item that has an arrow is selected. Applications can nest menus as far as they'd like, although in general programmers should avoid nesting too deeply, since this can disorient the user.

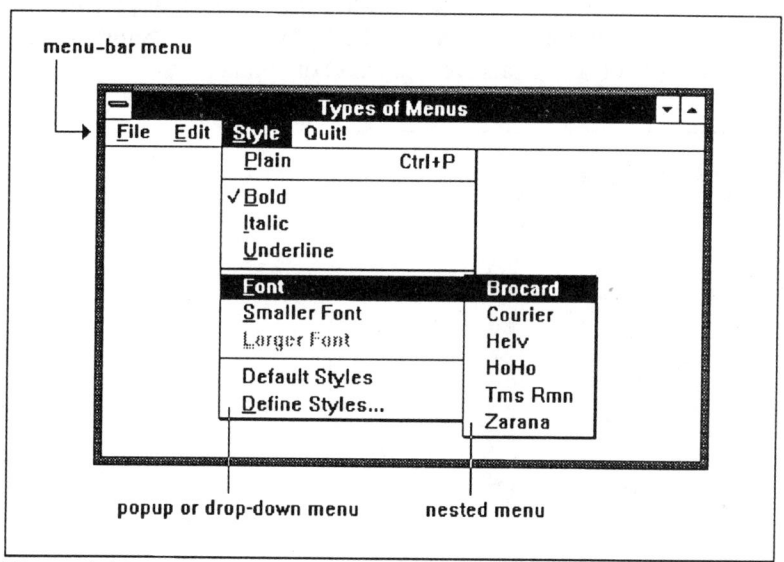

**Figure 1.13** Three types of menus

Figure 1.14 shows a tear-off menu positioned in the middle of a window. Tear-off menus can be made to appear anywhere in a window, and in fact anywhere on the display screen. They provide another alternative for programs that do not wish to rely solely on

## 22  An Introduction to Windows

menus that descend from the menu-bar menu. Thus, a menu can be made to appear when a specific object is clicked, or in response to a hot-key struck by the user on the keyboard.

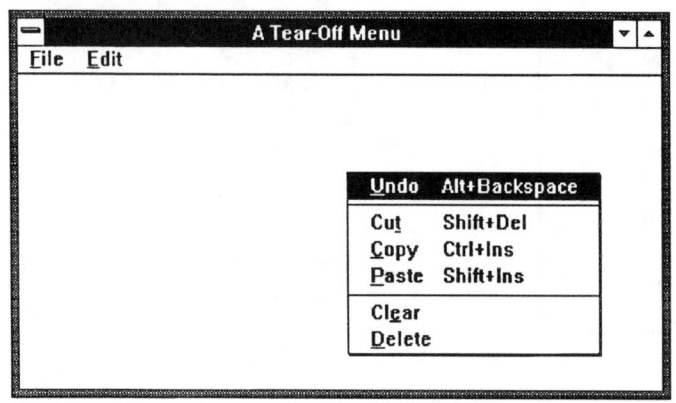

Figure 1.14  A tear-off menu

## Scroll Bars

When a scroll bar is shown in a window, the user knows that the data object is larger than the window. Scroll bars provide a means by which the user can control the display of such objects and also see at a glance the relative location of an object that is being viewed. Figure 1.15 shows the two types of scroll bars: vertical and horizontal.

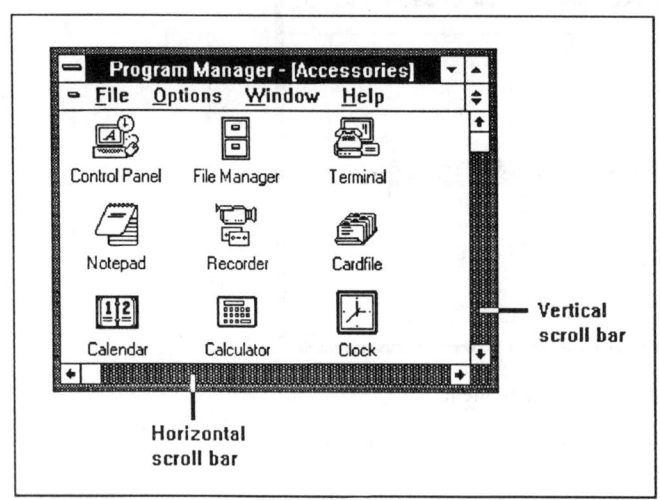

Figure 1.15  Vertical and horizontal scroll bars

## Cursors

A cursor is a bitmap that floats on the display screen in response to the movement of a mouse or other pointing device. Programs can change the shape of the cursor to indicate a change in the system. For example, programs often display an hourglass cursor to let the user know that some lengthy operation is taking place. Programs can also change the cursor to let the user know that a program has entered a specific mode. For example, drawing programs often change the cursor to reflect the type of object that can be drawn.

Using the Resource Workshop utility, which is included with the Turbo C++ compiler, programmers can create custom cursors. Cursors can also be created "on the fly," a process that we'll describe in Chapter 16. Of course, you may not need to create your own cursors, if the ones that Windows provides will serve your needs. All of Windows' built-in cursors are shown in Figure 1.16.

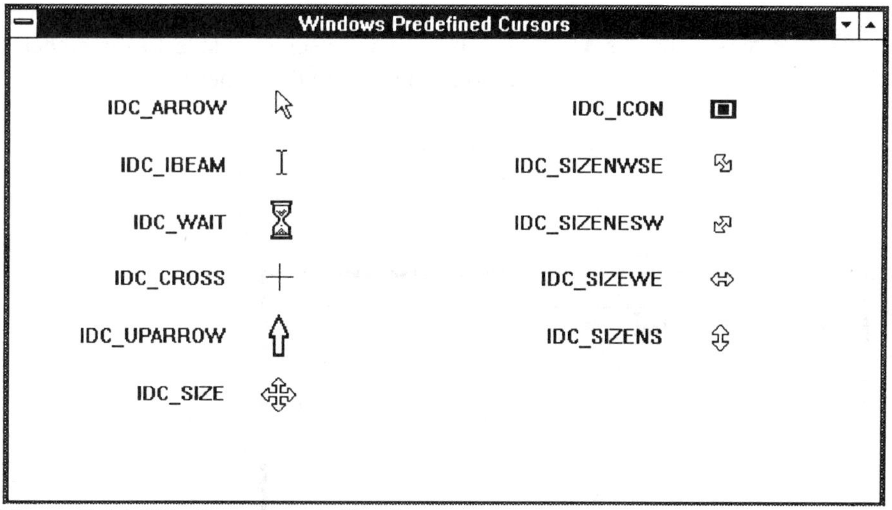

**Figure 1.16** Windows' predefined cursors

## Carets

A caret is a tiny bitmap that blinks and serves as a pointer for keyboard control. The window that has control of the keyboard (also known as the focus window) may create a caret to notify the user of this fact. Carets are quirky in two ways: the name and the control. The name is quirky because most other environments use the term "cursor" for the keyboard pointer. But in Windows, "cursor" is already used for the mouse pointer.

The second way that carets are quirky is in the way that programs must maintain them. The Windows user interface only supports a single caret at a time. Therefore, programs that wish to use a caret must create one upon receiving the keyboard focus and must destroy it on losing the keyboard focus. In Chapter 15, when we describe keyboard input, we'll look at what a program must do to properly maintain a caret.

## Dialog Boxes

Dialog boxes, also known as dialogs, provide a standard way to receive input from users. In particular, when a user has entered a command for which additional information is required, dialog boxes are the standard way to retrieve that input. While browsing through a Windows program, you often see an ellipsis (...) as part of a menu name. This indicates that a dialog box will appear when the menu item is selected.

One dialog box that is quite common is displayed whenever the user asks for a file to be opened. It is the file-open dialog box, shown in Figure 1.17. This dialog box provides the user with the opportunity of typing in a file name. It also shows two lists: one of file names and the other of directory names and disk drives. If the user is unable to remember a specific file name, she can browse the directories until she finds the desired file.

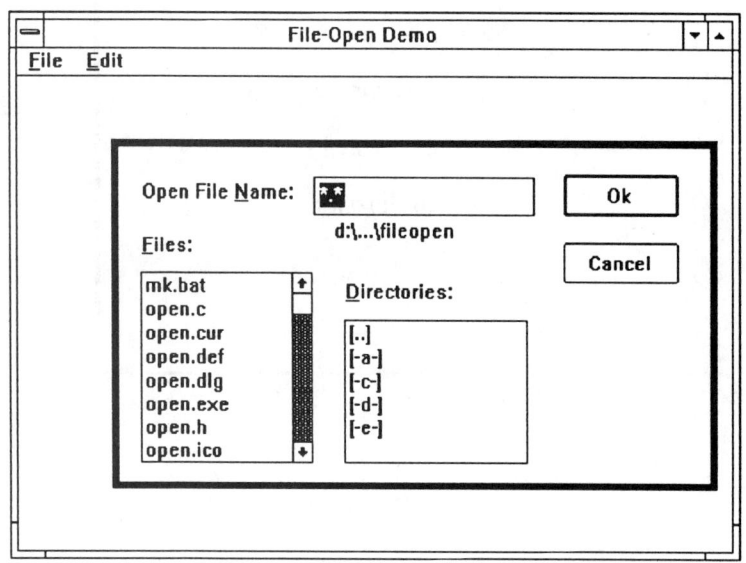

**Figure 1.17** A file-open dialog box

Notice that this dialog box has two pushbuttons: one marked "Ok" and the other marked "Cancel." In general, pushbuttons in dialog boxes are used to request an action. For this dialog box, there are two possible actions. The Ok pushbutton tells the program to accept the values that the user has entered. The Cancel pushbutton tells the program to ignore the values that have been entered in the dialog box. In general, wherever possible, programs should allow a user to withdraw a request without incurring any damage to files or data.

## Dialog Box Controls

Like all dialog boxes, the file-open dialog is a window that holds individual windows that either display information or accept input from the user. Each of these tiny windows is called a dialog box control. For example, the file-open dialog contains nine dialog box controls: two pushbuttons (Ok and Cancel), two listboxes, an edit control, and four static text controls. Windows has six predefined window classes from which dialog box controls are created: button, combobox, edit, listbox, scroll bar, and static.

In Chapter 14, we're going to investigate the creation of dialog boxes. You will see that dialog box controls do a lot of the work of interacting with the user. Edit controls, for example, handle all of the keyboard input without your having to intercede. And, once a listbox has received its list of items, it will happily display and scroll the items in a list without your having to intervene to assist it. You will see that, like many other parts of Windows, dialog boxes and dialog box controls are primarily message driven.

In summary, then, there are three conceptual hurdles to overcome to learn Windows programming: message-driven programming, controlling graphic output, and using user-interface objects. These three areas are the focus of parts 2, 3, and 4 of this book.

The next few chapters discuss Windows event-driven nature in the context of a minimum Windows program. You may be surprised at the size of this program, but it represents the *minimum* required to respond both to messages that are buffered and to messages that don't wait to be invited in. The minimum Windows program creates a single window and demonstrates how message traffic must be handled in a Windows program. As we look at each piece in the program, we'll describe how it fits in the overall architecture of Windows itself.

# PART TWO

# A Minimum Windows Program

# 2
# A Minimum Windows Program

This chapter introduces a minimum Windows program, MIN.EXE. MIN serves as the basis for every other program in this book. Figure 2.1 shows the window that MIN creates. The window can be moved, resized, closed, *minimized* (made into an icon), or *maximized* (enlarged to fill the screen). In other words, to an experienced Windows user, the window created by this program does all of the "right" things.

**Figure 2.1 The window created by our minimum Windows program**

**Table 2.1** Files that make up the minimum Windows program

| | |
|---|---|
| MAKEFILE.MAK | Make file, automates program build process. |
| MIN.LNK | Linker command line file. |
| MIN.CPP | C++ source code. |
| MIN.RC | Resource file, for user-interface data objects. |
| MIN.DEF | Module definition file, used by the linker. |
| MIN.ICO | Icon file, a resource. |
| MIN.CUR | Cursor file, another resource. |

The seven files that make up our minimum Windows program are listed in Table 2.1. Five are text files (MAKEFILE.MAK, MIN.LNK, MIN.CPP, MIN.RC, and MIN.DEF) and appear in the listings which accompany this discussion. The other two files contain graphic images (MIN.CUR and MIN.ICO). Figure 2.2 shows the contents of these files inside Borland's Resource Workshop. MIN.CUR contains a mouse cursor in the shape of a hand. MIN.ICO contains the icon displayed when our program is minimized.

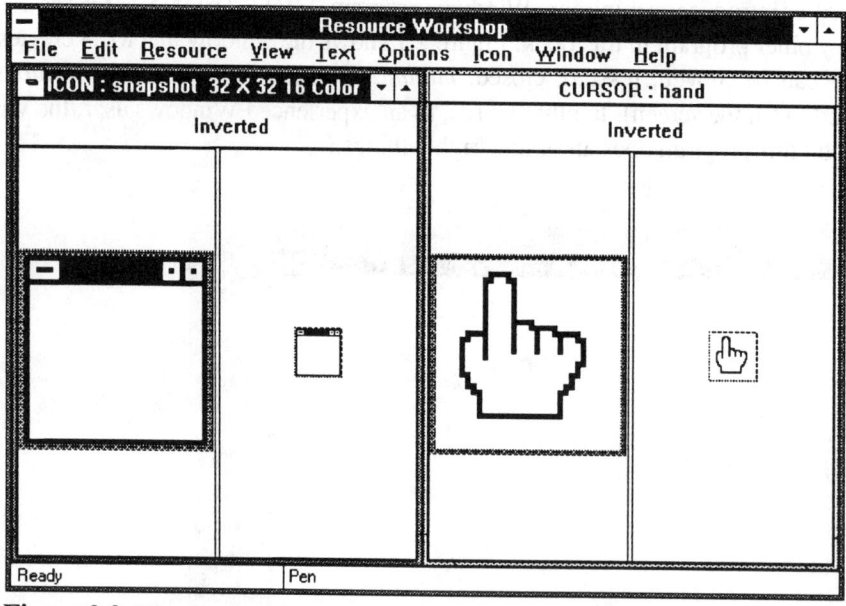

**Figure 2.2** The icon and cursor of our minimum Windows program

# MAKEFILE.MAK

```
.AUTODEPEND

#    Translator Definitions
INC=\BORLANDC\OWL\INCLUDE;\BORLANDC\CLASSLIB\INCLUDE;\BORLANDC\INCLUDE
CC = bcc -c -D_CLASSDLL -H -ml -WS -w -I$(INC)

#    Implicit Rules
.c.obj:
  $(CC) {$< }

.cpp.obj:
  $(CC) {$< }

#    Explicit Rules
Min.exe: Min.res Min.def Min.obj
    tlink /c/C/n/P-/Twe/x @Min.LNK
    RC Min.res Min.exe

#    Individual File Dependencies
Min.obj: Min.cpp

Min.res: Min.rc Min.cur Min.ico
    RC -R -FO Min.res -i$(INC) Min.RC
```

# MIN.LNK

```
\borlandc\lib\c0wl.obj+
min.obj
min,min
\borlandc\classlib\lib\tclasdll.lib+
\borlandc\owl\lib\owl.lib+
mathwl.lib+
import.lib+
crtldll.lib
min.def
```

# MIN.CPP

```
/*-------------------------------------------------------------*\
|   MIN.CPP   A Minimum C++ Windows Program.  MIN displays a    |
|             window which can be moved, sized, minimized, and  |
|             maximized.                                        |
\*-------------------------------------------------------------*/
#define WIN31
#define STRICT
#include <owl.h>
#include <WindowsX.h>
/*-------------------------------------------------------------*\
|                    Class Declarations.                        |
\*-------------------------------------------------------------*/
class TMinApplication : public TApplication
   {
   public:
```

## A Minimum Windows Program

```
        TMinApplication (LPSTR lpszName, HINSTANCE hInstance,
                         HINSTANCE hPrevInstance, LPSTR lpszCmdLine,
                         int nCmdShow);
      virtual void InitMainWindow ();
    };

class TMinWindow : public TWindow
    {
    public:
      TMinWindow (PTWindowsObject pwParent, LPSTR lpszTitle,
                  PTModule pmModule);
      virtual LPSTR GetClassName ();
      virtual void  GetWindowClass (WNDCLASS&);
    };

/*--------------------------------------------------------------*\
|                 Main Function:  WinMain.                       |
\*--------------------------------------------------------------*/
int PASCAL WinMain (HINSTANCE hInstance,   HINSTANCE hPrevInstance,
                    LPSTR    lpszCmdLine, int      nCmdShow)
    {
    TMinApplication Min ("MIN", hInstance, hPrevInstance,
                         lpszCmdLine, nCmdShow);
    Min.Run ();
    return Min.Status;
    }

/*--------------------------------------------------------------*\
|                 Application Class Member.                      |
\*--------------------------------------------------------------*/
TMinApplication::TMinApplication (LPSTR lpszName, HINSTANCE hInstance,
                  HINSTANCE hPrevInstance, LPSTR lpszCmdLine,
                  int nCmdShow)
              :TApplication (lpszName, hInstance, hPrevInstance,
                             lpszCmdLine, nCmdShow)
    {
    /*  Application specific initialization goes here.  */
    }

/*--------------------------------------------------------------*\
|                 Application Class Member.                      |
\*--------------------------------------------------------------*/
void TMinApplication::InitMainWindow ()
    {
    MainWindow = new TMinWindow (NULL, "Minimum", NULL);
    }

/*--------------------------------------------------------------*\
|                 TMinWindow Class Member.                       |
\*--------------------------------------------------------------*/
TMinWindow::TMinWindow (PTWindowsObject pwParent,
             LPSTR lpszTitle, PTModule pmModule)
          :TWindow (pwParent, lpszTitle, pmModule)
    {
    /*  Window specific initialization goes here.  */
    }

/*--------------------------------------------------------------*\
|                 TMinWindow Class Member.                       |
\*--------------------------------------------------------------*/
LPSTR TMinWindow::GetClassName ()
```

```
        {
        return "MIN:MAIN";
        }
/*----------------------------------------------------------*\
|                   TMinWindow Class Member.                 |
\*----------------------------------------------------------*/
void TMinWindow::GetWindowClass (WNDCLASS& wc)
        {
        TWindow::GetWindowClass (wc);
        wc.hIcon=LoadIcon (wc.hInstance, "snapshot");
        wc.hCursor=LoadCursor (wc.hInstance, "hand");
        }
```

## MIN.RC

```
snapshot icon min.ico

hand cursor min.cur
```

## MIN.DEF

```
NAME MIN

EXETYPE WINDOWS

DESCRIPTION 'Min -- Minimum Windows Program'

CODE MOVEABLE DISCARDABLE
DATA MOVEABLE MULTIPLE

HEAPSIZE  512
STACKSIZE 5120
```

If you look closely, you'll see that these source files make use of Borland's command line compiler, BCC.EXE. Borland also provides an integrated development environment called the Programmer's Platform which allows you to edit, compile, and link your source files. Unfortunately, the project files created by this program are binary files and therefore cannot be reprinted in this book. For details on setting up the Programmer's Platform to build Windows programs, refer to Appendix G.

You may be surprised at the size of our minimum program. With about 80 lines of source code, MIN.CPP may be the longest *minimum* program you have ever encountered. The size reflects the amount of work that a program must do to tap into the Windows 3.0 libraries and the OWL class libraries. But once a program has made the necessary connections, Windows and OWL work together to do a substantial amount of work for you.

For example, Windows provides default support for the different parts of our window. Consider the system menu, with its seven commands: *Restore*, *Move*, *Size*, *Minimize*, *Maximize*, *Close*, and *Switch To*. Windows does all the right things to make these commands operational, with only a minimum of effort required of our program. The OWL libraries, in turn, are structured so that the messages generated by these menu selections are delivered to the correct place to make the right things happen.

Each *part* of this minimum program is required to allow the OWL objects to interact properly with Windows. The *structure* of this program is extensible so that, when we create more sophisticated programs later in this book, we can use MIN as the starting point. The structure of this program is important because it embodies the structure of every Windows program built using the OWL libraries.

Because you may be eager to compile and run this program, we'll start by talking about the tools that you'll need to build Windows programs. You are already familiar with some tools, such as the Borland C++ Compiler and the Linker. You'll need to pay special attention to the compiler switches in order to generate Windows-compatible code. As for the linker, it needs a special input file: the **module definition.def file**. Other tools that we'll describe are specific to the Windows development environment, such as the Resource Compiler and the Resource Workshop.

After we describe the development tools, we're going to take a minor detour in the next chapter to talk about some of the conventions that have been adopted for Windows programming. This includes the **Hungarian Naming Convention**, which is used to name data structures and variables. And, we'll introduce the various include files that you'll need to take advantage of the Windows and OWL libraries: WINDOWS.H and OWL.H to name just two. These files contain the required symbolic constants, data structures, function prototypes, and C++ class definitions.

Subsequent chapters will look at the code from our minimum Windows program. We'll start with a look at the application object, as defined by the `TApplication` class. An instance of this class is created in `WinMain`, the function which serves as the entry point for every Windows program. `WinMain` typically creates an application object, and then starts it running in an (almost) endless loop to retrieve hardware-related **messages**. A message is a unit of input to a Windows program, as well as the "time-slice" that makes Windows' nonpreemptive multitasking system work.

In Chapter 5, we're going to review `TWindow` and `TObjectWindow`, the two classes which are the ancestors of MIN's window class object. The three member functions of MIN's window object seem to do very little, and yet they play an important role in every Windows program. We'll look at the way that MIN uses the `TWindow` and `TWindowObject` classes to connect a window to the Windows libraries. In particular, we'll look at the **default window procedure**. This is a Windows library routine which provides the minimum heartbeat required to bring a window to life. We'll also look at the member functions which you'll most likely want to override in order to create interesting and useful Windows programs.

We'll conclude this section of the book with an in-depth look at the different types of messages that you'll encounter in your Windows programming career. As you'll see, about 250 different messages are defined in WINDOWS.H. We create eight categories in our "Taxonomy of Messages."

Let's begin with a look at the development tools that are used to build our minimum Windows program.

## The Mechanics of Compiling and Linking MIN.EXE

When you write Windows programs, you use development tools that you are familiar with from other environments: a language compiler and a linker. Other tools are specific to the Windows environment, like the **Resource Compiler** and the **Resource Workshop**. These tools are used to create user-interface objects and merge them into a program's executable file. Almost every Windows program that you write will require the use of resources. In Chapters 11 and 14, for example, you'll see how resources are used to create menus and dialog boxes. MIN contains just two resources: a cursor and an icon.

➤ *Note to Apple Macintosh Programmers:*

*Windows resources are similar to Macintosh resources. Unlike a Macintosh program, however, a Windows program* cannot *alter the disk-image of its resources. In other words, Windows resources contain* read-only data.

If you're using Borland's integrated development environment, the Programmer's Platform, you won't need to worry about compiler or linker switches. Instead, turn to Appendix G to review the setup of the Programmer's Platform. Otherwise, if you're like us and are addicted to the "old-fashioned" way of using command line entries to build programs, read on. The first tool we're going to discuss is the MAKE utility, which coordinates the operation of the C++ compiler, the linker, and the resource compiler.

## The MAKE Utility

Borland's **MAKE** utility is descended from the Unix utility of the same name. In general, MAKE utilities automate the program creation process to minimize redundant processing: MAKE only compiles or links the program files that have changed. To be this smart, MAKE uses an input file (called a **make file**) that describes the relationship of each program file to the output file. Borland's MAKE also has the ability to determine the dependency relationship between source code files (.CPP) and include files (.H) based on information in the compiled object files (.OBJ). Here is the make file that MIN uses, MAKEFILE.MAK:

## 36  A Minimum Windows Program

```
        .AUTODEPEND

        #    Translator Definitions
        INC=\BORLANDC\OWL\INCLUDE;\BORLANDC\CLASSLIB\INCLUDE;\BORLANDC\INCLUDE
        CC = bcc -c -D_CLASSDLL -H -ml -WS -w -I$(INC)

        #    Implicit Rules
        .c.obj:
          $(CC) {$< }

        .cpp.obj:
          $(CC) {$< }

        #    Explicit Rules
        Min.exe: Min.res Min.def Min.obj
             tlink /c/C/n/P-/Twe/x @Min.LNK
             RC Min.res Min.exe

        #    Individual File Dependencies
        Min.obj: Min.cpp

        Min.res: Min.rc Min.cur Min.ico
             RC -R -FO Min.res -i$(INC) Min.RC
```

A file is referenced in the make file, the linker command line file, MIN.LNK, shown here:

```
        \borlandc\lib\c0wl.obj+
        min.obj
        min,min
        \borlandc\classlib\lib\tclasdll.lib+
        \borlandc\owl\lib\owl.lib+
        mathwl.lib+
        import.lib+
        crtldll.lib
        min.def
```

The **.AUTODEPEND** statement in the make file instructs MAKE to read dependency information written by the compiler into the .OBJ files. This helps ensure that program files are recompiled if any include (.H) files referenced in the program have changed. This minimizes the need for you to watch to make sure that your make file is always correct and up to date.

You might have noticed that certain symbols have a special meaning in the make file. In particular, a pound sign (#) marks the beginning of a comment, which continues until the end of a line. The backslash (\) continues a line (although it doesn't continue a comment).

In general, MAKE determines the rules to follow by reading the make file. Sometimes rules can be expressed as **implicit rules**, such as

```
        .cpp.obj:
          $(CC) {$< }
```

## A Minimum Windows Program

This statement says that files with the extension of .OBJ are dependent on files with the extension of .CPP, provided that the two files share the same name. The command executed is the one stored in the variable **CC**, defined as follows:

```
CC = bcc -c -D_CLASSDLL -H -ml -WS -w -I$(INC)
```

An implicit rule gets called upon when a statement like this is encountered in the make file:

```
Min.obj: Min.cpp
```

Implicit rules are useful, for example, when you have many C++ source files, all compiled using the same command line(s). Sometimes it makes sense to use **explicit rules**. You'd use these for dependency relationships that occur only once in a make file, such as a call to the linker. Here is an explicit rule from our make file:

```
Min.exe: Min.res Min.def Min.obj
    tlink /c/C/n/P-/Twe/x @Min.LNK
    RC Min.res Min.exe
```

If there is a change to any of the three dependent files (MIN.RES, MIN.DEF, or MIN.OBJ), then MIN.EXE is updated by executing the two commands in the second and third lines of this rule. The commands run the linker (TLINK.EXE) and the resource compiler (RC.EXE).

## Compiler Switches

Let's take a close look at the switches we pass to the compiler. The name of the command line compiler we use is BCC.EXE. This compiler uses the DOS Protected Mode Interface (DPMI). DPMI gives programs access to extended memory (the memory above the 1-megabyte boundary on Intel 80286 and later processors). Let's look at the individual compiler switches themselves.

The **-c** switch tells the compiler to compile but not to link. The primary value of this switch is that it allows you to create your program in multiple C source files. But it's also necessary because Windows programs require special instructions to the linker.

The **-D** switch defines a symbol for the compiler's preprocessor. In this case, **-D_CLASSDLL** creates the symbol **_CLASSDLL**. As you probably know, defining a symbol like this lets you write code for conditional compilation. For example, the block of code between the #if and #endif statements is included only if _CLASSDLL is defined:

## 38  A Minimum Windows Program

```
#if defined (_CLASSDLL)
x = 15;
TextOut (hdc, x, y, "Only display if _CLASSDLL is defined", 36);
#endif
```

The _CLASSDLL statement, referenced in the main OWL include file, OWL.H, creates a Windows program which uses the OWL.DLL dynamic link library. (For details on dynamic versus static linking, refer to Chapter 19.)

The **-H** switch tells the compiler to make use of precompiled header (.H) files. This capability helps speed up compilations, particularly when using large include files. A compiler directive,

```
#pragma hdrstop
```

lets you draw a line between unchanging header files and commonly changed header files. All header files before this statement are included in the precompiled header; header files listed after this pragma are recompiled every time you recompile a source file.

The **-ml** switch requests the large **memory model**. A memory model describes the defaults used to address memory. The large memory model means that *far* pointers are generated by default for both code and data. At present, when you create Windows programs that use the OWL dynamic link libraries (OWL.DLL, BCRTL.DLL, and BWCC.DLL), you need to specify the large model.

The documentation describes the **-WS** switch as requesting "smart exports." This refers to the way that *far* functions set up the data segment (DS) register for your code to use. There are many cases in which the Windows libraries call into your code. For example, to support windows and dialog boxes, the Windows libraries are given the address of special call-back functions. When the Windows libraries wish to communicate with your windows or dialog boxes, a call-back function is called. Some mechanism—such as smart exports— is needed to bridge the gap between your code and your data. We'll take a closer look at smart exports in Chapter 19, when we describe the way that Windows' dynamic linking mechanism works.

The **-w** switch enables all warning messages. This helps you write more robust code. Certain warning messages are on by default. This switch enables all other warning messages.

The **-I** switch defines the path to be used to search for include (.H) files. The settings of these switches will depend, of course, on where you've decided to install the compiler and OWL library files. In our case, we use the default installation paths for both the compiler and the OWL class library files.

# The Resource File

MIN.RC lists the resources to be merged into MIN.EXE. To the Windows memory manager, a resource is a read-only data object. By separating a program's read-only data from its read-write data, a Windows program helps the Windows memory manager optimize the way memory is used. Since almost all user-interface objects are stored as resources, every Windows program (knowingly or not) helps optimize memory use. Table 2.2 lists the eight types of predefined resources. For this set, there are Windows functions which create and control these objects. If you use large blocks of read-only data, you can create custom resource types to further optimize memory use.

Resources are normally read into memory when needed, although you can make a resource `PRELOAD` so it will be resident at program startup. When read into memory, a resource usually resides in a `DISCARDABLE` memory block. Such memory can be purged if the Windows memory manager requires it.

**Table 2.2**  Windows' predefined resources

| *Resource Type* | *Covered In Depth* |
| --- | --- |
| Accelerator table | Chapter 11 |
| Bitmaps | |
| Cursors | Chapter 16 |
| Dialog box template | Chapter 14 |
| Fonts | Chapter 10 |
| Icons | |
| Menu template | Chapter 11 |
| String table | Chapter 18 |

Our minimum Windows program has two types of resources: an icon and a cursor. To create your own icons and cursors, use the Whitewater Resource Toolkit or the Borland Resource Workshop. We used the Resource Workshop for our icons and cursors.

Cursors are bitmaps that respond to the movement of the mouse. Cursors allow the user to "point to" different objects on the display screen. For our minimum Windows program, we created a pointer in the image of the human hand. We used **Paintbrush** (bundled with Windows) to create the picture, and then transferred the image to the Resource Workshop via the Windows clipboard.

## 40   *A Minimum Windows Program*

In creating MIN's icon, we took a slightly different approach. Since an icon reminds the user of a program's existence, we created our icon from a snapshot taken of MIN while it was running. We created the snapshot using a built-in capability of Windows. When you strike the [PrtSc] (print screen) key, Windows puts a snapshot of the *entire screen* onto the clipboard. When you strike [Alt] + [PrtSc], Windows limits the snapshot to the currently active window.

We used the [Alt] + [PrtSc] combination to capture a snapshot of MIN.EXE. Then we pasted it into the Resource Workshop. After a bit of cleanup, we had a ready-to-use icon. Next, we saved the icon and cursor to their own files and made entries into MIN.RC, indicating our name for the resource, the resource type, and the resource file name:

```
snapshot icon min.ico
hand cursor min.cur
```

When our program is built, the resource compiler copies each resource into MIN.EXE. This is done so that every Windows program is a stand-alone executable file, with a minimum dependence on external files.

**Hint** The Windows screen-capture capability will be very useful in creating documentation for your Windows programs. In fact, we used this method to create all of the screen shots for this book. We used a monochrome VGA display driver and an HP LaserJet II printer. We then pasted the screen shots into Microsoft Word for Windows, which allowed us to print the final results.

## The Linker

The job of the linker is to build an executable (.EXE) program file from the object (.OBJ) and library (.LIB) files. The command line linker which we use is TLINK.EXE, which is the Borland linker. It is called in MAKEFILE.MAK with the following command line:

```
tlink /c/C/n/P-/Twe/x @Min.LNK
```

The /c switch treats case as significant during the linking process. It seems likely that the Borland linker does not treat case as significant because Borland's flagship product—

*A Minimum Windows Program* 41

a Pascal compiler—doesn't. No problem, since this switch sets things up in the standard C/C++ way.

The `/C` switch treats imported and exported symbols as case sensitive. This is needed because C++ programs generate symbols that are uppercase and lowercase, while the linker itself is not normally case sensitive.

The `/n` switch tells the linker to ignore default linker libraries. Instead, we provide the linker with the names of required libraries.

The `/P-` switch disables code segment packing. By default, the linker combines code segments together. However, as we describe in Chapter 18, you'll want to control the segmentation of your program yourself—hence, we recommend this switch.

The `/Twe` switch tells the linker to create a Windows executable (.EXE) file. This switch is needed since the linker can also create Windows DLLs and DOS executable files.

The `/x` switch prevents the linker from creating a map file. A map file lists all the symbols in your program, and can be a useful reference for how a program actually uses memory. For now, though, we use this switch to save disk space and forego access to our map file.

The linker command line file, MIN.LNK, references the following files:

| | |
|---|---|
| C0WL.LIB | This contains the startup and termination code for a large-model Windows program. It performs some initialization and calls WinMain. After a program terminates, code from this object file performs cleanup. |
| TCLASDLL.LIB | Import library which notifies the linker about functions in TCLASS31.DLL, the Borland C++ container class dynamic link library (DLL). |
| OWL.LIB | Import library for OWL.DLL, the Object Windows Library DLL. |
| MATHWL.LIB | Static link library containing the Windows compatible large-model Borland math library. |
| IMPORT.LIB | Import library for the Windows 3.0 system dynamic link libraries (KERNEL.EXE, USER.EXE, and GDI.EXE). |
| CRTLDLL.LIB | C-runtime library. This file contains static link records as well as import library records for BC30RTL.DLL, a dynamic link library which contains the dynamically linkable C-runtime library routines. |

## The Linker and the Module Definition File

In addition to the .OBJ and .LIB files, the linker gets input from a **module definition file** (.DEF) when creating Windows programs. The role of a module definition file is to describe the structure and organization of a program. You can think of the .DEF file as a set of linker switches. Let's review each statement in our module definition file, MIN.DEF.

The first line in MIN.DEF is

```
NAME MIN
```

In Windows, all code and data are organized into **modules**. There are two types of modules: **executable programs** and **dynamic link libraries**. The `NAME` keyword designates a module as an executable program. (For a dynamic link library, use the `LIBRARY` keyword instead.) The module name is placed after the `NAME` (or `LIBRARY`) keyword. Our program's module name is MIN. Although previous versions of Windows used the module name to differentiate one module from another, in Windows 3.0 the file name has priority in how Windows distinguishes one module from another.

This statement tells the linker to create a Windows program:

```
EXETYPE WINDOWS
```

This statement is optional, since the `/Twe` switch already tells the linker to create a Windows program. Nevertheless, we like to use this switch in preparation for a future version of the linker which may create OS/2 programs. At that time, we'll substitute `OS2` for `WINDOWS`.

The `DESCRIPTION` statement inserts text into an executable file:

```
DESCRIPTION 'Min -- Minimum Windows Program.'
```

Usually, this is used for a program's copyright notice or for version information. To see the description of a Windows program (or dynamic link library), run the EXEHDR.EXE utility.

The `CODE` statement sets the default memory disposition for code segments in a Windows program:

```
CODE MOVEABLE DISCARDABLE
```

As we will discuss in Chapter 18, the use of the `SEGMENTS` statement allows you to specify the memory disposition for individual code segments. For now, the CODE statement by itself will work fine. MOVEABLE (versus FIXED) allows a segment to be relocated. The DISCARDABLE declaration means that, when memory is low, the code segment can be purged from system memory. The dynamic link mechanism allows code to be moved around in memory, as well as removed from memory, in a manner that is completely transparent to your program.

The DATA statement is similar to the CODE statement, except that it sets the memory disposition of a program's data segment:

```
DATA MOVEABLE MULTIPLE
```

MOVEABLE allows the data segment to move in memory. (When a message is delivered to a program, the data segment is locked in place to avoid unexpected results. This is only a concern in Real Mode Windows, but since the Borland compiler only creates protected mode applications, this isn't a concern for you.) The MULTIPLE declaration is the standard for Windows programs. It allows several copies of a single program to run at the same time.

STACKSIZE sets the size of a program's stack:

```
STACKSIZE 5000
```

The stack has three uses: storing of local variables, passing parameters to called functions, and saving return addresses to allow "anonymous calling." Windows programs must have a minimum stack size of 5K. (If a smaller amount is specified, the Windows loader automatically allocates a 5K stack.) Of this, 2K is meant for your program's use. The other 3K is for Windows' use. When a program calls a Windows library routine, the arguments to the routine are passed on the program's stack. Use a higher value for programs with a lot of local variables or for recursive operations.

The HEAPSIZE statement sets the initial size of a program's local heap. Our minimum program uses the following value:

```
HEAPSIZE 512
```

The local heap is one of two places from which dynamic memory allocation can occur. (The other place is the system's global heap.) The local heap is private to a program, and resides in the program's data segment. Figure 2.3 shows the layout of a program's data segment. The HEAPSIZE statement sets the initial size of the local heap. A heap can grow beyond its initial size, limited only by the restriction that a segment cannot be larger than 64K.

## 44  A Minimum Windows Program

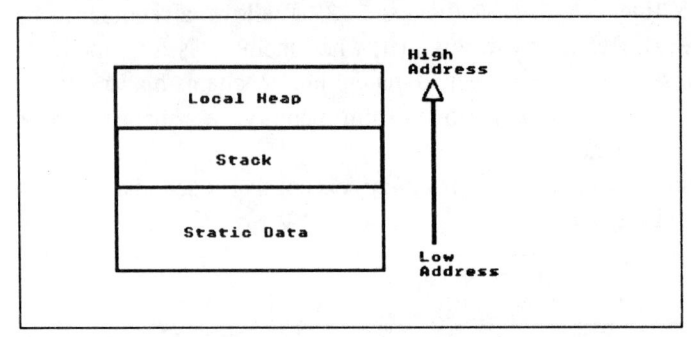

```
                  High
                  Address
   Local Heap       △
                    |
   Stack            |
                    |
   Static Data      |
                  Low
                  Address
```

**Figure 2.3  The layout of a program's data segment**

At this point, you have enough information to type in and create a minimum Windows program. We suggest you pause now and do so. It will give you an opportunity to check that your development environment is properly set up. It will also give you the chance to become familiar with this program before we delve into its inner workings.

In the next chapter, we're going to address some of the coding conventions of the Windows programming world, and the conventions used in the OWL class libraries.

# 3

# Windows and OWL Programming Conventions

Of all the things for a programmer to be concerned with, you'd probably put the creation of variable names near the bottom of the list. And yet, creating variable names is a task that every programmer must perform. We're going to introduce you to **Hungarian Naming**, a practice that permeates Windows programs. If you're like us, you may be puzzled by your first encounter with Hungarian. But over time, we have become so convinced of its value that we're going to talk about it first.

After we've covered the issues relating to Hungarian Naming, we'll talk about the various include files that your programs will need. You may have already noticed that one of the first lines in our Windows program is

```
#include <owl.h>
```

This include file brings in most of the needed OWL library files, and also WINDOWS. H.

WINDOWS.H is a very large—150K—data file which describes all the elements you'll need to connect to Windows. If you're like us, you might want to print out this important file and thumb through it. It contains the bare-bones definition of the Windows API as your program will see it.

We'll discuss **handles**, a data type you will encounter often in your Windows programming career. Handles have been referred to as "magic numbers," "magic cookies," and "claim check numbers." Whichever term you prefer, handles identify objects created by one part of the system or another. A handle is a number, but the meaning of the number is only known to the part of the system that created the object and issued the handle.

Finally, we'll touch on an issue that will concern you when you look at older Windows code: **casting**. While it used to be required in the earliest days of Windows programming, developments in language compilers have made this an obsolete practice. In fact, as we'll explain, the use of casts can be downright dangerous and can introduce hard-to-find errors into your code.

Let's get started with a look at Hungarian Naming.

## Hungarian Naming

Hungarian Naming is a convention for creating names of variables and functions. It is widely used by Windows programmers because it makes code easier to read and easier to maintain. Hungarian Naming, or Hungarian for short, gets its name from the nationality of the original developer, Charles Simonyi. The name is also a tongue-in-cheek description for the convention because programmers often find Hungarian to be initially confusing. Simonyi developed this naming convention as part of his doctoral dissertation on programmer productivity. It became widely used at Xerox PARC, where Simonyi was working when he developed this practice. It was adopted at Microsoft after Simonyi began working there, and has since become a standard of sorts among Windows programmers.

Creating *useful* variable names can be a real challenge. Should they be short and sweet? Short variable names are easy to type, but they can make your code hard to understand. You know what we mean if you've tried reading BASIC programs with very short variable names. What can you tell about the variables A and B in these lines of BASIC code?

```
20    LET B=10
30    FOR A=1 to 10
40    LET B=B+A
50    NEXT A
```

If short names are cryptic, perhaps we can create useful variable names by making them long and descriptive. Is there any doubt about how a variable called `loopindex` is used? And yet, this approach can lead to variable names that are long and unwieldy. Consider the names in this list:

```
countofcharacters
numberoffiles
temporaryfilename
windowhandle
pointertoarrayofcharacters
```

While such names may make code more readable, they put a burden on the programmer who has to type them. The use of long names also increases the chance that one will be mistyped.

## Windows and OWL Programming Conventions 47

Hungarian takes a middle road between these two extremes. In Hungarian, variable names are created by putting a short prefix in front of a longer, more descriptive name. The prefix describes the *type of data* referenced by the variable. In some cases, a prefix also describes the *way a variable is used*. For convenience, a prefix can be used alone as a variable name.

Here are some examples of Hungarian:

```
char       ch;
char       achFile[128];
char far * lpszName;
int        cbName;
```

Note that prefixes are lowercase, and long names combine uppercase and lowercase. The first variable, **ch**, is the prefix for character data. It is an example of a prefix used as a variable name. The prefix for **achFile** has two parts: a means this is an array, and ch tells us the type of data in the array, characters. The prefix for **lpszFirstName** also has two parts: lp means long pointer, and sz describes the data pointed to, a null-terminated string. The variable **cbName** contains the prefix cb to tell us that the variable contains a count of bytes.

Understanding Hungarian helps us read and understand these otherwise convoluted lines of code:

```
LPSTR      lpszName;
LPSTR      lpsz;
int        cbName;

for (lpsz = lpszName, cbName=0;
     lpsz != '\0';
     lpsz++, cbName++);
```

The prefix cb tells us that the variable **cbName** *must* contain a count of bytes. Since that's the case, it is pretty clear that the purpose of this code is to calculate the number of characters in the null-terminated string referenced by the pointer **lpszName**. Incidentally, the use of a Hungarian prefix by itself is quite common for "temporary" variables, which is what **lpsz** is used for.

In addition to helping you read code, Hungarian helps you avoid silly (but very common) programming errors. As you become familiar with Hungarian, you will come to recognize that

```
lpszName = achFile;
```

is a valid statement, while the following is not:

```
lpszName = cbName;
```

## 48  A Minimum Windows Program

After all, it makes sense to assign the address of an array to a pointer. But it does not make sense to assign a count of bytes to a pointer.

The trick to learning Hungarian is to learn the prefixes. Here is a list of the more common prefixes used in Windows programming:

| Prefix | Data Type |
| --- | --- |
| a    | Array (compound type) |
| ch   | Character |
| cb   | Count of bytes |
| dw   | Unsigned long, (WINDOWS.H typedef: DWORD) |
| h    | Handle—16-bit identifier |
| hdc  | Handle to a device context |
| hwnd | Handle to a window |
| i    | Index (compound) |
| l    | Long integer, (WINDOWS.H typedef: LONG) |
| lp   | Long (or far) pointer (compound type) |
| n    | Integer |
| np   | Near (or short) pointer (compound type) |
| pt   | An *x,y* point (WINDOWS.H typedef: POINT) |
| r    | A Rectangle structure (WINDOWS.H typedef: RECT) |
| sz   | Null-terminated string |
| w    | Unsigned integer, (WINDOWS.H typedef: WORD) |

Notice that some of these prefixes are "compound types." This means they are used as prefixes to other prefixes. The following code fragment shows how two compound prefixes, `a` and `i`, define variables that can be used together:

```
    char    ch;
    int     ich;           /* Index a character array. */
    char    achName[64];   /* Character array. */
    ...
    ch = achName[ich];
```

It is worth noting that there is no "official" list of prefixes. Since any given programming project is bound to have its own unique data types, prefixes can be created to reflect those types. In general, however, the usefulness of Hungarian comes from having a relatively small number of types and from agreement by the members of a development team on the meaning of each type.

Hungarian is also used for function names. There are several "dialects" that we have encountered. One use combines a verb and a noun to describe a function. For example, three Windows library routines are **CreateWindow**, **DrawText**, and **LoadIcon**. Within the Windows libraries, you can see other dialects: Some library routines consist of a noun by itself, such as `DialogBox`. For routines that convert from one type to another, the form XtoY is common. For example, the Windows library routine `DPtoLP` converts device points into logical points.

A special routine encountered in OWL programs is the message handler. Windows sends messages to your program when an event of interest occurs. For example, the `WM_PAINT` message tells you to repaint a window. A `WM_LBUTTONDOWN` message lets you know that the left mouse button has been pushed. All messages get sent to a window procedure. OWL sends these messages on to message handlers which you have defined. The name of a message handler is derived from the name of the message. For example, a `WMPaint` member function handles a `WM_PAINT` message, and a `WMLButtonDown` member function handles a `WM_LBUTTONDOWN` message.

If you choose to adopt Hungarian naming, it will help you write code that is easier to read and easier to maintain. Even if you don't adopt this convention, a familiarity with Hungarian will help you read sample code from this book and from other sources. It will also help you read and make sense of definitions that you encounter in the Windows include file, WINDOWS.H.

## OWL Naming Conventions

Borland's OWL libraries roughly follow Hungarian naming, with a few variations. The variations are mostly due to the fact that these libraries were ported to C++ from Pascal, so they have a Pascal flavor. Although this difference can sometimes be confusing, we find it helps distinguish the OWL parts of a program from the strictly Windows parts of a program.

The OWL libraries use an uppercase prefix to identify a class name: T, which stands for "type." Here are some of the classes defined in OWL:

`TApplication`
`TControl`
`TDialog`
`TWindow`
`TWindowsObject`

We'll use this convention in all our sample programs. For example, MIN contains two class definitions: `TMinApplication` and `TMinWindow`.

OWL class member functions follow the Hungarian convention of mixing uppercase and lowercase letters. You'll notice, however, that OWL strays from strict Hungarian in names given to class data members. Throughout this book, we've adopted Hungarian for class data members, since it helps distinguish OWL data members from our own. We suggest you do the same.

## Handles

A handle is an identifier. Handles are 16-bit unsigned integers. In the same way that MS-DOS issues file handles when a file is opened, Windows issues handles to identify objects. Keep in mind that the only use of a handle is as an identifier. It is just a number that has no meaning outside the context for which it was issued. You cannot, for example, cast a handle to a pointer and do any useful work with it. Quite a few Windows library routines return handles. When such routines fail, they return a "null handle" (that is, `handle == NULL`).

▼ **Warning!** Be careful—while a NULL value indicates an invalid handle from Windows, an invalid *file* handle has a value of −1. This is because file handles are issued by MS-DOS and not by Windows.

The two most important types of handles to a Windows programmer are **window handles** and **device context handles**.

A window handle identifies a window. Each window in the system has a unique handle. All window manipulation routines use a window handle as a parameter. Once you have a window's handle, you can move it, size it, make it invisible, and in general do anything you want with it.

Device context handles are used for controlling graphics output. All GDI drawing routines take a handle to a device context as the first parameter. When you wish to use the GDI graphics library to draw in a window or send output to a printer, you must first get a handle to a device context for the desired device.

Handles are used to identify other objects as well. User-interface objects have handles: menus, icons, and cursors. Drawing objects are identified by handles: pens, brushes, fonts, regions, and bitmaps. Even memory that is dynamically allocated is identified using a handle.

Let's take a look at the include file which every OWL program will reference: OWL.H.

## The OWL Include Files

A single include file, OWL.H, brings together the include files for basic OWL functionality. If you look at the file, you'll notice that it starts with two lines that may at first seem confusing:

```
#ifndef __OWL_H
#define __OWL_H
```

And then at the end of this file, the following statement can be found:

```
#endif
```

These statements help ensure that an include file is only used once. Otherwise, the compiler gets cranky and complains. You'll find statements like these in all of the OWL include files. You'll probably want to include these types of definitions in all your include files as well, since they eliminate the need to worry about avoiding redundant include statements.

Here is a list of the include files that OWL.H references (both directly and indirectly):

| Include File | Description |
| --- | --- |
| Applicat.H | Defines **TApplication**, the OWL application class. Also contains the prototype to **WinMain**, the entry point for every Windows application. |
| Dialog.H | Defines **TDialog**, OWL's dialog box class. |
| MDI.H | Defines the Multiple Document Interface (MDI) support classes, **TMDIClient**, **TMDIWindow**. |
| Module.H | Defines **TModule**, OWL's base module class and the parent of **TApplication**. |
| Object.H | Defines the abstract base class Object for the OWL libraries. Object is the root of the class hierarchy. |
| OwlDefs.H | Defines various symbolic constants for use by the OWL class libraries. |
| WindObj.H | Defines the **TWindowsObject** class, OWL's base window class and a parent of **TWindow** and **TDialog**. |
| Window.H | Defines **TWindow**, which can be subclassed to create an application's main window class. |
| Windows.H | The Windows library include file. This file (described later) contains the type definitions, symbolic constants, and data structure definitions needed to connect a program to the Windows APmI. |

In other chapters, we'll take a closer look at the classes defined in the OWL include files. For now, we're going to investigate the contents of the include file which describes the Windows API, WINDOWS.H.

## The Windows Include File

While C and C++ language libraries come with many small include files (STDIO.H, STRING.H, etc.), the Windows libraries come with a single, large (120K) include file: WINDOWS.H. This file needs to be referenced—directly or indirectly—by every source file that accesses the Windows API because of the definitions it contains. There are three basic types of definitions in WINDOWS.H: symbolic constants, data types, and library function prototypes. Let's take a moment to look at each of these in some detail.

### *Symbolic Constants*

In general, it's a bad practice to place "magic numbers" like 15 and 400 into a program. It makes your code hard to read. You should use symbolic constants instead. By convention, symbolic constants are written in uppercase to distinguish them from variable names. In C, the **#define** preprocessor statement creates symbolic constants:

```
#define MAXOPENFILES 15
```

Because WINDOWS.H is used for both C and C++ programs, only **define** statements are used instead of C++'s more advanced **const** statement.

In either language, symbolic constants improve the readability of a program and make program maintenance easier. Instead of hunting through a mountain of source code when numeric values change, only the single line of code that defines the value must be updated.

There are about 1,500 symbolic constants in WINDOWS.H. To help you sort them out, Hungarian Naming is used. For example, the symbols for window messages start with the prefix WM_ (as in **WM_CREATE** and **WM_DESTROY**). If a constant is only used with a single library function, the Hungarian prefix is derived from the function name. For example, you can only use the **CW_USEDEFAULT** constant with the **CreateWindow** function.

### *Data Type Definitions*

Quite a few data types are defined in WINDOWS.H. Some of them are little more than a convenient way to refer to commonly used C types. For example, the following statement appears in WINDOWS.H:

```
typedef char far * LPSTR;
```

This definition makes it easy to define a far pointer to a character string, since

```
LPSTR lpszName;
```

is equivalent to

```
char far * lpszName;
```

Here is a list of commonly used data types:

| WINDOWS.H Name | C Definition |
| --- | --- |
| BOOL | int |
| BYTE | unsigned char |
| DWORD | unsigned long |
| HANDLE | unsigned int |
| HDC | unsigned int |
| HWND | unsigned int |
| LONG | long |
| LPSTR | char far * |
| NPSTR | char near * |
| WORD | unsigned int |

Three types are defined as *unsigned int*: **HANDLE**, **HDC**, and **HWND**. Each defines a **handle**. Earlier in this chapter, we introduced handles as the method for identifying objects in Windows. The use of handles allows the complexity of an object to be hidden from your program. (In other words, Windows has data encapsulation!) Objects and object handles are very important to Windows programmers. When your program creates a window, for example, a handle is issued to identify the window: the HWND data type.

Although it may be tempting to use the "raw" data types, you'll want to stick with the uppercase WINDOWS.H types as much as possible. The reason is that it will help make your Windows program portable in the event that the Windows API is ported to another processor platform. If and when that happens, you can expect that Borland will most likely port the OWL libraries, so that your programs can be up and running quickly wherever Windows and OWL wander.

In addition to simple data types, WINDOWS.H holds a number of structure definitions. You might imagine that a rectangle structure would be useful in an environment that creates rectangular windows. You'd be right. Here is the rectangle data structure from WINDOWS.H:

```
typedef struct tagRECT
  {
```

## 54 A Minimum Windows Program

```
    int     left;
    int     top;
    int     right;
    int     bottom;
} RECT;
```

Since Windows allows the user to select objects with a mouse pointer, you might expect to find a data structure to record the location of the mouse pointer. Again, you'd be right on target. Here's the POINT data structure:

```
typedef struct tagPOINT
    {
    int     y;
    int     y;
    } POINT;
```

## *Function Prototypes*

An important feature of C++ is the ability to create **function prototypes**. Prototypes provide a means by which the compiler can perform some critical error checking for you. A function prototype tells the compiler how a routine should be called. Consider this prototype from WINDOWS.H:

```
BOOL    FAR PASCAL TextOut(HDC, int, int, LPSTR, int);
```

This declaration tells the compiler that the routine *must* be called with five parameters. A compiler error is generated if the function is called with too few (or too many) parameters. If you think about it, this capability alone makes the use of prototypes a recommended practice. How many times have you written a function, later added a parameter to the function definition, and then forgotten to change a line of code that calls the function? By doing so, you introduced a bug into your program. (Of course, this type of bug waits to appear until you demo your work to your boss...) A prototype lets the compiler complain about this type of problem so that you can find and correct it early.

A prototype tells the compiler about the expected *type* of each argument. When a type mismatch is encountered, a compiler error is generated. Consider this call to TextOut. It is clear that the fourth parameter is incorrect:

```
TextOut (hDC, 10, 20, 30, 2);
```

*Windows and OWL Programming Conventions* 55

Based on the prototype from WINDOWS.H, the fourth parameter should be a far pointer to a character string (`char far *`). When the compiler encounters the value of 30, it complains because the type is incorrect. Correcting this particular problem might require us to place quotes around the number, as in

```
TextOut (hDC, 10, 20, "30", 2);
```

Using prototypes, a C or C++ compiler can also check for the correct use of a function's return value. That is, it checks for type-mismatch errors. The prototype for **TextOut**, for example, defines the return value as **BOOL** in WINDOWS.H. This code causes the C compiler to complain:

```
char far * lpch;
lpch = TextOut (hDC, 10, 10, "Hello", 5);
```

Every Windows function has a prototype in WINDOWS.H, so that the C compiler can check your calls. Prototyping is useful for Windows library functions. Fortunately, it is also a requirement of any C++ code you write. Sometimes, developers combine C and C++ code. This is especially true when there is a large body of C code that is already in place. If you find yourself mixing C and C++ code, we recommend that you create prototypes for your C code, even if the compiler doesn't require it. This will save you a lot of grief.

The availability of function prototypes has made one practice obsolete: casting. And yet, a lot of code was written before function prototypes were available. For this reason, you need to be on the lookout for older Windows programs that may reflect an overuse of explicit casting.

## An Outdated Practice: Casting

One of the best ways to learn any new programming environment is to look at someone else's code. You need to be careful, though, not to be misled by an outdated practice that you might come across in some older Windows programming: **casting of pointers**. This is outdated because newer compilers support function prototypes, which allow the compiler to automatically generate the correct code.

A moment ago, we looked at the function prototype for the `TextOut` function:

```
BOOL FAR PASCAL TextOut(HDC, int, int, LPSTR, int);
```

## 56  A Minimum Windows Program

The earliest Windows programmers had to write code like the following:

```
TextOut (hDC, 10, 10, (LPSTR)"Hello World", 12);
```

Notice the cast to **LPSTR**. This forces the creation of a *far pointer*. It used to be that, in a small-model or medium-model program, the expression "`Hello World`" would cause a near pointer to be generated. But the function requires a far pointer, so a cast was required.

At first glance, this casting seems harmless enough. The only problem seems to be that a lot of extra keystrokes are wasted. However, there is a real danger to casting. If you were to follow the old-fashioned practice of casting every pointer, you might hide certain problems that the compiler would otherwise detect for you. Consider the following line of code:

```
TextOut (hDC, 10, 10, (LPSTR)30, 2);
```

Perhaps the programmer had meant to use the string 30 as the fourth parameter. Without the cast, the compiler notifies us of the type-mismatch error. But a cast forces the value to the correct type, hiding the error from the compiler. The cast tells the compiler, in effect, "I know what I'm doing. Please don't ask any questions."

The message should be clear: Avoid casting. It negates the compiler's automatic checking, and can hide problems from you.

This is not to say that casts are never needed. For example, they are often needed when working with Windows' dynamic memory allocation routines. These routines are prototyped to return character pointers. If you assign the return value to any other type, the compiler complains. The **GlobalLock** routine, for example, is defined as returning a LPSTR (char far *):

```
LPSTR  FAR PASCAL GlobalLock(HANDLE);
```

The following lines of code cause the compiler to complain:

```
int far * lpint;   /* Define an integer pointer. */
lpint = GlobalLock(hMem);   /* Compiler whines. */
```

The second line of code would be required if we had stored an array of integers in the block of memory referenced by the handle **hMem**. Even though the compiler complains, this line of code creates a correct result. However, it's a good practice to reserve compiler complaints for things that really matter. The cast in the following line of code produces the same result, except that the compiler is now happy that there is no type-mismatch error:

```
lpint = (LPINT)GlobalLock(hMem);
```

(Of course, you'll use `LPINT` instead of `int far *`, because it helps make your code more portable.)

So you see, there are times when casting is necessary. In general, however, the compiler will let you know when the time is right. The rule still stands: Avoid casting. Then, when the compiler complains, you can look at the offending code and determine whether or not a cast will fix your problem.

# Messages

Before you started writing object-oriented C++ code, you probably were used to a sequential, procedure-driven manner of coding. Windows borrows heavily from the world of object-oriented programming. However, you should take care not to be confused by the term "message." In the context of a C++ program, it really means "a call to an object's member function." In the context of Windows programming, it refers to something a little different.

Windows messages are generated in response to some change in the user interface, such as a window getting moved or the user striking a key on the keyboard. Messages are used to notify a program that a timer has gone off. Messages are also used for data sharing operations, which means the clipboard and the Dynamic Data Exchange (DDE).

From a programming point of view, a message is a 16-bit unsigned value that, for ease of reading, is given a parameter name that starts with `WM_`, like `WM_LBUTTONDOWN`. The `WM_LBUTTONDOWN` message means that the left button on the mouse has been pushed down. Another message will get sent when the left mouse button is released: `WM_LBUTTONUP`.

As you might guess, Windows messages are very important to a Windows programmer. Most of a Windows programmer's work involves deciding which messages to process and which messages to ignore. As with C++ messages, there is no predefined order to Windows messages.

To a certain extent, this is simply an implementation issue. Conceptually, a C++ message and a Windows message are the same. The only difference is that each C++ function handles one and only one message. On the other hand, a single function in a Windows program—known as a window procedure—handles all the messages sent to one type of window. When you start to work with a C++ class library, you learn about the public functions (messages) in the different classes. In the same way, learning to work with Windows' windows, you need to learn about the public messages that you'll get sent. To help you get started, we've included a "Taxonomy of Messages" at the end of Chapter 5 and also in Appendix A.

## 58  *A Minimum Windows Program*

Now that we've reviewed some of the basic conventions of Windows and C++ programming, it's time to take a closer look at MIN's source code. We're going to start by looking at all the parts which make up MIN's application object class, `TMinApplication`, including two classes defined by OWL: `TModule` and `TApplication`.

# 4

# The Application Object

You may have noticed that MIN has two object classes: **TMinApplication** and **TMinWindow**. In this chapter, we're going to focus our attention on **TMinApplication**, MIN's application object. In the next chapter, we'll explore the details of MIN's window object class, **TMinWindow**.

To get to the heart of **TMinApplication**, we're going to explore the role of two classes on which MIN's application class is based: **TApplication**, and its base class, **TModule**. In general, these two classes take care of application startup and termination. They also provide member functions that redirect Windows' message flow in a standard way. Figure 4.1 shows the place of **TMinApplication** in the class hierarchy.

Every Windows application—whether it is written in C++, C, Pascal, or assembler—has an application entry point named **WinMain**. Since this is the place where a typical OWL program creates its application object, we're going to start by looking at some of the things that **WinMain** shows us about Windows applications.

## WinMain Procedure Declaration

WinMain takes four parameters, defined as

```
int PASCAL WinMain (HINSTANCE hInstance,
                    HINSTANCE hPrevInstance,
                    LPSTR lpszCmdLine,
                    int   nCmdShow)
```

## 60 A Minimum Windows Program

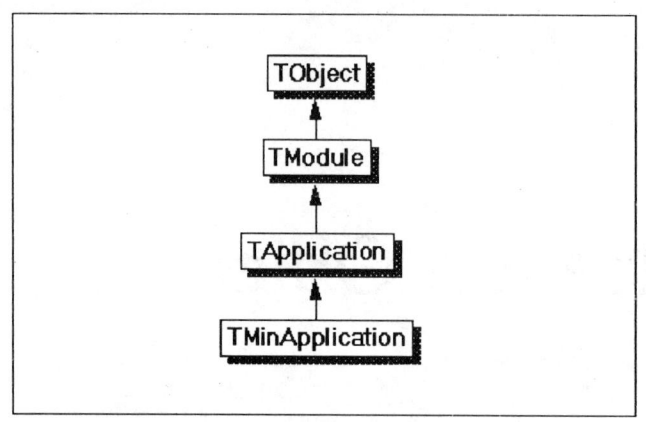

**Figure 4.1** MIN's application object hierarchy

When a program starts running, Windows gives it information about who it is and who it is related to. The **hInstance** parameter says who a program is. Think of it, if you'd like, as a program's name. Windows gives each program in the system a unique name. Of course, the name is not "Joe" or "Fred," but a 16-bit unsigned integer (the type for which HINSTANCE is defined in WINDOWS.H).

Windows tells a program its name because certain Windows library routines require this as a parameter. This allows Windows to know "who is calling." Although MIN's application object doesn't use this parameter, the **TWindow** member functions use **hInstance** to create our program's main window. It is also used by member functions that MIN subclasses to retrieve MIN's icon and cursor:

```
wc.hIcon=LoadIcon (wc.hInstance, "snapshot");
wc.hCursor=LoadCursor (wc.hInstance, "hand");
```

The second parameter, **hPrevInstance**, tells a program who it is related to. If it isn't related to any currently running program, the value of **hPrevInstance** is **NULL**. How does Windows decide if two programs are related? By name. In the same way that two people with the same last name are (often) related, two programs are related if either (1) the file names are the same, or (2) the **module names** are the same. Recall that MIN's module definition file, MIN.DEF, contains the following entry:

```
NAME MIN
```

When a user selects a program to run, Windows first looks at the file name to see if it matches the name of a currently running program. Then, it checks whether the module name—hidden in the executable file—matches the name of any currently running program. If a match is found for either, Windows starts up a second instance of the currently running program. It lets the program know that it has a relative already present by passing the name of the relative in the **hPrevInstance** parameter.

## The Application Object

Figure 4.2 shows four instances of MIN, three instances of CLOCK, two instances of REVERSI, and a single instance of PAINTBRUSH with a drawing of a partridge in a pear tree. When each subsequent instance of each program starts running, `hPrevInstance` has the name of the previous family member.

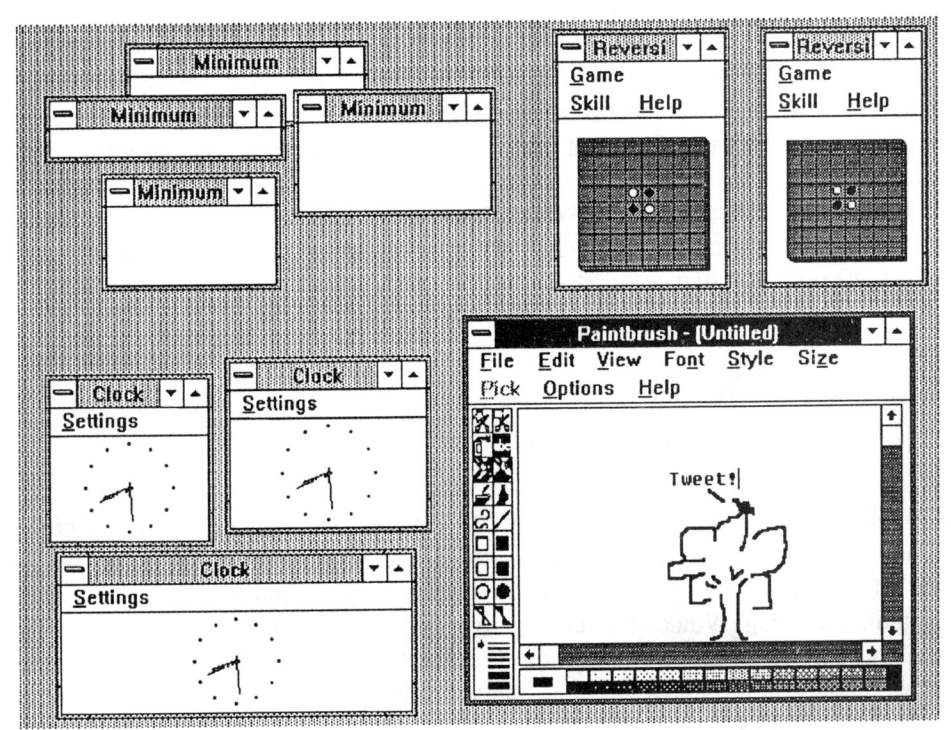

**Figure 4.2** Four instances of MIN, three of CLOCK, two of REVERSI, and one of Paintbrush

Why does a program want to know if it has relatives in town? One thing you should know about instances is that, like real-life relations, they share a lot of things. For example, to conserve memory, all instances of a program share code and resources. The only thing that is not shared, in fact, is the instance's data. The reason a Windows program is notified about its relatives is so that it can call them (that is, send them messages) to share even more things! Of course, you don't have to share. But if you want to share with your cousin Jim, you've got his number.

The third parameter to `WinMain`, `lpszCmdLine`, gives us the command line arguments for our program. There are a number of ways that command line arguments get created. The simplest involves putting the arguments after the program name in the Properties dialog box of the Program Manager. Like the `argv` parameter in the usual C or C++ program entry point

## 62  A Minimum Windows Program

```
main (int argc, char **argv)
```

the `lpszCmdLine` parameter allows a program to read its command line for arguments like file names, option switches, etc. Unlike `argv`, however, `lpszCmdLine` points to a single character string and not to an array of character pointers.

The final parameter, `nCmdShow`, tells a program what to do with its main window when it first starts. Should it be minimized? Should it be displayed full screen? When we talk about the `TWindow` and `TWindowObject` classes in the next chapter, you'll see that this parameter is passed by an application's main window object to Windows' `ShowWindow` library routine.

With an understanding of the four WinMain parameters under our belt, we're ready to look at the guts of the two objects on which our application object is built: `TModule` and `TApplication`. Let's start with `TModule`.

## The TModule Class

Since Windows is a multitasking system, there can be several programs in the system at the same time—MIN, CLOCK, REVERSI, and PAINTBRUSH in our earlier example. From OWL's point of view, each program is a module. There are other modules present in the system, including Windows' three main dynamic link libraries KERNEL.EXE, USER.EXE, and GDI.EXE, and the OWL dynamic link library, OWL.DLL. Still other modules include the device-driver dynamic link libraries: DISPLAY.DRV, MOUSE.DRV, KEYBOARD.DRV, etc.

Windows knows about two types of modules: application programs and dynamic link libraries (DLLs). The `TModule` class reflects the way the OWL class library represents a Windows module. When creating either type of module with OWL, you start by creating a `TModule` Object. Let's take a closer look at the `TModule` class. As defined in MODULE.H, here are `TModule`'s data members:

| Type | Name | Description |
|---|---|---|
| HINSTANCE | hInstance | A copy of the `WinMain` parameter for the application instance handle. |
| LPSTR | lpCmdLine | A copy of the `WinMain` parameter for the application command line string. |
| int | Status | Error flag. |
| LPSTR | Name | Application name. |

To access any of these data items, you first must get a pointer to your application object (which, after all, is a descendent of the `Module` class). You can do this by calling `GetApplicationObject()`. For example, here is how to retrieve the instance handle:

```
HINSTANCE hInstance;
PTApplication ptApplication;

ptApplication = GetApplicationObject();
hInstance = ptApplication->hInstance;
```

You'll want to retrieve a copy of **hInstance** to access resources, or to create user-interface objects which are stored as resources—menus, dialog boxes, cursors, icons, etc.

The **lpCmdLine** data member is a copy of the third parameter passed to **WinMain**.

**Status** is used by the application object to store error conditions that may occur during initialization, and for an application's return code when it terminates.

The **Name** data member holds a pointer to an ASCII text string that our program provided to the application object's constructor. Since this is available to every part of our application, this field provides a convenient string that can be used in message boxes and dialog boxes. Reusing a single copy of the application's name minimizes the memory overhead for strings in an OWL program.

**TModule** has 15 member functions. A complete discussion is beyond the scope of this book, since they serve mainly to support the inner workings of a module object.

| Function Name | Description |
| --- | --- |
| `TModule()` | `TModule` constructor. |
| `~TModule()` | `TModule` destructor. |
| `Error()` | Error reporting function. |
| `ExecDialog()` | Creates a modal dialog box, with error handling. |
| `GetClientHandle()` | Part of OWL's MDI support. Returns the window handle of an MDI client window. |
| `GetParentObject()` | Returns a pointer to an OWL window object from a Windows window handle. If not available, it creates one. |
| `hashValue()` | Object class virtual function to determine class hash value. |
| `isA()` | Object class virtual functions to determine an object's class. |
| `isEqual()` | Object class virtual function to test whether two references point to the same object. |
| `LowMemory()` | Checks whether memory safety pool has been tapped. |
| `MakeWindow()` | Creates a window or a modeless dialog box. |
| `nameOf()` | Object class virtual function to determine ASCII text class name. |

64 *A Minimum Windows Program*

| | |
|---|---|
| `printOn()` | Object class virtual function to display object information for debugging purposes. |
| `RestoreMemory()` | Increases the size of the heap. |
| `ValidWindow()` | Validates a pointer to a window object. |

The `MakeWindow` routine provides OWL's primary mechanism for creating Windows windows. We'll discuss this member function more completely in the next chapter when we look at the way the `TWindow` class operates. `MakeWindow` also creates modeless dialog boxes. A related function is `ExecDialog`, which creates modal dialog boxes. You'll hear more about both dialog box creating functions in Chapter 14.

Most of the interesting application-level activity is performed by a class that is derived from `TModule`, namely the `TApplication` class. We're going to explore this class next.

## The TApplication Class

OWL's `TApplication` class is the immediate parent class for MIN's Application Object class. `TApplication` handles the things a typical Windows application does: It initializes, creates a main window, and queries the system for messages. Let's take a close look at `TApplication` to help you see the work it—along with the Windows library functions—does for you.

`TApplication`'s data members, as defined in APPLICAT.H, are as follows:

| Type | Name | Description |
|---|---|---|
| HINSTANCE | `hPrevInstance` | A copy of the `WinMain` parameter for the previous instance handle. |
| int | `nCmdShow` | A copy of the `WinMain` parameter which describes how our application's main window should open. Passed to Windows' `ShowWindow` routine. |
| PTWindowsObject | `MainWindow` | A pointer to the OWL window object which is the application's main window. |
| HANDLE | `HAccTable` | Accelerator table handle, if application has one. |
| PTWindowsObject | `KBHandlerWnd` | Points to the `TWindowsObject` which is to receive keyboard input. |

*The Application Object* 65

The first two items in this list, **hPrevInstance** and **nCmdShow**, are copies of the second and fourth parameters passed to `WinMain`. An application typically uses these two parameters at startup time, and then never again.

The **MainWindow** data member is a pointer to a window object. From a Windows programming point of view, this makes sense because just about every Windows program has a single "main" window. The user expects an application to terminate when its main window is closed. This **TApplication** data member helps ensure that OWL programs behave this way.

The **HAccTable** data member is for an accelerator table handle. An **accelerator table** contains keyboard commands. For example, an accelerator table entry can convert a [Shift] + [Ins] key combination into an **Edit.Paste** command, for use with the clipboard. When we discuss accelerator tables more fully in Chapter 11, you'll see how the **TApplication** parent class simplifies accelerator support.

The **KBHandlerWnd** data member points to the **active** OWL window object. The active window is the one currently being worked with by the user. It might be a modeless dialog box, an application's main window, or an MDI frame window. A window lets the user know it is active by changing the color of its caption or its border. The OWL library uses this data member to support keyboard input. For example, using the [Tab] key, a user can move between child windows inside the currently active window.

Here are **TApplication**'s member functions:

| Function Name | Description |
| --- | --- |
| PUBLIC: | |
| **TApplication()** | TApplication constructor. |
| **~TApplication()** | TApplication destructor. |
| **CanClose()** | Query whether application can close. This unifies a query that requires a typical Windows program to monitor *two* Windows messages: WM_CLOSE and WM_QUERYENDSESSION. The application object queries the application's main window, which in turn queries each of its children to ensure—among other things—that no user data gets lost. |
| **isA()** | Object class virtual function to determine an object's class. |
| **nameOf()** | Object class virtual function to determine ASCII text class name. |
| **Run()** | Application's main function, which causes application object to do all of the initialization and processing required to run as a Windows program. |
| **SetKBHandler()** | Determines the window object which will handle keyboard input. |

## 66  *A Minimum Windows Program*

| | |
|---|---|
| PROTECTED: | |
| `IdleAction()` | Message loop subfunction for background processing. |
| `InitApplication()` | Initialization routine for an application's first instance. |
| `InitInstance()` | Initialization routine for every application instance. |
| `InitMainWindow()` | Initialization routine for the application's main window. |
| `MessageLoop()` | Application message loop. |
| `ProcessAccels()` | Message loop subfunction to handle keyboard accelerators. |
| `ProcessAppMsg()` | Message loop subfunction to handle application-specific tasks. |
| `ProcessDlgMsg()` | Message loop subfunction to handle modeless dialog box keyboard input. |
| `ProcessMDIAccels()` | Message loop subfunction to handle keyboard input for multiple document interface windows. |

**TApplication**'s work is strung together by a single member function: **TApplication::Run**, defined as

```
    void TApplication::Run()
    {
     if ( !hPrevInstance )
      InitApplication();
     if (Status == 0 )
      InitInstance();
     if (Status == 0)
      MessageLoop();
     else
      Error(Status);
    }
```

In its brevity, **Run** shows the four main parts required to run a Windows application:

1. Perform application-level initialization—that is, initialize for the first instance of MIN.
2. Perform instance-level initialization—that is, do whatever is going to be done for every instance of MIN.
3. Enter a tight message loop to poll for user input. Once initialization is finished, the program will spend the rest of its life in the message loop.
4. In case of initialization error, terminate.

Of these four member functions, the second and third are the most interesting, and we're going to explore them more fully. The first function, `InitApplication()`, is an empty placeholder which you can define to hold first instance initialization code. The last function, `Error()`, puts up a message box with the indicated error code, then terminates. This works well during the development of an OWL program, but you'll probably want to embed more sophisticated error handling in any software you distribute.

Figure 4.3 shows the hierarchy of functions called by `TApplication::InitInstance`. This diagram will help you sort out what is actually happening, since calls are made up and down the object hierarchy—and even to an object in another object class hierarchy (a `TWindow`/`TWindowsObject` object). In this diagram, the call to a Windows library function is shown as a member function to an imaginary class, `Win3`.

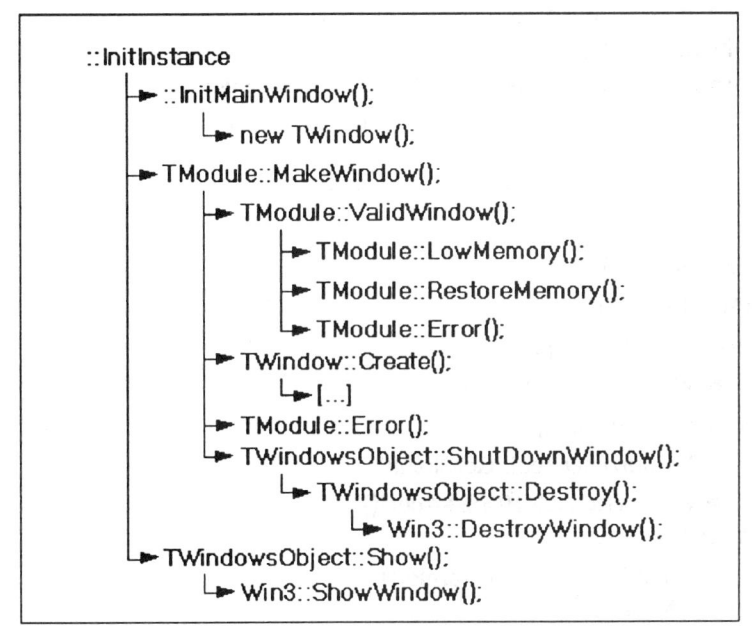

```
::InitInstance
    ::InitMainWindow();
        new TWindow();
    TModule::MakeWindow();
        TModule::ValidWindow();
            TModule::LowMemory();
            TModule::RestoreMemory();
            TModule::Error();
        TWindow::Create();
            [...]
        TModule::Error();
        TWindowsObject::ShutDownWindow();
            TWindowsObject::Destroy();
                Win3::DestroyWindow();
    TWindowsObject::Show();
        Win3::ShowWindow();
```

**Figure 4.3** Application object initialization performed by `TApplication::InitInstance`

`InitInstance` starts by calling `InitMainWindow`. Most OWL applications override this member function, since by default it creates an empty `TWindow` object. To bring life to your application, you'll define a class as a descendent of `TWindow`. That's the role of the `TMinWindow` class in MIN. MIN then creates an instance of this new window object in its `InitMainWindow` function:

```
void TMinApplication::InitMainWindow ()
  {
  MainWindow = new TMinWindow (NULL, "Minimum", NULL);
  }
```

Once the OWL window object has been constructed, the `TModule::MakeWindow` member function creates a Windows window. This module member function acts like a

## 68  A Minimum Windows Program

switchboard operator, calling between the various window object member functions and the Windows libraries. Along the way, it performs some basic error handling to make sure there is enough memory, and that a window gets created properly. The window object's `Create` member function does the actual window creation.

Once a window object and a window have been created, the final step in the initialization process is to make the window visible. That's the role of the `TWindowsObject::Show()` member function. As indicated in the diagram, it calls a Windows library routine, `ShowWindow`, passing it the `nCmdShow` parameter from our program's `WinMain` function. This allows MIN's main window to be opened properly, whether that be minimized, maximized, or as a normal open window.

Figure 4.4 shows the hierarchy of functions called by our application object's message processing routine, `TApplication::MessageLoop`. Once again, the Windows library routines are represented as belonging to the imaginary `Win3` object class.

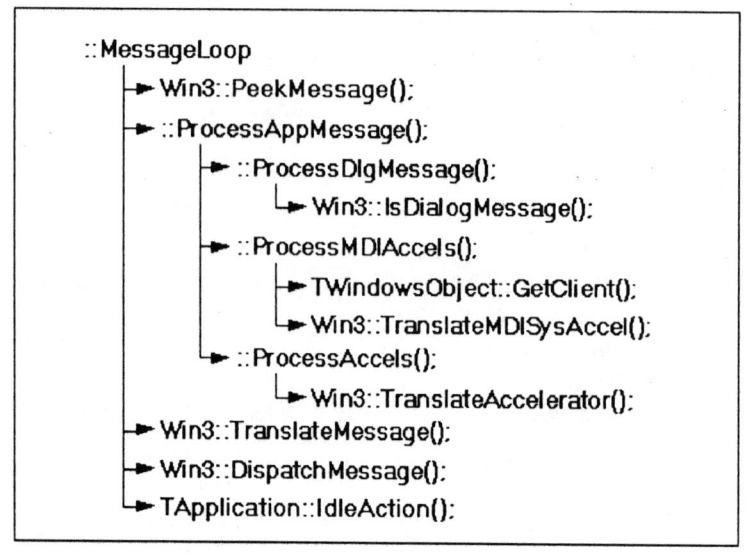

```
::MessageLoop
    ├─ Win3::PeekMessage();
    ├─ ::ProcessAppMessage();
    │      ├─ ::ProcessDlgMessage();
    │      │      └─ Win3::IsDialogMessage();
    │      ├─ ::ProcessMDIAccels();
    │      │      ├─ TWindowsObject::GetClient();
    │      │      └─ Win3::TranslateMDISysAccel();
    │      └─ ::ProcessAccels();
    │             └─ Win3::TranslateAccelerator();
    ├─ Win3::TranslateMessage();
    ├─ Win3::DispatchMessage();
    └─ TApplication::IdleAction();
```

Figure 4.4  Application object message loop in `TApplication::MessageLoop`

Once inside its message loop, a Windows program continually reads messages and sends them to the correct place. A message loop typically doesn't pay much attention to the content of the message, but instead leaves message processing to each window object. The exception to this rule occurs with three types of user-interface objects: modeless dialog boxes, MDI windows, and keyboard accelerators. These are represented by TApplication's three message loop subfunctions: `ProcessDlgMessage`, `ProcessMDISysAccels`, and `ProcessAccels`. We'll take a closer look at the

`ProcessDlgMessage` subfunction in Chapter 14 when we talk about modeless dialog boxes. We'll look at keyboard accelerator processing in Chapter 11.

Before we look at the ins and outs of message passing as it relates to the rest of `MessageLoop`, we're going to pause for a moment to look at the ways that MIN uses the `TApplication` class to create its own application object.

## MIN's TMinApplication Class

Life in a Windows program starts in the **WinMain** function. Most OWL programs will have a **WinMain** function that looks like MIN's:

```
int PASCAL WinMain (HINSTANCE hInstance,  HINSTANCE hPrevInstance,
              LPSTR lpszCmdLine, int   nCmdShow)
  {
  TMinApplication Min ("MIN", hInstance, hPrevInstance,
                  lpszCmdLine, nCmdShow);
  Min.Run();
  return Min.Status;
  }
```

An application object is created and run.

MIN uses the **TApplication** class as a base for its **TMinApplication** class. This class has two member functions: a constructor and a function to override a function in its parent class:

```
class TMinApplication : public TApplication
  {
  public:
   TMinApplication(LPSTR AName);
   virtual void InitMainWindow();
  };
```

The constructor function, **TMinApplication**, doesn't do anything. It's a placeholder for programs that use MIN as a starting point.

Almost every OWL program will override **InitMainWindow**. MIN's version looks like this:

```
void TMinApplication::InitMainWindow()
   {
   MainWindow = new TMinWindow (NULL, "Minimum");
   }
```

It creates a window object. If we didn't override **InitMainWindow**, the original version would create a **TWindow** object. Such a window would be empty, although it would function properly: Its system menu would work, as would its sizeable border, and its minimize and maximize buttons.

As MIN's application object creates itself, it creates a window object, displays the window, and enters a message loop. When the initialization is complete, the primary job of the application object is to keep messages flowing between the user and the window object.

Let's take a closer look at the messages which serve as the lifeblood of every Windows program. As we do, we're going to delve into a topic that may seem at first to be strangely out of place: Windows' multitasking capability. The two topics are related, however, because this capability is tightly interwoven into the fabric of the message delivery mechanism. Let's begin our study of messages, then, with a look at the relationship between messages and multitasking.

## Messages: Input Mechanism and Multitasking Time-Slice

In Chapter 1, we introduced the idea that Windows is a multitasking operating system. Unlike other multitasking systems, however, it does not interrupt one program to allow another to run. An interrupt-based approach to multitasking is sometimes called **preemptive multitasking**. Windows, on the other hand, is a **nonpreemptive** system. This means that programs are not interrupted by the operating system, but interrupt themselves to allow other programs to run. How can such a cooperative system be made to work?

Windows' multitasking switcher is embedded into Windows' message delivery system. Windows programs rely on messages to receive input from the user and from user-interface objects. Some messages are hardware related, and tell a program that the user has pointed with the mouse or typed a keystroke. Other messages come from user-interface objects like windows, menus, and scroll bars. To access the flow of messages, a program calls the message delivery system. It gets one message per call. If a program has no more messages, the message delivery system will start delivering messages to a program that *does* have messages to be delivered.

From this discussion, it is clear that a message serves a larger purpose than its namesake in the real world; that is, it does more than just communicate something. To a Windows program, messages are the unit of processing. They have the effect of creating time-slices during which a program runs. To get a clearer understanding about the dual role that messages play, let's take a closer look at the message delivery system.

A Windows program receives messages in two ways. The first way is by reading message buffers. Windows doesn't allow us direct access to its internal buffers, but rather reads a buffer for us when our program calls one of two Windows library routines:

`GetMessage` or `PeekMessage`. (There are subtle differences between these two functions, but for purposes of this discussion assume they behave the same.) As you'll recall, this second function is called in `TApplication`'s `MessageLoop` member function.

Two system buffers get read: the hardware event queue and the application message queue. The **hardware event queue** holds system-wide mouse and keyboard events. The **application message queue** holds application-specific messages. Each program has a message queue. In fact, every *instance* of every program has a message queue. If it finds a message for a program, `GetMessage` pulls the message into the program.

If `GetMessage` doesn't find messages for a program, it puts the program to sleep. At such times, the Window switcher takes over and transfers control to another program that does have messages waiting for it. The `GetMessage` routine, then, serves to make Windows' message-driven multitasking system work.

The second way a program receives messages is by a direct call to one of its window procedures. In C++ terms, a window procedure is a member function for every message sent to a class of windows. A window procedure is called as if it were a subroutine of Windows itself. In fact, you can think of a window procedure as an installable extension to Windows. Messages delivered by this mechanism don't wait in a message queue, but are processed immediately when a call is made.

Let's pause a moment and consider the implications of these two approaches. The first method, in which `GetMessage` (or `PeekMessage`) reads message buffers for us, is called **pull-model processing**. The name describes the active role our program plays in pulling a message from a buffer. The second method is called **push-model processing**. The name describes the passive role our program plays in waiting to be called and letting Windows *push* a message into our window procedure.

It may strike you as odd that Windows has *two* mechanisms for delivering messages. After all, other systems have been written that are strictly pull-model (the Apple Macintosh) or push-model (like the Xerox Star). Why two mechanisms? A little bit of history may make this clear.

Before Microsoft started shipping Windows in November 1985, it spent two years building the system. The earliest internal versions of Windows (1983–1984) were entirely push-model. In those days, a Windows program was just a subroutine package. For each window class, 10 member functions were defined, one for each of 10 different types of user-interface events. For example, one routine was called when a window was created, another to deliver mouse and keyboard input, and still another to draw in a window.

Things worked well, with the exception of mouse and keyboard input. The Microsoft engineers had trouble incorporating interrupt-driven hardware into push-model processing. After all, push-model processing does its work in a very orderly, synchronized manner. Interrupt-driven hardware, on the other hand, is quite chaotic. Depending on whether the user is typing at 60 words per minute, punching the function keys, or torturing the mouse, input arrives in a random order and at unpredictable times.

In a purely push-model system, each application requires time-critical interrupt handling code. Otherwise, if an application took too long processing a mouse or keyboard event, other mouse or keyboard events could be lost. Or, they might interrupt the application with a new hardware event before the previous hardware event has been handled. In either case, mouse and keyboard events aren't handled properly. The solution? Windows uses both push-model processing and pull-model processing.

The advantage of push-model processing is that it allows user-interface objects that are part of the operating system to directly interact with application programs. Can you think of a more direct way to be connected to an operating system than to be a *subroutine* to the operating system?

With pull-model processing, on the other hand, the unpredictable hardware events get stored in a system buffer. Incidentally, Windows' pull-model processing allows the creation of **modal loops**, during which time a program can filter out messages it doesn't want to handle. A simple example of a modal loop occurs in non-Windows programs when a message like the following is displayed:

```
Strike Any Key When Ready...
```

and all processing is suspended until the user types on the keyboard.

Used together, pull-model and push-model processing create a unique, hybrid system in Windows. Let's get back to the source code from the `TApplication` message loop to understand the implementation details of this hybrid approach.

## The Standard Message Loop

Every Windows program has a message loop allowing it to poll for messages. In this way, a program stays in touch with the supply of messages so vital to its proper operation. This is what a standard message loop in a Windows program looks like:

```
while (GetMessage(&msg, 0, 0, 0))
        {
        TranslateMessage(&msg);    /* Keyboard input.   */
        DispatchMessage(&msg);
        }
```

This loop runs during the life of the program. Each iteration represents the receipt of a single message from a message buffer. Except for the **WM_QUIT** message, each message causes **GetMessage** to return a value of **TRUE**. On receipt of **WM_QUIT**, a program drops out of its message loop and terminates. When we discuss MIN's window object in Chapter 5, you'll see how code in the `TWindowsObject` class sends a **WM_QUIT** message when the application's main window is destroyed. Without this message, a program won't terminate properly and the memory it occupies will be lost forever.

Let's look at each routine in this tiny message loop. A moment ago, we introduced the idea that **GetMessage** pulls messages into our program from system buffers—the hardware event queue and an application message queue. We can request **GetMessage** to filter messages by providing filter information in the second, third, and fourth parameters. Since we're interested in *all* messages, however, filtering is disabled by setting these to zero.

The most interesting parameter to us is the first parameter, a pointer to a structure that **GetMessage** fills with message data. Notice that a pointer to this structure is the sole parameter to the other routines in our message loop.

The **TApplication**'s member function, **MessageLoop()**, defines a local variable to hold message data as follows:

```
MSG Message;
```

For the definition of **MSG**, we can look in WINDOWS.H; and we find the following:

```
typedef struct tagMSG
  {
  HWND hwnd;
  UINT message;
  WPARAM wParam;
  LPARAM lParam;
  DWORD time;
  POINT pt;
  } MSG;
```

Let's look at each of the six elements in this structure:

- **hwnd**, an unsigned integer, contains a window handle. Every window in the system is given a unique handle. Like the instance handle we describe earlier, the window handle is simply a name given a window. The reason a window handle is associated with a message is that every message is directed at one window or another.

- **message**, another unsigned integer, contains the *type* of message, encoded as a 16-bit value. Starting on page 93, we'll take a look at all the different types of messages in Windows.

- **wParam** and **lParam** contain message data. The meaning depends on the type of message. For example, the menu command message uses wParam to identify the menu item that has been selected. Mouse messages pack the location of the mouse pointer into lParam. As far as the way these values are defined, wParam is an unsigned integer and lParam is an unsigned long. This gives us six bytes of data for each message.

- The last two items, `time` and `pt`, are rarely used by Windows programs. Both describe the state of the system when the message was put into the message queue: `time` holds the time, and `pt` holds the location of the mouse pointer.

`TranslateMessage` is the second function called in a typical message loop. This routine calls on the Windows keyboard driver to convert raw keystroke messages (`WM_KEYDOWN`) into cooked ASCII values, which are placed in the application message queue as `WM_CHAR` messages. This makes it easy for our program to tell the difference between "A" and "a" without having to get involved with the state of the shift key.

`TranslateMessage` also provides support for international keyboards. A British shopkeeper, for example, would probably use the £ symbol to quote you the special price of £35. If the shopkeeper used a Windows word processor to send you a note with this information, the word processor would call `TranslateMessage` to convert the keystroke to the proper symbol. As part of this translation process, `TranslateMessage` makes diacritics available; it allows Windows programs to display French words like *Voilà*, Spanish phrases like "*Hablo español*," and German city names like *München*.

The final routine in this loop, `DispatchMessage`, takes message data from the `MSG` structure and uses it to call the correct window procedure. It *pushes* the message into the window procedure for processing.

You might wonder whether you could speed things up by calling a window procedure directly rather than by calling `DispatchMessage`. The answer is, No. Windows must make all calls to our window procedure.

The reason has to do with the way data is addressed. A Windows program usually has its own data segment. The dynamic link library that controls the Windows user interface, USER, also has its own data segment. When USER calls a window procedure, it places the window procedure's data segment identifier into a special place: the AX register of the CPU.

The compiler generates the following code at the beginning of our window procedures:

```
PUSH DS         ; Save USER's data segment value
MOV DS, AX      ; Install our data segment value
```

At the very end of the window procedure, right before we return, we restore the USER module's data segment by saying

```
POP DS          ; Restore USER's data segment
```

For a Windows program to directly call into a window procedure, it would have to set up the AX register with the proper data segment value. Otherwise, the window procedure would not be able to access its data.

# The OWL Message Loop

We first showed you the standard message loop because you'll see it in other Windows programs. But that's not the message loop that OWL uses. The reason is that OWL gives you a framework to build more complex applications. Here is the `MessageLoop()` member function from the `TApplication` class:

```
void TApplication::MessageLoop()
{
 MSG Message;

 while ( TRUE )
 {
   if ( PeekMessage(&Message, 0, 0, 0, PM_REMOVE) )
   {
     if ( Message.message == WM_QUIT )
      break;
     if ( !ProcessAppMsg(&Message) )
     {
      TranslateMessage(&Message);
      DispatchMessage(&Message);
     }
   }
   else   // No message waiting.
     IdleAction();
 }
 Status = Message.wParam;
}
```

While this looks quite a bit more involved than the standard message loop, many of the components are the same. Messages are retrieved with a call to `PeekMessage`, keyboard support is provided by `TranslateMessage`, and messages are sent to the proper window procedure by `DispatchMessage`. As we mentioned earlier, `ProcessAppMsg` provides support for modeless dialog boxes, accelerators, and MDI windows.

Where this loop differs is in the call to `IdleAction`. This virtual member function of the base `TApplication` class is a placeholder. You can override this function and steal background processing cycles from the system. As we mentioned earlier, Windows is a nonpreemptive multitasking system. Therefore, you aren't (presently) able to create a background thread to do background work. But when an application retrieves messages with `PeekMessage`, it gets treated specially. In particular, when all message queues are empty, this function returns a value of `FALSE`. Windows programs which need to perform background processing often use a message loop like that shown in the accompanying code fragment. Notice that OWL's message loop requires special processing for the `WM_QUIT` message, since `PeekMessage` doesn't respond to this message in the same way that `GetMessage` does.

To do your own idle processing, start by defining an `IdleAction` routine. Within this routine, you can recalculate a spreadsheet, poll a device, paginate a document, or do whatever can be done without direct user interaction. Since scheduling is nonpreemptive, make sure you don't take too much time in this routine. Instead, break your background processing into small, manageable chunks. Of course, not every Windows program requires background processing. You can just as easily ignore this capability and create programs that get time-slices from regular messages.

At this point, our walk through MIN's application object is complete. Along the way, we have explored some of the fundamentals of the Windows architecture. But our journey is not over yet. We still have one more object to explore: our program's window object. This is the subject of our next chapter.

# 5

# OWL's Window Object Classes

In addition to application objects, OWL programs need window objects. OWL supports window objects through extensible classes that simplify interaction with the MS-Windows libraries. This chapter explores OWL's window object classes, while at the same time describing the way that our minimum OWL program, MIN, makes use of these classes.

OWL provides two window classes: **TWindow** and its parent, **TWindowsObject**. These classes handle the creation, destruction, and maintenance of windows. Much of your OWL development will involve building on the foundation provided by these two base classes. Figure 5.1 shows the place of MIN's window object class, **TMinWindow**, in the class hierarchy.

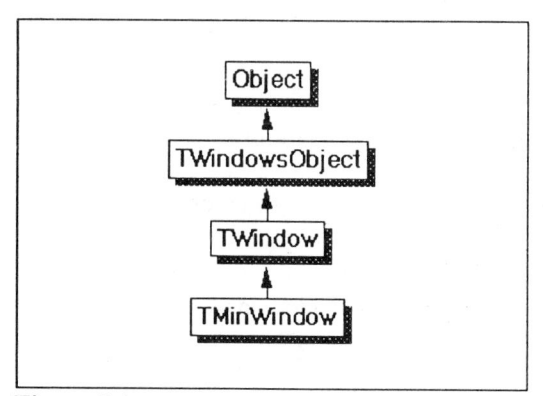

**Figure 5.1** MIN's window object hierarchy

OWL's base window objects contain a function that the Windows libraries call: a **window procedure**. Windows uses window procedures to communicate with you about your windows. OWL simplifies the communication process by allowing you to define a set of class member functions to handle incoming **messages**. Instead of having a single function do all the work, multiple message functions divide among themselves the tasks of supporting a window. It's like having a team of telephone operators to answer a large number of incoming lines. One operator could do the job, but by specializing on a subset of the total problem, each does a better job.

OWL hides the window procedure from you, and instead lets you create **message response functions**. With one per message, the task of writing code becomes easier. In hiding this complexity from you, however, OWL hides part of what makes Windows work. For this reason, we're going to dig a little deeper into Windows than you probably need to go. The added understanding should make it easier for you to push OWL and Windows to their limits.

Let's start, then, with a look at the `TWindowsObject` class.

## The TWindowsObject Class

Windows has two basic types of top-level windows: normal application windows and dialog boxes. The primary difference between these two is that dialog boxes are created from a dialog box template. Dialog box templates are static definitions created at program creation time and stored as a resource. Dialogs are created using OWL's `TDialog` class. You'll learn about `TDialog` in Chapter 14, when we discuss dialog boxes. A normal application window, like the one MIN uses, is created as a descendent of OWL's `TWindow` class. Both classes share a common base class: `TWindowsObject`.

Let's take a look at the data members and member functions which are defined in `TWindowsObject`. The data members are as follows:

| Type | Name | Description |
| --- | --- | --- |
| PUBLIC: | | |
| `HWND` | `HWindow` | Handle to associated Windows window. |
| `PTWindowsObject` | `Parent` | Points to parent window object—a main window has no parent. |
| `int` | `Status` | Error flag. |
| `LPSTR` | `Title` | Copy of the caption text. |
| PROTECTED: | | |
| `FARPROC` | `DefaultProc` | The window object's default message handler, which is called |

| | | |
|---|---|---|
| | | for all Windows messages not otherwise handled. |
| `Pvoid` | `TransferBuffer` | Points to a buffer for transferring dialog box data. |
| PRIVATE: | | |
| `PTApplication` | `Application` | Points to the `TApplication` object which created this window. |
| `PTWindowsObject` | `ChildList` | Points to a child window object which is at the head of the child list—MIN's main window has no children. |
| `WORD` | `CreateOrder` | For child windows, an integer describing the order of the window in the sibling list. |
| `WORD` | `Flags` | Window attribute flag, describing features such as auto-creation of children (for dialog boxes), whether the window is an MDI window, whether there is data to be transferred (for dialog boxes), and whether keyboard handling should be enabled/disabled. |
| `FARPROC` | `Instance` | Pointer to the window object instance block, which is part of the dynamic message dispatch mechanism (not to be confused with the `hInstance` parameter passed to `WinMain`). For more details, see Chapter 19. |
| `PTModule` | `Module` | Pointer to a module object. |
| `PTWindowsObject` | `SiblingList` | Pointer to the next sibling window (where sibling windows have a common parent window). |

`TWindowsObject` contains 84 member functions: 51 are public, 25 are protected, and 8 are private. Rather than list every member function, we're going to give you two short lists. One list contains commonly called member functions. The second gives the commonly overridden member functions. For more details, consult the OWL documentation. Or, you can refer to the "ultimate documentation," the OWL source code files.

80   *Borland C++ Programming for Windows*

**Commonly Called Member Functions:**

| *Function Name* | *Description* |
|---|---|
| `TWindowsObject()` | Constructor. |
| `~TWindowsObject()` | Destructor. |
| `CloseWindow()` | Closes a w.ndow, after first calling the `CanClose` member function to ensure that closing is allowed. |
| `GetApplication()` | Retrieves a pointer to the application object associated with a window object. |
| `GetModule()` | Returns a pointer to the module object. |
| `SetCaption()` | Puts new text into a window's caption. |
| `SetTransferBuffer()` | Provides a pointer to a buffer for use in transferring data between windows. |
| `Transfer()` | Transfers data to or from a window, such as a dialog box. |
| `TransferData()` | Sets the direction flag for the `Transfer` member function. |

**Commonly Overridden Member Functions:**

| *Function Name* | *Description* |
|---|---|
| `CanClose()` | Asks whether a window can close or not. Two Windows messages, `WM_CLOSE` and `WM_QUERYENDSESSION`, can cause a window to close. But sometimes it's not convenient to close—for example, if the data contained in the window hasn't been saved. By overriding this member function, a window object can make sure it can check with the user anytime there is potential risk of data loss. |
| `DefChildProc()` | Default message handler for child windows' `WM_COMMAND` notification messages. |
| `DefCommandProc()` | Performs default handling of the `WM_COMMAND` message. |
| `DefWndProc()` | Default message handler for a window. Default value is the Windows routine `DefWindowProc`. If you override this function, be sure to call `DefWindowProc` with your unwanted messages. |
| `Destroy()` | Destroys a window object and its associated Windows user-interface object. When overridding, be sure to call the overridden function *last* so it will accomplish the required cleanup. |

| | |
|---|---|
| `GetClassName()` | Use to provide unique names for your application's Windows window classes. *Never* call the overridden function. |
| `GetWindowClass()` | Override to modify a value in the `WNDCLASS` data structure for the Windows window class. Call the overridden function *first*, to initialize class data. |

In addition to these member functions, the `TWindowsObject` class supports a special type of member function called a **message response function**. This refers to a function which handles a single type of message. For example, you might have a message response function for the `WM_PAINT` message, another for the `WM_LBUTTONDOWN` message, and still a third for `WM_KEYDOWN`. Message response functions are built using a feature of the Borland's C++ compiler called **dynamic dispatch virtual tables** (DDVTs). These tables are arrays containing pairs of function index and function address values.

Dispatching Windows messages via a DDVT is quite fast. In particular, it's faster than the large `switch` statements typical of a Windows program written in C. A tiny assembly language routine scans the table of indices, dispatching to the correct message handler when it finds a match. If you're curious about the DDVT mechanism, look at the source code to the dispatch mechanism in DD.ASM.

To define a message response function, you provide an index number to the class definition. For example, here's how the PIXEL program from Chapter 7 defines the message response function for the `WM_PAINT` message:

```
class TPixelWindow : public TWindow
  {
  public:
...
    virtual void  WMPaint(TMessage& Msg) = [WM_FIRST + WM_PAINT];
  };
```

Since the value of `WM_FIRST` is zero, the same results are obtained from this definition:

```
    virtual void  WMPaint(TMessage& Msg) = [WM_PAINT];
```

As this code shows, PIXEL's window class, **TPixelWindow**, is not built directly on **TWindowsObject** but on **TWindow**, a descendent of **TWindowsObject**. But the principle is the same for both classes.

Message response functions can be used in other ways as well. For example, they can simplify the handing of menu and accelerator command (`WM_COMMAND`) messages. In particular, instead of having one member function for every menu and accelerator command, you can create one response function per command. OWL defines a symbolic constant, `CM_FIRST`, that you can use as the starting value for a range of `WM_COMMAND` function indices. We'll cover that in more detail in Chapter 11, when we discuss menus.

When a message response function hasn't been created for a specific message, the **TWindowsObject** class passes the message to a default handler. The class comes with its own default message handler, **DefWndProc()**. But, as with other class member functions, you can override this function to watch the flow of unprocessed messages through a window. Of course, you'll still want to send most messages to the overridden function. In turn, it will call the Windows default handler, **DefWindowProc()**, which gives every window in the system a similar "look and feel."

As we mentioned earlier, **TWindowsObject** is a base class for OWL's dialog box class, **TDialog**, as well as the normal application window class, **TWindow**. Dialogs differ from normal application windows in a number of ways. For one thing, dialogs are ordinarily created from preexisting window classes, and involve a single popup window containing a group of child windows. A dialog is ordinarily created from a resource definition. Dialogs come in two flavors: modal and modeless. A modal dialog disables input to its parent, while a modeless dialog allows its parent to continue normal operation. And finally, since a dialog box provides the user with access to application data, some mechanism is needed to initialize data values at dialog startup time, and to collect the results after the user has dismissed a dialog.

An application's window, on the other hand, is usually built from an application-specific window class. Its life is not so brief as a dialog, but rather it stays around for as long as the user wants access to the application. Application windows are never defined from resource definitions, but rather are created from scratch by the applications which need them. Although an application window can have child windows, they must be created from scratch rather than from any predefined resource definition.

We'll cover **TDialog** in Chapter 14 when we delve into the workings of OWL and Windows dialog box support. Right now, we're going to continue exploring MIN by examining the **TWindow** class.

## The TWindow Class

Since **TWindow** is derived from the **TWindowsObject** class, it inherits a number of data members and member functions. In addition, **TWindow** handles some of the things that every Windows application needs to do for a window: registration of an MS-Windows window class, scrolling, repainting, moving, and changing size. **TWindow** also taps into the Multiple Document Interface (MDI) support of Windows. As you build your own window objects, your goal will be to make these base classes work hard for you. Let's look at **TWindow**'s data members:

| Type | Name | Description |
|---|---|---|
| PUBLIC: | | |
| **TWindowAttr** | **Attr** | Contains window creation parameters to be passed to Windows' **CreateWindowEx** call: Style, ExStyle, X, Y, W, H, Menu, Id, and Param. |
| **PTScroller** | **Scroller** | Points to a scroller object. |
| **HANDLE** | **FocusChildHandle** | Stores the handle of the window which has the keyboard focus. This is the child window to whom all keyboard messages are sent. |

**TWindow** has a modest number of member functions, 26 in all: 10 public, 15 protected, and 1 private member function. While most of your work with a window will involve creating message response functions, here are some of the commonly called and commonly overridden member functions:

**Commonly Called Member Functions:**

| Function Name | Description |
|---|---|
| **TWindow()** | Constructor. |
| **~TWindow()** | Destructor. |
| **AssignMenu()** | Replaces the existing menu with a new menu. Two versions of this routine exist: one for menu resources with ASCII text names, and one for menu resources with numeric resource IDs. |

**Commonly Overridden Member Functions:**

| Function Name | Description |
|---|---|
| **Create()** | Creates an MS-Windows window, registering a window class if necessary. This function can create MDI document windows, as well as MDI frame windows. **TModule::MakeWindow** calls this function for you, and so you should never call **Create** directly yourself. If you override this function, be sure to call the original since it does a lot of work for you. |
| **GetClassName()** | Use to provide a unique name for your application's Windows window class. If you override, don't call the overridden function. |
| **GetWindowClass()** | Override to modify a value in the **WNDCLASS** data structure for the Windows window class. Call the overridden function *first*, since it fills in this structure with the required default values. |

To make our discussion of OWL's predefined window classes come alive, you have to look inside a program that uses them. For that reason, we're going to discuss how our minimum OWL program, MIN, uses these classes in its own window class.

## MIN's TMinWindow Class

Just about every OWL program that you create will contain at least one class derived from **TWindow**. MIN defines its **TMinWindow** class, with just a few changes from the solid foundation that OWL lays. Here is MIN's class declaration:

```
    class TMinWindow : public TWindow
  {
  public:
    TMinWindow (PTWindowsObject pwParent, LPSTR lpszTitle,
                PTModule pmModule);
    virtual LPSTR GetClassName ();
    virtual void  GetWindowClass (WNDCLASS&);
  };
```

That's it: a constructor and two functions which override the parent class. In fact, it's even simpler since the constructor is empty. We've included it because MIN is intended as a template for the more involved programs which will come later.

The other two class functions, **GetClassName** and **GetWindowClass**, play a part in providing MIN with a private window class complete with an icon and a cursor. Various parts of OWL call these functions to do what's needed to create an MS-Windows window for us. To help you understand exactly what's involved, let's dig deeper into the window creation process.

## Window Creation in MS-Windows

Creating a window using the native MS-Windows functions is a two- or three-step process. First, a window class is defined. Next, a window is created. Finally, the window is made visible.

A window class is somewhat like a C++ class. Code and data values are combined to define a class. The class serves as a template for the creation of actual objects. But the similarities end rather quickly since C++ classes are extensible and reusable in ways that window classes are not. Also, C++ classes provide more capability in terms of encapsulation, polymorphism, and inheritance.

A window class is defined by filling a **WNDCLASS** structure. This code shows what a typical Windows program does for itself. On the other hand, class registration is invisibly handled by OWL for you:

```
WNDCLASS wc;

    wc.lpszClassName  = "MIN:MAIN";
    wc.hInstance      = hInstance;
    wc.lpfnWndProc    = MinWndProc;
    wc.hCursor        = LoadCursor (hInstance, "hand");
    wc.hIcon          = LoadIcon (hInstance,"snapshot");
    wc.lpszMenuName   = NULL;
    wc.hbrBackground  = (HBRUSH)COLOR_WINDOW+1;
    wc.style          = NULL;
    wc.cbClsExtra     = 0;
    wc.cbWndExtra     = 0;

    RegisterClass( &wndclass);
```

Every OWL window object is associated with one and only one window class. Overriding the `GetClassName` function lets you tell OWL the name of that class. If it hasn't been registered already, OWL calls the `GetWindowClass` function to fill in the **WNDCLASS** data structure. OWL has a function which contains a reasonable set of defaults. But when you override it, as MIN does, you can change any value that suits you.

**RegisterClass** creates an entry in MS-Windows' **window class database**. At window creation time, the `CreateWindow` function references an entry in this database. This information becomes part of the identity of the window. Let's look at each element in **WNDCLASS** to better understand this process.

Every class has a name. You create the name, place it in a character string, and put a pointer to the string in the `lpszClasssName` element of the **WNDCLASS** structure. This is the key, or lookup value, for a class database entry. The `GetClassName` function defined by **TMinWindow** provides OWL with our window class name:

```
LPSTR TMinWindow::GetClassName ()
    {
    return "MIN:MAIN";
    }
```

If you create multiple window classes in your OWL programs, make sure each has a *unique* class name.

The `hInstance` value tells Windows who created the class definition. This is needed for Windows' internal housekeeping. When the last instance of a program terminates, Windows removes all associated class definitions.

The `lpfnWndProc` value gives Windows the address of a function to associate with a window class. This function is called a **window procedure**. The role of a window procedure can be simply stated: A window procedure processes messages. In a Windows program written in C, a single function handles the myriad messages sent to a window. In OWL programs, as we've already discussed, you define a different message response function for each message that you wish to handle. The OWL libraries contain a window procedure, since this is a requirement of MS-Windows. But this procedure takes care of calling the correct message response function depending on how we've defined our object window class.

The **hCursor** value identifies the default mouse cursor for a window class. Every time the cursor moves across our window, its shape will change to the one we define here. As we mentioned earlier, MIN's cursor was created using the Resource Workshop. The file that contains the cursor definition, MIN.CUR, is referenced in our resource file, MIN.RC, with the line **hand cursor min.cur**.

The **TMinWindow::GetWindowClass** member function installs the cursor handle into **WNDCLASS**. It calls **LoadCursor**, an MS-Windows function, which provides MIN with the required cursor handle:

```
wc.hCursor=LoadCursor (wc.hInstance, "hand");
```

The handle is assigned to the **hCursor** element in the **WNDCLASS** structure. Notice that the second parameter to **LoadCursor** is the name of the resource in MIN.RC, "hand."

The **hIcon** element of **WNDCLASS** is handled in a similar manner. We create an icon using the Resource Workshop, and store it in MIN.ICO. This file name, in turn, is referenced in the resource file, MIN.RC, as shown here:

```
snapshot icon min.ico
```

This declaration causes the icon resource data (along with the cursor resource we discussed earlier) to be bound into MIN.EXE at program creation time. MIN loads the resource into memory by making a call to a special routine:

```
wc.hIcon = LoadIcon (hInstance,"snapshot");
```

The class definition provides a place to define a menu for a window. Within OWL, code like the following sets up the default, which is to have no class menu:

```
wc.lpszMenuName = NULL;
```

The **hbrBackground** field of WNDCLASS asks for one thing, and is given something else! This requires a little explanation. This field defines the background color for a window. If we were to define a background color for this printed page, we would select white (since the book is printed black text on white paper). Before any drawing is done in a window, we often paint a window with the background color. This gives us a clean surface on which to draw.

The Hungarian prefix **hbr** says this is a "handle to a brush." In the next chapter, when we introduce the Graphics Device Interface (GDI), we'll talk about brushes. Briefly, a brush is the way a Windows program defines a color for filling areas. But our example doesn't use a brush for the background color (although one could have been given).

*OWL's Window Object Classes* 87

Instead, OWL—along with most Windows programs—provides a magic number to let Windows know we want the system's default background color. The user selects the background color using the Control Panel program. To make the default background color a part of our window class definition, we use the special **COLOR_WINDOW+1** value:

```
wc.hbrBackground = COLOR_WINDOW+1;
```

The definition that appears in WINDOWS.H is

```
#define COLOR_WINDOW            5
```

which is one of 19 system color constants that are defined. You might be wondering why we add one to this constant. It turns out that the first value in this group has the value zero. But zero is an invalid value for a brush handle (or any other handle, for that matter). So, to use these constants in place of a handle, we add one to make the entire range of system colors valid.

The next **WNDCLASS** structure member that we're going to look at is the **style** field. In the world of Windows programming, the term **style** refers to a collection of options that are each controlled by one or two bits. To conserve space, style fields combine these options into a two-byte (or four-byte) field. We'll delve into the meaning of each style bit in Chapter 13, where we'll cover all the aspects of creating windows. By default, OWL (like most Windows programs) turns all styles *off*:

```
wc.style        = NULL;
```

The last two fields in **WNDCLASS**, **cbClsExtra** and **cbWndExtra**, are used to request that extra space be allocated in the class database (**cbClsExtra**) and in a related database, the **window database** (**cbWndExtra**), which contains an entry for every window in the system. This allows you to attach your own, private data to a class or a window. Right now, this may seem like a strange thing to want to do. But, in the same way that a C++ program encapsulates data in a class instance, a window can encapsulate data in a window instance entry in the window database.

## Window Creation

We mentioned that window creation is a multistep process. Once a window class has been defined, the next step is to create a window. That's the job of the **CreateWindowEx** function. Here's how this function might be called in a C version of MIN:

```
hwnd = CreateWindowEx (0L,                  /* Extra style. */
                "MIN:MAIN",                 /* Class name.  */
                "Minimum",                  /* Title.       */
                WS_OVERLAPPEDWINDOW,        /* Style bits.  */
                CW_USEDEFAULT,              /* x - default. */
                0,                          /* y - default. */
```

```
                    CW_USEDEFAULT,         /* cx - default. */
                    0,                     /* cy - default. */
                    NULL,                  /* No parent.    */
                    NULL,                  /* Class menu.   */
                    hInstance,             /* Creator       */
                    NULL);                 /* Params.       */
```

In addition to `CreateWindowEx`, Windows has a second window creation routine: `CreateWindow`. The two routines are identical, except that `CreateWindowEx` has one extra parameter (the `Ex` stands for "extended"). This extra parameter is the very first parameter, not because it's the most important, but because this makes it easy to implement the older routine by calling the newer routine. Let's look at the parameters that these two routines take.

The first parameter, which is unique to `CreateWindowEx`, contains style bits. As you may recall from our discussion of class style bits, style fields combine several one- or two-bit-wide fields into a single two- or four-byte value. This extra parameter was needed because, quite frankly, the older `CreateWindow` call ran out of room in its style field. The original style field is the third parameter in the `CreateWindow` call and the fourth parameter in `CreateWindowEx`. OWL sets this to `0L` because a typical main window requires none of these styles.

The second parameter to `CreateWindow` specifies the class of window that we wish to create. In our example, the class name is `MIN:MAIN`.

The third parameter is the window title. The window title appears in the titlebar when a window is opened, and next to the window's icon when a window is minimized. This is a good place to put the name of our program. After a window has been created, your program can change the title by calling the `SetWindowText` routine. In `TMinWindow`, the window title is specified as the second parameter to the constructor:

```
    MainWindow = new TMinWindow (NULL, "Minimum", NULL);
```

The fourth parameter is for style bits. OWL uses the standard `WS_OVERLAPPEDWINDOW` definition for an application's main window. This definition combines together six simpler style values:

```
    #define WS_OVERLAPPEDWINDOW (WS_OVERLAPPED |
            WS_CAPTION | WS_SYSMENU | WS_THICKFRAME |
            WS_MINIMIZEBOX | WS_MAXIMIZEBOX)
```

The C-language bitwise OR operator, |, packs together these simpler bit definitions:

```
    #define WS_OVERLAPPED      0x00000000L
    #define WS_CAPTION         0x00C00000L
    #define WS_SYSMENU         0x00080000L
    #define WS_THICKFRAME      0x00040000L
    #define WS_MINIMIZEBOX     0x00020000L
    #define WS_MAXIMIZEBOX     0x00010000L
```

The definition of WS_OVERLAPPED has no bits turned on. This field has no effect when ORed with the other bit values. This style flag is available, however, to help distinguish the three types of windows that can be created. The other two types are created using the following style flags:

```
#define WS_POPUP      0x80000000L
#define WS_CHILD      0x40000000L
```

WS_OVERLAPPED is simply a placeholder so that at a glance you can tell what type of window is being created.

The other style bits that are part of the WS_OVERLAPPEDWINDOW definition serve to create the different parts of the window. Figure 5.2 shows the relationship of window-style bits to window parts. A complete discussion of all the different window-style bits is in Chapter 13.

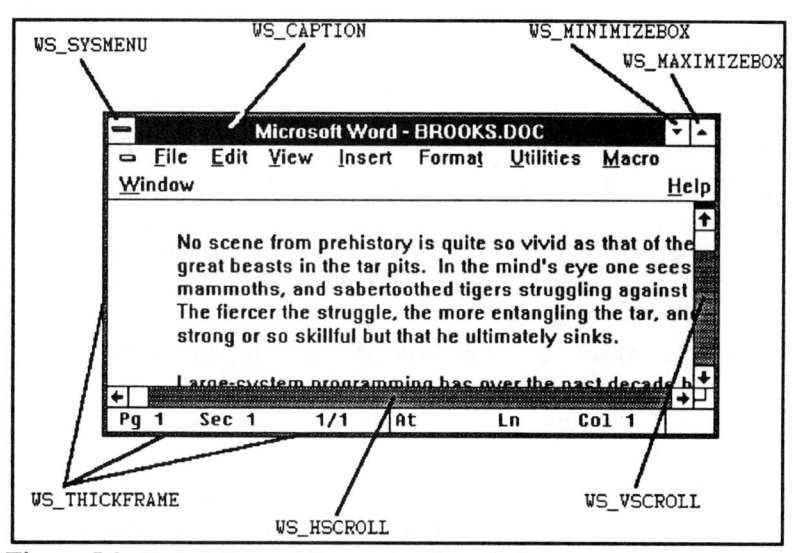

**Figure 5.2** Style bits and the parts of a window

The fifth, sixth, seventh, and eighth parameters are used to determine the starting size and location of our window. The X and Y values describe the location of the upper-left corner of our window relative to the upper-left corner of the display screen. The units for all four parameters are pixels. OWL, along with most Windows programs, takes the easy way out by asking Windows to create an appropriate size and location for our window with the **CW_USEDEFAULT** flag. This flag must be set in the X and CX fields of **CreateWindow**. When it is used, the Y and CY values are ignored.

The ninth parameter defines a window's parent. While the term "parent" has lots of connotations, both in the real world and in the world of object-oriented programming, the meaning here is much simpler. It describes where a window lives (for a WS_CHILD window) and whether a window should be automatically shown/hidden/destroyed (for all types of windows). When a window is shown, hidden, or destroyed, its children share a common fate. Like the main window in most programs, OWL creates MIN's main window without a parent.

The tenth parameter allows us to attach a menu to a window. This is the second chance we have to specify a menu—the first was in the class definition. The **WNDCLASS** data structure lets us define a menu to be shared by every member of a class. If our class definition had a menu name, we would automatically get the class menu by specifying NULL in this parameter. If a window has a private menu, it can use this field to establish that fact. By default, OWL defines MIN's main window to be without a menu, and sets the ninth parameter to **CreateWindow** to NULL as well.

The eleventh parameter, an instance handle, identifies the window owner. This lets Windows know which instance of our program has created the window. The reason for this parameter is subtle, but essentially it allows Windows to set up the data segment register correctly when it calls our window procedure. See the box on page 88 for more details on this mechanism, and Chapter 19 for an in-depth discussion of the data-segment side of dynamic linking.

The twelfth parameter lets us pass a data pointer to our window procedure. The pointer is passed to our window procedure with the very first message, WM_CREATE. This is used for providing window initialization data. OWL sets this value to NULL, indicating there is no initialization data to pass.

The **CreateWindowEx** function returns an identifier to the window created, a window handle. OWL dutifully stores this value for us in the **HWindow** data member of our window object.

After the return from **CreateWindowEx**, Windows has created all the internal information needed to support a window. That is, it has created an entry in the window database. But our window hasn't appeared on the screen yet. For this, a call to **ShowWindow** is required. When showing a window, a program should listen to the manner requested by the user. That's the role of **WinMain**'s **nCmdShow** parameter. Like most Windows applications, OWL programs use this parameter in **ShowWindow** like this:

```
ShowWindow (hwnd, nCmdShow);
```

Depending on the value of **nCmdShow**, our program might start out minimized as an icon, as a regular open window, or it might even start maximized. With the call to **ShowWindow**, the initialization of a window object is complete. This initialization sequence is typical for a Windows program. As we continue our exploration of the MS-Windows API, let's pause to investigate how an OWL program can more closely fine-tune the window creation process.

# Window Creation and OWL

You've seen how an OWL program can control window class registration. It can override the `GetWindowClass` function to change values in the `WNDCLASS` structure. That's how MIN added a custom cursor and icon to the class definition.

Overriding the parameters to `CreateWindowEx` is just as simple. Recall that one of the data members of `TWindow` is `Attr`. This data member is a structure of type `TWindowAttr`. If you look at the OWL sources, you see this structure defined as

```
struct _CLASSTYPE TWindowAttr {
    DWORD Style;
    DWORD ExStyle;
    int X, Y, W, H;
    LPSTR Menu;    // Menu name
    int Id ;       // Child identifier
    LPSTR Param;
};
```

These are the parameters to be used in calling `CreateWindowEx`.

`TWindow`'s constructor fills this structure with a reasonable set of default values. Since a derived class's constructor is called after the base class's constructor, you can change any value in your constructor and it will be used in the window creation call. For example, MIN would create a window 200 pixels tall by 300 pixels wide by changing `TMinWindow`'s constructor to

```
TMinWindow::TMinWindow (PTWindowsObject pwParent,
            LPSTR lpszTitle, PTModule pmModule)
        :TWindow (pwParent, lpszTitle, pmModule)
    {
    Attr.H = 200;
    Attr.W = 300;
    }
```

By changing the other values in the `Attr` data member, you can change the way your windows are created.

One of the values passed to the `RegisterClass` routine is the address of a function known as a window procedure. When you program using OWL, you don't define this type of function yourself, because OWL provides one for you. OWL's window procedure calls your window object's member functions. And yet, because window procedures are a central part of Windows programming, we're going to introduce them to you.

## The Window Procedure Declaration

Every window procedure—whether in OWL or in a Windows program written in C—must be defined like this:

```
long FAR PASCAL MinWndProc (HWND hwnd,
                            UINT msg,
                            WPARAM wParam,
                            LPARAM lParam)
```

The procedure name as well as the name of each parameter is, of course, up to you. But the number and type of parameters as well as the procedure declaration must appear as shown here. You don't write the code that calls this routine. Instead, a window procedure serves as the push-model part of a Windows program, meaning that this routine is called directly by Windows.

The return value for all window procedures is a long value. The meaning of the return value depends on the message. For example, the WM_QUERYENDSESSION message expects a TRUE (nonzero) or FALSE (zero) value. This particular message lets programs vote on whether Windows should honor the user's request to shut down the system (Windows can be very democratic). The WM_GETTEXT message, on the other hand, expects to receive a far pointer to a string (char far *) as a return value.

Every window procedure has exactly four parameters: a window handle (**hWnd**), a message identifier (**msg**), and two parameter values (**wParam** and **lParam**).

The window handle, **hWnd**, identifies the window associated with a message. This is a necessary parameter because a single window procedure can support several different windows at the same time. The window handle identifies the window that is "calling" a window procedure. Of course, this parameter is less interesting in an OWL program, since window objects already contain the window handle value in the **HWindow** data member.

The second parameter, **msg**, is the window message. If the window handle tells us "who is calling," then the message value tells us "what they want." Perhaps it is to announce that a window has been born (WM_CREATE), lives in a new location (WM_MOVE), has grown up (or shrunk) (WM_SIZE), needs a facelift (WM_PAINT), or has passed away (WM_DESTROY).

The **wParam** and **lParam** parameters give some more information about a given message. **wParam** is defined as a WORD value, which in WINDOWS.H is defined as a 16-bit unsigned integer. **lParam** is defined as a LONG value, which is a 32-bit unsigned value. The meanings of **wParam** and **lParam** depend on the message type. For example, the WM_COMMAND message, which is sent when a menu item is selected, uses **wParam** to identify the specific menu item that was selected. Mouse messages, like WM_LBUTTONDOWN and WM_MOUSEMOVE, use **lParam** to store the location of the mouse cursor in the window's client area.

The **PASCAL** keyword causes a function to use the Pascal Calling Convention. This keyword is not part of ANSI Standard C, but instead is a C-language extension. It takes advantage of a quirk in the Intel architecture that generates smaller and faster code than the C compiler's default calling convention. In fact, all of the Windows API routines (with the exception of **wsprintf**) use this calling convention.

The **FAR** keyword is needed because a window procedure is always called using an intersegment call. A related keyword is **NEAR**, which defines a reference to something in the same segment. Programmers often work hard to minimize the number of FAR references because they have a higher overhead than NEAR references. For more information, refer to Appendix H.

OWL's window objects provide a window procedure so you should never have to create your own. Understanding a window procedure will help your orient yourself when looking at sample Windows code written in C. It certainly will help you appreciate how OWL hides some of the complexity of Windows from you.

Although you'll never have to create a window procedure, you certainly will create message response functions. You may recall from our earlier discussion that these are functions that you'll define as part of your window objects to handle specific messages. Let's take a look at what's required for a typical message response function.

## OWL Message Response Functions

For each message that a window object wants to process, you'll create a message response function. As you may recall, a message response function is a member function of a window object's class. In some sense, each is a tiny, specialized window procedure. After all, OWL's window procedure is little more than a telephone operator which transfers messages to message response functions.

Where a message response function differs from a window procedure is in the declaration. Both provide access to the same four parameters, but they are packaged a little differently. For example, here is how a message response function is defined in one of our GDI sample programs, LINES (in Chapter 8):

```
void TLinesWindow::WMLButtonDown( TMessage& Msg )
```

This repackaging of parameters requires a bit of an explanation. First of all, the OWL window procedure, **StdWndProc**, copies the window procedure parameters into a structure of type **TMessage**, defined in WINDOBJ.H as:

```
struct TMessage {
  HWND Receiver;
  WORD Message;
  union {
    WORD WParam;
        struct tagWP {
```

```
                BYTE Lo;
                BYTE Hi;
            } WP;
    };
    union {
            DWORD LParam;
            struct tagLP {
                WORD Lo;
                WORD Hi;
            } LP;
    };
    long Result;
};
```

Essentially, a standard set of window procedures parameters are present: **Receiver, Message, WParam,** and **LParam**. A fifth structure parameter, **Result**, provides a place to store a message's return value. The meaning of a return value depends on the type of message. For example, the WM_GETTEXT message expects a far pointer to the character string.

If you're new to C++ programming, the use of & in the parameter to **WMLButtonDown** might seem odd. It is a "reference parameter," which means the parameter provides direct access to the actual memory location used by the caller. This is quite different from the "call by value" approach that C programmers are used to. This latter parameter passing method uses temporary variables for parameters.

A reference parameter, on the other hand, operates much like a passed pointer. Passing pointers to functions is something every C programmer has dealt with. For example, the standard **memcpy** function receives two pointers, as in

```
char * pchInBuffer;
char * pchOutBuffer;
int cbBuffer;

memcpy (pchOutBuffer, pchInBuffer, cbBuffer)
```

The syntax of a reference parameter is a little different from a passed pointer. In particular, the "->" operator is not used. Instead, the called function uses the dot operator ".", as if the structure were declared by the called function itself.

Since this is the case, a message response function like **WMLbuttonDown** will access the members of **TMessage** using the dot operator. Here, for example, is how all five members of **TMessage** can be accessed:

```
HWND    hWnd;
UINT    wMessage;
WPARAM  wParam;
LPARAM  lParam
hWnd     = TMessage.Receiver
wMessage = TMessage.Message
wParam   = TMessage.WParam
lParam   = TMessage.LParam

TMessage.Result = 0L;
```

This code fragment underscores the difference between ordinary Hungarian and the convention that has been adopted in OWL. While this may at first be annoying, we've found that the slight variation provided by OWL is helpful in distinguishing OWL variables from our own.

Within a message response function, there are two ways to access the window handle. First, it's stored in the **HWindow** data member of **TWindowsObject**. Also, it's provided in the **Receiver** field of the **TMessage** structure. It makes no difference which you reference, since they will be the same. From a performance point of view, the same machine instructions are used to access each of the two variables. The choice, then, depends on your personal preference. In general, we've tended to choose the **HWindow** data member.

From time to time, you'll want to access *part* of a message parameter. For example, mouse messages combine the X and Y cursor location in the **lParam** parameter (Y is in the high word, X is in the low word). While there are macros that let you separate these values, the definition of **TMessage** makes it easy. Here's how to get the high word of the **lParam** parameter:

```
WORD wHigh;
wHigh = Msg.LP.Hi
```

The chief benefit to using a reference parameter in message response functions is speed. After all, less overhead is required to pass the reference pointer (4 bytes) than the entire **TMessage** structure (14 bytes). Given the number of messages that pass through the system, this savings can add up to a significant savings.

Every message response function will be defined like the one in our example. Therefore, you can use it as a template for every OWL program you write. As you'll see, that's the template that we have used for all the code samples in this book. One slight variation worth mentioning is the use of **RTMessage** in place of **TMessage&**, as in

```
       void TLinesWindow::WMLButtonDown( RTMessage Msg )
```

You'll see this in quite a few of the example OWL programs that Borland ships with OWL. The two expressions are equivalent. Feel free to use the one that suits you.

At this point, you understand the basics of using the OWL window objects to create Windows programs. There's one crucial topic, however, that we still haven't covered: proper program termination. Although this might seem at first the job of an application object, in fact program termination in Windows is usually tied to the life of a program's main window. Let's see how an OWL window object should handle program termination.

## Program Termination

An important issue for every Windows program is proper termination. Proper termination is necessary to allow the cleanup and reclamation of memory and other resources used by a program. In our discussion of the application object, we introduced the WM_QUIT message. When the message loop detects this message, it causes the "infinite message loop" (and our program) to terminate. Let's see how the WM_QUIT message gets into our message queue.

Program termination usually occurs when the program's main window is closed. A user can close a window in any number of ways. Two of the more common ways are by selecting the Close item on the system menu or by striking the [Alt] + [F4] key combination. Each of these actions causes a stream of messages to be sent to our window procedure. Here is a list of messages that are sent to our window procedure when MIN's window is closed using the [Alt] + [F4] key combination:

| Message | Comment |
| --- | --- |
| WM_SYSKEYDOWN | [Alt] key was struck |
| WM_SYSKEYDOWN | [F4] key was struck |
| WM_SYSCOMMAND | System Command generated |
| WM_CLOSE | Window is told to close |
| WM_NCACTIVATE | Turn off titlebar (nonclient area) highlight |
| WM_ACTIVATE | Window is becoming inactive |
| WM_ACTIVATEAPP | Application is becoming inactive |
| WM_KILLFOCUS | Window is losing the keyboard |
| WM_DESTROY | Window has been destroyed |
| WM_NCDESTROY | Time to cleanup nonclient area data |

The first thing to be said about this stream of messages is that the default window procedure handles the bulk of the work to make the "right things" happen. For example, it takes the first two messages, which are raw keystroke messages, and translates them into the third message: a system command. The system command message is handled by the default window procedure to implement system level commands.

A system command is a generic request for some action to occur (move a window, size a window, etc.). A window object usually does not process these messages. Instead, it looks for more specific messages to respond to. In this case, that message is WM_CLOSE, a request to close our window.

The **TWindowsObject** class has a member function to handle this message: **WMClose**. This function first asks if it's OK to close the window. It does so by calling one of two different member functions named **CanClose**. If dealing with an application's main window, the application object's `CanClose` function is called. If dealing with any other window, it calls the window object's `CanClose` function. For both application object and window object, this member function returns one of two values: TRUE (nonzero) to allow the window to close, or FALSE (zero) to prevent the window from closing.

The default action of `TApplication::CanClose` is to call the main window's `CanClose` function. For this reason, we think it makes sense to think of this member function only in terms of its window object incarnation. The application object's version makes it easy to request application shutdown from any part of an application.

A typical `CanClose` member function might check for an unsaved file in our window. If one exists, our window object might display a message box like that shown in Figure 5.3 to warn the user of the possible loss of data. A `CanClose` member function makes sure that no harmful results will come from closing the window. In the sample message box, `CanClose` would return a TRUE (OK to close) message if the user clicked "Yes" or "No" On the other hand, if the user clicked "Cancel," `CanClose` would return FALSE to prevent the window from closing.

`TWindowsObject` handles the WM_QUERYENDSESSION message, in its `WMQueryEndSession` member function. Windows sends this message to the main window of every program when the user goes to shut down the system. Essentially, a vote is taken. A unanimous reply is needed to allow Windows to terminate. Once again, `CanClose` is called to ensure against loss of user data. First, the application's `CanClose` is called, which in turn calls the main window's `CanClose` member function.

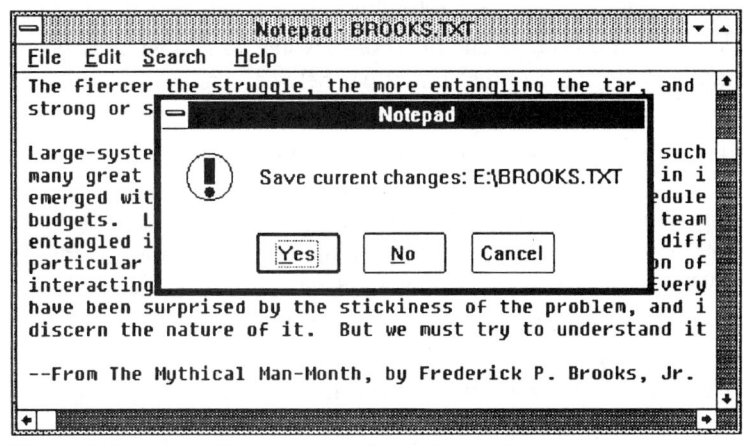

**Figure 5.3** Protecting the user from loss of data

When `CanClose` says it's OK to close, the `Destroy` member function is called. This is a `TWindowsObject` member function which cleans up the MDI document windows which have been created. Next it calls the MS-Windows routine `DestroyWindow`. This routine completely and irrevocably eliminates a window. It sends a "death certificate," in the form of a `WM_DESTROY` message.

Once again, `TWindowsObject` has a member function to handle this important message. Its `WMDestroy` member function does the job. If it's an application's main window, it calls the Windows `PostQuitMessage` routine, which puts a `WM_QUIT` message onto an application's message queue. It is this message, you will recall, that is responsible for terminating an application's message loop so that the program itself can terminate.

As you can see, most of program termination is taken care of for us by the OWL libraries. Of course, we can intervene at any point simply by overriding the base class member functions. Another component that helps out is Windows' own default window procedure. Let's focus our attention on this important workhorse.

## Default Message Handling

As we discussed in Chapter 1, the chief reason for the attractiveness of Windows comes from the consistent "look and feel" of the Windows user interface. Even the most casual Windows user notices the remarkable uniformity between programs. For example, menus work the same between two otherwise unrelated programs, and windows in different programs respond in the same way to the same actions.

Deep in the bowels of Windows, it is the work of the default window handler that accounts for this high degree of uniformity. The flood of messages that a window object diverts to the default handler is the cause of the similarities between programs. While a C program will rely heavily on the default window procedure, an OWL program gets many of these services from the base OWL objects. But even the OWL programs rely, to some degree, on the work done by the default window procedure.

While this work is being done for us, there is still something that we must do. A window object plays the role of traffic cop for messages. After all, the default message handler is never called directly by Windows. Instead, our window objects always receive messages first. To keep the user interface working properly, OWL passes messages on to the default window procedure.

There may, in fact, be times when we wish to vary the behavior of a window away from the default behavior. For example, we might wish to prevent the user from picking up a window by the titlebar. (This is a typical way for a user to move a window.) It is a simple matter to trap the messages associated with this action, and prevent them from arriving at the default window handler. For the most part, however, we'll allow the default window procedure to do its work for us, so that our program can participate in the consistency that makes Windows so usable.

In looking at the different parts of our minimum Windows program, we have talked a lot about the flow of messages through the system. We have also identified a few messages that are important. In order for you to fully understand how the message pipeline can work to your advantage, it will help you to know the types of messages that flow through these pipes. For this reason, we're going to conclude this chapter with an in-depth look at the types of messages in Windows.

# A Taxonomy of Messages

There are about 250 predefined messages in Windows. Fortunately, you do not have to be familiar with every single one of them, because most have very specialized uses. For example, a large number of messages are specific to one type of window. Other messages are used for very special purposes, like sharing data or implementing the **Multiple Document Interface** (MDI) standard. Still other messages float through our message pipeline but are never documented for our use. These are internal messages that Windows creates for its own purposes.

To help you come to terms with messages, we'll divide the messages into eight categories. These categories are intended as a framework in which to begin understanding messages. But this won't be the last you hear about messages. Almost every chapter in this book will provide details on the messages that apply to the different parts of Windows. So let's get started on our look at Windows messages.

Messages have names. Message names are defined in WINDOWS.H like this:

```
#define WM_COMMAND 0x0111
```

The `WM_` Hungarian prefix tells us that a symbol is a "window message." In spoken language, the prefix is ignored, so that programmers often refer to `WM_COMMAND` as a "command message." These symbolic names stand in for the raw numeric value of a message: a 16-bit unsigned integer. Besides the `WM_` prefix, there are other Hungarian prefixes for messages: `EM_`, `BM_`, `DM_`, `LB_`, and `CB_` (like `EM_GETSEL`, `BM_GETCHECK`, etc.). These are private messages, which don't concern us at this moment, except that they show that you can create your *own* private messages as you need them.

A useful tool for learning about messages is `WinSight`. Borland provides this utility with version 3.0 and later of the Borland C++ compiler. It's provided to help you eavesdrop on the message traffic for a window—even if you didn't write the program! When you use `WinSight`, you will be surprised at the number of messages encountered. For example, Figure 5.4 shows the messages generated by the simple action of making a menu selection. Even without knowing what specific messages do, you can tell that this is a lot of messages. A little experimentation with `WinSight` will demonstrate that this is typical for other user actions as well.

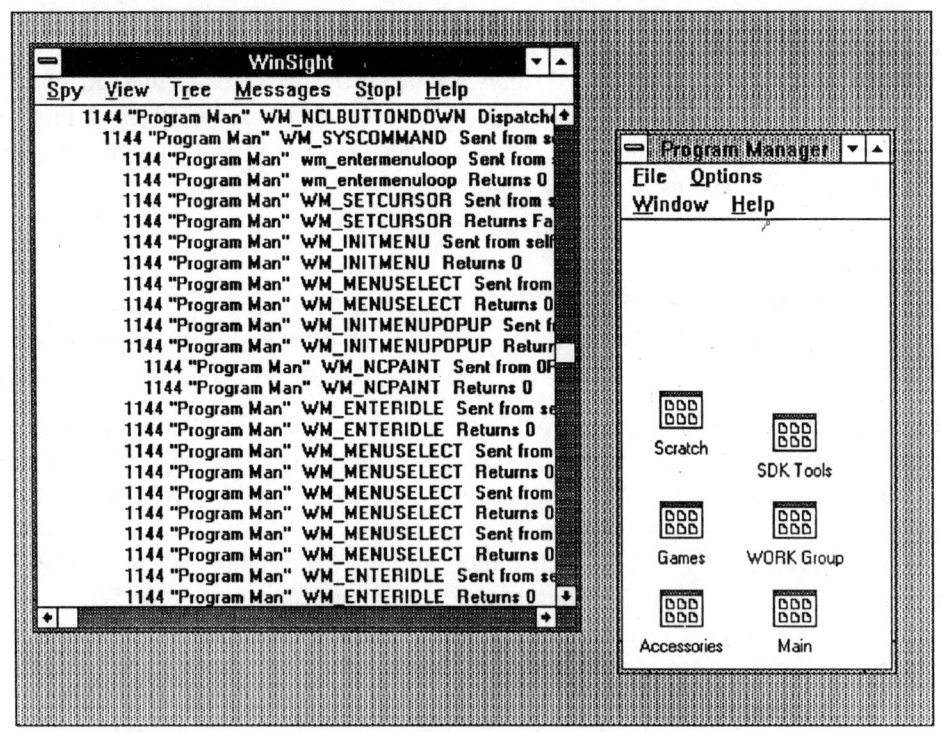

**Figure 5.4** WinSight showing messages generated by making a menu selection

Why so many messages? Some messages are for Windows' internal use, to synchronize events in different parts of the system. These messages are passed along to the default window procedure, which we introduced a short time ago. Other messages notify the window procedure of actions taken by the user. Messages guarantee that a window procedure will always have the latest information about what the user is doing. Once you understand the type of messages that are generated, messages ultimately mean less work on your part to keep in touch with a lot of information. It's like having a daily paper delivered to your door: "All the Messages Fit to Print."

Table 5.1 shows the eight categories of messages. As we review each category, we'll list the specific messages that are in the category. Since some of the categories are quite specialized, we'll limit our discussion to a brief introduction and omit a list of specific messages. All messages from all categories are listed in Appendix A, in case you're curious about what it is that we're omitting. Let's start with our first message category: hardware messages.

**Table 5.1** The eight types of messages

| Type | Description |
| --- | --- |
| Hardware | Mouse and keyboard input |
| Window Maintenance | Notification, request for action, query |
| User-Interface Maintenance | Menu, mouse pointer, scroll bar, dialog boxes, MDI |
| Termination | Application or system shutdown |
| Private | Dialog box controls: edit, button, list box, combobox |
| System Resource Notification | Color changes, fonts, spooler, device modes |
| Data Sharing | Clipboard and Dynamic Data Exchange (DDE) |
| Internal System | Undocumented messages |

## *Hardware Messages*

A window procedure receives messages generated by three different pieces of hardware: the keyboard, the mouse, and the system timer. Each of these generates hardware interrupts. Since Windows' scheduling is not interrupt-oriented, hardware events have to be buffered. This ensures that hardware events are processed in the order in which they occur.

For example, when you strike the "H" key, an interrupt notifies the system that keyboard input is ready. The Windows keyboard device driver retrieves this input and creates an entry into the **hardware event queue**. When its turn comes, messages bearing "H" key information are delivered to the proper window procedure. The mouse and timer messages are handled in a similar fashion. Table 5.2 shows the 29 messages that are generated in response to hardware activity.

**Table 5.2** Hardware messages

*Mouse Messages: In a window's client area*

| | |
|---|---|
| WM_LBUTTONDBLCLK | Left button double-click |
| WM_LBUTTONDOWN | Left button down |
| WM_LBUTTONUP | Left button up |
| WM_MBUTTONDBLCLK | Middle button double-click |
| WM_MBUTTONDOWN | Middle button down |
| WM_MBUTTONUP | Middle button up |
| WM_MOUSEMOVE | Mouse move |
| WM_RBUTTONDBLCLK | Right button double-click |
| WM_RBUTTONDOWN | Right button down |
| WM_RBUTTONUP | Right button up |

*Mouse Messages: In a window's non-client area*

| | |
|---|---|
| WM_NCLBUTTONDBLCLK | Left button double-click |
| WM_NCLBUTTONDOWN | Left button down |
| WM_NCLBUTTONUP | Left button up |
| WM_NCMBUTTONDBLCLK | Middle button double-click |
| WM_NCMBUTTONDOWN | Middle button down |
| WM_NCMBUTTONUP | Middle button up |
| WM_NCMOUSEMOVE | Mouse move |
| WM_NCRBUTTONDBLCLK | Right button double-click |
| WM_NCRBUTTONDOWN | Right button down |
| WM_NCRBUTTONUP | Right button up |

*Keyboard Messages*

| | |
|---|---|
| WM_CHAR | Character input |
| WM_DEADCHAR | Dead-character (umlaut, accent, etc.) |
| WM_KEYDOWN | Key has been depressed |
| WM_KEYUP | Key has been released |
| WM_SYSCHAR | System character input |

*(Continued)*

**Table 5.2**   Continued

|   |   |
|---|---|
| WM_SYSDEADCHAR | System dead-character |
| WM_SYSKEYDOWN | System key has been depressed |
| WM_SYSKEYUP | System key has been released |

*Timer Message*

|   |   |
|---|---|
| WM_TIMER | Timer has gone off. |

### ➤ *Caution:*

Like mouse and keyboard messages, timer messages are queued. This means that Windows timers are not exact. This is necessary since an interrupt-driven timer message would conflict with the nonpreemptive nature of Windows. The usefulness of a timer is that it lets you know that a minimum amount of time has passed.

With mouse messages, a distinction is made between the mouse messages generated in a window's client area and those generated in the nonclient area. (Remember: The nonclient area of a window includes its border, system menu, titlebar, menu, etc.) In general, an application only pays attention to client area mouse messages and lets the default window procedure process nonclient area mouse messages.

While we're on the subject of mouse messages, the WM_MOUSEMOVE message deserves some special attention. The WM_MOUSEMOVE message is handled in a special way to keep the hardware event queue from overflowing. After all, if you move the mouse quickly, you can easily create hundreds of mouse interrupts. To minimize the disruption this might cause, Windows keeps only *one* mouse move message at a time. When a new mouse move message arrives, Windows checks if one already exists. If so, the old message is updated with the new location information. A new entry is made only if a mouse move message isn't already present.

There are two basic types of keyboard messages: regular and system. In general, you can ignore system keyboard messages, which have names like WM_SYSCHAR and WM_SYSKEYDOWN. The default window procedure turns these into the proper system command. The regular keyboard messages are intended for application use. We'll discuss the details of all keyboard messages in Chapter 15, when we talk about getting input from the user.

## Window Maintenance Messages

This group has 27 messages. It seems that this is the trickiest group of messages, mostly because it takes a long time to learn the subtle nuances of each. Unfortunately, the names of the messages do not help very much.

To begin with, there are three types of window maintenance messages: notification, request for action, and queries. Table 5.3 lists all the window maintenance messages, sorted into these three types.

**Table 5.3** Window maintenance messages

*Window Messages: Notification*

| | |
|---|---|
| WM_ACTIVATE | Window is active. |
| WM_ACTIVATEAPP | Application is active. |
| WM_CREATE | Window has been created. |
| WM_DESTROY | Window has been destroyed. |
| WM_ENABLE | Input to the window has been enabled. |
| WM_KILLFOCUS | Window has lost keyboard control. |
| WM_MOUSEACTIVATE | Notifies a window that it is going to become active because of a mouse click. |
| WM_MOVE | Window has been moved. |
| WM_SETFOCUS | Window has gained keyboard control. |
| WM_SIZE | Window has changed size. |

*Window Messages: Request for action*

| | |
|---|---|
| WM_CLOSE | Close (destroy) window |
| WM_ERASEBKGND | Erase background |
| WM_ICONERASEBKGND | Erase background of iconic window |
| WM_NCACTIVATE | Change title bar to show active state |
| WM_NCCREATE | Create non-client area data |

*(Continued)*

**Table 5.3   Continued**

| | |
|---|---|
| WM_NCDESTROY | Destroy non-client area data |
| WM_NCPAINT | Redraw non-client area |
| WM_PAINT | Redraw client area |
| WM_PAINTICON | Redraw iconic window client area |
| WM_SETREDRAW | Inhibit redrawing of window |
| WM_SETTEXT | Change window text |
| WM_SHOWWINDOW | Change window visibility |

*Window Messages: Query*

| | |
|---|---|
| WM_GETMINMAXINFO | What are min/max sizes for window? |
| WM_GETTEXT | What is the window text? |
| WM_GETTEXTLENGTH | What is the length of the window text? |
| WM_NCCALCSIZE | How big should the client area be? |
| WM_QUERYNEWPALETTE | Do you have a new palette? |
| WM_QUERYOPEN | Can iconic window be opened? |

---

A notification message tells a window procedure that the state of a window has changed. Nothing is required from the window procedure to perform the action implied by the message name. The WM_MOVE message, for example, is *not* a request for your program to move anything. Instead, it is an after-the-fact message to tell you that your window has already been moved. It is worth noting that nothing in the message tells us how our window was moved. Maybe the user moved a window with the mouse. Or perhaps another program moved our window. Whichever is the case, notification messages are one-way communication to a window procedure.

A request for action message requires that some action take place. Without the action, a hole is created in the user interface. For example, the WM_PAINT message is sent to a window procedure when a window has been damaged and needs to be redrawn. If the window procedure doesn't repair the window, it stays broken. For the most part, the default window procedure provides the needed minimum action. There are times, however, when you must intercept and process one of these messages yourself—as is the case with the

`WM_PAINT` message we brought up a moment ago. When you do, be sure that you mimic the actions of the default handler. Finding out what this means is simpler than you might think: Just look at the source code to `DefWindowProc`.

For your convenience, we have duplicated a listing of `DefWindowProc` in Appendix B of this book for version 3.0 of the Software Development Kit. Check with your software dealer for the latest version of the Software Development Kit, since the listing we provide in the appendix of this book is subject to revision.

A query message requires an answer. This is used for two-way communication between Windows and your program. Like the request for action messages, you can rely on the default window procedure to give a reasonable answer for most cases. You may decide to intercept one if you want to change the default answer. For example, you will get a `WM_QUERYOPEN` message when the user tries to open a minimized window. If you want a program to run only in an iconic state, you simply answer `FALSE` instead of the default answer of `TRUE`.

## User-Interface Messages

This group contains messages for the other user-interface objects, including the application menu, mouse pointer, scroll bar, dialog boxes, and dialog box controls. It also includes a group of messages used to support the Multiple Document Interface (MDI). See Table 5.4. This is a user-interface convention that was first seen in Microsoft's Excel spreadsheet program. Since then, it has become something of a standard, so that Windows now includes built-in support for MDI. The use of MDI is beyond the scope of this book, but we'll cover the other types of messages elsewhere: menu messages in Chapter 11, mouse pointer messages in Chapter 16, scroll bar messages in Chapter 20, and dialog box messages in Chapter 14.

**Table 5.4** User Interface Messages

*Menu Messages*

| | |
|---|---|
| `WM_COMMAND` | Menu item has been selected. |
| `WM_INITMENU` | Initialize menu bar menu. |
| `WM_INITMENUPOPUP` | Initialize popup menu. |
| `WM_MENUCHAR` | Mnemonic key used to select menu. |
| `WM_MENUSELECT` | User is browsing through menus. |

*(Continued)*

**Table 5.4**  Continued

*System Commands: System Menu, Min/Max Buttons, Titlebar, etc.*

| | |
|---|---|
| WM_SYSCOMMAND | A system command has been selected. |

*Mouse Pointer Messages*

| | |
|---|---|
| WM_NCHITTEST | Query: Where is mouse on the window? |
| WM_SETCURSOR | Request: Change pointer to correct shape. |

*Scroll Bar Messages*

| | |
|---|---|
| WM_HSCROLL | Horizontal scrollbar has been clicked. |
| WM_VSCROLL | Vertical scrollbar has been clicked. |

*Dialog Box and Dialog Box Control Messages*

| | |
|---|---|
| WM_COMMAND | Control communicating with Dialog Box. |
| WM_COMPAREITEM | Sent to the parent of an owner-draw dialog box control, asking to compare two items for the purpose of sorting. |
| WM_CTLCOLOR | Control asking for colors to be set. |
| WM_DELETEITEM | Notification to an owner-draw listbox or an owner-draw combobox that an item has been deleted. |
| WM_DRAWITEM | Request to the parent of an owner-draw control, or owner-draw menu, to draw. |
| WM_GETDLGCODE | Query control: Want keyboard input? |
| WM_GETFONT | Query control: What font are you using? |
| WM_INITDIALOG | Initialize dialog. |
| WM_MEASUREITEM | Request to the parent of an owner-draw control or an owner-draw item to provide the dimensions of the item that is going to be drawn. |
| WM_SETFONT | Request to control: Use this font. |

*(Continued)*

**Table 5.4   Continued**

*Multiple Document Interface Messages*

| | |
|---|---|
| WM_CHILDACTIVATE | Notifies a parent window that a child is active. |
| WM_MDIACTIVATE | Notifies an MDI child window that it is either gaining or losing activation. |
| WM_MDICASCADE | Request to arrange the open MDI child windows in a cascading, stair-step fashion. |
| WM_MDICREATE | Requests an MDI client window to create an MDI child window. |
| WM_MDIDESTROY | Request to an MDI client window to destroy an MDI child window. |
| WM_MDIGETACTIVE | Query an MDI client window for the currently active MDI child window. |
| WM_MDIICONARRANGE | Request to arrange the iconic MDI child windows in an orderly fashion. |
| WM_MDIMAXIMIZE | Request to maximize, or zoom, an MDI child window so that it occupies all of its parent's client area. |
| WM_MDINEXT | Request to activate the next MDI child window. |
| WM_MDIRESTORE | Request to restore an MDI child window to its previous state≈iconic, normal, or zoomed. |
| WM_MDISETMENU | Adjusts the menu on an MDI frame window. |
| WM_MDITILE | Request to arrange the open MDI child windows in a tiled fashion in the MDI parent's client window. |

# Termination Messages

This is the smallest group of messages. See Table 5.5. But these messages are very important, since they are used to control the termination of a Windows program (WM_QUIT), as well as the termination processing for the system (WM_QUERYENDSESSION and WM_ENDSESSION). We covered the WM_QUIT message earlier.

**Table 5.5** Termination Messages

*Application and System Termination*

| | |
|---|---|
| WM_QUIT | Request that a program should terminate. |
| WM_QUERYENDSESSION | A Query: Ready for system shutdown? |
| WM_ENDSESSION | Notification of results of shutdown query. |

## Private Messages

Private window messages are for use with a specific window class. The predefined private messages in WINDOWS.H are used with the following window classes: edit, button, listbox, and combobox.

The use of private messages by predefined window types is a pretty good clue that we can use this technique for our own windows. Why would you want to do this? You might find that existing messages do not provide the required functionality. It is a simple matter to define your own private message types and use them for communicating between different windows that you create. Even though 250 message types have already been defined, message variables are unsigned integers, which means that there is room for 65,535 different message types. When you define a private message, you should use the range starting at WM_USER, which is defined in WINDOWS.H as follows:

```
#define WM_USER    0x0400
```

If we wrote a window procedure for windows that display numbers, we might control how numbers appear with the following private messages (PM_ is Hungarian for "private message"):

```
#define PM_DECIMAL      WM_USER + 0
#define PM_BINARY       WM_USER + 1
#define PM_HEX          WM_USER + 2
#define PM_OCTAL        WM_USER + 3
#define PM_NODECIMAL    WM_USER + 4
#define PM_DOLLARS      WM_USER + 5
#define PM_WITHCOMMAS   WM_USER + 6
```

Other parts of our program (or other programs that we write) can control the number display window simply by sending messages.

## System Resource Notification

There are eight system resource notification messages. See Table 5.6. These are sent to the top-level window of every program when a change has been made to a system resource. For example, when fonts are added or removed from the system, a `WM_FONTCHANGE` message is distributed. When the user changes the system colors or the system time from the Control Panel program, the `WM_SYSCOLORCHANGE` or `WM_TIMECHANGE` messages are sent out. The typical response to a notification is to record the change.

**Table 5.6** System resource notification messages

*System Resources Notification Messages*

| | |
|---|---|
| `WM_COMPACTING` | Notification that system memory is low, and that the Memory Manager is trying to free up some memory. |
| `WM_DEVMODECHANGE` | Printer setup has changed. |
| `WM_FONTCHANGE` | Installed fonts in the system have changed. |
| `WM_PALETTECHANGED` | Hardware color palette has changed. |
| `WM_SPOOLERSTATUS` | Job has been removed from spooler queue. |
| `WM_SYSCOLORCHANGE` | One or more system colors has changed. |
| `WM_TIMECHANGE` | System time has changed. |
| `WM_WININICHANGE` | Initialization file, WIN.INI, changed. |

Of course, not every change is of interest to every program. For example, a clock program would probably check the new time when it receives a `WM_TIMECHANGE` message. But if it didn't use different fonts, it would probably ignore the `WM_FONTCHANGE` message.

Because most programs use the system colors, just about every program will respond to the `WM_SYSCOLORCHANGE` message. This is a notification that one or more system colors have changed. Ordinarily, system colors are changed by the Control Panel program under the direction of the user. When a change has been made, the Control Panel sends `WM_SYSCOLORCHANGE`. On receipt of this message, programs that use system colors respond by redrawing with the new colors.

## Data Sharing Messages

Data sharing plays an important role in Windows. So it's not surprising that there are messages that are used in data sharing. Both data sharing mechanisms, the clipboard and Dynamic Data Exchange (DDE), make extensive use of messages. A full discussion of data sharing is beyond the scope of this book; however, Windows' data sharing messages are listed in Table 5.7.

**Table 5.7** Data sharing messages

*Clipboard Messages*

| | |
|---|---|
| WM_ASKCBFORMATNAME | Asks for the name of a Clipboard format. |
| WM_CHANGECBCHAIN | Notification of a change in the viewing chain. |
| WM_DESTROYCLIPBOARD | Clipboard contents are being destroyed. |
| WM_DRAWCLIPBOARD | Clipboard contents have changed. |
| WM_HSCROLLCLIPBOARD | Horizonal scrolling of owner draw clipboard item. |
| WM_PAINTCLIPBOARD | Requests drawing of an owner draw clipboard item. |
| WM_RENDERALLFORMATS | Request to provide the data for all clipboard formats that have been promised. |
| WM_RENDERFORMAT | Request to provide data for a single clipboard format that has been promised. |
| WM_SIZECLIPBOARD | Notification to the owner of owner draw clipboard data that the size of the Clipboard viewer window has changed. |
| WM_VSCROLLCLIPBOARD | Vertical scrolling of an owner draw clipboard item. |

*Dynamic Data Exchange(DDE) Messages*

| | |
|---|---|
| WM_DDE_ACK | Acknowledgment. |
| WM_DDE_ADVISE | Request from a DDE client to establish a permanent data link. |
| WM_DDE_DATA | Send a data item from a DDE server to a DDE client. |
| WM_DDE_EXECUTE | Request a DDE server to execute a series of commands. |
| WM_DDE_INITIATE | Logon to a DDE server. |

*(Continued)*

**Table 5.7** Continued

| | |
|---|---|
| WM_DDE_POKE | Request by a client for a server to update a specific data item. |
| WM_DDE_REQUEST | One-time request by a DDE client for a piece of information. |
| WM_DDE_TERMINATE | Logoff from a DDE server. |
| WM_DDE_UNADVISE | Terminate a permanent data link that was initiated with the WM_DDE_ADVISE message. |

## Internal System Messages

A large group of messages are defined in WINDOWS.H but not described in any documentation. These are internal system messages, the last group of messages we are going to discuss. Windows uses these messages for its own purposes. This is the same idea as private messages, with the exception that private messages are meant for only one class of window. Internal messages are encountered in the context of every window class.

If we don't know the reason for a message, why is it sent to a window procedure? Like other message types, if a window procedure does not process it, the message is passed on to the default message handler. The default message handler does the right thing with this group of messages.

Since you have the source code to the default message handler, you might think that you could reverse-engineer some of these messages and use them for your own purpose. You can do this, but be careful. A future version of Windows may change the way internal messages are used, or eliminate some altogether! It has been our experience that "undocumented goodies" are interesting to look at, but dangerous to include in software that is intended for general distribution.

# PART THREE

# Introduction to the Graphics Device Interface

# 6

# Overview of GDI

For the next few chapters, we're going to focus on issues relating to the creation of graphical output. We're going to be discussing various types of drawing that can be done using Windows' **Graphics Device Interface (GDI)**. Since Borland's OWL class libraries do not have any support for GDI functions, the next few chapters will focus exclusively on GDI. However, we'll provide sample C++ programs using the OWL application framework, to help you see where the GDI calls fit in.

In this chapter, we're going to start by looking at some of the basic concepts and capabilities of GDI. The next few chapters will build on this beginning, by looking at pixels, lines, filled areas, and text. Let's roll up our sleeves, then, and take a look at Windows' pixel-powered graphic output engine.

## An Overview of the Graphics Device Interface

GDI is Windows' graphic output library. GDI handles graphic output for the display screen as well as hard-copy devices like printers and plotters. GDI creates every line, letter, and mark displayed by a Windows program. Windows itself uses GDI to assemble the pieces that make up the user interface: windows, icons, menus, dialog boxes, etc.

## GDI Capabilities

Figure 6.1 shows some of the types of graphic objects that GDI can draw: lines, filled figures, and text of different shapes and sizes. This chapter and the chapters that follow introduce the basic concepts and programming techniques needed to take advantage of the capabilities that GDI has to offer.

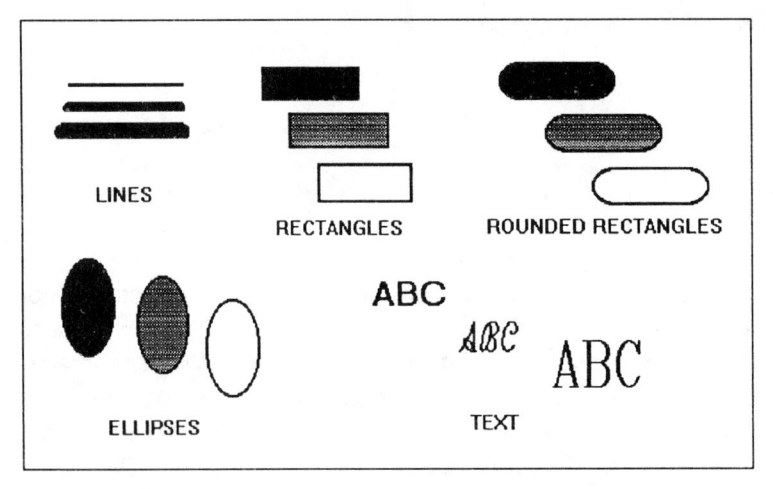

**Figure 6.1** A sample of GDI lines, filled figures, and text

## GDI Devices

GDI can draw on many different types of devices: display screens, laser printers, dot-matrix printers, plotters, etc. For GDI to work with a specific device, it depends on a special piece of software: a **device driver**. A GDI device driver converts drawing requests into the specific actions needed to draw on a specific device. For example, when a Windows program draws a picture of the space shuttle on an EGA display, GDI calls the EGA device driver to turn on the correct pixels. And when a program generates output on an HP LaserJet printer, GDI calls another device driver for help: the HP printer driver. In addition to performing this work, a device driver provides GDI with a set of **device capability bits**. These are flags that let GDI know about a device's built-in drawing ability. There are five sets of flags: a set for curves, lines, polygons, bitmaps, and text. These sets of flags tell GDI when to give a high-level drawing request directly to a device and when it must convert such requests into an equivalent set of low-level drawing requests.

At a minimum, a GDI device must be able to do two things: turn on pixels and draw solid lines. For a device with these minimum capabilities, GDI (with the help of a device driver) is able to do the rest. GDI has a set of built-in software simulations that take a high-level drawing request, like "draw a filled polygon," and convert it into a series of line and pixel operations. The software simulations are one reason that GDI is referred to as a **device-independent** graphics library. For devices with capabilities beyond the minimum, such as a PostScript printer, GDI uses the capability bits to determine when to send a high-level drawing request directly to the device driver.

In addition to physical devices like video screens and printers, GDI supports logical or **pseudodevices**. Pseudodevices are used for picture storage. Unlike physical devices, which display pictures using dedicated hardware, pseudodevices capture a picture in RAM or on disk. GDI supports two types of pseudodevices: **bitmaps** and **metafiles**.

In Windows, bitmaps are always rectangular. A bitmap stores a picture in memory in the same way that a display adapter uses memory to hold graphic images. For this reason, bitmaps provide a fast way to make a copy of a picture. Bitmaps are also used to store images that must be drawn quickly onto the screen. For example, Windows itself uses bitmaps to store icons and cursors, as well as the tiny symbols used to draw system menus, minimize/maximize icons, parts of a scroll bar, and even the check mark inside menus.

Another use of bitmaps is to store scanned images, such as company logos. A scanned image is created by running a paper copy of a logo through a device called a **scanner**. A scanner digitizes an image, making it suitable for storage in a bitmap. Figure 6.2 shows a bitmap that was created using a hand-held scanner and then placed into a PageMaker document.

Figure 6.2 A scanned image in a Pagemaker document

Metafiles are created by GDI's record-and-playback facility. A metafile is cheaper than a bitmap, in terms of memory use, but is slower in terms of drawing time.

A metafile is like a cassette tape. To create a metafile, you place the tape into GDI's cassette deck and push the "Record" button. GDI calls are recorded onto the metafile until you press the "Stop" button. Once a metafile has been created, it can be stored on disk, or passed to another program. For example, the clipboard is often used to pass GDI metafiles between programs. To recreate the drawing, GDI is given the metafile "tape" and told to replay its contents.

As you get started with GDI programming, you'll probably concentrate most of your efforts on learning to draw on physical devices. After all, there are a number of subtle issues that you need to learn about before you can make effective use of display screens and printers. When you are comfortable drawing on these devices, you will then be ready to begin exploring the ways that the pseudodevices can be used to enhance your program's graphic output.

## The Programming Interface

With the variety of devices and pseudodevices that GDI supports, you might be concerned that this somehow translates into a complicated and hard-to-use graphics library. After all, some graphics libraries provide two sets of routines: one for display screens and one for printers. If GDI were like that, you might have *four* different sets of drawing routines to worry about: one each for displays, printers, bitmaps, and metafiles.

But GDI is not like that: GDI has one set of routines for all devices. The `SetPixel` routine, for example, draws a single pixel on all devices that GDI supports. The `Polyline` routine draws a series of connected lines on any GDI-supported device or pseudodevice. In this chapter, we're going to focus our attention on writing output to the display screen. Nevertheless, the material in this chapter applies to all of the different devices that GDI supports.

## Drawing Coordinates

Before you can use GDI to create any output, you need to understand how GDI interprets drawing coordinates. GDI gives you quite a bit of control over drawing coordinates. For example, you can ask GDI to use inches, millimeters, or hybrid units that you specify. For the most control over your drawing, GDI lets you specify units that correspond to a device's native pixels. GDI uses the term **mapping mode** to refer to the different coordinate systems that it supports. Table 6.1 shows the eight mapping modes available in GDI.

**Table 6.1** GDI mapping modes

| Mapping Mode Name | 1 Logical Unit | Inches | Millimeters |
|---|---|---|---|
| MM_TEXT | 1 pixel | — | — |
| MM_HIMETRIC | 0.01 mm | 0.000394 | 0.01 |
| MM_TWIPS | 1/1440 inches | 0.000694 | 0.0176 |
| MM_HIENGLISH | 0.001 inches | 0.001 | 0.0254 |
| MM_LOMETRIC | 0.1 mm | 0.00394 | 0.1 |
| MM_LOENGLISH | 0.01 inches | 0.01 | 0.254 |
| MM_ISOTROPIC | } Scaling based on ratio between two device context | | |
| MM_ANISOTROPIC | } attribute values: window and viewport extents | | |

In this chapter, we're going to limit ourselves to GDI's default mapping mode: MM_TEXT. In this mapping mode, a unit refers to a pixel—that is, to the smallest "picture element" that a device can draw. This mapping mode gives us the greatest control over graphic output and avoids rounding errors that other mapping modes can create. It is often used for programs that require absolute precision. For example, Aldus PageMaker, a page layout program, uses the MM_TEXT mapping mode to ensure that objects aligned on the display screen match the alignment on the printer.

One drawback to MM_TEXT, however, is that it requires additional effort to avoid writing device-specific programs. That's the key advantage to the other mapping modes: They provide a way to draw in a device-independent manner.

An advantage of MM_TEXT coordinates is that they are identical to the coordinates that are used for mouse input. This coordinate system is called **client area coordinates**. In client area coordinates, the origin (0,0) is located at the upper-left corner of the client area. Unlike the Cartesian coordinate system that you may remember from your high school days, the value of $y$ increases as we move downward. Figure 6.3 shows the location of the origin and the directions in which $x$ and $y$ values increase.

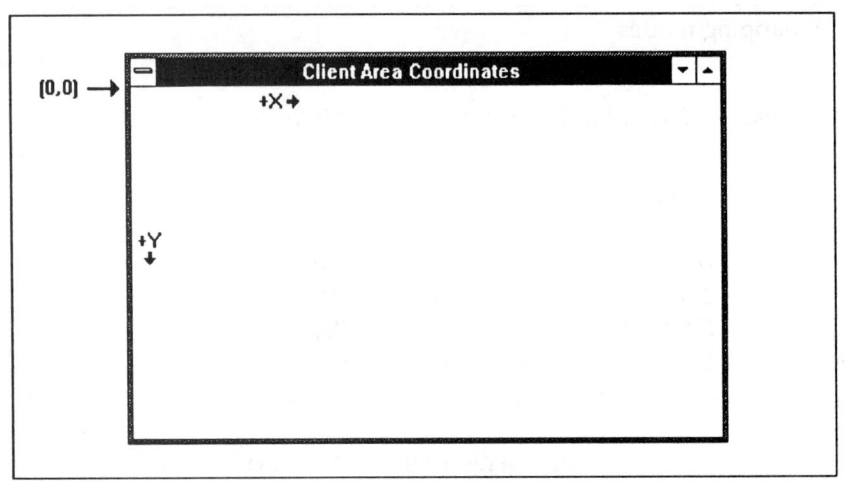

**Figure 6.3** GDI's default coordinate system

## Logical Drawing Objects

One of the means that GDI uses to achieve device independence is through the use of logical drawing objects. A logical drawing object describes how output should appear: It is a high-level, device-independent request. GDI supports the following logical drawing objects: pens (to draw lines), brushes (to fill areas), fonts (to display text), and logical colors (to describe color).

When a logical drawing object is created, it can be used on any device. But the results may differ from one device to another, since devices have different capabilities. For example, a red pen might draw a red line on a 16-color EGA display but draw a black line on a monochrome dot-matrix printer. It's the device driver's job to interpret a logical drawing object in a way that makes sense given a specific device's capabilities.

As we introduce each type of GDI drawing primitive, we'll describe the use of different logical drawing objects, and provide sample code to show how to use them.

# The Device Context

To get an idea of how GDI works with different types of devices, let's take a look at a GDI drawing routine: **TextOut**. This routine displays a single line of text on any GDI-supported device. This line of code writes the word "Hello":

```
TextOut (hdc, 10, 10, "Hello", 5);
```

Notice the first parameter: **hdc**. This is a commonly used Hungarian prefix for an important GDI data type: a **handle to a device context.** Recall what we have already said about handles: They are 16-bit unsigned integers used to identify objects. The object identified by this handle plays a key role whenever a Windows program wishes to draw on any device: It is a **device context** (or DC, for short).

A device context is a combination of several things rolled into one. It is a toolbox full of drawing tools, a connection to a specific device, and a permission slip to help GDI control the use of different devices by different programs. GDI never gives a program direct access to a device context. Instead, it provides a handle to identify a specific DC. Like the **TextOut** routine, every GDI drawing routine takes a DC handle as its first parameter.

As a toolbox, the DC is a set of **drawing attributes** that include one pen to draw lines, one brush to fill areas, and one font to display text. At any time while drawing, you can change the tools in a DC to give you, for example, red lines, green areas, and bold text. Put together, drawing attributes give you total control over the appearance and location of your program's output.

Every DC is a toolbox with 20 drawing attributes. By storing these in the DC, GDI hides complexity from you. There is a slight drawback to this approach, but we think you'll agree in the long run that it makes GDI easier to work with.

The drawback is that, until you become familiar with what they do for you, hidden attributes can be confusing. For example, consider the **TextOut** routine. We'll add some comments to explain the parameters:

```
TextOut (hdc,    /* Handle to DC.          */
         10,     /* X-location of text.    */
         10,     /* Y-location of text.    */
         "Hello",/* Text to display.       */
         5);     /* Text length.           */
```

From this code, can you tell what color the letters will be? Will they be red, blue, or black? And what type of font will be used—will it be 14-point bold Times Roman, or 24-point italicized Helvetica? Because this information is part of the DC, you can't answer these questions by simply reading this line of code.

## 122  Introduction to the Graphics Device Interface

When the **TextOut** routine draws, it plucks the drawing attributes it needs from the DC. These attributes determine the appearance and location of the displayed text (including text color and font). As we introduce the different GDI drawing routines, we'll describe the DC attributes that each set of routines depends upon.

By hiding their drawing attributes in a DC, GDI routines can get by with a minimum number of parameters. In practical terms, this means less typing for you when you write code that calls GDI. After all, drawing attributes tend to stay the same from one call to the next. To get an idea of the work that might be required in a world without a DC, consider what the **TextOut** function might look like:

```
/* Mythical TextOut in a world without a DC. */
TextOut (10,          /* X-location of text.       */
         10,          /* Y-location of text.       */
         "Hello",     /* Text to display.          */
         5,           /* Length of text.           */
         coFore,      /* Foreground text color.    */
         coBack,      /* Background text color.    */
         hClip,       /* Clipping Region.          */
         hPalette,    /* Color Palette.            */
         hFont,       /* Text Font.                */
         iSpace,      /* Intercharacter spacing.   */
         mmMapMode,   /* Mapping mode.             */
         xyViewExt,   /* Viewport extent.          */
         xyViewOrg,   /* Viewport origin.          */
         xyWinExt,    /* Window extent.            */
         xyWinOrg);   /* Window origin.            */
```

Even without knowing the meaning of each drawing attribute, you can tell that 15 is a lot more than the five parameters that **TextOut** actually needs. In a world without DCs, you'd have a lot of work to do just to say "Hello."

What's in a DC? Table 6.2 lists all the drawing attributes in a DC. For your convenience, we have indicated the type of primitive that uses each attribute.

**Table 6.2**  Drawing attributes in a DC

| Drawing Attribute | Default Value | Lines | Filled Areas | Text | Raster | Comments |
|---|---|---|---|---|---|---|
| Background color | White | x | x | x |  | Styled pen, hatch brush, text |
| Background mode | OPAQUE | x | x | x |  | On/off switch |
| Brush handle | White brush |  | x |  | x | Filled areas |
| Brush origin | (0,0) |  | x |  | x | Hatch and dithered brushes |

*(Continued)*

| | | | | | | |
|---|---|---|---|---|---|---|
| Clipping region handle | Entire surface | x | x | x | x | |
| Color palette handle | Default palette | x | x | x | | |
| Current pen position | (0,0) | x | | | | For `LineTo` routine |
| Drawing mode | R2_COPYPEN | x | x | | | Boolean mixing |
| Font handle | System font | | | x | | |
| Intercharacter spacing | 0 | | | x | | |
| Mapping mode | MM_TEXT | x | x | x | x | One unit = 1 pixel |
| Pen handle | Black pen | x | x | | | |
| Polygon-filling mode | Alternate | | x | | | For `Polygon` routine |
| Stretching mode | Black on white | | | | x | For `StretchBlt` routine |
| Text alignment | Left and top | | | x | | |
| Text color | Black | | x | x | | Foreground color for text and for monochrome pattern brushes |
| Text justification | 0,0 | | | x | | Break extra and character extra |
| Viewport extent | (1,1) | x | x | x | x | Coordinate mapping |
| Viewport origin | (0,0) | x | x | x | x | Coordinate mapping |
| Window extent | (1,1) | x | x | x | x | Coordinate mapping |
| Window origin | (0,0) | x | x | x | x | Coordinate mapping |

Not every drawing attribute in the DC is used by every drawing routine. For example, the text color is never used to draw lines. Instead, each drawing routine takes the attributes it needs from the DC. Let's look at the other roles played by the DC.

The second role of a DC is that it connects a program to a specific drawing surface. For example, a program that wants to draw on the system display must gain access to a DC for the system display (we'll describe how this is done in a moment). To draw on a printer, or on a pseudodevice like a bitmap, a program obtains a DC to connect to each of these drawing surfaces.

The connection that the DC provides is a logical connection and not a physical one. Windows, after all, is a multitasking system. If programs had direct access to the physical device, it would cause confusion both for the user and for the Windows programs. As each program fought to maintain control of a given device, the result would be mixed up graphical nonsense.

To understand what we mean by a physical connection, consider the way an MS-DOS program like Quattro Pro works. When it draws on the display, it writes directly to the memory buffers on the video adapter board. It directly manipulates the hardware registers to cause the hardware to perform the necessary tricks to display the desired spreadsheet or graph. To support this capability, it requires a private device driver so that it can tell the difference between the CGA, VGA, and 8514/a display cards. Lotus 1-2-3 is able to do this because MS-DOS is a single-tasking operating system. There isn't any danger that other programs might be disrupted.

But Windows is multitasking, so programs cannot access a physical output device without disrupting other programs. Instead, a Windows program must use the logical connection represented by the DC. All Windows programs use this approach, so that GDI can resolve the conflicts that might otherwise disrupt the system when two programs access the same device. This introduces the third role of a DC: its role as a permission slip.

To avoid conflicts on shared devices, a DC is a permission slip that a program must have before it can draw on any device. The permission system works in one of two ways, depending on the type of device. On hard-copy devices, the process is known as **spooling**. On video display devices, the permission system is called **clipping**.

On printers and plotters, GDI borrows a technique from mainframe computers: Output is spooled to disk. The Windows spooler, also known as the Print Manager, plays the role of a traffic cop to direct the flow of output to hard-copy devices. Otherwise, the output of one program might get mixed in with the pages of another. For spooled output, the DC helps GDI keep different print jobs separate.

On the display screen, Windows takes a different approach to separate the output from different programs. The method is called **clipping**. Clipping involves the creation of imaginary fences around a program's drawing area. To paraphrase an old saying: "Good fences make good Windows programs."

My next-door neighbor has a fence around his yard that prevents his dog from running away. The dog can go where he wants inside the yard, but cannot stray into my yard. The fences that GDI creates provide the same type of boundary enforcement. When a program wants to draw in a window, it gets a DC from the Window Manager that has a built-in fence around the window's client area. Inside the fence, a program is free to draw what it wants. But the fence prevents the program from letting its drawing stray.

An example might clarify exactly what we mean by clipping. Figure 6.4 shows two programs sharing the display screen: NOTEPAD and CLOCK. Before either program draws, a fence is built to prevent the program from drawing outside its client area.

The NOTEPAD program's fence forms a rectangle. Notice that the fence prevents NOTEPAD from drawing on the face of the CLOCK. It also prevents NOTEPAD from drawing on the nonclient area of its own window. After all, like most Windows programs, NOTEPAD doesn't maintain the nonclient area of its window; it leaves that work to Windows.

The clipping for CLOCK is a little more complex. But we know that the clipping works because CLOCK's sweeping second hand doesn't brush NOTEPAD away. Instead, the clock hands appear to go "behind" the NOTEPAD window. Figure 6.5 shows the shape of the fence that prevents NOTEPAD from drawing outside its client area.

You might imagine that CLOCK has its work cut out for it to avoid drawing on NOTEPAD. In fact, CLOCK doesn't even know that NOTEPAD is present. The DC that CLOCK gets from the Window Manager is the key to this magic. When CLOCK calls different GDI drawing routines, the DC handle lets GDI check the location of the fence to make sure that no drawing is done out of bounds. Hence, there is very little work that CLOCK must do; GDI does it all.

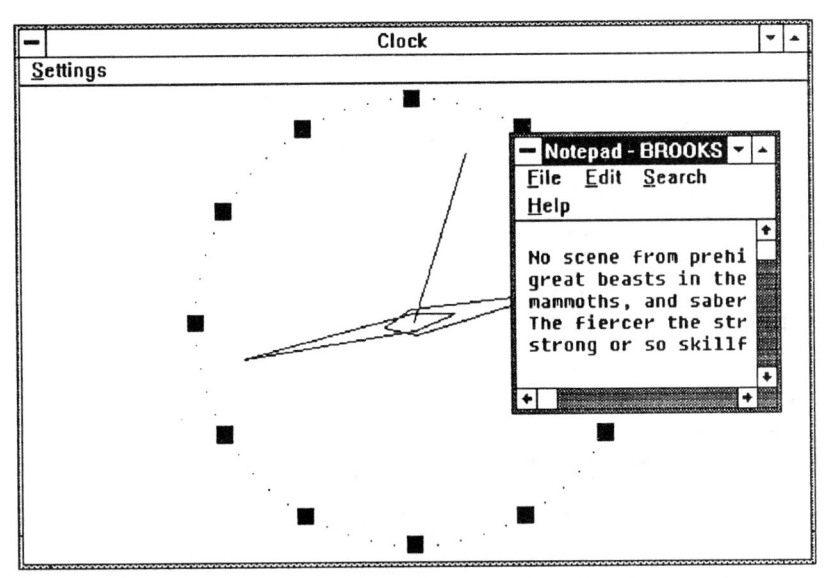

**Figure 6.4** Output from Clock and Notepad are kept separate through clipping

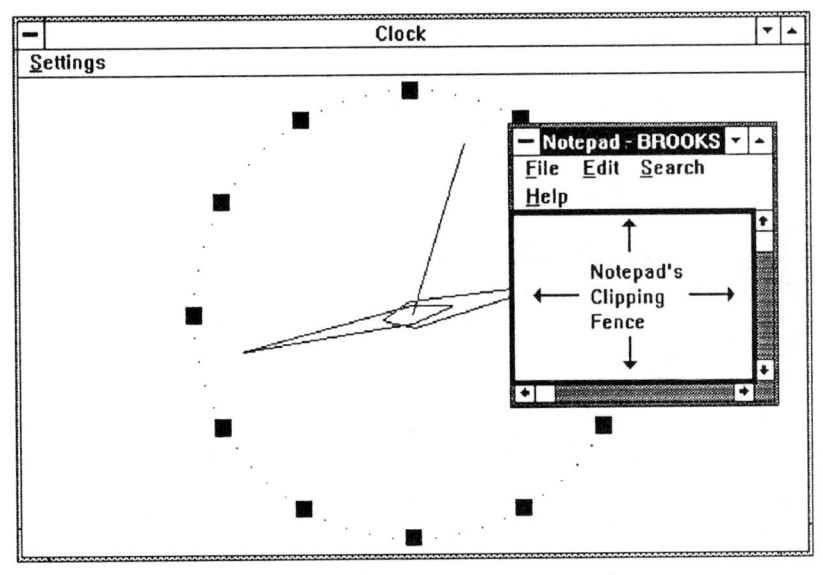

**Figure 6.5** The shape of the fence around Notepad

126  *Introduction to the Graphics Device Interface*

How does GDI perform boundary checking? Let's look at the simpler case: the way GDI clips NOTEPAD's output to the rectangle that makes up NOTEPAD's client area. GDI works with the device driver to establish a rectangular fence, which is defined in terms of four coordinates: top side, left side, bottom side, and right side. The boundaries of this fence are part of a drawing attribute in the DC: the **clipping region**. Every GDI drawing routine checks these boundaries when it draws. As you can tell by looking at the NOTEPAD window, this means that letters might be chopped in half. But this is necessary to make windowing a reality.

The more complex clipping we observe in CLOCK can be understood in terms of this simpler case. Namely, GDI defines clipping for CLOCK in terms of the four rectangles shown in Figure 6.6. Now instead of the four boundaries for one rectangle, GDI works with 16 boundaries for four rectangles. The principle is the same, even though GDI does four times as much work. To handle clipping like this, GDI treats each drawing operation like four separate drawing operations, with one for each clipping rectangle.

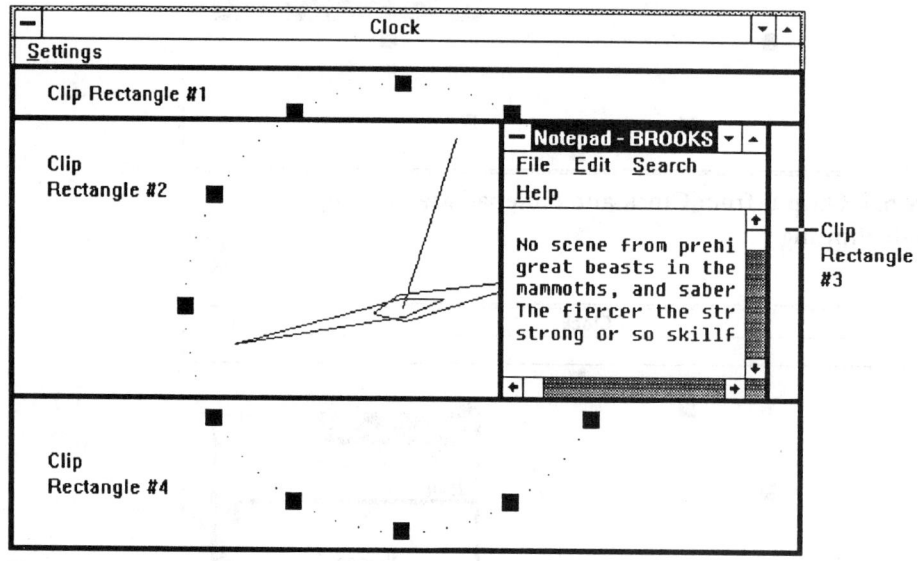

**Figure 6.6** The four clip rectangles for Clock

This complex clipping gives us a clue to how GDI stores clipping information. A set of one or more rectangles is combined into a data structure called a clipping region. As we mentioned earlier, a clipping region is an attribute that is part of the DC. This means that clipping can be performed on any GDI device. A clipping region might contain the entire drawing surface. Or, as we have seen, it might contain a set of one or more rectangles.

While clipping can be done on any device, clipping on the display screen is special. The reason is that Windows provides the clipping information to keep one program from accidentally overwriting another program's output. The part of Windows that takes care of display screen clipping is the part of Windows responsible for creating windows: the Window Manager.

## Clipping and the Window Manager

From our discussion of the interaction between NOTEPAD and CLOCK, it is clear that GDI's ability to perform clipping is what makes windowing possible. It lets programs share the display screen without requiring programs to worry about stepping on each other's toes.

Although GDI routines provide the clipping service, GDI itself does not set window boundaries. That job belongs to the Window Manager. When we introduced the Window Manager in Chapter 1, we said it was responsible for the user interface. Since the user interface resides on the display screen, the Window Manager builds and maintains all the display screen "fences."

The Window Manager owns a set of DCs for drawing on the system display. When a program wants to draw in a window, it borrows one of these DCs. Before it lends a DC to a program, the Window Manager installs a clipping region. There are three different Window Manager routines that a program can use to borrow a DC. For each of them, a different clipping region is installed in the DC. These routines are shown in Table 6.3, along with the routine that is used to return the DC to the Window Manager. When a program borrows a DC from the Window Manager, it must be careful to return the DC when it is finished. As you'll see shortly, this is the role of the "Sandwich" code construction.

Table 6.3  Routines to borrow and return system display DCs

| Borrowing Routine | Returning Routine | Description |
| --- | --- | --- |
| BeginPaint | EndPaint | Clip to invalid part of client area |
| GetDC | ReleaseDC | Clip to entire client area |
| GetWindowDC | ReleaseDC | Clip to entire window (client and non-client areas) |

## 128  *Introduction to the Graphics Device Interface*

Figure 6.7 gives an example of how clipping is set for each of these three routines.

The first routine, `BeginPaint`, allows a program to respond to requests by the Window Manager to draw in a window or repair damage that has been done to part of a window. The Window Manager sends the **WM_PAINT** message to let a program know that a window needs to be repaired. As you'll see, this message plays a central role in the maintenance of a window's client area.

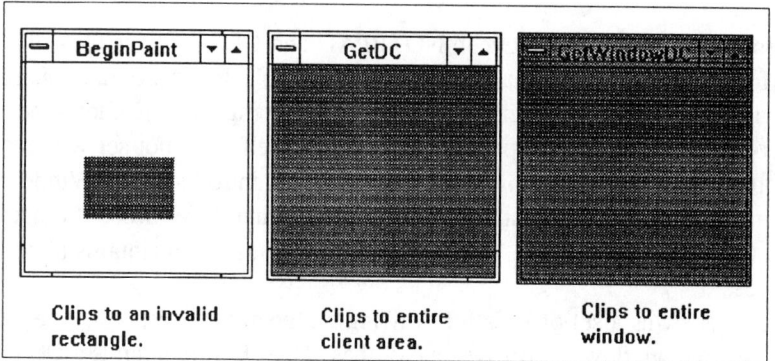

**Figure 6.7** Three ways that the Window Manager sets clipping

The second routine, `GetDC`, allows a program to draw in the client area of a window. The clipping fence keeps output in the client area, even if another program's window is lying on top of the client area, as we saw in the CLOCK-NOTEPAD example. This routine is used for most drawing *outside* the **WM_PAINT** message. For example, in response to a **WM_CHAR** message, we might wish to echo the character typed.

The third routine, `GetWindowDC`, sets clipping to allow drawing anywhere in a window, including the nonclient area. This routine is called by the Window Manager itself to draw the nonclient parts of a window. After all, a Windows program typically does not do this work itself, but lets the default window procedure take care of it.

This introduction to GDI may have left you hungering for some sample code to provide a framework for understanding all of the concepts that we've introduced. In our next chapter, we're going to look at a program that illuminates a single pixel, but it will also introduce you to one of the most important messages that Windows programs work with: WM_PAINT. We'll also discuss how Windows handles color, and we'll enhance GDI's drawing primitives by creating one of our own to draw markers.

# 7

# Pixels and Markers

The first program that we're going to look at lights up a single pixel. In doing so, it introduces you to the most important message for any program that draws on the display: **WM_PAINT**. Figure 7.1 shows three instances of PIXEL running. As you can see, the program illuminates a pixel in the very center of the client area.

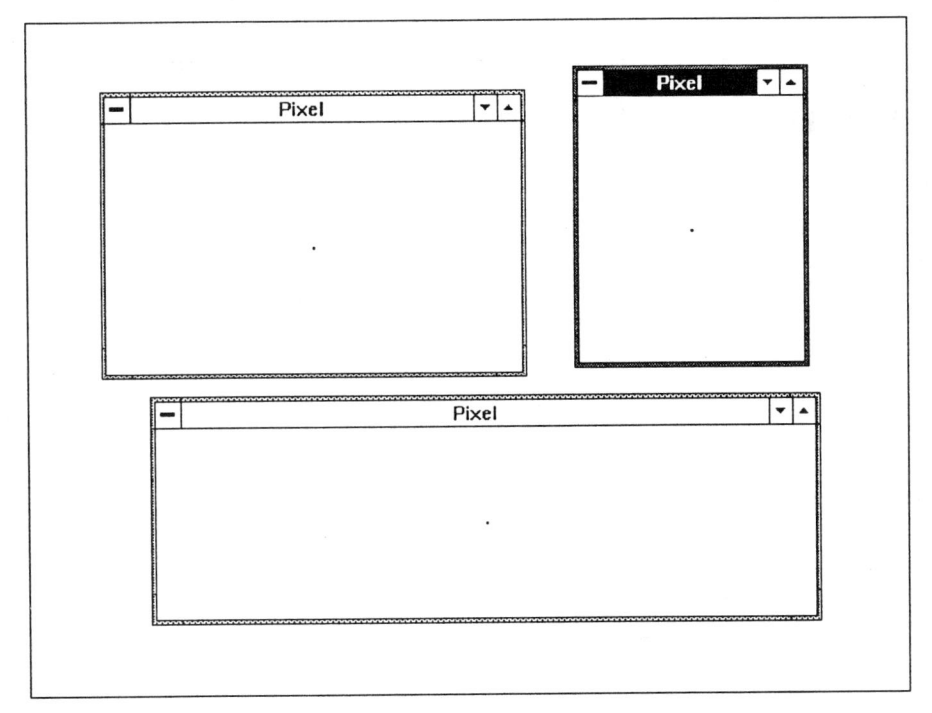

**Figure 7.1** Three instances of PIXEL

## 130  *Introduction to the Graphics Device Interface*

Like other programs in this book, MIN serves as a starting point for this program. Here is the source listing for the files that make up PIXEL.

# MAKEFILE.MAK

```
.AUTODEPEND

#    Translator Definitions
INC=\BORLANDC\OWL\INCLUDE;\BORLANDC\CLASSLIB\INCLUDE;\BORLANDC\INCLUDE
CC = bcc -c -D_CLASSDLL -H -ml -WS -w -I$(INC)

#    Implicit Rules
.c.obj:
   $(CC) {$< }

.cpp.obj:
   $(CC) {$< }

#    Explicit Rules
Pixel.exe: Pixel.res Pixel.def Pixel.obj
     tlink /c/C/n/P-/Twe/x @Pixel.LNK
     rlink Pixel.res Pixel.exe

#    Individual File Dependencies
Pixel.obj: Pixel.cpp

Pixel.res: Pixel.rc Pixel.cur Pixel.ico
     brcc -FO Pixel.res -i$(INC) Pixel.RC
```

# PIXEL.LNK

```
\borlandc\lib\c0wl.obj+
Pixel.obj
Pixel,Pixel
\borlandc\classlib\lib\tclasdll.lib+
\borlandc\owl\lib\owl.lib+
mathwl.lib+
import.lib+
crtldll.lib
Pixel.def
```

# PIXEL.CPP

```
/*----------------------------------------------------------*\
|   PIXEL.CPP    Illuminates a group of pixels in the center  |
|                of the client area.                          |
\*----------------------------------------------------------*/
#define WIN31
#define STRICT
#include <owl.h>
#include <WindowsX.h>
```

```
/*--------------------------------------------------------------*\
|                    Class Declarations.                         |
\*--------------------------------------------------------------*/
class TPixelApplication : public TApplication
  {
  public:
    TPixelApplication (LPSTR lpszName, HINSTANCE hInstance,
                       HINSTANCE hPrevInstance, LPSTR lpszCmdLine,
                       int nCmdShow);
    virtual void InitMainWindow ();
  };

class TPixelWindow : public TWindow
  {
  public:
    TPixelWindow (PTWindowsObject pwParent, LPSTR lpszTitle,
                  PTModule pmModule);
    virtual LPSTR GetClassName ();
    virtual void  GetWindowClass (WNDCLASS&);
    virtual void  WMPaint(TMessage& Msg) = [WM_FIRST + WM_PAINT];
  };

/*--------------------------------------------------------------*\
|                  Main Function:  WinMain.                      |
\*--------------------------------------------------------------*/
int PASCAL WinMain (HINSTANCE hInstance,   HINSTANCE hPrevInstance,
                    LPSTR    lpszCmdLine, int    nCmdShow)
    {
    TPixelApplication Pixel ("Pixel", hInstance, hPrevInstance,
                             lpszCmdLine, nCmdShow);
    Pixel.Run();
    return Pixel.Status;
    }

/*--------------------------------------------------------------*\
|                  Application Class Member.                     |
\*--------------------------------------------------------------*/
TPixelApplication::TPixelApplication (LPSTR lpszName,
                  HINSTANCE hInstance, HINSTANCE hPrevInstance,
                  LPSTR lpszCmdLine, int nCmdShow)
                :TApplication (lpszName, hInstance,
                  hPrevInstance, lpszCmdLine, nCmdShow)
    {
    /* Application specific initialization goes here.  */
    }

/*--------------------------------------------------------------*\
|                  Application Class Member.                     |
\*--------------------------------------------------------------*/
void TPixelApplication::InitMainWindow ()
    {
    MainWindow = new TPixelWindow (NULL, "Pixel", NULL);
    }

/*--------------------------------------------------------------*\
|                  TPixelWindow Class Member.                    |
\*--------------------------------------------------------------*/
TPixelWindow::TPixelWindow (PTWindowsObject pwParent,
             LPSTR lpszTitle, PTModule pmModule)
          :TWindow (pwParent, lpszTitle, pmModule)
    {
    /* Window specific initialization goes here.  */
    }
```

```
/*-------------------------------------------------------------*\
|                   TPixelWindow Class Member.                  |
\*-------------------------------------------------------------*/
LPSTR TPixelWindow::GetClassName ()
    {
    return "Pixel:MAIN";
    }

/*-------------------------------------------------------------*\
|                   TPixelWindow Class Member.                  |
\*-------------------------------------------------------------*/
void TPixelWindow::GetWindowClass (WNDCLASS& wc)
    {
    TWindow::GetWindowClass (wc);
    wc.hIcon=LoadIcon (wc.hInstance, "snapshot");
    wc.hCursor=LoadCursor (wc.hInstance, "hand");
    wc.style= CS_HREDRAW | CS_VREDRAW;
    }

/*-------------------------------------------------------------*\
|                   TPixelWindow Class Member.                  |
\*-------------------------------------------------------------*/
void TPixelWindow::WMPaint(TMessage&)
    {
    int         x, y;
    PAINTSTRUCT ps;
    RECT        rClient;

    BeginPaint(HWindow, &ps);
    GetClientRect (HWindow, &rClient);
    x = rClient.right  / 2;
    y = rClient.bottom / 2;

    SetPixel (ps.hdc, x, y, RGB (0, 0, 0));

    EndPaint(HWindow, &ps);
    }
```

## PIXEL.RC

```
snapshot icon Pixel.ico

hand cursor Pixel.cur
```

## PIXEL.DEF

```
NAME PIXEL

EXETYPE WINDOWS

DESCRIPTION 'Pixel -- SetPixel sample program'

CODE MOVEABLE DISCARDABLE
DATA MOVEABLE MULTIPLE

HEAPSIZE  512
STACKSIZE 5120
```

PIXEL's `WinMain` function is essentially the same as MIN's. And its application object and window object initialization code is basically the same as well. There is one change worth mentioning, however. We have added two new style bits to the window class definition:

```
wc.style=CS_HREDRAW | CS_VREDRAW;
```

These style bits direct the Window Manager to generate a **WM_PAINT** message when the size of the window changes, in either the vertical direction (**CS_VREDRAW**) or in the horizontal direction (**CS_HREDRAW**). These style bits cause the entire window to be redrawn (via the **WM_PAINT** message) whenever the window size changes to ensure that the pixel is always at the center of our window.

The **WM_PAINT** message is the most important message for any program that draws in a window. Like a bull in a china shop, the user can cause quite a bit of damage as he tromps across the display screen: Windows are moved, resized, opened, and closed. Dialog boxes are brought up and dismissed, and data is scrolled inside various windows.

Each of these actions can cause holes to appear in the user interface. Windows does its best to patch these holes, but in many cases Windows can't do it alone. In particular, when the client area of a window has been overwritten, Windows has a limited ability to repair the damage.

There are occasions when Windows is able to anticipate that an object (like a dialog box or a menu) will overwrite a window for a very short period of time. In these cases, Windows takes a snapshot of the area that is about to be overwritten. When the short-term guest disappears, Windows restores the screen without any outside help.

But such snapshots are quite memory intensive, so Windows only does this when it is critical to the performance of the user interface. For example, a snapshot is taken of the area under a menu to allow popup menus to appear and disappear very quickly. If this critical part of the user interface ran slowly, it would make the entire system seem sluggish.

Most of the time, Windows calls on your program to help repair holes in the user interface via the **WM_PAINT** message. In response to **WM_PAINT**, your window object obtains a DC, which gives it the drawing tools, device access, and permission slip it needs to draw in—and repair—the contents of the window.

# The BeginPaint Routine

The `BeginPaint` routine provides the required DC. `BeginPaint` borrows a DC from the supply that the Window Manager maintains. This routine is specially designed to work with the **WM_PAINT** message, because it installs a clipping region in the DC that corresponds to the damaged part of our window. This area is sometimes referred to as a window's **invalid region** or **invalid rectangle** (if the region is defined as a simple rectangle).

The invalid region might consist of the entire client area of our window, but in many cases it includes only a portion of the client area. For example, Figure 7.2 shows CLOCK and PIXEL sharing the display screen, with one corner of CLOCK covering part of PIXEL's client area. When we click on PIXEL to activate its window, the covered part of PIXEL's client area must be redrawn. That's the job of the `WM_PAINT` message. The dotted lines in the figure show the shape of the clipping region that is installed in the DC that **BeginPaint** returns. By making the invalid region a subset of the total client area, the Window Manager helps minimize the amount of effort that is required to repair a damaged window.

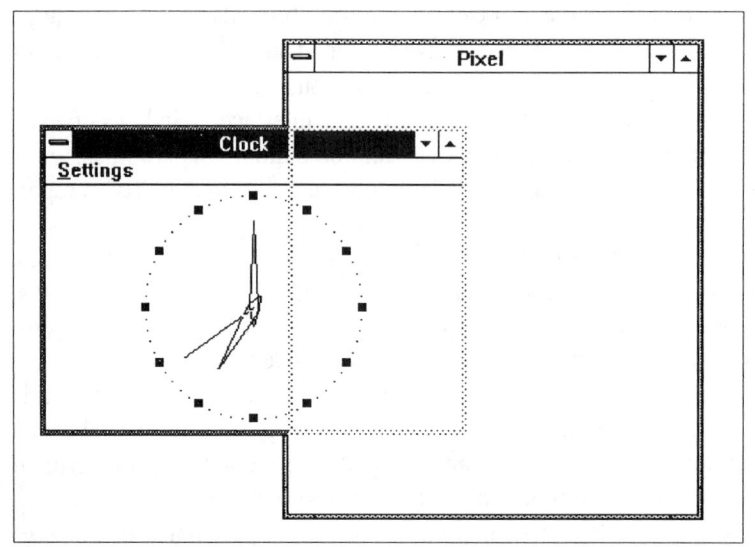

**Figure 7.2 CLOCK covering part of PIXEL's client area**

From our earlier discussion on clipping, you may recall that the clipping rectangle shown in Figure 7.2 only allows drawing inside the boundaries of the clipping fence. Outside the fence, no drawing is allowed. Why is clipping set in this manner?

Recall that the purpose of a **WM_PAINT** message is to repair damage to a window. As shown in the example, the clipping fence surrounds the *exact* part of the window that has been damaged. On the one hand, this is the only area in which our program will be allowed to draw. But on the other hand, this is the only part into which we need to draw. By definition, we don't need to repair the undamaged part of a window in response to a **WM_PAINT** message.

Let's take a closer look at the code involved with handling the **WM_PAINT** message, to get a better idea of what is involved.

`BeginPaint` takes two parameters: a window handle and a pointer to a `PAINTSTRUCT` data structure. The window handle identifies the window whose client area is to be repaired.

The `PAINTSTRUCT` structure is defined in WINDOWS.H as

```
typedef struct tagPAINTSTRUCT
  {
    HDC     hdc;
    BOOL    fErase;
    RECT    rcPaint;
    BOOL    fRestore;
    BOOL    fIncUpdate;
    BYTE    rgbReserved[16];
  } PAINTSTRUCT;
```

Of the six fields in this data structure, only the first and third are really useful. The first field, `hdc`, is a DC handle that we'll pass to GDI drawing routines. According to the *ObjectWindows for C++ Reference Guide*, the second field, `fErase`, is a flag that is supposed to tell us if our window needs erasing or not. In fact, this field always has the value of zero. The fourth, fifth, and sixth fields are all used internally by Windows.

The `rcPaint` field describes a rectangle that bounds the damaged area of our window—that is, the invalid region of our window. While most programs ignore this field, it serves as a hint that a program can use to minimize the amount of work it forces GDI to do. For example, if a program did a lot of drawing in a window, it might use this rectangle to decide exactly what needed repairing. By preclipping to this rectangle, drawing-intensive programs can get a substantial performance improvement.

`BeginPaint` gives us a handle to a DC, which is all we need to draw our pixel. Let's look at the other routines that our window procedure calls in response to the `WM_PAINT` message.

## GetClientRect Routine

Earlier, we compared a window to a canvas on which an artist draws. Unlike an artist's canvas, however, a window can change size. To help you cope with that change, the `GetClientRect` routine allows you to determine the size of a window's client area (saving this information from the `WM_SIZE` message also does the trick). `GetClientRect` takes two parameters:

- **A window handle.** We use the window handle data member, `HWindow`, inherited by our window class.

- **A pointer to a rectangle (RECT) data structure.** The size of the client area, in pixels, is returned in this structure.

The RECT structure is defined in WINDOWS.H as shown here:

```
typedef struct tagRECT
  {
    int  left;
    int  top;
    int  right;
    int  bottom;
  } RECT;
```

One aspect of **GetClientRect** is that it always returns zero in two of these fields—**left** and **top**—so they can be safely ignored. To determine the client area size, we rely on the **right** and **bottom** fields. We position the pixel in the middle of the client area using the values **r.right/2** and **r.bottom/2** as *x* and *y* coordinates.

## SetPixel Routine

The SetPixel routine takes four parameters:

```
SetPixel (hDC, X, Y, crColor);
```

- **Handle to a device context.** We use the handle provided by **BeginPaint**.
- ***x* and *y* coordinates.** We positioned the pixel in the middle of the client area by dividing the values returned in **GetClientRect** by two.
- **Color.** GDI provides three ways to specify color: an RGB triplet, a palette index, and a palette-relative RGB triplet.

An RGB triplet gets its name from its three parts: a red value, a green value, and a blue value. An RGB triplet is always an unsigned long integer, that is, a four-byte-wide, 32-bit value. Three of the bytes are used to store the red, green, and blue intensity of the color you are looking for. With one byte per color, that means there are 256 intensities for each color, and over 16 million unique combinations.

The **RGB** macro in WINDOWS.H provides the easiest means for creating an RGB triplet. The syntax for this macro is

```
rgbColor = RGB (bRed, bGreen, bBlue)
```

where `bRed`, `bGreen`, and `bBlue` are integers between 0 and 255. The **RGB** macro packs the intensity of all three colors into a single unsigned long integer.

Although you can specify over 16 million different RGB combinations, the actual color that is produced will depend on the device. For example, the 16-color EGA adapter will map the RGB values to the nearest available physical color. When we talk about pens, we'll talk about how GDI **dithers** to simulate many more colors on a device. But for pixels, the only colors that are available are the physical, or "pure," colors. Two RGB triplets have guaranteed results: RGB (0,0,0) is always black, and RGB (255,255,255) is always white.

A second way to specify color is with a palette index. A palette is a table of RGB triplets. Therefore, at first glance, a palette index is another way to specify an RGB triplet.

But unlike RGB triplets, palettes allow a program to specify the exact physical color that should be represented. For example, the VGA and 8514/a display adapters have hardware that supports 262,144 different colors. But only 256 of these colors are available at any one moment. The device driver selects a palette that is distributed evenly across the color range. But this isn't good enough for some uses. Palettes allow a program to select the exact colors to be used in the 256 available slots.

On devices that support GDI palettes, a program can actually change the hardware registers of a device to represent the exact set of colors that are required. For example, if a program wants to display a color bitmap of a woodland scene, it might need 150 shades of green to show all the subtle nuances in the grasses, trees, and shrubs. Or a color bitmap of skiers on a snow-covered mountain might require 100 shades of white, 50 shades of hot-pink and orange, and 10 shades of blue. Palettes allow a program to show images like these on a display screen with near picture-perfect representation.

Like RGB triplets, palette indices are unsigned long integers. The only difference is that a flag is set in the fourth, unused byte to indicate that the value is a palette index and not an actual RGB triplet. The **PALETTEINDEX** macro selects a palette index value. For example, to select color number 137, you would use the following:

```
PALETTEINDEX (137);
```

The third and final way to specify color is with a palette-relative RGB index. Like an RGB triplet, this allows you to specify a red, green, and blue portion of a color. But a palette-relative RGB color is never dithered. Instead, GDI finds the nearest pure color in the existing palette, and uses it. The **PALETTERGB** macro creates this type of color reference:

```
PALETTERGB (0, 128, 255);
```

### EndPaint Routine

After all the drawing for the `WM_PAINT` message is done, a program calls the `EndPaint` routine to return the display DC to the Window Manager. When the Window Manager receives the DC, it restores all the drawing attributes to the default state so that the DC is ready to be loaned to the next program that needs to draw in a window.

The `EndPaint` routine also notifies the Window Manager that the damaged window has been repaired. In Windows' terms, the *invalid* part of a window has been made *valid*. Later in this chapter, you'll see that a program can call the `InvalidateRect` routine to declare a client area damaged, which causes a `WM_PAINT` message to be generated. The `EndPaint` routine calls another Windows library routine, `ValidateRect`, which tells the Window Manager to recognize that the window has been repaired.

If a program does not call `EndPaint` in response to a `WM_PAINT` message, the Window Manager will send a constant stream of `WM_PAINT` messages. Until the Window Manager is told that a window has been repaired, it will continue to ask you to repair it—which it does via the `WM_PAINT` message.

The use of the `BeginPaint/EndPaint` pair is the standard way that programs respond to `WM_PAINT`. As you'll see, the use of a pair of routines like this is common in other parts of Windows programming: for locking memory, reading files, and accessing the clipboard. We call this construction the **Windows sandwich**. Let's take a moment to describe this construction in more detail.

### The Windows Sandwich

A construction that you will encounter often in your Windows programming career is what we call the Windows sandwich. While this term is not something you will read about in any book on structured programming, it is important in Windows programming.

Like its culinary counterpart, the Windows sandwich has three parts: two outside pieces (the bread) which serve to hold the third part: the filling. When I was a child, my mother made sandwiches with two pieces of wheat bread and a filling of peanut butter and jelly. All three ingredients were important to the proper creation of my lunchtime meal. When making a sandwich for lunch, it's important to remember all three ingredients. It is also important to arrange the three ingredients in the proper order.

Figure 7.3 shows the three parts of the Windows programming sandwich. The first piece of bread represents a line of code that grabs a resource. The second piece of bread is the final line of code that returns the resource. In between, the filling is made up of one or more lines of code.

This construction is important because there are certain resources that you must share with every other program that's running. Windows is a multitasking system, after all. Programs must cooperate with each other to share the scarce resources of the system. The sandwich represents the most common way that this is done.

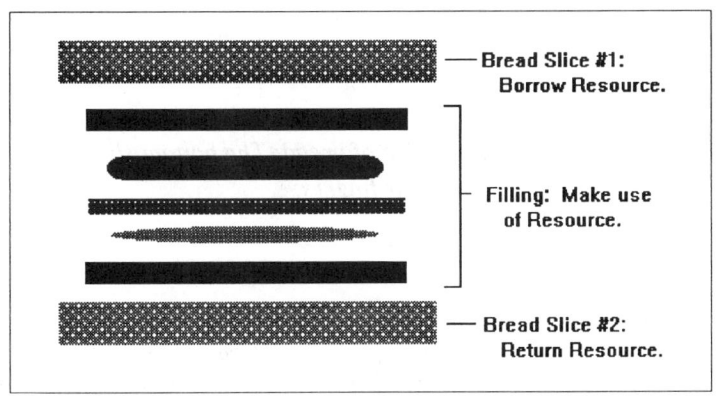

**Figure 7.3** The Windows programming sandwich

The resource we borrow might be a connection to a graphics output device, a disk file, or the Windows clipboard. In general, a sandwich holds the resource for the duration of a single message, like the DC that we borrow in response to the **WM_PAINT** message:

```
void TSampleWindow::WMPaint(TMessage&)
    {
    PAINTSTRUCT ps;

    BeginPaint(HWindow, &ps);    /* Top slice.    */
        .
        .                        /* Filling.      */
        .
    EndPaint (HWindow, &ps);     /* Bottom slice. */
    }
```

The **BeginPaint** call borrows the DC from the Window Manager. A handle to that resource is stored in the **hdc** member of the PAINTSTRUCT structure. From that line until the **EndPaint** line, the program has complete use of the DC. The filling of this sandwich in our PIXEL program drew a single pixel on the display. Once the **EndPaint** routine returns the DC, we no longer have access to it. Our program should not try to draw in the window after the second slice of bread.

*You don't have to be a chef at a four-star restaurant to tell that these sandwiches have been made incorrectly. The problem with this first sandwich is that the filling is outside the bread. You have jelly on your fingers:*

```
/* Don't do this: jelly on your fingers.  */
    void TSampleWindow::WMPaint(TMessage&)
        {
        PAINTSTRUCT ps;

        BeginPaint(HWindow, &ps);                    // Top Slice
        EndPaint (HWindow, &ps);                     // Bottom Slice
        SetPixel (ps.hdc, x, y, RGB (0, 0, 0));      // Filling
        }
```

*This sandwich is only made from a single slice of bread: The bottom slice of bread is missing. Again, you have jelly on your fingers:*

```
/* Don't do this: only one slice of bread.  */
    void TSampleWindow::WMPaint(TMessage&)
        {
        PAINTSTRUCT ps;

        BeginPaint(HWindow, &ps);                    // Top Slice
        SetPixel (ps.hdc, x, y, RGB (0, 0, 0));      // Filling
        }
```

*This sandwich is made without any bread at all. Peanut butter and jelly everywhere. Yuck.*

```
/* Don't do this: No bread at all.  */
    void TSampleWindow::WMPaint(TMessage&)
        {
        PAINTSTRUCT ps;

        SetPixel (ps.hdc, x, y, RGB (0, 0, 0));      // Filling
        }
```

A few sandwich constructions span multiple messages. You might call this a double-decker sandwich, or a Dagwood sandwich (named for the cartoon character who liked to make huge sandwiches). An example involves the capture of the mouse pointer. Sometimes, it is advantageous for a program to request exclusive use of the mouse pointer. Here is the code structure for such a sandwich:

```
void TSampleWindow::WMLButtonDown(TMessage& Msg)
    {
    SetCapture(HWindow);    // Top slice.
    .
    .
    }

void TSampleWindow::WMMouseMove(TMessage& Msg)
    {
    .                       // Filling.
```

```
            }
void TSampleWindow::WMLButtonUp(TMessage& Msg)
            {
            .
            .
            ReleaseCapture();      // Bottom slice.
            }
```

We'll take a closer look at this double-decker sandwich in Chapter 16, when we discuss mouse input. Let's move on to our next drawing primitive. This is not actually a GDI primitive, but one that we're going to build on top of the **SetPixel** routine.

## Creating Markers

Our second GDI program introduces a type of drawing primitive that is not native to GDI: **markers**. The most obvious use of a marker is on a graph, like the one in Figure 7.4. Each "+" symbol is a marker. In this example, each marker represents a population value for a given year.

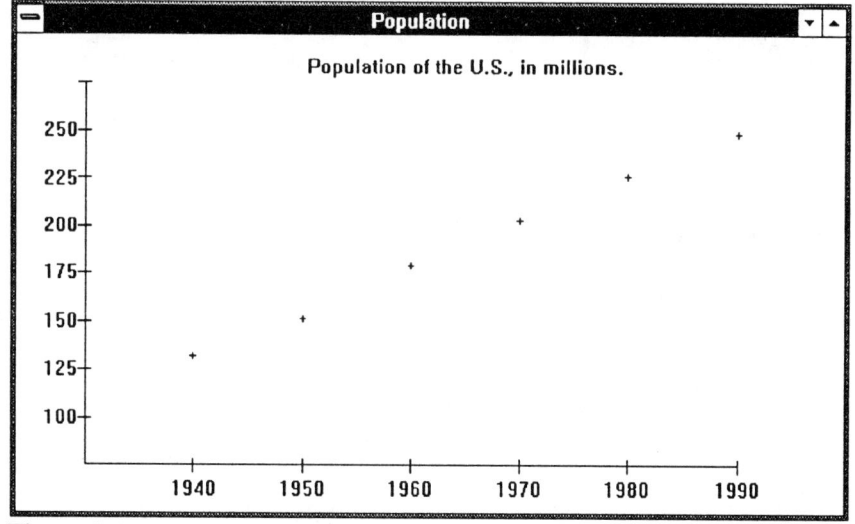

**Figure 7.4** Markers highlight points in a graph

At first glance, you might wonder why markers are special. After all, from the chart it is clear that GDI can display text. What's the difference between a marker and a text character?

142    *Introduction to the Graphics Device Interface*

As you'll see in Chapter 10, GDI text routines make it easy to work with different sizes and styles of text on a variety of devices. This very flexibility makes it difficult to guarantee that a specific letter will be centered on a specific location.

For example, if you used GDI letters to mark the location of buried treasure on a map, you introduce a margin of error. The location of the cross-hairs on the letter X, for example, will move depending on the font you are using.

Markers overcome this limitation since a marker is guaranteed to be centered over an exact location. That's the reason that markers are used for graphs. In the chapters that follow, you'll see that we use markers to help explain all of the GDI drawing routines.

One way to mark a location is with the `SetPixel` routine that we introduced in the preceding section. But a single pixel is often hard to see. For this reason, we create our "+" marker by grouping several pixels together.

When we introduce other GDI drawing primitives, we're going to use markers to show the relationship between the coordinates we specify when we call a drawing primitive and the resulting output. This will help clarify GDI's "inclusive-exclusive" drawing approach, and help you see how GDI creates lines, filled areas, and text output.

Figure 7.5 shows a sample of the output produced by our marker program, MARKER.CPP. This program uses mouse input to place markers.

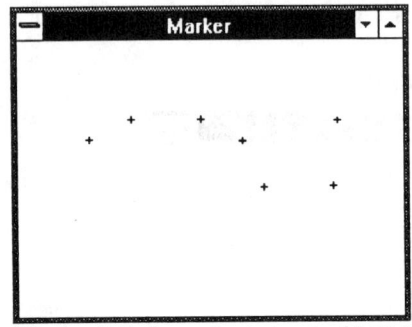

**Figure 7.5  Sample output of MARKER**

Here are the source files to MARKER:

# MAKEFILE.MAK

```
.AUTODEPEND

#       Translator Definitions
INC=\BORLANDC\OWL\INCLUDE;\BORLANDC\CLASSLIB\INCLUDE;\BORLANDC\INCLUDE
CC = bcc -c -D_CLASSDLL -H -ml -WS -w -I$(INC)

#       Implicit Rules
.c.obj:
   $(CC) {$< }
```

```
.cpp.obj:
    $(CC) {$< }

#    Explicit Rules
Marker.exe: Marker.res Marker.def Marker.obj
    tlink /c/C/n/P-/Twe/x @Marker.LNK
    rlink Marker.res Marker.exe

#    Individual File Dependencies
Marker.obj: Marker.cpp

Marker.res: Marker.rc Marker.cur Marker.ico
    brcc -FO Marker.res -i$(INC) Marker.RC
```

# MARKER.LNK

```
\borlandc\lib\c0wl.obj+
Marker.obj
Marker,Marker
\borlandc\classlib\lib\tclasdll.lib+
\borlandc\owl\lib\owl.lib+
mathwl.lib+
import.lib+
crtldll.lib
Marker.def
```

# MARKER.CPP

```
/*--------------------------------------------------------------*\
| Marker.CPP   Draws a marker in response to a mouse click.      |
\*--------------------------------------------------------------*/
#define WIN31
#define STRICT
#include <owl.h>
#include <WindowsX.h>

#define MOUSEX(arg)  (arg.LP.Lo)
#define MOUSEY(arg)  (arg.LP.Hi)

/*--------------------------------------------------------------*\
|                       Constants.                               |
\*--------------------------------------------------------------*/
const int MAXPOINTS   = 32;
const int MARKERSIZE  = 3;

/*--------------------------------------------------------------*\
|                    Class Declarations.                         |
\*--------------------------------------------------------------*/
class TMarkerApplication : public TApplication
    {
    public:
      TMarkerApplication (LPSTR lpszName, HINSTANCE hInstance,
                          HINSTANCE hPrevInstance, LPSTR lpszCmdLine,
```

```
                              int nCmdShow);
        virtual void InitMainWindow ();
    };

class TMarkerWindow : public TWindow
    {
public:
    TMarkerWindow (PTWindowsObject pwParent, LPSTR lpszTitle,
                   PTModule pmModule);
    virtual LPSTR GetClassName ();
    virtual void  GetWindowClass (WNDCLASS&);
    virtual void  WMLButtonDown(TMessage& Msg) = [WM_LBUTTONDOWN];
    virtual void  WMPaint(TMessage& Msg) = [WM_PAINT];
    int cpt;
    POINT pt[MAXPOINTS];
    };
/*----------------------------------------------------------------*\
|                    Function Prototypes.                          |
\*----------------------------------------------------------------*/
void DrawMarker (HDC hDC, int x, int y);

/*----------------------------------------------------------------*\
|                  Main Function:  WinMain.                        |
\*----------------------------------------------------------------*/
int PASCAL WinMain (HINSTANCE hInstance,   HINSTANCE hPrevInstance,
                    LPSTR lpszCmdLine, int    nCmdShow)
    {
    TMarkerApplication Marker ("Marker", hInstance,
                               hPrevInstance, lpszCmdLine,
                               nCmdShow);

    Marker.Run();
    return Marker.Status;
    }

/*----------------------------------------------------------------*\
|                  Application Class Member.                       |
\*----------------------------------------------------------------*/
TMarkerApplication::TMarkerApplication (LPSTR lpszName,
                  HINSTANCE hInstance, HINSTANCE hPrevInstance,
                  LPSTR lpszCmdLine, int nCmdShow)
                :TApplication (lpszName, hInstance,
                   hPrevInstance, lpszCmdLine, nCmdShow)
    {
    /* Application specific initialization goes here.  */
    }

/*----------------------------------------------------------------*\
|                  Application Class Member.                       |
\*----------------------------------------------------------------*/
void TMarkerApplication::InitMainWindow ()
    {
    MainWindow = new TMarkerWindow (NULL, "Marker", NULL);
    }

/*----------------------------------------------------------------*\
|                  TMarkerWindow Class Member.                     |
\*----------------------------------------------------------------*/
TMarkerWindow::TMarkerWindow (PTWindowsObject pwParent,
             LPSTR lpszTitle, PTModule pmModule)
           :TWindow (pwParent, lpszTitle, pmModule)
    {
    cpt = 0;
    }
```

```
/*--------------------------------------------------------------*\
 |                  TMarkerWindow Class Member.                  |
 \*--------------------------------------------------------------*/
LPSTR TMarkerWindow::GetClassName ()
    {
    return "Marker:MAIN";
    }

/*--------------------------------------------------------------*\
 |                  TMarkerWindow Class Member.                  |
 \*--------------------------------------------------------------*/
void TMarkerWindow::GetWindowClass (WNDCLASS& wc)
    {
    TWindow::GetWindowClass (wc);
    wc.hIcon=LoadIcon (wc.hInstance, "snapshot");
    wc.hCursor=LoadCursor (wc.hInstance, "hand");
    }

/*--------------------------------------------------------------*\
 |                  TMarkerWindow Class Member.                  |
 \*--------------------------------------------------------------*/
void TMarkerWindow::WMLButtonDown( TMessage& Msg )
    {
    if (cpt < MAXPOINTS)
        {
        pt[cpt].x = MOUSEX(Msg);
        pt[cpt].y = MOUSEY(Msg);
        InvalidateRect (HWindow, NULL, TRUE);
        cpt++;
        }
    }

/*--------------------------------------------------------------*\
 |                  TMarkerWindow Class Member.                  |
 \*--------------------------------------------------------------*/
void TMarkerWindow::WMPaint(TMessage&)
    {
    int i;
    PAINTSTRUCT ps;

    BeginPaint(HWindow, &ps);
    for (i=0; i<cpt; i++)
        {
        DrawMarker (ps.hdc, pt[i].x, pt[i].y);
        }
    EndPaint(HWindow, &ps);
    }

/*--------------------------------------------------------------*\
 |                    Marker Drawing Function.                   |
 \*--------------------------------------------------------------*/
void DrawMarker (HDC hdc, int x, int y)
    {
    DWORD dwColor;
    int i;

    dwColor = GetPixel (hdc, x, y);
    dwColor = ~dwColor;
    SetPixel (hdc, x, y, dwColor);

    for (i=1;i<=MARKERSIZE; i++)
```

146  *Introduction to the Graphics Device Interface*

```
        {
        dwColor = GetPixel (hdc, x+i, y);
        dwColor = ~dwColor;
        SetPixel (hdc, x+i, y, dwColor);

        dwColor = GetPixel (hdc, x-i, y);
        dwColor = ~dwColor;
        SetPixel (hdc, x-i, y, dwColor);

        dwColor = GetPixel (hdc, x, y+i);
        dwColor = ~dwColor;
        SetPixel (hdc, x, y+i, dwColor);

        dwColor = GetPixel (hdc, x, y-i);
        dwColor = ~dwColor;
SetPixel (hdc, x, y-i, dwColor);
        }
    }
```

## MARKER.RC

```
snapshot icon Marker.ico

hand cursor Marker.cur
```

## MARKER.DEF

```
NAME MARKER

EXETYPE WINDOWS

DESCRIPTION 'Marker - Marker demo.'

CODE MOVEABLE DISCARDABLE
DATA MOVEABLE MULTIPLE

HEAPSIZE  512
STACKSIZE 5120
```

Our marker program has subclassed the standard window class, **TWindow**, to process two messages: **WM_LBUTTONDOWN**, and **WM_PAINT**. As with MIN and PIXEL, the **TWindow** class handles the necessary initialization and shutdown required of every Windows program.

**WM_LBUTTONDOWN** is a mouse message. MARKER creates a message processing function, **WM_LButtonDown**, to handle this message. A **WM_LBUTTONDOWN** message is sent when two things happen at the same time: The mouse cursor is in our client area, and the user pushes the left mouse button. (You can receive this message when the mouse cursor is outside your window's client area, when the mouse has been captured. For details, see Chapter 16.)

*Pixels and Markers* 147

Every time our window object receives this mouse message, it records the *x* and *y* location of the mouse cursor. For all mouse messages, the cursor location is provided in the **LParam** parameter, in client area coordinates. As you may recall, this coordinate system has its origin (0,0) at the upper-left corner of the client area.

The window object stores the *x* and *y* location of the mouse cursor in an array of **POINT** structures. The **POINT** data type is defined in WINDOWS.H as

```
typedef struct tagPOINT
   {
     int    x;
     int    y;
   } POINT;
```

MARKER uses two macros to retrieve the *x* and *y* mouse locations from **LParam**: **MOUSEX** and **MOUSEY**. These macros are defined in MARKER.CPP as follows:

```
#define MOUSEX(arg)   (arg.LP.Lo)
#define MOUSEY(arg)   (arg.LP.Hi)
```

The primary advantage of using this type of macro to retrieve message parameters is that it will help you port your Windows 3.0 programs to run on other operating systems which support the Windows API. As you'll see in the rest of this book, we define this type of macro anytime we need to make use of a message parameter value.

Once a new point has been added to the array, our window object forces the window itself to be redrawn:

```
InvalidateRect (HWindow, NULL, TRUE);
```

This routine causes a **WM_PAINT** message to be generated by telling Windows that "the window is completely damaged."

**InvalidateRect** takes three parameters:

- Handle of the window to be redrawn.
- A far pointer to a rectangle that is being declared damaged. NULL means that the entire window is to be redrawn.
- An "erase first" flag. TRUE means erase the background before redrawing; FALSE means do not erase.

In response to the **WM_PAINT** message, our MARKER program uses the **BeginPaint/EndPaint** sandwich to borrow a DC from the Window Manager. The filling of the sandwich is a loop that calls our marker routine, **DrawMarker**, giving the *x* and *y* location of every point in the array pt.

148  *Introduction to the Graphics Device Interface*

The marker routine, **DrawMarker**, is built using two GDI routines: **GetPixel** and **SetPixel**. In general, if you don't find a GDI drawing routine that creates the exact output that you need, it is often a simple matter to write a routine that builds on top of existing GDI routines, as we've done here.

Our last program, PIXEL, wrote a single black pixel by calling **SetPixel** multiple times using parameters like the following:

```
SetPixel (hdc, r.right/2, r.bottom/2, RGB (0,0,0));
```

We could draw a black marker by simply making several calls like this. But what happens when we try to draw a marker on an area that is already black? The marker disappears.

Our marker routine solves this problem with Boolean algebra. Before we write a pixel, we read a pixel with the **GetPixel** routine. **GetPixel** returns an RGB triplet that lets us know the color of the pixel. We perform a bitwise negation of the RGB value to invert the color, and write a pixel with a call to **SetPixel**. Here is a code fragment to show what we mean:

```
dwColor = GetPixel (hdc, x, y);
dwColor = ~dwColor;
SetPixel (hdc, x, y, dwColor);
```

By making a series of calls like this, we draw a marker that will show up on just about any surface, regardless of its original color.

The ~ operator performs a one's complement on the operand, which in this case is an RGB triplet value. All of the zeros are turned into ones, and all of the ones into zeros. While this might seem strange, in fact this type of Boolean arithmetic is very useful in the world of graphics. Later on, we'll describe how **drawing modes** let us perform a logical operation when we draw lines, fill areas, or copy bitmaps.

For now, though, you can rest assured that this approach will be effective in making a mark on a display surface. This approach has one shortcoming: Two markers placed at the same location have the effect of negating each other. The markers disappear! Can you think of a way to solve this problem?

One way around this problem would require your program to walk the list of points every time it draws. If it finds a duplicate point, it simply ignores it instead of drawing it. Another way to avoid this problem might involve walking the list of points every time the user clicks the mouse. If a point has already been highlighted, a program could beep at the user to announce that the point is invalid.

We introduced the marker routine to help describe how native GDI routines work. Let's use our markers to learn about GDI's line drawing capabilities. This is the subject of the next chapter.

# 8

# Drawing Lines

Before we begin to draw lines with GDI routines, let's stop to consider: *What exactly is a line, anyway*? A line is a geometric figure created by joining a set of points. Lines are considered **open figures**, meaning that our interest is in the line itself, and not the area around the line. In the next chapter, we're going to look at **closed figures**, in which a line plus the area it surrounds make up a single geometric figure.

A GDI line is a geometric figure drawn by a GDI line drawing routine. Every GDI line has a starting point and an ending point. GDI draws lines using what graphics programmers refer to as an **inclusive/exclusive algorithm**. That is, the starting point is *included* in the line, but the ending point is *excluded*.

The MAGNIFY utility can convince you that this is the case. MAGNIFY stretches pixels on the display screen so they can be inspected more closely. (Appendix H contains the source code to MAGNIFY.) Figure 8.1 shows a GDI line with markers to highlight the end points. In this figure, you can see one effect of inclusive/exclusive drawing.

The white pixel at the marker cross-hair shows that the starting point is *included* in the line. After all, the marker is drawn by inverting pixels. For the ending point, the pixel at the marker cross-hair is black. This indicates that the ending point has been *excluded* from the line.

Although inclusive/exclusive drawing may seem odd at first, it lets you draw complex figures by making many simple line drawing calls. Each new figure picks up where the other left off. And as we'll see in Chapter 16, when we create dragable objects for the mouse pointer, this is especially important when using different drawing modes.

All of GDI's line drawing routines use inclusive/exclusive drawing. Let's tour the available routines, to see what GDI can do for us. In the process, we'll review the DC attributes that affect line drawing.

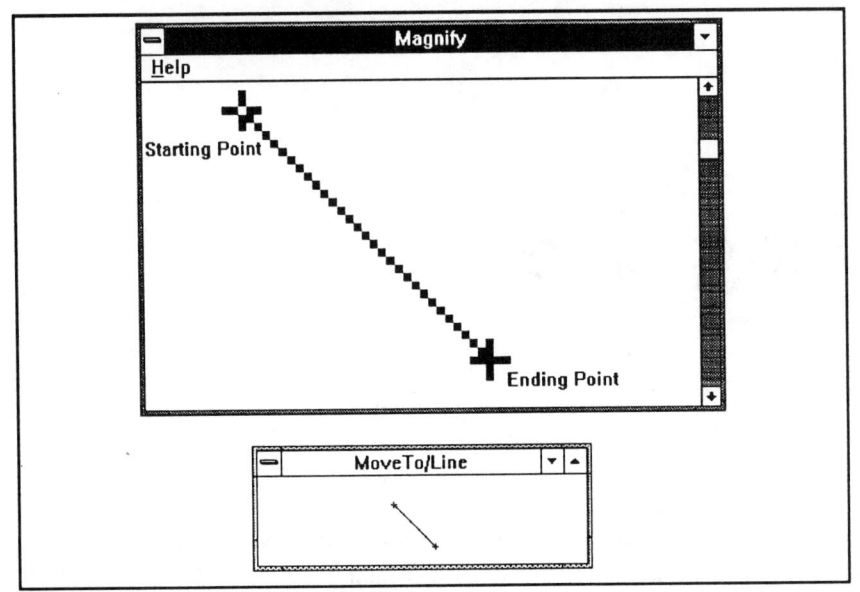

**Figure 8.1** Magnify shows GDI's inclusive/exclusive line drawing

# Line Drawing Primitives

GDI has four line drawing routines: **MoveTo**, **LineTo**, **Polyline**, and **Arc**. We'll consider each in turn. Let's start with the first two routines, which are always used together, **MoveTo** and **LineTo**.

## *MoveTo and LineTo*

Our first routine, **MoveTo**, doesn't actually draw lines. Instead, it stores a pair of *x* and *y* values in a DC attribute called the **current position**. The second routine, **LineTo**, uses this value as a starting point for a line. The **LineTo** function itself provides the ending point as a parameter. Here is how you use these routines to draw a line from point X1, Y1 to point X2, Y2:

```
MoveTo (hdc, X1, Y1);
LineTo (hdc, X2, Y2);
```

After the **LineTo** function has drawn a line, it updates the value of the current position in the DC to reflect the end point of the line. You can connect a series of points by making calls like the following:

```
MoveTo (hdc, X1, Y1);
LineTo (hdc, X2, Y2);
LineTo (hdc, X3, Y3);
LineTo (hdc, X4, Y4);
```

When these routines are called in this way, they produce the same result as our next routine, the **Polyline** function. You might wonder why GDI has this kind of redundancy.

It is partly a question of convenience. You will find that **MoveTo/LineTo** requires less work, since each takes an *x,y* value as a parameter. The **Polyline** function, on the other hand, requires the *x,y* values to be stored in an array of points.

Although it requires its parameters in a special format, the **Polyline** routine is the obvious choice when performance is important. The speed advantage is a direct result of the overhead incurred when a function is called. One **Polyline** call will draw many lines. Using **MoveTo/LineTo**, many calls would be required to draw the same lines.

Like the **MoveTo/LineTo** pair, **Polyline** draws straight lines. Unlike this pair, however, **Polyline** does not use the current position value in the DC. Instead, it relies solely on an array of **points** that are passed as a parameter. If we store the points (x1, y1), (x2, y2), (x3, y3), and (x4, y4) in an array like this

```
POINTS pt[] = {x1, y1, x2, y2, x3, y3, x4, y4};
```

the following call to **Polyline** connects the points:

```
Polyline (hdc, pt, 4);
```

The **Arc** function draws a curved line. The parameters to **Arc** define three boundaries: a bounding box, a starting point, and an ending point (see Figure 8.2). If the starting point and the ending point are the same, the **Arc** function draws a complete ellipse (or a circle, if the bounding box is a square). Otherwise, **Arc** draws a portion of an ellipse.

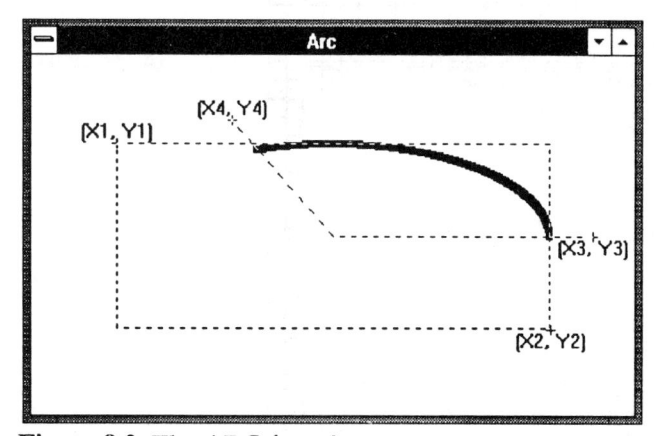

**Figure 8.2** The ARC function

152  *Introduction to the Graphics Device Interface*

With the other line drawing functions, the relationship of starting point to ending point was important, since GDI uses inclusive/exclusive drawing. This is also true for arcs. In addition, arcs are always drawn in a counterclockwise direction. Figure 8.3 shows how two different curves are drawn if the starting and ending points are swapped.

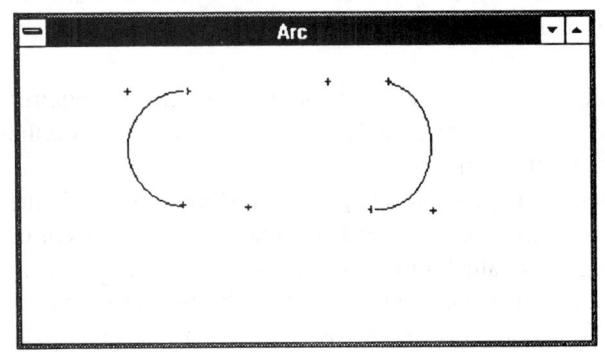

**Figure 8.3** Arcs are drawn counterclockwise

Our line drawing program uses all three types of line drawing primitives. You enter points by clicking the left mouse button in the client area. The first four points are used to draw two lines using `MoveTo/LineTo`. The second four points are used to draw a set of lines using `Polyline`. And finally, the last four points are used as input to the `Arc` function.

Figure 8.4 shows the output created by LINES, our line drawing program. A complete listing of LINES is shown below.

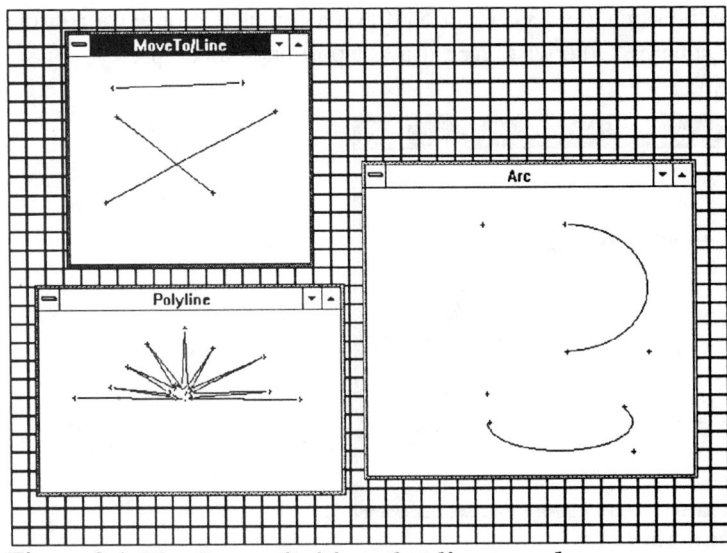

**Figure 8.4** The three primitives that lines can draw

# MAKEFILE.MAK

```
.AUTODEPEND

#       Translator Definitions
INC=\BORLANDC\OWL\INCLUDE;\BORLANDC\CLASSLIB\INCLUDE;\BORLANDC\INCLUDE
CC = bcc -c -D_CLASSDLL -H -ml -WS -w -I$(INC)

#       Implicit Rules
.c.obj:
  $(CC) {$< }

.cpp.obj:
  $(CC) {$< }

#       Explicit Rules
Lines.exe: Lines.res Lines.def Lines.obj
    tlink /c/C/n/P-/Twe/x @Lines.LNK
    rlink Lines.res Lines.exe

#       Individual File Dependencies
Lines.obj: Lines.cpp

Lines.res: Lines.rc Lines.cur Lines.ico
    brcc -FO Lines.res -i$(INC) Lines.RC
```

# LINES.LNK

```
\borlandc\lib\c0wl.obj+
Lines.obj
Lines,Lines
\borlandc\classlib\lib\tclasdll.lib+
\borlandc\owl\lib\owl.lib+
mathwl.lib+
import.lib+
crtldll.lib
Lines.def
```

# LINES.CPP

```
/*----------------------------------------------------------*\
 | LINES.CPP   Draws lines using MoveTo/LineTo, Polyline and |
 |             an Arc.                                       |
 \*----------------------------------------------------------*/
#define WIN31
#define STRICT
#include <owl.h>
#include <WindowsX.h>

#define MOUSEX(arg)  (arg.LP.Lo)
#define MOUSEY(arg)  (arg.LP.Hi)


/*----------------------------------------------------------*\
 |                       Constants.                          |
 \*----------------------------------------------------------*/
const int MAXPOINTS  = 12;
const int MARKERSIZE = 3;
```

```
/*--------------------------------------------------------------*\
|                    Class Declarations.                         |
\*--------------------------------------------------------------*/
class TLinesApplication : public TApplication
  {
  public:
    TLinesApplication (LPSTR lpszName, HINSTANCE hInstance,
                       HINSTANCE hPrevInstance, LPSTR lpszCmdLine,
                       int nCmdShow);
    virtual void InitMainWindow ();
  };

class TLinesWindow : public TWindow
  {
  public:
    TLinesWindow (PTWindowsObject pwParent, LPSTR lpszTitle,
                  PTModule pmModule);
    virtual LPSTR GetClassName ();
    virtual void  GetWindowClass (WNDCLASS&);
    virtual void  WMLButtonDown(TMessage& Msg) = [WM_LBUTTONDOWN];
    virtual void  WMPaint(TMessage& Msg) = [WM_FIRST + WM_PAINT];
  private:
    int cpt;
    POINT pt[MAXPOINTS];
  };

/*--------------------------------------------------------------*\
|                    Function Prototypes.                        |
\*--------------------------------------------------------------*/
void DrawMarker (HDC hDC, int x, int y);

/*--------------------------------------------------------------*\
|                 Main Function:  WinMain.                       |
\*--------------------------------------------------------------*/
int PASCAL WinMain (HINSTANCE hInstance,   HINSTANCE hPrevInstance,
                    LPSTR    lpszCmdLine, int      nCmdShow)
    {
    TLinesApplication Lines ("Lines", hInstance, hPrevInstance,
                             lpszCmdLine, nCmdShow);
    Lines.Run();
    return Lines.Status;
    }

/*--------------------------------------------------------------*\
|                   Application Class Member.                    |
\*--------------------------------------------------------------*/
TLinesApplication::TLinesApplication (LPSTR lpszName,
                  HINSTANCE hInstance, HINSTANCE hPrevInstance,
                  LPSTR lpszCmdLine, int nCmdShow)
                 :TApplication (lpszName, hInstance,
                  hPrevInstance, lpszCmdLine, nCmdShow)
    {
    /*  Application specific initialization goes here.  */
    }

/*--------------------------------------------------------------*\
|                   Application Class Member.                    |
\*--------------------------------------------------------------*/
void TLinesApplication::InitMainWindow ()
    {
    MainWindow = new TLinesWindow (NULL, "Lines", NULL);
    }
```

```
/*-------------------------------------------------------------*\
|                    TLinesWindow Class Member.                 |
\*-------------------------------------------------------------*/
TLinesWindow::TLinesWindow (PTWindowsObject pwParent,
               LPSTR lpszTitle, PTModule pmModule)
            :TWindow (pwParent, lpszTitle, pmModule)
    {
    cpt = 0;
    }

/*-------------------------------------------------------------*\
|                    TLinesWindow Class Member.                 |
\*-------------------------------------------------------------*/
LPSTR TLinesWindow::GetClassName ()
    {
    return "Lines:MAIN";
    }

/*-------------------------------------------------------------*\
|                    TLinesWindow Class Member.                 |
\*-------------------------------------------------------------*/
void TLinesWindow::GetWindowClass (WNDCLASS& wc)
    {
TWindow::GetWindowClass (wc);
    wc.hIcon=LoadIcon (wc.hInstance, "snapshot");
    wc.hCursor=LoadCursor (wc.hInstance, "hand");
    }

/*-------------------------------------------------------------*\
|                    TLinesWindow Class Member.                 |
\*-------------------------------------------------------------*/
void TLinesWindow::WMLButtonDown( TMessage& Msg )
    {
    if (cpt < MAXPOINTS)
        {
        pt[cpt].x = MOUSEX(Msg);
        pt[cpt].y = MOUSEY(Msg);
        InvalidateRect (HWindow, NULL, TRUE);
        cpt++;
        }
    }

/*-------------------------------------------------------------*\
|                    TLinesWindow Class Member.                 |
\*-------------------------------------------------------------*/
void TLinesWindow::WMPaint(TMessage&)
    {
    int i;
    PAINTSTRUCT ps;

    BeginPaint(HWindow, &ps);
    /*
     * Draw lines with MoveTo / LineTo.
     */
    if (cpt > 1)
        {
        MoveTo (ps.hdc, pt[0].x, pt[0].y);
        LineTo (ps.hdc, pt[1].x, pt[1].y);
        }
    if (cpt > 3)
        {
```

```
            MoveTo (ps.hdc, pt[2].x, pt[2].y);
            LineTo (ps.hdc, pt[3].x, pt[3].y);
            }
        /*
         * Draw lines using Polyline.
         */
        if (cpt > 7)
            Polyline (ps.hdc, &pt[4], 4);

        /*
         * Draw an arc.
         */
        if (cpt == 12)
            Arc (ps.hdc, pt[8].x,  pt[8].y,
                         pt[9].x,  pt[9].y,
                         pt[10].x, pt[10].y,
                         pt[11].x, pt[11].y);

        /*
         * Highlight control points with markers.
         */
        for (i=0; i<cpt; i++)
            {
            DrawMarker (ps.hdc, pt[i].x, pt[i].y);
            }

        EndPaint(HWindow, &ps);
        }

/*--------------------------------------------------------------*\
|                   Marker Drawing Function.                     |
\*--------------------------------------------------------------*/
void DrawMarker (HDC hdc, int x, int y)
    {
    DWORD dwColor;
    int i;

    dwColor = GetPixel (hdc, x, y);
    dwColor = ~dwColor;
    SetPixel (hdc, x, y, dwColor);

    for (i=1;i<=MARKERSIZE; i++)
        {
        dwColor = GetPixel (hdc, x+i, y);
        dwColor = ~dwColor;
        SetPixel (hdc, x+i, y, dwColor);

        dwColor = GetPixel (hdc, x-i, y);
        dwColor = ~dwColor;
        SetPixel (hdc, x-i, y, dwColor);

        dwColor = GetPixel (hdc, x, y+i);
        dwColor = ~dwColor;
        SetPixel (hdc, x, y+i, dwColor);

        dwColor = GetPixel (hdc, x, y-i);
        dwColor = ~dwColor;
        SetPixel (hdc, x, y-i, dwColor);
        }

    }
```

## LINES.RC

```
snapshot icon Lines.ico
hand cursor Lines.cur
```

## LINES.DEF

```
NAME LINES

EXETYPE WINDOWS

DESCRIPTION 'Lines -- Sample Line Drawing Program'

CODE MOVEABLE DISCARDABLE
DATA MOVEABLE MULTIPLE

HEAPSIZE   512
STACKSIZE  5120
```

Now that we've looked at GDI's line drawing routines, let's examine the DC attributes that deal with lines.

# DC Attributes

Five DC attributes are used by GDI to draw lines:

| Drawing Attribute | Comments |
| --- | --- |
| Background color | Second color for nonsolid pens |
| Background mode | Turns on/off background color |
| Current position | $(x,y)$ position for **LineTo** routine |
| Drawing mode | Boolean drawing operation |
| Pen | Line color, width, and style |

Without a doubt, the most important attribute is the pen, which determines the appearance of the line in terms of color, width, and style (or pattern, such as solid or dotted). The term **styled lines** is often used for lines with a nonsolid style: dotted, dashed, etc.

The second most important attribute is the **drawing mode**, which lets us specify a Boolean operator to use in a drawing operation. More on that later.

Of the other three attributes, two affect *styled* lines, but not solid lines: background color and background mode. GDI uses the background color for the spaces between the lines—that is, between the foreground dashes or dots. The background mode toggles whether the background part of a styled line should be filled in or left alone. Keep in mind while using these two attributes that they also affect filled areas—when a hatched brush is used—and text.

The background color is set using the **SetBkColor** routine, defined as follows:

SetBkColor (hDC, crColor)

- hDC is a handle to a DC.
- crColor is a color reference value; it is (a) an RGB triplet, (b) a palette index, or (c) a palette-relative RGB value.

The following line of code sets the background color to blue:

```
SetBkColor (hDC, RGB(0, 0, 0xFF));
```

To set the background mode, you call the **SetBkMode** routine, whose syntax is

SetBkMode (hDC, nBkMode)

- hDC is a handle to a DC.
- nBkMode is the on/off switch: Set to OPAQUE to enable background color, and to TRANSPARENT to disable background color.

The final attribute, the current position, is a DC attribute that we discussed in relation to the **MoveTo/LineTo** routines. It is an *x,y* value that is used by these routines as part of their drawing: **MoveTo** sets the current position; **LineTo** uses it as the starting point for the line to draw. **LineTo** updates the current position to the end point of the line it draws.

Let's take a close look at pens, and the way they are created and manipulated.

## About Pens

A pen is a DC drawing attribute that describes how lines are drawn. Pens have three qualities: color, width, and style. If you'd like, you can think of each of these qualities as a drawing attribute in its own right. In the world of graphics programming, when drawing attributes are grouped in this way, the group is called an **attribute bundle**. Attribute bundles are convenient because they let you refer to several drawing attributes at the same time.

GDI is very flexible in the way it lets you share pens: Pens can be shared between programs and between devices. GDI has a set of stock pens that any program can use, or a program can create a set of custom pens and let different devices share them. The net effect of this sharing is that GDI minimizes the amount of memory needed to store drawing attributes. GDI is thrifty with memory because earlier versions of Windows had to run in only 640K of RAM.

## *Pens and Device Independence*

How can pens be used for different devices? The term **logical pen** describes how this is possible. A pen is a request to a device to create lines with a particular appearance. When GDI is ready to draw on a specific device, it makes a request to the device to **realize** a pen. Only at this time does the device driver create the data structures needed to draw lines with the desired qualities. This aspect is hidden in the GDI device-driver interface, but it allows a program to share pens between devices.

## *Creating and Using Pens*

When Windows starts up, GDI creates a set of pens that can be shared by all programs. These are known as **stock pens**. GDI has three stock pens: one black, one white, and one null (invisible ink) pen. The null pen is a placeholder, since every DC must contain a valid pen. The other two pens draw solid lines with a width of one pixel.

Pens are identified by a handle. To get the handle of a stock pen, you call the `GetStockObject` routine, as shown here:

```
HPEN hpen;

hpen = GetStockObject (BLACK_PEN);  /* or */
hpen = GetStockObject (WHITE_PEN);  /* or */
hpen = GetStockObject (NULL_PEN);
```

Once you have a pen handle, you call another GDI routine to install the pen into the DC:

```
SelectObject (hdc, hpen);
```

After a pen has been selected into a DC, it is used for all subsequently drawn lines. This includes lines drawn with `MoveTo`/`LineTo`, `Polyline`, and `Arc`.

One thing about a DC is that it only has room for a single pen at any point in time. Therefore, by selecting one pen into a DC, you automatically remove the old pen. For your convenience, the `SelectObject` routine returns the handle of the pen being removed. For example, the following leaves the DC unchanged:

```
/* No Change to DC. */
hpenOld = SelectObject (hdc, hpenNew);
SelectObject (hdc, hpenOld);
```

If the three stock pens do not provide you with all the line drawing capability that you need, GDI has two routines for creating pens: **CreatePen** and **CreatePenIndirect**. The only difference between these two routines is in the way parameters are specified. The syntax for **CreatePen** is:

```
hpen = CreatePen (nPenStyle, nWidth, crColor);
```

- **nPenStyle** selects a pen style from the flags shown in Figure 8.5.
- **nWidth** sets the width in the *x* direction. Since we're limiting ourselves to pixels, the units are in pixels. But when we discuss coordinate transformations, you'll see that the width value reflects the coordinate system installed in the DC into which the pen is installed.
- **crColor** is a color reference; as before, it is (a) an RGB triplet, (b) a color palette index, or (c) a palette-relative RGB value.

So to create a black pen that draws lines one unit wide, you say

```
hpen = CreatePen (PS_SOLID, 1, RGB (0, 0, 0));
```

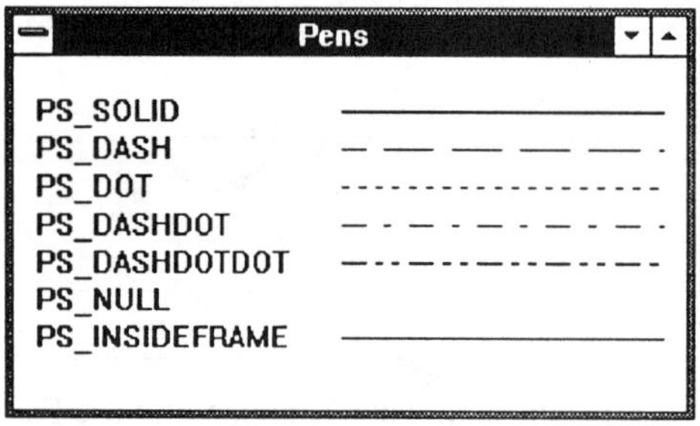

**Figure 8.5** GDI's seven pen styles

The syntax for **CreatePenIndirect**, on the other hand, is

```
LOGPEN logpen;

hpen = CreatePenIndirect (&logpen)
```

LOGPEN is defined in WINDOWS.H as

```
typedef struct tagLOGPEN
   {
      WORD    lopnStyle;
```

```
    POINT lopnWidth;
    DWORD lopnColor;
} LOGPEN;
```

One difference between `CreatePen` and `CreatePenIndirect` is that the `LOGPEN` structure uses a `POINT` structure to hold the pen width. As you may recall, the `POINT` structure has two members, one for an *x* value and one for a *y* value. To create the same black pen as above, you say

```
LOGPEN logpen;
logpen.lopnStyle = PS_SOLID;
logpen.lopnWidth.x = 1;
logpen.lopnColor = RGB (0, 0, 0));
hpen = CreatePenIndirect (&logpen)
```

GDI supports seven pen styles, as illustrated in Figure 8.5. The last style, `PS_INSIDEFRAME`, provides the same results as the `PS_SOLID` style with two important differences: color, and use in filled figures. This is the only line style that uses dithered colors. All other pens are only available in solid colors.

In the context of filled figures, the `PS_INSIDEFRAME` style has some unique features. As you'll see when we discuss filled figures, a pen with the style `PS_INSIDEFRAME` draws on the inside of the boundaries. Other pens are centered on the boundary so that half is inside the border and half is outside.

You specify the width of a pen in logical units. This corresponds to the units of the current mapping mode in the *x*-axis. Since we are using the `MM_TEXT` mapping mode, our units are pixels. If you specify a pen width of zero, then regardless of the mapping mode, you will get a pen that is exactly one pixel wide.

Most GDI devices currently do not support *wide* styled lines—that is, styled lines that have a width greater than 1. For this reason, if you ask for a six-unit-wide *dotted* pen, you will most likely get a six-unit-wide *solid* pen. As hardware gets smarter, however, you'll see wide-styled lines on more devices. Until then, you should assume that if you want a nonsolid pen, you'll have to settle for those that are one pixel wide.

Like pixel colors, pen colors are defined using one of three methods: an RGB triplet, a palette index value, or a palette-relative RGB triplet. Whichever you choose, pens are ordinarily created from solid colors. The exception is pens with the `PS_INSIDEFRAME` style. The color of such a pen can include dithered colors.

Dithered colors are created by combining two or more colors. In the real world, color mixing is nothing new. If you go to buy paint, for example, the store clerk might mix a little bit of black into a can of white paint to create a shade of gray.

GDI creates dithered colors by combining two (or more) colors in a regular pattern to create the illusion of hundreds of colors on 16-color devices, like EGA and VGA display adapters. On monochrome devices, like the Hercules and CGA display adapters, dozens of shades of gray can be created using this technique. Dithering works so well that, without the aid of a special program like MAGNIFY, it is often hard to tell a dithered color from a pure color.

Because dithered colors require a little more work from a device driver, only one pen style supports dithering: **PS_INSIDEFRAME**. Usually, dithering is reserved for brushes—a subject we'll cover when we discuss the creation of filled figures.

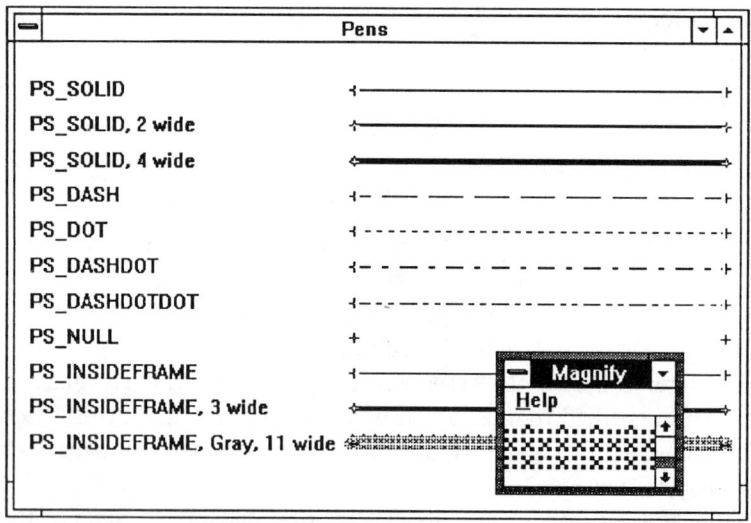

Figure 8.6 Lines drawn using GDI pens

Figure 8.6 shows the output of our PENS program. Ten lines are drawn using all the pen styles. Each line has a marker to highlight the end points. Notice for the wide lines that the markers appear in the middle of each line. In addition, notice that the end of each line is rounded. To GDI, a pen is a round drawing object. With the help of MAGNIFY, you can see that the **PS_INSIDEFRAME** line is, in fact, dithered. Here is the listing of our PENS program:

## MAKEFILE.MAK

```
.AUTODEPEND

#   Translator Definitions
INC=\BORLANDC\OWL\INCLUDE;\BORLANDC\CLASSLIB\INCLUDE;\BORLANDC\INCLUDE
CC = bcc -c -D_CLASSDLL -H -ml -WS -w -I$(INC)

#   Implicit Rules
.c.obj:
  $(CC) {$< }

.cpp.obj:
  $(CC) {$< }
```

```
#       Explicit Rules
Pens.exe: Pens.res Pens.def Pens.obj
        tlink /c/C/n/P-/Twe/x @Pens.LNK
        rlink Pens.res Pens.exe

#       Individual File Dependencies
Pens.obj: Pens.cpp

Pens.res: Pens.rc Pens.cur Pens.ico
        brcc -FO Pens.res -i$(INC) Pens.RC
```

## PENS.LNK

```
\borlandc\lib\c0wl.obj+
Pens.obj
Pens,Pens
\borlandc\classlib\lib\tclasdll.lib+
\borlandc\owl\lib\owl.lib+
mathwl.lib+
import.lib+
crtldll.lib
Pens.def
```

## PENS.CPP

```
/*--------------------------------------------------------------*\
|  PENS.CPP    Draws various types of GDI pens.                  |
\*--------------------------------------------------------------*/
#define WIN31
#define STRICT
#include <owl.h>
#include <WindowsX.h>

/*--------------------------------------------------------------*\
|                         Constants.                             |
\*--------------------------------------------------------------*/
const int PENCOUNT   = 11;
const int MARKERSIZE =  3;

/*--------------------------------------------------------------*\
|                   Data Structure Definitions.                  |
\*--------------------------------------------------------------*/
typedef struct tagPENDATA {
    WORD     wStyle;
    int      iWidth;
    COLORREF crColor;
    char *   pchName;
    } PENDATA;

PENDATA pens[PENCOUNT] = {
{ PS_SOLID, 1, RGB (0,0,0), "PS_SOLID"},
        { PS_SOLID, 2, RGB (0,0,0), "PS_SOLID, 2 wide"},
{ PS_SOLID, 4, RGB (0,0,0), "PS_SOLID, 4 wide"},
{ PS_DASH, 1, RGB (0,0,0), "PS_DASH"},
{ PS_DOT, 1, RGB (0,0,0), "PS_DOT"},
{ PS_DASHDOT, 1, RGB (0,0,0), "PS_DASHDOT"},
{ PS_DASHDOTDOT, 1, RGB (0,0,0), "PS_DASHDOTDOT"},
{ PS_NULL, 1, RGB (0,0,0), "PS_NULL"},
```

```
    { PS_INSIDEFRAME, 1, RGB (0,0,0), "PS_INSIDEFRAME"},
    { PS_INSIDEFRAME, 3, RGB (0,0,0),
                                "PS_INSIDEFRAME, 3 wide"},
    { PS_INSIDEFRAME, 11, RGB (180,180,180),
                                "PS_INSIDEFRAME, Gray, 11 wide   "}};
HPEN hpen[PENCOUNT];

/*-------------------------------------------------------------*\
|                   Class Declarations.                         |
\*-------------------------------------------------------------*/
class TPensApplication : public TApplication
    {
    public:
      TPensApplication (LPSTR lpszName, HINSTANCE hInstance,
                        HINSTANCE hPrevInstance, LPSTR lpszCmdLine,
                        int nCmdShow);
      virtual void InitMainWindow ();
    };

class TPensWindow : public TWindow
    {
    public:
      TPensWindow (PTWindowsObject pwParent, LPSTR lpszTitle,
                   PTModule pmModule);
      ~TPensWindow();
      virtual LPSTR GetClassName ();
      virtual void  GetWindowClass (WNDCLASS&);
      virtual void  WMPaint(TMessage& Msg) = [WM_PAINT];
    };

/*-------------------------------------------------------------*\
|                   Function Prototypes.                        |
\*-------------------------------------------------------------*/
void DrawMarker (HDC hDC, int x, int y);

/*-------------------------------------------------------------*\
|                   Main Function:  WinMain.                    |
\*-------------------------------------------------------------*/
int PASCAL WinMain (HINSTANCE hInstance,   HINSTANCE hPrevInstance,
                    LPSTR  lpszCmdLine, int    nCmdShow)
    {
    TPensApplication Pens ("Pens", hInstance, hPrevInstance,
                            lpszCmdLine, nCmdShow);
    Pens.Run();
    return Pens.Status;
    }

/*-------------------------------------------------------------*\
|                   Application Class Member.                   |
\*-------------------------------------------------------------*/
TPensApplication::TPensApplication (LPSTR lpszName,
                HINSTANCE hInstance, HINSTANCE hPrevInstance,
                LPSTR lpszCmdLine, int nCmdShow)
                :TApplication (lpszName, hInstance, hPrevInstance,
                               lpszCmdLine, nCmdShow)
    {
    /*  Application specific initialization goes here.  */
    }

/*-------------------------------------------------------------*\
|                   Application Class Member.                   |
\*-------------------------------------------------------------*/
```

```
void TPensApplication::InitMainWindow ()
    {
    MainWindow = new TPensWindow (NULL, "Pens", NULL);
    }
/*-------------------------------------------------------------*\
|                   TPensWindow Class Member.                   |
\*-------------------------------------------------------------*/
TPensWindow::TPensWindow (PTWindowsObject pwParent,
              LPSTR lpszTitle, PTModule pmModule)
           :TWindow (pwParent, lpszTitle, pmModule)
    {
    int i;

    for (i=0;i<PENCOUNT; i++)
        hpen[i] = CreatePen (pens[i].wStyle,
                             pens[i].iWidth,
                             pens[i].crColor);
    }

/*-------------------------------------------------------------*\
|                   TPensWindow Class Member.                   |
\*-------------------------------------------------------------*/
TPensWindow::~TPensWindow()
    {
    int i;
    for (i=0;i<PENCOUNT; i++)
        DeleteObject (hpen[i]);
    }

/*-------------------------------------------------------------*\
|                   TPensWindow Class Member.                   |
\*-------------------------------------------------------------*/
LPSTR TPensWindow::GetClassName ()
    {
    return "Pens:MAIN";
    }

/*-------------------------------------------------------------*\
|                   TPensWindow Class Member.                   |
\*-------------------------------------------------------------*/
void TPensWindow::GetWindowClass (WNDCLASS& wc)
    {
    TWindow::GetWindowClass (wc);
    wc.hIcon=LoadIcon (wc.hInstance, "snapshot");
    wc.hCursor=LoadCursor (wc.hInstance, "hand");
    }

/*-------------------------------------------------------------*\
|                   TPensWindow Class Member.                   |
\*-------------------------------------------------------------*/
void TPensWindow::WMPaint(TMessage&)
    {
    DWORD dwTextBox;
    int i;
    int xEnd, xStart, xText;
    int yIncr, yLine, yText;
    PAINTSTRUCT ps;
    RECT r;

    BeginPaint (HWindow, &ps);
```

```
    GetClientRect (HWindow, &r);
    yIncr = r.bottom/ (PENCOUNT+2);
    yText = yIncr;
    xText = 10;
    dwTextBox = GetTextExtent (ps.hdc, pens[10].pchName,
                               lstrlen(pens[10].pchName));

    for (i=0;i<PENCOUNT; i++)
        {
        TextOut (ps.hdc, xText, yText,
                 pens[i].pchName,
                 lstrlen(pens[i].pchName));

        xStart = xText + LOWORD(dwTextBox);
        xEnd   = r.right - 10;
        yLine  = yText + HIWORD(dwTextBox)/2;
        SelectObject (ps.hdc, hpen[i]);
        MoveTo (ps.hdc, xStart, yLine);
        LineTo (ps.hdc, xEnd, yLine);

        /* Draw Markers. */
        DrawMarker (ps.hdc, xStart, yLine);
        DrawMarker (ps.hdc, xEnd, yLine);
        yText += yIncr;
        }

    EndPaint (HWindow, &ps);
    }
/*-----------------------------------------------------------*\
|                  Marker Drawing Function.                   |
\*-----------------------------------------------------------*/
void DrawMarker (HDC hdc, int x, int y)
    {
    DWORD dwColor;
    int i;

    dwColor = GetPixel (hdc, x, y);
    dwColor = ~dwColor;
    SetPixel (hdc, x, y, dwColor);

    for (i=1;i<=MARKERSIZE; i++)
        {
        dwColor = GetPixel (hdc, x+i, y);
        dwColor = ~dwColor;
        SetPixel (hdc, x+i, y, dwColor);

        dwColor = GetPixel (hdc, x-i, y);
        dwColor = ~dwColor;
        SetPixel (hdc, x-i, y, dwColor);

        dwColor = GetPixel (hdc, x, y+i);
        dwColor = ~dwColor;
        SetPixel (hdc, x, y+i, dwColor);

        dwColor = GetPixel (hdc, x, y-i);
        dwColor = ~dwColor;
        SetPixel (hdc, x, y-i, dwColor);
        }

    }
```

## PENS.RC

```
snapshot icon Pens.ico

hand cursor Pens.cur
```

## PENS.DEF

```
NAME PENS

EXETYPE WINDOWS

DESCRIPTION 'Pens -- Draws with various GDI pens'

CODE MOVEABLE DISCARDABLE
DATA MOVEABLE MULTIPLE

HEAPSIZE   512
STACKSIZE  5120
```

This program creates 10 pens in response to the **WM_CREATE** message and destroys them in response to **WM_DESTROY**. This is important. Every Windows program must take care to dispose of its pens (and other drawing objects) properly. The problem actually results from one of the nice features of pens: They can be shared.

To allow GDI objects to be shared, Windows doesn't clean up leftover objects. If a program terminates without cleaning up its pens, that memory is lost forever (at least until the computer is turned off). So take care to always destroy your pens when you no longer need them.

We're now going to investigate the last DC drawing attribute that affects lines: the drawing mode. In the process, we'll give you a preview of our mouse input program from Chapter 16.

## Drawing Modes and Lines

A **drawing mode** is a Boolean operation that directs GDI how to draw pixels, lines, and filled figures. The drawing mode, sometimes called a raster operation, or "ROP" for short, determines how source pixels will interact with destination pixels.

With lines, a drawing mode describes how pens interact with pixels already present on the display surface. In the physical world, a ballpoint pen overwrites whatever surface it touches. While some drawing modes produce this effect, drawing modes provide a much richer set of effects than are available with a ballpoint pen. In an earlier chapter, the MARKER program used the NOT operator to ensure that a marker is visible. A drawing

168  *Introduction to the Graphics Device Interface*

mode provides a faster, convenient means to get the same effect. It is faster since the logic is built into the device driver.

Another use of drawing modes lets us draw shapes that seem to "float" on the display screen. This is the technique used for the mouse cursor, which wanders everywhere without leaving a trail of dirty pixels. In Chapter 16, we'll write a program that uses drawing modes to drag objects across the display. Figure 8.7 illustrates object dragging.

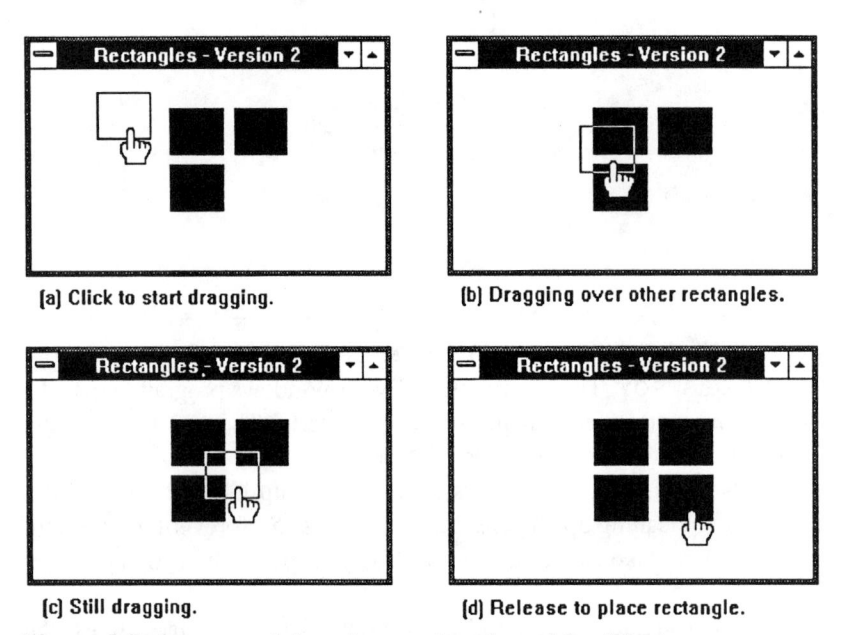

[a] Click to start dragging.

[b] Dragging over other rectangles.

[c] Still dragging.

[d] Release to place rectangle.

**Figure 8.7 One use of drawing modes: dragable objects**

It may seem strange that we want to perform Boolean algebra on graphic output. And yet, in a digital computer, every piece of data is encoded as a number. RGB triplets, for example, are numbers that describe colors. In the depths of graphics devices like the EGA display, numbers make up the pixels of a graphic image.

Drawing modes take advantage of this to allow the application of Boolean operations. And since a computer's CPU uses Boolean algebra as part of its day-to-day operation, it is a simple matter to apply Boolean operations to graphic images.

Figure 8.8 shows the 16 raster operations that GDI supports, along with the lines that are created with a white and with a black pen. Notice how every drawing mode is different. If you'd like, you can inhibit output with the **R2_NOP** mode, or guarantee that something will be drawn using the **R2_NOT** mode. Notice that two of the modes, **R2_BLACK** and **R2_WHITE**, ignore the pen color.

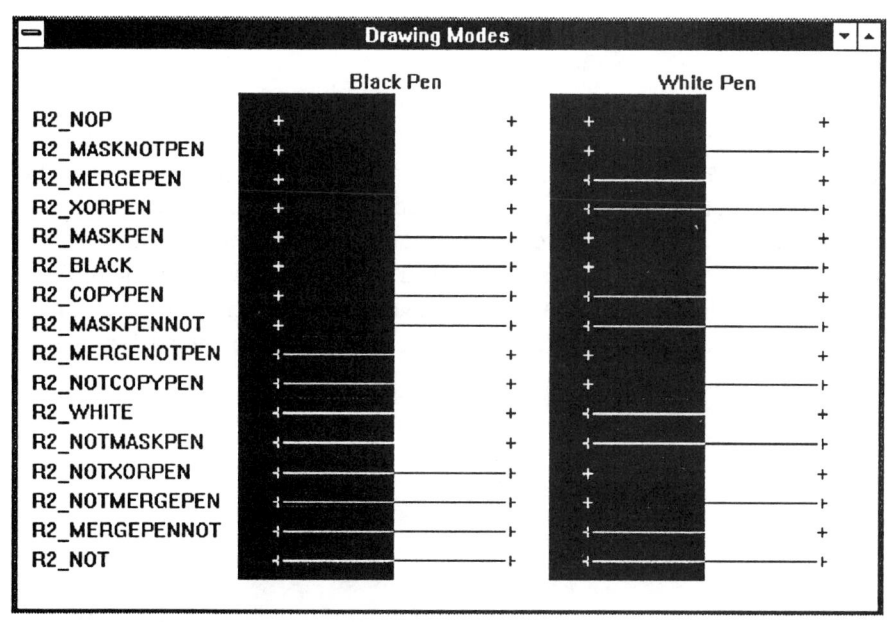

**Figure 8.8** GDI's sixteen drawing modes

One thing to keep in mind about drawing attributes is that they affect more than just lines: They affect the output of pixels (`SetPixel` routine) and filled geometric figures (the primitives we discuss in the next chapter). GDI doesn't use drawing modes when drawing text, however. The reason has to do with performance. Even though raster operations are implemented at the level of the device driver and are quite fast, they slow down the output of text and so are not used by GDI's text drawing routines.

To find out the current setting of the drawing mode, you call the `GetROP2` routine. To set a new drawing mode value in the DC, you call the `SetROP2` routine, as in

```
SetROP2 (hdc, R2_XORPEN);
```

Here is a newer, faster version of our marker routine, done using ROP codes:

```
VOID DrawMarker (HDC hdc, int x, int y)
    {
    int i;
    int rop;

    rop = SetROP2 (hdc, R2_NOT);
    SetPixel (hdc, x, y, RGB(0, 0, 0));

    for (i=1;i<<=MARKERSIZE; i++)
        {
        SetPixel (hdc, x+i, y, RGB(0, 0, 0));
        SetPixel (hdc, x-i, y, RGB(0, 0, 0));
        SetPixel (hdc, x, y+i, RGB(0, 0, 0));
        SetPixel (hdc, x, y-i, RGB(0, 0, 0));
```

170   *Introduction to the Graphics Device Interface*

```
        }
    SetROP2 (hdc, rop);
    }
```

As you recall, the `SetPixel` routine illuminates a pixel with the color specified by the last parameter. In this routine, `RGB(0, 0, 0)` selects black. But since we're using the `R2_NOT` drawing mode, GDI ignores the color we specify and inverts the destination pixel.

In our next chapter, we're going to discuss filled figures. Every filled figure has a border, which is simply a line drawn as an outline. As you will see, everything that we have discussed dealing with line drawing applies equally well to the creation of borders on GDI filled figures.

# 9

# Drawing Filled Figures

The next set of GDI drawing routines that we're going to look at are those that create filled figures. A filled figure has two parts: an area and a border around the area. Filled figures are sometimes referred to as **closed figures** because the border closes in on itself. In line drawing terms, the starting and ending points are the same.

Figure 9.1 shows some examples of the types of filled figures that GDI can draw. Notice the variation in the thickness and style of different borders. These are the result of different pens. After all, a border is simply a line, and GDI uses pens to draw lines.

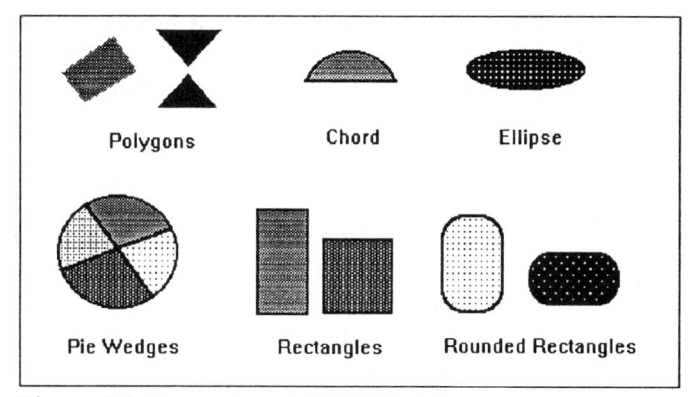

**Figure 9.1** Examples of GDI filled figures

Notice also the variation in the interior area of the figures in the illustration. This is the result of another GDI drawing object: a **brush**. In the same way that different pens draw different types of lines, different brushes create different filled areas.

To understand the way that GDI draws filled figures, it is important to understand how coordinates are interpreted. Filled figure coordinates are slightly different from those used

172  *Introduction to the Graphics Device Interface*

in line drawing. If you draw both types of figures, you will need to make adjustments to ensure that figures are aligned in an expected manner.

In the world of graphics programming, there are two primary ways to interpret a coordinate. Put simply, the issue is: Do coordinates lie in the center of pixels or at the intersections of a grid surrounding the pixels? Figure 9.2 illustrates pixel-centered and grid-intersection coordinates.

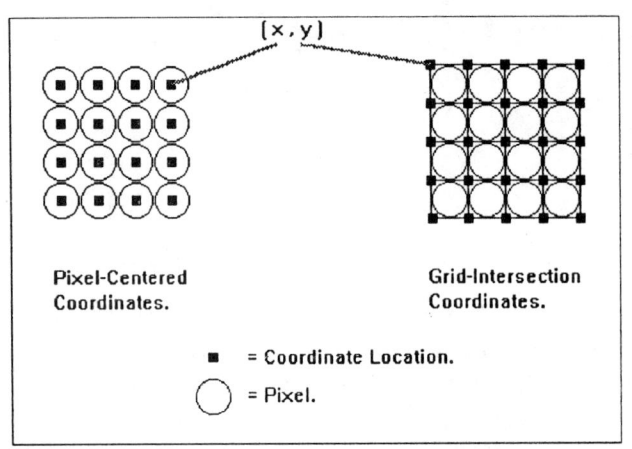

**Figure 9.2** Pixel-centered and grid-intersection coordinates

All of GDI's line drawing primitives use **pixel-centered coordinates**. Of GDI's seven area filling primitives, two use pixel-centered coordinates and five use **grid-intersection coordinates**. While this may seem odd, each type of coordinate has its own use that makes sense in its own right. Table 9.1 shows GDI's seven area filling primitives, and the type of coordinates that each uses:

**Table 9.1** GDI's area filling routines

| Routine | Coordinates | Description |
| --- | --- | --- |
| `Polygon` | Pixel-centered | A filled polyline |
| `PolyPolygon` | Pixel-centered | Multiple polygons |
| `Chord` | Grid-intersection | Partial arc joined by a straight line |
| `Ellipse` | Grid-intersection | Full arc |
| `Pie` | Grid-intersection | Pie wedge |
| `Rectangle` | Grid-intersection | Rectangle |
| `RoundRect` | Grid-intersection | Rectangle with rounded corners |

*Drawing Filled Figures* 173

Two of the filled figure routines use pixel-centered coordinates: `Polygon` and `PolyPolygon`. You can think of these routines as extensions to `Polyline`, one of GDI's line primitives. It's easy to use these routines with line drawing routines, since they use the same types of coordinates.

The other five routines use grid-intersection coordinates. These are the coordinates that GDI uses to define clipping regions. This makes it easy to use these routines with GDI's clipping routines.

GDI uses pixel-centered coordinates when the emphasis of a routine is line drawing, and grid-intersection coordinates when the emphasis is a two-dimensional area. However, if you wish to use both types of routines, it's usually a simple matter to modify the coordinates of one type of routine to fit in with the other type of routine.

The visible effect of grid-intersection coordinates is that filled figures seem to be one pixel smaller than expected. With the help of MAGNIFY, you can see this in Figure 9.3.

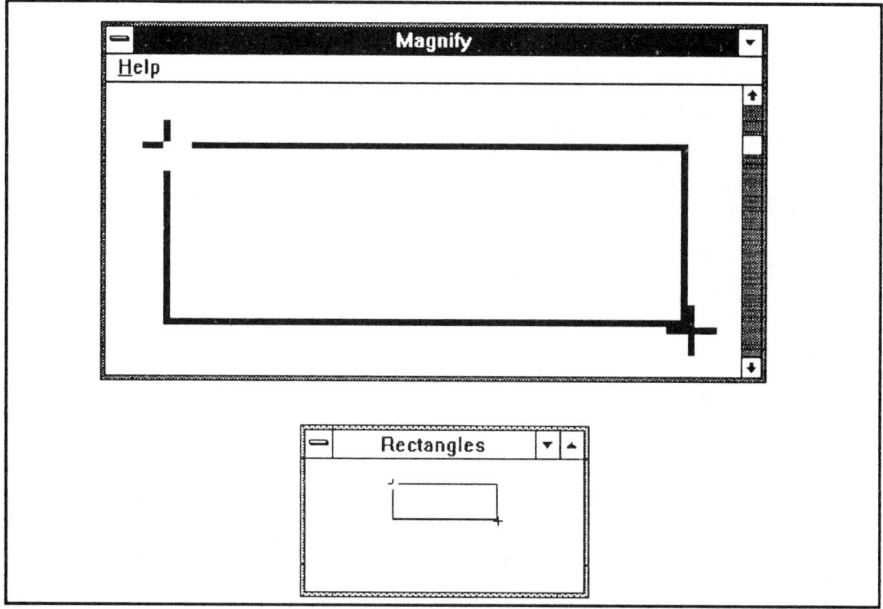

**Figure 9.3** Grid-intersection coordinates seem to be one pixel off

The program that created this output is RECT. This program uses two mouse messages to draw a rectangle: **WM_LBUTTONDOWN** and **WM_LBUTTONUP**. Each message provides one of the two pairs of points that are required by the `Rectangle` routine. `Rectangle` takes five parameters:

```
Rectangle (hDC, X1, Y1, X2, Y2);
```

- hDC is a handle to a device context.
- The coordinates (X1, Y1) define one corner of a rectangle.
- The coordinates (X2, Y2) define a second corner of a rectangle.

*174    Introduction to the Graphics Device Interface*

The rectangle drawn by this routine has borders which are parallel to the *x*- and *y*-axes, which is why only two points are required (and not four). The two corners are "opposite" each other on the resulting rectangle.

Here is the source code for our rectangle drawing program:

# MAKEFILE.MAK

```
.AUTODEPEND

#    Translator Definitions
INC=\BORLANDC\OWL\INCLUDE;\BORLANDC\CLASSLIB\INCLUDE;\BORLANDC\INCLUDE
CC = bcc -c -D_CLASSDLL -H -ml -WS -w-par -I$(INC)

#    Implicit Rules
.c.obj:
  $(CC) {$< }

.cpp.obj:
  $(CC) {$< }

#    Explicit Rules
Rect.exe: Rect.res Rect.def Rect.obj
     tlink /c/C/n/P-/Twe/x @Rect.LNK
     rlink Rect.res Rect.exe

#    Individual File Dependencies
Rect.obj: Rect.cpp

Rect.res: Rect.rc Rect.cur Rect.ico
     brcc -FO Rect.res -i$(INC) Rect.RC
```

# RECT.LNK

```
\borlandc\lib\c0wl.obj+
Rect.obj
Rect,Rect
\borlandc\classlib\lib\tclasdll.lib+
\borlandc\owl\lib\owl.lib+
mathwl.lib+
import.lib+
crtldll.lib
Rect.def
```

# RECT.CPP

```
/*------------------------------------------------------------*\
 | RECT.CPP   Draws a set of rectangles in response to mouse  |
 |            click messages.                                 |
 \*------------------------------------------------------------*/
#define WIN31
#define STRICT
#include <owl.h>
#include <WINDOWSX.H>
```

```
#define MOUSEX(arg)  (arg.LP.Lo)
#define MOUSEY(arg)  (arg.LP.Hi)

/*-------------------------------------------------------------*\
|                       Constants.                              |
\*-------------------------------------------------------------*/
const int MAXRECTANGLES = 50;
const int MARKERSIZE = 3;

/*-------------------------------------------------------------*\
|                    Class Declarations.                        |
\*-------------------------------------------------------------*/
class TRectApplication : public TApplication
   {
   public:
     TRectApplication (LPSTR lpszName, HINSTANCE hInstance,
                  HINSTANCE hPrevInstance, LPSTR lpszCmdLine,
                  int nCmdShow);
     virtual void InitMainWindow ();
   };

class TRectWindow : public TWindow
   {
   public:
     TRectWindow (PTWindowsObject pwParent, LPSTR lpszTitle,
              PTModule pmModule);
     virtual LPSTR GetClassName ();
     virtual void  GetWindowClass (WNDCLASS&);
     virtual void  Paint(HDC hdc, PAINTSTRUCT& ps);
     virtual void  WMLButtonDown(TMessage& Msg)=[WM_LBUTTONDOWN];
     virtual void  WMLButtonUp(TMessage& Msg)=[WM_LBUTTONUP];
   private:
     RECT arRectangles[MAXRECTANGLES];
     int  cRects;
   };

/*-------------------------------------------------------------*\
|                    Function Prototypes.                       |
\*-------------------------------------------------------------*/
void DrawMarker (HDC hDC, int x, int y);

/*-------------------------------------------------------------*\
|                  Main Function: WinMain.                      |
\*-------------------------------------------------------------*/
int PASCAL WinMain (HINSTANCE hInstance,   HINSTANCE hPrevInstance,
               LPSTR  lpszCmdLine, int    nCmdShow)
    {
    TRectApplication Rect ("Rect", hInstance, hPrevInstance,
                    lpszCmdLine, nCmdShow);
    Rect.Run();
    return Rect.Status;
    }

/*-------------------------------------------------------------*\
|                  Application Class Member.                    |
\*-------------------------------------------------------------*/
TRectApplication::TRectApplication (LPSTR lpszName, HINSTANCE hInstance,
              HINSTANCE hPrevInstance, LPSTR lpszCmdLine,
              int nCmdShow)
                 :TApplication (lpszName, hInstance, hPrevInstance,
                    lpszCmdLine, nCmdShow)
    {
    /*  Application specific initialization goes here.  */
    }
```

```
/*---------------------------------------------------------------*\
|                     Application Class Member.                   |
\*---------------------------------------------------------------*/
void TRectApplication::InitMainWindow ()
    {
    MainWindow = new TRectWindow (NULL, "Rectangles", NULL);
    }

/*---------------------------------------------------------------*\
|                     TRectWindow Class Member.                   |
\*---------------------------------------------------------------*/
TRectWindow::TRectWindow (PTWindowsObject pwParent,
              LPSTR lpszTitle, PTModule pmModule)
         :TWindow (pwParent, lpszTitle, pmModule)
    {
    cRects = 0;
    }

/*---------------------------------------------------------------*\
|                     TRectWindow Class Member.                   |
\*---------------------------------------------------------------*/
LPSTR TRectWindow::GetClassName ()
    {
    return "Rect:MAIN";
    }

/*---------------------------------------------------------------*\
|                     TRectWindow Class Member.                   |
\*---------------------------------------------------------------*/
void TRectWindow::GetWindowClass (WNDCLASS& wc)
    {
    TWindow::GetWindowClass (wc);
    wc.hIcon=LoadIcon (wc.hInstance, "snapshot");
    wc.hCursor=LoadCursor (wc.hInstance, "hand");
    }

/*---------------------------------------------------------------*\
|                     TRectWindow Class Member.                   |
\*---------------------------------------------------------------*/
void TRectWindow::WMLButtonDown(TMessage& Msg)
    {
    arRectangles[cRects].left = MOUSEX(Msg);
    arRectangles[cRects].top  = MOUSEY(Msg);
    }

/*---------------------------------------------------------------*\
|                     TRectWindow Class Member.                   |
\*---------------------------------------------------------------*/
void TRectWindow::WMLButtonUp(TMessage& Msg)
    {
    arRectangles[cRects].right  = MOUSEX(Msg);
    arRectangles[cRects].bottom = MOUSEY(Msg);
    cRects++;
    if (cRects == MAXRECTANGLES)
        cRects = 0;
    InvalidateRect (HWindow, NULL, TRUE);
    }

/*---------------------------------------------------------------*\
|                     TRectWindow Class Member.                   |
\*---------------------------------------------------------------*/
```

```
void TRectWindow::Paint(HDC hdc, PAINTSTRUCT& ps)
    {
    int i;

    for (i = 0; i < cRects ; i++ )
        {
        Rectangle (hdc, arRectangles[i].left,
                        arRectangles[i].top,
                        arRectangles[i].right,
                        arRectangles[i].bottom);

        DrawMarker (hdc, arRectangles[i].left,
                         arRectangles[i].top);
        DrawMarker (hdc, arRectangles[i].right,
                         arRectangles[i].bottom);
        }
    }

/*----------------------------------------------------------------*\
|                    Marker Drawing Function.                      |
\*----------------------------------------------------------------*/
void DrawMarker (HDC hdc, int x, int y)
    {
    int i;
    int rop;

    rop = SetROP2 (hdc, R2_NOT);
    SetPixel (hdc, x, y, RGB(0, 0, 0));

    for (i=1;i<=MARKERSIZE; i++)
        {
        SetPixel (hdc, x+i, y, RGB(0, 0, 0));
        SetPixel (hdc, x-i, y, RGB(0, 0, 0));
        SetPixel (hdc, x, y+i, RGB(0, 0, 0));
        SetPixel (hdc, x, y-i, RGB(0, 0, 0));
        }

    SetROP2 (hdc, rop);
    }
```

## RECT.RC

```
snapshot icon Rect.ico

hand cursor Rect.cur
```

## RECT.DEF

```
NAME RECT

EXETYPE WINDOWS

DESCRIPTION 'Rect -- Rectangle Drawing'

CODE MOVEABLE DISCARDABLE
DATA MOVEABLE MULTIPLE

HEAPSIZE  512
STACKSIZE 5120
```

To store the points that describe each rectangle, we allocate an array of type RECT:

```
RECT    arRectangles[MAXRECTANGLES];
```

**RECT** is defined in WINDOWS.H as

```
typedef struct tagRECT
  {
    int  left;
    int  top;
    int  right;
    int  bottom;
  } RECT;
```

The elements of this array are named in a somewhat odd fashion, reflecting the use of this structure for clipping rectangles. The `left` and `right` fields contain *x* values, and the `top` and `bottom` fields contain *y* values.

We use the **MAKEPOINT** macro to copy the mouse location from the `lParam` parameter of a mouse message to a `POINT` variable. When the user pushes the left mouse button, a `WM_LBUTTONDOWN` message is generated. When our window object receives this message, it stores the mouse location in the `left` and `top` fields of `arRectangles`. Later, when the user releases the left mouse button, a `WM_LBUTTONUP` message is generated. The window object responds to this message by storing the mouse location information in the `right` and `bottom` fields of `arRectangles`.

In response to the `WM_LBUTTONUP` message, our window object declares the entire window to be damaged with the `InvalidateRect` routine. As you recall, this causes a `WM_PAINT` message to be generated. This allows us to put all our rectangle drawing code in one place.

In response to the `WM_PAINT` message, the `TWindow`'s `WMPaint` member does all the "standard" work required for this message. Then, it calls the `Paint` member function, which our window object has overridden so we can point in our own window. As you may recall from the last chapter, the minimum work required for `WM_PAINT` is to call `BeginPaint` and `EndPaint`. In between these calls, a window can draw to its heart's content.

Our `Paint` member function runs through the array of rectangles, drawing each in turn. After a rectangle has been drawn, a marker is placed at the two points that defined the rectangle.

This brief introduction to the `Rectangle` routine, and GDI's two different types of coordinates, has gotten us ready to look at the rest of GDI's filled figure routines.

# GDI Filled Figure Routines

Let's take a close look at each of GDI's filled figure routines. GDI has seven such routines: `Polygon`, `PolyPolygon`, `Chord`, `Ellipse`, `Pie`, `Rectangle`, and `RoundRect`.

We'll begin with the two routines that use pixel-centered coordinates.

## *Polygon and PolyPolygon*

The `Polygon` routine is defined

`Polygon (hDC, lpPoints, nCount)`

- hDC is a handle to a device context.
- lpPoints is a pointer to an array of type POINT. It is the points to connect.
- nCount is the number of points to connect.

Like the `Polyline` routine that we encountered in the last chapter, this routine connects a series of points using the pen that is currently installed in the DC. In addition, if the first and last points are not the same, a line is drawn to close the figure, and the area inside the figure is filled using the brush currently installed in the DC.

`Polygon` is GDI's most flexible filled area routine, since you can use it to draw any filled figure. As a simple example, Figure 9.4 shows rectangles drawn using `Polygon`. Unlike the normal `Rectangle` routine, `Polygon` can draw *rotated* rectangles.

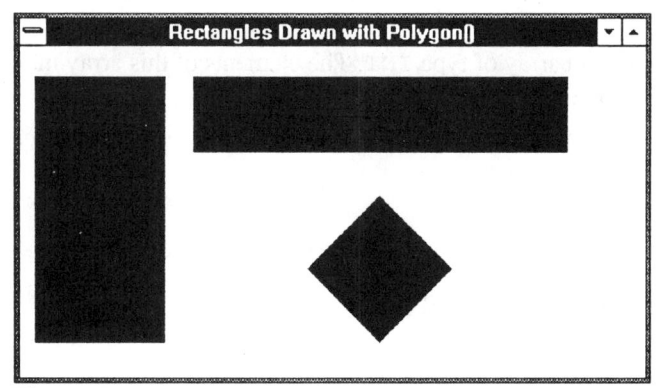

**Figure 9.4** Rectangles drawn with the Polygon routine

180 *Introduction to the Graphics Device Interface*

Here is the code fragment that created this illustration:

```
void TSampleWindow::Paint(HDC hdc, PAINTSTRUCT& ps)
    {
    SelectObject (hdc, GetStockObject (BLACK_BRUSH));

    apt[0].x =  10;   apt[0].y =  20;
    apt[1].x = 100;   apt[1].y =  20;
    apt[2].x = 100;   apt[2].y = 200;
    apt[3].x =  10;   apt[3].y = 200;
    Polygon (hdc, apt, 4);

    apt[0].x = 120;   apt[0].y =  20;
    apt[1].x = 380;   apt[1].y =  20;
    apt[2].x = 380;   apt[2].y =  70;
    apt[3].x = 120;   apt[3].y =  70;
    Polygon (hdc, apt, 4);

    apt[0].x = 200;   apt[0].y = 150;

    apt[1].x = 250;   apt[1].y = 100;
    apt[2].x = 300;   apt[2].y = 150;
    apt[3].x = 250;   apt[3].y = 200;
    Polygon (hdc, apt, 4);
    }
```

The **PolyPolygon** routine lets us draw many polygons with a single call. This routine is an extension of the **Polygon** routine. Programs that draw many polygons will run faster if they call **PolyPolygon** than if they make many separate calls to **Polygon**. The speed advantage is a result of the overhead involved with making a function call.

**PolyPolygon** is defined as follows:

PolyPolygon (hDC, lpPoints, lpPolyCount, nCount);

- hDC is a handle to a device context.
- lpPoints is a pointer to an array of type **POINT**. It is the points to connect to create the various polygons.
- lpPolyCount is a pointer to an array of type **INT**. The elements of this array indicate the number of points in each polygon.
- nCount is an integer for the number of points in the lpPolyCount array. In other words, it is the number of polygons to draw.

Here is the code that draws the previous figure using a single call to **PolyPolygon**:

```
void TSampleWindow::Paint(HDC hdc, PAINTSTRUCT& ps)
    {
    SelectObject (hdc, GetStockObject (BLACK_BRUSH));

    /*  First Rectangle.  */
    apt[0].x =  10;   apt[0].y =  20;
    apt[1].x = 100;   apt[1].y =  20;
```

```
        apt[2].x =  100;   apt[2].y = 200;
        apt[3].x =   10;   apt[3].y = 200;
        apt[4].x =   10;   apt[4].y =  20;
        ai[0] = 5;

        /* Second Rectangle. */
        apt[5].x = 120;   apt[5].y = 20;
        apt[6].x = 380;   apt[6].y = 20;
        apt[7].x = 380;   apt[7].y = 70;
        apt[8].x = 120;   apt[8].y = 70;
        apt[9].x = 120;   apt[9].y = 20;
        ai[1] = 5;

        /* Third Rectangle. */
        apt[10].x = 200;   apt[10].y = 150;
        apt[11].x = 250;   apt[11].y = 100;
        apt[12].x = 300;   apt[12].y = 150;
        apt[13].x = 250;   apt[13].y = 200;
        apt[14].x = 200;   apt[14].y = 150;
        ai[2] = 5;

        PolyPolygon (hdc, apt, ai, 3);
        }
```

When we talk about polygons, we normally think of figures with flat sides—like the rectangles we drew in our sample code. But we can also use the **Polygon** routines to draw curves, as long as we provide enough points. In fact, that's how GDI simulates curves—with a series of short lines. Of course, if we want to draw curves in this way, we have our work cut out for us. We'd have to calculate all of the points along the curve.

GDI has a set of routines that do this work for us and make it easy to draw filled figures with curved sides. Let's take a look at those routines.

## *Ellipse, Chord, and Pie*

GDI has three routines that create filled figures with curved sides. As you'll see in a moment, you can think of these routines as extensions of the **Arc** routine that we covered in the last chapter. Each routine uses a bounding rectangle to draw a curve.

Here is the definition of the Ellipse function:

`Ellipse (hDC, X1, Y1, X2, Y2)`

- hDC is a handle to a device context.
- (X1, Y1) is a corner of the bounding rectangle.
- (X2, Y2) is the opposite corner of the bounding rectangle.

The **Ellipse** function creates an ellipse whose perimeter is tangent to the sides of the bounding rectangle, as illustrated in Figure 9.5.

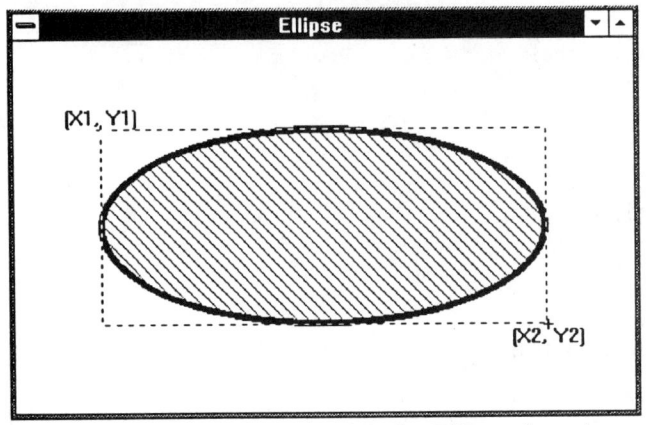

**Figure 9.5** A figure drawn with the Ellipse function

The `Chord` function also makes use of a bounding rectangle to draw a partial arc connected with a line segment. This function is defined as follows:

```
Chord (hDC, X1, Y1, X2, Y2, X3, Y3, X4, Y4)
```

- hDC is a handle to a device context.
- (X1, Y1) and (X2, Y2) define the bounding rectangle.
- (X3, Y3) is the starting point of the line segment.
- (X4, Y4) is the ending point of the line segment.

Figure 9.6 shows a chord drawn with this function, with notation to show the bounding box and the line segment coordinates.

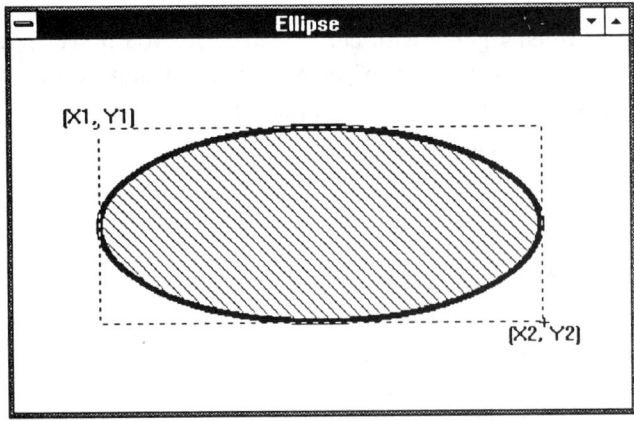

**Figure 9.6** A figure drawn with the chord function

The **Pie** function takes the same parameters as the **Chord** function. This function draws a wedge of a pie instead of a chord. The function is defined as follows:

```
Pie (hDC, X1, Y1, X2, Y2, X3, Y3, X4, Y4)
```

- hDC is a handle to a device context.
- (X1, Y1) and (X2, Y2) define the bounding rectangle.
- (X3, Y3) is the starting point of the wedge.
- (X4, Y4) is the ending point of the wedge.

Figure 9.7 shows a pie wedge, with the bounding box, starting point, and ending point shown.

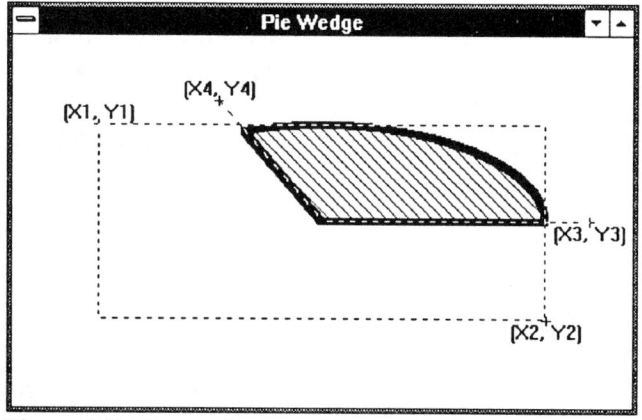

**Figure 9.7** Figure drawn with the Pie function

## *Rectangle and RoundRect*

We have seen the **Rectangle** function before, but for completeness sake, here is the function definition:

```
Rectangle (hDC, X1, Y1, X2, Y2)
```

- hDC is a device context handle.
- (X1, Y1) is one corner of the rectangle.
- (X2, Y2) is the opposite corner of the rectangle.

Like other GDI filled figure routines, **Rectangle** uses the pen from the DC to draw the rectangle border and the brush to fill the interior. This routine only draws rectangles

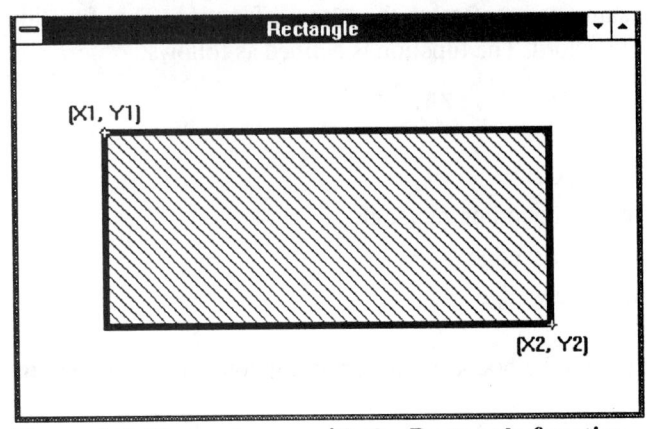

184   *Introduction to the Graphics Device Interface*

**Figure 9.8** Figure drawn with the Rectangle function

with sides that are parallel with the *x-* and *y*-axes. For rotated rectangles, you must use either the `Polygon` function or the `PolyPolygon` function. Figure 9.8 illustrates the relationship of the two control points to the rectangle that is drawn.

The `RoundRect` routine draws a rectangle with rounded corners. It is defined as follows:

```
RoundRect (hDC, X1, Y1, X2, Y2, X3, Y3)
```

- hDC is a device context handle.
- (X1, Y1) is one corner of the rectangle.
- (X2, Y2) is the opposite corner of the rectangle.
- (X3, Y3) define a bounding box for an ellipse that is used to draw the rounded corners.

Figure 9.9 shows an example of the type of output that `RoundRect` can be used to create.

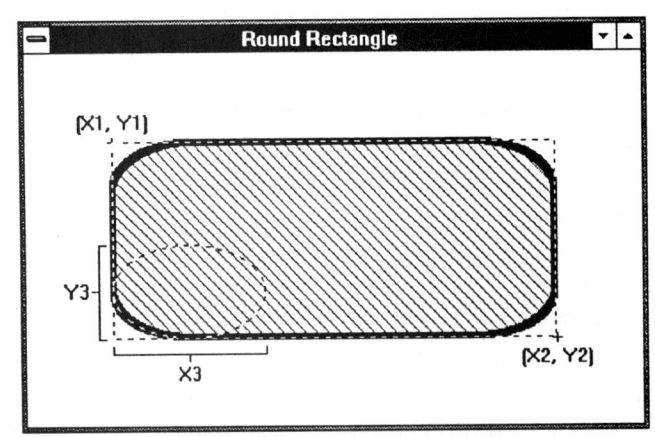

**Figure 9.9** Sample of RoundRect output

# DC Attributes

As with other GDI drawing primitives, we must visit the device context to fully understand how much control GDI gives us over filled figures. Here is a list of the attributes that affect filled figures:

| Drawing Attribute | Comments |
| --- | --- |
| Background color | Second color for hatched brushes and nonsolid pens |
| Background mode | Turns on/off background color |
| Brush | Color for filling interior |
| Brush origin | Alignment of hatched brushes |
| Drawing mode | Boolean drawing operation |
| Pen | Border color, width, and style |
| Polygon-filling mode | For `Polygon` and `PolyPolygon` routines |

Since the borders of filled figures are lines, all of the DC attributes that affect lines are also used for the borders of filled figures: background color, background mode, drawing mode, and pen. An important point to note is that, when used to draw a border, a pen is always *centered* on the border. For example, a nine-pixel-wide pen will draw a border with four pixels inside the figure, four pixels outside the figure, and one pixel on the border itself.

Pens created with a style of `PS_INSIDEFRAME`, however, never draw borders that extend beyond the border of the figure. A nine-pixel-wide `PS_INSIDEFRAME` pen, for example, will draw a border that has one pixel on the exact border and eight pixels inside the figure. This can be useful when drawing a figure which *must* occupy a specific area, and not grow beyond the rectangle which bounds the area.

Three attributes are specific to filled areas: brush, brush origin, and polygon-filling mode. Before we discuss GDI brushes, we're going to briefly discuss two of these: polygon-filling mode and drawing mode.

The names of drawing modes seem to imply that they only affect lines. For example, the default drawing mode, `R2_COPYPEN`, includes the word "pen," the line drawing attribute. In spite of this unfortunate choice of names, drawing modes affect filled figures: both the inside area and the border. Drawing modes affect pens and brushes equally.

The polygon-filling mode determines how to fill complex figures created by two routines: `Polygon` and `PolyPolygon`. For simple figures, like squares and rectangles, the polygon-filling mode has no effect. For complex figures, like the star in Figure 9.10, the polygon-filling mode determines which areas to fill.

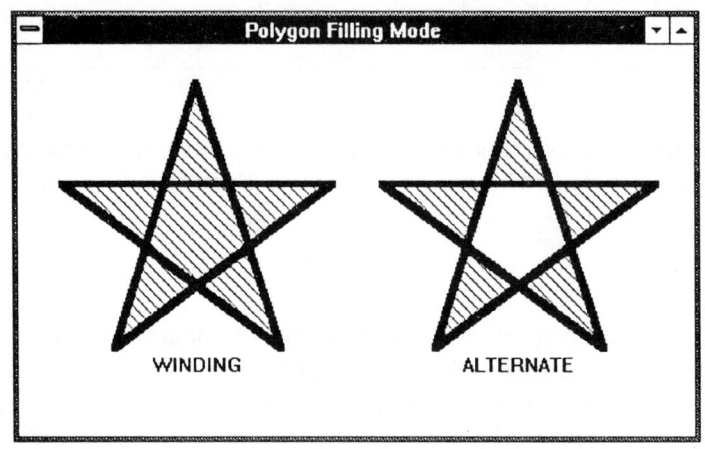

**Figure 9.10** Polygon filling modes only affect complex Polygons

The winding mode fills all areas inside the border. The alternate mode, on the other hand, fills only the odd areas. That is, if you were to draw a line segment through a figure, filling is turned *on* after odd boundary crossings (1, 3, 5, etc.), and turned *off* after even boundary crossings (2, 4, 6). GDI has no provision for filling the even areas, though you can achieve this effect by drawing the same figure twice.

The `SetPolyFillMode` routine, which sets this drawing attribute, is defined as follows:

```
SetPolyFillMode (hDC, nPolyFillMode)
```

- hDC is a handle to a device context.
- nPolyFillMode is either **ALTERNATE** or **WINDING**.

Now let's turn our attention to the attribute that has the most effect on the appearance of filled figures: GDI brushes.

## About Brushes

A brush is a DC drawing attribute for filling areas. Three qualities make up a brush: a style, a color, and a pattern. The size of a brush is eight pixels by eight pixels. When we discussed GDI pens, we mentioned that attribute bundles allow a convenient way for a program to refer to several attributes at the same time. The convenience factor is certainly one of the reasons for brushes.

We mentioned earlier that pens can be shared between programs and between devices. The same is true of brushes. Just as there are stock pens, there are stock brushes. That is, GDI creates a set of brushes for use by any program. If stock brushes don't provide what you need, it is a simple matter to create your own brushes. And finally, like pens, you must be sure to clean up all of the brushes that you create. Otherwise, the memory is lost from the system. Let's look at some of the details surrounding the creation and use of brushes.

## Creating and Using Brushes

At system startup time, GDI creates the following stock brushes: black, dark gray, gray, light gray, white, and null (or hollow). Like the null pen, a null brush is a placeholder. You can think of a null brush as one having a transparent color.

The **GetStockObject** routine provides a handle to stock brushes. To use a brush, install it into a DC with the **SelectObject** routine. Here is one way to draw a rectangle with a gray interior:

```
brush = GetStockBrush (GRAY_BRUSH);// macro for GetStockObject
SelectBrush (hdc, brush);          // macro for SelectObject
Rectangle (hdc, X1, Y1, X2, Y2);
```

To supplement the stock brushes, you can create custom brushes. There are three types of custom brushes: solid, hatched, and pattern. Figure 9.11 shows examples of each type. GDI provides five routines to create brushes: **CreateBrushIndirect**, **CreateDIBPatternBrush**, **CreateHatchBrush**, **CreatePatternBrush**, and **CreateSolidBrush**.

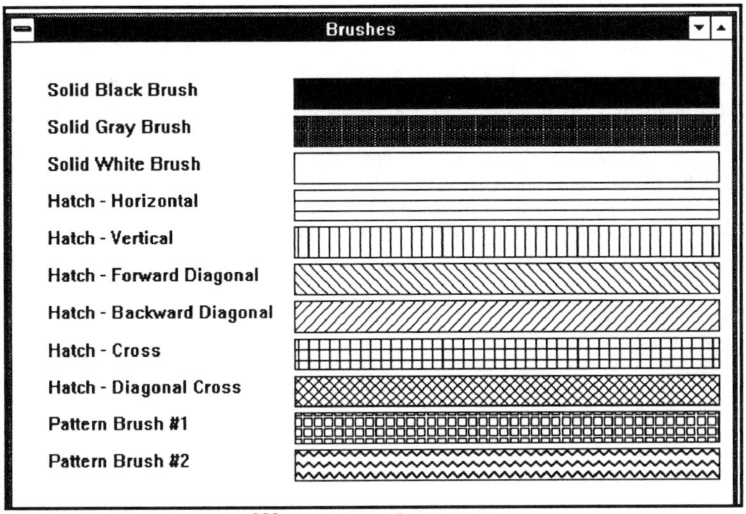

**Figure 9.11 Eleven different brushes**

We're going to take a close look at the last three routines in this list. Let's take a moment, though, to look at the other two routines. The first, **CreateBrushIndirect**, is able to do the job of any of the other routines. It is unique in that it takes as a parameter a pointer to a data structure that can describe any brush: a **LOGBRUSH** (logical brush). The second routine in this list, **CreateDIBPatternBrush**, creates a brush from a device-independent bitmap, also known as a DIB. DIBs are bitmaps whose color information is stored in a standard format. The colors in a DIB can be correctly interpreted on any GDI device.

Let's now turn our attention to the three types of bitmaps: solid, hatched, and pattern. As we examine each, we'll look at the three routines that we use in our sample program to create these types of brushes: **CreateSolidBrush**, **CreateHatchBrush**, and **CreatePatternBrush**.

A **solid brush** is a brush that is created from either a pure or a dithered color. We introduced dithered colors in the last chapter in our discussion of dithered pens. Dithered colors are created by mixing pure colors.

For example, the device that created Figure 9.11 has just two colors: black and white. By dithering, we can create many different shades of gray, like the one that was used to draw the rectangle labeled "Solid Gray Brush" in our figure.

The **CreateSolidBrush** routine lets you create these brushes. It is defined as

```
HBRUSH CreateSolidBrush (crColor)
```

- crColor is a color reference. This can be an RGB triplet, a palette index, or a palette-relative RGB value.

For example, here's how to create a white brush:

```
hbr = CreateSolidBrush (RGB (255, 255, 255));
```

A **hatch brush** fills areas with a pattern created with hatch marks. GDI provides six built-in hatch patterns, as shown in Figure 9.11. The **CreateHatchBrush** routine is the easiest way to create a hatch brush (although the **CreateBrushIndirect** routine can be used as well).

The syntax of **CreateHatchBrush** is as follows:

```
HBRUSH CreateSolidBrush (nIndex, crColor)
```

- nIndex can be any one of six values:
    - HS_BDIAGONAL
    - HS_CROSS
    - HS_DIAGCROSS
    - HS_FDIAGONAL

```
HS_HORIZONTAL
HS_VERTICAL
```
- `crColor` is a color reference. This can be an RGB triplet, a palette index, or a palette-relative RGB value.

A **pattern brush** is a brush created from a bitmap pattern. If the six styles of hatch brushes aren't enough for you, a pattern brush can be created with just about any hatch pattern you'd like to use. A pattern brush can also be made to resemble a solid brush, although this is usually more work than it's worth.

To create a pattern brush, you use the **CreatePatternBrush** routine. It's syntax is as follows:

```
HBRUSH CreatePatternBrush (hBitmap)
```

- `hBitmap` is a handle to a bitmap.

To create a pattern brush, you first need a bitmap. There are many ways to create a bitmap. For now, let's look at the two methods we use in our sample program.

The first method involves using a graphic editor, such as the Resource Workshop, to draw a bitmap pattern like that shown in Figure 9.12. This pattern is saved to a file (SQUARE.BMP in our sample program). To incorporate this bitmap into our program, we make an entry in the resource script file, like the following:

```
square bitmap square.bmp
```

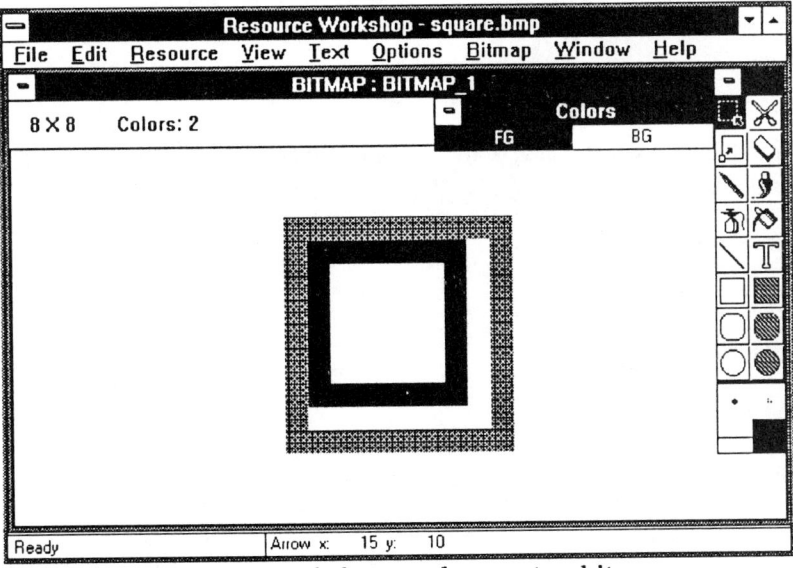

**Figure 9.12** Resource Workshop used to create a bitmap

## 190  *Introduction to the Graphics Device Interface*

The following lines of code read this bitmap into memory, and use it to create a pattern brush:

```
hbm = LoadBitmap (hInst, "square");
hbr[9] = CreatePatternBrush (hbm);
```

This brush is now ready to be selected into a DC for use in filling the inside of a GDI filled figure.

A second method that can be used to create a bitmap is to call the `CreateBitmap` routine with a pointer to the bits to include in the bitmap. The `CreateBitmap` routine is defined as follows:

```
HBITMAP CreateBitmap (nWidth, nHeight, nPlanes,
                      nBitCount, lpBits)
```

- `nWidth` and `nHeight` are the width and height of the bitmap in pixels. Since all GDI brushes are eight pixels wide by eight pixels high, the value of both fields must be set to 8.
- `nPlanes` is the number of planes in the bitmap. Planes provide one means to store color information (for example, the EGA display adapter uses this method). We're going to create a monochrome bitmap, so we'll use the value 1 here.
- `nBitCount` is the number of bits per color. Packed pixels provide a second way to store color information (some modes of the CGA display adapter use this method). Since we are creating a monochrome bitmap, we set this to 1.
- `lpBits` is a pointer to the bits to use to initialize the bitmap.

Our program creates its second pattern bitmap by making the following calls:

```
hbm = CreateBitmap (8, 8, 1, 1, acPattern);
hbr[10] = CreatePatternBrush (hbm);
```

The last parameter of the `CreateBitmap` call is a pointer to an array of character values. It is defined in our program as

```
static unsigned char acPattern[] =
        {0xFF, 0,  /* 1 1 1 1 1 1 1 1  */
         0xE7, 0,  /* 1 1 1 0 0 1 1 1  */
         0xC3, 0,  /* 1 1 0 0 0 0 1 1  */
         0x99, 0,  /* 1 0 0 1 1 0 0 1  */
         0x3C, 0,  /* 0 0 1 1 1 1 0 0  */
         0x7E, 0,  /* 0 1 1 1 1 1 1 0  */
         0xFF, 0,  /* 1 1 1 1 1 1 1 1  */
         0xFF, 0}; /* 1 1 1 1 1 1 1 1  */
```

Our array is defined with hexadecimal values, but for your convenience the comment shows the values in binary. The 1's represent white pixels and the 0's represent black pixels. Since

*Drawing Filled Figures* 191

bitmap data is expected to be aligned on 16-bit boundaries, we have an additional zero byte between each of our bitmap byte values.

Each of these routines creates a **logical brush**. Like logical pens, logical brushes are requests that can be passed to any device. When asked to use a brush, the device driver *realizes* the brush—that is, it converts the logical request to a form that matches the capabilities of the specific device.

All the source files to our brush creation program, BRUSHES, are shown here:

# MAKEFILE.MAK

```
.AUTODEPEND

#    Translator Definitions
INC=\BORLANDC\OWL\INCLUDE;\BORLANDC\CLASSLIB\INCLUDE;\BORLANDC\INCLUDE
CC = bcc -c -D_CLASSDLL -H -ml -WS -w-par -I$(INC)

#    Implicit Rules
.c.obj:
  $(CC) {$< }

.cpp.obj:
  $(CC) {$< }

#    Explicit Rules
Brushes.exe: Brushes.res Brushes.def Brushes.obj
    tlink /c/C/n/P-/Twe/x @Brushes.LNK
    rlink Brushes.res Brushes.exe

#    Individual File Dependencies
Brushes.obj: Brushes.cpp

Brushes.res: Brushes.rc Brushes.cur Brushes.ico
    brcc -FO Brushes.res -i$(INC) Brushes.RC
```

# BRUSHES.LNK

```
\borlandc\lib\c0wl.obj+
Brushes.obj
Brushes,Brushes
\borlandc\classlib\lib\tclasdll.lib+
\borlandc\owl\lib\owl.lib+
mathwl.lib+
import.lib+
crtldll.lib
Brushes.def
```

## 192 Introduction to the Graphics Device Interface
# BRUSHES.CPP

```cpp
/*-------------------------------------------------------------*\
|   BRUSHES.CPP   Shows different types of GDI brushes.         |
\*-------------------------------------------------------------*/
#define WIN31
#define STRICT
#include <owl.h>
#include <WindowsX.h>

/*-------------------------------------------------------------*\
|                         Constants.                            |
\*-------------------------------------------------------------*/
const int BRUSHCOUNT  = 11;
const int PATTERNSIZE = 16;

/*-------------------------------------------------------------*\
|                     Class Declarations.                       |
\*-------------------------------------------------------------*/
class TBrushesApplication : public TApplication
    {
    public:
       TBrushesApplication (LPSTR lpszName, HINSTANCE hInstance,
                    HINSTANCE hPrevInstance, LPSTR lpszCmdLine,
                    int nCmdShow);
       virtual void InitMainWindow ();
    };

class TBrushesWindow : public TWindow
    {
public:
    TBrushesWindow (PTWindowsObject pwParent, LPSTR lpszTitle,
                    PTModule pmModule);
    ~TBrushesWindow();
    virtual LPSTR GetClassName ();
    virtual void  GetWindowClass (WNDCLASS&);
    virtual void  Paint(HDC hdc, PAINTSTRUCT& ps);
  private:
    HBRUSH hbr[BRUSHCOUNT];
    char * apszDesc[BRUSHCOUNT];
    unsigned char acPattern[PATTERNSIZE];
    };

/*-------------------------------------------------------------*\
|                   Main Function:  WinMain.                    |
\*-------------------------------------------------------------*/
int PASCAL WinMain (HINSTANCE hInstance,   HINSTANCE hPrevInstance,
               LPSTR  lpszCmdLine, int   nCmdShow)
    {
    TBrushesApplication Brushes ("Brushes", hInstance,
                                 hPrevInstance, lpszCmdLine,
                                 nCmdShow);
    Brushes.Run();
    return Brushes.Status;
    }

/*-------------------------------------------------------------*\
|                   Application Class Member.                   |
\*-------------------------------------------------------------*/
TBrushesApplication::TBrushesApplication (LPSTR lpszName,
                      HINSTANCE hInstance, HINSTANCE hPrevInstance,
                      LPSTR lpszCmdLine, int nCmdShow)
```

```
                    :TApplication (lpszName, hInstance,
                       hPrevInstance, lpszCmdLine, nCmdShow)
    {
    /* Application specific initialization goes here. */
    }
/*---------------------------------------------------------------*\
|                   Application Class Member.                     |
\*---------------------------------------------------------------*/
void TBrushesApplication::InitMainWindow ()
    {
    MainWindow = new TBrushesWindow (NULL, "Brushes", NULL);
    }
/*---------------------------------------------------------------*\
|                   TBrushesWindow Class Member.                  |
\*---------------------------------------------------------------*/
TBrushesWindow::TBrushesWindow (PTWindowsObject pwParent,
              LPSTR lpszTitle, PTModule pmModule)
           :TWindow (pwParent, lpszTitle, pmModule)
    {
    HBITMAP hbm;

    /*
     * Initialize array for dynamic bitmap creation.
     */
    acPattern[0]  = 0xff;
    acPattern[1]  = 0;
    acPattern[2]  = 0xe7;     /* 1 1 1 1 1 1 1 1 */
    acPattern[3]  = 0;        /* 1 1 1 0 0 1 1 1 */
    acPattern[4]  = 0xc3;     /* 1 1 0 0 0 0 1 1 */
    acPattern[5]  = 0;        /* 1 0 0 1 1 0 0 1 */
    acPattern[6]  = 0x99;     /* 0 0 1 1 1 1 0 0 */
    acPattern[7]  = 0;        /* 0 1 1 1 1 1 1 0 */
    acPattern[8]  = 0x3c;     /* 1 1 1 1 1 1 1 1 */
    acPattern[9]  = 0;        /* 1 1 1 1 1 1 1 1 */
    acPattern[10] = 0x7e;
    acPattern[11] = 0;
    acPattern[12] = 0xff;
    acPattern[13] = 0;
    acPattern[14] = 0xff;
    acPattern[15] = 0;

    /*
     * Create brushes.
     */
    apszDesc[0] = "Solid Black Brush";
    hbr[0]  = CreateSolidBrush (RGB (0, 0, 0));

    apszDesc[1] = "Solid Gray Brush";
    hbr[1]  = CreateSolidBrush (RGB (64, 64, 64));

    apszDesc[2] = "Solid White Brush";
    hbr[2]  = CreateSolidBrush (RGB (255, 255, 255));

    apszDesc[3] = "Hatch - Horizontal";
    hbr[3]  = CreateHatchBrush (HS_HORIZONTAL , RGB(0, 0, 0));

    apszDesc[4] = "Hatch - Vertical";
    hbr[4]  = CreateHatchBrush (HS_VERTICAL , RGB(0, 0, 0));
```

```
    apszDesc[5] = "Hatch - Forward Diagonal";
    hbr[5]   = CreateHatchBrush (HS_FDIAGONAL , RGB(0, 0, 0));

    apszDesc[6] = "Hatch - Backward Diagonal    ";
    hbr[6]   = CreateHatchBrush (HS_BDIAGONAL, RGB(0, 0, 0));

    apszDesc[7] = "Hatch - Cross";
    hbr[7]   = CreateHatchBrush (HS_CROSS , RGB(0, 0, 0));

    apszDesc[8] = "Hatch - Diagonal Cross";
    hbr[8]   = CreateHatchBrush (HS_DIAGCROSS , RGB(0, 0, 0));

    apszDesc[9] = "Pattern Brush #1";
    hbm = LoadBitmap (GetApplication()->hInstance, "square");
    hbr[9]   = CreatePatternBrush (hbm);
    DeleteBitmap (hbm);

    apszDesc[10] = "Pattern Brush #2";
    hbm = CreateBitmap (8, 8, 1, 1, (LPSTR)&acPattern[0]);
    hbr[10] = CreatePatternBrush (hbm);
    DeleteBitmap (hbm);
    }

/*----------------------------------------------------------------*\
|               TBrushesWindow Class Member.                       |
\*----------------------------------------------------------------*\
TBrushesWindow::~TBrushesWindow()
    {
    int i;

    for (i=0;i<BRUSHCOUNT; i++)
        DeleteBrush (hbr[i]);
}

/*----------------------------------------------------------------*\
|               TBrushesWindow Class Member.                       |
\*----------------------------------------------------------------*/
LPSTR TBrushesWindow::GetClassName ()
    {
    return "Brushes:MAIN";
    }

/*----------------------------------------------------------------*\
|               TBrushesWindow Class Member.                       |
\*----------------------------------------------------------------*/
void TBrushesWindow::GetWindowClass (WNDCLASS& wc)
    {
    TWindow::GetWindowClass (wc);
    wc.hIcon=LoadIcon (wc.hInstance, "snapshot");
    wc.hCursor=LoadCursor (wc.hInstance, "hand");
    }

/*----------------------------------------------------------------*\
|               TBrushesWindow Class Member.                       |
\*----------------------------------------------------------------*/
void TBrushesWindow::Paint(HDC hdc, PAINTSTRUCT& ps)
    {
    DWORD dw;
    int i;
    int xStart, xEnd, xText;
    int yIncr, yLine, yText;
    int cxWidth;
```

```
        RECT r;
        TEXTMETRIC tm;

        /* Divide available client area.  */
        GetClientRect (HWindow, &r);
        yIncr = r.bottom/ (BRUSHCOUNT+2);
        yText = yIncr;

        /* Get measurements to indent text 4 spaces. */
        GetTextMetrics (hdc, &tm);
        xText = tm.tmAveCharWidth * 4;

        /* Get measurements of longest text string. */
        dw = GetTextExtent (hdc, apszDesc[6],
                            lstrlen(apszDesc[6]));
        cxWidth = LOWORD(dw);

        /* Calculate width of rectangles. */
        xStart = xText + cxWidth;
        xEnd   = r.right - 10;

        /* Loop through all brushes. */
        for (i=0;i<BRUSHCOUNT; i++, yText += yIncr)
            {
            TextOut (hdc, xText, yText,apszDesc[i],
                    lstrlen(apszDesc[i]));

            SelectBrush (hdc, hbr[i]);
            yLine  = yText + yIncr - tm.tmHeight/4;
            Rectangle (hdc, xStart, yText, xEnd, yLine);
            }
        }
```

## BRUSHES.RC

```
snapshot icon Brushes.ico

hand cursor Brushes.cur

square bitmap square.bmp
```

## BRUSHES.DEF

```
NAME BRUSHES

EXETYPE WINDOWS

DESCRIPTION 'Brushes - Sample GDI Brushes'

CODE MOVEABLE DISCARDABLE
DATA MOVEABLE MULTIPLE

HEAPSIZE   512
STACKSIZE  5120
```

BRUSHES does its work in response to three events: window creation, window destruction, and window painting. In C++ terms, our window object class has three member functions: a constructor, a destructor, and a function to handle the **WM_PAINT** message.

At window creation time, our window creates the GDI brushes it needs. It's common for a window object to create GDI brushes in its constructor, and hold onto them for the life of the window. Although brushes take up memory, this approach allows for the fastest **WM_PAINT** processing.

Anytime you create a GDI object, you must be sure to clean it up when you're done. Since we created brushes in the constructor, it makes sense to destroy the brushes in our window object's destructor. If you overlook any GDI objects, you risk losing system memory.

In response to the **WM_PAINT** message, a default message response function calls our window object's **Paint** member function. This function divides up the available client area into 11 parts. Each part displays a rectangle that has been drawn with a different brush.

In the course of this program, we call three GDI text routines: **GetTextMetrics**, **GetTextExtent**, and **TextOut**. **GetTextMetrics** provides measurement information for the current font, or text pattern table. **GetTextExtent** is used to determine the width and height of a specific line of text. And **TextOut** displays a line of text.

In the next chapter, we're going to take a closer look at these routines and all of the other facilities that GDI provides for the creation of text output.

# 10

# Drawing Text

In most programs, text serves as the primary output media. And yet, we have postponed a discussion of text until now because text output in GDI is quite different from text output in traditional programming environments. GDI treats text as a type of graphic object.

You may have written programs with **line-oriented output**. This method was first used on the earliest interactive computer systems, which used typewriters to display output and receive input. With today's display screens, this type of output causes lines of text to roll off the top of a screen into an imaginary "bit bucket." Interaction is simple: The computer displays a request, the user responds. Beginning C programmers always start with this type of output, because it is part of the standard C library. Here is an example:

```
printf ("Enter first number:");
scanf ("%i", &iValue);
```

The next step up is **screen-oriented output**, which treats the display screen as a grid of character cells. Programs like word processors and full screen editors typically use this method. One popular MS-DOS database language, dBase, uses commands like these to write text and receive input on the display screen:

```
@ 10, 25 SAY "Please Enter Your Name:"
@ 10, 49 GET NAME
```

GDI's approach to text can be described as **pixel-oriented**, since GDI has no built-in idea of the size of a character cell. Instead, GDI lets you position text using the same pixel grid that you use for lines, rectangles, and other geometric shapes. This gives you a great deal of control over text placement and makes it easy to mix text with geometric figures. You can even mix different sizes and styles of text with a minimum of effort.

Unlike other graphic objects, text is not drawn using simple geometric equations. Instead, **fonts** are required to create text output. A font is a database of patterns that describe the shape and size of every letter, number, and punctuation mark. Each GDI device supports one or more fonts. Figure 10.1 shows some of the VGA display adapter's base fonts. The following box discusses GDI's base fonts.

---

### GDI Base Fonts

*Every GDI display driver is equipped with a set of base fonts, like those shown in Figure 10.1. A common set of base fonts ensures a minimum level of support will be available on all video displays.*

*Microsoft carefully chose the following fonts as part of the base set:*

Courier: *Provides fixed-pitch fonts for typewriter-like output.*

Tms Rmn: *A set of proportional, serif fonts available in a fairly wide range of sizes. This set can be used as a "stand-in" for other serif fonts for programs that wish to mimic a printer's output on a display screen.*

Helv: *A set of proportional, sans-serif Helvetica-like fonts, also available in a wide range of sizes. Like Tms Rmn, they are meant for use in programs that mimic a printer's output on a display screen.*

Symbol: *An alternative character set can be used in a font; this font uses Greek letters.*

Roman, Modern, and Script: *Vector fonts, in which the letter patterns are represented as sequences of vectors, or line segments.*

---

The available fonts can be extended beyond this base set. An end user can purchase fonts and install them using the Windows Control Panel. Programmers can create custom fonts and incorporate them into Windows programs. Microsoft plans to incorporate a whole new kind of font in a version 3.1 of Windows, using the **TrueType** "font engine." As of this writing, this technology is still being built in the development labs of Microsoft and Apple Computer.

Placing text often involves determining the **font metrics**, which is a table of values that tells you height and width information for a specific font.

If you wish to think in terms of a 25-line, 80-column output area, GDI gives you the tools to do so. You will find, however, that there are a few more things that you have to keep in mind—like the size of your output area (windows can shrink or grow) and the size of your text (every display has over 20 sizes and styles to choose from). And you'll want to do all of this in a way that allows your program to run on any display or printer—you'll want to do this in a device-independent manner.

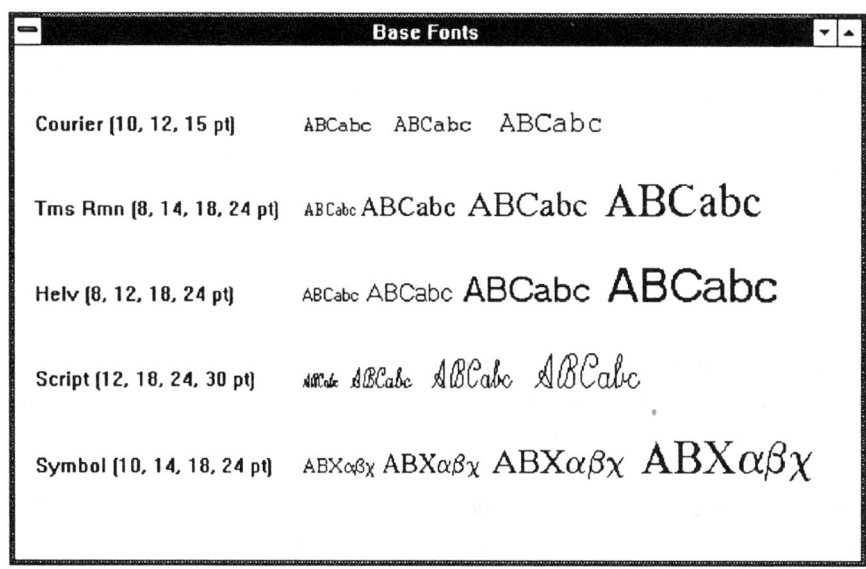

**Figure 10.1** A sampling of VGA base fonts

Although it may seem strange at first to position text in a framework of pixels, this is necessary to allow you to freely mix text with other types of graphic objects. In GDI, text is positioned using the same pixel-oriented grid that we used to draw markers, lines, and rectangles.

We're going to start by reviewing the available text routines. We'll then look at the DC attributes that affect text and give special attention to the most important attribute: the font. We'll conclude this chapter with a discussion of text metrics, which is important to create device-independent text output.

## Text Drawing Primitives

There are five routines for outputting text: **DrawText**, **ExtTextOut**, **GrayString**, **TabbedTextOut**, and **TextOut**. Strictly speaking, three of these are not part of GDI, but instead are part of the Window Manager. These routines are **DrawText**, **GrayString**, and **TabbedTextOut**. Even though these routines are not GDI routines, they provide some useful enhancements to GDI and so are worth considering in our discussion.

Let's begin by looking at **TextOut**, probably the most widely used GDI text routine.

## TextOut

**TextOut** is GDI's simplest text routine: It draws a single line of text. We used this routine to write labels in some of our earlier programs, but now it's time to give it a closer look. **TextOut** is defined as

```
TextOut (hDC, x, y, lpString, nCount)
```

- **hDC** is a DC handle. It tells GDI the device to draw on and the drawing attributes to use.
- **x** and **y** are integers that specify a **control point** used to position the text. The control point is a location in the coordinate system as defined in the DC. Since we're limiting ourselves to the MM_TEXT coordinate system, our units are pixels.
- **lpString** is a far pointer to a character string. This does not have to be a null-terminated string, since **TextOut** gets the string size from the nCount parameter.
- **nCount** is the number of characters in the text string.

By default, GDI positions a line of text with the upper-left corner at the control point. Figure 10.2 demonstrates this with a marker. Later in this chapter, when we talk about DC attributes, we'll describe other text alignment choices.

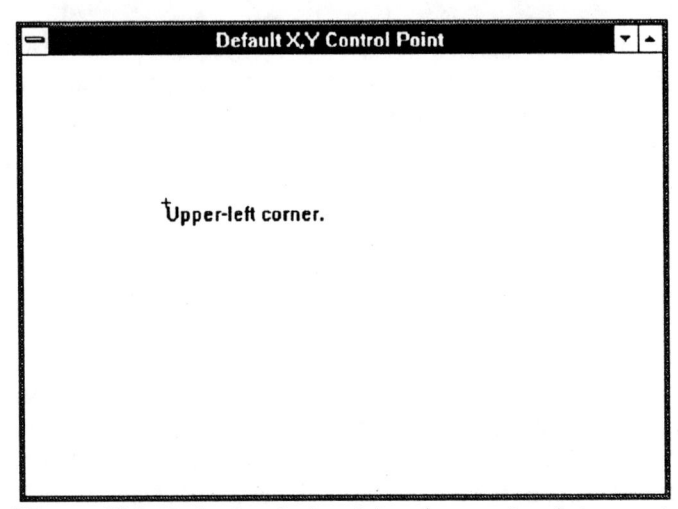

**Figure 10.2** Default relationship of control point to text

It is often convenient to call **TextOut** like this:

```
static char ac[] = "Display This Text.";
BeginPaint (hwnd, &ps);
TextOut (ps.hdc, X, Y, ac, lstrlen(ac));
EndPaint (hwnd, &ps);
```

This code calculates string length "on the fly" using `lstrlen`, a Windows routine that mimics the standard **strlen** function.

Some programmers prefer to split length calculation from drawing, as in

```
static char ac[] = "Display This Text.";
static int  cb = sizeof(ac) - 1;
BeginPaint (hwnd, &ps);
TextOut (ps.hdc, X, Y, ac, cb);
EndPaint (hwnd, &ps);
```

so that text length is calculated at compile time and not at runtime. The result is faster drawing. In many cases, the time saved is hardly noticed. But when performance is critical, every little bit helps.

The next text routine is similar to **TextOut**, but provides some extra features.

## ExtTextOut

Like **TextOut**, **ExtTextOut** draws a single line of text, but adds three options: character width control, clipping, and an opaque rectangle. You can mix and match these options as your needs require. Figure 10.3 shows text drawn with each of these options.

**ExtTextOut** is defined as follows:

```
ExtTextOut (hDC, X, Y, wOptions, lpRect, lpString,
            nCount, lpDx);
```

- **hDC** is a DC handle. It tells GDI the device to draw on and the drawing attributes to use.
- **x** and **y** are integers that specify a **control point** used to position the text. The control point is a location in the coordinate system as defined in the DC. Since we're limiting ourselves to the MM_TEXT coordinate system, our units are pixels.
- **wOptions** is a flag for two of the three extras that this routine provides. It can be 0, **ETO_CLIPPED**, **ETO_OPAQUE**, or a combination: **ETO_CLIPPED | ETO_OPAQUE**. We'll explain these options in a moment.
- **lpRect** is a pointer to a rectangle. Depending on the value of **wOptions**, **lpRect** may point to a clip rectangle, an opaque rectangle, or both.

- **lpString** is a far pointer to a character string. This does not have to be a null-terminated string, since **TextOut** gets the string size from the nCount parameter.
- **nCount** is the number of characters in the text string.
- **lpDx** points to an array of character width values.

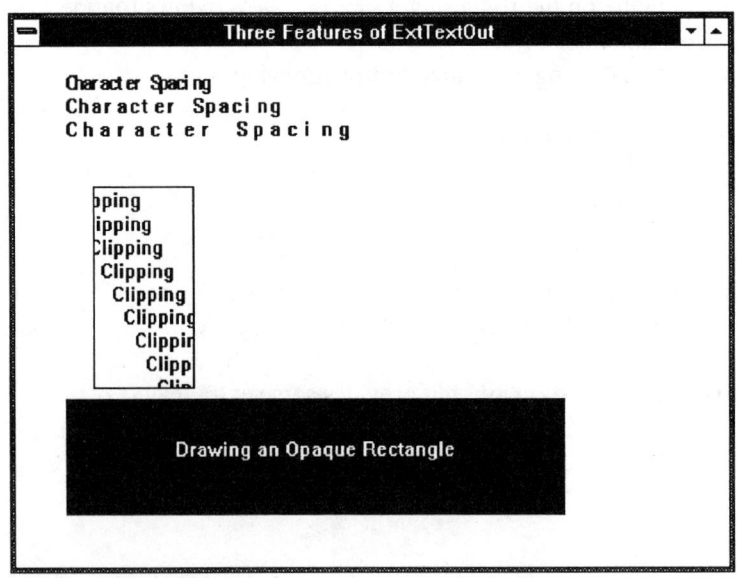

**Figure 10.3** *ExtTextOut*

The first option that we're going to discuss is character spacing, which gives you total control over the amount of space between characters. Unlike **TextOut**, which uses the default spacing defined in a font, **ExtTextOut** lets you specify your own width values for each character. You specify width values by passing an array of integers. The last parameter, **lpDx**, points to this array.

Here is source code to our sample program, EXTTEXT:

## MAKEFILE.MAK

```
.AUTODEPEND

#    Translator Definitions
INC=\BORLANDC\OWL\INCLUDE;\BORLANDC\CLASSLIB\INCLUDE;\BORLANDC\INCLUDE
CC = bcc -c -D_CLASSDLL -H -ml -WS -w-par -I$(INC)

#    Implicit Rules
.c.obj:
  $(CC) {$< }
```

```
        .cpp.obj:
          $(CC) {$< }

     #    Explicit Rules
     ExtText.exe: ExtText.res ExtText.def ExtText.obj
          tlink /c/C/n/P-/Twe/x @ExtText.LNK
          rlink ExtText.res ExtText.exe

     #    Individual File Dependencies
     ExtText.obj: ExtText.cpp

     ExtText.res: ExtText.rc ExtText.cur ExtText.ico
          brcc -FO ExtText.res -i$(INC) ExtText.RC
```

# EXTTEXT.LNK

```
    \borlandc\lib\cOwl.obj+
    ExtText.obj
    ExtText,ExtText
    \borlandc\classlib\lib\tclasdll.lib+
    \borlandc\owl\lib\owl.lib+
    mathwl.lib+
    import.lib+
    crtldll.lib
    ExtText.def
```

# EXTTEXT.CPP

```
    /*-----------------------------------------------------------*\
    |  EXTTEXT.CPP  Program to show capabilities of ExtTextOut.   |
    \*-----------------------------------------------------------*/
    #define WIN31
    #define STRICT
    #include <owl.h>
    #include <WindowsX.h>

    /*-----------------------------------------------------------*\
    |                    Class Declarations.                      |
    \*-----------------------------------------------------------*/
    class TExtTextApplication : public TApplication
       {
       public:
         TExtTextApplication (LPSTR lpszName, HINSTANCE hInstance,
                       HINSTANCE hPrevInstance, LPSTR lpszCmdLine,
                       int nCmdShow);
         virtual void InitMainWindow ();
       };

    class TExtTextWindow : public TWindow
       {
       public:
         TExtTextWindow (PTWindowsObject pwParent, LPSTR lpszTitle,
                   PTModule pmModule);
         virtual LPSTR GetClassName ();
         virtual void  GetWindowClass (WNDCLASS&);
```

## 204  Introduction to the Graphics Device Interface

```
        virtual void  Paint(HDC hdc, PAINTSTRUCT& ps);
    };
/*--------------------------------------------------------------*\
|                     Function Prototypes.                       |
\*--------------------------------------------------------------*/
void NEAR PASCAL ExtTextClipping(HDC hdc);
void NEAR PASCAL ExtTextOpaqueRect(HDC hdc, HWND hwnd);
void NEAR PASCAL ExtTextSpacing(HDC hdc);

/*--------------------------------------------------------------*\
|                   Main Function:  WinMain.                     |
\*--------------------------------------------------------------*/
int PASCAL WinMain (HINSTANCE hInstance,   HINSTANCE hPrevInstance,
                    LPSTR   lpszCmdLine, int    nCmdShow)
    {
    TExtTextApplication ExtText ("ExtText", hInstance,
                                 hPrevInstance, lpszCmdLine,
                                 nCmdShow);
    ExtText.Run();
    return ExtText.Status;
    }

/*--------------------------------------------------------------*\
|                    Application Class Member.                   |
\*--------------------------------------------------------------*/
TExtTextApplication::TExtTextApplication (LPSTR lpszName,
                   HINSTANCE hInstance, HINSTANCE hPrevInstance,
                   LPSTR lpszCmdLine, int nCmdShow)
                  :TApplication (lpszName, hInstance,
                      hPrevInstance, lpszCmdLine, nCmdShow)
    {
    /* Application specific initialization goes here. */
    }

/*--------------------------------------------------------------*\
|                    Application Class Member.                   |
\*--------------------------------------------------------------*/
void TExtTextApplication::InitMainWindow ()
    {
    MainWindow = new TExtTextWindow (NULL,
                             "Three Features of ExtTextOut",
                             NULL);
    }

/*--------------------------------------------------------------*\
|                    TExtTextWindow Class Member.                |
\*--------------------------------------------------------------*/
TExtTextWindow::TExtTextWindow (PTWindowsObject pwParent,
               LPSTR lpszTitle, PTModule pmModule)
              :TWindow (pwParent, lpszTitle, pmModule)
    {
    /* Window specific initialization goes here. */
    }

/*--------------------------------------------------------------*\
|                    TExtTextWindow Class Member.                |
\*--------------------------------------------------------------*/
LPSTR TExtTextWindow::GetClassName ()
    {
    return "ExtText:MAIN";
    }
```

```
/*----------------------------------------------------------------*\
|                   TExtTextWindow Class Member.                   |
\*----------------------------------------------------------------*/
void TExtTextWindow::GetWindowClass (WNDCLASS& wc)
    {
    TWindow::GetWindowClass (wc);
    wc.hIcon=LoadIcon (wc.hInstance, "snapshot");
    wc.hCursor=LoadCursor (wc.hInstance, "hand");
    }

/*----------------------------------------------------------------*\
|                   TExtTextWindow Class Member.                   |
\*----------------------------------------------------------------*/
void TExtTextWindow::Paint(HDC hdc, PAINTSTRUCT& ps)
    {
    ExtTextSpacing(hdc);
    ExtTextClipping(hdc);
    ExtTextOpaqueRect(hdc, HWindow);
    }

/*----------------------------------------------------------------*\
|    ExtTextClipping: Demonstrate ExtTextOut Clipping.             |
\*----------------------------------------------------------------*/
void NEAR PASCAL ExtTextClipping(HDC hdc)
    {
    static char ach[] = "Clipping";
    static int  cch   = sizeof (ach) - 1;
    int x;
    int y;
    int yHeight;
    RECT r;
    TEXTMETRIC tm;

    GetTextMetrics (hdc, &tm);
    yHeight = tm.tmHeight + tm.tmExternalLeading;
    x = tm.tmAveCharWidth * 5;
    y = yHeight * 6;

    r.top = y;
    r.left   = x + 20;
    r.right  = x + 90;
    r.bottom = y + tm.tmHeight * 8 + tm.tmHeight/2;
    Rectangle (hdc, r.left-1, r.top-1,
               r.right+1, r.bottom+1);
    while (y< r.bottom)
        {
        ExtTextOut (hdc, x, y, ETO_CLIPPED, &r, ach, cch, NULL);
        y += yHeight;
        x += 8;
        }
    }

/*----------------------------------------------------------------*\
|   ExtTextOpaqueRect: Demonstrate ExtTextOut opaque               |
|                      rectangle.                                  |
\*----------------------------------------------------------------*/
void NEAR PASCAL ExtTextOpaqueRect(HDC hdc, HWND hwnd)
    {
    static char ach[] = "Drawing an Opaque Rectangle";
    static int  cch   = sizeof (ach) - 1;
    int x;
    int y;
```

## 206  Introduction to the Graphics Device Interface

```
    int yHeight;
    RECT r;
    TEXTMETRIC tm;

    GetTextMetrics (hdc, &tm);
    yHeight = tm.tmHeight + tm.tmExternalLeading;
    x = tm.tmAveCharWidth * 5;
    y = yHeight * 15;

    GetClientRect (hwnd, &r);
    r.top = y;
    r.bottom = r.top + (5 * tm.tmHeight);
    r.left = x;
    r.right = x + tm.tmAveCharWidth * 50;
    SetBkColor (hdc, RGB (0, 0, 0));
    SetTextColor (hdc, RGB (255, 255, 255));
    SetTextAlign (hdc, TA_CENTER | TA_BASELINE);
    x = (r.left + r.right) / 2;
    y = (r.top  + r.bottom) / 2;
    ExtTextOut (hdc, x, y, ETO_OPAQUE, &r, ach, cch, NULL);
    }

/*----------------------------------------------------------------*\
| ExtTextSpacing: Demonstrate ExtTextOut character                 |
|                 spacing.                                         |
\*----------------------------------------------------------------*/
void NEAR PASCAL ExtTextSpacing(HDC hdc)
    {
    static char ac1[] = "Character Spacing";
    static int  cb1   = sizeof (ac1) - 1;
    static int  ai1[] = {6, 6, 6, 6, 6, 6, 6, 6,
                         6, 6, 6, 6, 6, 6, 6};
    static int  ai2[] = {9, 9, 9, 9, 9, 9, 9, 9,
                         9, 9, 9, 9, 9, 9, 9};
    static int  ai3[] = {12, 12, 12, 12, 12, 12, 12, 12,
                         12, 12, 12, 12, 12, 12, 12};
    int x;
    int y;
    int yHeight;
    TEXTMETRIC tm;

    GetTextMetrics (hdc, &tm);
    yHeight = tm.tmHeight + tm.tmExternalLeading;
    x = tm.tmAveCharWidth * 5;
    y = yHeight;

    ExtTextOut (hdc, x, y, 0, NULL, ac1, cb1, ai1);
    y += yHeight;
    ExtTextOut (hdc, x, y, 0, NULL, ac1, cb1, ai2);
    y += yHeight;
    ExtTextOut (hdc, x, y, 0, NULL, ac1, cb1, ai3);
    y += yHeight;
    }
```

# EXTTEXT.RC

```
snapshot icon ExtText.ico

hand cursor ExtText.cur
```

## EXTTEXT.DEF

```
NAME EXTTEXT

EXETYPE WINDOWS

DESCRIPTION 'ExtText - ExtTextOut Demo'

CODE MOVEABLE DISCARDABLE
DATA MOVEABLE MULTIPLE

HEAPSIZE  512
STACKSIZE 5120
```

Each of the subroutines—**ExtTxtSpacing**, **ExtTxtClipping**, and **ExtTxtOpaqueRect**—demonstrates a different feature of **ExtTextOut**.

In our example (Figure 10.3), we display "Character Spacing" using arrays with three different widths: 6, 9, and 12 pixels. Notice that the third line is twice as wide as the first line. This option is used to justify text. Text justification lets us expand lines of text to the left and right margins. For example, the text on this page is justified text. Depending on how we fill the character width array, we could fit a line of text into just about any margin. Here is the code for the text in our example:

```
/*------------------------------------------------------------*\
| ExtTextSpacing: Demonstrate ExtTextOut character             |
|                 spacing.                                     |
\*------------------------------------------------------------*/
void NEAR PASCAL ExtTextSpacing(HDC hdc)
    {
    static char ac1[] = "Character Spacing";
    static int  cb1   = sizeof (ac1) - 1;
    static int  ai1[] = {6, 6, 6, 6, 6, 6, 6, 6,
                         6, 6, 6, 6, 6, 6, 6, 6};
    static int  ai2[] = {9, 9, 9, 9, 9, 9, 9, 9,
                         9, 9, 9, 9, 9, 9, 9, 9};
    static int  ai3[] = {12, 12, 12, 12, 12, 12, 12, 12,
                         12, 12, 12, 12, 12, 12, 12, 12};
    int x;
    int y;
    int yHeight;
    TEXTMETRIC tm;

    GetTextMetrics (hdc, &tm);
    yHeight = tm.tmHeight + tm.tmExternalLeading;
    x = tm.tmAveCharWidth * 5;
    y = yHeight;

    ExtTextOut (hdc, x, y, 0, NULL, ac1, cb1, ai1);
    y += yHeight;
    ExtTextOut (hdc, x, y, 0, NULL, ac1, cb1, ai2);
    y += yHeight;
    ExtTextOut (hdc, x, y, 0, NULL, ac1, cb1, ai3);
    y += yHeight;
    }
```

Our character array has 17 characters, which means there are 16 spaces between letters. For this reason, our character width array has 16 values. Each value defines the width of one character cell. While it requires some extra work to maintain a character width array, it also means that you have a tremendous amount of control over the placement of each letter in a line of text.

Notice the call to **GetTextMetrics**. This provides measurement information for the current font. We use the values returned by this routine to position our first line of text one line from the top of the window, and five spaces from the left side of the window. We'll explore this routine more fully later in this chapter.

The second option available with **ExtTextOut** lets you specify a clip rectangle for text. When we introduced the DC, we said that every DC comes equipped with a clipping region. With the **ETO_CLIPPED** option, **ExtTextOut** lets you specify an additional clipping rectangle. This option provides a way to create a window of text without incurring the overhead of creating an actual window. Here is the code for the clipped text in our example:

```
/*-------------------------------------------------------------*\
|       ExtTextClipping: Demonstrate ExtTextOut Clipping.       |
\*-------------------------------------------------------------*/
void NEAR PASCAL ExtTextClipping(HDC hdc)
    {
    static char ach[] = "Clipping";
    static int  cch   = sizeof (ach) - 1;
    int x;
    int y;
    int yHeight;
    RECT r;
    TEXTMETRIC tm;

    GetTextMetrics (hdc, &tm);
    yHeight = tm.tmHeight + tm.tmExternalLeading;
    x = tm.tmAveCharWidth * 5;
    y = yHeight * 6;

    r.top = y;
    r.left  = x + 20;
    r.right = x + 90;
    r.bottom = y + tm.tmHeight * 8 + tm.tmHeight/2;
    Rectangle (hdc, r.left-1, r.top-1,
               r.right+1, r.bottom+1);
    while (y< r.bottom)
        {
        ExtTextOut (hdc, x, y, ETO_CLIPPED, &r, ach, cch, NULL);
        y += yHeight;
        x += 8;
        }
    }
```

Once again, we rely on the **GetTextMetrics** routine to help us decide where to draw lines of text. In this case, we start six lines from the top of the window and five spaces from the left side of the window.

We have arbitrarily made our clip rectangle 70 pixels wide and eight and one half lines high. The coordinates used in a clip rectangle are **grid-intersection coordinates**, which we first encountered in the context of drawing filled areas in Chapter 9. To make the clip rectangle more readily apparent, we draw a rectangle just outside its border.

**ExtTextOut**'s third option creates an opaque rectangle; it is like having a free call to the **Rectangle** routine. This option lets you erase a background area when drawing a line of text. As indicated in our sample code, the background color is selected by making a call to **SetBkColor**, which sets a DC attribute value that is used by all text drawing routines. We'll explore this and other DC attributes later in this chapter.

Here is the code that created the opaque rectangle:

```
/*-------------------------------------------------------------*\
|    ExtTextOpaqueRect: Demonstrate ExtTextOut opaque           |
|                      rectangle.                               |
\*-------------------------------------------------------------*/
void NEAR PASCAL ExtTextOpaqueRect(HDC hdc, HWND hwnd)
    {
    static char ach[] = "Drawing an Opaque Rectangle";
    static int  cch   = sizeof (ach) - 1;
    int x;
    int y;
    int yHeight;
    RECT r;
    TEXTMETRIC tm;

    GetTextMetrics (hdc, &tm);
    yHeight = tm.tmHeight + tm.tmExternalLeading;
    x = tm.tmAveCharWidth * 5;
    y = yHeight * 15;

    GetClientRect (hwnd, &r);
    r.top = y;
    r.bottom = r.top + (5 * tm.tmHeight);
    r.left = x;
    r.right = x + tm.tmAveCharWidth * 50;
    SetBkColor (hdc, RGB (0, 0, 0));
    SetTextColor (hdc, RGB (255, 255, 255));
    SetTextAlign (hdc, TA_CENTER | TA_BASELINE);
    x = (r.left + r.right) / 2;
    y = (r.top  + r.bottom) / 2;
    ExtTextOut (hdc, x, y, ETO_OPAQUE, &r, ach, cch, NULL);
    }
```

Once again, we rely on the **GetTextMetrics** routine to help us place the text and its black opaque background. In this case, the top of the rectangle is situated 15 lines from the top of the window and 5 spaces from the left side.

We set the size of our rectangle to be 5 character cells high and 50 character cells wide. To make the opaque rectangle visible, we changed two DC attributes: the text color (set to white) and the background color (set to black). We used a third DC attribute, text alignment, to center the text inside the rectangle.

## *TabbedTextOut*

Our third text drawing primitive draws a single line of text, but expands tabs to tab stops. This provides a convenient way to align columns of data. Microsoft included this routine in the Windows library for listboxes to make it easy to create lists of column-oriented data. But it's a simple matter to use this routine in your programs to achieve the same benefit.

Figure 10.4 shows an example of text drawn with this routine. Given an array of strings like those at the bottom of the page,

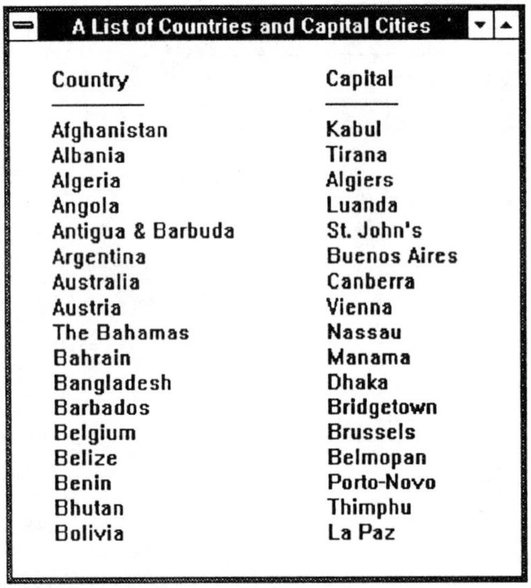

**A List of Countries and Capital Cities**

| Country | Capital |
| --- | --- |
| Afghanistan | Kabul |
| Albania | Tirana |
| Algeria | Algiers |
| Angola | Luanda |
| Antigua & Barbuda | St. John's |
| Argentina | Buenos Aires |
| Australia | Canberra |
| Austria | Vienna |
| The Bahamas | Nassau |
| Bahrain | Manama |
| Bangladesh | Dhaka |
| Barbados | Bridgetown |
| Belgium | Brussels |
| Belize | Belmopan |
| Benin | Porto-Novo |
| Bhutan | Thimphu |
| Bolivia | La Paz |

**Figure 10.4  TabbedTextOut**

```
#define COUNT 19
    static char *apch[]= {"Country \tCapital",
                          "--------------- \t------------",
                          "Afghanistan \tKabul",
                          "Albania \tTirana",
                          "Algeria \tAlgiers",
                          "Angola \tLuanda",
                          "Antigua & Barbuda \tSt. John's",
                          "Argentina \tBuenos Aires",
                          "Australia \tCanberra",
                          "Austria \tVienna",
                          "The Bahamas \tNassau",
                          "Bahrain \tManama",
                          "Bangladesh \tDhaka",
                          "Barbados \tBridgetown",
                          "Belgium \tBrussels",
                          "Belize \tBelmopan",
                          "Benin \tPorto-Novo",
                          "Bhutan \tThimphu",
                          "Bolivia \tLa Paz"};
```

here is code that a window object's `Paint` function would use to create the output shown:

```
void TSampleWindow::Paint (HDC hdc, PAINTSTRUCT& ps)
    {
    DWORD dwSize;
    int i;
    int xTab;
    int xText;
    int yText;
    int yHeight;

    dwSize = GetTextExtent (hdc, "X", 1);
    yHeight = yText = HIWORD(dwSize);
    xText = 3 * LOWORD (dwSize);
    xTab  = 20 * LOWORD (dwSize);

    for (i=0;i<COUNT;i++, yText += yHeight)
        {
        TabbedTextOut (hdc, xText, yText,
                       apch[i], lstrlen(apch[i]),
                       1, &xTab, xText);
        }
    }
```

This code calls `GetTextExtent` to determine the width and height of the letter "X" in the current (system) font. In previous examples, we've used the `GetTextMetrics` routine to determine this information, but for the sake of variety we have chosen this alternative method. Notice the use of the `HIWORD` and `LOWORD` macros, which filter out the desired part of this routine's return value.

We use the results to calculate three values: the *x* and *y* starting position of the text (one line from the top and three characters from the left) and the location of the tab-stop. In this case, we have placed the tab-stop at approximately 20 spaces from the *x* and *y* starting point. If there had been more than a single tab-stop, we would have had to allocate an array to hold them. As it is, we get by with allocating a single integer value and then passing this value to our routine.

## *DrawText*

Like `TabbedTextOut`, `DrawText` provides some formatting capability. In our opinion, the most useful option is the ability to perform word wrapping for multiple lines of text (although this is just one of several things that `DrawText` will do for you).

Figure 10.5 shows three instances of a sample program that uses `DrawText` to display a long line of text in an area of different sizes and shapes. Given an array of characters defined like this:

```
static char *apchDesc = "The DT_WORDBREAK flag makes "
                       "DrawText split a long string "
                       "into several lines of text. "
                       "As you can tell, the split is "
                       "only performed at normal word "
                       "breaks.";
```

window object's `Paint` member function would look like this:

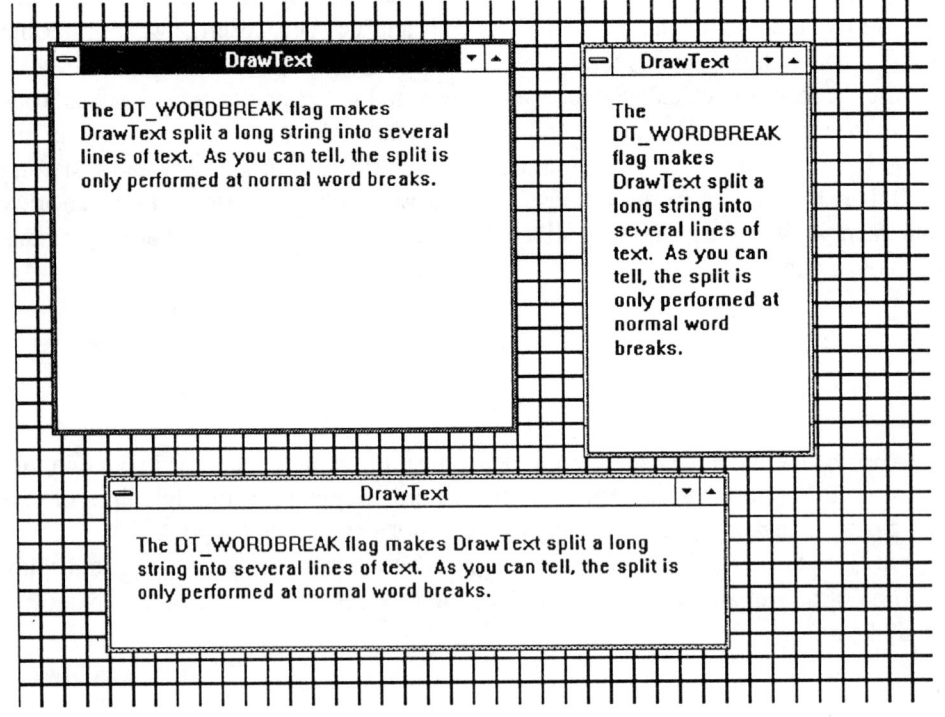

```
void TSampleWindow::Paint (HDC hdc, PAINTSTRUCT& ps)
  {
  DWORD dwSize;
  RECT r;

  dwSize = GetTextExtent(hdc, "X", 1);

  GetClientRect (hwnd, &r);
  r.top    += HIWORD (dwSize);
  r.bottom -= HIWORD (dwSize);
  r.left   += LOWORD (dwSize) * 2;
  r.right  -= LOWORD (dwSize) * 2;

  DrawText (hdc, apchDesc, lstrlen (apchDesc),
            &r, DT_WORDBREAK);
  }
```

**Figure 10.5 DrawText**

Once more, we use `GetTextExtent` to determine the width and height of the letter "X." We use these values to offset the dimensions of our client area so that there is a margin around our text.

The `GetClientRect` routine gets the dimensions of the client area into a RECT variable. We then modify the values in this structure to create margins on all four sides of the text. The resulting rectangle is passed to **DrawText**, which uses the values to determine where to position the text.

## *GrayString*

The text produced by this routine is best described as checkered. But the name of the routine describes the primary reason that Microsoft created this routine: to create text with a gray appearance.

The Window Manager uses this routine for disabled menu items and disabled dialog box controls. If you write your own custom dialog box controls (discussed in Chapter 14) or create owner-drawn menu items (discussed in Chapter 12), then this routine may be quite useful to you. Figure 10.6 shows an example of a gray string.

**Figure 10.6** GrayString

Given the following data definitions:

```
static char acString[] = "This is a Gray String";
static int   cb = sizeof (acString) - 1;
```

this is what a window object's **Paint** member function would do to create output like that shown:

```
void TSampleWindow::Paint (HDC hdc, PAINTSTRUCT& ps)
    {
    DWORD dwSize;
    int xText, yText;
    TEXTMETRIC tm;

    GetTextMetrics (hdc, &tm);
    xText = tm.tmAveCharWidth * 3;
    yText = tm.tmHeight * 2;

    GrayString (hdc, GetStockObject (BLACK_BRUSH),
```

```
                    NULL, (DWORD)(LPSTR)acString, cb,
                    xText, yText, 0, 0);
    }
```

As in earlier examples, we depend on the results of **GetTextMetrics** to give us some size information to help us position lines of text. Here, we place the gray string two lines from the top of the window and three character widths from the left margin.

This is the only text drawing routine that uses a brush. The color of the brush determines the foreground color of the checkered text: In this case we use a black brush, which gives the text a grayed appearance. If we had chosen a red brush, it would give the appearance of red and white checkered text.

This concludes our tour of the different GDI text drawing routines. As you can see, there are quite a few different effects that you can achieve by making a single call to one of these routines. But the library routines are only half of the story. To get the complete picture of the amount of control that GDI allows you over text drawing, we need to address the issue of DC attributes that affect text appearance.

## DC Attributes for Text Drawing

Six attributes affect the appearance and positioning of text:

| *Attribute* | *Description* |
| --- | --- |
| Background color | Color of "empty space" in text |
| Background mode | Turns on/off background color |
| Font | Text style and size |
| Intercharacter spacing | Extra pixels between characters for text justification |
| Text alignment | Relationship of text to control point |
| Text color | Color of letters themselves |

The most important of these attributes is the font, which determines the shape and size of the individual characters. Before we delve into the way GDI handles fonts, let's explore some of the other text attributes, starting with those that control color.

## *Color*

Three different DC attributes deal with the color of text: text color, background color, and background mode. Text can only be drawn with *pure* colors, and not dithered colors like those available for filled areas. Like pixel, pen, and brush colors, you can use any of three methods to define colors: an RGB triplet, a palette index, or an RGB palette-relative value.

The text color attribute determines the actual color of the letters. If GDI had been used to create the letters on this page, it would have been with text color set to black. To set the text color, you must call the **SetTextColor** routine. Its parameters are

```
SetTextColor (hDC, crColor);
```

- **hDC** is a DC handle. It tells GDI the device to draw on and the drawing attributes to use.
- **crColor** is the desired text color.

The **crColor** parameter is a color reference value, using one of the three methods. Here is how to set text color to blue, using an RGB triplet:

```
SetTextColor (hDC, RGB (0, 0, 0xFF));
```

The background color attribute determines the color of the areas inside character cells not touched by the text color. From GDI's point of view, the text on this page has a white background, since that's the color of the space between letters and the area inside hollow letters like "O" and "Q."

As you may have noticed, the background color attribute is also used for hatched brushes and styled lines to set, respectively, the color *between* the hatches and the blank area *inside* the pattern of a style line.

To set the background color, call **SetBkColor**, which takes the same two parameters as **SetTextColor**:

```
SetBkColor (hDC, crColor);
```

- **hDC** is a DC handle. It tells GDI the device to draw on and the drawing attributes to use.
- **crColor** is the desired background color.

For example, here is how to request a green background:

```
SetBkColor (hDC, RGB (0, 0xFF, 0));
```

Our third color attribute, background mode, is a toggle switch for the background color. The routine that controls this attribute, **SetBkMode**, takes two parameters:

SetBkMode (hDC, nBkMode);

- **hDC** is a DC handle. It tells GDI the device to draw on and the drawing attributes to use.
- **nBkMode** is the desired background mode, either **OPAQUE** or **TRANSPARENT**.

When **nBkMode** is **OPAQUE**, the background color is turned *on*. When set to **TRANSPARENT**, the background color is turned *off*.

Figure 10.7 shows three lines of text, using different foreground and background colors. Notice that the second line of text is unreadable, because we set both foreground and background colors to black. Given the following data definitions:

```
char acFirst[]  = "Black on White (default)";
char acSecond[] = "Black on Black (invisible)";
char acThird[]  = "White on Black (inverted)";
```

here is **Paint** code that creates the output in the figure:

```
void TSampleWindow::Paint (HDC hdc, PAINTSTRUCT& ps)
    {
    int X;
    int Y;
    TEXTMETRIC tm;

    GetTextMetrics (hdc, &tm);
    X = tm.tmAveCharWidth * 3;
    Y = tm.tmHeight * 2;

    TextOut (hdc, X, Y, acFirst, lstrlen (acFirst));
    Y += tm.tmHeight * 2;

    SetBkColor (hdc, RGB (0, 0, 0));
    TextOut (hdc, X, Y, acSecond,
             lstrlen (acSecond));
    Y += tm.tmHeight * 2;

    SetTextColor (hdc, RGB (255, 255, 255));
    TextOut (hdc, X, Y, acThird, lstrlen (acThird));
    }
```

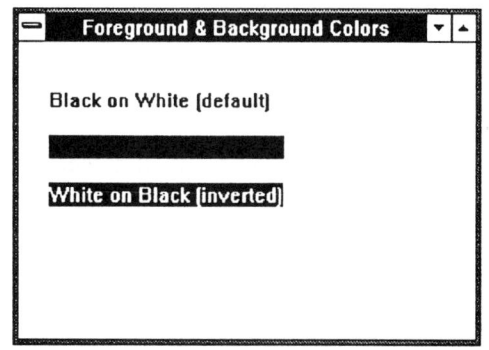

**Figure 10.7** Three different foreground/background colors

Although our example is in black and white, it is a simple matter to create red or green text on devices that support color: Supply the appropriate color reference, and GDI does the rest.

## Text Alignment

The text alignment attribute lets you change the relationship between the control point, which is the (x,y) pair that is passed to each routine, and the text to be displayed. Figure 10.8 shows the nine possible ways to align text, with a marker at each control point to emphasize the alignment.

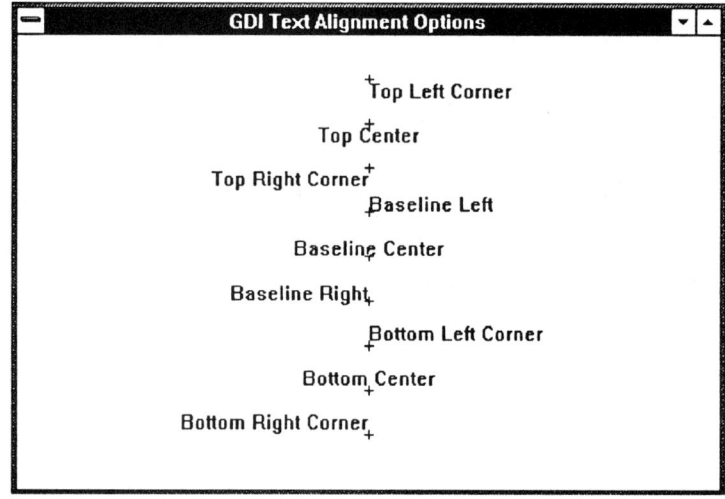

**Figure 10.8** Nine different text alignments

## 218  *Introduction to the Graphics Device Interface*

To set text alignment, you call the `SetTextAlign` routine, which has the following syntax:

```
SetTextAlign (hDC, wFlags);
```

As indicated in the example, there are nine possible alignments. Select an alignment by combining two flags from the following table, with one flag taken from each of the two categories:

| *Horizontal Flag* | *Vertical Flag* |
|---|---|
| TA_LEFT | TA_TOP |
| TA_CENTER | TA_BASELINE |
| TA_RIGHT | TA_BOTTOM |

The default alignment is **TA_LEFT | TA_TOP**. To set alignment to the bottom right, you say

```
SetTextAlign (hDC, TA_BOTTOM | TA_RIGHT);
```

Our illustration was created with the following code fragments. Given the following data definitions:

```
#define LINECOUNT 9
    static char * apchDesc[LINECOUNT] =
            { "Top Left Corner",
              "Top Center",
              "Top Right Corner",
              "Baseline Left",
              "Baseline Center",
              "Baseline Right",
              "Bottom Left Corner",
              "Bottom Center",
              "Bottom Right Corner"};
    static int   fAlign [LINECOUNT] =
            {
            TA_LEFT   | TA_TOP ,
            TA_CENTER | TA_TOP ,
            TA_RIGHT  | TA_TOP ,
            TA_LEFT   | TA_BASELINE ,
            TA_CENTER | TA_BASELINE,
            TA_RIGHT  | TA_BASELINE ,
            TA_LEFT   | TA_BOTTOM ,
            TA_CENTER | TA_BOTTOM ,
            TA_RIGHT  | TA_BOTTOM };
```

the drawing was done as follows:

```
void TSampleWindow::Paint (HDC hdc, PAINTSTRUCT& ps)
    {
    int i;
    int xText;
    int yText;
    int yLineHeight;
    RECT r;

    GetClientRect (hwnd, &r);
    xText = r.right/2;
    yLineHeight = r.bottom/ (LINECOUNT+1);
    yText = yLineHeight;

    for (i = 0; i < LINECOUNT; i++)
        {
        SetTextAlign (hdc, fAlign[i]);

        TextOut (hdc, xText, yText, apchDesc[i],
                 lstrlen(apchDesc[i]));
        DrawMarker (hdc, xText, yText);
        yText += yLineHeight;

        }
    }
```

In this code, we have departed from our usual practice of spacing lines. Instead of using the **GetTextMetrics** or **GetTextExtent** routines, we have split the available space in the window into 10 areas, with one line per area. Since GDI treats text as a graphic object, there is nothing to stop you from devising interesting and useful methods like this to take advantage of available screen real estate when you draw text.

## *Intercharacter Spacing*

Intercharacter spacing allows you to insert extra pixels between characters. It provides another option (besides the **ExtTextOut** routine) to expand a line of text to fit an arbitrary margin. Figure 10.9 shows six lines of text, with extra spacing varying from zero to five pixels. It is difficult to detect the difference from one line to the next, but between the top and bottom lines the difference is quite apparent.

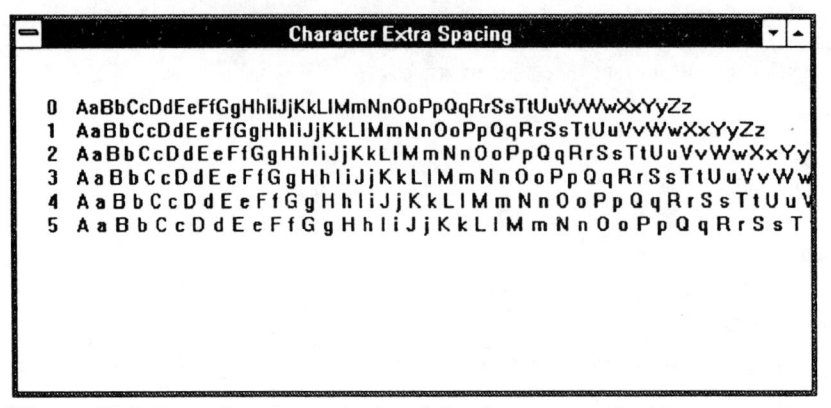

**Figure 10.9** Intercharacter spacing (also known as character extra spacing)

The code which created this drawing is as follows. First of all, we need the following data items:

```
#define COUNT 6
    static char acLine[] = "AaBbCcDdEeFfGgHhIiJjKkLlMm"
                           "NnOoPpQqRrSsTtUuVvWwXxYyZz";
    static char *apch[] = {"0", "1", "2", "3", "4", "5"};
    static int  cbLine = sizeof (acLine) - 1;
```

Next, here is the **Paint** code to draw these lines:

```
void TSampleWindow::Paint (HDC hdc, PAINTSTRUCT& ps)
    {
    int i;
    int xText;
    int xText2;
    int yText;
    TEXTMETRIC tm;

    GetTextMetrics (hdc, &tm);
    xText  = tm.tmAveCharWidth * 3;
    xText2 = tm.tmAveCharWidth * 6;
    yText = tm.tmHeight * 2;
    for (i=0;i<COUNT;i++)
        {
        SetTextCharacterExtra (hdc, i);
        TextOut (hdc, xText, yText,
                 apch[i], lstrlen (apch[i]));
        TextOut (hdc, xText2, yText,
                 acLine, cbLine);
        yText += tm.tmHeight;
        }

    }
```

We have one more DC attribute to describe, which plays the most important role in determining the shape and size of letters that GDI draws: the font.

## *About Fonts*

A font is a collection of patterns used to create text output. Fonts come in all shapes, sizes, and styles. Fonts have a lot in common with other GDI drawing objects, like pens and brushes. For one thing, fonts can be shared between programs. And like these other GDI objects, fonts are referenced using a handle. When a program is ready to use a specific font, it selects the font handle into a DC using the `SelectObject` routine:

```
SelectObject (hDC, hFont);
```

Internally, GDI recognizes two types of fonts: **logical fonts** and **physical fonts**. A logical font describes text in a standard, device-independent manner. As we'll see in a moment, a logical font consists of the set of values in the data structure `LOGFONT`. By itself, a logical font isn't enough information to draw text on a device. Instead, like other logical drawing objects, a logical font is a *request* for text with a specific appearance.

The GDI **font mapper** selects a physical font from the description contained in a logical font. The mapping is done when a logical font handle is selected into a DC. A physical font is a device-*dependent* set of patterns. These patterns are used to create the letters, numbers, and punctuation marks that we normally associate with text. A physical font might live in the device hardware, which is typical for printer fonts. Or, it may be kept in memory by GDI.

Physical fonts are device-dependent, because every font is created with a specific type of device in mind. Two measurements are used to match fonts to devices: resolution (pixels per inch) and aspect ratio (the *squareness* of the pixels). By default, the GDI mapper only selects physical fonts that match the metrics of a given device. Otherwise, the results might be very odd.

For example, a VGA display has approximately 72 pixels per inch. Today's typical laser printer has 300 pixels per inch. If you tried to mix fonts between these two devices, the results would be strange: VGA fonts on a laser printer would create text that is too small to be readable. Going the other way, if you used laser printer fonts to create text on a VGA, the resulting text would be too large.

If a program needs precise control over its text selection, it can ask for a list of available physical fonts that a device can support. This process is called **font enumeration**. When a device driver enumerates fonts, it provides a logical font description for each physical font. When a program wishes to use a specific font, it turns the process around: It gives the logical font description to GDI, which in turn makes the connection to the physical font.

Many programs don't need a lot of control over the appearance of text. Such programs can use the default fonts. Every device has a default font. And not surprisingly, the default font is the default selection in the DC.

On a video display, the default font is also called the **system font**. Windows 1.x and 2.x used a fixed-pitch system font—that is, a font in which every character is the same width. Starting with Windows 3.0, the system font is proportionally spaced: Some characters are wider than others. "W," for example, is given more room than "i." Microsoft made this

222 *Introduction to the Graphics Device Interface*

change because proportionally spaced text is easier to read than fixed-pitch text and gives a better overall appearance.

Windows uses the system font for menus, titlebars, dialog box controls, and, of course, as the default font in any DC that a program gets its hands on. Microsoft has decreed that every Windows display driver must provide a system font that allows a minimum of 25 lines and 80 columns of text to be displayed. This guarantees that Windows programs will be able to display at least as much text as their MS-DOS counterparts.

To maintain compatibility with programs written for earlier versions of Windows (versions 1.x and 2.x), every display driver also maintains a fixed-pitch system font. When GDI detects that a program was written for an older version of Windows, it provides a system font that these programs expect.

Table 10.1 lists the characteristics of the default font on four popular displays and four popular printers.

**Table 10.1** Default fonts

| Device | Size of Drawing Surface | Default Font Height | Width (avg) |
|---|---|---|---|
| CGA display | 640 × 200 | 8 | 7 |
| EGA display | 640 × 350 | 12 | 7 |
| VGA display | 640 × 480 | 16 | 7 |
| 8514/a display | 1024 × 768 | 20 | 9 |
| Apple Imagewriter II printer | 2550 × 3300 | 42 | 25 |
| Epson LQ-1050 (24-pin) printer | 3060 × 1980 | 25 | 36 |
| HP LaserJet II printer | 2550 × 3300 | 50 | 30 |
| Okidata ML 320 (9-pin) printer | 1020 × 792 | 10 | 12 |

As you can see, the size of the default font can vary quite widely from one device to another. To make sure the text created by your program looks good on every device, it's important to ask GDI about the size of a font before you start drawing. GDI provides two routines for this purpose: `GetTextExtent` and `GetTextMetrics`.

## GetTextExtent

The `GetTextExtent` routine calculates the size of a line of text using the font currently selected in a DC. For example, here is how to calculate the width and height of the phrase "Device Independent":

```
DWORD dwSize;
WORD  yHeight, xWidth;

dwSize  = GetTextExtent (hDC, "Device Independent", 18);
yHeight = HIWORD (dwSize);
xWidth  = LOWORD (dwSize);
```

This routine takes three parameters: a DC handle, a long pointer to a string, and the count of characters. The return value is a single `DWORD` (`unsigned long`) value, in which are packed the height and width of the text. The `HIWORD` and `LOWORD` macros separate these two values.

## GetTextMetrics

A more complete set of font measurements is provided by the `GetTextMetrics` routine. Every physical font has a header record that includes font metric information. There are 20 fields, defined by the data structure `TEXTMETRIC`. Here is a call that retrieves the metrics of the font currently selected in a DC:

```
TEXTMETRIC tm;

GetTextMetrics (hDC, &tm);
```

Figure 10.10 shows five of the key fields in this data structure.

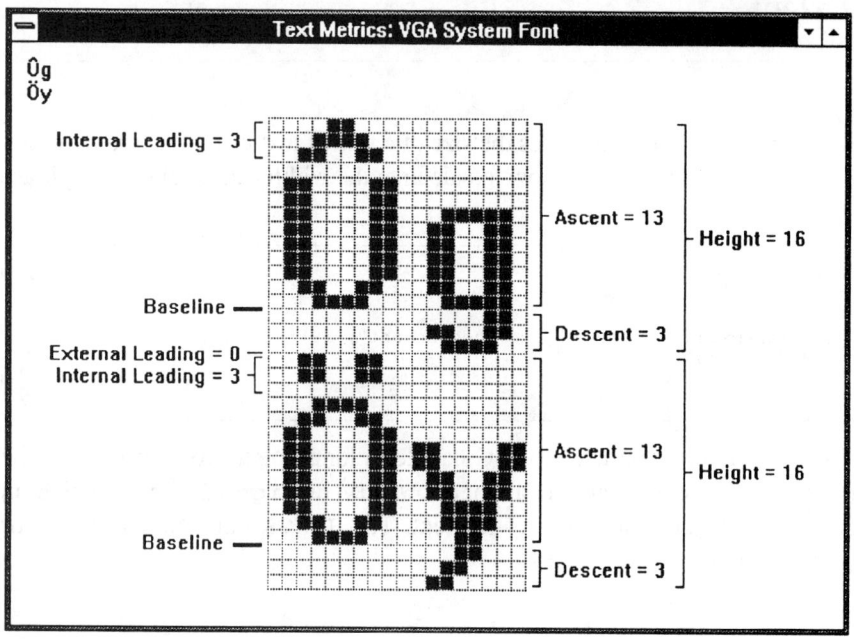

224  *Introduction to the Graphics Device Interface*

**Figure 10.10** Key TextMetric fields visually defined

The **tmHeight** field defines the size of the characters in the font in pixels (since we're using the **MM_TEXT** mapping mode) or in the units of the currently selected mapping mode. Notice that this field has two components: **tmAscent**, which is the height above the baseline, and **tmDescent**, which is the height below the baseline for characters like "g" and "y."

The **tmInternalLeading** field describes the size of the area for diacritic marks, such as accents, umlauts, etc. Notice that, with two lines of text, the top of the diacritic marks can touch the bottom of descenders. This is normal for many fonts.

If, however, a font designer wants to avoid this situation, he does so with the **tmExternalLeading** field. The value in this field is the suggested width to place between lines of text. Notice that in our example, this field is zero. The term "leading" comes from the days when type was cast in lead and set by hand. To separate lines of text, typesetters would add a thin bar of lead between rows of type.

You may have noticed that many of our sample programs combine **tmHeight** and **tmExternalLeading** for the height of a line, as in

```
int yLineHeight;
TEXTMETRIC tm;
GetTextMetrics (hDC, &tm);
yLineHeight = tm.tmHeight + tm.tmExternalLeading;
```

This is a very common method for spacing lines of text.

*Drawing Text* 225

All this theory about fonts is well and good, but now it's time to do something practical. We're going to explore the use of different fonts and the display of multiple lines of text.

## Creating and Using Logical Fonts

As we discussed earlier, a logical font is a request. It provides a way for a program to describe the physical font it wants to use. Two routines create logical fonts: `CreateFont` and `CreateFontIndirect`. The results of both are the same: The difference is in the way parameters are passed. `CreateFont` takes 14 parameters. `CreateFontIndirect` takes a single parameter: a pointer to a structure filled with the same 14 values. We're going to limit our discussion to `CreateFontIndirect`, since it is somewhat easier to use.

`CreateFontIndirect` takes one parameter: a pointer to a `LOGFONT` structure. `LOGFONT` is defined in WINDOWS.H as

```
typedef struct tagLOGFONT
   {
   int    lfHeight;         /* Character Height */
   int    lfWidth;          /* Average width   */
   int    lfEscapement;     /* Text angle */
   int    lfOrientation;    /* Individual character angle */
   int    lfWeight;         /* Average pixels/1000 */
   BYTE   lfItalic;         /* Flag != 0 if italic */
   BYTE   lfUnderline;      /* Flag != 0 if underlined */
   BYTE   lfStrikeOut;      /* Flag != 0 if strikeout */
   BYTE   lfCharSet;        /* Character set: ANSI, OEM */
   BYTE   lfOutPrecision;   /* Mapping precision-unused */
   BYTE   lfClipPrecision;  /* Clip precision - unused */
   BYTE   lfQuality;        /* Draft or proof quality */
   BYTE   lfPitchAndFamily; /* Flags for font style */
   BYTE   lfFaceName[LF_FACESIZE]; /* Typeface name */
   } LOGFONT;
```

There are quite a few fields in this structure, but let's look at the fields used in our sample program: `lfFaceName`, `lfHeight`, `lfWidth`, `lfItalic`, and `lfUnderline`.

`lfFaceName` is a 32-character-wide field for the font name. A program can use font names to tell users about available fonts. In this way, a user can select fonts by name. Here is a list of the face names for the Windows base fonts:

Courier    Helv      Modern    Roman
Script     Symbol    System    Terminal
Tms Rmn

Each font is available in different sizes and styles.

The `lfHeight` field is identical to the `tmHeight` field in the **TEXTMETRIC** data structure. Since we're dealing with the **MM_TEXT** mapping mode, the units are pixels. When another coordinate system is used, GDI converts the values to the mapping mode currently selected in the DC.

The `lfWidth` field is the average width of characters in the font. There is also a field in the **TEXTMETRIC** data structure that contains the identical information, `tmAveCharWidth`.

The `lfItalic` field is a flag: A nonzero value requests an italic font. The `lfUnderline` field is also a flag: A nonzero value requests an underlined font.

Our next program displays text using three different fonts. The first font is the system font, which is already installed in the DC for us. The other two are fonts that we request by defining a logical font: a Times Roman font (Tms Rmn) and a Helvetica font (Helv).

The program displays the first eight **TEXTMETRIC** fields for each of the fonts, as shown in Figure 10.11. The name of each font is also included, for ease of reference.

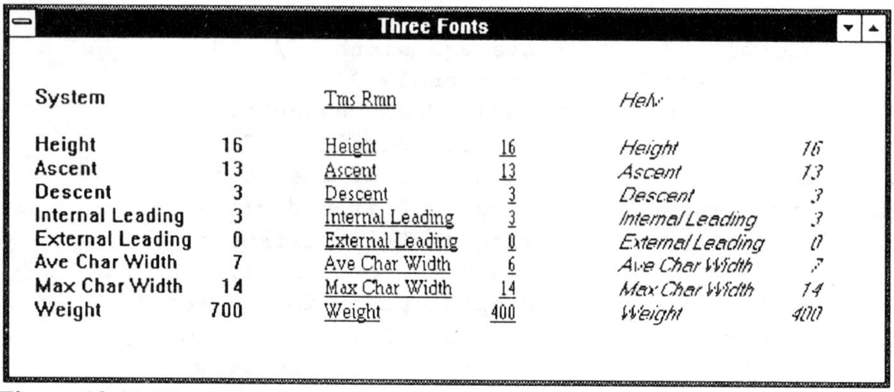

```
Three Fonts

System                          Tms Rmn                         Helv

Height              16          Height              16          Height              16
Ascent              13          Ascent              13          Ascent              13
Descent              3          Descent              3          Descent              3
Internal Leading     3          Internal Leading     3          Internal Leading     3
External Leading     0          External Leading     0          External Leading     0
Ave Char Width       7          Ave Char Width       6          Ave Char Width       7
Max Char Width      14          Max Char Width      14          Max Char Width      14
Weight             700          Weight             400          Weight             400
```

**Figure 10.11** Three fonts

Here is the code to our program:

# MAKEFILE.MAK

```
.AUTODEPEND

#       Translator Definitions
INC=\BORLANDC\OWL\INCLUDE;\BORLANDC\CLASSLIB\INCLUDE;\BORLANDC\INCLUDE
CC = bcc -c -D_CLASSDLL -H -ml -WS -w-par -I$(INC)

#       Implicit Rules
.c.obj:
  $(CC) {$< }

.cpp.obj:
  $(CC) {$< }

#       Explicit Rules
TxtLines.exe: TxtLines.res TxtLines.def TxtLines.obj
     tlink /c/C/n/P-/Twe/x @TxtLines.LNK
     rlink TxtLines.res TxtLines.exe

#       Individual File Dependencies
TxtLines.obj: TxtLines.cpp

TxtLines.res: TxtLines.rc TxtLines.cur TxtLines.ico
     brcc -FO TxtLines.res -i$(INC) TxtLines.RC
```

# TXTLINES.LNK

```
\borlandc\lib\c0wl.obj+
TxtLines.obj
TxtLines,TxtLines
\borlandc\classlib\lib\tclasdll.lib+
\borlandc\owl\lib\owl.lib+
mathwl.lib+
import.lib+
crtldll.lib
TxtLines.def
```

# TXTLINES.CPP

```
/*--------------------------------------------------------------*\
 |  TXTLINES.CPP   Text output sample of three fonts.           |
 \*--------------------------------------------------------------*/
#define WIN31
#define STRICT
#include <owl.h>
#include <WindowsX.h>

/*--------------------------------------------------------------*\
 |                    Class Declarations.                       |
 \*--------------------------------------------------------------*/
```

```
class TTxtLinesApplication : public TApplication
   {
public:
   TTxtLinesApplication (LPSTR lpszName, HINSTANCE hInstance,
                   HINSTANCE hPrevInstance, LPSTR lpszCmdLine,
                   int nCmdShow);
   virtual void InitMainWindow ();
  };

class TTxtLinesWindow : public TWindow
   {
   public:
     TTxtLinesWindow (PTWindowsObject pwParent, LPSTR lpszTitle,
              PTModule pmModule);
     ~TTxtLinesWindow ();
     virtual LPSTR GetClassName ();
     virtual void  GetWindowClass (WNDCLASS&);
     virtual void  Paint(HDC hdc, PAINTSTRUCT& ps);
    private:
     HFONT hfontTmsRmn;
     HFONT hfontHelv;
    };

/*---------------------------------------------------------------*\
|                    Function Prototypes.                         |
\*---------------------------------------------------------------*/
void NEAR PASCAL TxtWriteTextMetrics (HDC hdc, int xText,
                                      int yText);

/*---------------------------------------------------------------*\
|                    Main Function:  WinMain.                     |
\*---------------------------------------------------------------*/
int PASCAL WinMain (HINSTANCE hInstance,   HINSTANCE hPrevInstance,
                LPSTR  lpszCmdLine, int    nCmdShow)
    {
    TTxtLinesApplication TxtLines ("TxtLines", hInstance,
                                   hPrevInstance, lpszCmdLine,
                                   nCmdShow);
    TxtLines.Run();
    return TxtLines.Status;
    }

/*---------------------------------------------------------------*\
|                  Application Class Member.                      |
\*---------------------------------------------------------------*/
TTxtLinesApplication::TTxtLinesApplication (LPSTR lpszName,
                   HINSTANCE hInstance, HINSTANCE hPrevInstance,
                   LPSTR lpszCmdLine, int nCmdShow)
                :TApplication (lpszName, hInstance,
                    hPrevInstance, lpszCmdLine, nCmdShow)
    {
    /* Application specific initialization goes here.  */
    }

/*---------------------------------------------------------------*\
|                  Application Class Member.                      |
\*---------------------------------------------------------------*/
void TTxtLinesApplication::InitMainWindow ()
    {
    MainWindow = new TTxtLinesWindow (NULL, "Three Fonts", NULL);
    }
```

```
/*--------------------------------------------------------------*\
|                 TTxtLinesWindow Class Member.                  |
\*--------------------------------------------------------------*/
TTxtLinesWindow::TTxtLinesWindow (PTWindowsObject pwParent,
                   LPSTR lpszTitle, PTModule pmModule)
                :TWindow (pwParent, lpszTitle, pmModule)
    {
    LOGFONT lf;

    memset (&lf, 0, sizeof (LOGFONT));
    lf.lfHeight = 16;
    lf.lfWidth = 6;
    lf.lfUnderline = 1;
    lstrcpy ((LPSTR)&lf.lfFaceName[0], (LPSTR)"Tms Rmn");
    hfontTmsRmn = CreateFontIndirect (&lf);

    memset (&lf, 0, sizeof (LOGFONT));
    lf.lfHeight = 16;
    lf.lfWidth = 7;
    lf.lfItalic = 1;
    lstrcpy ((LPSTR)&lf.lfFaceName[0], (LPSTR)"Helv");
    hfontHelv  = CreateFontIndirect (&lf);
    }

/*--------------------------------------------------------------*\
|                 TTxtLinesWindow Class Member.                  |
\*--------------------------------------------------------------*/
TTxtLinesWindow::~TTxtLinesWindow()
    {
    DeleteFont (hfontTmsRmn);
    DeleteFont (hfontHelv);
    }

/*--------------------------------------------------------------*\
|                 TTxtLinesWindow Class Member.                  |
\*--------------------------------------------------------------*/
LPSTR TTxtLinesWindow::GetClassName ()
    {
    return "TxtLines:MAIN";
    }

/*--------------------------------------------------------------*\
|                 TTxtLinesWindow Class Member.                  |
\*--------------------------------------------------------------*/
void TTxtLinesWindow::GetWindowClass (WNDCLASS& wc)
    {
    TWindow::GetWindowClass (wc);
    wc.hIcon=LoadIcon (wc.hInstance, "snapshot");
    wc.hCursor=LoadCursor (wc.hInstance, "hand");
    }

/*--------------------------------------------------------------*\
|                 TTxtLinesWindow Class Member.                  |
\*--------------------------------------------------------------*/
void TTxtLinesWindow::Paint(HDC hdc, PAINTSTRUCT& ps)
    {
    DWORD dwSize;
    int xText;
    int yText;
    RECT r;

    GetClientRect (HWindow, &r);
```

## 230 Introduction to the Graphics Device Interface

```
        dwSize = GetTextExtent (hdc, "X", 1);
        yText = HIWORD (dwSize) * 2;
        xText = LOWORD (dwSize) * 2;
        TxtWriteTextMetrics (hdc, xText, yText);

        SelectFont (hdc, hfontTmsRmn);
        xText += r.right/3;
        TxtWriteTextMetrics (hdc, xText, yText);

        SelectFont (hdc, hfontHelv);
        xText += r.right/3;
        TxtWriteTextMetrics (hdc, xText, yText);
        }
/*----------------------------------------------------------------*\
|   TxtWriteTextMetrics - Writes metrics of currently selected   |
|                         font.                                  |
\*----------------------------------------------------------------*/
void NEAR PASCAL TxtWriteTextMetrics (HDC hdc, int xText,
                                      int yText)
    {
    char        buffer[80];
    DWORD       dwSize;
    int         nLength;
    int         yLineHeight;
    int         xIndent;
    TEXTMETRIC  tm;
    static char *apchLabel[] =
                { "Height",             /* [0] */
                  "Ascent",             /* [1] */
                  "Descent",            /* [2] */
                  "Internal Leading",   /* [3] */
                  "External Leading",   /* [4] */
                  "Ave Char Width",     /* [5] */
                  "Max Char Width",     /* [6] */
                  "Weight"};            /* [7] */

    GetTextMetrics (hdc, &tm);
    yLineHeight = tm.tmHeight + tm.tmExternalLeading;

    nLength = GetTextFace (hdc, sizeof(buffer) - 1, buffer);
    TextOut (hdc, xText, yText, buffer, nLength);
    yText += yLineHeight * 2;

    dwSize = GetTextExtent (hdc, apchLabel[4],
                            lstrlen (apchLabel[4]));
    xIndent = LOWORD (dwSize);
    dwSize = GetTextExtent (hdc, "XXXX", 4);
    xIndent += LOWORD (dwSize);

    /*  Height.  */
    TextOut (hdc, xText, yText, apchLabel[0],
             lstrlen (apchLabel[0]));
    nLength = wsprintf (buffer, "%d", tm.tmHeight);
    SetTextAlign (hdc, TA_RIGHT);
    TextOut (hdc, xText + xIndent, yText, buffer, nLength);
    SetTextAlign (hdc, TA_LEFT);
    yText += yLineHeight;

    /*  Ascent.  */
    TextOut (hdc, xText, yText, apchLabel[1],
```

```
                lstrlen (apchLabel[1]));
    nLength = wsprintf (buffer, "%d", tm.tmAscent);
    SetTextAlign (hdc, TA_RIGHT);
    TextOut (hdc, xText + xIndent, yText, buffer, nLength);
    SetTextAlign (hdc, TA_LEFT);
    yText += yLineHeight;

    /* Descent. */
    TextOut (hdc, xText, yText, apchLabel[2],
            lstrlen (apchLabel[2]));
    nLength = wsprintf (buffer, "%d", tm.tmDescent);
    SetTextAlign (hdc, TA_RIGHT);
    TextOut (hdc, xText + xIndent, yText, buffer, nLength);
    SetTextAlign (hdc, TA_LEFT);
    yText += yLineHeight;

    /* Internal Leading. */
    TextOut (hdc, xText, yText, apchLabel[3],
            lstrlen (apchLabel[3]));
    nLength = wsprintf (buffer, "%d", tm.tmInternalLeading);
    SetTextAlign (hdc, TA_RIGHT);
    TextOut (hdc, xText + xIndent, yText, buffer, nLength);
    SetTextAlign (hdc, TA_LEFT);
    yText += yLineHeight;

    /* External Leading. */
    TextOut (hdc, xText, yText, apchLabel[4],
            lstrlen (apchLabel[4]));
    nLength = wsprintf (buffer, "%d", tm.tmExternalLeading);
    SetTextAlign (hdc, TA_RIGHT);
    TextOut (hdc, xText + xIndent, yText, buffer, nLength);
    SetTextAlign (hdc, TA_LEFT);
    yText += yLineHeight;

    /* Average Character Width. */
    TextOut (hdc, xText, yText, apchLabel[5],
            lstrlen (apchLabel[5]));
    nLength = wsprintf (buffer, "%d", tm.tmAveCharWidth);
    SetTextAlign (hdc, TA_RIGHT);
    TextOut (hdc, xText + xIndent, yText, buffer, nLength);
    SetTextAlign (hdc, TA_LEFT);
    yText += yLineHeight;

    /* Max Character Width. */
    TextOut (hdc, xText, yText, apchLabel[6],
            lstrlen (apchLabel[6]));
    nLength = wsprintf (buffer, "%d", tm.tmMaxCharWidth);
    SetTextAlign (hdc, TA_RIGHT);
    TextOut (hdc, xText + xIndent, yText, buffer, nLength);
    SetTextAlign (hdc, TA_LEFT);
    yText += yLineHeight;

    /* Weight. */
    TextOut (hdc, xText, yText, apchLabel[7],
            lstrlen (apchLabel[7]));
    nLength = wsprintf (buffer, "%d", tm.tmWeight);
    SetTextAlign (hdc, TA_RIGHT);
    TextOut (hdc, xText + xIndent, yText, buffer, nLength);
    SetTextAlign (hdc, TA_LEFT);
}
```

## TXTLINES.RC

```
snapshot icon TxtLines.ico

hand cursor TxtLines.cur
```

## TXTLINES.DEF

```
NAME TXTLINES

EXETYPE WINDOWS

DESCRIPTION 'TxtLines - Sample text output'

CODE MOVEABLE DISCARDABLE
DATA MOVEABLE MULTIPLE

HEAPSIZE   512
STACKSIZE  5120
```

To create a logical font, this program sets the desired fields in a **LOGFONT** structure and calls **CreateFontIndirect**. This routine ignores zero values and creates a font request using the fields we have explicitly set. That is the reason we call the C library routine memset to initialize all fields to zero.

Like other GDI objects, logical fonts take up memory, which must be explicitly freed to avoid keeping system memory from other uses. In response to the **WM_DESTROY** message, the program removes the logical fonts with calls to **DeleteFont**.

Most of the work in our program is done in response to the **WM_PAINT** message. It starts by getting the width of the window, using **GetClientRect**, and splitting the window into three columns. We first display the metric information for the system font before proceeding to the Times Roman and Helvetica fonts. It is worth noting that, although the logical font has already been created, the physical font is not determined until the logical font handle is selected into the DC, as in

`SelectFont (hDC, hfontTmsRmn);`

Our routine, TxtWriteTextMetrics, displays the first eight fields in the **TEXTMETRIC** data structure for each of the fonts. To obtain the name of each font face, we call the **GetTextFace** routine, which is defined as

`GetTextFace (hDC, nCount, lpFaceName);`

in which hDC is a handle to a device context, nCount is the size of the buffer to receive the font face name, and lpFaceName is a long pointer to a character buffer.

We call **GetTextExtent** twice, to determine the width of the widest field name, "External Leading," and then again to determine the width of "XXXX." The variable xIndex holds the sum of these two widths and is used as a margin between the field names and the value.

Notice that for each **TEXTMETRIC** field, we display the field name and then call on the **wsprintf** routine to convert the numeric value into a text string suitable for display with the **TextOut** routine. **wsprintf** behaves in the same way as the C library **sprintf** routine, except that it overcomes some of the incompatibilities of that routine in the Windows environment.

Notice also that we use the text alignment attribute (via **SetTextAlign**) to create a table with neatly left-justified text and right-justified numeric values.

As you can see, GDI treats text as a graphic object. This means that you get a great deal of control over the placement, sizing, and color of text. You can freely mix text and geometric shapes, and combine text of different sizes and styles on the same page. We think you'll find that the extra effort required is well worth the device-independent punch that GDI packs in text creation.

For programmers who don't need a lot of variety in text, GDI guarantees that you will find a default font for every GDI device. This will provide reasonable-looking text output with a minimum of effort on your part.

# PART FOUR

# USER INTERFACE OBJECTS

# 11

# Commands: Menu and Accelerator Basics

Windows has built-in support for two user-interface objects that retrieve command input from users: menus and accelerators. Menus allow a program to show users available actions and options, and encourage users to explore the capabilities of a program. Menus help beginners by eliminating the need to memorize commands. More advanced users can take advantage of accelerators, which translate keystrokes into program commands. To bridge the gap between menus and accelerators, programs often list accelerator keys inside menus. Figure 11.1 shows a menu with a description of the accelerator keys that correspond to each menu item. In this example, a user can press the [Shift] and [Del] keys instead of selecting the *Cut* menu item.

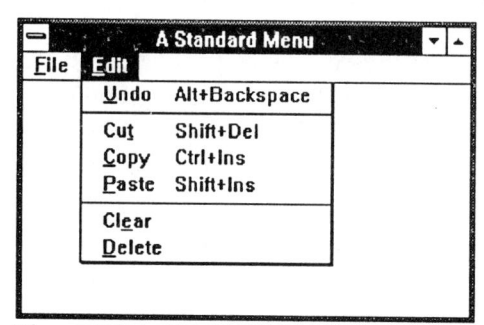

**Figure 11.1** A menu with accelerator key entries

Programs that adhere to the Windows standards for accelerators and menus are easier for users to learn than programs that do not. Therefore, it's important for programmers who plan to design menus to first learn these standards. There are two things you can do that will help you become familiar with these standards: You can use Windows, and you can read the style guidelines that Microsoft includes with the software development kit. Learning the standards is time well spent, since it will minimize the time required for a user to become comfortable with your program. Users who are familiar with the "look and feel" that pervades Windows programs will be put off by programs that ignore widely accepted standards.

Let's start with a quick look at some of the things that users expect to find in menus.

## User-Interface Standards

Users expect to find two types of items in a menu: **actions** and **options**. A menu action is usually expressed as a verb, or as a noun-verb combination. For example, many programs have an *Open* menu item inside a "File" menu. Menu actions usually act on a specific object that the user has selected. But menu actions can also cause a change that will affect an entire program. The *Close* item in a system menu, for example, can cause a program to terminate when the window being closed is the program's main, top-level window.

Options are toggle switches. Unlike menu actions, which create a short-lived response, options have a more long-lasting effect that is usually reversible. Programs often display check marks in menus to indicate whether an option is active or not. For example, the Program Manager has an Options menu that lets the user enable and disable two features: "Auto Arrange" and "Minimize on Use." While certain important options are set inside menus, most large programs make use of dialog boxes to allow the user to control a program's settable options. In other words, you don't need to put every available option inside menus. The less frequently required options can be placed into dialog boxes, which we'll discuss in more detail in Chapter 14.

Users expect to see **visual clues** in menus. Visual clues can be subtle, like the ellipses (...) that appear when the selection of a menu item causes a dialog box to appear. Or, can be as obvious as the way menu items are grouped. Here is a list of some of the different visual clues that can be incorporated into menus to indicate special handling of menu items:

- **Accelerator keystrokes** tell the user the accelerator key that matches the menu selection.
- An **arrow** indicates that a menu item is a doorway to a nested menu. The nested menu appears when the user touches the menu item, either by dragging the mouse or moving to the menu selection using keyboard cursor keys.
- A **separator** divides longer menus into smaller groups of menu items.
- A **check mark** next to a menu item indicates that the option has been turned on.

*Commands: Menu and Accelerator Basics* 239

- An **ellipsis** (...) after a menu item tells the user to expect a dialog box when the menu item is selected.
- An **exclamation point** at the end of a menu item in a top-level menu indicates that the menu item causes an action and will not cause a popup menu to appear.
- A **grayed** menu item is unavailable. In the system menu, for example, several menu items are grayed when a window is maximized.
- An **underlined** *letter* in the menu item text indicates the letter can be used to select the menu item. Such a letter is called a **mnemonic**. To make a popup menu appear, the [Alt] key is pressed with the mnemonic of the popup menu. Once a popup has appeared, menu items can be selected by pressing the mnemonic corresponding to the desired menu item.

Figure 11.2 shows a menu with an example of each of these different visual clues.

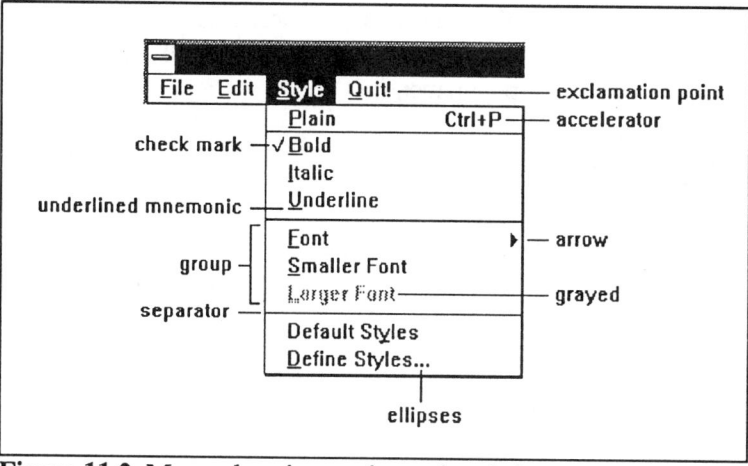

**Figure 11.2** Menu showing various visual clues

Users expect every program to have a **system menu**. From a programming point of view, this is easily accomplished, since Windows creates and maintains the system menu for you. In general, programs should not alter the contents of the system menu without a very good reason. A program may *add* certain items to the system menu. In particular, programs which only run in a minimized (or iconic) state can add private menu items to the system menu. The system menu, after all, is the only menu to appear when a program is iconic. Tiny utility and toy applications can add items to the system menu as well, to avoid the fuss of creating private menus. It's not something you'll do often, but under certain conditions it makes sense to. Figure 11.3 shows a standard system menu.

240   User Interface Objects

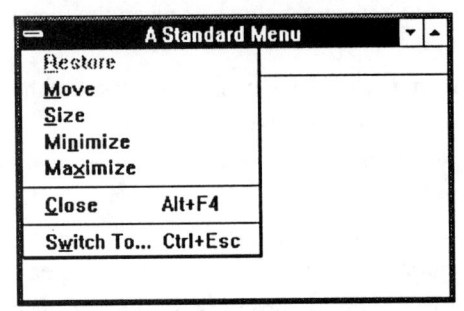

```
┌─────────────────────────────┬───┬───┐
│      A Standard Menu        │ ▼ │ ▲ │
├─────────────────────────────┴───┴───┤
│ Restore                             │
│ Move                                │
│ Size                                │
│ Minimize                            │
│ Maximize                            │
├─────────────────────────────────────┤
│ Close              Alt+F4           │
├─────────────────────────────────────┤
│ Switch To...   Ctrl+Esc             │
└─────────────────────────────────────┘
```

**Figure 11.3 The standard system menu**

In programs that work with data files, users expect to find a **File** popup menu. This menu provides access to the commands involved with opening, closing, and printing files. Notice, as shown in Figure 11.4, the *Exit* menu item is a standard part of the File menu. When selected, this item causes the program to terminate. While this duplicates the *Close* menu item in the system menu of a top-level window, it is a standard that users have come to expect. If you write a program that does *not* have a File menu, you'll still want to put an *Exit* menu item at the bottom of your first popup menu.

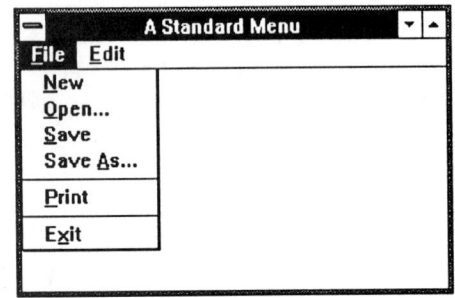

```
┌─────────────────────────────┬───┬───┐
│      A Standard Menu        │ ▼ │ ▲ │
├──────┬──────────────────────┴───┴───┤
│ File │ Edit                         │
├──────┴──────┐                       │
│ New         │                       │
│ Open...     │                       │
│ Save        │                       │
│ Save As...  │                       │
├─────────────┤                       │
│ Print       │                       │
├─────────────┤                       │
│ Exit        │                       │
└─────────────┴───────────────────────┘
```

**Figure 11.4 A typical file menu**

Another standard menu that users expect is the **Edit** popup menu. This menu lists general-purpose editing actions, including clipboard control, search and replace, undo previous actions, and repeat previous actions. A program can add other items to the standard Edit menu to allow an application-specific object to be manipulated. For example, a word processing program might list an action in its Edit menu to allow a user to edit the header or footer of a document. Figure 11.5 shows a typical Edit menu, which is part of the first program we're going to write.

Menus can be accessed using any combination of mouse and keyboard input. For example, after a mouse click makes a popup menu appear, users can browse through menu items by pressing arrow keys and can select a menu item by pressing the return key. As an alternative, users can activate a popup menu from the keyboard by pressing the [Alt] or the [F10] key. Menu browsing and selection can then be done with the mouse.

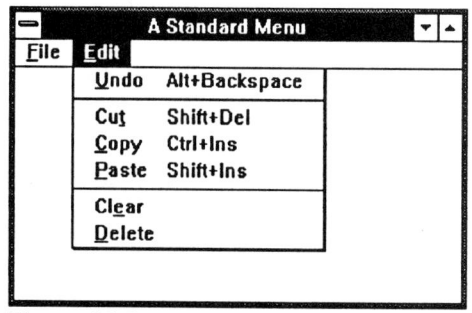

**Figure 11.5** A typical edit menu

This ability to choose between the mouse and the keyboard for menu operations is part of a larger plan to allow these devices to be used interchangeably in other actions as well. Of course, there are limits—entering characters with the mouse is difficult. But aside from these extremes, this ability to choose is important for program designers to keep in mind. Some users will rely solely on the keyboard—either because they don't have a mouse or because they prefer the keyboard. Others may switch between the two input methods, depending on the operation and their personal preference. In Chapters 15 and 16, when we discuss mouse and keyboard input in more detail, we'll reiterate this choice as an important part of the overall design for Windows programs. For now, let's get into the programming details of creating menus.

# Menu Programming Issues

Windows has a very robust, flexible menuing system that is, at the same time, quite easy to work with. While menus are easy to create for Windows programmers, the creation of the menuing system proved one of the most challenging tasks in the creation of Windows. The code that supports menuing has been reworked, tuned, and rewritten more than any other part of the system. One of the reasons has to do with performance: From the beginning, menus had to be snappy. Otherwise, the system itself would risk appearing sluggish. To help menus disappear quickly with minimum performance impact, a bitmap "snapshot" is taken of the screen where a menu is going to be drawn. When a user has finished using a menu, the snapshot is used to restore the area where the menu had been.

After all of Microsoft's efforts to make menus work quickly and efficiently, you'll be happy to know that menu creation is easy. As we'll see shortly, the quickest way to create a menu involves writing a short menu description in a program's resource file. When a window class is registered, a **WNDCLASS** parameter accepts a menu name. When a window of that class is created, a menu is created as well. The only other thing that a programmer must do is to process the **WM_COMMAND** messages that the menu sends to the window procedure.

Since we're working with a message-driven system, it probably won't surprise you to learn that menus created in Windows use messages to communicate with your program. Or, more precisely, messages are used to communicate with your *window procedure*. The most important menu message is the **WM_COMMAND** message, which is sent to notify you that a menu item has been selected.

Table 11.1 shows the different steps in the operation of a menu, the mouse and keyboard actions that lead to each step, and the associated messages. Notice that identical message traffic occurs whether the mouse or the keyboard is used. The details of the interaction between the user and your menus are hidden in the menu system, so that your program can simply respond to the messages with complete trust that the menuing system is taking care of the rest.

**Table 11.1**   Menu operation and menu messages

| Menu Operation | Mouse Action | Keyboard Action | Message |
| --- | --- | --- | --- |
| Initiate menu use | n/a | F10 or Alt key | WM_INITMENU |
| Display a popup | n/a | arrow or mnemonic keys | WM_INITMENUPOPUP |
| Initiate and display popup | \<Click\> | Alt + mnemonic key | WM_INITMENU and WM_INITMENUPOPUP |
| Browse a menu item | \<Drag\> | arrow keys | WM_MENUSELECT |
| Select a menu item | \<Release\> | Enter key or mnemonic key | WM_COMMAND |

While the **WM_COMMAND** message is the most useful, you'll want to understand the role of the other messages since there are times that they can be useful as well. For example, if a program wishes to initialize a top-level menu before the user makes a selection, it would respond to the **WM_INITMENU** message. To initialize a popup menu before it appears, a program would respond to **WM_INITMENUPOPUP**. Programs that use the clipboard often respond to one of these initialization messages to let the user know, for example, whether or not there is data on the clipboard that can be pasted. If there is, the *Paste* item in the Edit menu is enabled. Otherwise, it is grayed.

As the user browses through the items in a menu, the **WM_MENUSELECT** message tells a program the specific menu item that the user is highlighting at every moment in time. This information can be used to support an "information area" to display hints about the meaning of each menu item. This might be another window on the screen where information is displayed for the user to see. Quite a few commercial Windows programs provide this feature to assist in the selection of menu items. In Chapter 13, where we discuss issues relating to windowing, we'll show you a program that creates a window and processes **WM_MENUSELECT** messages in this way.

## Menu Template

The simplest menus start with a menu template. A menu template defines the popup menus and menu items that make up a menu. A menu template is a hierarchical data structure, like the DOS file system with its root directory and subdirectories. At the top of the hierarchy—the root directory—are the items for the menu bar, also known as the **action bar**. At this top level, items can be either menu items, which send command messages when selected, or the tops of popup menus. As a side note, it's something of a curiosity that another term used to refer to a popup menu is **pull-down menu**.

Popup menus are like subdirectories that are one level below the root directory in the DOS file hierarchy. And in the same way that subdirectories can themselves contain *other* subdirectories, a popup menu can contain other popup menus. There isn't any limit to the number of nested menu levels that the menu subsystem will provide. But common sense would indicate that three levels of menus—the main menu bar and two levels of popup menus—is the deepest you will most likely want to go. Otherwise, you risk losing your user in a sea of menus.

The quickest and easiest way to create a menu template is from within the Resource Workshop. As shown in Figure 11.6, this editor makes it easy to change a menu, since it lets you instantly see the results of a change. You can also create a menu template using a text editor. Whichever method you choose, our discussion will give you all the details of menu template creation:

```
menuID MENU [load option] [memory option]
BEGIN
    MENUITEM or POPUP statement
    MENUITEM or POPUP statement
      .
      .
      .
END
```

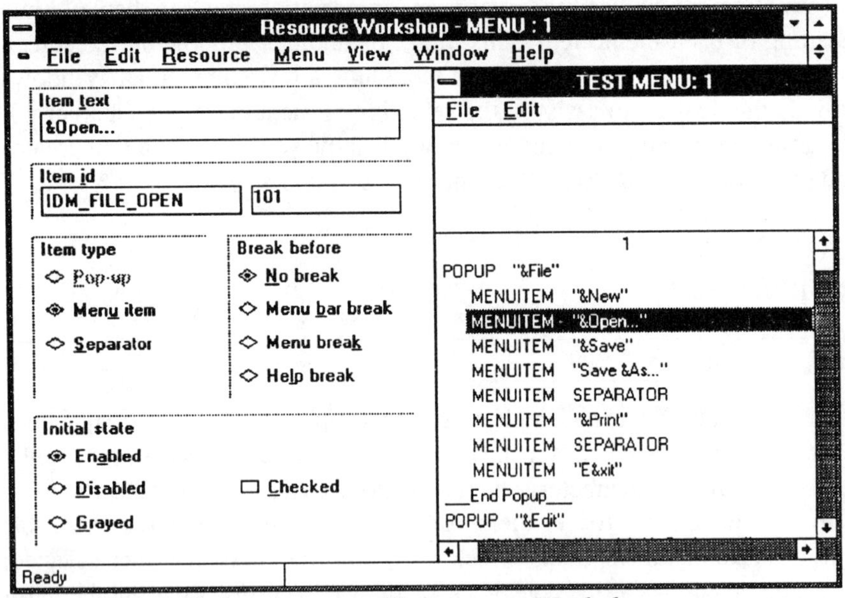

## 244  User Interface Objects

**Figure 11.6** Defining a menu with Resource Workshop

The [load option] can be either PRELOAD or LOADONCALL, and the [memory option] can be FIXED, MOVEABLE, or DISCARDABLE. These describe how the menu data itself is handled as a memory object. PRELOAD causes a menu resource to be loaded into memory before a program starts running. LOADONCALL causes the menu item to be loaded only when it is needed. The other three options, FIXED, MOVEABLE, and DISCARDABLE, describe how the memory object should behave once it has been loaded into memory. In Chapter 17, we'll describe in detail the meaning of these three options. Since the default behavior of LOADONCALL and the memory option of DISCARDABLE are good enough for now, we won't bother specifying these options in our menu examples.

Each MENUITEM statement defines a menu item that, when selected, causes a WM_COMMAND message to be sent. Each POPUP statement starts the definition of a popup menu, with a BEGIN and an END statement to bracket other MENUITEM or POPUP statements. Incidentally, if you want to save yourself some typing, you can use the C language squiggly brackets "{" and "}" in place of the BEGIN and END statements. Here is the menu definition for the File and Edit menus that we discussed earlier in this chapter:

```
7 MENU
    {
    POPUP "&File"
        {
        MENUITEM "&New",            1
        MENUITEM "&Open...",        2
        MENUITEM "&Save",           3
```

```
            MENUITEM "Save &As...",           4
            MENUITEM SEPARATOR
            MENUITEM "&Print",                5
            MENUITEM SEPARATOR
            MENUITEM "E&xit",                 6
        }
    POPUP "&Edit"
        {
        MENUITEM "&Undo\tAlt+Backspace",      7
        MENUITEM SEPARATOR
        MENUITEM "Cu&t\tShift+Del",           8
        MENUITEM "&Copy\tCtrl+Ins",           9
        MENUITEM "&Paste\tShift+Ins",        10
        MENUITEM SEPARATOR
        MENUITEM "Cl&ear",                   11
        MENUITEM "&Delete",                  12
        }
    }
```

The menu identifier is the number 7. Although we could have specified an ASCII text string, using a number is more efficient. This identifier is our name for the menu; it is how we'll identify this menu definition to Windows. Each ampersand (&) defines a mnemonic, which is a letter used in the keyboard interface to menus. The \t causes a tab character to be generated, to separate an accelerator keystroke name from a menu item name.

Perhaps the most important value in the definition of each menu item is the command result code. This is the number at the end of each of these **MENUITEM** statements that distinguishes one menu item from another. The menu system uses the result code to identify menu items for the **WM_COMMAND** and **WM_MENUSELECT** messages.

The general syntax of the **POPUP** statement is

```
POPUP text [,optionlist]
```

and the **MENUITEM** statement has the following syntax:

```
MENUITEM text, result-code [,optionlist]
```

The big difference between the two statements is that a **MENUITEM** statement has a result code and the **POPUP** statement does not. As far as [optionlist] goes, there are five options that can be selected. The first three select the initial state of the menu item:

- **CHECKED**. Places a check mark next to the popup or menu item name. This only affects items inside a popup menu, and not items in the top-level menu.
- **GRAYED**. Item is initially grayed and inactive.
- **INACTIVE**. Item appears normally, but cannot be selected. The **GRAYED** option is better, since it provides the user with visual feedback that a menu item isn't available.

246   *User Interface Objects*

The other two options change the physical layout of the menu itself:

- **MENUBREAK**. Causes a menu break. For horizontal (top-level) menus, this means a break in the vertical direction. For vertical (popup) menus, this means a break in the horizontal direction. If used with wild abandon, you could have vertical top-level and horizontal popup menus.
- **MENUBARBREAK**. Causes a menu break. In popup menus, the break is accompanied by a vertical bar.

In a top-level menu, these last two options have the same effect, which is to cause a menu item to start on a new line. For example, consider the following menu definition:

```
7 MENU
    {
    MENUITEM "Item-1",  1
    MENUITEM "Item-2",  2, MENUBREAK
    MENUITEM "Item-3",  3
    MENUITEM "Item-4",  4
    MENUITEM "Item-5",  5, MENUBARBREAK
    MENUITEM "Item-6",  6
    }
```

As depicted in Figure 11.7, the two break statements, **MENUBREAK** and **MENUBARBREAK**, cause the menu to wrap on the second and the fifth menu items. Windows itself will break top-level menus when the window is too narrow. But if you want to control when and how this occurs, these options are what you'll need.

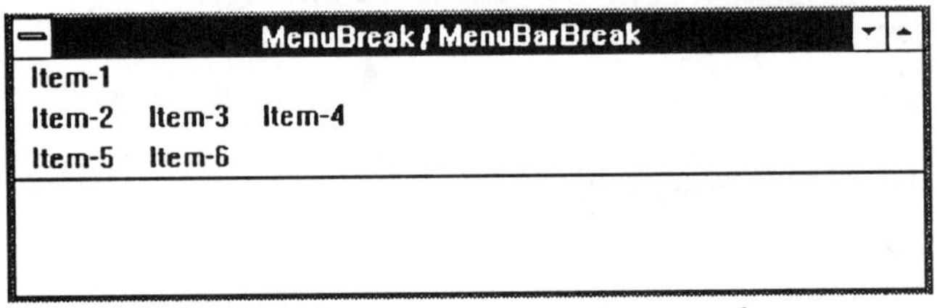

**Figure 11.7** Results of a MENUBREAK and MENUBARBREAK option on a top-level menu

To see the effect of these two options in a popup menu, consider the following menu template:

```
7 MENU
    {
    POPUP "Popup"
        {
        MENUITEM "Item-1", 1
```

```
            MENUITEM "Item-2",  2, MENUBREAK
            MENUITEM "Item-3",  3
            MENUITEM "Item-4",  4
            MENUITEM "Item-5",  5, MENUBARBREAK
            MENUITEM "Item-6",  6
            }
    }
```

Figure 11.8 shows the resulting popup menu. Notice that both options cause the menus to begin a new column, but that the **MENUBARBREAK** option adds a vertical bar to separate the different columns of menu items that are created.

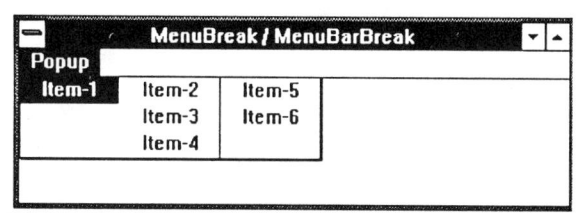

**Figure 11.8** Results of a MENUBREAK and a MENUBARBREAKoption in a popup menu

An additional option is listed in the documentation—**HELP**—but it no longer applies to the current standard for menus and so it has no effect. The old standard put the Help menu on the far right side of the top-level menu, with a vertical bar separating it from the other menu items. The current standard simply calls for making the Help menu the last item on the top-level menu. If you experiment with this option, you'll see that the menu system simply ignores it. On the other hand, if you want popup menus to appear on the right side of the menu bar, you'll need to create the menu dynamically and use the MF_HELP flag.

Let's take a look at a full-blown program that incorporates a menu. The menus we'll use are the standard File and Edit menus that we looked at earlier.

## A Sample Program: STANMENU

This program shows all of the pieces that must be put together to get a working menu. The menu itself is defined in the resource file, STANMENU.RC. But a resource by itself is just a data definition. To bring it into a program and make it work requires some code. There is room in the window class data structure, **WNDCLASS**, for a menu name. And so, we add one as follows:

```
wc.lpszMenuName = "#1";
```

248    User Interface Objects

The number sign indicates that we've used a numeric value in our menu definition. This is one of the easiest and most efficient ways to reference a menu. A regular ASCII name could have been used, but this would waste memory and take more time to use.

If we did not want to associate this menu with our window class, we could have placed a reference to our menu in the **Attr** structure in our window object's constructor. As you may recall, this structure is a data member which our window object class inherits from the **TWindow** class. The Menu member takes a `LPSTR (char far *)` value of the menu name. For example, if we had a menu named "ShortMenus," we could install this at window creation time by adding the following line to our window class constructor:

`Attr.Menu = "ShortMenus";`

Here is the code to our sample menu program, STANMENU:

# MAKEFILE.MAK

```
.AUTODEPEND

#    Translator Definitions
INC=\BORLANDC\OWL\INCLUDE;\BORLANDC\CLASSLIB\INCLUDE;\BORLANDC\INCLUDE
CC = bcc -c -D_CLASSDLL -H -ml -WS -w -I$(INC)

#    Implicit Rules
.c.obj:
  $(CC) {$< }

.cpp.obj:
  $(CC) {$< }

#    Explicit Rules
StanMenu.exe: StanMenu.res StanMenu.def StanMenu.obj
     tlink /c/C/n/P-/Twe/x @StanMenu.LNK
     rlink StanMenu.res StanMenu.exe

#    Individual File Dependencies
StanMenu.obj: StanMenu.cpp

StanMenu.res: StanMenu.rc StanMenu.cur StanMenu.ico
     brcc -FO StanMenu.res -i$(INC) StanMenu.RC
```

# STANMENU.LNK

```
\borlandc\lib\c0wl.obj+
StanMenu.obj
StanMenu,StanMenu
\borlandc\classlib\lib\tclasdll.lib+
\borlandc\owl\lib\owl.lib+
mathwl.lib+
import.lib+
crtldll.lib
StanMenu.def
```

# STANMENU.CPP

```
/*----------------------------------------------------------------*\
|  STANMENU.CPP     Program showing a standard File and Edit       |
|                   menu.                                          |
\*----------------------------------------------------------------*/
#define WIN31
#define STRICT
#include <owl.h>
#include <WindowsX.h>
#include "stanmenu.h"

#define COMMANDMSG(arg) (arg.WParam)

/*----------------------------------------------------------------*\
|                   Class Declarations.                            |
\*----------------------------------------------------------------*/
class TStanMenuApplication : public TApplication
   {
   public:
     TStanMenuApplication (LPSTR lpszName, HINSTANCE hInstance,
                           HINSTANCE hPrevInstance,
                           LPSTR lpszCmdLine, int nCmdShow);
     virtual void InitMainWindow ();
   };

class TStanMenuWindow : public TWindow
   {
   public:
     TStanMenuWindow (PTWindowsObject pwParent, LPSTR lpszTitle,
                  PTModule pmModule);
     virtual LPSTR GetClassName ();
     virtual void  GetWindowClass (WNDCLASS&);
     virtual void  WMCommand(TMessage& Msg) = [WM_COMMAND];
   };

/*----------------------------------------------------------------*\
|                   Main Function:  WinMain.                       |
\*----------------------------------------------------------------*/
int PASCAL WinMain (HINSTANCE hInstance,   HINSTANCE hPrevInstance,
                LPSTR  lpszCmdLine, int    nCmdShow)
    {
    TStanMenuApplication StanMenu ("StanMenu", hInstance,
                               hPrevInstance, lpszCmdLine,
                               nCmdShow);
    StanMenu.Run();
    return StanMenu.Status;
    }

/*----------------------------------------------------------------*\
|                   Application Class Member.                      |
\*----------------------------------------------------------------*/
TStanMenuApplication::TStanMenuApplication (LPSTR lpszName,
                        HINSTANCE hInstance, HINSTANCE hPrevInstance,
                        LPSTR lpszCmdLine, int nCmdShow)
                       :TApplication (lpszName, hInstance,
                            hPrevInstance, lpszCmdLine, nCmdShow)
    {
    /* Application specific initialization goes here.  */
    }
```

250  User Interface Objects

```
/*--------------------------------------------------------------*\
|                   Application Class Member.                    |
\*--------------------------------------------------------------*/
void TStanMenuApplication::InitMainWindow ()
    {
    MainWindow = new TStanMenuWindow (NULL, "A Standard Menu",
                                      NULL);
    }

/*--------------------------------------------------------------*\
|                   TStanMenuWindow Class Member.                |
\*--------------------------------------------------------------*/
TStanMenuWindow::TStanMenuWindow (PTWindowsObject pwParent,
                LPSTR lpszTitle, PTModule pmModule)
            :TWindow (pwParent, lpszTitle, pmModule)
    {
    /* Window specific initialization goes here.  */
    }

/*--------------------------------------------------------------*\
|                   TStanMenuWindow Class Member.                |
\*--------------------------------------------------------------*/
LPSTR TStanMenuWindow::GetClassName ()
    {
    return "StanMenu:MAIN";
    }

/*--------------------------------------------------------------*\
|                   TStanMenuWindow Class Member.                |
\*--------------------------------------------------------------*/
void TStanMenuWindow::GetWindowClass (WNDCLASS& wc)
    {
    TWindow::GetWindowClass (wc);
    wc.hIcon=LoadIcon (wc.hInstance, "snapshot");
    wc.hCursor=LoadCursor (wc.hInstance, "hand");
    wc.lpszMenuName = "#1";
    }

/*--------------------------------------------------------------*\
|                   TStanMenuWindow Class Member.                |
\*--------------------------------------------------------------*/
void TStanMenuWindow::WMCommand(TMessage& Msg)
    {
    char buffer[80];

    if (COMMANDMSG(Msg) == IDM_FILE_EXIT)
        SendMessage (HWindow, WM_SYSCOMMAND, SC_CLOSE, 0L);
    else
        {
        wsprintf (buffer, "Command = %d", COMMANDMSG(Msg));
        MessageBox (HWindow, buffer, "WM_COMMAND", MB_OK);
        }
    }
```

# STANMENU.RC

```
#include "stanmenu.h"

snapshot icon StanMenu.ico
```

## Commands: Menu and Accelerator Basics 251

```
hand cursor StanMenu.cur

1 MENU
    {
    POPUP "&File"
        {
        MENUITEM "&New",           IDM_FILE_NEW
        MENUITEM "&Open...",       IDM_FILE_OPEN
        MENUITEM "&Save",          IDM_FILE_SAVE
        MENUITEM "Save &As...",    IDM_FILE_SAVEAS
        MENUITEM SEPARATOR
        MENUITEM "&Print",         IDM_FILE_PRINT
        MENUITEM SEPARATOR
        MENUITEM "E&xit",          IDM_FILE_EXIT
        }
    POPUP "&Edit"
        {
        MENUITEM "&Undo\tAlt+Backspace",  IDM_EDIT_UNDO
        MENUITEM SEPARATOR
        MENUITEM "Cu&t\tShift+Del",       IDM_EDIT_CUT
        MENUITEM "&Copy\tCtrl+Ins",       IDM_EDIT_COPY
        MENUITEM "&Paste\tShift+Ins",     IDM_EDIT_PASTE
        MENUITEM SEPARATOR
        MENUITEM "Cl&ear",                IDM_EDIT_CLEAR
        MENUITEM "&Delete",               IDM_EDIT_DELETE
        }
    }
```

## STANMENU.DEF

```
NAME STANMENU

EXETYPE WINDOWS

DESCRIPTION 'StanMenu - Sample Standard Menu'

CODE MOVEABLE DISCARDABLE
DATA MOVEABLE MULTIPLE

HEAPSIZE   512
STACKSIZE  5120
```

As menu items are selected, a **WM_COMMAND** message is sent to our program to let us know. When a **WM_COMMAND** message arrives, the **wParam** parameter contains a result code that lets us know exactly which menu item has been selected. As you might expect, you'll want to make each value different so that you can tell the difference between different menu items. In STANMENU, we don't do very much when a **WM_COMMAND** message arrives:

```
void TStanMenuWindow::WMCommand(TMessage& Msg)
    {
    char buffer[80];

    if (COMMANDMSG(Msg) == IDM_FILE_EXIT)
    SendMessage (HWindow, WM_SYSCOMMAND, SC_CLOSE, 0L);
```

## 252  User Interface Objects

```
        else
            {
            wsprintf (buffer, "Command = %d", COMMANDMSG(Msg));
            MessageBox (HWindow, buffer, "WM_COMMAND", MB_OK);
            }
        }
```

If the menu result code is `IDM_FILE_EXIT`, which is the value of the *Exit* item in the File menu, we terminate our program by sending a system command message to close our application's main window. Otherwise, we display a message box that displays the menu item result code. One way to handle a **WM_COMMAND** is to create a switch statement, with a case for each command result code.

As an alternative, you can define a set of message response functions, with one per command. As you may recall from our discussion in Chapter 5, a message response function is a member function of a **TWindowsObject** descendent class. Each response function has a unique ID associated with it. For functions that handle a single message, such as **WM_PAINT** or **WM_LBUTTONDOWN**, the numeric value of the message itself provides the unique ID. For example, **WM_PAINT** is defined as 15 and **WM_LBUTTONDOWN** has a value of 513.

Message response functions for specific **WM_COMMAND** commands are defined at the high end of the range, between `0xA0000` and `0xFFFF`. For your convenience an OWL include file, OWLDEFS.H, defines the symbolic constant **CM_FIRST** at the beginning of this range. For example, here is how **TStanMenu** would be defined if we created one message dispatch function per menu item:

```
    class TStanMenuWindow : public TWindow
       {
       public:
           TStanMenuWindow (PTWindowsObject pwParent, LPSTR lpszTitle,
                        PTModule pmModule);
           virtual LPSTR GetClassName ();
           virtual void  GetWindowClass (WNDCLASS&);

           void CmdFileNew(TMessage& Msg)    =[CM_FIRST+IDM_FILE_NEW];
           void CmdFileOpen(TMessage& Msg)   =[CM_FIRST+IDM_FILE_OPEN];
           void CmdFileSave(TMessage& Msg)   =[CM_FIRST+IDM_FILE_SAVE];
           void CmdFileSaveAs(TMessage& Msg) =[CM_FIRST+IDM_FILE_SAVEAS];
           void CmdFilePrint(TMessage& Msg)  =[CM_FIRST+IDM_FILE_PRINT];
           void CmdFileExit(TMessage& Msg)   =[CM_FIRST+IDM_FILE_EXIT];

           void CmdEditUndo(TMessage& Msg)   =[CM_FIRST+IDM_EDIT_UNDO];
           void CmdEditCut(TMessage& Msg)    =[CM_FIRST+IDM_EDIT_CUT];
           void CmdEditCopy(TMessage& Msg)   =[CM_FIRST+IDM_EDIT_COPY];
           void CmdEditPaste(TMessage& Msg)  =[CM_FIRST+IDM_EDIT_PASTE];
           void CmdEditClear(TMessage& Msg)  =[CM_FIRST+IDM_EDIT_CLEAR];
           void CmdEditDelete(TMessage& Msg) =[CM_FIRST+IDM_EDIT_DELETE];
       };
```

Since each menu command result code (like `IDM_FILE_NEW`) is unique, the dispatch table index for each message response function will be unique. You can treat each command as if each was its own, separate message.

The simple menu in STANMENU has enough sophistication for most Windows programs. However, you may decide you need to get more involved with the handling of a menu. This would be the case if you wanted to change your menu at runtime: to add a menu item, or to make a menu item grayed or checked. For programs (and programmers) that demand more, Windows has 26 menu support routines that you can use. To help you get a grasp of them, we've divided these routines into six main types. We're going to discuss each type in turn.

## Menu Support Routines

Windows has 26 menu support routines, which can be divided into six categories. Each category describes a different type of activity that can be performed on a menu. The categories are creation, connect to a window, destruction, modification, query, and tracking. When you need more than just the simplest menu operations, you'll find that you can go to each group of routines and find one or more that will help you with whatever problem you have. Table 11.2 summarizes the various categories of menu functions.

Table 11.2  A summary of menu functions

| Category | Routine | Description |
| --- | --- | --- |
| Creation (4) | CreateMenu | Creates an empty menu in memory. |
| | CreatePopupMenu | Creates an empty popup menu in memory. |
| | LoadMenu | Creates a menu from a disk-based (.EXE or .DLL file) menu resource. |
| | LoadMenuIndirect | Creates a menu from a memory-based menu resource. |
| Connect to a Window (1) | SetMenu | Attaches a top-level menu to a window. |

*(Continued)*

254  User Interface Objects

**Table 11.2**  Continued

| Category | Routine | Description |
| --- | --- | --- |
| Destruction (2) | DeleteMenu | Removes a menu item from a top-level or popup menu, and destroys any associated popup menus. |
| | DestroyMenu | Destroys a specific top-level or popup menu and all the menus below it. |
| Modification (10) | AppendMenu | Adds items to the end of a top-level or popup menu. |
| | ChangeMenu | Old Windows 1.x and 2.x menu modification function. |
| | CheckMenuItem | Toggles a checkmark inside a popup menu. |
| | DrawMenuBar | Forces the top-level menu to be redrawn after it has been changed. |
| | EnableMenuItem | Enables, disables, and grays menu items. |
| | HiliteMenuItem | Toggles highlighting of an item in a top-level menu. |
| | InsertMenu | Puts a new item into a menu. |
| | ModifyMenu | Changes an item in a menu. |
| | RemoveMenu | Removes a menu item or a popup menu. After a popup menu is removed, it is not destroyed, which means it can be reused. |
| | SetMenuItemBitmaps | Defines two bitmaps to be used in place of the default checked and unchecked display. |
| Query (8) | GetMenu | Retrieves the menu handle for a window's top-level menu. |
| | GetMenuCheckMarkDimensions | Gets the size of the default menu check mark, as set by the display driver. |

*(Continued)*

**Table 11.2**   Continued

| Category | Routine | Description |
| --- | --- | --- |
| | GetMenuItemCount | Returns the number of items in a top-level or popup menu. |
| | GetMenuItemID | Finds the menu ID for a given menu item. |
| | GetMenuState | Returns the flags that are set for a given menu item. |
| | GetMenuString | Returns the label of a menu item. |
| | GetSubMenu | Retrieves the menu handle of a popup menu. |
| | GetSystemMenu | Retrieves a handle to a system menu. |
| Tracking (1) | TrackPopupMenu | Creates a floating popup menu to appear anywhere on the display screen. |

Let's look at each type of menu routine, starting with the menu creation routines.

## *Menu Creation*

To the user, menus are user-interface objects that sit inside windows. All of the work that Windows does to support a menu remains hidden behind the scenes. It's the programmer's job, however, to understand what goes on behind the scenes, to make sure that things operate smoothly and efficiently. From a programmer's point of view, menu support requires that certain data structures be created that define the shape and behavior of a menu. Most programs take the easy route to menu creation by attaching a menu resource to a window class. As the window is created, the menu is automatically created as well.

But a program can become more intimately involved in a menu's internal data structures. We have already seen that a program can call **LoadMenu** to request that a menu resource be loaded. Let's see what other possibilities are available.

Using the **CreateMenu** and **CreatePopup** routines, a program can build empty menus, which can then be filled with menu command items and connected to other popup menus. Adding a menu item can involve any of several of the menu modification routines. In the following example, we've decided to use **AppendMenu**. This code fragment creates from scratch a menu like the one that STANMENU built using a menu resource:

```
{
HMENU hSub;
HMENU hTop;
hTop = CreateMenu ();
hSub = CreatePopupMenu ();
AppendMenu (hSub, MF_STRING, 1, "&New");
AppendMenu (hSub, MF_STRING, 2, "&Open...");
AppendMenu (hSub, MF_STRING, 3, "&Save");
AppendMenu (hSub, MF_STRING, 4, "Save &As...");
AppendMenu (hSub, MF_SEPARATOR, 0, 0);
AppendMenu (hSub, MF_STRING, 5, "&Print");
AppendMenu (hSub, MF_SEPARATOR, 0, 0);
AppendMenu (hSub, MF_STRING, 6, "E&xit");
AppendMenu (hTop, MF_POPUP, hSub, "&File");
hSub = CreatePopupMenu ();
AppendMenu (hSub, MF_STRING, 7, "&Undo\tAlt+Backspace");
AppendMenu (hSub, MF_SEPARATOR, 0, 0);
AppendMenu (hSub, MF_STRING, 8, "Cu&t\tShift+Del");
AppendMenu (hSub, MF_STRING, 9, "&Copy\tCtrl+Ins");
AppendMenu (hSub, MF_STRING,10, "&Paste\tShift+Ins");
AppendMenu (hSub, MF_SEPARATOR, 0, 0);
AppendMenu (hSub, MF_STRING,11, "Cl&ear");
AppendMenu (hSub, MF_STRING,12, "&Delete");
AppendMenu (hTop, MF_POPUP, hSub, "&Edit");
SetMenu (hwnd, hTop);
}
```

The **AppendMenu** routine provides the glue to put the different menu pieces together. It attaches menu items to menus and connects popup menus to top-level menus. **AppendMenu** is defined as

```
BOOL AppendMenu (hMenu, wFlags, wIDNewItem, lpNewItem)
```

- **hMenu** is a handle to a menu, either a popup or a top-level menu.
- **wFlags** is a combination of one or more of the MF_ flags, as described below.
- **wIDNewItem** is the result code delivered with the **WM_COMMAND** message, or a handle to a popup menu when a popup menu is being appended.
- **lpNewItem** is a long value that can contain three different types of values. When inserting a string, it is a long pointer to a text string. When inserting a bitmap, it is a bitmap handle. Otherwise, if you are creating an **owner-draw** menu item, it identifies the specific item that you wish to draw.

**AppendMenu** has several different uses, depending on whether you are attaching a regular menu item or a popup menu, and whether the new item will display a string, a bitmap, or an owner-draw menu item. To put a new string item in a menu for a regular command item, you can call **AppendMenu** like this:

```
AppendMenu (hMenu, MF_STRING, wID, "Open...");
```

The value of `wID` is the command result code that will be sent with the **WM_COMMAND** message when the user selects the menu item, which will be identified by the label "Open..."

Alternatively, **AppendMenu** can be used to attach a popup menu to a top-level menu (or a popup menu to another popup menu). In such cases, it could be called like this:

```
AppendMenu (hMenuTop, MF_POPUP, hMenuPopup, "File");
```

In this case, the value of the third parameter, **hMenuPopup**, is not a command result code, but it is a handle to a popup menu that is to be appended to the end of the menu identified by the `hMenuTop` menu handle. When the popup is added, it will be identified with the string "File."

AppendMenu can also be used to install a bitmap in place of a string as the label that is displayed for a menu item. When a bitmap is used, the last parameter is used to hold the bitmap handle, instead of a long pointer to a string. In the following example, the variable **hbm** is a bitmap handle, and it is packed into the last parameter using the **MAKELONG** macro:

```
AppendMenu (hMenu, MF_BITMAP, wID, MAKELONG(hbm, 0));
```

Of the 12 flags for the **wFlags** field, 10 duplicate features that can be requested from a resource file entry. The other two are only available for dynamically generated menus: **MF_BITMAP** and **MF_OWNERDRAW**. In Chapter 12, you'll find sample programs that show how to use these two types of menu items. Table 11.3 lists and describes each menu flag. To put these flags into a slightly different perspective, there are four general categories of flags: type of object, checked or not, enabled or not, and menu break or not. Table 11.4 lists each of the categories and the flags that are in each. The top item in each list is the default value.

Table 11.3 The MF–Menu creation flags

| Menu Flag | Available in a Resource | Description |
|---|---|---|
| MF_BITMAP | No | Displays a GDI bitmap instead a text string for a menu item. It provides one way that graphic images can be displayed in a menu. The other way involves an MF_OWNERDRAW menu item. |
| MF_CHECKED | Yes | Puts a checkmark next to a menu item. |

*(Continued)*

**Table 11.3** Continued

| Menu Flag | Available in a Resource | Description |
|---|---|---|
| MF_DISABLED | Yes | Disables a menu item. Use the MF_GRAYED flag instead, since it provides the user with visual feedback. |
| MF_ENABLED | Yes | Enables a menu item. |
| MF_GRAYED | Yes | Disables and grays a menu item. |
| MF_MENUBARBREAK | Yes | Creates a menu break, and a vertical bar for items inside a popup menu. |
| MF_MENUBREAK | Yes | Creates a menu break. |
| MF_OWNERDRAW | No | The creator of the menu is sent a message, WM_DRAWITEM, which includes a handle to a device context to be used for drawing custom menu labels using GDI drawing calls. Cannot be used for top-level menu items. |
| MF_POPUP | Yes | A popup menu is being attached to a top-level menu, or to another popup. |
| MF_SEPARATOR | Yes | A horizontal separator should be created in a menu item. |
| MF_STRING | Yes | A text string is being supplied for a menu item label. |
| MF_UNCHECKED | Yes | Menu item should be drawn without a check mark. |

**Table 11.4** Four categories of menu flags

| Type of Object | Checked | Enabled | Menu Break |
|---|---|---|---|
| MF_STRING | MF_UNCHECKED | MF_ENABLED | <none> |
| MF_POPUP | MF_CHECKED | MF_GRAYED | MF_MENUBARBREAK |
| MF_BITMAP |  | MF_DISABLED | MF_MENUBREAK |
| MF_SEPARATOR |  |  |  |
| MF_OWNERDRAW |  |  |  |

The only menu creation routine we have not investigated is `LoadMenuIndirect`. This routine builds a menu from a memory-resident menu template. This routine is just like `LoadMenu`, except that `LoadMenu` creates a menu from a disk-based menu template.

`LoadMenuIndirect` creates a menu using data that is memory-resident. Thus, you can create a menu template "on the fly" and give it to the menu system for use in creating a menu. Doing this requires that you duplicate what the resource compiler does in creating a memory object that describes a menu. The data structures in WINDOWS.H that have been defined for this purpose include the `MENUITEMTEMPLATEHEADER` and `MENUITEMTEMPLATE`.

The next routine that we're going to cover is `SetMenu`. This routine provides the one and only way to attach a menu to a window.

## Connect to a Window

A single Windows function supports the placement of a menu in a window: `SetMenu`. This single function gets its own category because it provides the only way to replace a top-level menu. In addition, there are some system memory cleanup issues that this routine raises, which we'll describe in a moment. The syntax of this routine is

```
BOOL SetMenu (hWnd, hMenu)
```

- **hWnd** is a window handle to a `WS_OVERLAPPED` or `WS_POPUP` window. A menu cannot be attached to a `WS_CHILD` window.
- **hMenu** is the handle of a top-level menu to be attached to a window.

A program can create several menus and make a different menu available to the user at different times during the operation of a program. There are several reasons why a program might want to do this. One has to do with supporting different levels of users. A beginner might only want to see short menus, with a program's most basic commands. More advanced users can set a program option to allow them to view a program's longer, more complete menus.

Another reason for a program to have multiple menus involves program security. Different menus can be used to enforce privilege levels in a program. For example, a program might ask for a password at program startup time. The menu that is installed will depend on which password is used. A regular user might get an abbreviated set of menus, while more privileged users get a more complete set of menus giving them the ability to do more privileged operations.

Yet another reason for a program to have different menus is to support the Multiple Document Interface (MDI) standard. This user-interface standard opens a new document window for each new document that a user asks to work with. Different types of documents may need different menus. For example, Microsoft's Excel spreadsheet has two types of documents: worksheets and charts. There are two menus, one for each type of document. Excel switches between the two menus, depending on the type of document with which the user is working.

Whatever your reason for having different menus, `SetMenu` lets you quickly switch from one menu to another. If you do this, however, a word of caution is in order. When you remove a menu from a window, Windows forgets about the menu. If your program terminates without explicitly destroying this menu, the memory taken up by the menu is lost forever (or until the user exits Windows). Therefore, be sure to destroy menus that have been detached from a window. Otherwise, your program will inadvertently waste system memory (in the USER module's data segment) every time it runs. The next section discusses how to destroy menus.

---

**Hint** If you replace a menu by calling `SetMenu`, be sure to hold onto the handle of the old menu. Then, when your program exits, destroy the menu since menus that aren't attached to windows are not cleaned up automatically.

---

## *Menu Destruction*

Windows has two routines that destroy menus and free the memory associated with them: `DestroyMenu` and `DeleteMenu`.

The `DestroyMenu` routine destroys menus that are *not* connected to any window. If you pass it the menu handle for a menu connected to a window, your program will crash. `DestroyMenu` is defined as follows:

```
BOOL DestroyMenu (hmenu)
```

- **hmenu** is the handle of a top-level or popup menu that is to be destroyed. The menu specified and all associated popup menus are destroyed.

Here is code that will determine the currently installed menu, remove it from the window, and destroy it:

```
HMENU hmenu;

hmenu = GetMenu(hwnd);     /* Find out menu handle. */
SetMenu (hwnd, NULL);      /* Remove menu.          */
DestroyMenu (hmenu);       /* Destroy the menu.     */
```

You don't have to do this for every menu you create, though, because a menu that is attached to a window is automatically destroyed when the window is destroyed.

The second menu destruction routine, **DeleteMenu**, actually does two things: It removes a menu item from a menu and destroys whatever popup menus are associated with the menu item. This routine frees the memory used by the menu in the same way that **DestroyMenu** does.

**DeleteMenu** is defined as

BOOL DeleteMenu (hMenu, nPosition, wFlags)

- **hMenu** is a handle to either a top-level or a popup menu.
- **nPosition** identifies the menu item of interest. The meaning of this field depends on the value of the last parameter, **wFlags**.
- **wFlags** is either **MF_BYPOSITION** or **MF_BYCOMMAND**.

If **wFlags** is **MF_BYPOSITION**, then the menu item is selected by its relative position in the menu: The first item in a menu has an offset of zero, the next has an offset of one, and so forth. This is necessary to reference popup menus, which don't have an associated result code. Here is one way to remove the Edit popup menu from the top-level menu in the STANMENU program:

```
HMENU hmenu;
...
hmenu = GetMenu (hwnd);
DeleteMenu (hmenu, 1, MF_BYPOSITION);
DrawMenuBar (hwnd);
```

As we'll discuss in the next section, the call to **DrawMenuBar** is necessary whenever the top-level menu changes, to request that it be completely redrawn.

The **MF_BYPOSITION** flag also can be used to remove an item in a popup menu. But you must first get a handle to the popup menu that contains the item by calling **GetSubMenu**. For example, here is how to delete the *Copy* command, which is the fourth item in our standard menu:

```
HMENU hmenu;
HMENU hmenuEdit;
hmenu = GetMenu (hwnd);
hmenuEdit = GetSubMenu (hMenu, 1);
DeleteMenu (hmenuEdit, 3, MF_BYPOSITION);
```

Menu items can also be deleted by using the command result code, by using the **MF_BYCOMMAND** flag in **DeleteMenu**'s last parameter. For deleting items in popup menus, using the command result code is faster than using the relative position, since the command result code lets you reference any item in the menu hierarchy by referencing the handle to the top-level menu. For example, here is another way to remove the *Copy* command from the Edit menu in STANMENU:

```
HMENU hmenu;
...
hmenu = GetMenu (hwnd);
DeleteMenu (hmenu, 9, MF_BYCOMMAND);
```

Our discussion of `DeleteMenu` has introduced two more menu flags: **MF_BYCOMMAND** and **MF_BYPOSITION**. These two, plus the 12 flags that were introduced in the discussion of the `AppendMenu` routine, bring to 14 the total number of menu flags that we have encountered. These 14 form the core set that you will use in just about all of the work you do with menus.

The next set of routines that we're going to look at are used to modify a menu once it has been created.

## *Menu Modification*

Once a program has created a menu and attached it to a window, there is no reason for the menu to remain unchanged. In fact, Windows provides 10 routines that let you fiddle with menus as much as you need to. We've looked at one of them already, `AppendMenu`. Four other routines change the structure of an existing menu: `ChangeMenu`, `InsertMenu`, `ModifyMenu`, and `RemoveMenu`. In general, the `ChangeMenu` routine should be avoided since it was created for an earlier version of Windows and is somewhat clumsy and complicated to use. More to the point, its capabilities are replaced by the other three menu modification routines.

`InsertMenu` installs a new menu item or popup menu into an existing menu. Unlike `AppendMenu`, which can only create new items at the *end* of a menu, `InsertMenu` creates new items anywhere. The `ModifyMenu` routine *changes* an existing menu item. For example, it can be used to change the menu string, change the command result code, enable a grayed menu item, or gray and disable a menu item. The `RemoveMenu` routine detaches a popup menu from a top-level menu or other popup menus. This routine leaves the internal menu structure intact, so that a menu can be reused later. Of course, if you remove a menu item from a menu, you must remember to destroy the menu item before your program exits, since otherwise the memory will be lost to the system.

Our first routine, `InsertMenu`, is defined as follows:

```
BOOL InsertMenu( hMenu, nPosition, wFlags, wID, lpNew)
```

- `hMenu` is a handle to a popup or top-level menu.
- `nPosition` indicates the menu item before which the new item is to be created. This value can be either the relative position of a menu item or the result code of a menu

item, depending on whether the `MF_BYPOSITION` or `MF_BYCOMMAND` flag is selected.

- `wFlags` is a combination of the 12 menu flags that were described earlier with the AppendMenu routine. Two other flags indicate how the new item location is selected: `MF_BYPOSITION` and `MF_BYCOMMAND`.
- `wID` is the result code for a new menu item and is the value delivered with the `WM_COMMAND` message. Or, when a popup menu is being inserted, it is a popup menu handle.
- `lpNew` is a long value that can contain three different types of values. When inserting a string, it is a long pointer to a text string. When inserting a bitmap, it is a bitmap handle. Otherwise, if you are creating an owner-draw menu item, it identifies the specific item that you wish to draw.

Here is one way to add a *Close* command to the File menu, underneath the *Open* ... menu item:

```
HMENU hmenu;
HMENU hmenuFile;
...
hmenu = GetMenu (hwnd);
hmenuFile = GetSubMenu (hmenu, 0);
InsertMenu (hmenuFile, 2, MF_BYPOSITION, 13, "&Close");
```

This code fragment uses the `MF_BYPOSITION` method to specify the location of the new menu item. Since we're inserting a menu item in a popup menu, this approach requires us to get a handle to the popup menu. The `GetMenu` routine gets a handle to the top-level menu. The `GetSubMenu` routine gets a handle to the File menu, since it's the first (zeroth) item in the top-level menu. Once we have a handle to the correct popup menu, the `InsertMenu` routine inserts a new menu command that will produce a result code of 13. The second parameter, 2, specifies that the menu item is to be inserted *before* menu item 2. In zero-based counting, that means before the *third* item. Figure 11.9 shows the File menu with the newly added *Close* menu item.

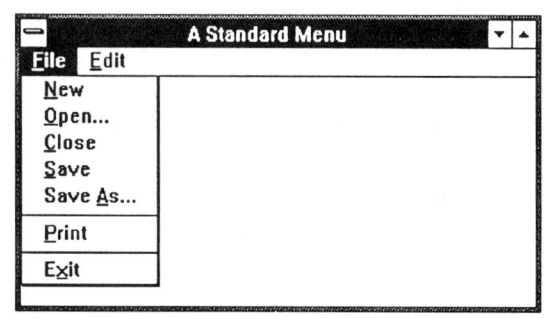

**Figure 11.9** File menu with newly added Close menu item

Another slightly simpler way to add this menu item involves using the **MF_BYCOMMAND** option to specify the position for the new menu item. This approach is simpler, since it can be done using a handle to the top-level menu instead of requiring a handle to the specific popup where we're going to insert our new item:

```
HMENU hmenu;
...
hmenu = GetMenu (hwnd);
InsertMenu (hmenu, 3, MF_BYCOMMAND, 13, "&Close");
```

This code fragment also creates a Close menu item in the File menu. This time, however, the **MF_BYCOMMAND** parameter lets us specify the location using a command result code. In this case, the value of 3 is chosen since this is the result code for the *Save* menu item, before which we wish to have a menu item inserted.

The **ModifyMenu** routine, which can change any aspect of a menu item, takes the same parameters and flags as **InsertMenu**. This routine uses the same two methods for specifying a specific menu item: **MF_BYPOSITION** and **MF_BYCOMMAND**. Of course, since this routine modifies existing menu items instead of inserting new menu items, the way an item is specified is a little different. With **InsertMenu**, we point to the item that will follow the new menu item. **ModifyMenu**, on the other hand, requires us to point to the item itself.

**ModifyMenu** can put a new label on a menu item, gray a regular menu item, or enable a grayed menu item. It can be used to change a regular menu item into a bitmap or into an owner-draw menu item. In brief, anything that can be added to a menu with **InsertMenu** or **AppendMenu** can be changed using **ModifyMenu**. For example, here is how **ModifyMenu** can be used to change the labels on a menu item. We're going to change the Edit menu's *Cut*, *Copy*, and *Paste* menu items so that each menu item displays the equivalent French phrase instead. Using the **MF_BYPOSITION** option, we would say

```
HMENU hmenu;
HMENU hmenuEdit;
...
hmenu = GetMenu (hwnd);
hmenuEdit = GetSubMenu (hmenu, 1);
ModifyMenu (hmenuEdit, 2, MF_BYPOSITION, 8,  "Couper");
ModifyMenu (hmenuEdit, 3, MF_BYPOSITION, 9,  "Copier");
ModifyMenu (hmenuEdit, 4, MF_BYPOSITION, 10, "Coller");
```

As we saw in earlier examples, the **MF_BYPOSITION** option requires us to get the handle of the specific menu or submenu that contains the item of interest. A simpler approach involves using the **MF_BYCOMMAND** option. Here is how to use the **MF_BYCOMMAND** option to achieve the same results as in our previous example, except it requires no call to **GetSubMenu**:

```
HMENU hmenu;
...
hmenu = GetMenu (hwnd);
ModifyMenu (hmenu,  8, MF_BYCOMMAND,  8, "Couper");
ModifyMenu (hmenu,  9, MF_BYCOMMAND,  9, "Copier");
ModifyMenu (hmenu, 10, MF_BYCOMMAND, 10, "Coller");
```

Our next menu modification function, **RemoveMenu**, removes items from a menu. If an item is a command, it is removed and the memory associated with it is freed. However, if an item is a popup menu, it is not destroyed so that it can be used again. **RemoveMenu** is defined as

```
BOOL RemoveMenu (hMenu, nPosition, wFlags)
```

- **hMenu** is a handle to a popup or top-level menu.
- **nPosition** indicates the menu item to be removed. This value is either the relative position of a menu item or the result code of a menu item, depending on whether the **MF_BYPOSITION** or **MF_BYCOMMAND** flag is selected.
- **wFlags** is either **MF_BYPOSITION** or **MF_BYCOMMAND**.

Using the **MF_BYCOMMAND** flag, we could delete the *Clear* menu item with

```
HMENU hmenu;
...
hmenu = GetMenu (hwnd);
RemoveMenu (hmenu, 11, MF_BYCOMMAND);
```

If we wanted to remove the entire Edit menu, we would have to use the **MF_BYPOSITION** flag as shown here:

```
HMENU hmenu;
...
hmenu = GetMenu (hwnd);
hmenuEdit = GetSubMenu (hmenu, 1);
RemoveMenu (hmenu, 1, MF_BYPOSITION);
DrawMenuBar (hwnd);
```

Since we are removing a popup menu from the menu hierarchy, unless we attach it later on we're going to have to be sure to destroy the menu before our program terminates:

```
DestroyMenu (hmenuEdit);
```

so that the memory associated with the Edit menu is freed.

You may have noticed the call to **DrawMenuBar** after the popup menu is removed. Whenever a change is made to a top-level menu, **DrawMenuBar** should be called. The reason is that the menu modification routines *only* change the internal data structures that support a menu. For the user to see the change, `DrawMenuBar` must be called to redraw the newly modified menu. Otherwise, the change does not appear to the user, which is sure to result in some confusion.

All of the remaining routines in this group are used to change the state of existing menu items. `CheckMenuItem`, for example, is used to place a check mark next to a menu item, or to remove a check mark. Incidentally, if you don't like the shape of the default check mark, you can create a bitmap that has an image that you do like and associate it with a menu item by calling `SetMenuItemBitmaps`. This routine also lets you select the bitmap to be displayed when a menu item is not checked. In Chapter 12, when we discuss how to enhance menu items using graphics, we'll show you exactly how this is done.

The `EnableMenuItem` routine lets you pick one of three enable states for a menu item: enabled, disabled, and grayed. As we mentioned earlier, because the disabled state provides no visual feedback to the user, it is probably best to avoid using it. For the other two, *enabled* is the default state of a menu in which it can be selected and manipulated in a normal manner. A *grayed* menu item, on the other hand, is displayed in a grayed text and cannot be selected by the user.

A final routine, `HiliteMenuItem`, lights up items in the top-level menu. This routine is used by the keyboard accelerator support code when a keyboard accelerator is pressed. The top-level menu item that is associated with the selected menu item is highlighted for a moment. Unless you plan to simulate this functionality yourself, you'll probably not find occasion to use this routine.

Our next set of routines perform a query—that is, they ask the menu system for some information.

## *Query*

The Query routines let you ask for information about menus. There are two types of routines: one set returns a handle to a menu, the other provides menu attribute information. In general, if you can set a value or a flag, there is a query routine to let you know the currently selected value or flag associated with a menu item.

Three query routines give you menu handle information: `GetMenu`, `GetSubMenu`, and `GetSystemMenu`. Figure 11.10 gives a graphic depiction of the menu handles returned by these three routines. `GetMenu` gives you a handle to the top-level menu that is attached to a window. Here is how it is called:

*Commands: Menu and Accelerator Basics* 267

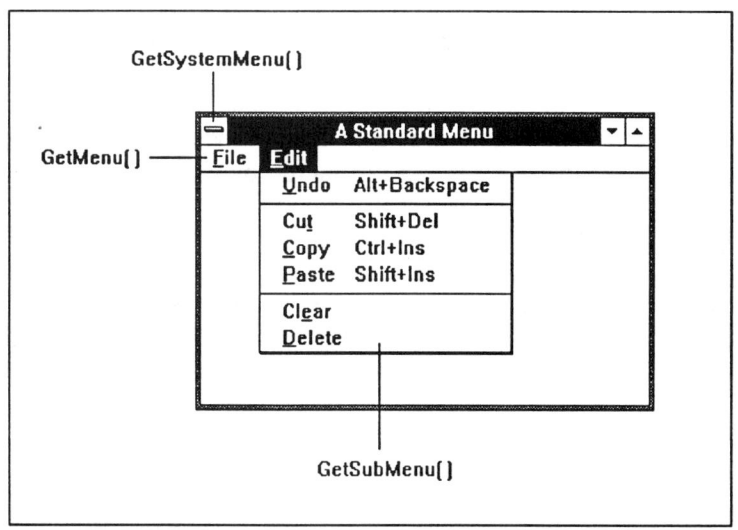

**Figure 11.10** Three query routines return menu handles

`hmenuTop = GetMenu (hwnd);`

Once you have the handle to a top-level menu, you get a handle to one of its popups by calling

`hmenu = GetSubMenu (hmenuTop, nPosition);`

where `nPosition` is the zero-based index of the popup in the top-level menu, or the index of a popup within another popup menu. Once you have a popup menu handle, it can be used with any of the menu modification routines to add, remove, or modify any item in the menu.

The **GetSystemMenu** routine has two uses to handle the special nature of the system menu. Most programs will use the default system menu, and so Windows only maintains a single copy. However, a copy is automatically created for a window if it calls **GetSystemMenu** like this:

`hmenuSys = GetSystemMenu (hwnd, 0);`

The zero in the second parameter tells the menu system to give you a handle to a private system menu that you can modify. If, after changing the system menu, you decide that you want to return to the original system menu, you make a call like this:

`hmenuSys = GetSystemMenu (hwnd, 1);`

A nonzero value in the second parameter attaches the default system menu to your window, which cannot be modified by you.

## 268   User Interface Objects

The other five query routines return menu attribute information. Figure 11.11 shows the specific attribute for four of the routines. To find out the number of items in a menu, you call

```
w = GetMenuItemCount (hMenu);
```

where hMenu is either a top-level menu handle or a popup menu handle. The number of items includes the vertical separators that appear in the menu. If you need to find out the result code for a menu item command, you can call

```
w = GetMenuItemID (hMenu, nPosition);
```

This routine can't tell you about a popup menu item, since they don't have result codes. If you ask for the result code for a popup menu, you get a -1. To find out the handle of a popup menu, you need to call **GetSubMenu**.

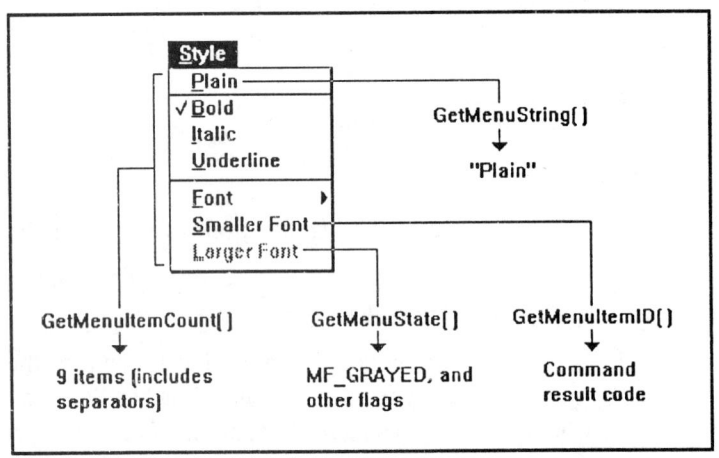

**Figure 11.11** Menu attributes that a program can query

Another menu query routine is **GetMenuState**, which tells you the current settings for various menu flags. If you want to test for a specific menu flag, you use the logical AND function. For example, this code fragment gets the flags for the menu command item that has a result code of 38, then checks to see if the menu item is grayed or not:

```
WORD wFlags;
...
wFlags = GetMenuState (hmenu, 38, MF_BYCOMMAND);
if (wFlags & MF_GRAYED)
    {
    .
    .
    .
```

Be careful when using this routine, however. All of the default flags (**MF_STRING**, **MF_UNHILITE**, **MF_ENABLED**, and **MF_UNCHECKED**) have a value of zero. You really can't test for them with the logical AND, since ANDing with zero always gives a result of zero. Instead, to test for any of the default flags, you need to check whether the flags that represent the opposite are present. For example, here is how to check whether or not a menu is enabled:

```
WORD wFlags
...
wFlags = GetMenuState (hmenu, 38, MF_BYCOMMAND);
if (!(wFlags & (MF_DISABLED | MF_GRAYED)))
    {
    .
    .
    .
```

If the disabled and grayed flags are not set, this conditional statement returns a value of true. While it may seem like an odd way to test for the presence of a flag, it is necessary because of the way that the default flag information is stored. Notice that the **GetMenuState** routine lets you choose between the **MF_BYCOMMAND** and **MF_BYPOSITION** flags for picking a specific menu item.

If you have a menu item that displays a string (as opposed to a separator, a bitmap, or an owner-draw item), you can retrieve a copy of the string by calling

```
cbSize = GetMenuString (hmenu, wID, lpBuff, bufsize, wFlag);
```

where hmenu is a menu handle, wID is either a command result code or the relative position of an item, lpBuff is a long pointer to a character buffer, bufsize is the buffer size, and wFlag is either **MF_BYCOMMAND** or **MF_BYPOSITION**. The return value, cbSize, is the number of bytes that were copied.

Our last menu query routine has perhaps the longest routine name in Windows: **GetMenuCheckMarkDimensions**. As indicated in Figure 11.12, this routine returns the width and height of a default menu check mark. This is useful for programs that wish to install custom check marks to replace the default check mark. In addition, a program can install a mark that is displayed when the menu item is *not* checked. This routine returns a four-byte value that must be split apart to yield the two size values:

```
DWORD dwCheck;
int cxWidth;
int cyHeight;
dwCheck  = GetMenuCheckMarkDimensions();
cxWidth  = LOWORD (dwCheck);
cyHeight = HIWORD (dwCheck);
```

As indicated in the code example, this routine takes no parameters.

There is one more category to look at that deals with tracking, which is the support of a popup menu outside a window's regular menu.

270   User Interface Objects

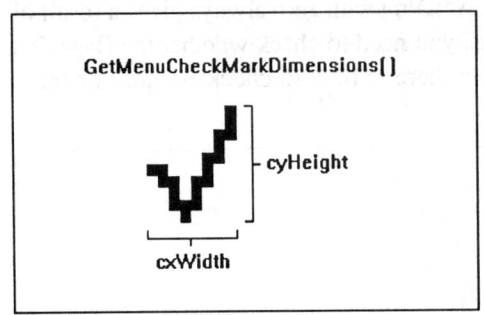

**Figure 11.12** Check-mark dimensions returned by GetMenuCheckMark

## Tracking

Our final category of menu routines is made up of a single routine that is used for menu tracking. This routine, `TrackPopupMenu`, allows a program to create a popup menu anywhere on the display screen. Menus that are not attached to a top-level menu are sometimes referred to as **tear-off** menus, since they look like regular popup menus, except that they can appear anywhere. `TrackPopupMenu` is defined as

```
BOOL TrackPopupMenu (hMenu, 0, x, y, 0, hWnd, 0L)
```

- **hMenu** is a handle to a popup menu.
- **x** is the *x* value of the upper-left corner of the menu, in screen coordinates.
- **y** is the *y* value of the upper-left corner of the menu, in screen coordinates.
- **hWnd** is a handle of the window to which the `WM_COMMAND` and other menu messages are sent.
- The second, fifth, and seventh parameters are reserved values and must be zero, as shown here.

An important point to keep in mind with this routine is that the popup menu is *not* positioned in client area coordinates but in **screen coordinates**. Like client area coordinates, screen coordinates are a pixel-based coordinate system. However, the origin (0,0) in screen coordinates is always the upper-left corner of the display screen. If you wish to put a popup menu in your client area, you must convert client area coordinates to screen coordinates. The `ClientToScreen` routine does this for you quite nicely. Here is how a left-button-up mouse message can be used to trigger a tear-off menu at the point where the user clicks the mouse:

```
case WM_LBUTTONUP:
    {
    HMENU hmenu;
    HMENU hmenuEdit;
    POINT pt;
    hmenu = GetMenu (hwnd);
    hmenuEdit = GetSubMenu (hmenu, 1);
    pt = MAKEPOINT (lParam);
    ClientToScreen(hwnd, &pt);
    TrackPopupMenu (hmenuEdit, /* Popup menu handle. */
                    0,         /* Reserved.          */
                    pt.x,      /* X-coordinate.      */
                    pt.y,      /* Y-coordinate.      */
                    0,         /* Reserved.          */
                    hwnd,      /* Hwnd to send msgs. */
                    0L);       /* Reserved.          */
    }
    break;
```

This code fragment makes the Edit menu from STANMENU appear anywhere in the client area.

The popup menu created by the **TrackPopupMenu** routine is just like a regular popup menu. An important difference, however, is that a **WM_INITMENUPOPUP** message is *not* sent before this menu is displayed. Instead, the only menu initialization message that you receive is the **WM_INITMENU** message.

The reason is that a tear-off menu created by **TrackPopupMenu** is treated as a top menu in a menu hierarchy. From the point of view of the menu system, then, it has equal status with the menu-bar menu displayed under a window's caption bar. The **WM_INITMENU** message is reserved for the initialization of all top-level menus, including the popup menu displayed by **TrackPopupMenu**. But if a tear-off menu created by **TrackPopupMenu** were to have any nested popup menus, a **WM_INITMENUPOPUP** message is sent to tell you to perform whatever initialization is required for these lower level, nested menus.

Although menus allow a program to show the user the commands that are available, some users prefer to enter keyboard commands. To help you give these users what they want, Windows supports the creation of keyboard accelerators. Keyboard accelerators provide a virtually seamless connection between keyboard input and menu commands. The connection is so good that accelerator commands even cause a menu item to be briefly illuminated to let the user know that a command has been selected. Let's take a look at the capabilities that are available with keyboard accelerators and see how they can be incorporated into a Windows program.

## Keyboard Accelerators

Keyboard accelerator support was one of the last pieces to be put in place when Microsoft was getting ready to ship the first version of Windows in 1985. Windows' original design called for a user interface that relied primarily on the mouse for command input. But after taking a second look at the existing base of computers—most of which didn't have a mouse—Microsoft had second thoughts. Another factor that strongly influenced their decision to put accelerator support into Windows was feedback from software developers who were considering the use of Windows for their applications. Some of the software developers had successful DOS programs that relied heavily on a keyboard interface, and they were concerned about the suitability of Windows for their products. Microsoft's response was to provide keyboard accelerators.

Keyboard accelerators tie together keyboard input and menu command selection. For users who don't have a mouse, or who prefer to use the keyboard to enter commands, accelerators link keystrokes with the creation of messages that match the menu messages we described earlier in this chapter. For programmers, this means that a minimum amount of effort is required to incorporate accelerator support in a Windows program.

Microsoft did such a good job of creating accelerator support that programmers usually think of accelerators as little more than an extension to the menu system. In fact, it is a separate part of Windows that can support commands that have no menu equivalent. Carried to an extreme, you could even write programs that rely *solely* on accelerator keystrokes for command input, and which make no use of menus. Of course, you probably won't want to do this since the presence of *both* menus and accelerators makes for a very flexible user interface.

In Chapter 15, when we discuss keyboard input, you'll see that keyboard input goes through a *two-step* translation process. Keyboard hardware generates **scan codes** to report keyboard activity. In fact, every key on the keyboard has *two* scan codes: one that says the key is being pressed and another that says the key is being released. A scan code lets the keyboard hardware report that a change has taken place. In general, scan codes are not interesting to most programs since they are too low-level to work with, and because Windows' keyboard driver translates scan codes into more useful information.

The first translation process converts scan codes into **virtual key codes**. Virtual key codes get us one step closer to character information, but they don't distinguish, for example, between a capital "A" and a lowercase "a." This is because virtual key codes don't represent characters, but keyboard keys. From the point of view of accelerators, virtual key codes are the most useful way to think about keyboard input. After all, when a user enters a keyboard command such as [Ctrl]+[A], it should have the same effect whether or not the [Caps Lock] key is active. In other words, there shouldn't be a difference between [Ctrl]+[A] (capital "A") and [Ctrl]+[a] (lowercase"a").

The second translation process converts virtual key codes into the extended ASCII character set that Windows supports. Programs that wish to receive character input—such as a word processor—are most interested in ASCII characters and ignore scan codes and virtual key codes. From the point of view of accelerators, a program *can* incorporate ASCII characters as accelerators. But this could be very limiting, for example, to a word processing program if certain letters were command keys and not interpreted as data. Of course, if you're writing a program that uses keyboard input *only* for command input, there is no reason not to use ASCII characters.

Windows lets you define accelerator keys using either virtual key code information or ASCII characters. Virtual keys are the more common type of accelerator, because they do not rely on the state of shift keys, such as the [Caps Lock] key. But if you wish to create a case-sensitive command key, then ASCII character accelerators are what you need.

For a program to get access to accelerators, an accelerator table must be created. Programs can have more than one accelerator table, but only one can be active at any moment. Acclerator tables are created by making an entry in a program's resource file using the **ACCELERATORS** keyword. As shown in Figure 11.13, the Resource Workshop has a built-in accelerator editor which makes it easy to create an accelerator table. Or, you can use a text editor to create your accelerator definitions.

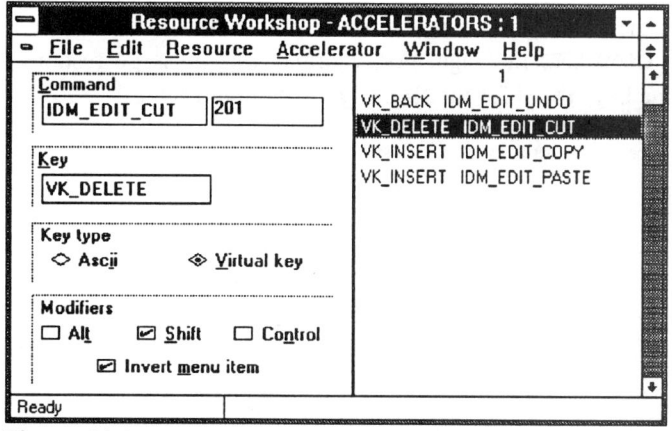

**Figure 11.13** The Resource Workshop's Accelerator Editor

Here's a template showing the two basic types of accelerator table entries. Each line in the table represents a different keyboard accelerator:

```
table-name ACCELERATORS
    {
    <key>,<cmd>,VIRTKEY,   [,NOINVERT][,ALT][,SHIFT][,CONTROL]
    <key>,<cmd>,ASCII      [,NOINVERT][,ALT][,SHIFT][,CONTROL]
    }
```

- `<key>` is the key, either text in quotes, "A," or a virtual key constant from WINDOWS.H, like `VK_F1`. It can also be a numeric value, like `58` or `0x6C`.
- `<cmd>` is the command result code to be included with the `WM_COMMAND` message to notify a program that an accelerator key combination has been pressed.
- `VIRTKEY` specifies that the value of `<key>` represents a virtual key code.
- `ASCII` specifies that `<key>` is an ASCII key code.
- `NOINVERT` inhibits the automatic highlighting of the related menu command.
- `ALT` indicates that an accelerator uses the [Alt] key.
- `SHIFT` indicates that an accelerator uses the [Shift] key.
- `CONTROL` indicates that an accelerator uses the [Ctrl] key.

Here is an example of an accelerator table containing only ASCII values:

```
AscKeys ACCELERATORS
    {
    "A", 25, ASCII
    "a", 26, ASCII
    "1", 27, ASCII
    }
```

The command result code is the value sent to the window procedure in the **wParam** parameter as part of the `WM_COMMAND` message. For example, this message response function traps and processes the keystrokes for the `AscKeys` accelerator table:

```
void TSampleWindow::WMCommand(TMessage& Msg)
    {
    switch (COMMANDMSG(msg))
        {
        case 25:
            .
            .
        case 26:
            .
            .
        case 27:
            .
            .
        }
    }
```

This approach would allow you to write a program that uses regular character values as commands. Notice, though, that the use of ASCII makes your commands case sensitive. The capital A command is created when either the [Shift] key is pressed *or* [Caps Lock] is on. As you're probably aware, when both keys are active, they cancel each other out, to create lowercase letters.

Instead of using ASCII accelerators, most programs use virtual key code accelerators. Virtual key codes let you define accelerators in a case-insensitive fashion. They also allow

*Commands: Menu and Accelerator Basics*   275

you to combine keys with any combination of the [Alt], [Shift], and [Ctrl] keys. Here is another accelerator table showing how virtual key accelerators can be defined:

```
VirtKeys ACCELERATORS
    {
    "A",    35, VIRTKEY, CONTROL
    VK_F1,  36, VIRTKEY
    VK_F8,  37, VIRTKEY, ALT, CONTROL, SHIFT
    }
```

This table defines three virtual key accelerators: [Ctrl]+[A], [F1], and [Alt]+[Ctrl]+[Shift]+[F8]. Because virtual key codes are tied to keyboard *keys* and not ASCII code values, the [Ctrl]+[A] accelerator ignores the state of the [Caps Lock] key. For this reason, virtual key accelerators are less confusing to the user. The second accelerator in this table causes the [F1] function key to send a **WM_COMMAND** message with a value of 36 in the **wParam** parameter. The last accelerator in this table shows that an accelerator can be defined using all three shift keys: [Alt], [Ctrl], and [Shift]. Of course, it's probably *not* a good idea to use all three shift keys in a single accelerator, since you'd be asking your user to press four keys simultaneously just to make a command selection. Of course, if you *do* need this capability, you will sleep better at night knowing that it's available.

Certain key combinations should not be used as accelerator keys. Some of them are shown in this accelerator table:

```
AvoidThese ACCELERATORS
    {
    VK_TAB,      99, VIRTKEY, ALT       ; switch programs
    VK_SPACE,   100, VIRTKEY, ALT       ; system menu
    VK_F10,     101, VIRTKEY            ; menu hot key
    VK_F4,      102, VIRTKEY, ALT       ; close window
    VK_ESCAPE,  103, VIRTKEY, CONTROL   ; get task list
    VK_ESCAPE,  104, VIRTKEY, ALT       ; switch programs

    VK_MENU,    105, VIRTKEY            ; Alt key
    VK_SHIFT,   106, VIRTKEY            ; Shift key
    VK_CONTROL, 107, VIRTKEY            ; Control key

    VK_DELETE,  108, VIRTKEY, CONTROL, ALT  ; Reboot!
    }
```

The first set of accelerator definitions are key combinations that are reserved for Windows' use. If you create an accelerator key for one of them, you will prevent that key combination from playing its standard role in the user interface. The second set of accelerator keys involves the use of the [Alt], [Shift], and [Ctrl] keys alone. The keyboard accelerator system ignores these keys when used alone, since they are reserved for use with other keys. The very last accelerator key in this table needs no further explanation other than to say that you will never use it as an accelerator key command.

You'll want to avoid another set of accelerator key combinations, except when you need them for the actions for which they are reserved. [Shift]+[Del], for example, is reserved for the *Edit/Cut* menu item, a standard menu item for programs that use the clipboard. Table

11.5 summarizes these reserved accelerator keys and describes the use of each. From this set, you can see that the number of reserved accelerator keys is small and that you are left with a very wide range of keyboard combinations to choose from.

**Table 11.5** Reserved accelerator key combinations

| Key Combination | Description |
| --- | --- |
| Alt + Backspace | Edit / Undo menu item. |
| Shift + Del | Edit / Cut menu item to remove an item to the clipboard. |
| Ctrl + Ins | Edit / Copy to place a copy of an item on the clipboard. |
| Shift + Ins | Edit / Paste to copy the contents of the clipboard into a document. |
| Del | Edit / Clear or Edit / Delete to remove data without affecting the contents of the clipboard. |
| F1 | Help. |
| F6 | Switch to a different panel in a split window. |
| Ctrl + F6 | Switch to a different window under the multiple document interface. |

If you are creating a Windows program that may someday be translated for use in a different language, you will probably want to avoid creating any accelerators that combine [Alt] with a letter key, for example, [Alt] + [A.] Such accelerators create the possibility of a conflict with mnemonic keystrokes. As we discussed earlier, a mnemonic keystroke lets the user strike [Alt] + a letter key to call up a popup menu. If an accelerator is defined for such a keystroke, like [Alt] + [A], and a popup menu uses the letter as a mnemonic, the mnemonic is disabled because accelerator key combinations have a higher priority.

At first glance, you might think that the solution would be simply to avoid creating accelerators that conflict with mnemonic letters. Consider a program with two popups: File and Edit. If [Alt]+[F] and [Alt]+[E] are the only two mnemonic keystrokes that the program uses, you might think that you can use [Alt]+[T] without any problem. But when the time comes for you to convert your product to be used in Finland, where the word for file is "Tiedosto," you will find that your accelerator, [Alt]+[T], has collided with the most obvious mnemonic for this menu. See Figure 11.14 for an example of how a Finnish program might appear.

As you can see from looking at this program, either an [Alt]+[T] or [Alt]+[M] accelerator would collide with the mnemonics in the Finnish version of our program for the File

(Tiedosto) or Edit (Muokkaus) menus. The easiest way to avoid this problem is simply to avoid creating accelerator keys that consist of [Alt] and a letter key alone.

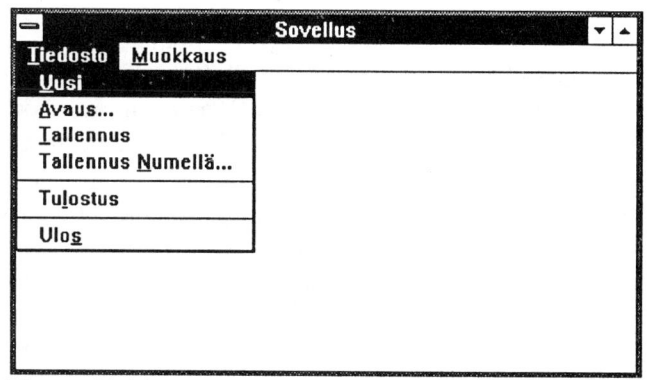

**Figure 11.14** A sample Finnish program

Once an accelerator table has been defined in the resource file, bringing it into a program requires a call to the **LoadAccelerators** routine. This is defined as

HANDLE LoadAccelerators (hInstance, lpTableName)

- **hInstance** is an instance handle passed to a program as a parameter to **WinMain**.
- **lpTableName** is a long pointer to a character string containing the name of an accelerator table in the program's resource file.

The return value is a handle to an accelerator table, which identifies the specific set of accelerator keystrokes to be used. You would load an accelerator table named VIRTKEYS as shown here:

HANDLE hAccel;
hAccel = LoadAccelerators (hInstance, "VIRTKEYS");

Just like other resources (such as the menus described earlier), a numeric value can be used to identify an accelerator table, as in

```
23 ACCELERATORS
    {
    "A",   35, VIRTKEY, CONTROL
     .
     .
    }
```

To load this accelerator table into memory, you would make a call like this:

hAccel = LoadAccelerators (hInstance, "#23");

278    User Interface Objects

Or, the **MAKEINTRESOURCE** macro can be used to package the value in another way so that it is recognized as a numeric identifier:

```
hAccel=LoadAccelerators(hInstance,MAKEINTRESOURCE(23));
```

Once an accelerator table has been loaded, using it requires calling **TranslateAccelerator** in a message loop. Since the OWL application object already calls this routine for us, you don't need to know too much about it. If you're curious about the details, though, you can learn about **TranslateAccelerator** in the accompanying boxed discussion.

Accelerator keys generate the same messages as a corresponding menu selection. In particular, the **WM_COMMAND** message brings the command to a window object. As with menu commands, you can create a single message response function to handle all **WM_COMMAND** messages. Or, you can create a different message response function for each command. If you do, be sure to use the **CM_FIRST** value as the first command function index.

---

### Acclerator Translation

Acclerator keystrokes are automatically translated into their menu equivalents by the **TranslateAccelerator** routine, when it is embedded in a program's message loop. The OWL application object already calls this routine for us, in its message loop. **TranslateAccelerator** is defined as

```
int TranslateAccelerator (hWnd, haccTable, lpMsg)
```

- **hWnd** is a handle of the window that is to receive the command and menu control messages created by keyboard accelerators. This window will normally have a menu attached, so that menu and accelerator support can be seamlessly integrated.
- **haccTable** is a handle to an accelerator table loaded with the **LoadAccelerators** routine.
- **lpMsg** is a long pointer to an **MSG** data structure.

The most common way to use accelerators is to modify the standard **GetMessage** loop in your **WinMain** function. Here is the standard **GetMessage** loop:

```
while (GetMessage(&msg, 0, 0, 0))
    {
    TranslateMessage(&msg);   /* Keyboard input. */
    DispatchMessage(&msg);
    }
```

TranslateAccelerator can check the message traffic received by **GetMessage** and convert it to the appropriate menu messages. If it performs a translation, it provides a return code of TRUE. Otherwise, the return code is FALSE. Here is the most common way to incorporate this routine into a standard message loop:

```
while (GetMessage(&msg, 0, 0, 0))
    {
    if (!TranslateAccelerator(hwnd, hAccel, &msg))
        {
        TranslateMessage(&msg);    /*  Kbd input. */
        DispatchMessage(&msg);
        }
    }
```

If **TranslateAccelerator** does not find an accelerator, it returns a value of FALSE. This causes the message to be handled normally by **TranslateMessage** and **DispatchMessage**. Otherwise, if an accelerator was found, then no other steps are required by the **GetMessage** loop, since it is handled entirely by **TranslateAccelerator**.

Here is a complete program that shows how an accelerator table can be implemented. This program is built on the standard menu program we introduced at the beginning of this chapter, STANMENU. We have added the four standard accelerators that support the standard clipboard operations: *undo*, *cut*, *copy*, and *paste*.

# MAKEFILE.MAK

```
.AUTODEPEND

#    Translator Definitions
INC=\BORLANDC\OWL\INCLUDE;\BORLANDC\CLASSLIB\INCLUDE;\BORLANDC\INCLUDE
CC = bcc -c -D_CLASSDLL -H -ml -WS -w -I$(INC)

#    Implicit Rules
.c.obj:
  $(CC) {$< }

.cpp.obj:
  $(CC) {$< }

#    Explicit Rules
Accel.exe: Accel.res Accel.def Accel.obj
    tlink /c/C/n/P-/Twe/x @Accel.LNK
    rlink Accel.res Accel.exe

#    Individual File Dependencies
Accel.obj: Accel.cpp

Accel.res: Accel.rc Accel.cur Accel.ico
    brcc -FO Accel.res -i$(INC) Accel.RC
```

# ACCEL.LNK

```
\borlandc\lib\c0wl.obj+
Accel.obj
Accel,Accel
\borlandc\classlib\lib\tclasdll.lib+
\borlandc\owl\lib\owl.lib+
mathwl.lib+
import.lib+
crtldll.lib
Accel.def
```

# ACCEL.CPP

```cpp
/*----------------------------------------------------------*\
 |  ACCEL.CPP    Demo showing creation of keyboard accelerators.  |
\*----------------------------------------------------------*/
#include <owl.h>
#include "Accel.H"

#define COMMANDMSG(arg) (arg.WParam)

/*----------------------------------------------------------*\
 |                  Class Declarations.                      |
\*----------------------------------------------------------*/
class TAccelApplication : public TApplication
   {
   public:
     TAccelApplication (LPSTR lpszName, HINSTANCE hInstance,
                        HINSTANCE hPrevInstance,
                        LPSTR lpszCmdLine, int nCmdShow);
     virtual void InitMainWindow ();
   };

class TAccelWindow : public TWindow
   {
    public:
     TAccelWindow (PTWindowsObject pwParent, LPSTR lpszTitle,
                   PTModule pmModule);
     virtual LPSTR GetClassName ();
     virtual void  GetWindowClass (WNDCLASS&);
     virtual void  WMCommand(TMessage& Msg) = [WM_COMMAND];
   };

/*----------------------------------------------------------*\
 |              Main Function:  WinMain.                     |
\*----------------------------------------------------------*/
int PASCAL WinMain (HINSTANCE hInstance,   HINSTANCE hPrevInstance,
                   LPSTR   lpszCmdLine, int    nCmdShow)
    {
    TAccelApplication Accel ("Accel", hInstance,
                             hPrevInstance, lpszCmdLine,
                             nCmdShow);
    Accel.Run();
    return Accel.Status;
    }
```

```
/*----------------------------------------------------------------*\
|                  Application Class Member.                        |
\*----------------------------------------------------------------*/
TAccelApplication::TAccelApplication (LPSTR lpszName,
                   HINSTANCE hInstance, HINSTANCE hPrevInstance,
                   LPSTR lpszCmdLine, int nCmdShow)
                :TApplication (lpszName, hInstance,
                   hPrevInstance, lpszCmdLine, nCmdShow)
    {
    HAccTable = LoadAccelerators (hInstance, "#1");
    }

/*----------------------------------------------------------------*\
|                  Application Class Member.                        |
\*----------------------------------------------------------------*/
 void TAccelApplication::InitMainWindow ()
    {
    MainWindow = new TAccelWindow (NULL, "Accelerators", NULL);
    }

/*----------------------------------------------------------------*\
|                  TAccelWindow Class Member.                       |
\*----------------------------------------------------------------*/
TAccelWindow::TAccelWindow (PTWindowsObject pwParent,
            LPSTR lpszTitle, PTModule pmModule)
         :TWindow (pwParent, lpszTitle, pmModule)
    {
    /* Window specific initialization goes here. */
    }

/*----------------------------------------------------------------*\
|                  TAccelWindow Class Member.                       |
\*----------------------------------------------------------------*/
LPSTR TAccelWindow::GetClassName ()
    {
    return "Accel:MAIN";
    }

/*----------------------------------------------------------------*\
|                  TAccelWindow Class Member.                       |
\*----------------------------------------------------------------*/
void TAccelWindow::GetWindowClass (WNDCLASS& wc)
    {
    TWindow::GetWindowClass (wc);
    wc.hIcon=LoadIcon (wc.hInstance, "snapshot");
    wc.hCursor=LoadCursor (wc.hInstance, "hand");
    wc.lpszMenuName = "#1";
    }

/*----------------------------------------------------------------*\
|                  TAccelWindow Class Member.                       |
\*----------------------------------------------------------------*/
void TAccelWindow::WMCommand(TMessage& Msg)
    {
    char buffer[80];

    if (COMMANDMSG(Msg) == IDM_FILE_EXIT)
        SendMessage (HWindow, WM_SYSCOMMAND, SC_CLOSE, 0L);
    else
        {
        wsprintf (buffer, "Command = %d", COMMANDMSG(Msg));
        MessageBox (HWindow, buffer, "WM_COMMAND", MB_OK);
        }
    }
```

282  User Interface Objects

# ACCEL.RC

```
#include <Windows.H>
#include "Accel.h"

snapshot icon Accel.ico

hand cursor Accel.cur
1 MENU
    {
    POPUP "&File"
        {
        MENUITEM "&New",          IDM_FILE_NEW
        MENUITEM "&Open...",      IDM_FILE_OPEN
        MENUITEM "&Save",         IDM_FILE_SAVE
        MENUITEM "Save &As...",   IDM_FILE_SAVEAS
        MENUITEM SEPARATOR
        MENUITEM "&Print",        IDM_FILE_PRINT
        MENUITEM SEPARATOR
        MENUITEM "E&xit",         IDM_FILE_EXIT
        }
    POPUP "&Edit"
        {
        MENUITEM "&Undo\tAlt+Backspace", IDM_EDIT_UNDO
        MENUITEM SEPARATOR
        MENUITEM "Cu&t\tShift+Del",     IDM_EDIT_CUT
        MENUITEM "&Copy\tCtrl+Ins",     IDM_EDIT_COPY
        MENUITEM "&Paste\tShift+Ins",   IDM_EDIT_PASTE
        MENUITEM SEPARATOR
        MENUITEM "Cl&ear",              IDM_EDIT_CLEAR
        MENUITEM "&Delete",             IDM_EDIT_DELETE
        }
    }

1 ACCELERATORS
    {
    VK_BACK,    IDM_EDIT_UNDO,  VIRTKEY, ALT
    VK_DELETE,  IDM_EDIT_CUT,   VIRTKEY, SHIFT
    VK_INSERT,  IDM_EDIT_COPY,  VIRTKEY, CONTROL
    VK_INSERT,  IDM_EDIT_PASTE, VIRTKEY, SHIFT
    }
```

# ACCEL.DEF

```
NAME ACCEL

EXETYPE WINDOWS

DESCRIPTION 'Accel - Sample Accelerator'

CODE MOVEABLE DISCARDABLE
DATA MOVEABLE MULTIPLE

HEAPSIZE 512
STACKSIZE 5120
```

All of the accelerator processing in our code is done in our application object's constructor function, **TAccelApplication**. This function loads the accelerator table into memory. The message loop in the OWL application object has built-in accelerator keyboard support. In particular, the **TranslateAccelerator** routine scans for accelerator keys and diverts the flow of messages as appropriate.

You may have also noticed that, instead of using numeric constants in our resource file, we have defined a set of symbolic constants in an include file, ACCEL.H. This allows you to use a more meaningful value, like `IDM_NEW`, instead of "magic numbers" that can't explain what they are used for. With the set of values defined in the include file, both the resource file and our C source files can access this file with the familiar include statement:

```
#include "Accel.H"
```

Windows gives you a comprehensive set of menu creation and management routines and lets you create accelerator keystrokes to define keyboard commands. It communicates via messages each action taken by the user with menus. The menu system is robust, fast, and flexible. You can create static menu templates, build menus on the fly, or change any part of an existing menu.

In the next chapter, we're going to see how we can get a little more sparkle out of our menus by adding graphics. We're going to explore three techniques to allow us to use GDI drawing routines to change the appearance of menu items: owner-draw menu items, bitmaps in menus, and custom check marks.

# 12

# Enhancing Menus with Graphics

Windows uses the system font, a bold, Helvetica-like, proportionally spaced font, to draw the text inside menus. This default font was chosen because it is easy to read and has a slick, modern look. However, there may be times when you want to use another font inside a menu. Or, you might want to create a menu that contains geometric figures or graphic images. When you want to do this, Windows lets you hook into its menu creation mechanism so that you can enhance the look of your menus with graphical objects. In this chapter, we're going to look at three methods that are available to you: owner-draw menu items, bitmaps in menus, and custom check marks.

## Owner-Draw Menu Items

All of the menus that we've created up to now have used a text label drawn with the system font. For most applications, this is a reasonable approach to take. But there may be times when you wish to replace the text with a graphic object. Or, you may wish to change the font that is used. Owner-draw menu items give you the ability to create graphical menu images using GDI drawing calls. Thus, instead of just *telling* users what a menu item will produce, you can *show* them. A drawing program might use this capability to show the user the different lines, shapes, and fonts that are available. A flowchart program might put different flowchart elements into menus to provide instant feedback on which flowchart elements are available.

Because the resource compiler does not provide any support for owner-draw menu items, you have to dynamically create the menu items by calling one of the menu modification routines we discussed in the last chapter. If you want an owner-draw menu item to appear in your menu the first time your window appears, you'll probably want to add the menu item in response to the **WM_CREATE** message. You won't be able to add owner-draw menu items at window object creation time (i.e., in your window object constructor) since the MS-Windows window hasn't been created yet.

After an owner-draw menu item has been inserted into a menu, two messages will be sent to the window procedure to measure and draw the menu item: **WM_MEASUREITEM** and **WM_DRAWITEM**. The **WM_MEASUREITEM** message arrives before the menu item is ever drawn. Your program must respond to this message by filling in a data structure that describes the width and height of your menu item in pixels. The second message, **WM_DRAWITEM**, is sent whenever drawing is needed for the menu item. Drawing is needed when a menu is displayed and when the menu item is highlighted to provide the user with visual feedback while menu items are browsed.

Before we look at the handling of these two messages in detail, it's worth mentioning that these two messages are also sent for the other types of owner-draw objects: buttons, comboboxes, and listboxes. As you'll see, there are elements of the owner-draw mechanism, intended for use with the other owner-draw objects, that can be safely ignored when dealing with owner-draw menu items. As we look at each part of this mechanism, we'll be sure to identify these elements for you.

## The WM_MEASUREITEM Message

An owner-draw item can be as small or as large as you would like to make it. The **WM_MEASUREITEM** message provides a way for you to let the menu system know the exact size that you need to draw the menu item. The units are in pixels, but since you're going to use GDI routines to draw, you can use GDI's coordinate mapping system.

When calculating the size of the area that you'll need in an owner-draw menu item, you need to take into account space for a margin around the menu item. For one thing, you'll want to allow enough space between your menu item and other menu items. It's also a good idea to reserve space for a check mark on the left side of your menu. You can call the **GetMenuCheckMarkDimensions** routine for information about the default width and height of a check mark. Even if you don't use a check mark for your owner-draw menu item, you'll still want to do this. The width of a check mark is the standard left margin of a menu item; using this value will help give your owner-draw menu items a consistent look with normal menu items.

To accommodate the higher resolution of devices that we may see some day, it's a good idea to avoid hard-coding any specific sizes for owner-draw menu items. Instead, you should make your drawing relative to the size of system objects, because they are automatically scaled for different device resolutions. Icons are a type of system object that can serve as a good reference point for owner-draw menu items. Icon dimensions are determined by the system display device driver. To determine the dimensions of an icon, you call **GetSystemMetrics**. If you wanted to make your menu items the same size as an icon, here's how you could do it:

```
DWORD dwCheckMark;
int cxWidth, cyHeight;

cxWidth  = GetSystemMetrics (SM_CXICON); /* Width.  */
cyHeight = GetSystemMetrics (SM_CYICON); /* Height. */

/* Adjust for check mark.  */
dwCheckMark = GetMenuCheckMarkDimensions();
cxWidth  +=      LOWORD(dwCheckMark);
cyHeight = max (HIWORD(dwCheckMark), cyHeight);
```

We add a value for the width of the check mark, and we also update `cyHeight` to make sure that it can accommodate the height of a check mark.

As an alternative, you can base the size of your owner-draw items on the metrics of the system font. When we discuss dialog boxes in Chapter 14, you'll see that the dialog box manager uses this approach to provide device-independent **dialog box coordinates**. To calculate the dimensions of an owner-draw menu item that is twice as tall as the system font, and which has a width equal to that of 15 characters, you can say

```
DWORD dwCheckMark;
HDC hdc
int cxWidth, cyHeight;
TEXTMETRIC tm;

hdc = GetDC (hwnd);
GetTextMetrics (hdc, &tm);
ReleaseDC (hwnd, hdc);

cxWidth  = tm.tmMaxCharWidth * 15;
cyHeight = tm.tmHeight * 2;

/* Adjust for check mark. */
dwCheckMark = GetMenuCheckMarkDimensions();
cxWidth  +=      LOWORD(dwCheckMark);
cyHeight = max (HIWORD(dwCheckMark), cyHeight);
```

The **GetTextMetrics** routine, which we first discussed in Chapter 10, gets the metrics of the font that is currently installed in a DC. In the absence of special window class styles (discussed in Chapter 13), **GetDC** returns a DC with the system font installed. As in the earlier example, this code includes the dimensions of a menu check mark in the overall dimensions of the owner-draw item.

Whichever method you choose, one **WM_MEASUREITEM** message is sent for each owner-draw menu item. When it arrives, the **lParam** parameter contains a long pointer to a structure of type **MEASUREITEMSTRUCT**. This structure is defined in WINDOWS.H as

```
typedef struct tagMEASUREITEMSTRUCT
  {
    WORD    CtlType;     /* ODT_MENU              */
    WORD    CtlID;       /* Ignore for menus.     */
    WORD    itemID;
    WORD    itemWidth;   /* Return width.         */
    WORD    itemHeight;  /* Return height.        */
    DWORD   itemData;
  } MEASUREITEMSTRUCT;
```

When you get a **WM_MEASUREITEM** message, the two fields that you use to return the width and height of your owner-draw item are **itemWidth** and **itemHeight**. The other fields in this data structure help you identify a specific owner-draw item, since you will have one **WM_MEASUREITEM** message for each owner-draw menu item that you have. When working with owner-draw menu items, one of these fields can be ignored since it's only used for owner-draw dialog box controls: **CtlID**.

The **CtlType** field describes the type of owner-draw item. It is set to **ODT_MENU** for menus. The presence of this field means a single body of code can support owner-draw objects in menus, listboxes, or comboboxes.

**itemID** is the command result code for a menu item. It is the value that gets sent in the wParam parameter of a **WM_COMMAND** message. As we'll see in a moment, this value is set when a menu item is created.

The **itemData** field provides another way to identify an owner-draw menu item. It is a 32-bit field that you create and provide when you create an owner-draw menu item. When you create an owner-draw popup menu (as opposed to a regular command menu item), this field provides the only way to distinguish one owner-draw popup menu from another, since popup menu items do not have a command result code.

If you create an owner-draw menu item by calling **AppendMenu** like this:

```
AppendMenu (hmenu, MF_OWNERDRAW, 38, (LPSTR)200);
```

it creates a menu item with an **itemID** of 38 and an **itemData** value of 200. The last parameter is cast as an **LPSTR** because that is how this routine is prototyped. Otherwise, the compiler issues an unnecessary warning message. If the variables **cxWidth** and **cyHeight** contained the desired dimensions of this menu item, we could respond to the **WM_MEASUREITEM** message like this:

```
case WM_MEASUREITEM:
    {
    LPMEASUREITEMSTRUCT lpmi;

    lpmi = (LPMEASUREITEMSTRUCT)lParam;
```

```
        if (lpmi->itemID == 38)
            {
            lpmi->itemWidth  = cxWidth;
            lpmi->itemHeight = cyHeight;
            }
```

Another approach involves checking **itemData** for the specific owner-draw menu item:

```
case WM_MEASUREITEM:
    {
    LPMEASUREITEMSTRUCT lpmi;

    lpmi = (LPMEASUREITEMSTRUCT)lParam;

    if (lpmi->itemData == 200)
        {
        lpmi->itemWidth  = cxWidth;
        lpmi->itemHeight = cyHeight;
        }
    }
```

A program only receives a single **WM_MEASUREITEM** message for each owner-draw item. After that, the menu system remembers the dimensions of the menu item and sends a **WM_DRAWITEM** message whenever it needs a menu item to be drawn.

## The WM_DRAWITEM Message

A **WM_DRAWITEM** message is sent to your window procedure when a popup menu is opened that contains an owner-draw menu item. Then, as the user browses through a menu, this message is sent to toggle menu highlighting. As you'll see in a moment, the **WM_DRAWITEM** message provides flags that let you know the effect that the menu system requires.

When the **WM_DRAWITEM** message is sent, the window procedure's lParam parameter contains a long pointer to a structure of type **DRAWITEMSTRUCT**, defined in WINDOWS.H as follows:

```
typedef struct tagDRAWITEMSTRUCT
    {
    WORD    CtlType;    /* ODT_MENU.                 */
    WORD    CtlID;      /* Ignore for menus.         */
    WORD    itemID;
    WORD    itemAction; /* Ignore for menus.         */
    WORD    itemState;  /* Selected, grayed, checked.*/
    HWND    hwndItem;   /* Handle to popup menu.     */
    HDC     hDC;
```

290  User Interface Objects

```
    RECT    rcItem;      /* Bounding rectangle.        */
    DWORD   itemData;
} DRAWITEMSTRUCT;
```

Four of the items in this data structure are identical to items in the data structure that is sent with the **WM_MEASUREITEM** message: `CtlType`, `CtlID`, `itemID`, and `itemData`.

The `CtlType` field describes the type of owner-draw item. It is set to **ODT_MENU** for menus.

The `CtlID` field can be ignored for owner-draw menu items, since it is only used for owner-draw dialog box controls.

`itemID` is the command result code for a menu item, which is the value sent to a window procedure in the `wParam` parameter of a **WM_COMMAND** message.

The `itemData` field provides another way to identify an owner-draw menu item and is the only way to distinguish one owner-draw popup menu from another.

The `itemAction` field describes the action the menu system wants you to perform. However, since menu items are drawn to reflect the menu item state, you can usually ignore this field and determine the menu state from the next field.

The `itemState` field defines the current state of the menu item, as shown here:

| Value | Menu Item State |
|---|---|
| ODS_CHECKED | Check mark is to appear in the menu. |
| ODS_DISABLED | Menu to be drawn disabled. |
| ODS_FOCUS | Ignore—not used for menus. |
| ODS_GRAYED | Menu to be drawn grayed. |
| ODS_SELECTED | Menu to be drawn selected. |

The most important flag is **ODS_SELECTED**. When this bit is set, it indicates that the menu item needs to be highlighted. A highlighted menu item is drawn in a different color from a regular menu item to provide visual feedback while the user is browsing a menu. You should draw highlighted menu items using two system colors that are defined for this purpose. To obtain the RGB values of the required system colors, call the **GetSysColor** routine. Here are the color indices that you should use for menu highlights:

| Value | Description |
|---|---|
| COLOR_HIGHLIGHT | Background color of the highlighted object. |
| COLOR_HIGHLIGHTTEXT | Foreground color of the highlighted object. |

If you plan to set the state of an owner-draw menu item to checked, or if you plan to gray the menu item, your response to the **WM_DRAWITEM** message must provide for this. You will need to test the value in the `itemState` field and change the way you draw your menu item according to the desired effect. For example, you might use a shade of gray in your drawing to indicate a grayed menu item. You can draw a check mark using a bitmap that is built into the display driver. Here is one way to obtain a handle to that bitmap, and draw with it:

```
hbm = LoadBitmap (NULL,MAKEINTRESOURCE(OBM_CHECK));
hdcBitmap = CreateCompatibleDC (hDC);
hbmOld = SelectBitmap (hdcBitmap, hbm);

dwDimensions = GetMenuCheckMarkDimensions();
cxWidth  = LOWORD(dwDimensions);
cyHeight = HIWORD(dwDimensions);

BitBlt (ps.hdc, 0, 0, cxWidth, cyHeight,
        hdcBitmap, 0, 0, SRCCOPY);

SelectBitmap (hdcBitmap, hbmOld);
DeleteDC (hdcBitmap);
```

In spite of its name, the **hwndItem** field is not a window handle but instead is a popup menu handle for the menu that contains the owner-draw item. Its name comes from its use with owner-draw dialog box controls, when it does contain a window handle. When a program receives a **WM_DRAWITEM** message, it might wish to use the popup menu handle to call a menu query routine to find out, for example, the number of items that are in the current menu, or the state of other menu items.

The **hDC** field is a handle to a device context for drawing in the menu. Be sure to restore the DC to its initial state when you are done, otherwise you risk causing problems for the menu system when it draws other parts of your menu.

The **rcItem** field defines a rectangle within which you can draw your menu item. You should not go beyond this rectangle, since doing so risks overwriting other menu items.

The owner-draw items supported by these messages and data structures give a program a remarkable amount of flexibility in deciding how a menu item should appear. Let's look at a sample program that shows how to put these messages and data structures to work for you.

## *A Sample Program: OWNDRAW*

Our sample program, OWNDRAW, shows how owner-draw menu items can be used to display different fonts in a menu. The menu from OWNDRAW is shown in Figure 12.1. Not only is the user provided with the *name* of the font, but also with the *image* of the font itself. This would be a useful technique in any program that lets the user select a font. If you do this, you should keep in mind the fact that only display fonts can be used to draw in menus. Therefore, if you wish to show a user the printer fonts that are available, you would be limited in some cases to the name of the font. Of course, with the coming of TrueType font technology in a future version of Windows, the differences between display and printer fonts are going to be substantially reduced.

292    *User Interface Objects*

**Figure 12.1  An owner-drawn menu showing three fonts**

Here is the source listing of OWNDRAW. To write this program, we used the STANMENU program as a base and added the items needed for our owner-draw items.

# MAKEFILE.MAK

```
.AUTODEPEND

#    Translator Definitions
INC=\BORLANDC\OWL\INCLUDE;\BORLANDC\CLASSLIB\INCLUDE;\BORLANDC\INCLUDE
CC = bcc -c -D_CLASSDLL -H -ml -WS -w -I$(INC)

#    Implicit Rules
.c.obj:
  $(CC) {$< }

.cpp.obj:
  $(CC) {$< }

#    Explicit Rules
OwnDraw.exe: OwnDraw.res OwnDraw.def OwnDraw.obj
     tlink /c/C/n/P-/Twe/x @OwnDraw.LNK
     rlink OwnDraw.res OwnDraw.exe

#    Individual File Dependencies
OwnDraw.obj: OwnDraw.cpp

OwnDraw.res: OwnDraw.rc OwnDraw.cur OwnDraw.ico
     brcc -FO OwnDraw.res -i$(INC) OwnDraw.RC
```

# OWNDRAW.LNK

```
\borlandc\lib\cOwl.obj+
OwnDraw.obj
OwnDraw,OwnDraw
\borlandc\classlib\lib\tclasdll.lib+
\borlandc\owl\lib\owl.lib+
mathwl.lib+
import.lib+
crtldll.lib
OwnDraw.def
```

# OWNDRAW.CPP

```cpp
/*--------------------------------------------------------------*\
|  OWNDRAW.CPP - A sample owner draw menu.                       |
\*--------------------------------------------------------------*/
#define WIN31
#define STRICT
#include <owl.h>
#include <WindowsX.h>
#include "OwnDraw.H"

#define max(a,b)             (((a) > (b)) ? (a) : (b))
#define COMMANDMSG(arg) (arg.WParam)

/*--------------------------------------------------------------*\
|                   Class Declarations.                          |
\*--------------------------------------------------------------*/
class TOwnDrawApplication : public TApplication
   {
   public:
     TOwnDrawApplication (LPSTR lpszName, HINSTANCE hInstance,
                          HINSTANCE hPrevInstance, LPSTR lpszCmdLine,
                          int nCmdShow);
     virtual void InitMainWindow ();
   };

class TOwnDrawWindow : public TWindow
   {
   public:
     TOwnDrawWindow (PTWindowsObject pwParent, LPSTR lpszTitle,
             PTModule pmModule);
     ~TOwnDrawWindow();
     virtual LPSTR GetClassName ();
     virtual void GetWindowClass (WNDCLASS&);
     virtual void WMCommand(TMessage& Msg)= [WM_COMMAND];
     virtual void WMCreate(TMessage& Msg)= [WM_CREATE];
     virtual void WMDrawItem(TMessage& Msg)= [WM_DRAWITEM];
     virtual void WMMeasureItem (TMessage& Msg)= [WM_MEASUREITEM];
   private:
     HFONT hfontTmsRmn;
     HFONT hfontHelv;
     HFONT hfontCour;
     COLORREF crHighlight;
     COLORREF crHighlightText;
   };

/*--------------------------------------------------------------*\
|                   Main Function:  WinMain.                     |
\*--------------------------------------------------------------*/
int PASCAL WinMain (HINSTANCE hInstance,   HINSTANCE hPrevInstance,
                 LPSTR  lpszCmdLine, int    nCmdShow)
    {
    TOwnDrawApplication OwnDraw ("OwnDraw", hInstance,
                                 hPrevInstance, lpszCmdLine,
                                 nCmdShow);
    OwnDraw.Run();
    return OwnDraw.Status;
    }

/*--------------------------------------------------------------*\
|                   Application Class Member.                    |
\*--------------------------------------------------------------*/
```

## 294    User Interface Objects

```c
TOwnDrawApplication::TOwnDrawApplication (LPSTR lpszName,
                    HINSTANCE hInstance, HINSTANCE hPrevInstance,
                    LPSTR lpszCmdLine, int nCmdShow)
                :TApplication (lpszName, hInstance,
                    hPrevInstance, lpszCmdLine, nCmdShow)
    {
    /*  Application specific initialization goes here.  */
    }
/*----------------------------------------------------------------*\
|                   Application Class Member.                      |
\*----------------------------------------------------------------*/
void TOwnDrawApplication::InitMainWindow ()
    {
    MainWindow = new TOwnDrawWindow (NULL, "Owner Draw Menu",
                                     NULL);
    }


/*----------------------------------------------------------------*\
|                   TOwnDrawWindow Class Member.                   |
\*----------------------------------------------------------------*/
TOwnDrawWindow::TOwnDrawWindow (PTWindowsObject pwParent,
                LPSTR lpszTitle, PTModule pmModule)
            :TWindow (pwParent, lpszTitle, pmModule)
    {
    HDC         hdc;
    LOGFONT     lf;
    TEXTMETRIC  tm;

    /*
     * Create three logical fonts, with different
     * sizes and styles.
     */
    memset (&lf, 0, sizeof (LOGFONT));

    hdc = CreateDC ("DISPLAY", 0, 0, 0);
    GetTextMetrics (hdc, &tm);
    DeleteDC (hdc);


    // Font 1:  Bold Courier.
    lf.lfWeight = 700;
    lstrcpy ((LPSTR)&lf.lfFaceName[0], "Courier");
    lf.lfHeight = tm.tmHeight;
    hfontCour = CreateFontIndirect (&lf);

    // Font 2:  Times Roman
    lstrcpy ((LPSTR)&lf.lfFaceName[0], "Tms Rmn");
    lf.lfHeight = tm.tmHeight + tm.tmHeight/4;
    hfontTmsRmn = CreateFontIndirect (&lf);

    // Font 3:  Helv
    lstrcpy ((LPSTR)&lf.lfFaceName[0], "Helv");
    lf.lfHeight = tm.tmHeight + tm.tmHeight/2;
    hfontHelv = CreateFontIndirect (&lf);

    /*
     * Get system colors for our owner draw items.
     */
    crHighlight = GetSysColor (COLOR_HIGHLIGHT);
    crHighlightText = GetSysColor (COLOR_HIGHLIGHTTEXT);
    }
```

```
/*--------------------------------------------------------------*\
|                   TOwnDrawWindow Class Member.                 |
\*--------------------------------------------------------------*/
TOwnDrawWindow::~TOwnDrawWindow()
    {
    SelectFont (hfontTmsRmn);
    SelectFont (hfontHelv);
    SelectFont (hfontCour);
    }

/*--------------------------------------------------------------*\
|                   TOwnDrawWindow Class Member.                 |
\*--------------------------------------------------------------*/
LPSTR TOwnDrawWindow::GetClassName ()
    {
    return "OwnDraw:MAIN";
    }

/*--------------------------------------------------------------*\
|                   TOwnDrawWindow Class Member.                 |
\*--------------------------------------------------------------*/
void TOwnDrawWindow::GetWindowClass (WNDCLASS& wc)
    {
    TWindow::GetWindowClass (wc);
    wc.hIcon=LoadIcon (wc.hInstance, "snapshot");
    wc.hCursor=LoadCursor (wc.hInstance, "hand");
    wc.lpszMenuName = "#1";
    }

/*--------------------------------------------------------------*\
|                   TOwnDrawWindow Class Member.                 |
\*--------------------------------------------------------------*/
void TOwnDrawWindow::WMCommand(TMessage& Msg)
    {
    char buffer[80];

    if (COMMANDMSG(Msg) == IDM_FILE_EXIT)
        SendMessage (HWindow, WM_SYSCOMMAND, SC_CLOSE, 0L);
    else
        {
        wsprintf (buffer, "Command = %d", COMMANDMSG(Msg));
        MessageBox (HWindow, buffer, "WM_COMMAND", MB_OK);
        }
    }

/*--------------------------------------------------------------*\
|                   TOwnDrawWindow Class Member.                 |
\*--------------------------------------------------------------*/
void TOwnDrawWindow::WMCreate(TMessage& Msg)
    {
    HMENU       hmenu;
    HMENU       hmenuPopup;

    /*
     * Create a menu with three owner-draw items.
     */
    hmenu = GetMenu (Msg.Receiver);
    hmenuPopup = CreatePopupMenu();
    AppendMenu (hmenu, MF_POPUP, (UINT) hmenuPopup, "Fo&nt");

    AppendMenu (hmenuPopup,
                MF_OWNERDRAW,
```

## 296  User Interface Objects

```
                            IDM_FONT_COURIER,
                            MAKEINTRESOURCE(IDM_FONT_COURIER));
        AppendMenu (hmenuPopup,
                            MF_OWNERDRAW,
                            IDM_FONT_TMSRMN,
                            MAKEINTRESOURCE(IDM_FONT_TMSRMN));
        AppendMenu (hmenuPopup,
                            MF_OWNERDRAW,
                            IDM_FONT_HELV,
                            MAKEINTRESOURCE(IDM_FONT_HELV));

    }

/*----------------------------------------------------------------*\
|                   TOwnDrawWindow Class Member.                   |
\*----------------------------------------------------------------*/
void TOwnDrawWindow::WMDrawItem(TMessage& Msg)
    {
    char buff[80];
    COLORREF crFore;
    COLORREF crBack;
    DWORD dwCheckMark;
    HFONT hfontOld;
    HFONT hfont;
    int fSwapColors;
    int xText,yText;
    int cxCheck;
    LPDRAWITEMSTRUCT lpdi;

    lpdi = (LPDRAWITEMSTRUCT)Msg.LParam;

    switch (lpdi->itemID)
        {
        case IDM_FONT_COURIER:
            lstrcpy (buff, "Courier");
            hfont = hfontCour;
            break;
        case IDM_FONT_TMSRMN:
            lstrcpy (buff, "Times Roman");
            hfont = hfontTmsRmn;
            break;
        case IDM_FONT_HELV:
            lstrcpy (buff, "Helvetica");
            hfont = hfontHelv;
            break;
        }
    hfontOld = SelectFont (lpdi->hDC, hfont);

    /*
     * If current menu item should be highlighted,
     * install the correct system colors.
     */
    if (lpdi->itemState & ODS_SELECTED)
        {
        crFore = SetTextColor (lpdi->hDC,
                                crHighlightText);
        crBack = SetBkColor (lpdi->hDC,
                                crHighlight);
        fSwapColors= TRUE;
        }
    else
        fSwapColors= FALSE;
```

```
    /*
     * Get width of checkmark.
     */
    dwCheckMark = GetMenuCheckMarkDimensions();
    cxCheck = LOWORD (dwCheckMark);
    xText = lpdi->rcItem.left + cxCheck;
    yText = lpdi->rcItem.top;


    /*
     * Display line of text.
     */
    ExtTextOut (lpdi->hDC, xText, yText,
                ETO_OPAQUE,
                &lpdi->rcItem,
                buff,
                lstrlen(buff),
                NULL);

    /*
     * Restore DC before we send it home.
     */
    SelectFont (lpdi->hDC, hfontOld);      // Restore Font.
    if (fSwapColors)
        {
        SetTextColor (lpdi->hDC, crFore);  // Restore Colors.
        SetBkColor (lpdi->hDC, crBack);
        }
    }
/*----------------------------------------------------------------*\
|                TOwnDrawWindow Class Member.                      |
\*----------------------------------------------------------------*/
void TOwnDrawWindow::WMMeasureItem (TMessage& Msg)
    {
    char buff[80];
    DWORD dwSize;
    DWORD dwCheckMark;
    HDC   hdc;
    HFONT hfont;
    int   cxWidth, cyHeight;
    int   cxCheck, cyCheck;
    LPMEASUREITEMSTRUCT lpmi;

    lpmi = (LPMEASUREITEMSTRUCT)Msg.LParam;
    switch (lpmi->itemID)
        {
        case IDM_FONT_COURIER:
            lstrcpy (buff, "Courier");
            hfont = hfontCour;
            break;
        case IDM_FONT_TMSRMN:
            lstrcpy (buff, "Times Roman");
            hfont = hfontTmsRmn;
            break;
        case IDM_FONT_HELV:
            lstrcpy (buff, "Helvetica");
            hfont = hfontHelv;
            break;
        }

    /* Find size of string.                              */
```

```
        hdc = GetDC (HWindow);
        SelectObject (hdc, hfont);
        dwSize = GetTextExtent (hdc, buff, lstrlen(buff));
        ReleaseDC (HWindow, hdc);
        /*  Start with string size information.         */
        cxWidth  = LOWORD(dwSize);
        cyHeight = HIWORD(dwSize);

        /*  Add in check mark size information.         */
        dwCheckMark = GetMenuCheckMarkDimensions();
        cxCheck = LOWORD (dwCheckMark);
        cyCheck = HIWORD (dwCheckMark);

        lpmi->itemWidth  = cxWidth + cxCheck;
        lpmi->itemHeight = max (cyHeight, cyCheck);
        }
```

# OWNDRAW.H

```
/*-------------------------------------------------------------*\
|   Owndraw.H - Include file for Owndraw.cpp                    |
\*-------------------------------------------------------------*/


#define IDM_FILE_NEW        100
#define IDM_FILE_OPEN       101
#define IDM_FILE_SAVE       102
#define IDM_FILE_SAVEAS     103
#define IDM_FILE_PRINT      104
#define IDM_FILE_EXIT       105

#define IDM_EDIT_UNDO       200
#define IDM_EDIT_CUT        201
#define IDM_EDIT_COPY       202
#define IDM_EDIT_PASTE      203
#define IDM_EDIT_CLEAR      204
#define IDM_EDIT_DELETE     205

#define IDM_FONT_TMSRMN     300
#define IDM_FONT_HELV       301
#define IDM_FONT_COURIER    302
```

# OWNDRAW.RC

```
#include "OwnDraw.H"

snapshot icon OwnDraw.ico

hand cursor OwnDraw.cur

1 MENU
    {
    POPUP "&File"
        {
        MENUITEM "&New",        IDM_FILE_NEW
        MENUITEM "&Open...",    IDM_FILE_OPEN
```

```
                MENUITEM "&Save",         IDM_FILE_SAVE
                MENUITEM "Save &As...",   IDM_FILE_SAVEAS
                MENUITEM SEPARATOR
                MENUITEM "&Print",        IDM_FILE_PRINT
                MENUITEM SEPARATOR
                MENUITEM "E&xit",         IDM_FILE_EXIT
            }
        POPUP "&Edit"
            {
            MENUITEM "&Undo\tAlt+Backspace", IDM_EDIT_UNDO
            MENUITEM SEPARATOR
            MENUITEM "Cu&t\tShift+Del",      IDM_EDIT_CUT
            MENUITEM "&Copy\tCtrl+Ins",      IDM_EDIT_COPY
            MENUITEM "&Paste\tShift+Ins",    IDM_EDIT_PASTE
            MENUITEM SEPARATOR
            MENUITEM "Cl&ear",   IDM_EDIT_CLEAR
            MENUITEM "&Delete",  IDM_EDIT_DELETE
            }
```

## OWNDRAW.DEF

```
NAME OWNDRAW

EXETYPE WINDOWS

DESCRIPTION 'OwnDraw - Owner draw menus'

CODE MOVEABLE DISCARDABLE
DATA MOVEABLE MULTIPLE

HEAPSIZE   512
STACKSIZE  5120
```

As with the other programs you've encountered up to now, this program has two objects: an application object and a window object. We pretty much use the OWL application object as is. It performs all the required initialization for us, and manages our message loop.

As expected, the window object's constructor initializes the window object's various data members. This includes creating three GDI fonts and retrieving color information that the window object will use to draw its owner-draw menu items. While a real-world application would more likely create an owner-draw menu object, we've simplified things to keep with the stated aim of this book: helping you understand how Windows works.

In response to the **WM_CREATE** message, OWNDRAW creates three owner-draw menu items and attaches them to the window. You won't be able to attach a menu to a window in the window object's constructor, since the MS-Windows window doesn't exist yet. Instead, like OWNDRAW, you'll need to rely on the WM_CREATE message to initialize an owner-draw menu item. In fact, the same holds true for any object that you wish to attach to a window.

Once the measurement information has been provided, our window procedure starts to receive **WM_DRAWITEM** messages. Since we're not interested in grayed or disabled items,

OWNDRAW doesn't check for these flags. We also don't check whether or not the item should display a check mark. If we wanted a check mark, we would have to draw it ourselves in response to the **WM_DRAWITEM** message. That is to say, if we are going to draw *part* of a menu item, we must draw the *entire* menu item.

Keyboard mnemonics are not supported in owner-draw menu items. In general, this makes sense, since a graphic image can hardly be expected to have an associated keyboard keystroke. However, the presence of text inside these owner-draw menu items creates the paradox that, even though our owner-draw items could certainly use a mnemonic keystroke as graphic objects, Windows does not provide mnemonic keystroke support for owner-draw items. If this is important to you, there is a way for an owner-draw menu item to simulate a mnemonic. You start by underlining the mnemonic letter in each of the font names. Then, in response to the **WM_MENUCHAR** message, you would check for the mnemonic letters and indicate either an error or a menu selection in the return value. The **WM_MENUCHAR** message is sent when the user strikes a keystroke that doesn't correspond to any mnemonic or accelerator key. When the default window procedure receives this message, it provides a return value that tells the menu system to beep at the user. But processing this message yourself would allow you to provide the necessary return value so that the menu system would handle the keystroke as a regular mnemonic.

Since our window object created three fonts in its constructor, it must clean them up in its destructor. After all, these are GDI drawing objects that take up memory in GDI's local heap. This is a good example of one way that C++ really benefits the Windows programmer. In general, any time you create an MS-Windows data object in a constructor, just be sure to destroy the object in the destructor. The following code in OWNDRAW's window object class destructor cleans up the fonts:

```
DeleteFont (hfontTmsRmn);
DeleteFont (hfontHelv);
DeleteFont (hfontCour);
```

The use of owner-draw items gives a program the greatest control and flexibility in the appearance of menu items. From one moment to the next, a menu item may change in response to some outside event. But you may not need this much flexibility in the graphic images you put in a menu. You have a second choice, which in some respects is easier to implement than owner-draw menu items. It involves the creation of a GDI bitmap. Such a bitmap can be associated with a menu item and automatically displayed by the menu system without any intervention required on your part. Let's take a look at what is involved in putting bitmaps into menu items.

# Bitmaps in Menus

In Chapter 6, in our introduction to GDI, we discussed how bitmaps are useful for storing graphic images. Once a graphic image has been created in a bitmap, it can be incorporated into a menu as an alternative to the text that is normally displayed in menus. Bitmaps in menus provide a somewhat easier method than owner-draw menu items for getting graphic images into menus.

To take advantage of this capability, we need to start by describing how a Windows program goes about creating and using GDI bitmaps. The clearest way to understand what GDI expects is to examine a code fragment that shows how all the pieces are brought together. Here is one way to create a GDI bitmap that can be displayed in a menu:

```
HDC     hdcScreen;
HDC     hdcBitmap;
HBITMAP hbm;
HBITMAP hbmOld;

hdcScreen = GetDC (hwnd);
hdcBitmap = CreateCompatibleDC (hdcScreen);
hbm = CreateCompatibleBitmap (hdc, cxWidth, cyHeight);
ReleaseDC (hwnd, hdcScreen);
hbmOld = SelectBitmap (hdcBitmap, hbm);
```

Using a bitmap requires that two objects be created and connected together: a bitmap and a device context. Creating a bitmap requires us to specify the size of the rectangular display image that we wish to store. GDI responds by allocating the required memory. We need a device context because, as you're aware, every GDI drawing routine takes a handle to a DC as its first parameter. Without this special "membership card," the bitmap won't be admitted to the private club that all GDI devices belong to. But *with* the DC, a bitmap becomes a full participant in all the drawing capabilities that GDI has to offer.

The quickest and easiest way to create a DC involves asking GDI to clone an existing DC, by calling `CreateCompatibleDC`. This routine takes a single parameter, a handle to an existing DC. Since our bitmap is going to be copied to the display screen, we pass a display DC that we obtained by calling `GetDC`. To create a bitmap that is compatible with the display screen, we call a related routine, `CreateCompatibleBitmap`. This routine also takes a DC handle as a parameter, along with a width and a height value for the size of the drawing surface to create.

The only thing missing is a way to connect the bitmap and the DC. The routine we use is shown below:

```
hbmOld = SelectBitmap (hdcBitmap, hbm);
```

## User Interface Objects

You probably remember that we use this routine to install pens, brushes, and fonts into DCs. Here you see it has another use: connecting a bitmap to a device context. Once this connection has been made, we can use any GDI drawing routines to draw in our bitmap. For example, we could draw an ellipse in the bitmap with the following call:

```
Ellipse (hdcBitmap, x1, y1, x2, y2);
```

Or we could make any other call to a GDI drawing routine.

When you have finished drawing into the bitmap, you place the bitmap into a menu by calling one of these routines: **AppendMenu**, **InsertMenu**, or **ModifyMenu**. Here is a call to **AppendMenu** that inserts the bitmap at the end of a popup menu, and gives the new menu item a command result code of 23:

```
HMENU hmenu;
HMENU hmenuPopup;

hmenu = GetMenu (hwnd);
hmenuPopup = GetSubMenu (hmenu, 1);

AppendMenu (hmenuPopup, MF_BITMAP, 23,
            MAKEINTRESOURCE(hbm));
```

Once the bitmap has been installed into the menu, our DC isn't needed anymore, so we destroy it. But first, we must remove the bitmap handle from the DC. When we installed the bitmap handle into our DC, **SelectBitmap** returned a value that we stored in **hbmOld**. This value represents a placeholder for a bitmap. Before we can destroy the DC, we must first break the connection between the DC and the bitmap. This is accomplished by another call to **SelectObject** (hidden in the SelectBitmap macro):

```
SelectBitmap (hdcBitmap, hbmOld);
```

after which, we can destroy the DC with this call:

```
DeleteDC (hdcBitmap);
```

Figure 12.2 shows a menu that was created by attaching five bitmaps to five different menu items. Each menu item represents a different brush that the user can select to draw with. This menu was created by our next sample program, BITMENU.

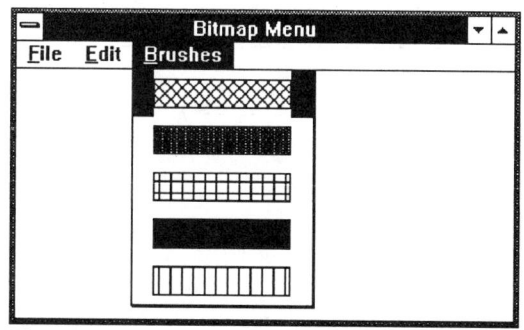

**Figure 12.2** *Menu containing bitmaps with GDI brush images*

# MAKEFILE.MAK

```
.AUTODEPEND

#    Translator Definitions
INC=\BORLANDC\OWL\INCLUDE;\BORLANDC\CLASSLIB\INCLUDE;\BORLANDC\INCLUDE
CC = bcc -c -D_CLASSDLL -H -ml -WS -w -I$(INC)

#    Implicit Rules
.c.obj:
  $(CC) {$< }

.cpp.obj:
  $(CC) {$< }

#    Explicit Rules
BitMenu.exe: BitMenu.res BitMenu.def BitMenu.obj
     tlink /c/C/n/P-/Twe/x @BitMenu.LNK
     rlink BitMenu.res BitMenu.exe

#    Individual File Dependencies
BitMenu.obj: BitMenu.cpp

BitMenu.res: BitMenu.rc BitMenu.cur BitMenu.ico
    brcc -FO BitMenu.res -i$(INC) BitMenu.RC
```

# BITMENU.LNK

```
\borlandc\lib\c0wl.obj+
BitMenu.obj
BitMenu,BitMenu
\borlandc\classlib\lib\tclasdll.lib+
\borlandc\owl\lib\owl.lib+
mathwl.lib+
import.lib+
crtldll.lib
BitMenu.def
```

## 304　User Interface Objects

# BITMENU.CPP

```cpp
/*--------------------------------------------------------------*\
 | BITMENU.CPP   - Demo showing creation of bitmaps in a menu.  |
\*--------------------------------------------------------------*/
#define WIN31
#define STRICT
#include <owl.h>
#include <WindowsX.h>
#include "Bitmenu.H"

#define COMMANDMSG(arg)  (arg.WParam)

/*--------------------------------------------------------------*\
 |                        Constants.                            |
\*--------------------------------------------------------------*/
const int COUNT = 5;

/*--------------------------------------------------------------*\
 |                    Class Declarations.                       |
\*--------------------------------------------------------------*/
class TBitmenuApplication : public TApplication
   {
   public:
      TBitmenuApplication (LPSTR lpszName, HINSTANCE hInstance,
                           HINSTANCE hPrevInstance, LPSTR lpszCmdLine,
                           int nCmdShow);
      virtual void InitMainWindow ();
   };

class TBitmenuWindow : public TWindow
   {
   public:
      TBitmenuWindow (PTWindowsObject pwParent, LPSTR lpszTitle,
                      PTModule pmModule);
      ~TBitmenuWindow();
      virtual LPSTR GetClassName ();
      virtual void  GetWindowClass (WNDCLASS&);
      virtual void  WMCommand(TMessage& Msg) = [WM_COMMAND];
      virtual void  WMCreate(TMessage& Msg) = [WM_CREATE];
   private:
      HBITMAP  hbm[COUNT];
      HBRUSH   hbr[COUNT];
      int      cxBitmapWidth;
      int      cyBitmapHeight;
   };

/*--------------------------------------------------------------*\
 |                   Main Function: WinMain.                    |
\*--------------------------------------------------------------*/
int PASCAL WinMain (HINSTANCE hInstance,  HINSTANCE hPrevInstance,
                    LPSTR  lpszCmdLine, int    nCmdShow)
   {
   TBitmenuApplication Bitmenu ("Bitmenu", hInstance,
                                hPrevInstance, lpszCmdLine,
                                nCmdShow);
   Bitmenu.Run();
   return Bitmenu.Status;
   }

/*--------------------------------------------------------------*\
 |                  Application Class Member.                   |
\*--------------------------------------------------------------*/
```

```
TBitmenuApplication::TBitmenuApplication (LPSTR lpszName,
                    HINSTANCE hInstance, HINSTANCE hPrevInstance,
                    LPSTR lpszCmdLine, int nCmdShow)
                :TApplication (lpszName, hInstance,
                    hPrevInstance, lpszCmdLine, nCmdShow)
    {
    /* Application specific initialization goes here. */
    }

/*-------------------------------------------------------------*\
|                   Application Class Member.                   |
\*-------------------------------------------------------------*/
void TBitmenuApplication::InitMainWindow ()
    {
    MainWindow = new TBitmenuWindow (NULL, "Bitmap Menu", NULL);
    }

/*-------------------------------------------------------------*\
|                   TBitmenuWindow Class Member.                |
\*-------------------------------------------------------------*/
TBitmenuWindow::TBitmenuWindow (PTWindowsObject pwParent,
                LPSTR lpszTitle, PTModule pmModule)
            :TWindow (pwParent, lpszTitle, pmModule)
    {
    COLORREF crBackground;
    HBITMAP  hbmOld;
    HBRUSH   hbrBackground;
    HBRUSH   hbrOld;
    HDC      hdcScreen;
    HDC      hdcBitmap;
    int      i;

    // Calculate bitmap size information.
    cxBitmapWidth  = GetSystemMetrics (SM_CXICON) * 3;
    cyBitmapHeight = GetSystemMetrics (SM_CYICON);

    // Create the background brush to initialize bitmaps.
    crBackground = GetSysColor (COLOR_MENU);
    hbrBackground = CreateSolidBrush (crBackground);

    // Create the needed GDI objects: DCs and bitmaps.
    hdcScreen = CreateDC ("DISPLAY", 0, 0, 0);
    hdcBitmap = CreateCompatibleDC (hdcScreen);
    hbrOld = SelectBrush (hdcBitmap, hbrBackground);

    for (i=0;i<COUNT;i++)
        {
        hbm[i] = CreateCompatibleBitmap (hdcScreen, cxBitmapWidth,
                                    cyBitmapHeight);
        if (i==0)
            hbmOld = SelectBitmap (hdcBitmap, hbm[0]);
        else
            SelectBitmap (hdcBitmap, hbm[i]);
        PatBlt (hdcBitmap, 0, 0, cxBitmapWidth, cyBitmapHeight,
                PATCOPY);
        }

    // Clean up all GDI objects we've created.
    SelectBitmap (hdcBitmap, hbmOld);
    SelectBrush (hdcBitmap, hbrOld);
    DeleteDC (hdcBitmap);

    DeleteDC (hdcScreen);
```

## 306   User Interface Objects

```
        DeleteBrush (hbrBackground);
        // Create the brushes we're going to use.
        hbr[0] = CreateHatchBrush (HS_DIAGCROSS , RGB(0, 0, 0));
        hbr[1] = CreateSolidBrush (RGB (64, 64, 64));
        hbr[2] = CreateHatchBrush (HS_CROSS , RGB(0, 0, 0));
        hbr[3] = CreateSolidBrush (RGB (0, 0, 0));
        hbr[4] = CreateHatchBrush (HS_VERTICAL , RGB(0, 0, 0));
        }
/*----------------------------------------------------------------*\
|                  TBitmenuWindow Class Member.                    |
\*----------------------------------------------------------------*/
TBitmenuWindow::~TBitmenuWindow()
    {
    int i;
    for (i=0;i<COUNT;i++)
        {
        DeleteBrush (hbr[i]);
        DeleteBitmap (hbm[i]);
        }
    }

/*----------------------------------------------------------------*\
|                  TBitmenuWindow Class Member.                    |
\*----------------------------------------------------------------*/
LPSTR TBitmenuWindow::GetClassName ()
    {
    return "Bitmenu:MAIN";
    }

/*----------------------------------------------------------------*\
|                  TBitmenuWindow Class Member.                    |
\*----------------------------------------------------------------*/
void TBitmenuWindow::GetWindowClass (WNDCLASS& wc)
    {
    TWindow::GetWindowClass (wc);
    wc.hIcon=LoadIcon (wc.hInstance, "snapshot");
    wc.hCursor=LoadCursor (wc.hInstance, "hand");
    wc.lpszMenuName="#1";
    }

/*----------------------------------------------------------------*\
|                  TBitmenuWindow Class Member.                    |
\*----------------------------------------------------------------*/
void TBitmenuWindow::WMCommand(TMessage& Msg)
    {
    char buffer[80];

    if (COMMANDMSG(Msg) == IDM_FILE_EXIT)
        SendMessage (HWindow, WM_SYSCOMMAND, SC_CLOSE, 0L);
    else
        {
        wsprintf (buffer, "Command = %d", COMMANDMSG(Msg));
        MessageBox (HWindow, buffer, "WM_COMMAND", MB_OK);
        }
    }

/*----------------------------------------------------------------*\
|                  TBitmenuWindow Class Member.                    |
\*----------------------------------------------------------------*/
void TBitmenuWindow::WMCreate(TMessage& Msg)
    {
```

```
    HBITMAP   hbmOld;
    HBRUSH    hbrOld;
    HDC       hdcScreen;
    HDC       hdcBitmap;
    HMENU     hmenu;
    HMENU     hmenuPopup;
    int       i;
    int       cyOffset;

    cyOffset = cyBitmapHeight - cyBitmapHeight/5;

    // Create the needed GDI objects: a bitmap DC
    hdcScreen = GetDC (HWindow);
    hdcBitmap = CreateCompatibleDC (hdcScreen);
    ReleaseDC (HWindow, hdcScreen);
    // Create an empty popup menu, and attach it to menu-bar.
    hmenuPopup =CreatePopupMenu();
    hmenu = GetMenu (Msg.Receiver);
    AppendMenu (hmenu, MF_POPUP, (UINT) hmenuPopup, "&Brushes");

    // Save original GDI objects.
    hbrOld = SelectBrush (hdcBitmap, hbr[0]);
    hbmOld = SelectBitmap (hdcBitmap, hbm[0]);

    /* Put a brush into the DC, attach the DC to a bitmap,
     * and then draw a rectangle into the bitmap.  Finally,
     * create a new menu item using the bitmap.
     */
    for (i=0;i<COUNT;i++)
        {
        SelectBrush (hdcBitmap, hbr[i]);
        SelectBitmap (hdcBitmap, hbm[i]);
        Rectangle (hdcBitmap,
                   0,
                   cyOffset,
                   cxBitmapWidth,
                   cyBitmapHeight-cyOffset);
        AppendMenu (hmenuPopup, MF_BITMAP, IDM_MENU_FREE+i,
                    MAKEINTRESOURCE(hbm[i]));
        }

    // Clean up bitmap DC.
    SelectBrush (hdcBitmap, hbrOld);
    SelectBitmap (hdcBitmap, hbmOld);
    DeleteDC (hdcBitmap);
    }
```

# BITMENU.H

```
/*----------------------------------------------------------*\
|  Bitmenu.H - Include file for Bitmenu.cpp                  |
\*----------------------------------------------------------*/

#define IDM_FILE_NEW       100
#define IDM_FILE_OPEN      101
#define IDM_FILE_SAVE      102
#define IDM_FILE_SAVEAS    103
#define IDM_FILE_PRINT     104
```

```
#define IDM_FILE_EXIT       105

#define IDM_EDIT_UNDO       200
#define IDM_EDIT_CUT        201
#define IDM_EDIT_COPY       202
#define IDM_EDIT_PASTE      203
#define IDM_EDIT_CLEAR      204
#define IDM_EDIT_DELETE     205

#define IDM_MENU_FREE       300
```

# BITMENU.RC

```
#include "Bitmenu.H"

snapshot icon BitMenu.ico

hand cursor BitMenu.cur

1 MENU
    {
    POPUP "&File"
        {
        MENUITEM "&New",            IDM_FILE_NEW
        MENUITEM "&Open...",        IDM_FILE_OPEN
        MENUITEM "&Save",           IDM_FILE_SAVE
        MENUITEM "Save &As...",     IDM_FILE_SAVEAS
        MENUITEM SEPARATOR
        MENUITEM "&Print",          IDM_FILE_PRINT
        MENUITEM SEPARATOR
        MENUITEM "E&xit",           IDM_FILE_EXIT
        }
    POPUP "&Edit"
        {
        MENUITEM "&Undo\tAlt+Backspace", IDM_EDIT_UNDO
        MENUITEM SEPARATOR
        MENUITEM "Cu&t\tShift+Del",     IDM_EDIT_CUT
        MENUITEM "&Copy\tCtrl+Ins",     IDM_EDIT_COPY
        MENUITEM "&Paste\tShift+Ins",   IDM_EDIT_PASTE
        MENUITEM SEPARATOR
        MENUITEM "Cl&ear",   IDM_EDIT_CLEAR
        MENUITEM "&Delete",  IDM_EDIT_DELETE
        }
    }
```

# BITMENU.DEF

```
NAME BITMENU

EXETYPE WINDOWS

DESCRIPTION 'BitMenu - Bitmap in a menu'

CODE MOVEABLE DISCARDABLE
DATA MOVEABLE MULTIPLE
```

```
HEAPSIZE   512
STACKSIZE  5120
```

Most of BITMENU's work is split between two of the window object's member functions: the constructor, and the message response function for the **WM_CREATE** message, **WMCreate()**. As with the owner-draw menu item, it might have been better to create a separate "bitmap menu object" to hide menu complexity from the window object. To help you better understand bitmaps in menus, the two are together.

In its constructor, BITMENU's window object starts by calling **GetSystemMetrics** to determine the display driver's icon size settings. These values are used to calculate the size of the bitmaps. As we mentioned earlier, it's a good idea to avoid hard-coded sizes, since they can produce unexpected results on high-resolution displays. BITMENU creates bitmaps that are sized relative to the system icons:

```
cxBitmapWidth   = GetSystemMetrics (SM_CXICON) * 3;
cyBitmapHeight  = GetSystemMetrics (SM_CYICON);
```

When a memory bitmap is created, GDI does not initialize the drawing surface to any particular color. Before we can draw on the bitmap, we need to erase the surface to avoid the appearance of random colors. In the same way that the OWNDRAW program called **GetSysColors** to find the correct menu colors to use, BITMENU makes the same call and uses the resulting color to create a solid brush to erase the bitmap backgrounds:

```
crBackground = GetSysColor (COLOR_MENU);
hbrBackground = CreateSolidBrush (crBackground);
```

As you may recall from our discussion of the OWNDRAW program, GDI can be called to draw on a bitmap only when a DC has been created and connected to the bitmap. We call **CreateDC** to get a display DC, then clone this DC for use with a bitmap by calling **CreateCompatibleDC**. Next, we install the background brush into the DC so it is ready to initialize the bitmaps:

```
hdcScreen = CreateDC ("DISPLAY", 0, 0, 0);
hdcBitmap = CreateCompatibleDC (hdcScreen);
hbrOld = SelectBrush (hdcBitmap, hbrBackground);
```

Then, the window object constructor creates bitmaps and initializes them to the color of the brush we just created, **hbrBackground**. As each bitmap is created, **PatBlt** paints the brush colors onto each bitmap:

```
    for (i=0;i<COUNT;i++)
    {
    hbm[i]= CreateCompatibleBitmap (hdcScreen,
                                    cxWidth, cyHeight);
    if (i == 0)
        hbmOld = SelectBitmap (hdcBitmap, hbm[0]);
    else
               SelectBitmap (hdcBitmap, hbm[i]);
```

```
        PatBlt (hdcBitmap,0,0, cxWidth, cyHeight, PATCOPY);
    }
```

This code brings up an important point about GDI: When creating DCs, you must restore the DC to its original state before deleting the DC. That's the reason this code stores in **hbmOld** the handle of the first bitmap selected *out* of the DC. Before destroying the DC, we'll select this bitmap back into the DC. After the bitmaps have been initialized, we clean up all the GDI objects we created:

```
SelectBitmap (hdcBitmap, hbmOld);
SelectBrush (hdcBitmap, hbrOld);
DeleteDC (hdcBitmap);

DeleteDC (hdcScreen);
DeleteBrush (hbrBackground);
```

The constructor finally creates brushes for the different bitmap patterns:

```
hbr[0] = CreateHatchBrush (HS_DIAGCROSS, RGB(0,0,0));
hbr[1] = CreateSolidBrush (RGB(64, 64, 64));
hbr[2] = CreateHatchBrush (HS_CROSS, RGB(0, 0, 0));
hbr[3] = CreateSolidBrush (RGB(0, 0, 0));
hbr[4] = CreateHatchBrush (HS_VERTICAL, RGB(0, 0, 0));
```

When it is done, the constructor has initialized every data member in BITMENU's window object. They lie in wait like the pit crew waiting for a car race to begin. The **WM_CREATE** message serves as the starting flag for the window object's race, and the pit crew rushes in to install a popup menu complete with several bitmaps. First, a DC is created to be used with the bitmaps:

```
hdcScreen = GetDC (HWindow);
hdcBitmap = CreateCompatibleDC (hdcScreen);
ReleaseDC (HWindow, hdcScreen);
```

Then, an empty popup menu is created and attached to the top-level menu:

```
hmenuPopup = CreatePopupMenu ();
hmenu = GetMenu (hwnd);
AppendMenu (hmenu, MF_POPUP,  (UINT)hmenuPopup, "&Brushes");
```

As before, we save a copy of the original GDI objects in our DC for use when we delete the DC:

```
hbrOld = SelectBrush (hdcBitmap, hbr[0]);
hbmOld = SelectBitmap (hdcBitmap, hbm[0]);
```

Next, we loop through the bitmaps, calling **SelectBitmap** to connect each bitmap in turn to the bitmap DC. **SelectBrush** is called to connect brushes to the DC. With that done, we draw an image of the brush in the bitmap by calling the `Rectangle` routine. As you may recall, this routine draws a rectangle using the currently installed pen for the border and the currently installed brush for the inside area. Once this is done, the bitmap is ready to be added to the menu, which is accomplished by calling `AppendMenu`:

```
for (i=0;i<COUNT;i++)
    {
    SelectBrush (hdcBitmap, hbr[i]);
    SelectBitmap (hdcBitmap, hbm[i]);
    Rectangle (hdcBitmap,
               0,
               cyOffset,
               cxWidth,
               cyHeight-cyOffset);
    AppendMenu (hmenuPopup, MF_BITMAP, IDM_FIRST+i,
                MAKEINTRESOURCE(hbm[i]));
    }
```

Once the bitmaps have been created and attached to a menu, we must clean up GDI objects that were created. The only object we have to worry about is the bitmap DC. First, we must sever connections with the brushes and bitmaps that have been created. Only then can the DC be safely destroyed, without fear of leaving unaccounted for objects in the system:

```
SelectBrush (hdcBitmap, GetStockBrush(BLACK_BRUSH));
SelectBitmap (hdcBitmap, hbmOld);
DeleteBrush (hbrBackground);
```

Once this is done, two sets of GDI objects remain in memory: the bitmaps and the brushes. Our window object retains these objects during its entire life. The bitmaps can't be destroyed until the menu that uses them is destroyed. The brushes are retained, on the other hand, since we may want to use them to draw the objects selected by the user from the bitmap menu items.

These objects are finally cleaned up by the window object's destructor:

```
for (i=0;i<COUNT;i++)
    {
    DeleteBrush (hbr[i]);
    DeleteBitmap (hbm[i]);
    }
```

Bitmaps in menus and owner-draw menu items are just two ways that you can incorporate graphical objects in your menus. We're going to look at the third type now: custom check marks.

## Creating Custom Menu Check Marks

In the last chapter, we mentioned that check marks provide one type of visual clue in menus. Although the standard check mark is useful in many situations, you may want to use a different symbol in your menus. You can call GDI routines to create your own custom check marks and install them into menus. When you do this, the menu system lets you attach *two* different bitmaps to every menu item. One bitmap is displayed when the menu item is in a *checked* state; the other is for the *unchecked* state.

Creating a check mark bitmap starts with the creation of a regular GDI bitmap. We discussed how to do this in the context of the BITMENU program earlier in this chapter. You must create a bitmap, create a DC, and then connect the two. From there, you use GDI routines to draw whatever figure you wish to use to reflect the checked and unchecked states. You have to be careful, though, because your drawing has to be small enough to fit in the space that the menu system has set aside for check marks.

To determine the proper size to use, you call `GetMenuCheckMarkDimensions`. This routine takes no parameters, but returns a `DWORD` (unsigned long) value into which is packed the required dimensions of a check mark bitmap. Here is how to extract the dimension information from the return value:

```
DWORD dwCheck;
int cxWidth, cyHeight;

dwCheck  = GetMenuCheckMarkDimension();
cxWidth  = LOWORD (dwCheck);
cyHeight = HIWORD (dwCheck);
```

Using the size information provided by this routine, you can create a pair of bitmaps, draw checked and unchecked images that you wish to use, and attach the bitmap to the specific menu items that you wish to have use the check marks. Since bitmaps are shared GDI objects, you can create a single pair of check mark bitmaps and use them in many different menu items. To attach a bitmap to a menu item, you call the `SetMenuItemBitmaps` routine, which is defined:

```
BOOL SetMenuItemBitmaps (hMenu, nPosition, wFlags,
                        hbmUnchecked, hbmChecked)
```

- `hMenu` is a menu handle.
- `nPosition` identifies the menu item to which the pair of bitmaps are to be attached. If the next parameter, `wFlags`, is `MF_BYCOMMAND`, then `nPosition` is a command result code. If it is `MF_BYPOSITION`, `nPosition` is the relative position of the menu item in the menu identified by `hMenu`.
- `wFlags` is either `MF_BYCOMMAND` or `MF_BYPOSITION`.

- **hbmUnchecked** is a handle of a GDI bitmap to be displayed when the menu is not checked.
- **hbmChecked** is a handle of a GDI bitmap to be displayed when the menu item is checked.

Once the check mark bitmaps are attached to a menu item, they are used automatically without requiring any additional effort from your program. All you need to do at this point is call **CheckMenuItem** to set the checked state to either **MF_CHECKED** or **MF_UNCHECKED**.

If, at any time, you wish to remove a custom check mark, you call **SetMenuItemBitmaps** with a NULL value in the bitmap handle parameter corresponding to the bitmap that you wish to have removed. Figure 12.3 shows two sets of custom check marks created by CHEKMENU, our sample program.

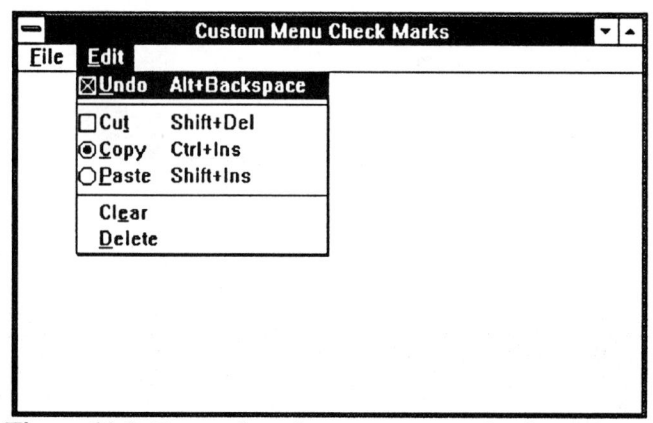

**Figure 12.3** Two pairs of custom menu check marks

CHEKMENU creates two pairs of custom menu check marks. One pair uses a square box, with an X in the box for the checked state and an empty box for the unchecked state. The second pair is a circle check mark, with a filled interior for the checked state and an empty interior for the unchecked state. Having created these two pairs of check mark bitmaps, we could then use them for any or all of the menu items in our menu. As you can tell by looking at Figure 12.3, CHEKMENU uses the standard menu that we created in the last chapter.

## 314  User Interface Objects

# MAKEFILE.MAK

```
.AUTODEPEND

#    Translator Definitions
INC=\BORLANDC\OWL\INCLUDE;\BORLANDC\CLASSLIB\INCLUDE;\BORLANDC\INCLUDE
CC = bcc -c -D_CLASSDLL -H -ml -WS -w -I$(INC)

#    Implicit Rules
.c.obj:
  $(CC) {$< }

.cpp.obj:
  $(CC) {$< }

#    Explicit Rules
ChekMenu.exe: ChekMenu.res ChekMenu.def ChekMenu.obj
    tlink /c/C/n/P-/Twe/x @ChekMenu.LNK
    rlink ChekMenu.res ChekMenu.exe

#    Individual File Dependencies
ChekMenu.obj: ChekMenu.cpp

ChekMenu.res: ChekMenu.rc ChekMenu.cur ChekMenu.ico
    brcc -FO ChekMenu.res -i$(INC) ChekMenu.RC
```

# CHEKMENU.LNK

```
\borlandc\lib\c0wl.obj+
ChekMenu.obj
ChekMenu,ChekMenu
\borlandc\classlib\lib\tclasdll.lib+
\borlandc\owl\lib\owl.lib+
mathwl.lib+
import.lib+
crtldll.lib
ChekMenu.def
```

# CHEKMENU.CPP

```
/*------------------------------------------------------------*\
| CHEKMENU.CPP   - Demo showing custom menu checkmarks.        |
\*------------------------------------------------------------*/
#define WIN31
#define STRICT
#include <owl.h>
#include <WindowsX.h>
#include "Chekmenu.h"

#define COMMANDMSG(arg)  (arg.WParam)

/*------------------------------------------------------------*\
|                        Constants.                            |
\*------------------------------------------------------------*/
```

```
const int COUNT = 4;
/*-------------------------------------------------------------*\
|                   Class Declarations.                         |
\*-------------------------------------------------------------*/
class TChekMenuApplication : public TApplication
   {
   public:
     TChekMenuApplication (LPSTR lpszName, HINSTANCE hInstance,
                           HINSTANCE hPrevInstance,
                           LPSTR lpszCmdLine, int nCmdShow);
     virtual void InitMainWindow ();
   };

class TChekMenuWindow : public TWindow
   {
   public:
     TChekMenuWindow (PTWindowsObject pwParent, LPSTR lpszTitle,
                      PTModule pmModule);
     ~TChekMenuWindow();
     virtual LPSTR GetClassName ();
     virtual void  GetWindowClass (WNDCLASS&);
     virtual void  WMCommand(TMessage& Msg) = [WM_COMMAND];
     virtual void  WMCreate(TMessage& Msg) = [WM_CREATE];
   private:
     HBITMAP hbmCheck[COUNT];
   };

/*-------------------------------------------------------------*\
|                  Main Function:   WinMain.                    |
\*-------------------------------------------------------------*/
int PASCAL WinMain (HINSTANCE hInstance,   HINSTANCE hPrevInstance,
                    LPSTR lpszCmdLine, int    nCmdShow)
    {
    TChekMenuApplication ChekMenu ("ChekMenu", hInstance,
                                   hPrevInstance, lpszCmdLine,
                                   nCmdShow);
    ChekMenu.Run();
    return ChekMenu.Status;
    }

/*-------------------------------------------------------------*\
|                  Application Class Member.                    |
\*-------------------------------------------------------------*/
TChekMenuApplication::TChekMenuApplication (LPSTR lpszName,
                      HINSTANCE hInstance, HINSTANCE hPrevInstance,
                      LPSTR lpszCmdLine, int nCmdShow)
                    :TApplication (lpszName, hInstance,
                      hPrevInstance, lpszCmdLine, nCmdShow)
    {
    /* Application specific initialization goes here. */
    }

/*-------------------------------------------------------------*\
|                  Application Class Member.                    |
\*-------------------------------------------------------------*/
void TChekMenuApplication::InitMainWindow ()
     {
     MainWindow = new TChekMenuWindow (NULL,
                                       "Custom Menu Checkmarks",
                                       NULL);
     }
```

```
/*---------------------------------------------------------------*\
|                  TChekMenuWindow Class Member.                  |
\*---------------------------------------------------------------*/
TChekMenuWindow::TChekMenuWindow (PTWindowsObject pwParent,
             LPSTR lpszTitle, PTModule pmModule)
         :TWindow (pwParent, lpszTitle, pmModule)
    {
    COLORREF  crBackground;
    DWORD     dwCheck;
    HBRUSH    hbrBackground;
    HBRUSH    hbrOld;
    HBITMAP   hbmOld;
    HDC       hdcScreen;
    HDC       hdcBitmap;
    int       xMin, xMax;
    int       yMin, yMax;
    int       cxCheckWidth;
    int       cyCheckHeight;
    int       cxFourth;
    int       cyFourth;
    int       cxMargin;
    int       i;

    //  Get checkmark dimension information.
    dwCheck  = GetMenuCheckMarkDimensions();
    cyCheckHeight = HIWORD (dwCheck);
    cxCheckWidth  = LOWORD (dwCheck);

    //  Calculate a margin based on border widths.
    cxMargin = GetSystemMetrics (SM_CXBORDER);

    xMin = cxMargin;
    xMax = cxCheckWidth - cxMargin;
    yMin = cxMargin;
    yMax = cyCheckHeight - cxMargin;
    cxFourth = cxCheckWidth/4;
    cyFourth = cyCheckHeight/4;

    //  Create the background brush to initialize bitmaps.
    crBackground = GetSysColor (COLOR_MENU);
    hbrBackground = CreateSolidBrush (crBackground);

    //  Create a DC and a set of bitmaps.
    hdcScreen = CreateDC ("DISPLAY", 0, 0, 0);
    hdcBitmap = CreateCompatibleDC (hdcScreen);
    hbrOld = SelectBrush (hdcBitmap, hbrBackground);

    for (i=0;i<COUNT;i++)
        {
        hbmCheck[i] = CreateCompatibleBitmap (hdcScreen,
                   cxCheckWidth, cyCheckHeight);
        if (i == 0)
            hbmOld = SelectBitmap (hdcBitmap, hbmCheck[i]);
        else
            SelectObject (hdcBitmap, hbmCheck[i]);
        PatBlt (hdcBitmap, 0, 0, cxCheckWidth, cyCheckHeight,
                PATCOPY);
        }

    //  Draw first unchecked menu item.
    SelectBitmap (hdcBitmap, hbmCheck[0]);
    Rectangle (hdcBitmap, xMin, yMin,
                          xMax, yMax);
```

```
    //  Draw first checked menu item.
    SelectBitmap (hdcBitmap, hbmCheck[1]);
    Rectangle (hdcBitmap, xMin, yMin,
                          xMax, yMax);

    MoveTo (hdcBitmap, xMin, yMin);
    LineTo (hdcBitmap, xMax, yMax);
    MoveTo (hdcBitmap, xMin, yMax-1);
    LineTo (hdcBitmap, xMax-1, yMin);

    //  Draw second unchecked menu item.
    SelectBitmap (hdcBitmap, hbmCheck[2]);
    Ellipse (hdcBitmap, xMin, yMin,
                        xMax, yMax);

    //  Draw second checked menu item.
    SelectBitmap (hdcBitmap, hbmCheck[3]);
    Ellipse (hdcBitmap, xMin, yMin,
                        xMax, yMax);
    SelectBrush (hdcBitmap, GetStockBrush (BLACK_BRUSH));

    Ellipse (hdcBitmap, xMin+cxFourth, yMin+cyFourth,
                        xMax-cxFourth, yMax-cyFourth);

    //  Clean up the GDI objects we've created.
    SelectBrush (hdcBitmap, hbrOld);
    SelectBitmap (hdcBitmap, hbmOld);
    DeleteDC (hdcBitmap);
    DeleteBrush (hbrBackground);
    DeleteDC (hdcScreen);
    }

/*----------------------------------------------------------------*\
|                 TChekMenuWindow Class Member.                    |
\*----------------------------------------------------------------*/
TChekMenuWindow::~TChekMenuWindow()
    {
    int i;

    for (i=0;i<COUNT;i++)
        DeleteBitmap (hbmCheck[i]);
    }

/*----------------------------------------------------------------*\
|                 TChekMenuWindow Class Member.                    |
\*----------------------------------------------------------------*/
LPSTR TChekMenuWindow::GetClassName ()
    {
    return "ChekMenu:MAIN";
    }

/*----------------------------------------------------------------*\
|                 TChekMenuWindow Class Member.                    |
\*----------------------------------------------------------------*/
void TChekMenuWindow::GetWindowClass (WNDCLASS& wc)
    {
    TWindow::GetWindowClass (wc);
    wc.hIcon=LoadIcon (wc.hInstance, "snapshot");
    wc.hCursor=LoadCursor (wc.hInstance, "hand");
    wc.lpszMenuName="#1";
    }
```

## User Interface Objects

```
/*----------------------------------------------------------------*\
|                  TChekMenuWindow Class Member.                   |
\*----------------------------------------------------------------*/
void TChekMenuWindow::WMCommand(TMessage& Msg)
    {
    char buffer[80];

    if (COMMANDMSG(Msg) == IDM_FILE_EXIT)
        SendMessage (HWindow, WM_SYSCOMMAND, SC_CLOSE, 0L);
    else
        {
        wsprintf (buffer, "Command = %d", COMMANDMSG(Msg));
        MessageBox (HWindow, buffer, "WM_COMMAND", MB_OK);
        }
    }

/*----------------------------------------------------------------*\
|                  TChekMenuWindow Class Member.                   |
\*----------------------------------------------------------------*/
void TChekMenuWindow::WMCreate(TMessage& Msg)
    {
    HMENU    hmenu;

    //  Get handle to top-level menu.
    hmenu = GetMenu (Msg.Receiver);

    //  Attach check marks to four menu items.

    //  (1) Edit-Undo, and set it to checked.
    SetMenuItemBitmaps (hmenu, IDM_EDIT_UNDO, MF_BYCOMMAND,
                        hbmCheck[0], hbmCheck[1]);
    CheckMenuItem (hmenu, IDM_EDIT_UNDO,
                   MF_BYCOMMAND | MF_CHECKED);

    //  (2) Edit-Cut, and leave it unchecked.
    SetMenuItemBitmaps (hmenu, IDM_EDIT_CUT, MF_BYCOMMAND,
                        hbmCheck[0], hbmCheck[1]);

    //  (3) Edit-Copy, and set it to checked.
    SetMenuItemBitmaps (hmenu, IDM_EDIT_COPY, MF_BYCOMMAND,
                        hbmCheck[2], hbmCheck[3]);
    CheckMenuItem (hmenu, IDM_EDIT_COPY,
                   MF_BYCOMMAND | MF_CHECKED);

    //  (4) Edit-Paste, and leave it unchecked.
    SetMenuItemBitmaps (hmenu, IDM_EDIT_PASTE, MF_BYCOMMAND,
                        hbmCheck[2], hbmCheck[3]);
    }
```

# CHEKMENU.H

```
/*----------------------------------------------------------------*\
|  Chekmenu.H - Include file for Chekmenu.cpp                      |
\*----------------------------------------------------------------*/


#define IDM_FILE_NEW     100
#define IDM_FILE_OPEN    101
#define IDM_FILE_SAVE    102
```

```
#define IDM_FILE_SAVEAS    103
#define IDM_FILE_PRINT     104
#define IDM_FILE_EXIT      105

#define IDM_EDIT_UNDO      200
#define IDM_EDIT_CUT       201
#define IDM_EDIT_COPY      202
#define IDM_EDIT_PASTE     203
#define IDM_EDIT_CLEAR     204
#define IDM_EDIT_DELETE    205
```

## CHEKMENU.RC

```
#include "Chekmenu.H"

snapshot icon ChekMenu.ico

hand cursor ChekMenu.cur

1 MENU
    {
    POPUP "&File"
        {
        MENUITEM "&New",            IDM_FILE_NEW
        MENUITEM "&Open...",        IDM_FILE_OPEN
        MENUITEM "&Save",           IDM_FILE_SAVE
        MENUITEM "Save &As...",     IDM_FILE_SAVEAS
        MENUITEM SEPARATOR
        MENUITEM "&Print",          IDM_FILE_PRINT
        MENUITEM SEPARATOR
        MENUITEM "E&xit",           IDM_FILE_EXIT
        }
    POPUP "&Edit"
        {
        MENUITEM "&Undo\tAlt+Backspace", IDM_EDIT_UNDO
        MENUITEM SEPARATOR
        MENUITEM "Cu&t\tShift+Del",      IDM_EDIT_CUT
        MENUITEM "&Copy\tCtrl+Ins",      IDM_EDIT_COPY
        MENUITEM "&Paste\tShift+Ins",    IDM_EDIT_PASTE
        MENUITEM SEPARATOR
        MENUITEM "Cl&ear",   IDM_EDIT_CLEAR
        MENUITEM "&Delete",  IDM_EDIT_DELETE
        }
    }
```

## CHEKMENU.DEF

```
NAME CHEKMENU

EXETYPE WINDOWS

DESCRIPTION 'ChekMenu - Custom menu checkmarks'

CODE MOVEABLE DISCARDABLE
DATA MOVEABLE MULTIPLE
```

```
HEAPSIZE   512
STACKSIZE 5120
```

CHEKMENU combines menu functionality into the window object. As with the other programs in this chapter, this was done to focus on the Windows API considerations rather than to demonstrate object-oriented design principles.

The initialization and creation of check marks in the menu were divided into two parts: In the window object constructor, bitmaps were created for both the checked and the unchecked states. In response to the WM_CREATE message, these bitmaps were attached to the menus and—for the sake of demonstration—some menu items were checked and some were left unchecked.

The window object constructor starts by asking the system for the expected size of a check mark:

```
//   Get checkmark dimension information.
dwCheck  = GetMenuCheckMarkDimensions();
cyHeight = HIWORD (dwCheck);
cxWidth  = LOWORD (dwCheck);
```

With this information in hand, CHEKMENU calculates a border around the edges of our check mark. This is necessary because the area that we are given actually touches the left border of a menu. The creation of a margin avoids the crowded appearance this might cause. We calculate our border by calling **GetSystemMetrics** with the **SM_CXBORDER** parameter, to get the width of a thin window border to use as a check mark margin:

```
/* Calculate a margin based on border widths.    */
cxMargin = GetSystemMetrics (SM_CXBORDER);
xMin = cxMargin;
xMax = cxWidth - cxMargin;
yMin = cxMargin;
yMax = cyHeight - cxMargin;
cxFourth = cxWidth/4;
cyFourth = cyHeight/4;
```

Since we're going to create a bitmap, we're going to want to initialize the bitmap background. We call **GetSysColor** for the menu background color, then use that color to create a brush:

```
/* Create the background brush to initialize bitmaps.*/
crBackground = GetSysColor (COLOR_MENU);
hbrBackground = CreateSolidBrush (crBackground);
```

As we saw in the BITMENU program, to draw in a bitmap you need a DC. Here is how CHEKMENU creates a DC, creates a set of bitmaps, and uses the background brush to initialize our bitmaps to the menu background color:

```
/* Create a DC and a set of bitmaps.           */
hdcScreen = GetDC (hwnd);
hdcBitmap = CreateCompatibleDC (hdcScreen);
hbrOld = SelectBrush (hdcBitmap, hbrBackground);

for (i=0;i<COUNT;i++)
    {
    hbmCheck[i] = CreateCompatibleBitmap (hdcScreen,
                                cxWidth, cyHeight);
    if (i==0)
        hbmOld = SelectBitmap (hdcBitmap, hbmCheck[0]);
    else
        SelectBitmap (hdcBitmap, hbmCheck[i]);
    PatBlt (hdcBitmap, 0, 0, cxWidth, cyHeight, PATCOPY);
    }
ReleaseDC (hwnd, hdcScreen);
```

Drawing the four check mark images is as simple as calling a few GDI routines. Of course, our four bitmaps share a DC, so **SelectBitmap** is needed to create the connection to each bitmap:

```
// Draw first unchecked menu item.
SelectBitmap (hdcBitmap, hbmCheck[0]);
Rectangle (hdcBitmap, xMin, yMin,
                      xMax, yMax);

// Draw first checked menu item.
SelectBitmap (hdcBitmap, hbmCheck[1]);
Rectangle (hdcBitmap, xMin, yMin,
                      xMax, yMax);

MoveTo (hdcBitmap, xMin, yMin);
LineTo (hdcBitmap, xMax, yMax);
MoveTo (hdcBitmap, xMin, yMax-1);
LineTo (hdcBitmap, xMax-1, yMin);

// Draw second unchecked menu item.
SelectBitmap (hdcBitmap, hbmCheck[2]);
Ellipse (hdcBitmap, xMin, yMin,
                    xMax, yMax);

// Draw second checked menu item.
SelectBitmap (hdcBitmap, hbmCheck[3]);
Ellipse (hdcBitmap, xMin, yMin,
                    xMax, yMax);

SelectBrush (hdcBitmap, GetStockBrush (BLACK_BRUSH));
Ellipse (hdcBitmap, xMin+cxFourth, yMin+cyFourth,
                    xMax-cxFourth, yMax-cyFourth);
```

The constructor concludes by cleaning up all of the GDI objects which have been created along the way. This involves making sure that connections to any GDI objects have first been removed:

```
// Clean up the GDI objects we've created.
SelectBrush (hdcBitmap, hbrOld);
SelectBitmap (hdcBitmap, hbmOld);
DeleteDC (hdcBitmap);
DeleteBrush (hbrBackground);

DeleteDC (hdcScreen);
```

The menu check marks are attached to our window object's menu in response to the **WM_CREATE** message. First, however, we need a handle to our window's top-level menu:

```
// Get handle to top-level menu.
hmenu = GetMenu (Msg.Receiver);
```

Then, it makes four calls to **SetMenuItemBitmaps**:

```
// Attach check marks to four menu items.

// (1) Edit-Undo, and set it to checked.
SetMenuItemBitmaps (hmenu, IDM_EDIT_UNDO, MF_BYCOMMAND,
                    hbmCheck[0], hbmCheck[1]);
CheckMenuItem (hmenu, IDM_EDIT_UNDO,
               MF_BYCOMMAND | MF_CHECKED);

// (2) Edit-Cut, and leave it unchecked.
SetMenuItemBitmaps (hmenu, IDM_EDIT_CUT, MF_BYCOMMAND,
                    hbmCheck[0], hbmCheck[1]);

// (3) Edit-Copy, and set it to checked.
SetMenuItemBitmaps (hmenu, IDM_EDIT_COPY, MF_BYCOMMAND,
                    hbmCheck[2], hbmCheck[3]);
CheckMenuItem (hmenu, IDM_EDIT_COPY,
               MF_BYCOMMAND | MF_CHECKED);

// (4) Edit-Paste, and leave it unchecked.
SetMenuItemBitmaps (hmenu, IDM_EDIT_PASTE, MF_BYCOMMAND,
                    hbmCheck[2], hbmCheck[3]);
```

That's all there is to it. At this point, we can check/uncheck the menu items, and the menu system will take care of displaying the right bitmap.

There is one more issue to contend with. Since we've created GDI bitmaps, we have to make sure we clean them up when we're done using them. Since we created them in the window object constructor, it makes sense to destroy them in the window object's destructor. That's just what CHEKMENU does:

```
TChekMenuWindow::~TChekMenuWindow()
    {
    int i;

    for (i=0;i<COUNT;i++)
        DeleteBitmap (hbmCheck[i]);
    }
```

The creation of custom check marks is straightforward, although it requires an understanding of how to create and manipulate GDI bitmaps. Once a bitmap has been created and attached to a DC, drawing in the bitmap involves calling the various GDI drawing routines: `PatBlt` to erase the background. Then `Rectangle`, `Ellipse`, `MoveTo`, and `LineTo` draw the actual check mark images. As we have shown in our sample programs, it is important to clean up GDI drawing objects you have created.

Our next chapter returns to a subject that we first touched on in Chapter 2 when we introduced our minimum Windows program. The issue is that of window creation. While a program doesn't have to create more than a single window to be useful, there are times when more windows are indispensable for providing a good user interface. And even if you never create more than one window in your windows programs, some of Windows' special capabilities are hidden in the window creation process. Let's roll up our sleeves and take a look at what those capabilities are.

# 13

# Windowing

Up to now, every program in this book has had a single top-level window. While you could use this approach for all of your Windows programs, there are times when it makes sense for a program to have more than a single window. For example, programs that use the **Multiple Document Interface** (MDI) standard create a new window for every new document. Programs that use dialog boxes also use multiple windows, since dialog boxes themselves are windows, as are the pushbuttons, listboxes, and other controls that live inside dialog boxes. We'll describe dialog boxes further in Chapter 14.

A program might create multiple windows to divide a single window into smaller work areas. For example, programs often place scroll bars, which are windows, inside other windows so the user can control which portion of the data is visible. Consider a terminal emulation program, which might use a tiny text window to display communication status information. Another type of application, such as a word processing program, might show a document's margin and tab settings inside a small window resting next to a larger document window. There are as many possibilities as there are types of applications.

To help you understand how to use multiple windows effectively, we're going to discuss the implementation details that make Windows' windows unique. We're going to start by looking at the two-step process for creating a window: window class registration and window creation. We'll then discuss what size to make an application's top-level window. And finally, we'll cover the creation of a child window as an application "status window." Among other tasks, this window will output details to help users browse through a program's menus. And, in keeping with the spirit of this book, we'll provide working samples to help you with your own programming projects.

## The Window Creation Process

In Chapter 2, we introduced the minimum Windows program. At the time, we said that window creation was a two-step process. We introduced you to the two routines that control the operation of each of those steps, **RegisterClass** and **CreateWindow**; but we refrained from going into more detail until now. As you'll see, the window creation process is quite involved and gives you quite a few choices over the shape, size, style, and behavior of a window. When we first described the window creation process, you probably suspected that we were holding out on you. In particular, the sheer number of fields in the **WNDCLASS** data structure and the number of parameters that are passed to **CreateWindow** hint at more possibilities than we told you.

OK. It's time for us to come clean with you. Let's start by looking at the first part of the window creation process, which revolves around a single data structure: the window class.

## *Window Classes*

In the same way that a C++ class is a template to create instances of different objects, a window class is a template for creating windows. While a C++ class can have multiple member functions, a window class has only *one* function, called a window procedure. The structure of the OWL application framework lets you define a set of message response functions, to redirect the flow of window messages. Nonetheless, it's important for you to understand the way Windows itself is working for you.

Let's take a closer look at the window class registration process to understand what data members are associated with a window class. Here is how a non-OWL program would handle registering a window class:

```
WNDCLASS wc;

    wc.lpszClassName = "MIN:MAIN";
    wc.hInstance     = hInstance;
    wc.lpfnWndProc   = MinWndProc;
    wc.hCursor       = LoadCursor(hInstance, "hand");
    wc.hIcon         = LoadIcon(hInstance,"snapshot");
    wc.lpszMenuName  = NULL;
    wc.hbrBackground = COLOR_WINDOW+1;
    wc.style         = NULL;
    wc.cbClsExtra    = 0;
    wc.cbWndExtra    = 0;

    RegisterClass( &wndclass );
```

The **lpszClassName** field defines an ASCII text string for the class name. Although in earlier versions of Windows there was a problem creating names that were identical with existing class names, in Windows 3.0 and later all window classes are **private classes** by default. A private window class is only accessible from a single program. This means that you can use any name you'd like and know that it won't interfere with the class names of other programs. Avoid the predefined dialog box classes to avoid interfering with dialog boxes: **button, combobox, edit, listbox, scroll bar,** and **static**. In addition, to avoid getting in the way of Windows' MDI support, don't create a class with the name **mdiclient**.

The `hInstance` field tells Windows which program created the window class. The primary reason has to do with internal housekeeping. After every instance of a program has terminated, then Windows de-registers the classes that the program created.

The `lpfnWndProc` field identifies the function that will process messages for the windows in the class. A window procedure can support multiple windows because each window has a unique window handle. When a message is delivered to a window procedure, the window handle tells the window procedure exactly *which* window is sending the message. If you want to treat different windows in a different manner, you can look at the window handle to know who is calling.

The `hCursor` field is a handle to a cursor shared by all members of a window class. The default window procedure uses this to install the correct cursor whenever it receives a **WM_SETCURSOR** message. If you want a window to have a *private* cursor, different from the class cursor, you need to process this message. If you need further information, skip ahead to Chapter 16, which covers issues relating to the mouse, mouse message traffic, and custom cursors.

The `hIcon` field is a handle to an icon that is displayed when a window in the class is minimized. Not every kind of window will use its icon. Icons are only displayed for top-level windows (windows that have no parents) and document windows in programs that use the MDI. The typical way for a program to define an icon handle is to load the icon, as shown here:

```
wc.hIcon   =   LoadIcon(hInstance,"snapshot");
```

A program can also draw an icon on the fly by defining a null icon:

```
wc.hIcon = NULL;
```

When the window is iconized, it appears as a tiny, empty window. Creating a drawing for the icon is surprisingly simple: You handle the **WM_PAINT** message just as you would when the window is *not* iconized. The only difference is that you need to be prepared to draw into a very tiny area. Here is a sample code fragment that draws an icon when the window is minimized:

```
    void TSample::Paint(HDC hdc, PAINTSTRUCT& ps)
        {
        char ach[40];
        HBRUSH hbr;
        POINT apt[4];
        RECT r;
        TEXTMETRIC tm;
```

328  User Interface Objects

```
    if (IsIconic (hwnd))
        {
        GetTextMetrics (hdc, &tm);
        GetClientRect (hwnd, &r);
        r.bottom -= tm.tmHeight/2;

        /*  Draw a rectangle.                             */
        Rectangle (hdc, 0, 0, r.right, r.bottom);

        /*  Draw an ellipse.                              */
        hbr = GetStockBrush (GRAY_BRUSH);
        SelectBrush (hdc, hbr);
        Ellipse (hdc, 0, 0, r.right, r.bottom);

        /*  Draw a triangle.                              */
        hbr = GetStockBrush (BLACK_BRUSH);
        SelectBrush (hdc, hbr);
        apt[0].x = r.right/2;    apt[0].y = 0;
        apt[1].x = 0;            apt[1].y = r.bottom;
        apt[2].x = r.right;      apt[2].y = r.bottom;
        apt[3].x = r.right/2;    apt[3].y = 0;

        Polygon (hdc, apt, 4);
        }
    }
```

The icon created by this code fragment is shown in Figure 13.1. It creates our on-the-fly icon by drawing a rectangle, an ellipse, and a triangle.

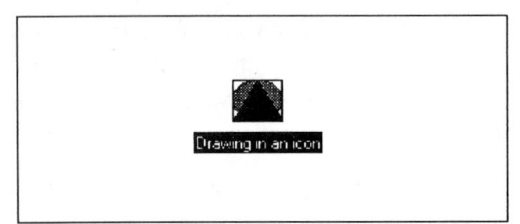

**Figure 13.1**  *Drawing in a NULL icon*

A window created from a window class with a null icon has one more issue to deal with. That issue involves the choice of icons to display when the user drags the iconic program. When the user drags a program that does have an icon, the mouse cursor changes to the shape of that icon. But when a program's window doesn't have an icon, it has two choices: It can let the system display a default icon, or it can provide one in response to the **WM_QUERYDRAGICON** message. Here, for example, is what a program without an icon might do when sent this message:

```
    void TSample::WMQueryDragIcon(HDC hdc, PAINTSTRUCT& ps)
        {
        HANDLE hIcon;

        hIcon = LoadIcon (hInstance, "DRAGICON");
        return (MAKELONG(hIcon, 0));
        }
        ...
```

A top-level window without an icon will see other message traffic that is different from that which is sent to windows that *do* have an icon. As our earlier code fragment indicates, a top-level window without an icon will receive a **WM_PAINT** message when it's time to draw its iconized image. Top-level windows *with* icons receive a **WM_PAINTICON** message instead. The default window procedure responds to this message by displaying the icon for the window class. A program that had a class icon that wanted to draw a custom icon could respond to the **WM_PAINTICON** message and create an on-the-fly icon if it wanted to.

The **lpszMenuName** field identifies the class menu by name. As we discussed in Chapter 11 when we introduced menus, this value can take one of three forms. For a menu resource defined like this:

```
15 MENU
    {
    POPUP "File"
        {
        MENUITEM "New", IDM_NEW
        ...
```

the menu name can be a character string preceded by a # sign:

`wc.lpszMenuName   = "#15";`

Alternatively, the **MAKEINTRESOURCE** macro can be used to sneak in an integer value in place of a long pointer to a string. Here is an example showing how the **MAKEINTRESOURCE** macro can be used:

`wc.lpszMenuName   = MAKEINTRESOURCE(15);`

A third choice, but a less attractive one because it consumes more memory and is slower, involves using a regular character string:

```
MyMenu MENU
    {
    POPUP "File"
        {
        MENUITEM "New", IDM_NEW
        .
        .
        .
```

To load this menu into memory, you provide the name of the menu in the **WNDCLASS** data structure, as shown here:

`wc.lpszMenuName   = "MyMenu";`

The disadvantage to this approach is that a string takes up more space than an integer. This means that this approach takes more memory. When the time comes to load the menu, an integer identifier allows faster loading than a string identifier since an integer compare is faster than a string compare. From the point of view of performance and memory use, integer values are better.

The **hbrBackground** field is a handle to a brush that is used to fill the background before any drawing is done. The default window procedure fills in the background in response to the **WM_ERASEBACKGROUND** message. This seems like a funny name for the messages, since in fact the background is really *painted* and not erased. However, it *does* suggest the idea that whatever was in the window before is removed to provide a clean surface on which to draw. There are two types of values that can be placed in this field: a brush handle and an index to a system color. Here is how to use a stock black brush for the background:

```
wc.hbrBackground = GetStockObject (BLACK_BRUSH);
```

A better alternative, however, involves using a "magic number" for the background color, like this:

```
wc.hbrBackground = COLOR_WINDOW+1;
```

When the default window procedure sees this value, it uses the default window background color that the user has defined from the Control Panel.

The **cbClsExtra** field defines the number of bytes that are added at the end of the class definition as a reserved data area. These bytes are known as **class extra bytes**. This data area can be used by a program for any purpose, but Windows does not provide a pointer to the data area itself. Instead, you must set these values using the **SetClassWord** and **SetClassLong** routines, and retrieve them using the **GetClassWord** and **GetClassLong** routines. If you don't plan to use class extra bytes, be sure to initialize **cbClsExtra** to zero. If you don't explicitly initialize this field to zero, it is possible that some random, large value will be passed as the number of bytes to be allocated. Initializing to zero avoids an accidental waste of memory.

The **cbWndExtra** field, like the **cbClsExtra** field, defines a reserved data area for the private use of your application. These bytes are referred to as **window extra bytes**. Unlike class extra bytes, which are shared by every window in a class, window extra bytes are reserved for the private use of each individual window. They provide a way for a window to have its own "bank account" for bytes that it wishes to use—like having a Swiss bank account. To read the value of the window extra bytes, a program calls either **GetWindowWord** or **GetWindowLong**. These routines take a window handle as a parameter to identify exactly whose bytes are to be accessed. To write values into the window extra bytes, a program must call the **SetWindowWord** or **SetWindowLong** routines. These routines also take a window handle, which lets the Window Manager know into whose bank account you wish to make a deposit.

The **style** field is a 16-bit field that contains a set of flags that describe various features of the window class. There are 13 style flags, as shown in Figure 13.2. Let's look at each of the window class style bits in detail.

*Windowing* 331

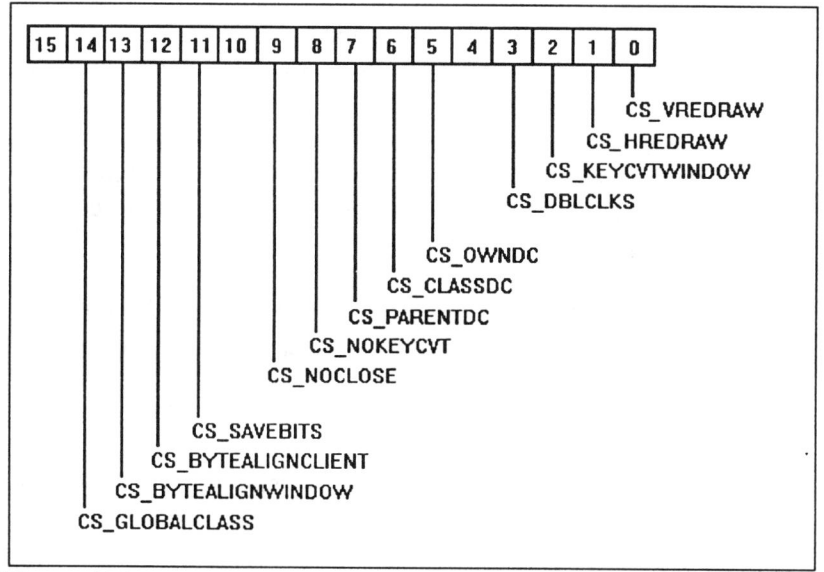

```
┌─────────────────────────────────────────────────┐
│ │15│14│13│12│11│10│ 9│ 8│ 7│ 6│ 5│ 4│ 3│ 2│ 1│ 0│ │
│                                           │    │
│                                           CS_VREDRAW
│                                        CS_HREDRAW
│                                    CS_KEYCVTWINDOW
│                                 CS_DBLCLKS
│                           CS_OWNDC
│                        CS_CLASSDC
│                     CS_PARENTDC
│                  CS_NOKEYCVT
│               CS_NOCLOSE
│         CS_SAVEBITS
│      CS_BYTEALIGNCLIENT
│   CS_BYTEALIGNWINDOW
│ CS_GLOBALCLASS
└─────────────────────────────────────────────────┘
```

**Figure 13.2** The thirteen WNDCLASS style bits

## *Window Class Style Bits*

A lot of the subtlety in creating windows actually comes from certain class style bits that you can select. Let's take a look at all of them, to try to understand where they can be useful in a Windows program.

The **CS_VREDRAW** and **CS_HREDRAW** styles determine whether the window should be completely redrawn when the user changes the window size in either the vertical (**CS_VREDRAW**) or horizontal (**CS_HREDRAW**) direction. In other words, they determine whether a call is made like the following when a window's size changes:

```
InvalidateRect (hwnd, NULL, TRUE);
```

As you probably remember, the `InvalidateRect` routine is used to mark a portion of a window as damaged, which means that a **WM_PAINT** message will eventually be generated to repair the window. A `NULL` value in the second parameter declares the *entire* window to be damaged. The `TRUE` value in the last parameter requests that the damaged area (in this case, the entire window) be erased before being redrawn.

Two style bits are referenced in WINDOWS.H but not mentioned in the documentation: **CS_KEYCVTWINDOW** and **CS_NOKEYCVT**. They seem to be remnants of support for a Kanji conversion window for Japanese Windows. However, Microsoft has created a separate version of Windows for the Japanese market, which also requires its own special version of the Windows Software Development Kit. Therefore, even though these style bits promise built-in Kanji support, you must obtain the special Software Development Kit to develop Windows programs for the Japanese-speaking market.

If you want a window to receive double-click mouse messages (`WM_LBUTTONDBLCLK`, `WM_MBUTTONDBLCLK`, or `WM_RBUTTONDBLCLK`), then you must use the `CS_DBLCLKS` style bit. As we'll show in Chapter 16, when we discuss mouse input, this special style bit causes a timer to be set when an initial mouse click is received. A double-click message is generated only when a second click is received before the timer runs out. The presence of this style bit helps the Window Manager to decide when to start the timer in response to a mouse click message.

Two style bits allow a window to have a private device context (DC): `CS_OWNDC` and `CS_CLASSDC`. When we introduced the device context in Chapter 6, we mentioned that most programs borrow a DC from the system DC cache. But because of the overhead associated with checking out and returning a DC, some programs prefer to have their own. In the same way that library books require more effort than books that you own, borrowed DCs require more effort. Of course, like private book collections, private DCs cost more in terms of memory required.

How much *does* a private DC cost? Although there has been talk among Windows programmers for some years that a DC is 800 bytes, in fact the actual size is about 200 bytes, all of which are allocated from GDI's local heap. While this doesn't seem like a lot, the allocation of a private DC has to be weighed against the fact that, as we'll discuss in Chapter 18, GDI's local heap space is a shared resource that all programs compete for. Therefore, avoid allocating a private DC unless you really need it.

So when is the cost of a private DC justified? In general, programs that do a lot of drawing, and programs that interact with the user *while* drawing, may run faster with a private DC. A word processor program, for example, that displays text as the user types may get a performance boost by getting its own, private DC. Or a drawing package that interacts with the user to interactively draw pictures may get a slight performance benefit from a private DC. In general, in a program that uses keystrokes or mouse clicks to draw, you might find that a private DC is faster to work with than a shared, system DC.

The `CS_OWNDC` style bit gives a private DC to *every window* in a class. This type of DC is the most expensive, in terms of memory used, but gives the fastest response. It is the most expensive because one DC is allocated for each window in a class. It is fastest because you don't incur the overhead of borrowing and returning the DC every time you draw. As illustrated in the following code fragment, a window created from a class with the `CS_OWNDC` style bit can get a DC handle during the `WM_CREATE` message and use it when it needs to draw for any other message:

```
class TSample : TWindow
    {
    ...
    HDC hdc;
    ...
    }
```

```
void TSample::WMCreate(TMessage& Msg)
{
    hdc = GetDC (hwnd);
}

void TSample::WMLButtonDown(TMessage& Msg)
    {
    TextOut (hdc, ...);
    ...
    }

void TSample::WMChar(TMessage& Msg)
    {
    TextOut (hdc, ...);
    ...
    }
```

Besides the **WM_CREATE** message, the only other time this window procedure asks for a DC is in response to a **WM_PAINT** message, when a regular `BeginPaint/EndPaint` sandwich is used. This contrasts sharply with the approach that programs must take when they use a system DC. As shown in this code fragment, such programs must borrow and return a DC for each message:

```
class TSample : TWindow
    {
    ...
    }

void TSample::WMLButtonDown(TMessage& Msg)
    {
    hdc = GetDC (hwnd);
    TextOut (hdc, ...);
    ...
    ReleaseDC (hwnd, hdc);
    }

void TSample::WMChar(TMessage& Msg)
    {
    hdc = GetDC (hwnd);
    TextOut (hdc, ...);
    ...
    ReleaseDC (hwnd, hdc);
    }
```

From this, you can see that one advantage of a private DC is that programs don't have to borrow a DC every time they wish to draw. A second advantage is that a program can set up the DC's drawing attributes and then not have to worry about them again. In contrast with this is the way programs must work with system DCs. Every time a system DC is borrowed, its drawing attributes are reset to their initial, default state. Programs that use a system DC have to set up the DC drawing attributes every time they wish to draw.

Programs with a private DC must still use a `BeginPaint/EndPaint` sandwich in response to a **WM_PAINT** message. This is because the **WM_PAINT** message can only be turned off by the use of these two routines. `BeginPaint` is smart enough to recognize when a window has a private DC, and it returns the correct DC handle inside the **PAINTSTRUCT** structure. The only difference is that the DC will have a clipping region installed to limit drawing to the damaged part of the window.

The `CS_CLASSDC` style provides a DC that is similar to a private DC except that it is shared by an entire class of Windows and not owned by a single window. Like a private DC, the drawing attributes in a class DC are not reset every time the DC is returned. This gives us a slight performance improvement over a regular system DC, in which drawing attributes *are* reset. Therefore, a class DC has some of the benefits of a private DC except that it is shared between several windows of the same class. Because it is shared between windows, a class DC must be handled like a system DC. In other words, it must be borrowed when needed—using either `GetDC` or `BeginPaint`—and returned when it is not needed—using either `ReleaseDC` or `EndPaint`.

The `CS_PARENTDC` style can also help improve performance when drawing in a window. Unlike the private DC and the class DC, however, a parent DC does not cause a new DC to be allocated in the system. Instead, a window with this style bit will receive a regular DC from the system's DC cache.

The difference lies in the way that clipping is set in the DC. Unlike a regular DC, in which clipping is set either to the visible part of the client area (by `GetDC`) or to the damaged part of a window (by `BeginPaint`), clipping in a parent DC is set to the boundaries of the parent window. Figure 13.3 compares the clipping that is set up in a regular system DC and in a parent DC. With the parent DC, the child window can draw anywhere in the client area of its parent's window. If you have children, this may sound like a familiar state of affairs. Even if your children have their own rooms, they certainly are not shy about wandering into other rooms in your home.

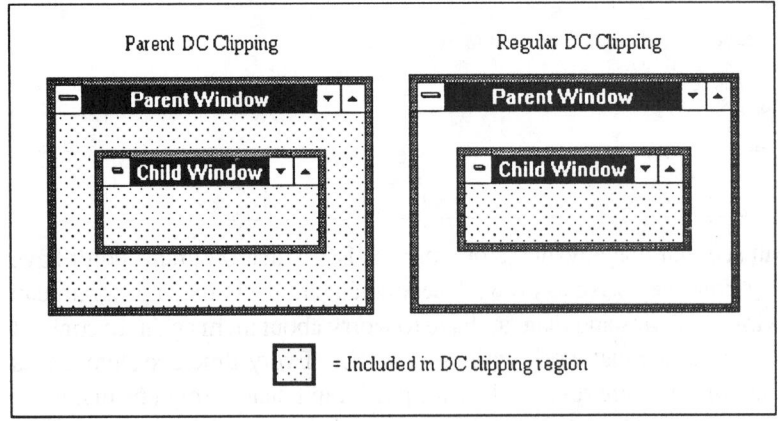

**Figure 13.3** Comparison of clipping in a system cache DC and in a parent DC

You might be wondering why on earth anyone would give a child window the ability to draw into its parent's client area. This is a performance optimization to help in situations when the child is drawing in a very small space and may accidentally draw outside its own border (kids will be kids).

The parent DC style bit is set for the predefined classes that create Windows' dialog box controls. As you will see when we discuss dialog boxes in Chapter 14, dialog box controls are given a size and a position using a special set of coordinates called **dialog box coordinates**. Since there can be some degree of imprecision with these coordinates, the parent DC style bit gives the dialog box controls room to maneuver. If you create your own custom dialog box controls, you may wish to use the `CS_PARENTDC` style bit for them as well.

The `CS_PARENTDC` style bit is not compatible with the `WS_CLIPCHILDREN` style that we'll discuss when we look at `CreateWindow` style bits. If the parent window has this window style bit set, then its child windows cannot draw in the parent's window. You might call this the "Aunt Edna" style bit, since the kids don't run around as much (or at all) when your Aunt Edna comes over (she has a way with kids).

The `CS_NOCLOSE` class style removes the *Close* item from the system menu. You use this with windows that have a system menu, which shouldn't be closed by the user. Of course, as we discussed in Chapter 11, another way to achieve the same result involves modifying the system menu using the various menu modification routines. This style bit provides a simpler way to achieve the same end, providing that you need this behavior for every window in the window class.

The `CS_SAVEBITS` class style is a performance bit that you set for windows that visit the display screen for very short periods of time. The save-bits style asks the Window Manager to take a snapshot of the bits that the window overwrites when it appears. You may recall that this is how menus are able to make a graceful exit when they leave. After a menu disappears, a window never gets a `WM_PAINT` message to redraw the area that the menu had occupied. Menus are very polite: They don't damage any window on the display screen.

The save-bits style asks every window in a class to provide the same courtesy. The class of windows that are used to create dialog boxes are set up this way. For the most part, when a dialog box visits your window, it can disappear quickly and easily without requiring your window to be sent a `WM_PAINT` message to redraw. But sometimes things happen that thwart the save-bits style. For example, if the dialog box moves, the bitmap snapshot of the area behind the dialog box can no longer be used to restore the area after the dialog box is removed. Or, if any drawing is done underneath the dialog box, then the bitmap snapshot will also be unusable to restore the area covered by the dialog box. In both cases, a `WM_PAINT` message is generated to repair the damage caused by the exit of the dialog box (or the other window).

Two class style bits are used to specify how a window should be positioned on the display screen: `CS_BYTEALIGNWINDOW` and `CS_BYTEALIGNCLIENT`. These style bits never affect the height of a window or its placement on the *y*-axis. However, they *do* affect the width of a window and its placement on the *x*-axis. As the names suggest, these style bits force either a window or its client area to be aligned on a byte boundary. This allows a performance improvement for certain types of operations: moving the window, drawing menu items, and drawing into the window.

Byte-aligned drawing is faster on certain types of devices: monochrome displays and color displays that use multiple planes to represent color. In fact, the only kind of device that doesn't really benefit from byte-aligned drawing is a color display that uses a packed pixel approach to storing data. Since all of the most popular display devices are either monochrome or color with multiple planes (including EGA, VGA, and 8514), the byte-aligned style can give a program a slight performance improvement.

The **CS_GLOBALCLASS** class style is used for window classes that are going to be shared among different programs. For example, if you are going to create a custom dialog box control, you'll want to register the window class of your dialog box control as a global class. This allows a single window class to be shared among several programs. For example, you could use your custom dialog box control to create your spreadsheet program, your word processing program, and even for your database program.

Once a window class has been registered, you can create as many copies of the window as you like. There are two Windows library routines that do this for you, which is what we're going to look at next.

## Creating a Window

In general, an OWL program creates a window by creating a window object. In every program in this book, an application object member function—**InitMainWindow**—creates a window object (and an MS-Windows window) with a statement like this:

```
MainWindow = new TMinWindow (NULL, "Minimum", NULL);
```

To get the most from an MS-Windows window, though, you need to understand all the capabilities which are embodied in the window creation routines.

First, let's take a brief look at the **TWindowAttr** structure. Every descendent of **TWindow** has a data member of this type called **Attr**. You control the MS-Windows window creation process by changing values in this data structure. For the changes to affect the window creation process, the changes must be made in a window object's constructor. Here is **TWindowAttr**, as defined in WINDOW.H:

```
struct _CLASSTYPE TWindowAttr {
    DWORD Style;
    DWORD ExStyle;
    int X, Y, W, H;
    LPSTR Menu;     // Menu name
    int Id ;        // Child identifier
    LPSTR Param;
};
```

These parameters are passed to one of the MS-Windows window creation routines, **CreateWindowEx**. Let's examine both window creation routines.

Two Windows library routines create a window: **CreateWindow** and **CreateWindowEx**. The "Ex" at the end of the second routine's name stands for "extended." The extended routine does all of the things that the first routine can do, plus a little more. The **CreateWindowEx** routine was created because Windows ran out of style bits in the **CreateWindow** routine. This being the case, we're going to start by looking at the parameters to these routines and then consider all of the available style bits—both regular and extended.

**CreateWindow** is defined as follows:

```
CreateWindow (lpClassName, lpWindowName,
              dwStyle, X, Y, nWidth, nHeight,
              hWndParent, hMenu, hInstance, lpParaml)
```

The extended style bits parameter is the first one in **CreateWindowEx**, which is defined as

```
CreateWindowEx (dwExStyle, lpClassName, lpWindowName,
                dwStyle, X, Y, nWidth, nHeight,
                hWndParent, hMenu, hInstance, lpParaml)
```

The value of **dwExStyle** is an unsigned long (**DWORD**) value of the extended style bits for use with the **CreateWindowEx** routine. We'll discuss the regular and extended style bits in a moment.

The **lpClassName** parameter is a long pointer to a character string for the class name. This is the class name that you defined using the **RegisterClass** routine, or it can be the name of a public window class that was created by someone else. For example, Windows makes available the following public window classes: **button, combobox, edit, listbox, scroll bar,** and **static**. We'll take a closer look at each of these classes when we discuss dialog boxes in Chapter 14. There isn't a **TWindowAttr** data member for the window class. The reason is that the window class name is provided by the **GetClassName** member function, which you'll need to override to define the window class for your window object.

The **lpWindowName** parameter is a long pointer to a character string for the window text. The window text is displayed in the titlebar (also known as a caption bar) for windows that have a titlebar. When a window is minimized—is put into an iconic state—the window text is displayed as a label for the icon. Certain types of windows that don't have a titlebar, like pushbuttons, use the window text as a window label.

The **dwStyle** parameter is an unsigned long (**DWORD**) value that contains a set of flags to define the shape, size, and behavior of the window you wish to create. We'll discuss style bits, along with the extended style bits, in a moment.

The **X** and **Y** parameters identify the $x$ and $y$ coordinates of the upper-left corner of the window. For top-level windows—that is, windows that don't have parents—this location is relative to the upper-left corner of the display screen, also known as **screen coordinates**. For child windows, this is relative to the upper-left corner of the parent window's client area, also known as client area coordinates.

338    User Interface Objects

The Window Manager calculates the location of a top-level window when the value of the *x* coordinate is set to `CW_USEDEFAULT`. When this option is used, each subsequent top-level window is given an initial position that cascades from the previous window. This option arranges top-level windows in an orderly fashion, like soldiers in a row. Figure 13.4 shows the cascading effect created by this flag.

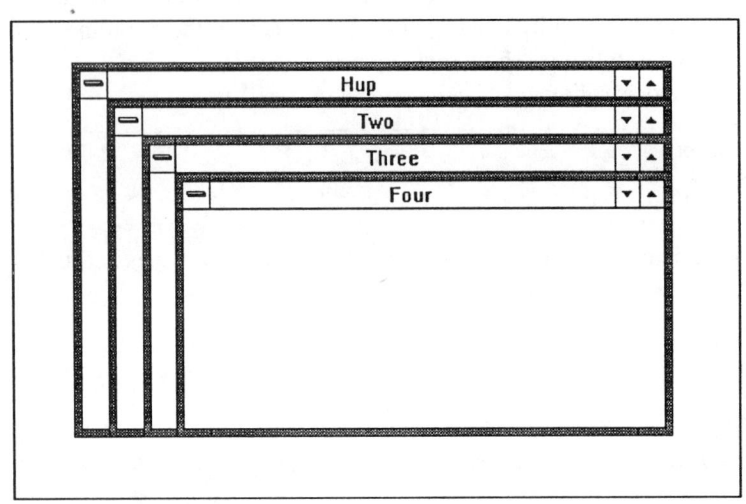

**Figure 13.4** Cascading effect of the CW_USEDEFAULT FLAG

The `nWidth` and `nHeight` fields allow you to define the width and height of a window. For top-level windows, you can set `nWidth` to `CW_USEDEFAULT`. This tells the Window Manager to set the size of your window for you. But this feature is not available for child windows, so you will have to calculate their size yourself.

When you calculate the size of a window—whether it is a child window or a top-level window—you'll need to keep in mind that `CreateWindow` and `CreateWindowEx` expect the size of the *entire* window and not just the client area. Many programmers make the mistake of calculating the size of the client area and using those dimensions. But an additional step is required: You must add in the size of the various nonclient area objects. When we discuss the issue of window metrics later in this chapter, we'll describe two different ways to calculate the size of the actual window to get a client area of the desired size.

The `hwndParent` parameter identifies the window that is to be the parent of the newborn window. Windows that don't have a parent can pass a NULL value in this field, which effectively makes the window a child of the desktop window. Children of the desktop are considered top-level windows and are shown in the Task List window that appears with the [Ctrl] + [Esc] key combination.

When we discuss window style bits, you'll see that there are three different kinds of windows: overlapped, popup, and child. When you create a child window, it *must* have a parent window. This agrees with the way we think of human parents and children: Children

*Windowing* 339

depend on their parents for their well-being. The other two types of windows do not require a parent.

The `hMenu` parameter identifies the menu that is to be associated with a window. We have already seen that a menu name can be supplied in the `lpszMenuName` field when we register a window class. But, to use a menu that is different from the default class menu, we can specify a menu handle in this field. As we discussed in Chapter 11 when we introduced menus, the `LoadMenu` routine provides one way to obtain a menu handle when a menu has been defined in a program's resource file:

```
HANDLE hMenu;
hMenu = LoadMenu (hInstance, "MENUNAME");
```

The OWL libraries call `LoadMenu` for you, which is why you provide a menu name (and not a handle) *both* when you register a window class *and* when in the `Attr` window creation structure.

The `hInstance` parameter is a handle to an instance. Earlier, we said that this identifies the instance currently running. When we discuss dynamic linking in Chapter 19, you'll see that the instance handle is actually a memory handle that identifies a program's default data segment. The presence of this value in the parameter list plays a part in making sure that the window procedure is able to access its data segment correctly.

While this may seem like an odd issue when you are creating a window, keep in mind that a window procedure is a call-back function that is, in effect, a subroutine used exclusively by Windows. The part of Windows that calls this subroutine—Windows' USER module—has its own data segment. When a call is made into the window procedure, it goes through a gateway that uses the value of `hInstance` to store the value of our data segment into the CPU's AX register. As we'll discuss in more detail in Chapter 19, the compiler, linker, and Windows' loader work together so that this value ends up in the CPU's DS or data segment register.

Fortunately, this mechanism is transparent to you. Your window procedure is able to access your program's static data without having to do anything special—it only requires that you use the right compiler switches and that you list your window procedure in the EXPORTS section of the module definition (.DEF) file. All the rest is taken care of for you through the magic of dynamic linking.

The `lpParam` parameter is an optional, four-byte-long value that you can use to pass private data to your window procedure along with the `WM_CREATE` message. If you translate this Hungarian notation into English, this field is intended to hold a long pointer, presumably to a private parameter block. But if you only have, say, two bytes of private data to pass, then you don't need to use it as a long pointer but can simply pass the two bytes inside the pointer field.

If you *do* wish it to pass a parameter block, here is an example to show you how to go about doing it. We start by allocating a data block and passing a pointer to the block in the last parameter of `CreateWindow`:

## 340  User Interface Objects

```
LPSTR  lp;
RECT   rPrivate;

rPrivate.left  = 10;   rPrivate.top    = 20;
rPrivate.right = 200;  rPrivate.bottom = 100;

lp = (LPSTR)&rPrivate;

hwnd = CreateWindow("MIN:MAIN",      /* Class name.   */
           "Minimum",                /* Title.        */
           WS_OVERLAPPEDWINDOW,      /* Style bits.   */
           CW_USEDEFAULT,            /* x - default.  */
           0,                        /* y - default.  */
           CW_USEDEFAULT,            /* cx - default. */
           0,                        /* cy - default. */
           NULL,                     /* No parent.    */
           NULL,                     /* Class menu.   */
           hInstance,                /* Creator.      */
           lp);                      /* Params.       */
```

In this example, our data block is simply a **RECT** structure containing two (*x,y*) pairs that presumably are of interest to our window procedure. A pointer to this structure is placed in the lpParam parameter, which is the last parameter of **CreateWindow**.

Within the OWL framework, you'll pass the data block by defining it in the **Param** member of the **TWindowAttr** data structure, like this:

`Attr.Param = lp`

The time to get a pointer to our data block is during the processing for the **WM_CREATE** message. The **lParam** parameter of our window procedure will contain a pointer to a data structure defined in WINDOWS.H as **CREATESTRUCT**. It is defined in WINDOWS.H as:

```
typedef struct tagCREATESTRUCT
    {
    LPSTR    lpCreateParams;
    HANDLE   hInstance;
    HANDLE   hMenu;
    HWND     hwndParent;
    int      cy;
    int      cx;
    int      y;
    int      x;
    LONG     style;
    LPSTR    lpszName;
    LPSTR    lpszClass;
    DWORD    dwExStyle;
    } CREATESTRUCT;
```

The first item in this structure, **lpCreateParams**, is the value that we passed as our last parameter to **CreateWindow**. Here is one way to create a pointer to our rectangle data:

```
void TSample::WMCreate(TMessage& Msg)
    {
    int xTop;
    LPCREATESTRUCT lpcs;
    LPRECT lpr;

    lpcs = (LPCREATESTRUCT)Msg.LParam;
    lpr  = (LPRECT)lpcs->lpCreateParams;

    xTop = lpr -> top;  /* =20    */
    ...
```

If you pass a pointer to a data block, you'll want to make a local copy of the data block for your window procedure, since the pointer may not be valid after the conclusion of the **WM_CREATE** message. As we'll discuss in Chapter 17 when we discuss memory issues, when Windows is operating in Real Mode, pointers can become invalid since the address of data objects can move. The pointer may also become invalid if the caller decides to free the memory that had been allocated to hold the data object.

At this point, we have discussed all of the parameters to `CreateWindow` and `CreateWindowEx`. To get a complete picture of what these routines have to offer, we need to dig a little deeper and investigate the different style bits that can be passed in the `dwExStyle` and `dwStyle` parameters.

## Window Creation Style Bits

There are five categories of style bits to control window creation for `CreateWindow` and `CreateWindowEx`: type of window, window border, nonclient area components, the window's initial state, and performance bits. These are summarized in Table 13.1.

Table 13.1  Summary of CreateWindow and CreateWindowEx style bits

| Category | Style Bit | Description |
|---|---|---|
| Type of Window (3) | WS_OVERLAPPED | Create an overlapped window, suitable for use as a top-level window. Overlapped windows always have a caption whether or not you specify the WS_CAPTION style. And they always have a border. A border of type |

*(Continued)*

**Table 13.1** Continued

| Category | Style Bit | Description |
|---|---|---|
| | | WS_BORDER is used if no other type has been requested. |
| | WS_POPUP | Create a popup window, suitable for use as a dialog box or secondary window. |
| | WS_CHILD | Create a child window, suitable for dividing up the area of overlapped, popup, and other child windows into smaller functional areas. |
| Window Border (4) | WS_BORDER | Window is to have a thin border. This is the default when a caption bar has been requested (with the WS_CAPTION style). |
| | WS_DLGFRAME | Window is to have a thick, solid border. In previous versions of Windows, this was the standard for dialog boxes. The WS_EX_DLGMODALFRAME style bit is used in Windows 3.0 instead. |
| | WS_THICKFRAME | Window is to have a thick frame. The presence of this border indicates that a window can be resized. The WS_CAPTION style must accompany this selection. |
| | WS_EX_DLGMODALFRAME | Window is to have an extended dialog frame, to include a system menu and caption bar, if requested. This is the standard style for dialog boxes. |
| Non-Client Components (6) | WS_CAPTION | Window has a caption, also known as a titlebar. A caption is always accompanied by a border, with the WS_BORDER selected by default. |
| | WS_HSCROLL | Specifies to create the window with a horizontal scroll bar. Scroll bars created using this style bit are always on the bottom edge of the window. To place a scroll bar in another part of a |

*(Continued)*

**Table 13.1** Continued

| Category | Style Bit | Description |
|---|---|---|
| | | window, you must create a scroll bar control. |
| | WS_MAXIMIZEBOX | Window is to have a maximize box. The WS_CAPTION style must accompany this selection. |
| | WS_MINIMIZEBOX | Window is to have a minimize box. The WS_CAPTION style must accompany this selection. |
| | WS_SYSMENU | Window is to have a system menu. The WS_CAPTION style must accompany this selection. |
| | WS_VSCROLL | Window is to have a vertical scroll bar. Scroll bars created using this style bit are always placed on the right edge of the window. To locate a scroll bar at another location, you must create a scroll bar control. |
| Initial State (5) | WS_DISABLED | Window is initially disabled, which means that mouse and keyboard input is not delivered to the window. If the user tries to click on a disabled window, a warning beep is generated. |
| | WS_ICONIC | Window is initially iconic or minimized, which means that window is closed, and only its icon is displayed. |
| | WS_MAXIMIZE | Window is initially maximized. For top-level windows, this means it occupies the complete display screen. For child windows, it means it occupies its parent's entire client area. |
| | WS_MINIMIZE | Window is initially iconic. This style bit is the same as the WS_ICONIC style bit. |
| | WS_VISIBLE | Window is initially visible. This is a very important style bit, since without it a window will not appear. |

*(Continued)*

**Table 13.1** Continued

| Category | Style Bit | Description |
| --- | --- | --- |
| Performance Bits (3) | WS_CLIPCHILDREN | Clipping in software is expensive; therefore, a parent window usually does not clip, to avoid drawing in its children. However, if you wish a parent window to avoid overwriting its children, the parent must have this style set. |
| | WS_CLIPSIBLINGS | Clipping in software is expensive; therefore, sibling windows≈that is, windows that have the same parent≈do not make any extra effort to avoid drawing over each other. This style bit ensures that siblings do not overwrite each other. It prevents what some Windows programmers refer to as "sibling rivalry." |
| | WS_EX_NOPARENTNOTIFY | By default, a child window sends quite a few notification messages to its parent, in the form of the WM_PARENTNOTIFY message. Notification messages are sent when the child is created, when it receives mouse click messages, and when it is destroyed. This style bit prevents a child from writing so many letters home. This decreased message traffic helps improve performance. Dialog box controls, for example, are always created with this style. |

## Type of Window

The best way to explain the three types of windows is to describe the intended use of each. The **WS_OVERLAPPED** window, for example, is meant to serve as a program's main, top-level window. A window created with the **WS_POPUP** style has some things in common with overlapped windows, and this style is intended for dialog boxes and other secondary "free-floating" windows outside a program's main window. **WS_CHILD** windows are used to organize the use of overlapped, popup, and other child windows into functional areas. An example of child window use is as a dialog box control (pushbutton, listbox, etc.) in a dialog box.

When you create a window with the **WS_OVERLAPPED** style, the Window Manager gives you some help in making sure that the window meets the minimum standards required of a top-level window. For one thing, it makes sure that your window has a caption bar and a border. (But you'll still need to specify the **WS_CAPTION** style if you wish to create a system menu or other caption bar elements.) Since overlapped windows are expected to serve as the top-level windows, the Window Manager will automatically size and position an overlapped window using the **CW_USEDEFAULT** flag. And finally, an overlapped window is always positioned in screen coordinates. This means that, even if an overlapped window has a parent, it is positioned independent of its parent.

A window created with the **WS_POPUP** style is a popup window. In many respects, a popup window behaves like an overlapped window: It can reside anywhere on the display screen and is positioned in screen coordinates. So why have two different styles? It's mostly an accident of history.

Version 1.x of Windows used *tiled windows* as main program windows. Popup windows were the only kind of overlapping window that could be created, and these were used for dialog boxes. Starting with version 2.x of Windows, overlapping windows replaced tiled windows as the style used for main program windows. Since then, the differences between overlapped and popup windows have been mostly cosmetic, since they behave in exactly the same way.

With Windows 3.x, the differences between the two types have been reduced even further. For one thing, starting with Windows 3.x, dialog boxes have titlebars. So then, what's the difference between the two? It is mostly an issue of conventional usage. As we said earlier, overlapped windows are intended for a program's main window. Popup windows are intended for dialog boxes. Presumably, if a difference should appear between these two uses in a future version of Windows, programs that follow this convention will have no problem running with whatever convention is adopted.

A window created with the **WS_CHILD** style is a child window. Child windows are used to divide other windows—overlapped, popup, and other child windows—into smaller functional areas. Since this is the case, a child window *must* have a parent. At window creation time, the parent is the window whose handle is passed as the **hwndParent** parameter of the **CreateWindow** and **CreateWindowEx** routines. Like human children, child windows require a parent because the parent provides a place to live. A child window is only visible when positioned inside the client area of its parent. If it is moved outside the client area by either a program or by a user action, any portion that lies outside of the parent's client area will not be visible.

## Window Border

Figure 13.5 shows the four types of borders that are available. Notice that, among the different window border styles, only the `WS_DLGFRAME` cannot be used with a caption. This is an older style that has been replaced by the `WS_EX_DLGMODALFRAME` border for dialog boxes but is still present to maintain compatibility with programs created for older versions of Windows.

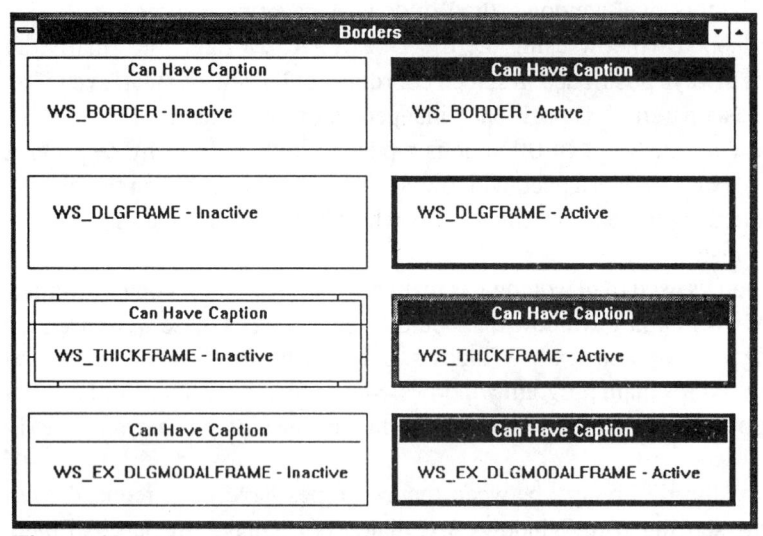

**Figure 13.5** The four types of borders, shown in both inactive and active states

As we mentioned earlier, a `WS_OVERLAPPED` window must have a border. If a border is not specified, the thin `WS_BORDER` is automatically created for the window. The other types of windows do not require a border, which is convenient when you wish to use a child window to invisibly divide up a larger window. However, it doesn't make sense to create a popup window without a border. Without a border, a popup can easily be lost as windows are shuffled around the screen.

The border of a window and the caption bar change colors to let the user see a difference between active windows and inactive windows, as shown in Figure 13.5. The borders of top-level windows are changed automatically by the system, which sends a `WM_NCACTIVATE` message to inform a window to redraw its nonclient area to reflect either an active or an inactive state. However, this message is not sent for child windows. If you wish to change a child window's border and caption to reflect an active state, you can use the following line of code to transmit your message:

```
SendMessage (hwndChild, WM_NCACTIVATE, TRUE, 0L);
```

Changing the border and caption to reflect an inactive state involves the same message, with a zero or **FALSE** value for the **wParam**:

```
SendMessage (hwndChild, WM_NCACTIVATE, FALSE, 0L);
```

## Nonclient Area Components

Figure 13.6 shows a window with all of the nonclient area components with a style flag labeling the corresponding part. With the exception of the two scroll bars, each nonclient area component is managed by the default window procedure. This means, of course, that a window procedure must forward the various nonclient area messages on to the window procedure for these components to work properly. But this is hardly a new requirement, since you are used to the idea that the messages you don't process yourself are always sent on to the default window procedure.

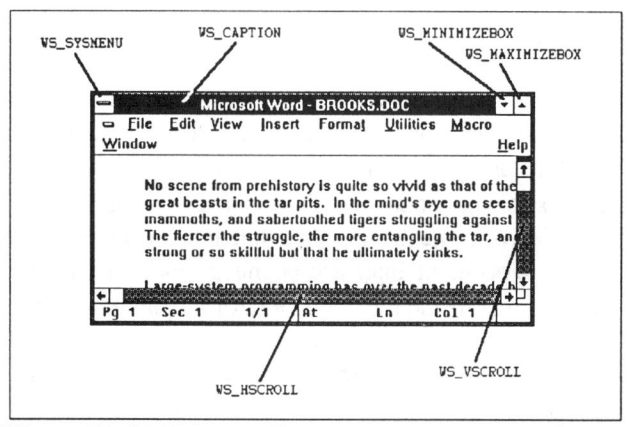

**Figure 13.6** The non-client area components of a window

The one exception involves scroll bars. Scroll bars send messages that let a window know how the user is interacting with the scroll bar. There are two messages that scroll bars send: A **WM_HSCROLL** message is sent by horizontal scroll bars, and **WM_VSCROLL** is sent by vertical scroll bars.

## Initial State

Of the four style bits that set a window's initial state, perhaps the most important is the **WS_VISIBLE**. Without this style bit, a window does not appear at creation time. Of course, a window can be created invisible and later made visible by calling routines like **ShowWindow**, but it is often easier for you to simply make a window visible at window creation time. One exception to this, of course, is the way that top-level windows are ordinarily handled in a program's `WinMain` function. Every OWL program, in fact, creates an invisible top-level window and then calls `ShowWindow` to make it appear, by calling these two routines:

```
hwnd = CreateWindow("MIN:MAIN",     /* Class name.    */
            "Minimum",              /* Title.         */
            WS_OVERLAPPEDWINDOW,    /* Style bits.    */
            CW_USEDEFAULT,          /* x - default.   */
            0,                      /* y - default.   */
            CW_USEDEFAULT,          /* cx - default.  */
            0,                      /* cy - default.  */
            NULL,                   /* No parent.     */
            NULL,                   /* Class menu.    */
            hInstance,              /* Creator.       */
            NULL                    /* Params.        */
            ) ;

ShowWindow (hwnd, cmdShow);
```

As we discussed earlier, the `cmdShow` parameter is the value passed as the last parameter in the `WinMain` function, which tells a program how its top-level window should first appear.

The `WS_MINIMIZE` and `WS_MAXIMIZE` style bits describe whether a window should be initially minimized (iconic) or maximized (zoomed). This is usually limited to a program's top-level window, since users have come to expect a single top-level window in an application. Of course, the Multiple Document Interface changes this a bit, since a document window can be minimized and rest inside the client area of its parent window. The Program Manager provides a good example of how windows other than a program's top-level window can be managed when either minimized or maximized. In older Windows programs, you may see the `WS_ICONIC` style used instead of `WS_MINIMIZE`. If you check WINDOWS.H, you'll notice that these two flags have identical values, and therefore can be used interchangeably.

The `WS_DISABLED` style bit lets you create a window that may be visible but is not available for user interaction. This is like having a door that is locked and that displays a "Closed" sign. All of the predefined dialog box controls take on a grayed appearance when they are disabled. In this way, not only is the user locked out from using the window, but the window provides visual feedback to make this aspect clear. You may wish to use this same approach if you plan to have windows that are visible, but not accessible. The two pushbuttons in Figure 13.7 show one way to let the user know that a window is not available.

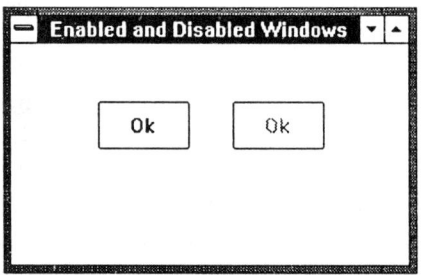

**Figure 13.7** A disabled push button displays its label in grayed text

## Performance Bits

When we discussed the various style bits that are available for window classes, we looked at several style flags that we referred to as performance bits. In those cases, each of those performance bits provided a way to give a bit of a boost in speed for certain types of operations.

Of the three flags that we call performance bits, only one of them actually improves the performance of the system. The other two actually cause things to slow down a bit, although from your viewpoint they mean that less effort is required by your program to make things work right. For this reason, we feel justified in calling them performance bits, although perhaps a better term would be "performance-*related*" style bits.

The first two styles, **WS_CLIPCHILDREN** and **WS_CLIPSIBLINGS**, control the amount of clipping that is set up in the DC when drawing in a window. In Chapter 6, when we first discussed the role of clipping, we mentioned that clipping allows windowing. Without clipping, one program might accidentally overwrite another program's window. Between two windows that don't belong to the same program, clipping is automatically provided.

But between windows that belong to the same program, clipping is not so strictly enforced. In particular, there is no automatic mechanism to prevent a parent window from overwriting a child (**WS_CHILD**) window. And between child windows, there is no automatic clipping to prevent one child window from overwriting another. The primary reason that clipping is turned *off* in these situations is performance. If a program has put a window in a particular spot, the Window Manager assumes that the program will not allow other windows to interfere with the operation of that window. This works well and eliminates the overhead that would otherwise occur when a window has more than a few child windows.

However, things begin to break down when the user is able to move windows. In this case, a program has less control over the placement of child windows. When there is the risk that the user will cause two windows to interfere with each other, the **WS_CLIPSIBLINGS** style bit should be used to avoid "sibling rivalry," which is a tongue-in-cheek term for what happens when two child windows don't respect each other's boundaries.

The other clipping style bit, **WS_CLIPCHILDREN**, is used to prevent a parent window from overwriting its children. This is required when (a) a user can pick up a child window and move it around and (b) the window's parent draws in its own client area. The fix involves using this style bit to force the Window Manager to do a little more work in setting up the clipping that will cause the parent window to respect the boundaries of its children.

The last performance bit is **WS_EX_NOPARENTNOTIFY**. This performance bit reduces the number of messages that a child window sends to its parent. By default, a child window sends its parent a message when it is created, when it receives mouse click messages, and when it is destroyed. This message prevents the **WM_PARENTNOTIFY** message from being sent when child windows are created and destroyed (but still sends notify messages for mouse clicks). While it seems like a lot of effort to eliminate two messages, when there are a lot of windows being created or destroyed at one time, it slows things down a bit. This is why, for example, dialog box controls use this style.

## Compound Window Styles

The last three styles that we're going to look at are values that have been defined in WINDOWS.H for the sake of convenience: **WS_OVERLAPPEDWINDOW**, **WS_POPUPWINDOW**, and **WS_CHILDWINDOW**. These compound styles are defined as follows:

```
#define WS_OVERLAPPEDWINDOW
                    (WS_OVERLAPPED | WS_CAPTION |
                    WS_SYSMENU | WS_THICKFRAME |
                    WS_MINIMIZEBOX | WS_MAXIMIZEBOX)
#define WS_POPUPWINDOW
                    (WS_POPUP | WS_BORDER | WS_SYSMENU)
#define WS_CHILDWINDOW
                    (WS_CHILD)
```

These values are available for the sake of convenience, to make it easier to select the most commonly selected style bits.

# Top-Level Window Considerations

A program's top-level window is the main doorway through which users access your program. When it first opens, it creates an initial impression of what a user can expect from your program. For this reason, it would seem that programmers would wish to make that initial impression a favorable one. And yet, that doesn't seem to be the case in many of today's programs. We're not interested in flashy graphics, spiffy logos, or sexy animation. What we're concerned with is much simpler than any special effects: A program will give a distinct impression based on the initial position and size of its main window.

On the one hand, quite a few programs use the **CW_USEDEFAULT** flag and let the Window Manager control the size and positioning of a program's main window. But, if you spend very much time using Windows, you soon find that this behavior can be annoying. Even though Windows creates this effect by keeping careful track of the location of each new top-level window that it positions, to the user the effect is one of chaos. The process of starting a program can seem to a user to be out of control, since programs seem to start up at seemingly random positions. The cascading effect creates more work for the user, since the first thing a user does is reposition the window of a newly started program to a convenient location.

If you agree that this is a problem, there are several possible solutions. One involves always creating your program's top-level window at a fixed location and with a fixed size. For example, a program might create its top-level window with a location of (10, 10) and make its window 320 pixels wide and 240 pixels high. The problem with hard-coding values like this is that the effect you produce is dependent on the type of display the user happens to be using. For example, a window of this size would occupy about one half of a CGA screen, which is 640 × 200 pixels. But on an 8514, which has a resolution of 1024 × 768, this window would only occupy one twelfth of the screen.

As an alternative, a program can call **GetSystemMetrics** to determine the size of the display screen and then set the size of the top-level window accordingly. Our next sample program, OWNSIZE, does just that. It creates a top-level window that is equal to the width of the display screen. It makes the window almost as tall as the display screen but leaves enough room at the bottom of the display screen so that program icons that are resting there are visible. Figure 13.8 shows our program's top-level window when it is first created.

352   User Interface Objects

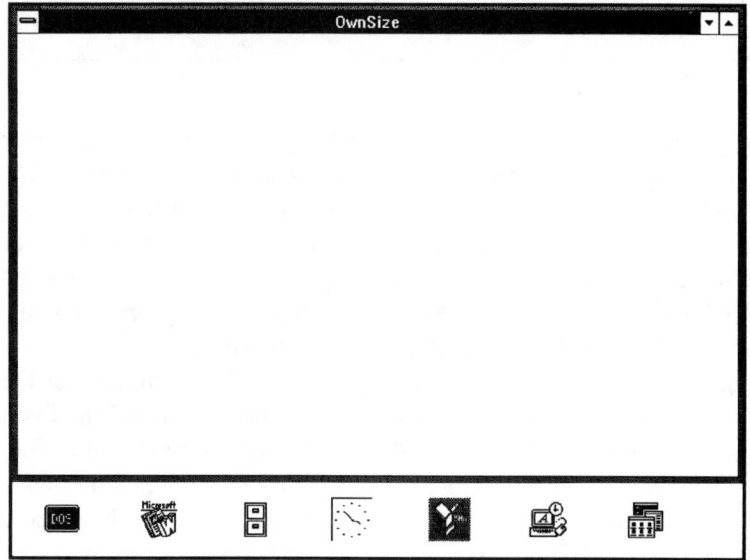

**Figure 13.8** *A top-level window that defines its own size*

Here is the source code to OWNSIZE:

# MAKEFILE.MAK

```
.AUTODEPEND

#    Translator Definitions
INC=\BORLANDC\OWL\INCLUDE;\BORLANDC\CLASSLIB\INCLUDE;\BORLANDC\INCLUDE
CC = bcc -c -D_CLASSDLL -H -ml -WS -w -I$(INC)

#    Implicit Rules
.c.obj:
  $(CC) {$< }

.cpp.obj:
  $(CC) {$< }

#    Explicit Rules
OwnSize.exe: OwnSize.res OwnSize.def OwnSize.obj
     tlink /c/C/n/P-/Twe/x @OwnSize.LNK
     rlink OwnSize.res OwnSize.exe

#    Individual File Dependencies
OwnSize.obj: OwnSize.cpp

OwnSize.res: OwnSize.rc OwnSize.cur OwnSize.ico
     brcc -FO OwnSize.res -i$(INC) OwnSize.RC
```

# OWNSIZE.LNK

```
\borlandc\lib\c0wl.obj+
OwnSize.obj
OwnSize,OwnSize
\borlandc\classlib\lib\tclasdll.lib+
\borlandc\owl\lib\owl.lib+
mathwl.lib+
import.lib+
crtldll.lib
OwnSize.def
```

# OWNSIZE.CPP

```cpp
/*-----------------------------------------------------------*\
|   OwnSize.CPP  - Demonstrates window creation using system  |
|                  metric values and use of profile file.     |
\*-----------------------------------------------------------*/
#define WIN31
#define STRICT
#include <owl.h>
#include <WindowsX.h>

/*-----------------------------------------------------------*\
|                        Constants.                           |
\*-----------------------------------------------------------*/
const int REOPEN_NORMAL  = 0;
const int REOPEN_ZOOM    = 1;
const int REOPEN_DEFAULT = 2;

/*-----------------------------------------------------------*\
|                       Static Data.                          |
\*-----------------------------------------------------------*/
char achPr[]   = "OWNSIZE";     /* Profile file key name. */
char achFile[] = "OWNSIZE.INI"; /* Profile file name.     */

/*-----------------------------------------------------------*\
|                   Class Declarations.                       |
\*-----------------------------------------------------------*/
class TOwnSizeApplication : public TApplication
  {
  public:
    TOwnSizeApplication (LPSTR lpszName, HINSTANCE hInstance,
                         HINSTANCE hPrevInstance, LPSTR lpszCmdLine,
                         int nCmdShow);
    virtual void InitMainWindow ();
  };

class TOwnSizeWindow : public TWindow
  {
  public:
    TOwnSizeWindow (PTWindowsObject pwParent, LPSTR lpszTitle,
                    PTModule pmModule);
    virtual LPSTR GetClassName ();
    virtual void  GetWindowClass (WNDCLASS&);
    virtual void  WMDestroy(TMessage& Msg) = [WM_DESTROY];
  };
```

```
/*--------------------------------------------------------------*\
|                  Main Function:  WinMain.                      |
\*--------------------------------------------------------------*/
int PASCAL WinMain (HINSTANCE hInstance,   HINSTANCE hPrevInstance,
                    LPSTR    lpszCmdLine, int       nCmdShow)
    {
    TOwnSizeApplication OwnSize ("OwnSize", hInstance,
                                  hPrevInstance, lpszCmdLine,
                                  nCmdShow);
    OwnSize.Run();
    return OwnSize.Status;
    }

/*--------------------------------------------------------------*\
|                  Application Class Member.                     |
\*--------------------------------------------------------------*/
TOwnSizeApplication::TOwnSizeApplication (LPSTR lpszName,
                      HINSTANCE hInstance, HINSTANCE hPrevInstance,
                      LPSTR lpszCmdLine, int nCmdShow)
                     :TApplication (lpszName, hInstance,
                       hPrevInstance, lpszCmdLine, nCmdShow)
    {
    /* Application specific initialization goes here. */
    }

/*--------------------------------------------------------------*\
|                  Application Class Member.                     |
\*--------------------------------------------------------------*/
void TOwnSizeApplication::InitMainWindow ()
    {
    MainWindow = new TOwnSizeWindow (NULL,
                 "Own Size: Self Sizing Window", NULL);
    }

/*--------------------------------------------------------------*\
|                  TOwnSizeWindow Class Member.                  |
\*--------------------------------------------------------------*/
TOwnSizeWindow::TOwnSizeWindow (PTWindowsObject pwParent,
                 LPSTR lpszTitle, PTModule pmModule)
               :TWindow (pwParent, lpszTitle, pmModule)
    {
    int iReopen;
    int x, y, cx, cy;

    if (!GetApplication()->hPrevInstance)
        {
        /*
         * For first instance, set position & size to that
         * of window when we last ran.
         */

        x = GetPrivateProfileInt (achPr, "x", 0, achFile);
        y = GetPrivateProfileInt (achPr, "y", 0, achFile);

        cx = GetSystemMetrics (SM_CXSCREEN);
        cx = GetPrivateProfileInt (achPr, "cx", cx, achFile);
        cy = GetSystemMetrics (SM_CYSCREEN) -
             GetSystemMetrics (SM_CYICON)   -
            (GetSystemMetrics (SM_CYCAPTION) * 2);
        cy = GetPrivateProfileInt (achPr, "cy", cy, achFile);

        iReopen = GetPrivateProfileInt (achPr, "Reopen", 0,
                                        achFile);
```

```
            if (iReopen == REOPEN_ZOOM)
                GetApplication()->nCmdShow = SW_SHOWMAXIMIZED;
            if (iReopen == REOPEN_DEFAULT)
                {
                x  = CW_USEDEFAULT;
                cx = CW_USEDEFAULT;
                }
        }
    else
        {
        /*  Other instances, use default position & size.      */
        x = cx = CW_USEDEFAULT;
        y = cy = 0;
        }

    Attr.X = x;
    Attr.Y = y;
    Attr.W = cx;
    Attr.H = cy;
    }
/*-----------------------------------------------------------*\
|                  TOwnSizeWindow Class Member.               |
\*-----------------------------------------------------------*/
 LPSTR TOwnSizeWindow::GetClassName ()
    {
    return "OwnSize:MAIN";
    }

/*-----------------------------------------------------------*\
|                  TOwnSizeWindow Class Member.               |
\*-----------------------------------------------------------*/
void TOwnSizeWindow::GetWindowClass (WNDCLASS& wc)
    {
    TWindow::GetWindowClass (wc);
    wc.hIcon=LoadIcon (wc.hInstance, "snapshot");
    wc.hCursor=LoadCursor (wc.hInstance, "hand");
    }

/*-----------------------------------------------------------*\
|                  TOwnSizeWindow Class Member.               |
\*-----------------------------------------------------------*/
void TOwnSizeWindow::WMDestroy(TMessage& Msg)
    {
    char ach[80];
    int  iReopen;

    //  Update window position information.

    wsprintf (ach, "%d",Attr.X);
    WritePrivateProfileString (achPr, "x", ach, achFile);

    wsprintf (ach, "%d",Attr.Y);
    WritePrivateProfileString (achPr, "y", ach, achFile);

    wsprintf (ach, "%u",Attr.W);
    WritePrivateProfileString (achPr, "cx", ach, achFile);

    wsprintf (ach, "%d",Attr.H);
    WritePrivateProfileString (achPr, "cy", ach, achFile);

    /*
```

```
            *  Write reopen flags for iconic/zoomed windows.
            */
           iReopen = REOPEN_NORMAL;
           if (IsZoomed (HWindow))   iReopen = REOPEN_ZOOM;
           if (IsIconic (HWindow))   iReopen = REOPEN_DEFAULT;

           wsprintf (ach, "%d", iReopen);
           WritePrivateProfileString (achPr, "Reopen", ach, achFile);

           TWindow::WMDestroy(Msg);
           }
```

## OWNSIZE.RC

```
    snapshot icon OwnSize.ico

    hand cursor OwnSize.cur
```

## OWNSIZE.DEF

```
        NAME OWNSIZE

    EXETYPE WINDOWS

    DESCRIPTION 'Self-sizing window & profile file'

    CODE MOVEABLE DISCARDABLE
    DATA MOVEABLE MULTIPLE

    HEAPSIZE   512
    STACKSIZE 5120
```

OWNSIZE demonstrates two programming techniques that may be interesting to you. First, it uses the **GetSystemMetrics** routine to determine the size of its top-level window when it is first run. When OWNSIZE is about to exit, it writes the size of its window to a private **profile file**. A profile file is an ASCII text file that a program can use to store values that it wants to remember. OWNSIZE uses a profile file to save the location and dimensions of its window, so the next time it is run it can start up with the same size. Also, the profile sets a flag if the window was zoomed, so that the next time the program is started it can make its window zoomed as well. The profile file provides a sense of continuity for a program.

The initial width of the window in OWNSIZE is set to the width of the display screen. To determine the width of the display screen, the window object's constructor calls **GetSystemMetrics** with the SM_CXSCREEN parameter, as shown here:

```
cx = GetSystemMetrics (SM_CXSCREEN);
```

The initial height of the window in OWNSIZE is set so that when the window is open, the row of icons at the bottom of the display screen is visible. To calculate the required value, we make three calls to **GetSystemMetrics**. The first determines the screen height; the second determines the height of an icon; and the third call determines the height of a caption, since each icon is accompanied by a caption. Here is the line of code that does this calculation:

```
cy = GetSystemMetrics (SM_CYSCREEN) -
    GetSystemMetrics (SM_CYICON)   -
    (GetSystemMetrics (SM_CYCAPTION) * 2);
```

The caption height is multiplied by two just to make sure there is enough room.

**GetSystemMetrics** provides measurement information for quite a few objects that make up the Windows user interface. Included are the sizes of cursors, icons, menus, and captions, as well as the widths of the different types of borders. Let's take a moment to look at some of the different measurement values that this routine can provide.

## *System Metrics*

Table 13.2 lists all of the system metrics that are defined for Windows, along with the symbolic value for the index. To give a better idea of what each value represents, Figures 13.9 through 13.11 provide the same information in a visual form.

**Table 13.2**  Windows system metrics

| Type | Index | Description |
| --- | --- | --- |
| Screen Metrics (4) | SM_CXSCREEN | Screen width in pixels. |
|  | SM_CYSCREEN | Screen height in pixels. |
|  | SM_CXFULLSCREEN | Screen width in pixels. |
|  | SM_CYFULLSCREEN | Screen height in pixels minus the height of a window caption. |
| Border Sizes (6) | SM_CXBORDER | Width of a border created with the WS_BORDER style. |
|  | SM_CYBORDER | Height of a border created with the WS_BORDER style. |
|  | SM_CXFRAME | Width of a border on a window created with the WS_THICKFRAME style bit. |

*(Continued)*

**Table 13.2** *Continued*

| Type | Index | Description |
| --- | --- | --- |
| | SM_CYFRAME | Height of a border on a window created with the WS_THICKFRAME style bit. |
| | SM_CXDLGFRAME | Width of a border on a window with either a WS_EX_DLGMODALFRAME or WS_DLGFRAME style border. |
| | SM_CYDLGFRAME | Height of a border on a window with either a WS_EX_DLGMODALFRAME or WS_DLGFRAME style border. |
| Scroll Bar Metrics (6) | SM_CXVSCROLL | Width of the arrow bitmap in a vertical scroll bar. |
| | SM_CYHSCROLL | Height of the arrow bitmap in a horizontal scroll bar. |
| | SM_CYVSCROLL | Height of the arrow bitmap in a vertical scroll bar. |
| | SM_CXHSCROLL | Width of the arrow bitmap in a horizontal scroll bar. |
| | SM_CYVTHUMB | Height of the thumb in a vertical scroll bar. |
| | SM_CXHTHUMB | Width of the thumb in a horizontal scroll bar. |
| Window Components (8) | SM_CYCAPTION | Height of a caption bar. |
| | SM_CYMENU | Height of a single-line menu item. |
| | SM_CXICON | Width of an icon. |
| | SM_CYICON | Height of an icon. |
| | SM_CXCURSOR | Width of a cursor. |
| | SM_CYCURSOR | Height of a cursor. |
| | SM_CXSIZE | Width of the system menu, minimize and maximize icons. |

*(Continued)*

**Table 13.2** *Continued*

|  | SM_CYSIZE | Height of the system menu, minimize and maximize icons. |
|---|---|---|
| Window Tracking (4) | SM_CXMIN | Minimum width of a window. |
|  | SM_CYMIN | Minimum height of a window. |
|  | SM_CXMINTRACK | Minimum tracking width of a window. |
|  | SM_CYMINTRACK | Minimum tracking height of a window. |
| Miscellaneous Flags (4) | SM_DEBUG | Nonzero if the debug version of Windows is installed. |
|  | SM_SWAPBUTTON | Nonzero if the left and right mouse buttons are swapped. |
|  | SM_MOUSEPRESENT | Nonzero if a mouse is present. |
|  | SM_CMETRICS | Count of the number of system metric values. |

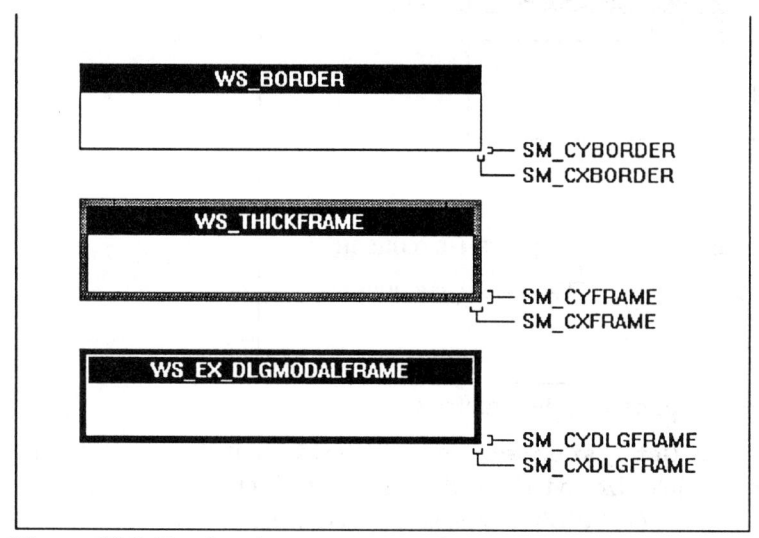

**Figure 13.9** Border size system metrics

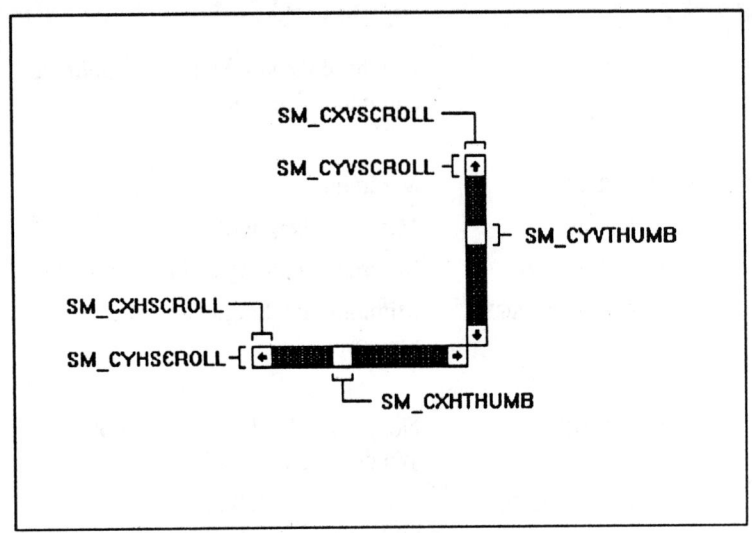

**Figure 13.10** Scroll bar system metrics

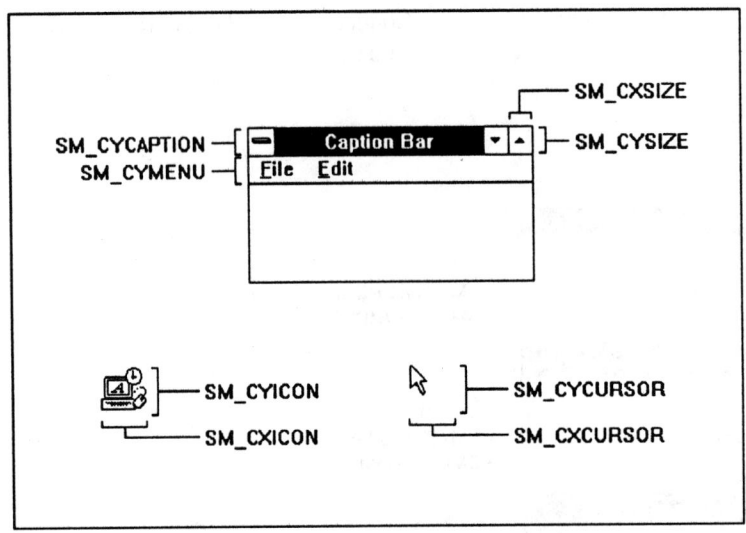

**Figure 13.11** Window component system metrics

By using the values from `GetSystemMetrics`, OWNSIZE initially creates its top-level window with a reasonable size and avoids the cascading effect that seems to serve only to confuse the user. When OWNSIZE terminates, it records its last size and position onto disk. It does this in response to the `WM_CREATE` message, like this:

```
    void TOwnSizeWindow::WMDestroy(TMessage& Msg)
    {
    char ach[80];
    int  iReopen;

    // Update window position information.

    wsprintf (ach, "%d",Attr.X);
    WritePrivateProfileString (achPr, "x", ach, achFile);

    wsprintf (ach, "%d",Attr.Y);
    WritePrivateProfileString (achPr, "y", ach, achFile);

    wsprintf (ach, "%u",Attr.W);
    WritePrivateProfileString (achPr, "cx", ach, achFile);

    wsprintf (ach, "%d",Attr.H);
    WritePrivateProfileString (achPr, "cy", ach, achFile);

    /*
     * Write reopen flags for iconic/zoomed windows.
     */
    iReopen = REOPEN_NORMAL;
    if (IsZoomed (HWindow))  iReopen = REOPEN_ZOOM;
    if (IsIconic (HWindow))  iReopen = REOPEN_DEFAULT;

    wsprintf (ach, "%d", iReopen);
    WritePrivateProfileString (achPr, "Reopen", ach,
                               achFile);

    TWindow::WMDestroy(Msg);
    }
```

It uses a set of routines that are part of the support Windows provides for private profile files.

## *Private Profile Files*

One way that a program can improve its rapport with a user is to remember the preferences that the user has expressed. This might mean remembering the menu options that were selected, the preferred color to use for negative numbers, or something as simple as the position of the program's top-level window. To help make this easy for you to do, Windows includes a set of routines that support the creation of private profile files, also known as private initialization files. Of course, you might prefer to keep user preference data in your own format, but the profile file support provides an easy way to read and write user preference information.

A profile file is an ASCII text file, which means that users can modify the file using a text editor. Here is the profile file that our program, OWNSIZE, created:

```
    [OWNSIZE]
    x=0
    y=0
    cx=640
    cy=408
    Reopen=0
```

As you can tell from this example, profile files have the following format:

```
    [application name]
    keyname1 = value1
    keyname2 = value2
    keyname3 = value3
```

OWNSIZE keeps four numeric values that correspond to the location and the dimensions of the window when OWNSIZE was last run. These are associated with the keynames x, y, cx, and cy. A fifth numeric value, associated with the keyname Reopen, is used when the window has been either zoomed or iconized (maximized or minimized), in which case the program provides special handling.

Windows provides six routines that can be used to read and write profile files. Three of them are for reading and writing WIN.INI, which is the profile file used by Windows and older Windows programs: **GetProfileInt**, **GetProfileString**, and **WriteProfileString**. The other three provide support for private initialization files: **GetPrivateProfileInt**, **GetPrivateProfileString**, and **WritePrivateProfileString**.

OWNDRAW writes into its private profile file, OWNDRAW.INI, by calling **WritePrivateProfileString**, which is defined

```
WritePrivateProfileString (lpApplication, lpKey,
                           lpString, lpFile)
```

- **lpApplication** is a long pointer to the application name. This is the name placed in square brackets in the profile file to identify a group of keyname/value pairs.
- **lpKey** is the long pointer to the name of the data identifier. That is, it is the string on the left of the equal sign in a keyname/value pair.
- **lpString** is a long pointer to the string to be placed on the right side of the equal sign in a keyname/value pair.
- **lpFile** is a long pointer to a character string for the file name to be used as a profile file. If no directory is given, the profile file is written into Windows' directory.

Here, for example, is how OWNSIZE writes the *x* location of the window:

```
    wsprintf (ach, "%d",Attr.X);
    WritePrivateProfileString (achPr, "x", ach, achFile);
```

When OWNDRAW starts up, it calls `GetPrivateProfileInt` to retrieve the various numeric values that it uses for the initial size and position of its window. This routine allows a program to establish a default value in case the requested integer value is not available. `GetPrivateProfileInt` is defined as follows:

```
WORD GetPrivateProfileInt (lpApp, lpKey, nDefault,
                           lpFile)
```

- `lpApplication` is a long pointer to the application name. This is the name placed in square brackets in the profile file to identify a group of keyname/value pairs.
- `lpKey` is the long pointer to the name of the data identifier. That is, it is the string on the left of the equal sign in a keyname/value pair.
- `nDefault` is the value to be used if the keyname is not available in the initialization file, or if the initialization file does not exist.
- `lpFile` is a long pointer to a character string for the file name to be used as a profile file. If no directory is given, the profile file is written into Windows' directory.

The return value is an unsigned integer value that is the value in the private profile file, or the default value if the profile entry could not be found. Here is how OWNDRAW retrieves the (x,y) location from the private profile file:

```
x = GetPrivateProfileInt (achPr, "x", 0, achFile);
y = GetPrivateProfileInt (achPr, "y", 0, achFile);
```

The next topic we're going to discuss is the use of child windows in a program's top-level window.

## Creating a Child Window

In our discussion of the `CreateWindow` and `CreateWindowEx` routines, we mentioned that there are three types of windows: overlapped, popup, and child. All of the windows that we have created up until now have been overlapped windows. In the next chapter, we'll create quite a few popup and child windows when we create dialog boxes. Right now, though, let's look at what is involved in creating a child window inside the client area of our program's main window.

The OWL application framework makes it easy to create a child window: You define a new window class as a descendent of `TWindow`. As with every window we create in this book, you'll want to override two member functions to define the window class information: `GetClassName` and `GetWindowClass`. Then, to fine-tune the window that is created, you'll want to fill in the `Attr` structure in your window object's constructor. And, of course, you'll create message response functions for each window message of interest. Finally, create a window object and voilà: You will have a window.

## 364   User Interface Objects

The next sample program that we're going to look at is STATLINE, which creates a child window to display status information about menu items as the user browses the menus.

## STATLINE: Menu Status Information

In Chapter 11, when we discussed the message traffic associated with menus, we mentioned that the **WM_MENUSELECT** message gets sent when the user browses through a menu. STATLINE responds to this message by displaying additional information about each menu item in a child window that resides at the bottom of the top-level window. Figure 13.12 shows STATLINE and the child window that displays menu status information.

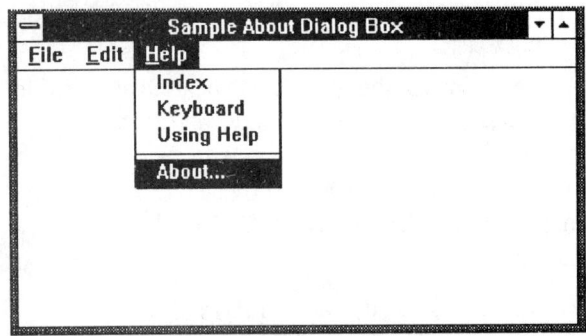

**Figure 13.12**  *STATLINE uses a child window to display menu selection information*

Here is the source code to STATLINE:

## MAKEFILE.MAK

```
.AUTODEPEND

#   Translator Definitions
INC=\BORLANDC\OWL\INCLUDE;\BORLANDC\CLASSLIB\INCLUDE;\BORLANDC\INCLUDE
CC = bcc -c -D_CLASSDLL -H -ml -WS -w -I$(INC)

#   Implicit Rules
.c.obj:
  $(CC) {$< }

.cpp.obj:
  $(CC) {$< }

#   Explicit Rules
StatLine.exe: StatLine.res StatLine.def StatLine.obj
     tlink /c/C/n/P-/Twe/x @StatLine.LNK
     rlink StatLine.res StatLine.exe

#   Individual File Dependencies
```

```
StatLine.obj: StatLine.cpp

StatLine.res: StatLine.rc StatLine.cur StatLine.ico
    brcc -FO StatLine.res -i$(INC) StatLine.RC
```

# STATLINE.LNK

```
\borlandc\lib\c0wl.obj+
StatLine.obj
StatLine,StatLine
\borlandc\classlib\lib\tclasdll.lib+
\borlandc\owl\lib\owl.lib+
mathwl.lib+
import.lib+
crtldll.lib
StatLine.def
```

# STATLINE.CPP

```
/*------------------------------------------------------------*\
|   STATLINE.CPP  - Demo showing creation of a status line    |
|                   child window.                             |
\*------------------------------------------------------------*/
#define WIN31
#define STRICT
#include <owl.h>
#include <WindowsX.h>
#include "statline.h"

#define SIZEMSGW(arg)          (LOWORD(arg.LParam))
#define SIZEMSGH(arg)          (HIWORD(arg.LParam))
#define MENUSELECTMSGID(arg)   (arg.WParam)
#define MENUSELECTMSGFLAG(arg) (LOWORD(arg.LParam))

/*------------------------------------------------------------*\
|                       Constants.                            |
\*------------------------------------------------------------*/
const int COUNT = 23;

/*------------------------------------------------------------*\
|                   Class Declarations.                       |
\*------------------------------------------------------------*/
class TStatLineApplication : public TApplication
  {
  public:
    TStatLineApplication (LPSTR lpszName, HINSTANCE hInstance,
                          HINSTANCE hPrevInstance, LPSTR lpszCmdLine,
                          int nCmdShow);
    virtual void InitMainWindow ();
  };

class TStatLineWindow : public TWindow
  {
  public:
    TStatLineWindow (PTWindowsObject pwParent, LPSTR lpszTitle,
```

```
                              PTModule pmModule);
      virtual LPSTR GetClassName ();
      virtual void  GetWindowClass (WNDCLASS&);
      virtual void  WMCreate(TMessage& Msg) = [WM_CREATE];
      virtual void  WMMenuSelect(TMessage& Msg) = [WM_MENUSELECT];
      virtual void  WMSize(TMessage& Msg) = [WM_SIZE];
    private:
      PTWindowsObject StatusWindow;
      int             cyChildHeight;
    };
class TStatusWindow : public TWindow
    {
    public:
      TStatusWindow(PTWindowsObject AParent, LPSTR ATitle);
      virtual LPSTR GetClassName();
      virtual void  GetWindowClass(WNDCLASS&);
      virtual void  WMCreate(TMessage& Msg) = [WM_CREATE];
      virtual void  WMMenuSelect(TMessage& Msg) = [WM_MENUSELECT];
    private:
      HMENU hmenuEdit;
      HMENU hmenuFile;
      HMENU hmenuSys;
    };

/*--------------------------------------------------------------*\
|                   Main Function:  WinMain.                     |
\*--------------------------------------------------------------*/
int PASCAL WinMain (HINSTANCE hInstance,   HINSTANCE hPrevInstance,
                    LPSTR lpszCmdLine, int    nCmdShow)
     {
     TStatLineApplication StatLine ("StatLine", hInstance,
                       hPrevInstance, lpszCmdLine, nCmdShow);
     StatLine.Run();
     return StatLine.Status;
     }

/*--------------------------------------------------------------*\
|                   Application Class Member.                    |
\*--------------------------------------------------------------*/
TStatLineApplication::TStatLineApplication (LPSTR lpszName,
                      HINSTANCE hInstance, HINSTANCE hPrevInstance,
                      LPSTR lpszCmdLine, int nCmdShow)
                    :TApplication (lpszName, hInstance,
                       hPrevInstance, lpszCmdLine, nCmdShow)
     {
     /*  Application specific initialization goes here.  */
     }

/*--------------------------------------------------------------*\
|                   Application Class Member.                    |
\*--------------------------------------------------------------*/
void TStatLineApplication::InitMainWindow ()
     {
     MainWindow = new TStatLineWindow (NULL, "Status Line", NULL);
     }

/*--------------------------------------------------------------*\
|                 TStatLineWindow Class Member.                  |
\*--------------------------------------------------------------*/
TStatLineWindow::TStatLineWindow (PTWindowsObject pwParent,
              LPSTR lpszTitle, PTModule pmModule)
           :TWindow (pwParent, lpszTitle, pmModule)
```

```
    {
    /* Window specific initialization goes here. */
    }

/*--------------------------------------------------------------*\
|                   TStatLineWindow Class Member.                |
\*--------------------------------------------------------------*/
LPSTR TStatLineWindow::GetClassName ()
    {
    return "StatLine:MAIN";
    }

/*--------------------------------------------------------------*\
|                   TStatLineWindow Class Member.                |
\*--------------------------------------------------------------*/
void TStatLineWindow::GetWindowClass (WNDCLASS& wc)
    {
    TWindow::GetWindowClass (wc);
    wc.hIcon=LoadIcon (wc.hInstance, "snapshot");
    wc.hCursor=LoadCursor (wc.hInstance, "hand");
    wc.lpszMenuName="#1";
    }

/*--------------------------------------------------------------*\
|                   TStatLineWindow Class Member.                |
\*--------------------------------------------------------------*/
void TStatLineWindow::WMCreate(TMessage& Msg)
    {
    HDC hdc;
    int cyBorder;
    TEXTMETRIC tm;

    StatusWindow = GetApplication()->MakeWindow(new
                     TStatusWindow (this, NULL) );
    hdc = GetDC (Msg.Receiver);
    GetTextMetrics (hdc, &tm);
    ReleaseDC (Msg.Receiver, hdc);

    cyBorder = GetSystemMetrics (SM_CYBORDER);

    cyChildHeight = tm.tmHeight + cyBorder * 2;
    }

/*--------------------------------------------------------------*\
|                   TStatLineWindow Class Member.                |
\*--------------------------------------------------------------*/
void TStatLineWindow::WMMenuSelect(TMessage& Msg)
    {
    SendMessage (StatusWindow->HWindow, Msg.Message, Msg.WParam,
                 Msg.LParam);
    }

/*--------------------------------------------------------------*\
|                   TStatLineWindow Class Member.                |
\*--------------------------------------------------------------*/
void TStatLineWindow::WMSize(TMessage& Msg)
    {
    int cxWidth;
    int cyHeight;
    int xChild;
    int yChild;
```

## 368 User Interface Objects

```
    cxWidth  = SIZEMSGW(Msg);
    cyHeight = SIZEMSGH(Msg);

    xChild = 0;
    yChild = cyHeight - cyChildHeight + 1;

    MoveWindow (StatusWindow->HWindow,
                xChild,
                yChild,
                cxWidth,
                cyChildHeight,
                TRUE);
    }

/*----------------------------------------------------------*\
|                  TStatusWindow Class Member.               |
\*----------------------------------------------------------*/
TStatusWindow::TStatusWindow( PTWindowsObject AParent,
              LPSTR ATitle) : TWindow (AParent, ATitle)
    {
    Attr.Style = WS_CHILD | WS_BORDER | WS_VISIBLE;
    Attr.X = 0;
    Attr.Y = 0;
    Attr.W = 0;
    Attr.H = 0;
    }

/*----------------------------------------------------------*\
|                  TStatusWindow Class Member.               |
\*----------------------------------------------------------*/
LPSTR TStatusWindow::GetClassName()
    {
    return "STATLINE:CHILD";
    }

/*----------------------------------------------------------*\
|                  TStatusWindow Class Member.               |
\*----------------------------------------------------------*/
void TStatusWindow::GetWindowClass(WNDCLASS& wc)
    {
    TWindow::GetWindowClass(wc);
    wc.hCursor=LoadCursor (wc.hInstance, "hand");
    }

/*----------------------------------------------------------*\
|                  TStatusWindow Class Member.               |
\*----------------------------------------------------------*/
void TStatusWindow::WMCreate(TMessage& Msg)
    {
    HMENU hmenu;
    HWND  hwndParent;

    hwndParent = GetParent (Msg.Receiver);
    hmenu = GetMenu (hwndParent);

    hmenuFile = GetSubMenu (hmenu, 0);
    hmenuEdit = GetSubMenu (hmenu, 1);
    hmenuSys  = GetSystemMenu (hwndParent, 0);
    }
```

```
/*----------------------------------------------------------------*\
|                  TStatusWindow Class Member.                     |
\*----------------------------------------------------------------*/
void TStatusWindow::WMMenuSelect(TMessage& Msg)
    {
    static STATUSDATA sd[COUNT] =
        {{ 0xffff, "" },
         { IDM_SYS,   "Move, size or close application window"},
         { IDM_FILE,  "Create, open, save, print, or quit"},
         { IDM_EDIT,  "Undo, cut, copy, paste and delete"},

         { IDM_NEW,    "Creates a new item"},
         { IDM_OPEN,   "Open an existing item"},
         { IDM_SAVE,   "Save existing item"},
         { IDM_SAVEAS, "Save the current item with a new name"},
         { IDM_PRINT,  "Prints the current item"},
         { IDM_EXIT,   "Quits Statline"},

         { IDM_UNDO,   "Reverse the last action"},
         { IDM_CUT,    "Cuts the selection to the Clipboard"},
         { IDM_COPY,   "Copies the selection to the Clipboard"},
         { IDM_PASTE,  "Copies the selection from the Clipboard"},
         { IDM_CLEAR,  "Erases the currently selected item"},
         { IDM_DELETE, "Erases the currently selected item"},

         { SC_SIZE,    "Changes window size"},
         { SC_MOVE,    "Changes window position"},
         { SC_MINIMIZE,"Reduces window to an icon"},
         { SC_MAXIMIZE,"Enlarges the active window to full size"},
         { SC_CLOSE,   "Quits Statline"},
         { SC_RESTORE, "Restores window to normal size"},
         { SC_TASKLIST,"Switches to the task list"}
        };
    HDC  hdc;
    int  isd;
    int  i;
    RECT rClient;
    WORD wFlag;
    WORD wId;

    wFlag = MENUSELECTMSGFLAG(Msg);
    wId   = MENUSELECTMSGID(Msg);

    isd=0;
    if (wFlag == 0xffff)
        isd=0;
    else if (wFlag & MF_POPUP)
        {
        if (hmenuSys == wId)
            isd = 1;
        if (hmenuFile == wId)
            isd = 2;
        if (hmenuEdit == wId)
            isd = 3;
        }
    else
        {
        for (i=0;i<COUNT;i++)
            {
            if (wId == sd[i].wCode)
```

```
                    {
                    isd = i;
                    break;
                    }
                }
            }

        GetClientRect (HWindow, &rClient);

        hdc = GetDC (HWindow);
        ExtTextOut (hdc,
                    0,                      /* X.                */
                    0,                      /* Y.                */
                    ETO_OPAQUE,             /* Opaque rectangle. */
                    &rClient,               /* Rectangle.        */
                    sd[isd].achMsg,         /* String.           */
                    lstrlen(sd[isd].achMsg), /* Length.          */
                    NULL);
        ReleaseDC (HWindow, hdc);
        }
```

# STATLINE.H

```
/*----------------------------------------------------------------*\
|    Statline.h -- include file for Statline.C.                    |
\*----------------------------------------------------------------*/

#define IDM_NEW         1
#define IDM_OPEN        2
#define IDM_SAVE        3
#define IDM_SAVEAS      4
#define IDM_PRINT       5
#define IDM_EXIT        6

#define IDM_UNDO        7
#define IDM_CUT         8
#define IDM_COPY        9
#define IDM_PASTE       10
#define IDM_CLEAR       11
#define IDM_DELETE      12

#define IDM_SYS         13
#define IDM_FILE        14
#define IDM_EDIT        15

typedef struct tagSTATUSDATA
    {
    WORD wCode;
    char achMsg[80];
    } STATUSDATA;
```

# STATLINE.RC

```
#include "statline.h"

snapshot icon StatLine.ico

hand cursor StatLine.cur

1 MENU
    {
    POPUP "&File"
        {
        MENUITEM "&New",          IDM_NEW
        MENUITEM "&Open...",      IDM_OPEN
        MENUITEM "&Save",         IDM_SAVE
        MENUITEM "Save &As...",   IDM_SAVEAS
        MENUITEM SEPARATOR
        MENUITEM "&Print",        IDM_PRINT
        MENUITEM SEPARATOR
        MENUITEM "E&xit",         IDM_EXIT
        }
    POPUP "&Edit"
        {
        MENUITEM "&Undo\tAlt+Backspace", IDM_UNDO
        MENUITEM SEPARATOR
        MENUITEM "Cu&t\tShift+Del",      IDM_CUT
        MENUITEM "&Copy\tCtrl+Ins",      IDM_COPY
        MENUITEM "&Paste\tShift+Ins",    IDM_PASTE
        MENUITEM SEPARATOR
        MENUITEM "Cl&ear",    IDM_CLEAR
        MENUITEM "&Delete",   IDM_DELETE
        }
    }
```

# STATLINE.DEF

```
NAME STATLINE

EXETYPE WINDOWS

DESCRIPTION 'Status Line window'

CODE MOVEABLE DISCARDABLE
DATA MOVEABLE MULTIPLE

HEAPSIZE   512
STACKSIZE  5120
```

Creating the child window in STATLINE starts with the defining two member functions which play a role in the window class registration: **GetClassName** and **GetWindowClass**. From Windows' point of view, here is what the class registration process looks like:

```
wc.lpszClassName = "STATLINE:CHILD";
wc.hInstance     = hInstance;
wc.lpfnWndProc   = StdWndProc;
```

## 372   User Interface Objects

```
wc.hCursor         = LoadCursor (hInstance,"hand");
wc.hIcon           = NULL;
wc.lpszMenuName    = NULL;
wc.hbrBackground   = COLOR_WINDOW+1;
wc.style           = NULL;
wc.cbClsExtra      = 0;
wc.cbWndExtra      = 0;

RegisterClass( &wc );
```

Of course, this is much simpler with OWL since we inherit all the normal default values and simply fill in the rest.

A window is automatically created when we create the window object. In the case of the status line window, that means

```
StatusWindow = GetApplication()->MakeWindow(new
                    TStatusWindow (this, NULL) );
```

This line is taken from the **WMCreate** message response function of STATLINE's main window. A few things require an explanation.

First of all, the status window is created as a child of our application's main window. After all, it is used to subdivide the main window's screen space. Although it might have made sense, we couldn't create the status window in the main window's constructor. The reason is that we need to identify the parent window when we create a child window.

The call to **MakeWindow** (a **TModule** member function) is required to create the MS-Windows window along with the window object. You haven't seen this routine before because OWL takes care of calling this function for you when creating an application's main window. Among other things, this function calls a window object's **Create** member function, and traps errors when a window cannot be created.

The status window object's constructor set the window creation parameters like this:

```
Attr.Style = WS_CHILD | WS_BORDER | WS_VISIBLE;
Attr.X = 0;
Attr.Y = 0;
Attr.W = 0;
Attr.H = 0;
```

The OWL library will use these parameters when it creates the MS-Windows window, making a call like the following:

```
CreateWindow("STATLINE:CHILD",/* Class Name.    */
        NULL,                 /* Title.         */
        WS_CHILD    |         /* Style bits.    */
        WS_BORDER   |
        WS_VISIBLE,
        0, 0, 0, 0,           /* Size/Location. */
        hwndMainWindow,       /* Parent.        */
        NULL,                 /* Class menu.    */
        hInstance,            /* Creator.       */
        NULL);                /* Params.        */
```

Every child window must have a parent. A child window needs a parent because it has to live in the pixels of another window. The status window's parent was defined by the first parameter of its constructor. OWL converts the pointer to the main window object into an MS-Windows window handle, which is what the **CreateWindow** function expects.

One thing that may seem odd to you is the initial size and location of our window. We used all zeros for the four parameters that define a window size: x, y, cx, and cy. We select a window with no size or location because we want to postpone calculating the size and location of our child window until we know the size of the parent window. We do this to make sure that the child window occupies the very bottom of the parent window.

In response to the **WM_SIZE** message, the parent window moves the status window to the bottom of the window. This approach does not represent an optimal object design. In particular, the status window object *should* take care of sizing itself. Unfortunately, there is no simple way for the child window to know when its parent changes size; therefore, we have adopted the approach you see here. An incremental improvement would be for the parent window to send the child window an application-defined message when it receives a WM_SIZE message. Then, the child window object would be able to behave like a grown-up and take care of itself.

In response to the size message, the parent window object resizes the status window as follows:

```
void TStatLineWindow::WMSize(TMessage& Msg)
    {
    int cxWidth;
    int cyHeight;
    int xChild;
    int yChild;

    cxWidth  = SIZEMSGW(Msg);
    cyHeight = SIZEMSGH(Msg);

    xChild = 0;
    yChild = cyHeight - cyChildHeight + 1;

    MoveWindow (StatusWindow->HWindow,
                xChild,
                yChild,
                cxWidth,
                cyChildHeight,
                TRUE);
    }
```

The **MoveWindow** routine changes the location of the child window to reflect the new size of the parent window. The **MoveWindow** routine is defined as

```
MoveWindow (hWnd, X, Y, cxWidth, cyHeight, bRepaint)
```

374    User Interface Objects

- **hWnd** identifies the window to be moved.
- **X** and **Y** are the new location of the window.
- **cxWidth** and **cyHeight** are the new width and height of the window.
- **bRepaint** is a Boolean flag. When set to TRUE, it causes the window to be completely redrawn in its new location. When set to FALSE, it prevents redrawing.

When the size of a window's client area changes, the window is sent a **WM_SIZE** message to notify it of the change.

As the user browses through a program's menus, messages are sent to the window that owns the menu. In the case of STATLINE, that means the top-level window. When the top-level window procedure receives the **WM_MENUSELECT** message, which is a notification that the user is browsing through a menu, it passes the message on to the window procedure of the child window by calling the **SendMessage** routine:

```
void TStatLineWindow::WMMenuSelect(TMessage& Msg)
    {
    SendMessage (StatusWindow->HWindow, Msg.Message,
            Msg.WParam, Msg.LParam);
    }
```

**SendMessage** delivers a message to a window procedure just as if it were directly calling the child window's window procedure. However, **SendMessage** should be used in place of a direct call, since Windows' dynamic link mechanism won't allow a direct call to a window procedure or to any other exported procedure.

In response to the **WM_MENUSELECT** message, the child window procedure checks to see what kind of menu selection is being made:

```
void TStatusWindow::WMMenuSelect(TMessage& Msg)
    {
    static STATUSDATA sd[COUNT] = {
    { 0xffff,     "" },
    { IDM_SYS,    "Move, size or close application window"},
    { IDM_FILE,   "Create, open, save, print, or quit"},
    { IDM_EDIT,   "Undo, cut, copy, paste and delete"},

    { IDM_NEW,    "Creates a new item"},
    { IDM_OPEN,   "Open an existing item"},
    { IDM_SAVE,   "Save existing item"},
    { IDM_SAVEAS, "Save the current item with a new name"},
    { IDM_PRINT,  "Prints the current item"},
    { IDM_EXIT,   "Quits Statline"},

    { IDM_UNDO,   "Reverse the last action"},
    { IDM_CUT,    "Cuts the selection to the Clipboard"},
    { IDM_COPY,   "Copies the selection to the Clipboard"},
    { IDM_PASTE,  "Copies selection from the Clipboard"},
    { IDM_CLEAR,  "Erases the currently selected item"},
    { IDM_DELETE, "Erases the currently selected item"},

    { SC_SIZE,    "Changes window size"},
```

```
    { SC_MOVE,     "Changes window position"},
    { SC_MINIMIZE,"Reduces window to an icon"},
    { SC_MAXIMIZE,"Enlarge the active window to full size"},
    { SC_CLOSE,    "Quits Statline"},
    { SC_RESTORE, "Restores window to normal size"},
    { SC_TASKLIST,"Switches to the task list"}
     };

    HDC  hdc;
    int  isd;
    int  i;
    RECT rClient;
    WORD wFlag;
    WORD wId;

wFlag = MENUSELECTMSGFLAG(Msg);
wId   = MENUSELECTMSGID(Msg);

    isd=0;
    if (wFlag == 0xffff)
        isd=0;
    else if (wFlag & MF_POPUP)
        {
        if (hmenuSys == wId)
            isd = 1;
        if (hmenuFile == wId)
            isd = 2;
        if (hmenuEdit == wId)
            isd = 3;
        }
    else
        {
        for (i=0;i<COUNT;i++)
            {
            if (wId == sd[i].wCode)
                {
                isd = i;
                break;
                }
            }
        }

    GetClientRect (HWindow, &rClient);

    hdc = GetDC (HWindow);
    ExtTextOut (hdc,
                0,                      /* X.               */
                0,                      /* Y.               */
                ETO_OPAQUE,             /* Opaque rectangle.*/
                &rClient,               /* Rectangle.       */
                sd[isd].achMsg,         /* String.          */
                lstrlen(sd[isd].achMsg), /* Length.         */
                NULL);
    ReleaseDC (HWindow, hdc);
    }
```

The **WM_MENUSELECT** message lets you know about three types of events: browsing a regular menu item, browsing the top of a popup menu, and terminating a menu browsing. To tell the difference between these three events, you must look in the low-order word of the **lParam**. When it is equal to **0xFFFF**, the browsing has terminated. When the

**MF_POPUP** bit is set, then the value in the **wParam** parameter is a popup menu handle. Otherwise, **wParam** is the command result code for the menu item that the user is currently viewing.

When STATLINE figures out exactly which menu is being browsed, it calls the **ExtTextOut** routine to display the description of the menu item. One of the nice features of this routine is the availability of the **ETO_OPAQUE** flag, which causes **ExtTextOut** to paint an opaque rectangle to erase whatever was drawn previously in the background.

The two sample programs in this chapter, OWNSIZE and STATLINE, provide a template that you can use to fine-tune the handling of windows in your own programming projects. But this is only the beginning of how you can take advantage of Windows' windows. In the next chapter, we're going to be looking at a part of the user interface that is built on top of windowing. What we are referring to, of course, is the topic of dialog boxes.

# 14

# Dialog Boxes

Dialog boxes are windows that provide a standard way for a program to ask users for additional information that may be required to complete a command. For example, a user may select the *Open...* menu item from a program's File popup menu. The ellipsis (...) at the end of the menu text indicates that a dialog box will appear. For the program to determine *which* file to open, it displays a dialog box. The user can either type the name of the file to be opened or select a file from a list. Figure 14.1 shows a standard file-open dialog box.

A dialog box itself is a window that contains child windows. In the context of dialog boxes, these child windows are called **dialog box controls**. Windows provides six window classes to support a wide range of dialog box controls. Dialog box controls can be created using the button, combobox, edit, listbox, scroll bar, and static window classes. And, if these predefined window classes don't provide the exact type of control that is needed, creating a custom dialog box control is as easy as creating a new window class.

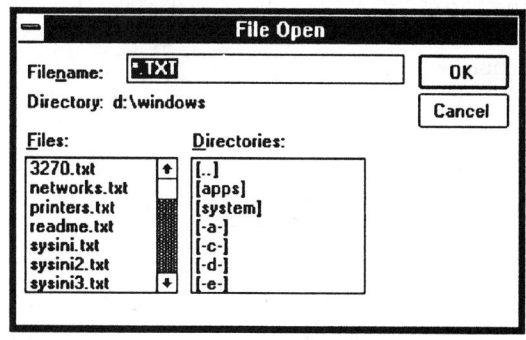

Figure 14.1 A standard file-open dialog box

Dialog boxes come in two flavors: modal and modeless. A **modal dialog box** prevents the user from interacting with other windows in a program. **System modal dialog boxes** are a special type of modal dialog box that prevents the user from interacting with any window in the *system*. A **modeless dialog box**, on the other hand, doesn't interfere with a user's interaction with other windows, but instead lets the user choose the window to work with.

Internally, the difference between the two has to do with the way the flow of messages is controlled. A modal dialog box cuts off the flow of mouse and keyboard messages to its parent and sibling windows by making its parent window **disabled**. If the user tries to interact with the disabled parent window by clicking the mouse in its client area, in its menu, or in any other part of its nonclient area, the system responds with a warning beep. A second way that modal dialog boxes control message flow is that each has its own message processing loop. Instead of using OWL's standard `PeekMessage` loop, a modal dialog box establishes its own. This means that keyboard accelerators, which depend on the call to `TranslateAccelerator` in the message loop, will be disabled when a modal dialog box is present.

A modeless dialog box, on the other hand, does not alter the flow of messages to any part of your program. Once a modeless dialog box has been opened, the user is free to work with other windows in your program or to access keyboard accelerators. Modeless dialog boxes act like the windows that a program can create by calling `CreateWindow`. In fact, this is how both modeless *and* modal dialog boxes are created. As we'll discuss, dialog box creation routines simply make a sequence of calls to `CreateWindow` on your behalf.

At first glance, modeless dialog boxes may seem more attractive than modal dialog boxes, since they give the user more choices over the structure of an interaction. In spite of this initial impression, most dialog boxes are modal. A modal dialog box provides an ideal way to focus the user's attention on the command he has selected. Once you have his attention, he must decide whether to complete the command or to cancel it. The ability to cancel a modal dialog box is one reason that modal dialogs can be so strict in their interactions with users.

Dialog boxes are an important part of the Windows user interface, and there is a standard set of dialog box controls that users quickly learn how to manipulate. The success of your dialog box programming depends to a large degree on how well you understand these conventions. We're going to start by looking at some of the conventions that have been developed for dialog boxes and dialog box controls.

## Dialog Box User-Interface Standards

Perhaps the first thing to be said about interacting with a dialog box is that, as we mentioned earlier, a user should be able to cancel a dialog box at any time without ill effects. For this reason, every dialog box should have a "Cancel" pushbutton. The user clicks this button with the mouse or uses the equivalent [Esc] keystroke to dismiss an unwanted dialog box.

A dialog box will have other pushbuttons as well, to allow the user to request different types of actions. A pushbutton marked "Ok" provides a standard way for the user to indicate that all data has been entered into the dialog box, and that the program should perform whatever action had been requested that first caused the dialog to be created. In the same way that a dialog box can be canceled by either mouse or keyboard action, the user can click with the mouse on the Ok button, or use the [Tab] key to position the keyboard focus indicator and strike [Enter] to push the Ok button. At a minimum, users expect to see two pushbuttons: one to accept the changes and one to reject them.

There are other types of pushbuttons that a programmer can create, including a pushbutton that displays a text label followed by an ellipsis (...). Like its counterpart in menus, this pushbutton causes a dialog box to be displayed. A variation on this theme is a pushbutton with a chevron (> >) after the button label. When such a button is pushed, it causes the dialog box to grow and reveal hidden dialog box controls. Figure 14.2 shows four types of pushbuttons: Ok, Cancel, ellipsis (...), and chevron (> >).

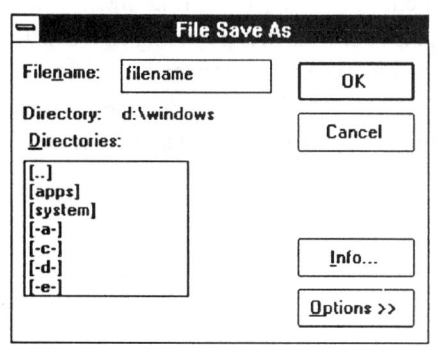

**Figure 14.2 Four pushbutton types, from the Paintbrush program's Save As dialog box**

Pushbuttons indicate the set of actions that users can request from a dialog box. When a dialog box opens, one pushbutton will be the default, which means it is selected when the user strikes the [Enter] key. The default pushbutton has a thicker border than normal, so that the user knows it at a glance. When the user strikes the [Tab] key to move between dialog box controls, the pushbutton that has the keyboard focus will always be the default pushbutton.

Two other types of buttons are **radio buttons** and **check boxes**. Radio buttons always come in groups. A group of radio buttons is like a question in a multiple-choice test: At least one of the answers must be correct. A check box is like an on/off switch: When it is checked, it is turned on and when it is not checked, it is turned off. Figure 14.3 shows a dialog box containing radio buttons and check boxes.

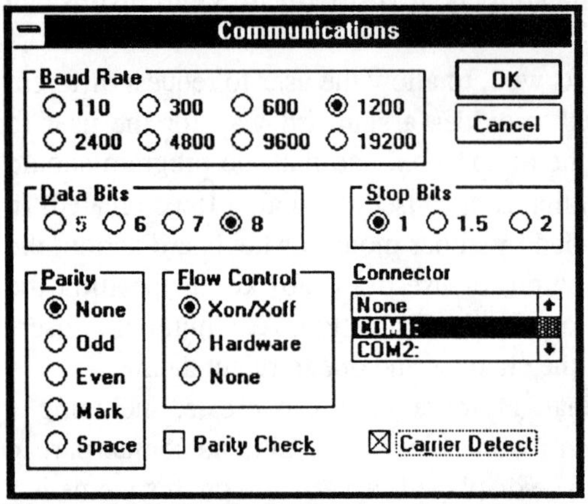

380    User Interface Objects

**Figure 14.3** Radio buttons and check boxes

An **edit control** lets the user enter and edit text. There are several different styles of edit controls, including single line and multiline, automatic conversion to either uppercase or lowercase, and character masking to hide text when entering passwords. Like most of the other standard parts of the Windows user interface, edit controls can be manipulated with the mouse or the keyboard. Either device can be used to select a character or a range of characters, or move the insertion point. A multiline edit control can be equipped with a scroll bar for when the text might not be able to fit into the area available in an edit control. Figure 14.4 shows a typical edit control.

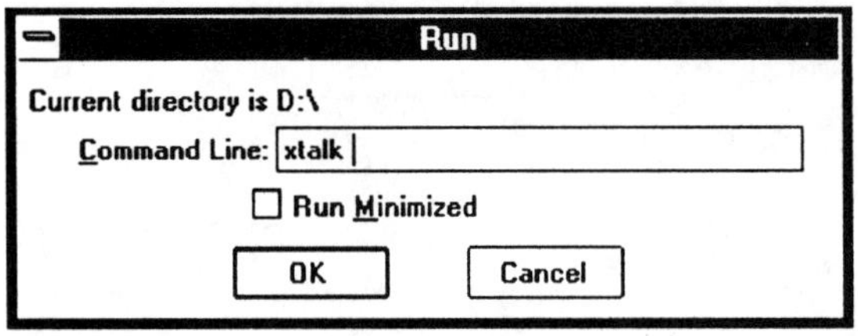

**Figure 14.4** An edit control from the File Manager

The **static** window class creates controls that are used to display icons, text labels, and empty and filled rectangles. Figure 14.5 shows a group of static controls in a dialog box.

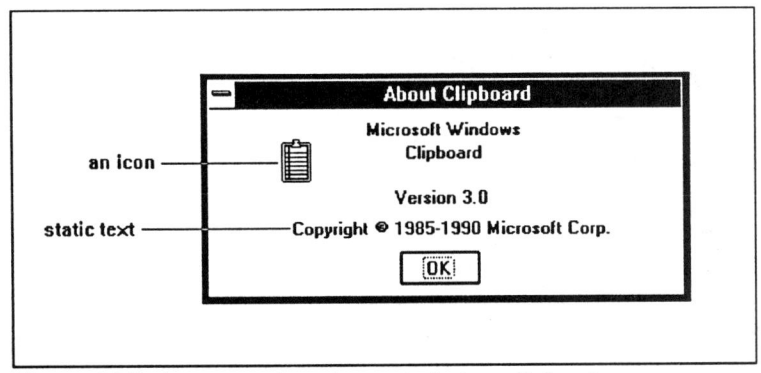

**Figure 14.5** A group of static controls in a dialog box

A **listbox** shows the user a set of choices that are available. The most common type of listbox contains text, but graphic images can also be drawn into a listbox when the set of choices is best represented by pictures instead of by words. Listboxes can have scroll bars, which are necessary when the items in a list cannot all be displayed simultaneously. Figure 14.6 shows a listbox.

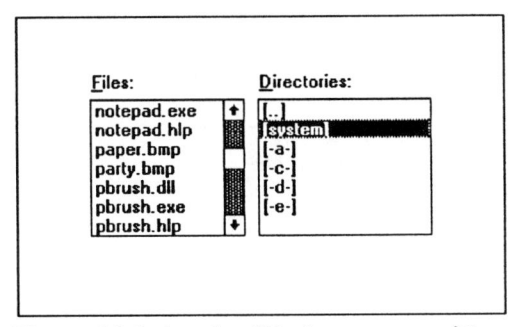

**Figure 14.6** A pair of listboxes: one with and one without a scroll bar

A **combobox** combines a listbox with an edit control or a listbox with a static text control. A combobox can hide its listbox until the user clicks on an arrow icon to call up the listbox. Like regular listboxes, a combobox can have a scroll bar and can display either text or graphic images. From a user's point of view, a combobox looks and acts exactly like a listbox paired with a static or edit control. From a programming point of view, however, a combobox is much easier to support. Figure 14.7 shows an example of a combobox.

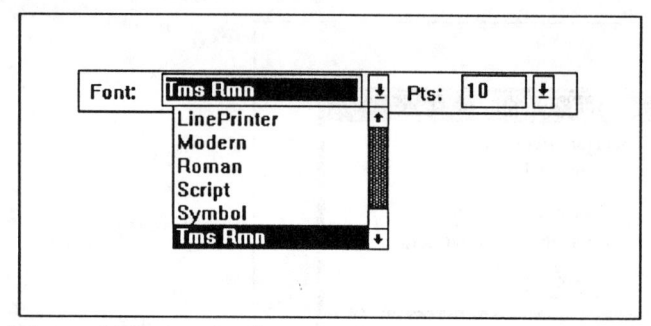

**Figure 14.7** A pair of comboboxes: one showing and one hiding a listbox

A **scroll bar** is a graphical representation of three related numbers: a minimum, a maximum, and a current value that lies between the two. You may recall that a scroll bar is installed in a regular window that was created with either the `WS_HSCROLL` or `WS_VSCROLL` style bits. Also, as we mentioned earlier, listboxes and edit controls can be created with a built-in scroll bar. However, you can request a stand-alone scroll bar as a dialog box control. Figure 14.8 shows a vertical and a horizontal scroll bar in the Program Manager application.

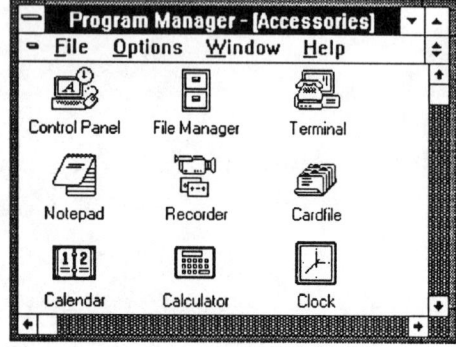

**Figure 14.8** Vertical and horizontal scroll bars

Programs that have special input requirements that cannot be met by Windows' predefined dialog box controls can provide their own. Custom dialog box controls can be incorporated into a dialog box alongside Windows' own dialog box controls.

Now that we've reviewed Windows' predefined dialog box controls, we're ready to look at what's involved in writing code to support a dialog box. What you'll find is that the predefined controls do most of the work for you. All the while, they issue notification messages that help your program keep track of the user's progress in entering data. We're going to start by looking at the creation of modal dialog boxes, because they are the more common. Then, we'll take a look at modeless dialog boxes.

## Modal Dialog Boxes

Creating a dialog box—whether modal or modeless—requires a combination of three ingredients: a dialog box template, code to create the dialog box, and code to maintain the dialog box. Each of these elements puts a different twist on the dialog box creation process, so we're going to look at them one at a time.

### *Dialog Box Template*

A dialog box template is a data object that defines the size of the dialog box, the type of controls in the dialog box, as well as the size and positioning of each dialog box control. The most common type of dialog box template is one built with a graphic editor like the one built into the Resource Workshop. The dialog box editor creates a template like this:

```
IDD_ABOUT DIALOG LOADONCALL MOVEABLE DISCARDABLE
              20, 24, 180, 84
STYLE WS_DLGFRAME | WS_POPUP
BEGIN
    CONTROL "A Sample About Box", IDD_TEXT1, "static",
            SS_CENTER | WS_CHILD, 47, 13, 84, 8
    CONTROL "Windows 3.0 Power Programming Techniques",
            IDD_TEXT2, "static", SS_CENTER | WS_CHILD,
            0, 30, 180, 8
    CONTROL "By Peter Norton and Paul Yao", IDD_TEXT3,
            "static", SS_CENTER | WS_CHILD,
            0, 42, 180, 8
    CONTROL "Ok", IDD_OK, "button",
            BS_DEFPUSHBUTTON | WS_TABSTOP | WS_CHILD,
            70, 64, 40, 16
    CONTROL "snapshot", IDD_ICON, "static",
            SS_ICON | WS_CHILD, 18, 8, 16, 16
END
```

The **DIALOG** statement is a lot like the **MENU** statement, which is the resource keyword for defining a menu. The syntax of the **DIALOG** statement is

`dialogID DIALOG [load option] [memory option] x, y, cx, cy`

- `dialogID` identifies the dialog box resource.

- **[load option]** is either **PRELOAD** or **LOADONCALL**. **PRELOAD** causes a dialog to be loaded into memory before a program starts running. **LOADONCALL** causes the dialog to be loaded only when it is needed.
- **[memory option]** is **FIXED**, **MOVEABLE**, or **DISCARDABLE**, and describes the behavior of the object once it has been loaded. For more details on these options, refer to the discussion in Chapter 18.
- **x** and **y** is the position of the dialog box window, in dialog box coordinates, relative to the client area of the dialog box's parent window.
- **cx** and **cy** are the width and height of the control, in dialog box coordinates.

Each **CONTROL** statement in the dialog box definition defines a different dialog box control. The general syntax of the **CONTROL** statement is

```
CONTROL <text>, nID, <class>, <styles>, x, y, cx, cy
```

- **<text>** is a character string in double quotes that later becomes the window text of the window that is created.
- **nID** is an integer value that uniquely identifies the dialog control window.
- **<class>** is the character string name of the window class from which a dialog control is to be created.
- **<styles>** are a set of generic window class styles and control-specific styles that are ORed together.
- **x** and **y** is the position of the control in the dialog box window, in dialog box coordinates.
- **cx** and **cy** are the width and height of the control, in dialog box coordinates.

You may have noticed that the position and size of the dialog box itself, and of each control in the dialog box, are specified in a coordinate system called **dialog box coordinates**. This coordinate system helps a dialog box definition be somewhat device-independent, since the units are defined relative to the size of the system font. In dialog box coordinates, units in the *x* direction are approximately 1/4 of the average width of the system font. In the *y* direction, they are 1/8 of the height of the system font. **GetDialogBoxUnits** provides the necessary base units, which can be used to convert between dialog box units and pixels using code like the following:

```
int    xBase,  yBase;
int    xDlg,   yDlg;
int    xPixel, yPixel;
LONG   lBase;

lBase = GetDialogBoxUnits();
xBase = LOWORD (lBase);
yBase = HIWORD (lBase);
```

```
xPixel = (xDlg * xBase)/4;
yPixel = (yDlg * yBase)/8;
```

The **STYLE** statement in the **DIALOG** statement lists the window styles that are part of the dialog box window when it is created. From this, you may have already guessed that the dialog box template is little more than a convenient way to list the parameters of the **CreateWindow** routine. Your guess would be correct. One of the tasks performed by the dialog box routines is to parse the dialog box template, making appropriate calls to **CreateWindow**.

If you find that you're a bit overwhelmed by all the details that are involved in the definition of the dialog box template, you'll be glad to know there is an easier way. Rather than messing with the creation of a dialog box template by hand, there is a tool that is part of the Borland Resource Workshop: the dialog box editor.

## *The Resource Workshop Dialog Box Editor*

The very first Windows programmers, back at the beginning of (Windows) time, had to create dialog box templates from scratch. This involved taking pencil to graph paper to create dialogs that looked somewhat reasonable. Getting a dialog box to look good required many hours of work. Fortunately, those days are long gone, and Windows programmers can take advantage of a graphic tool that allows them to draw dialog boxes and create dialog templates from these images.

Figure 14.9 shows the Resource Workshop's dialog box editor displaying the image of the dialog box definition that we saw earlier. The editor lets you adjust a dialog until it looks right. It supports all of the predefined types of dialog box controls, as well as custom controls which reside in a dynamic link library. The editor has quite a few convenient features.

To fine-tune a specific dialog box control, you select the Control.Style... menu or double-click on the control. This causes a customizing dialog box to appear, which allows you to change a control's text, its ID value, and the specific style bits that will control the appearance and behavior of the control. There is a different customizing dialog box for each class of dialog box control, since each class has its own, private style bits. Figure 14.10 shows the customizing dialog box that allows you to select the different styles available for static class dialog box controls.

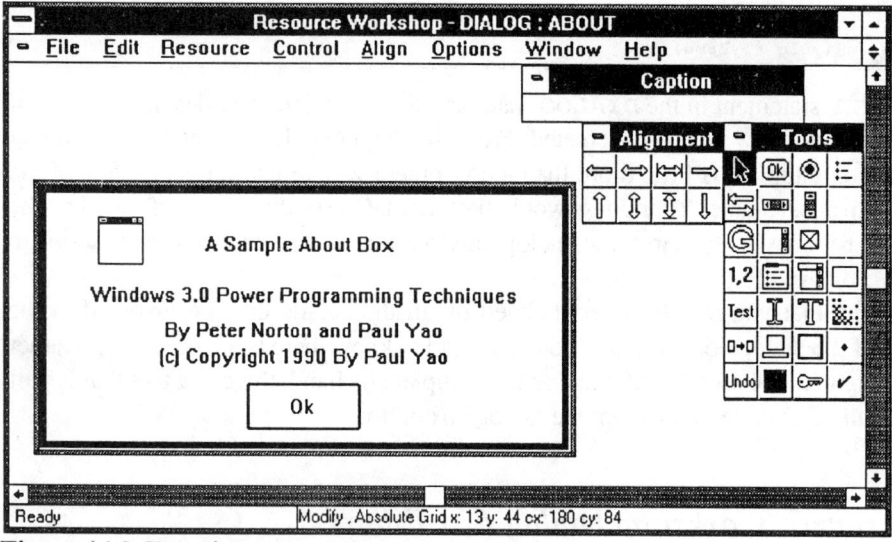

**Figure 14.9** The dialog box editor

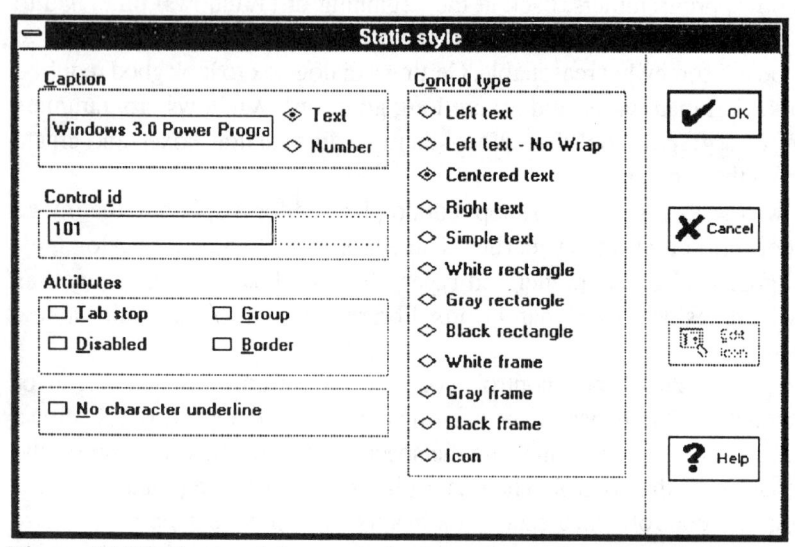

**Figure 14.10** Customizing a static class dialog box control

The dialog box editor also lets you edit include (.H) files. Select the Resource.Identifiers... menu to view and change the symbolic constants you have created for control command IDs. We always create a separate include file for each dialog box, to simplify the process of reusing templates for different projects.

Creating the dialog box template involves creating a resource object that describes the shape, size, and position of the dialog box itself and those of each control in a dialog box.

This object is placed into your program's resource file, along with the icon, resource, and menu definitions that are part of your application program. With the resource defined, the next ingredient that you'll need to create a dialog box is the actual code that triggers the dialog box creation.

## *Creating a Modal Dialog Box*

The creation of a modal dialog box is a two-step process. First, you create an OWL dialog object. Then, using the dialog object, you create an MS-Windows dialog box. The OWL dialog object maintains state information for the dialog. The MS-Windows dialog box handles the interaction with the user.

OWL has a dialog box class, **TDialog**, which can serve as a foundation for the dialog box classes you create in your applications. For simple dialog boxes (like the one we'll create first), you don't need to define a new class. Simply let **TDialog** handle everything. For more involved dialog boxes, of course, you'll want to derive classes from **TDialog**.

**TDialog** itself is derived from **TWindowsObject**. As you may recall from the discussion in Chapter 5, **TWindowsObject** is a base class for **TWindow**. This class, in turn, is a base class for the main window object in every application in this book.

**TDialog** has only a few data members:

| *Type* | *Name* | *Description* |
| --- | --- | --- |
| PUBLIC: | | |
| **TDialogAttr** | **Attr** | Structure for dialog box attributes. |
| **BOOL** | **IsModal** | Flag set if dialog box is modal. |

And, of course, the member it inherits from **TWindowsObject**. The **TDialogAttr** structure is defined in DIALOG.H, an OWL include file, as follows:

```
struct _CLASSTYPE TDialogAttr {
    LPSTR Name;
    DWORD Param;
};
```

Name refers to the resource ID for the dialog box template. This value is provided as a parameter to the constructor. **Param** provides a way to pass initialization data to a dialog box. You can assign a value to this field in the constructor of classes derived from **TDialog**.

**TDialog** contains 29 member functions: 17 are public, 11 are protected, and 1 is private. Here is a list of the more commonly called and more commonly overridden member functions:

388  User Interface Objects

**Commonly Called Member Functions:**

| Function Name | Description |
| --- | --- |
| `TDialog()` | Constructor. |
| `~TDialog()` | Destructor. |
| `Execute()` | Creates an MS-Windows modal dialog box from a resource template. You don't actually call this function, but rather call a member function of the application object, `ExecDialog()`. |
| `Create()` | Creates an MS-Windows *modeless* dialog box from a resource template. You don't actually call this function, but rather call a member function of the application object, `MakeWindow()`. |
| `CloseWindow()` | Closes a dialog box. |
| `GetItemHandle()` | Retrieves an MS-Windows handle for a dialog box control. |
| `SendDlgItemMsg()` | Sends a message to an MS-Windows dialog box control. |

**Commonly Overridden Member Functions:**

| Function Name | Description |
| --- | --- |
| `WMInitDialog()` | Respond to the `WM_INITDIALOG` message. Call the overridden function, since it performs some initialization processing as well. |
| `Ok()` | Override to process `WM_COMMAND` notification codes from an Ok pushbutton. |
| `Cancel()` | Override to process `WM_COMMAND` notification from a Cancel pushbutton. |

To create a dialog box object, you'll want to use the **new** keyword. This is the safest approach to take, since it works for both modal and modeless dialog boxes. Once a dialog box object has been created, you'll call one of two `TApplication` member functions to create the MS-Windows dialog box: `ExecDialog` (for a modal dialog box) or `MakeWindow` (for a modeless dialog box).

The application object's `ExecDialog` function calls `TDialog`'s `Execute` member function. This function, in turn, creates the MS-Windows dialog box itself by calling the `DialogBoxParam` API. For details on this routine, see the following boxed discussion.

## The `DialogBoxParam` Routine

Four MS-Windows routines create a modal dialog box: `DialogBox`, `DialogBoxIndirect`, `DialogBoxIndirectParam`, and `DialogBoxParam`. The OWL dialog box object, `TDialog`, calls the last of these routines to create an MS-Windows dialog box: `DialogBoxParam`. This routine is defined

```
int DialogBox (hInstance, lpszTemplate,
               hwndParent,lpDialogProc, dwParam);
```

- `hInstance` is the instance handle of the program or dynamic link library that owns the dialog box definition. The application object holds a copy of this for you.
- `lpszTemplate` is a far pointer to a character string for the name of the dialog box definition, as defined in the dialog box template. Alternatively, it can be an integer value wrapped inside the `MAKEINTRESOURCE` macro, when an integer is used in place of a character string to identify the dialog box template. `TDialog` gets the resource ID from your dialog box constructor.
- `hwndParent` is a handle to the parent window of the dialog box. The parent window of a modal dialog box is disabled when the dialog box is displayed. You identify the parent of a dialog box to `TDialog`'s constructor.
- `lpDialogProc` is a far pointer to a piece of code that maintains the dialog box while it is being displayed. This is a function that is referred to as a dialog box procedure. The address passed in this parameter is not the actual address of the routine itself, but the instance thunk created by the `MakeProcInstance` routine for the dialog box procedure. This mechanism is covered in detail in Chapter 19.
- `dwParam` is a DWORD (unsigned long) value for an (optional) parameter to be passed to the dialog box at creation time. This value is copied from the `Attr` data member of the `TDialog` class.

The first and third parameters are relatively straightforward, since we have encountered instance handles and window handles before. Let's take a closer look at the second and fourth parameters.

The second parameter to `DialogBox` is defined as an **LPSTR** value, which means it can hold a far pointer to a character string. The second parameter identifies the dialog box template from the resource file definition. This can be a regular character string for dialog box templates that are defined that way:

```
DialogBoxParam (hInst, "MYDIALOG", hwndParent,
                lpproc, 0L);
```

As an alternative, an integer value can be used to define a dialog box template. When this is the case, a program can use the **MAKEINTRESOURCE** macro to disguise an integer value in a character string position:

```
DialogBoxParam (hInst, MAKEINTRESOURCE(15),
                hwndParent, lpproc, 0L);
```

Or, instead of the **MAKEINTRESOURCE** macro, a pound sign can be placed in a character string to identify a dialog box template with a numeric identifier:

```
DialogBoxParam (hInst, "#15", hwndParent,
                lpproc, 0L);
```

The fourth parameter to `DialogBoxParam` identifies a function which maintains the dialog box while it is opened. This procedure, known as a **dialog box procedure**, processes messages for a dialog box in the same way that a window procedure processes messages for an MS-Windows window. OWL provides a dialog box procedure, and dispatches messages to an OWL program's **message response functions**. As you may recall from the discussion in Chapter 5, these are member functions of a `TWindowsObject`-derived class. Each message response function handles one message, or one specific type of `WM_COMMAND` message.

A non-OWL dialog box requires the creation of a **dialog box procedure**. This is a function defined to handle the MS-Windows messages sent to the dialog box. OWL programs, on the other hand, process MS-Windows dialog box messages by creating message response functions. As you may recall from our discussion of the window object classes in Chapter 5, these class member functions each process one MS-Windows message *or* one specific type of `WM_COMMAND` message.

Let's take a closer look at these member functions, since they play a key role in the maintenance of a dialog box.

## *Maintaining the Dialog Box*

Although a dialog box is a regular MS-Windows window, you'll deal with a different set of messages from those in a normal window. In particular, there are two messages which are interesting in a dialog box: **WM_INITDIALOG** and **WM_COMMAND**. To handle these messages, you'll create two member functions in a dialog box class: **WMInitDialog** and **WMCommand**. As with menu commands, you may decide to create a different message response function for each type of **WM_COMMAND** message you receive. Alternatively, you can create handlers in the child control objects to handle these messages.

The **WM_INITDIALOG** message is sent to the dialog box procedure after all of the dialog box control windows have been created, but before they have been made visible. In response to this message, a dialog box procedure initializes each of the dialog box controls to the correct initial state. For example, it might fill a listbox with the items to be viewed by the user. Or, it might set the state of radio buttons or check box buttons to a state that reflects the current settings. If there is an edit control in the dialog box, the dialog box procedure might insert a string at initialization time.

Once the dialog box controls have been given their initial settings, they work on their own to accept user input, modify the current settings, and keep out of each other's way. As they work, they send **WM_COMMAND** messages to the dialog box procedure to notify it of just about every action that the user takes. In some respects, dialog box controls are like children away at summer camp, who write home to tell their parents about the day's activities:

Dear Mom and Dad Window,

    Camp is fun. Today we went hiking, played volleyball, received the input focus from the user, and a mouse click or two.

        Your child window control,
        Check-Box

The **WM_COMMAND** notification messages allow the dialog box procedure to respond to the changes that take place in a dialog box control. In some respects, the **WM_COMMAND** message sent from a dialog box control is just like the **WM_COMMAND** message sent from a menu item when the user has made a menu selection. The **wParam** contains the value of the identifier assigned to the control in its resource file definition. The **lParam** parameter contains other information: The high-order word contains a **notification code**, and the low-order word contains the control's window handle. Figure 14.11 graphically depicts the contents of the parameters to the **WM_COMMAND** message.

## 392  User Interface Objects

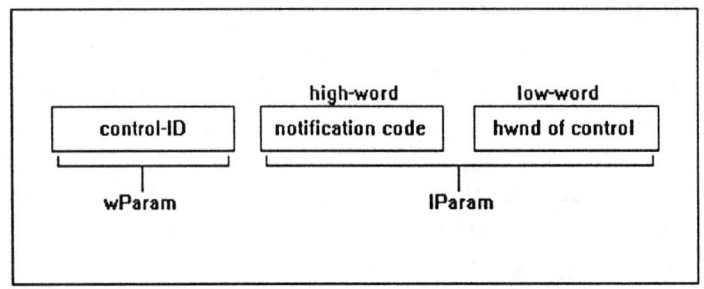

```
                 high-word        low-word
  control-ID   notification code  hwnd of control
  └─────┬────┘ └──────────────┬──────────────────┘
      wParam                lParam
```

**Figure 14.11  The parameters in a WM_COMMAND notification message**

Symbolic constants have been assigned for each control's notification codes. With some controls, only a few notification codes have been assigned. This is the case with pushbuttons, which only have two notification codes: `BN_CLICKED` and `BN_DOUBLECLICKED`. These notification codes communicate, respectively, that a button has been clicked and double-clicked with the mouse. Notifications for comboboxes start with `CBN_`, as in `CBN_DBLCLK`, `CBN_DROPDOWN`, `CBN_EDITCHANGE`, etc. Edit control notifications start with `EN_` (`EN_CHANGE`, `EN_HSCROLL`, etc.). Listbox notifications start with `LBN_` (`LBN_DBLCLK`, `LBN_KILLFOCUS`, etc.). For more details, refer to the Windows API documentation.

In addition to the messages that a dialog box procedure receives, you'll send quite a few messages *from* your dialog box objects *to* the dependent controls. Sending messages provides the primary mechanism by which your dialog box objects communicate with their controls. At initialization (`WM_INITDIALOG`) time, a dialog box object sets the initial state of controls by sending messages. As the dialog box object receives notification messages, it may send more messages to fine-tune the controls based on the content of the notifications.

A final issue that needs addressing is the termination of a dialog box. For both modal and modeless dialog boxes, `TDialog`'s `CloseWindow` member function does the work for you. If you've ever written dialog box support code in C, you might recall modal and modeless dialog boxes each require special handling. One of the niceties of the OWL libraries is that they hide these types of differences from you, allowing a single function to do all the dirty work for you.

Now that we've explored the basics of dialog box creation, let's take a look at a simple dialog box. This dialog box is so simple, in fact, that we're able to create it without creating our own dialog box class. Instead, we rely on OWL's built-in dialog box class, `TDialog`.

## A Simple Dialog Box: ABOUT

Our first, and simplest, dialog box will be an About box. This dialog box is displayed by programs to tell the user about a program: its creator, version number, and any copyright information. An About box is usually displayed by a program in response to a menu selection made from the standard Help menu, depicted in Figure 14.12. The About dialog box that our program displays is shown in Figure 14.13.

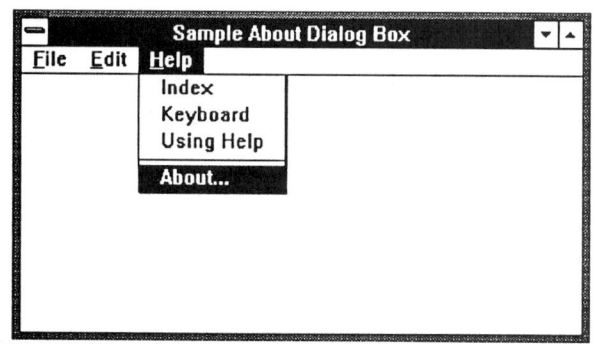

**Figure 14.12** A standard help menu

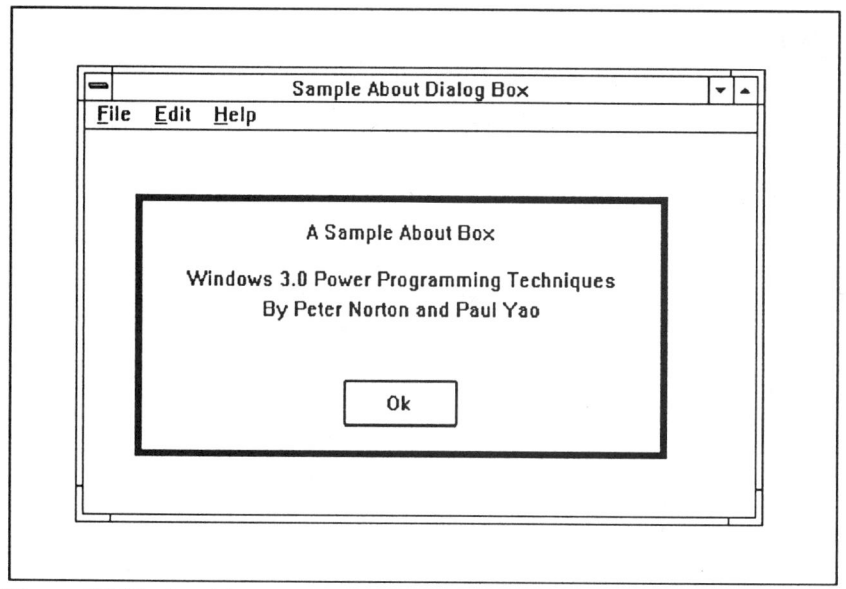

**Figure 14.13** An About dialog box

**User Interface Objects**

Here is the source code to our program:

# MAKEFILE.MAK

```
.AUTODEPEND

#    Translator Definitions
INC=\BORLANDC\OWL\INCLUDE;\BORLANDC\CLASSLIB\INCLUDE;\BORLANDC\INCLUDE
CC = bcc -c -D_CLASSDLL -H -ml -WS -w -I$(INC)

#    Implicit Rules
.c.obj:
  $(CC) {$< }

.cpp.obj:
  $(CC) {$< }

#    Explicit Rules
About.exe: About.res About.def About.obj
     tlink /c/C/n/P-/Twe/x @About.LNK
     rlink About.res About.exe

#    Individual File Dependencies
About.obj: About.cpp

About.res: About.rc About.cur About.ico
     brcc -FO About.res -i$(INC) About.RC
```

# ABOUT.LNK

```
\borlandc\lib\c0wl.obj+
About.obj
About,About
\borlandc\classlib\lib\tclasdll.lib+
\borlandc\owl\lib\owl.lib+
mathwl.lib+
import.lib+
crtldll.lib
About.def
```

# ABOUT.CPP

```
/*------------------------------------------------------------*\
 | ABOUT.CPP   - Sample About dialog box.                      |
\*------------------------------------------------------------*/
#define WIN31
#define STRICT
#include <owl.h>
#include <WindowsX.h>
#include "About.h"
#include "Aboutdlg.h"

#define COMMANDMSG(arg)   (arg.WParam)
```

```
/*-------------------------------------------------------------*\
|                  Class Declarations.                          |
\*-------------------------------------------------------------*/

class TAboutApplication : public TApplication
   {
   public:
     TAboutApplication (LPSTR lpszName, HINSTANCE hInstance,
                   HINSTANCE hPrevInstance, LPSTR lpszCmdLine,
                   int nCmdShow);
     virtual void InitMainWindow ();
   };

class TAboutWindow : public TWindow
   {
   public:
     TAboutWindow (PTWindowsObject pwParent, LPSTR lpszTitle,
              PTModule pmModule);
     virtual LPSTR GetClassName ();
     virtual void  GetWindowClass (WNDCLASS&);
     virtual void  WMCommand(TMessage& Msg) = [WM_COMMAND];
   };
/*-------------------------------------------------------------*\
|                  Main Function: WinMain.                      |
\*-------------------------------------------------------------*/
int PASCAL WinMain (HINSTANCE hInstance,   HINSTANCE hPrevInstance,
                  LPSTR  lpszCmdLine, int    nCmdShow)
     {
     TAboutApplication About ("About", hInstance, hPrevInstance,
                           lpszCmdLine, nCmdShow);
     About.Run();
     return About.Status;
     }

/*-------------------------------------------------------------*\
|                  Application Class Member.                    |
\*-------------------------------------------------------------*/
TAboutApplication::TAboutApplication (LPSTR lpszName,
                   HINSTANCE hInstance, HINSTANCE hPrevInstance,
                   LPSTR lpszCmdLine, int nCmdShow)
                :TApplication (lpszName, hInstance,
                   hPrevInstance, lpszCmdLine, nCmdShow)
     {
     /*  Application specific initialization goes here.  */
     }

/*-------------------------------------------------------------*\
|                  Application Class Member.                    |
\*-------------------------------------------------------------*/
void TAboutApplication::InitMainWindow ()
     {
     MainWindow = new TAboutWindow (NULL, "Sample About Box",
                                    NULL);
     }

/*-------------------------------------------------------------*\
|                  TAboutWindow Class Member.                   |
\*-------------------------------------------------------------*/
TAboutWindow::TAboutWindow (PTWindowsObject pwParent,
            LPSTR lpszTitle, PTModule pmModule)
            :TWindow (pwParent, lpszTitle, pmModule)
```

```
        {
        /* Window specific initialization goes here. */
        }
/*----------------------------------------------------------*\
|                 TAboutWindow Class Member.                 |
\*----------------------------------------------------------*/
LPSTR TAboutWindow::GetClassName ()
    {
    return "About:MAIN";
    }

/*----------------------------------------------------------*\
|                 TAboutWindow Class Member.                 |
\*----------------------------------------------------------*/
void TAboutWindow::GetWindowClass (WNDCLASS& wc)
    {
    TWindow::GetWindowClass (wc);
    wc.hIcon=LoadIcon (wc.hInstance, "snapshot");
    wc.hCursor=LoadCursor (wc.hInstance, "hand");
    wc.lpszMenuName="#1";
    }

/*----------------------------------------------------------*\
|                 TAboutWindow Class Member.                 |
\*----------------------------------------------------------*/
void TAboutWindow::WMCommand(TMessage& Msg)
    {
    switch (COMMANDMSG(Msg))
        {
        case IDM_FILE_EXIT:
            SendMessage (HWindow, WM_SYSCOMMAND, SC_CLOSE, 0L);
            break;
        case IDM_HELP_ABOUT:
            TDialog *PAbout;
            PAbout = new TDialog( this, "ABOUT" );
            GetApplication()->ExecDialog(PAbout);
            break;
        default:
            MessageBox (HWindow, "Feature not implemented",
                        "About", MB_OK);
        }
    }
```

# ABOUT.H

```
/*----------------------------------------------------------*\
| About.h - Include file for About.cpp.                      |
\*----------------------------------------------------------*/

#define IDM_FILE_NEW        100
#define IDM_FILE_OPEN       101
#define IDM_FILE_SAVE       102
#define IDM_FILE_SAVEAS     103
#define IDM_FILE_PRINT      104
#define IDM_FILE_EXIT       105

#define IDM_EDIT_UNDO       200
#define IDM_EDIT_CUT        201
#define IDM_EDIT_COPY       202
#define IDM_EDIT_PASTE      203
```

```
#define IDM_EDIT_CLEAR     204
#define IDM_EDIT_DELETE    205

#define IDM_HELP_INDEX     300
#define IDM_HELP_KEYS      301
#define IDM_HELP_USING     302
#define IDM_HELP_ABOUT     303
```

# ABOUTDLG.H

```
#define IDD_TEXT1     100
#define IDD_TEXT2     101
#define IDD_TEXT3     102
#define IDD_TEXT4     103
#define IDD_ICON      104

#define IDD_ABOUT     10
```

# ABOUT.RC

```
#include <Windows.h>
#include "About.h"
#include "Aboutdlg.h"

snapshot icon About.ico

hand cursor About.cur
#include "About.Dlg"

1 MENU
    {
    POPUP "&File"
        {
        MENUITEM "&New",            IDM_FILE_NEW
        MENUITEM "&Open...",        IDM_FILE_OPEN
        MENUITEM "&Save",           IDM_FILE_SAVE
        MENUITEM "Save &As...",     IDM_FILE_SAVEAS
        MENUITEM SEPARATOR
        MENUITEM "&Print",          IDM_FILE_PRINT
        MENUITEM SEPARATOR
        MENUITEM "E&xit",           IDM_FILE_EXIT
        }
    POPUP "&Edit"
        {
        MENUITEM "&Undo\tAlt+Backspace", IDM_EDIT_UNDO
        MENUITEM SEPARATOR
        MENUITEM "Cu&t\tShift+Del",      IDM_EDIT_CUT
        MENUITEM "&Copy\tCtrl+Ins",      IDM_EDIT_COPY
        MENUITEM "&Paste\tShift+Ins",    IDM_EDIT_PASTE
        MENUITEM SEPARATOR
        MENUITEM "Cl&ear",               IDM_EDIT_CLEAR
        MENUITEM "&Delete",              IDM_EDIT_DELETE
        }
    POPUP "&Help"
        {
        MENUITEM "Index",           IDM_HELP_INDEX
        MENUITEM "Keyboard",        IDM_HELP_KEYS
        MENUITEM "Using Help",      IDM_HELP_USING
```

```
            MENUITEM SEPARATOR
            MENUITEM "About...",            IDM_HELP_ABOUT
            }
    }
```

## ABOUT.DLG

```
ABOUT DIALOG LOADONCALL MOVEABLE DISCARDABLE
        20, 24, 180, 84
STYLE WS_DLGFRAME | WS_POPUP | WS_VISIBLE
BEGIN
    CONTROL "A Sample About Box", 100, "static",
            SS_CENTER | WS_CHILD, 47, 13, 84, 8
    CONTROL "Borland C++ Programming for Windows",
            101, "static", SS_CENTER | WS_CHILD, 0, 30, 180, 8
    CONTROL "Paul Yao", 102, "static",
            SS_CENTER | WS_CHILD, 0, 42, 180, 8
    CONTROL "(c) Copyright 1992 By Paul Yao", 103, "static",
            SS_CENTER | WS_CHILD, 0, 51, 180, 8
    CONTROL "Ok", IDOK, "button",
            BS_DEFPUSHBUTTON | WS_TABSTOP | WS_CHILD,
            70, 64, 40, 16
    CONTROL "snapshot", IDD_ICON, "static", SS_ICON | WS_CHILD,
            18, 8, 16, 16
END
```

## ABOUT.DEF

```
NAME ABOUT

EXETYPE WINDOWS

DESCRIPTION 'An About... dialog box'

CODE MOVEABLE DISCARDABLE
DATA MOVEABLE MULTIPLE

HEAPSIZE  512
STACKSIZE 5120
```

While reviewing the source code to ABOUT, you may notice that the dialog box template is in a separate file from the resource file. The resource file has a **#include** statement that causes the dialog box template to be loaded into the resource file when it is compiled: ABOUT.DLG. ABOUT also has a separate include file for this dialog's symbolic constants: ABOUTDLG.H. As we mentioned already, this helps make it easy to swipe this template for use in another Windows program.

The About dialog box is displayed when the user selects the *About...* item from the Help menu. Note that this is a standard way to bring up an About box. When this item is selected, a **WM_COMMAND** message is sent with the **IDM_HELP_ABOUT** command ID. In response, these lines of code create the dialog box:

```
TDialog *PAbout;

PAbout = new TDialog( this, "ABOUT" );
GetApplication()->ExecDialog(PAbout);
```

In review, the creation of a modal dialog box is a two-step process: Start by creating an OWL dialog box object, then create an MS-Windows dialog box object. The default dialog box object does a lot of work for you. But for most dialog boxes, you'll need to derive a class from `TDialog` to get the functionality that you require. In the next section, we'll look at such a dialog box and at the same time explore the creation of modeless dialog boxes.

## Modeless Dialog Boxes

The three elements needed to create a modeless dialog box are the same as those needed for a modal dialog box: a dialog template, code to create the dialog, and code to maintain the dialog once it has been created. From an MS-Windows point of view, modal and modeless dialog boxes are similar but different. The OWL libraries hide these differences from you, to simplify your programming tasks.

### *Dialog Box Template*

The dialog box template for a modeless dialog box is almost identical to the template you'd use for a modal dialog box. However, there are a few subtle things you'll want to change. For example, you'll want to set the dialog's window styles in a particular way. You do this from the Resource Workshop's Window Style dialog box, shown in Figure 14.14. You access this dialog by selecting the dialog box frame. Then, either select the *Control.Style...* menu item or double-click on the dialog box frame.

For a modeless dialog box, be sure to click the check box marked *Initially Visible*. This adds the `WS_VISIBLE` style to the dialog box templates. You don't need this style for a modal dialog box, since modal dialogs are automatically made visible. It makes sense: Otherwise, a modal dialog would disable its parent, then remain hidden. A modeless dialog without this style, on the other hand, simply would not appear—leaving you wondering what went wrong!

Another useful style is `WS_CAPTION`, which is controlled by the radio button marked *Caption* in the "Frame style" group. This gives users something to grab when they need to move a modeless dialog box out of the way, using the mouse. The *System Menu* check box

400  User Interface Objects

requests the `WS_SYSMENU` style. A system menu lets a user control a dialog using keyboard commands.

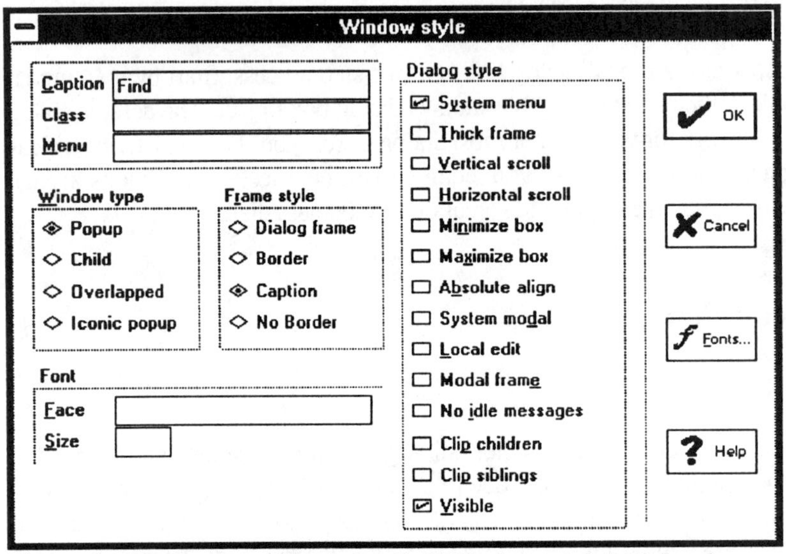

**Figure 14.14** Resource Workshop's "Window style" dialog box

Although it's not used in our programming example, notice that the "Window style" dialog box in Figure 14.14 lets you change the font used in a dialog box. This adds a `FONT` statement to a dialog template, causing the selected font to be used in all of the dialog's controls. The dialog and each of its controls change size to match the selected font's proportions.

For the dialog box template, the only difference between a modal and a modeless dialog box is the style bits. Let's look at how a modeless dialog differs from a modal dialog in its creation.

## *Creating a Modeless Dialog Box*

Creating a modeless dialog box is similar to creating a modal dialog box: First create a dialog box object, and then use this object to create an MS-Windows dialog box.

Like a modal dialog box, you can derive classes from the OWL `TDialog`. For example, this class would process the standard `WM_INITDIALOG` and `WM_COMMAND` messages:

```
class TSampleDialog : public TDialog
  {
  public:
```

```
TSampleDialog(PTWindowsObject ptParent, LPSTR lpszName);,

virtual void WMCommand(TMessage& Msg) = [WM_COMMAND];
virtual void WMInitDialog(TMessage& Msg)= [WM_INITDIALOG];
};
```

If we declare a pointer to this dialog, like this:

```
TSampleDialog * ptModelessDialog;
```

we can create an instance of this object using the **new** keyword:

```
ptModelessDialog = new TSampleDialog (ptParent, "DLGTEMP");
```

To create an MS-Windows *modeless* dialog box, we call an application object member function, **MakeWindow**, like this:

**GetApplication()->MakeWindow(ptModelessDialog);**

MakeWindow calls the **TDialog**'s **Create** member function. This routine, in turn, calls the MS-Windows **CreateDialogParam** routine. This routine creates a modeless dialog box from a dialog box resource definition. For details on this routine, see the following boxed discussion.

---

### The CreateDialogParam Routine

Four MS-Windows routines create a modeless dialog box: **CreateDialog**, **CreateDialogIndirect**, **CreateDialogIndirectParam**, and **CreateDialogParam**. OWL uses the last one to create a modeless dialog box. This routine is defined

```
int CreateDialog (hInstance, lpszTemplate,
                  hwndParent,lpDialogProc,
                  dwParam);
```

- **hInstance** is the instance handle of the program or dynamic link library that owns the dialog box definition.
- **lpszTemplate** is a far pointer to a character string for the name of the dialog box definition, as defined in the dialog box template. Alternatively, it can be an integer value wrapped inside the **MAKEINTRESOURCE** macro, when an integer is used in place of a character string to identify the dialog box template.
- **hwndParent** is a handle to the parent window of the dialog box. The parent window of a modal dialog box is disabled when the dialog box is displayed.

- **lpDialogProc** is a far pointer to a piece of code that maintains the dialog box while it is being displayed. This is a function that is referred to as a dialog box procedure. The address passed in this parameter is not the actual address of the routine itself, but the instance thunk created by the **MakeProcInstance** routine for the dialog box procedure. For details on thunks, see Chapter 19.
- **dwParam** is a DWORD (unsigned long) value for an (optional) parameter to be passed to the dialog box at creation time. This value is copied from the **Attr** data member of the **TDialog** class.

The parameters to **CreateDialog** are identical with those of **DialogBox** (discussed earlier). Even though you probably will never create a dialog box that is both modal and modeless, the similarity between these two routines makes it possible. One of the reasons for the similarity is that **DialogBox** itself calls **CreateDialog** to build the actual dialog box. The difference between the two, of course, is that **DialogBox** disables its parent and has its own message loop, while **CreateDialog** simply returns when the dialog box has been built.

As you can see, the creation of a modeless dialog box is quite similar to a modal dialog box. Where a modeless dialog box differs is in the fact that its parent window will be enabled. In other words, it can receive mouse and keyboard input. One issue this raises for modeless dialog is that you'll need to prevent *two* (or more) copies of a modeless dialog from being created. After all, with the parent enabled, the user can access the commands which will request a second dialog box. (This isn't a problem with *modal* dialogs, since the parent window—and its menu—is disabled.) To prevent this from happening, as you'll see in the FIND sample program, you simply need a flag. Before we look at our sample program, let's look at some of the message processing concerns of modeless dialog boxes.

## *Maintaining a Modeless Dialog Box*

As with a modal dialog box, a modeless dialog box will be mainly concerned with two messages: **WM_INITDIALOG** for initialization, and **WM_COMMAND** for handling dialog control notification codes. For these messages, you'll create message response functions **WMInitDialog** and **WMCommand**, assigning them the appropriate function index values.

One issue specific to modeless dialog boxes involves keyboard input. In particular, the [Tab], [Enter], and arrow keys have certain expected behavior in a dialog box. A *modal* dialog box, with its private message loop, already handles this. With a *modeless* dialog box, on the other hand, special handling is required. In particular, the message loop must be modified to make a call to the **IsDialogMessage** routine. Fortunately, as you may recall from our discussion of the message loop in Chapter 4, the OWL application object handles this for us. While you don't need to understand the particulars, if you're curious, you can read the accompanying boxed discussion.

---

The keyboard interface to a *modal* dialog box consists of support for several keys: [Tab], [Enter], [Esc], and the arrow keys. These keys allow the user to move between controls and dismiss the dialog box. They are automatically available for modal dialog boxes because, as you may recall, a modal dialog box has its own message loop. To get these keys to work in a *modeless* dialog box, you must modify your program's message loop to include a call to **IsDialogMessage**. This routine is defined as

BOOL IsDialogMessage (hDlg, lpMsg)

- **hDlg** is a handle to a modeless dialog box.
- **lpMsg** is a far pointer to a structure of type MSG.

**IsDialogMessage** returns TRUE when the message was for a dialog box or a dialog box control. In this case, **IsDialogMessage** makes the necessary calls to **TranslateMessage** and **DispatchMessage**. **IsDialogMessage** returns FALSE when the message was not for the dialog box or any control in the dialog box. In that case, the message loop can handle the message in the usual way.

Here is an example of a message loop that has been modified to correctly call **IsDialogMessage** to handle the keyboard interface for a modeless dialog box:

```
while (GetMessage(&msg, 0, 0, 0))
    {
    if (hwndFindDialog)
      if (IsDialogMessage(hwndFindDialog,&msg))
          continue;
    TranslateMessage(&msg);
    DispatchMessage(&msg);
    }
```

Notice that **IsDialogMessage** is only called if the value of **hwndFindDialog** is nonzero. This is the variable in which is stored either the window handle of a modeless dialog box or a zero when the modeless dialog box is not open.

To terminate a modeless dialog, call **TDialog**'s **CloseWindow** member function. This same routine closes modal dialogs. Under the hood, MS-Windows requires a different routine to be called to close each type of dialog. Once again, OWL simplifies the Windows programming interface for you.

Our next sample program introduces two new concepts. We're going to create a modeless dialog box by deriving a dialog box class from OWL's base class, **TDialog**. The dialog box we create is one that, as of this writing, will be incorporated in the common dialog boxes in version 3.1 of Windows. Whether the final, shipping version provides this or not, we think this dialog is still a useful sample program.

## A Modeless Dialog Box: FIND

The modeless dialog box that we're going to create is modeled after a modeless dialog box that is used by a program that is bundled with Windows: Write. It creates a modeless dialog box when the user selects the *Search.Find...* menu item. This dialog can be left open to support an ongoing string search function. The user can continue working with the word processing document and ignore the FIND dialog box; he can move the dialog box out of the way, or dismiss it entirely. Figure 14.15 shows the dialog box that our program creates.

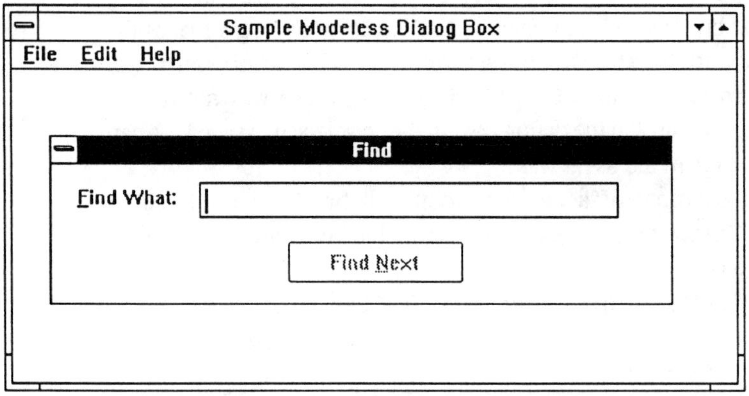

**Figure 14.15** A modeless dialog box

Here is the code to our modeless dialog box program:

## MAKEFILE.MAK

```
.AUTODEPEND

#    Translator Definitions
INC=\BORLANDC\OWL\INCLUDE;\BORLANDC\CLASSLIB\INCLUDE;\BORLANDC\INCLUDE
CC = bcc -c -D_CLASSDLL -H -ml -WS -w-par -I$(INC)

#    Implicit Rules
.c.obj:
  $(CC) {$< }

.cpp.obj:
  $(CC) {$< }

#    Explicit Rules
Find.exe: Find.res Find.def Find.obj
     tlink /c/C/n/P-/Twe/x @Find.LNK
     rlink Find.res Find.exe

#    Individual File Dependencies
Find.obj: Find.cpp

Find.res: Find.rc Find.cur Find.ico
     brcc -FO Find.res -i$(INC) Find.RC
```

## FIND.LNK

```
\borlandc\lib\c0wl.obj+
Find.obj
Find,Find
\borlandc\classlib\lib\tclasdll.lib+
\borlandc\owl\lib\owl.lib+
mathwl.lib+
import.lib+
crtldll.lib
Find.def
```

## FIND.CPP

```
/*-------------------------------------------------------------*\
 | FIND.CPP   - Sample modeless dialog box.                    |
 \*-------------------------------------------------------------*/
#define WIN31
#define STRICT
#include <owl.h>
#include <WindowsX.h>
#include "Find.h"
#include "Finddlg.h"

#define COMMANDMSG(arg) (arg.WParam)

/*-------------------------------------------------------------*\
 |                        Constants.                           |
 \*-------------------------------------------------------------*/
const int FINDBUFSIZE = 80;
```

## 406  User Interface Objects

```
/*--------------------------------------------------------------*\
|                     Class Declarations.                        |
\*--------------------------------------------------------------*/
class TFindApplication : public TApplication
    {
    public:
      TFindApplication (LPSTR lpszName, HINSTANCE hInstance,
                        HINSTANCE hPrevInstance, LPSTR lpszCmdLine,
                        int nCmdShow);
      virtual void InitMainWindow ();
    };

class TFindDialog : public TDialog
    {
    public:
      LPSTR lpBuffer;
      WORD  cbBuffer;

      TFindDialog(PTWindowsObject ptParent, LPSTR lpszName,
                  LPSTR lpFindData, WORD cbBufSize);

      virtual void Find(TMessage& Msg) = [ID_FIRST + IDD_FIND];
      virtual void Edit(TMessage& Msg) = [ID_FIRST + IDD_EDIT];
      virtual void WMCommand(TMessage& Msg) = [WM_COMMAND];
      virtual void WMInitDialog(TMessage& Msg) = [WM_INITDIALOG];
    };

class TFindWindow : public TWindow
    {
    public:
      char achFindText[FINDBUFSIZE];
      TDialog * ptFindDialog;

      TFindWindow (PTWindowsObject pwParent, LPSTR lpszTitle,
                   PTModule pmModule);
      virtual LPSTR GetClassName ();
      virtual void  GetWindowClass (WNDCLASS&);
      virtual void  WMCommand(TMessage& Msg) = [WM_COMMAND];
    };

/*--------------------------------------------------------------*\
|                     Main Function:  WinMain.                   |
\*--------------------------------------------------------------*/
int PASCAL WinMain (HINSTANCE hInstance,   HINSTANCE hPrevInstance,
                    LPSTR lpszCmdLine, int    nCmdShow)
    {
    TFindApplication Find ("Find", hInstance, hPrevInstance,
                           lpszCmdLine, nCmdShow);
    Find.Run();
    return Find.Status;
    }

/*--------------------------------------------------------------*\
|                     Application Class Member.                  |
\*--------------------------------------------------------------*/
TFindApplication::TFindApplication (LPSTR lpszName,
                   HINSTANCE hInstance, HINSTANCE hPrevInstance,
                   LPSTR lpszCmdLine, int nCmdShow)
               :TApplication (lpszName, hInstance,
                   hPrevInstance, lpszCmdLine, nCmdShow)
    {
    /*  Application specific initialization goes here.  */
```

```
        }
/*--------------------------------------------------------------*\
|                    Application Class Member.                   |
\*--------------------------------------------------------------*/
void TFindApplication::InitMainWindow ()
    {
    MainWindow = new TFindWindow (NULL,
                                  "Sample Modeless Dialog Box",
                                  NULL);
    }
/*--------------------------------------------------------------*\
|                    TFindWindow Class Member.                   |
\*--------------------------------------------------------------*/
TFindWindow::TFindWindow (PTWindowsObject pwParent,
              LPSTR lpszTitle, PTModule pmModule)
           :TWindow (pwParent, lpszTitle, pmModule)
    {
    ptFindDialog = (TFindDialog *)0L;
    }
/*--------------------------------------------------------------*\
|                    TFindWindow Class Member.                   |
\*--------------------------------------------------------------*/
LPSTR TFindWindow::GetClassName ()
    {
    return "Find:MAIN";
    }
/*--------------------------------------------------------------*\
|                    TFindWindow Class Member.                   |
\*--------------------------------------------------------------*/
void TFindWindow::GetWindowClass (WNDCLASS& wc)
    {
    TWindow::GetWindowClass (wc);
    wc.hIcon=LoadIcon (wc.hInstance, "snapshot");
    wc.hCursor=LoadCursor (wc.hInstance, "hand");
    wc.lpszMenuName="#1";
    }

/*--------------------------------------------------------------*\
|                    TFindWindow Class Member.                   |
\*--------------------------------------------------------------*/
void TFindWindow::WMCommand(TMessage& Msg)
    {
    switch (COMMANDMSG(Msg))
        {
        case IDM_FILE_EXIT:
            SendMessage (HWindow, WM_SYSCOMMAND, SC_CLOSE, 0L);
            break;

        case IDM_EDIT_FIND:
            /*
             *   If already present, activate.
             */
            if (ptFindDialog && IsWindow(ptFindDialog->HWindow))
                {
                SetActiveWindow (ptFindDialog->HWindow);
                }
            else
                {
                ptFindDialog = new TFindDialog( this, "FIND",
```

## 408  User Interface Objects

```
                                achFindText,FINDBUFSIZE);
                    GetApplication()->MakeWindow(ptFindDialog);
                    }
                break;
            case IDM_FIND_NOW:
                MessageBox (Msg.Receiver, achFindText,
                            "Find Request Received", MB_OK);
                break;

            default:
                MessageBox (HWindow, "Feature not implemented",
                            GetApplication()->Name, MB_OK);
            }
    }

/*----------------------------------------------------------------*\
|                   TFindDialog Class Member.                      |
\*----------------------------------------------------------------*/
TFindDialog::TFindDialog(PTWindowsObject ptParent, LPSTR lpszName,
                         LPSTR lpFindData, WORD cbBufSize)
            :TDialog(ptParent, lpszName)
    {
    lpBuffer = lpFindData;
    cbBuffer = cbBufSize;
    }

/*----------------------------------------------------------------*\
|                   TFindDialog Class Member.                      |
\*----------------------------------------------------------------*/

void TFindDialog::WMCommand(TMessage& Msg)
    {
    switch (Msg.WParam)
        {
        case IDD_FIND:
            {
            HWND hwndParent;

            // Copy data to parent's find buffer.
            GetDlgItemText (HWindow, IDD_EDIT, lpBuffer, cbBuffer);

            // Notify parent that find request has been made.
            hwndParent = GetParent (Msg.Receiver);
            SendMessage (hwndParent, WM_COMMAND, IDM_FIND_NOW, 0L);
            }
            break;

        case IDD_EDIT:
            {
            HWND hCtl;
            int  cc;
            WORD wNotifyCode;

            wNotifyCode = HIWORD (Msg.LParam);
            hCtl = LOWORD (Msg.LParam);
            if (wNotifyCode == EN_CHANGE)
                {
                cc = (int)SendMessage (hCtl,
                                        WM_GETTEXTLENGTH,
                                        0, 0L);
                hCtl = GetDlgItem (Msg.Receiver, IDD_FIND);
                EnableWindow (hCtl, cc);
```

```
                    }
                }
            break;
        }
    }
/*----------------------------------------------------------------*\
|                   TFindDialog Class Member.                      |
\*----------------------------------------------------------------*/
void TFindDialog::WMInitDialog(TMessage& Msg)
    {
    HWND hCtl;

    hCtl = GetItemHandle (IDD_FIND);
    EnableWindow (hCtl, FALSE);
    }
/*----------------------------------------------------------------*\
|                   TFindDialog Class Member.                      |
\*----------------------------------------------------------------*/
void TFindDialog::Find(TMessage& Msg)
    {
    }
/*----------------------------------------------------------------*\
|                   TFindDialog Class Member.                      |
\*----------------------------------------------------------------*/
void TFindDialog::Edit(TMessage& Msg)
    {
    HWND hCtl;
    int  cc;
    WORD wNotifyCode;

    wNotifyCode = HIWORD (Msg.LParam);
    hCtl = LOWORD (Msg.WParam);
    if (wNotifyCode == EN_CHANGE)
        {
        cc = (int)SendMessage (hCtl, WM_GETTEXTLENGTH, 0, 0L);
        hCtl = GetItemHandle (IDD_FIND);
        EnableWindow (hCtl, cc);
        }
    }
```

# FIND.H

```
/*----------------------------------------------------------------*\
| Find.h  - Include file for Find.cpp.                             |
\*----------------------------------------------------------------*/

#define IDM_FILE_NEW        100
#define IDM_FILE_OPEN       101
#define IDM_FILE_SAVE       102
#define IDM_FILE_SAVEAS     103
#define IDM_FILE_PRINT      104
#define IDM_FILE_EXIT       105

#define IDM_EDIT_UNDO       200
#define IDM_EDIT_CUT        201
#define IDM_EDIT_COPY       202
```

```
#define IDM_EDIT_PASTE     203
#define IDM_EDIT_CLEAR     204
#define IDM_EDIT_DELETE    205
#define IDM_EDIT_FIND      206

#define IDM_HELP_INDEX     300
#define IDM_HELP_KEYS      301
#define IDM_HELP_USING     302
#define IDM_HELP_ABOUT     303

#define IDM_FIND_NOW       400
#define IDM_FIND_DELETE    401
```

# FINDDLG.H

```
#define IDD_EDIT    101
#define IDD_FIND    102
```

# FIND.RC

```
#include <Windows.h>
#include "Find.h"
#include "Finddlg.h"

snapshot icon Find.ico

hand cursor Find.cur

#include "Find.Dlg"

1 MENU
    {
    POPUP "&File"
        {
        MENUITEM "&New",          IDM_FILE_NEW
        MENUITEM "&Open...",      IDM_FILE_OPEN
        MENUITEM "&Save",         IDM_FILE_SAVE
        MENUITEM "Save &As...",   IDM_FILE_SAVEAS
        MENUITEM SEPARATOR
        MENUITEM "&Print",        IDM_FILE_PRINT
        MENUITEM SEPARATOR
        MENUITEM "E&xit",         IDM_FILE_EXIT
        }
    POPUP "&Edit"
        {
        MENUITEM "&Undo\tAlt+Backspace", IDM_EDIT_UNDO
        MENUITEM SEPARATOR
        MENUITEM "Cu&t\tShift+Del",      IDM_EDIT_CUT
        MENUITEM "&Copy\tCtrl+Ins",      IDM_EDIT_COPY
        MENUITEM "&Paste\tShift+Ins",    IDM_EDIT_PASTE
        MENUITEM SEPARATOR
        MENUITEM "Cl&ear",               IDM_EDIT_CLEAR
        MENUITEM "&Delete",              IDM_EDIT_DELETE
        MENUITEM SEPARATOR
        MENUITEM "&Find...",             IDM_EDIT_FIND
        }
```

```
        POPUP "&Help"
          {
            MENUITEM "Index",              IDM_HELP_INDEX
            MENUITEM "Keyboard",           IDM_HELP_KEYS
            MENUITEM "Using Help",         IDM_HELP_USING
            MENUITEM SEPARATOR
            MENUITEM "About...",           IDM_HELP_ABOUT
          }
      }
```

## FIND.DLG

```
    FIND DIALOG LOADONCALL MOVEABLE DISCARDABLE
        9, 27, 216, 47
    CAPTION "Find"
    STYLE WS_BORDER | WS_CAPTION | WS_DLGFRAME | WS_SYSMENU |
         WS_VISIBLE | WS_POPUP
    BEGIN
        CONTROL "&Find What:", -1, "static",
                SS_LEFT | WS_CHILD, 9, 7, 39, 10
        CONTROL "", IDD_EDIT, "edit",
                ES_LEFT | WS_BORDER | WS_TABSTOP | WS_CHILD,
                52, 6, 146, 12
        CONTROL "Find &Next", IDD_FIND, "button",
                BS_DEFPUSHBUTTON | WS_TABSTOP | WS_CHILD,
                83, 26, 61, 14
    END
```

## FIND.DEF

```
    NAME FIND

    EXETYPE WINDOWS

    DESCRIPTION 'Modeless dialog box'

    CODE MOVEABLE DISCARDABLE
    DATA MOVEABLE MULTIPLE

    HEAPSIZE  512
    STACKSIZE 5120
```

The FIND modeless dialog box is displayed after the user selects the *Edit.Find...* menu item, depicted in Figure 14.16. This sends a **WM_COMMAND** message to the main window object, with a value of **IDM_FIND** in the **wParam**. The OWL message dispatcher delivers this message to FIND's **WMCommand** message response function, where it ends up running this code:

412   User Interface Objects

```
/*
 *    If already present, activate.
 */
if (ptFindDialog && IsWindow(ptFindDialog->HWindow))
    {
    SetActiveWindow (ptFindDialog->HWindow);
    }
else
    {
    ptFindDialog = new TFindDialog( this, "FIND",
                    achFindText,FINDBUFSIZE);
    GetApplication()->MakeWindow(ptFindDialog);
    }
```

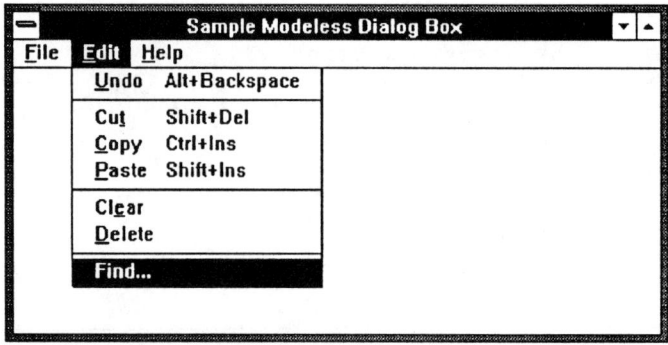

**Figure 14.16** The "Find" menu item triggers the creation of the modeless dialog box

The global variable, `ptFindDialog`, serves as the flag which lets us know if our modeless dialog has been created or not. If so, we activate the existing window. If not, a new modeless dialog is created.

The *Find* pushbutton in the modeless dialog box is initially grayed, to notify the user that it cannot be selected. Actually, our dialog box doesn't gray the control itself. Instead, it disables it with a call to `EnableWindow`. When disabled, the control grays its text to let the user know it's "out to lunch." `EnableWindow` is defined

```
BOOL EnableWindow (hwnd, bEnable)
```

- `hwnd` is a handle of the window to be enabled or disabled.
- `bEnable` is TRUE (nonzero) to enable a window and FALSE (zero) to disable it.

The dialog box object only enables the pushbutton when there are characters in the edit control.

The easiest way to detect characters in an edit control is to wait for the edit control's **EN_CHANGE** notification messages. As we mentioned earlier, notifications arrive as

**WM_COMMAND** messages, with the notification code in **lParam**'s high word. This notification is sent whenever characters are added to or deleted from an edit control.

To determine whether an edit control has characters or not, you send the edit control a **WM_GETTEXTLENGTH** message. It returns the count of characters. We can use this value as a parameter to **EnableWindow**, as shown here:

```
wNotifyCode = HIWORD (Msg.LParam);
hCtl = LOWORD (Msg.WParam);
if (wNotifyCode == EN_CHANGE)
    {
    cc = (int)SendMessage (hCtl, WM_GETTEXTLENGTH, 0, 0L);
    hCtl = GetItemHandle (IDD_FIND);
    EnableWindow (hCtl, cc);
    }
```

Only when there are characters in the edit control is the *Find* button enabled. At that time, the user can push the button. When pushed, the button sends a notification to the dialog box object: a **WM_COMMAND** message with the button's ID in **wParam**, and a **BN_CLICKED** notification code in the **lParam**'s high word. This causes the following code to be executed:

```
HWND hwndParent;

// Copy data to parent's find buffer.
GetDlgItemText (HWindow, IDD_EDIT, lpBuffer, cbBuffer);

// Notify parent that find request has been made.
hwndParent = GetParent (Msg.Receiver);
SendMessage (hwndParent, WM_COMMAND, IDM_FIND_NOW, 0L);
```

Thus, the parent window is sent a message letting it know that the user wishes to find some text.

Notice that the parent window gets sent what is effectively an internal command: **IDM_FIND_NOW**. From the parent window's point of view, it doesn't know whether this message comes from a menu selection, an accelerator key, or a dialog box. Like other command codes, this command code is something we invent and use through our program because of a definition like the following:

```
#define IDM_FIND_NOW 400
```

This modeless dialog box has shown how two dialog box controls can be interconnected: The pushbutton is grayed when the edit control is empty, and enabled when the edit control has character information. As you build dialog boxes that are more and more complex, you'll see that this is quite typical for dialog boxes. Our next programming example—a set of file handling dialog boxes—shows how you can take advantage of features which are built into the OWL libraries.

## File Open and Save As Dialog Boxes

Any program that reads and writes files to disk will require dialog boxes to allow the user to open and save files. Built into OWL are two such dialog boxes: one to select a file to open, and one to select the name of a file—and a directory—for saving a file.

Figure 14.17 shows the dialog boxes which are created by our FILEDLG program. Here is the source code:

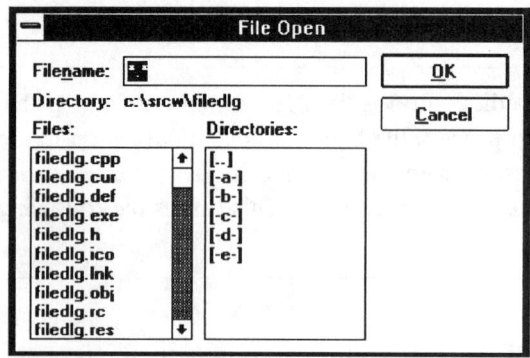

**Figure 14.17 Dialog box created by FILEDLG program**

### MAKEFILE.MAK

```
.AUTODEPEND

#    Translator Definitions
INC=\BORLANDC\OWL\INCLUDE;\BORLANDC\CLASSLIB\INCLUDE;\BORLANDC\INCLUDE
CC = bcc -c -D_CLASSDLL -H -ml -WS -w -I$(INC)

#    Implicit Rules
.c.obj:
  $(CC) {$< }

.cpp.obj:
  $(CC) {$< }

#    Explicit Rules
FileDlg.exe: FileDlg.res FileDlg.def FileDlg.obj
     tlink /c/C/n/P-/Twe/x @FileDlg.LNK
     rlink FileDlg.res FileDlg.exe

#    Individual File Dependencies
FileDlg.obj: FileDlg.cpp

FileDlg.res: FileDlg.rc FileDlg.cur FileDlg.ico
     brcc -FO FileDlg.res -i$(INC) FileDlg.RC
```

# FILEDLG.LNK

```
\borlandc\lib\c0wl.obj+
FileDlg.obj
FileDlg,FileDlg
\borlandc\classlib\lib\tclasdll.lib+
\borlandc\owl\lib\owl.lib+
mathwl.lib+
import.lib+
crtldll.lib
FileDlg.def
```

# FILEDLG.CPP

```
/*----------------------------------------------------------------*\
|   FILEDLG.CPP  - 'File.Open...' and 'File.Save As...' dialog     |
|                  demos.                                          |
\*----------------------------------------------------------------*/
#include <owl.h>
#include <string.h>
#include "FileDlg.h"

#include <filedial.h>

/*----------------------------------------------------------------*\
|                         Constants.                               |
\*----------------------------------------------------------------*/
const int MAXFILENAME = 80;

/*----------------------------------------------------------------*\
|                     Class Declarations.                          |
\*----------------------------------------------------------------*/
class TFileDlgApplication : public TApplication
   {
   public:
     TFileDlgApplication (LPSTR lpszName, HINSTANCE hInstance,
                          HINSTANCE hPrevInstance, LPSTR lpszCmdLine,
                          int nCmdShow);
     virtual void InitMainWindow ();
   };

class TFileDlgWindow : public TWindow
   {
   public:
     TFileDlgWindow (PTWindowsObject pwParent, LPSTR lpszTitle,
                     PTModule pmModule);
     virtual LPSTR GetClassName ();
     virtual void  GetWindowClass (WNDCLASS&);
     virtual void  CMFileOpen(TMessage& Msg) =
                             [CM_FIRST + IDM_FILE_OPEN];
     virtual void  CMSaveAs(TMessage& Msg) =
                             [CM_FIRST + IDM_FILE_SAVEAS];
   };
```

```
/*--------------------------------------------------------------*\
|                  Main Function:  WinMain.                      |
\*--------------------------------------------------------------*/
int PASCAL WinMain (HINSTANCE hInstance,   HINSTANCE hPrevInstance,
             LPSTR   lpszCmdLine, int    nCmdShow)
    {
    TFileDlgApplication FileDlg ("FileDlg", hInstance,
                                 hPrevInstance, lpszCmdLine,
                                 nCmdShow);
    FileDlg.Run();
    return FileDlg.Status;
    }

/*--------------------------------------------------------------*\
|                  Application Class Member.                     |
\*--------------------------------------------------------------*/
TFileDlgApplication::TFileDlgApplication (LPSTR lpszName,
              HINSTANCE hInstance, HINSTANCE hPrevInstance,
              LPSTR lpszCmdLine, int nCmdShow)
             :TApplication (lpszName, hInstance,
                 hPrevInstance, lpszCmdLine, nCmdShow)
    {
    /* Application specific initialization goes here. */
    }

/*--------------------------------------------------------------*\
|                  Application Class Member.                     |
\*--------------------------------------------------------------*/
void TFileDlgApplication::InitMainWindow ()
    {
    MainWindow = new TFileDlgWindow (NULL,
                                     "Open/Save Dialog Boxes",
                                     NULL);
    }

/*--------------------------------------------------------------*\
|                  TFileDlgWindow Class Member.                  |
\*--------------------------------------------------------------*/
TFileDlgWindow::TFileDlgWindow (PTWindowsObject pwParent,
           LPSTR lpszTitle, PTModule pmModule)
         :TWindow (pwParent, lpszTitle, pmModule)
    {
    /* Window specific initialization goes here. */
    }

/*--------------------------------------------------------------*\
|                  TFileDlgWindow Class Member.                  |
\*--------------------------------------------------------------*/
LPSTR TFileDlgWindow::GetClassName ()
    {
    return "FileDlg:MAIN";
    }

/*--------------------------------------------------------------*\
|                  TFileDlgWindow Class Member.                  |
\*--------------------------------------------------------------*/
void TFileDlgWindow::GetWindowClass (WNDCLASS& wc)
    {
    TWindow::GetWindowClass (wc);
    wc.hIcon=LoadIcon (wc.hInstance, "snapshot");
    wc.hCursor=LoadCursor (wc.hInstance, "hand");
```

```
        wc.lpszMenuName = "#1";
    }
/*---------------------------------------------------------------*\
|                   TFileDlgWindow Class Member.                  |
\*---------------------------------------------------------------*/
void TFileDlgWindow::CMFileOpen(TMessage& Msg)
    {
    char        achFile[MAXFILENAME];
    int         iRetVal;
    TFileDialog * ptFileOpen;

    // Set up wild-card & file path information.
    _fstrcpy (achFile, "*.*");

    // Create a dialog object
    ptFileOpen = new TFileDialog(this, SD_FILEOPEN, achFile,
                                 NULL);

    // Display File.Open dialog
    iRetVal = GetApplication()->ExecDialog (ptFileOpen);

    // What did user do?
    if (iRetVal == IDOK)
        {
        MessageBox (Msg.Receiver, achFile, "User Pressed OK",
                    MB_OK);
        }
    else
        {
        MessageBox (Msg.Receiver, achFile, "User Cancelled",
                    MB_OK);
        }
    }
/*---------------------------------------------------------------*\
|                   TFileDlgWindow Class Member.                  |
\*---------------------------------------------------------------*/
void TFileDlgWindow::CMSaveAs(TMessage& Msg)
    {
    char        achFile[MAXFILENAME];
    int         iRetVal;
    TFileDialog * ptFileSaveAs;

    // Set up default file name
    _fstrcpy (achFile, "WORK.DAT");

    // Create a dialog object
    ptFileSaveAs = new TFileDialog(this, SD_FILESAVE, achFile,
                                   NULL);

    // Display File.SaveAs dialog
    iRetVal = GetApplication()->ExecDialog (ptFileSaveAs);

    // What did user do?
    if (iRetVal == IDOK)
        {
        MessageBox (Msg.Receiver, achFile, "User Pressed OK",
                    MB_OK);
        }
    else
```

```
                {
                MessageBox (Msg.Receiver, achFile, "User Cancelled",
                            MB_OK);
                }
        }
```

# FILEDLG.H

```
/*----------------------------------------------------------------*\
|  FILEDLG.H    Include file for FILEDLG.CPP.                      |
\*----------------------------------------------------------------*/
#define IDM_FILE_NEW        100
#define IDM_FILE_OPEN       101
#define IDM_FILE_SAVE       102
#define IDM_FILE_SAVEAS     103
#define IDM_FILE_PRINT      104
#define IDM_FILE_EXIT       105


#define IDM_EDIT_UNDO       200
#define IDM_EDIT_CUT        201
#define IDM_EDIT_COPY       202
#define IDM_EDIT_PASTE      203
#define IDM_EDIT_CLEAR      204
#define IDM_EDIT_DELETE     205
```

# FILEDLG.RC

```
#include <Windows.h>
#include <Owlrc.h>

#include "FileDlg.h"

snapshot icon FileDlg.ico

hand cursor FileDlg.cur

rcinclude filedial.dlg

1 MENU
    {
    POPUP "&File"
        {
        MENUITEM "&New",            IDM_FILE_NEW
        MENUITEM "&Open...",        IDM_FILE_OPEN
        MENUITEM "&Save",           IDM_FILE_SAVE
        MENUITEM "Save &As...",     IDM_FILE_SAVEAS
        MENUITEM SEPARATOR
        MENUITEM "&Print",          IDM_FILE_PRINT
        MENUITEM SEPARATOR
        MENUITEM "E&xit",           IDM_FILE_EXIT
        }
    POPUP "&Edit"
        {
        MENUITEM "&Undo\tAlt+Backspace", IDM_EDIT_UNDO
        MENUITEM SEPARATOR
```

```
            MENUITEM "Cu&t\tShift+Del",       IDM_EDIT_CUT
            MENUITEM "&Copy\tCtrl+Ins",       IDM_EDIT_COPY
            MENUITEM "&Paste\tShift+Ins",     IDM_EDIT_PASTE
            MENUITEM SEPARATOR
            MENUITEM "Cl&ear",                IDM_EDIT_CLEAR
            MENUITEM "&Delete",               IDM_EDIT_DELETE
            }
    }
```

## FILEDLG.DEF

```
NAME FILEDLG

EXETYPE WINDOWS

DESCRIPTION 'File Open/Save Dialog Boxes'

CODE MOVEABLE DISCARDABLE
DATA MOVEABLE MULTIPLE

HEAPSIZE   512
STACKSIZE  5120
```

This program's File.Open and File.Save As... dialog boxes are provided courtesy of the OWL libraries. They require a minimum of coding effort, but because almost every application will require these dialogs, we decided this coding sample was well worth the time to discuss. You start by including the OWL file dialog include files in your C++ source files, like this:

`#include <filedial.h>`

Among other things, this file contains the class declaration for the **TFileDialog** class. This class supports *both* types of dialog boxes. Our program uses this class "as is."

Although not directly relevant to dialog boxes, our sample program's main window class defines two message response functions to handle the two menu selections that are of interest in this program:

```
virtual void CMFileOpen(TMessage& Msg) =
                    [CM_FIRST + IDM_FILE_OPEN];
virtual void CMSaveAs(TMessage& Msg) =
                    [CM_FIRST + IDM_FILE_SAVEAS];
```

Presumably, an OWL program would have one such response function for each menu command. To simplify matters, however, a window class can contain a **DefCommandProc** member function. This function would handle the **WM_COMMAND** messages which didn't have a reserved message response function.

The **TFileDialog** class has two constructors: a regular version and a stream version. We're only going to discuss the regular version. It is defined

```
TFileDialog(PTWindowsObject AParent, int ResourceId,
            LPSTR AFilePath, PTModule AModule)
```

- **AParent** points to a window object which is the parent of the file dialog box. This identifies the MS-Windows window which is to be disabled while the file dialog is open.
- **ResourceId** identifies the type of dialog box to be created. It can be either **SD_FILESAVE**, for the **File.Save As...** dialog, or **SD_FILEOPEN**, for the **File.Open...** dialog.
- **AFilePath** is a text buffer. It provides the initial file identifier (such as *.*, or *.TXT). It also provides the return value from the dialog box.
- **AModule** points to a current module object, and can be NULL to use the current module.

To create these dialogs, you perform the same two steps as for your own dialog classes: Create a dialog box object, then create an MS-Windows dialog box. This code creates the **File.Open...** dialog:

```
// Create a dialog object
ptFileOpen = new TFileDialog(this, SD_FILEOPEN, achFile,
                             NULL);

// Display File.Open dialog
iRetVal = GetApplication()->ExecDialog (ptFileOpen);
```

The return value, `iRetVal`, is provided by the dialog box procedure to let the caller know the results. It is **TRUE** if the user pushes the Ok button, and **FALSE** if the user pushes Cancel.

The final item worth noting is the dialog box template. Our application doesn't have to provide a resource definition (although it could). Instead, this line

```
rcinclude filedial.dlg
```

brings in the dialog box definitions expected by the **TFileDialog** class. If you decide to modify this file, it's a simple matter of copying the resource from the OWL include file to your own resource file.

At this point, you've seen several working examples of dialog boxes. This should provide a reasonable framework for building your own, application-specific dialog boxes. In addition, you should refer to the numerous OWL sample dialog box programs—since the creation and control of dialog boxes is so involved.

One of the nice features of dialog boxes and dialog box controls is that they handle the low-level input from the user. There are times, however, when your application needs direct access to keyboard or mouse input. This is the subject of the next chapters of this book.

# PART FIVE

# Message Driven Input

# 15

# Keyboard Input

In earlier chapters, we looked at the way a Windows program creates graphics output. The facilities available for graphics output can be considered quite high-level: Sophisticated drawing can be accomplished with a minimum of effort. In particular, this is the case if you consider how much code would be required to accomplish the same results without the help of GDI.

In this chapter and the one that follows, we're going to look at the way that Windows handles *input*. In contrast to GDI's high-level output, the form in which input arrives can be regarded as very low-level. That is, keyboard input arrives in the form of individual keystroke messages, with two or three messages generated per key typed. And the actions of the mouse are reported as a stream of messages that give a blow-by-blow account of the actions of this pointing device.

This chapter discusses keyboard input, leaving the next chapter to describe mouse input.

## How a Windows Program Receives Keyboard Input

Figure 15.1 shows all the pieces that play a role in handling keyboard input. The black lines represent data flow.

We'll start our study of keyboard input by tracing the flow of data from the keyboard, through the various software layers into a typical Windows program. Every Windows program has a `GetMessage` (or `PeekMessage`) loop which is responsible for pulling all keyboard messages into a program. But as you'll see, that's only half the story; once raw keyboard data arrives in a Windows program, a special Windows library routine must be called to cook the data to create truly useful character input. We introduced this routine in

424  *Message Driven Input*

Chapter 4, in the context of an OWL program's application object: `TranslateMessage`. This routine is a standard part of every Windows program's message loop. While Windows provides an abundant set of messages to describe keyboard activity, you will find that you can concentrate your efforts on a subset of these messages, which we'll describe as we follow the path of the wily keyboard messages. Keyboard input starts in the hardware of the keyboard, so that's where we'll begin.

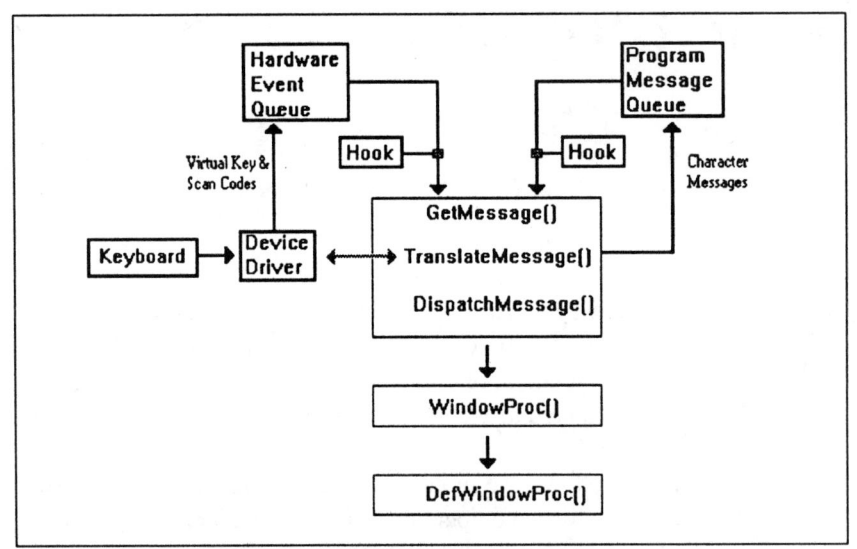

**Figure 15.1** The flow of keyboard data

## The Keyboard

Windows runs on IBM-compatible personal computers, and so the range of keyboards you're likely to encounter is small. Nonetheless, since IBM introduced its first PC in 1981, the keyboard has changed. The first IBM PC had an 83-key keyboard. IBM introduced a new keyboard with its PC/AT, which moved a few keys around and added the [SysReq] key, for a total of 84 keys. With its current line of PS/2 computers, IBM has adopted yet another keyboard, the Enhanced 101/102-key keyboard. This keyboard added two function keys, but most of the new keys were simply duplicates of keys already on the keyboard. With some minor variations, makers of IBM-compatible computers have adopted the same keyboard layout as IBM machines.

Although successive keyboards have moved a key here and added a key there, the basic operation of all keyboards has stayed the same. Every time you press or release a key, the keyboard hardware generates a one- or two-byte **scan code** that uniquely identifies the key. Every key produces two different scan codes, depending on whether the key is pressed or released. When you press a key, the value of the scan code is between 01H and 58H (for IBM-compatible keyboards). When you release the key, the value of the scan code is 80H higher. For example, when you press the letter "Z," the keyboard generates a scan code of 2CH. When it is released, the keyboard generates a scan code of ACH (2CH + 80H).

From the keyboard's point of view, the two scan codes are the only meaningful information associated with a given key. The meaning of the scan code is interpreted by the software that receives the keyboard input. In our case, that means the Windows keyboard device driver. Consider the two scan codes from the previous example: 2CH and ACH. When the keyboard driver is told that a US English keyboard is present, these codes are interpreted as the letter "Z." But the same scan codes will be interpreted as the letter "W" if the keyboard driver is told that a French keyboard is present. From this example, you can see how international support is provided: The keyboard driver simply needs the correct scan code to virtual key code and virtual key code to ASCII translation tables.

As keys are pressed and released, scan codes are sent via the keyboard cable to control circuitry on the system board of the computer. When the control circuitry senses that keyboard input is available, it generates a hardware interrupt 09H. When DOS is present, this interrupt results in a call to the ROM BIOS keyboard handler. But when Windows is present, another mechanism is put into place which meets the special requirements that Windows has for handling keyboard input. That mechanism is part of the Windows keyboard device driver, which we'll look at next.

## *The Windows Keyboard Device Driver*

During Windows startup, the Windows keyboard driver installs an interrupt handler to receive keyboard scan codes. The interrupt handler is called any time a key is pressed or released. It reads scan values from the keyboard port and maps these onto a set of **virtual key** values that make up the **Windows virtual keyboard**.

The virtual keyboard defines a standard set of keys for all keyboards currently on the market. It also defines keys that don't correspond to any current keyboard, to allow room for growth. Table 15.1 lists all of the keys in the virtual keyboard, along with the symbolic names as defined in WINDOWS.H.

**Table 15.1** The Windows virtual keys

| (hex) | (dec) | Symbolic Name | Key Pressed (US English 101/102 Keyboard) |
|---|---|---|---|
| 1 | 1 | VK_LBUTTON | |
| 2 | 2 | VK_RBUTTON | |
| 3 | 3 | VK_CANCEL | Ctrl+Break |

*(Continued)*

426   *Message Driven Input*

**Table 15.1**   *Continued*

| (hex) | (dec) | Symbolic Name | Key Pressed (US English 101/102 Keyboard) |
|---|---|---|---|
| 4 | 4 | VK_MBUTTON | |
| 8 | 8 | VK_BACK | Backspace |
| 9 | 9 | VK_TAB | Tab |
| C | 12 | VK_CLEAR | 5 on numeric keypad with Num Lock off |
| D | 13 | VK_RETURN | Enter |
| 10 | 16 | VK_SHIFT | Shift |
| 11 | 17 | VK_CONTROL | Ctrl |
| 12 | 18 | VK_MENU | Alt |
| 13 | 19 | VK_PAUSE | Pause (or Ctrl+Num Lock) |
| 14 | 20 | VK_CAPITAL | Caps Lock |
| 1B | 27 | VK_ESCAPE | Esc |
| 20 | 32 | VK_SPACE | Spacebar |
| 21 | 33 | VK_PRIOR | Page Up |
| 22 | 34 | VK_NEXT | Page Down |
| 23 | 35 | VK_END | End |
| 24 | 36 | VK_HOME | Home |
| 25 | 37 | VK_LEFT | Left Arrow |
| 26 | 38 | VK_UP | Up Arrow |
| 27 | 39 | VK_RIGHT | Right Arrow |
| 28 | 40 | VK_DOWN | Down Arrow |
| 29 | 41 | VK_SELECT | <unused> |
| 2A | 42 | VK_PRINT | <unused> |
| 2B | 43 | VK_EXECUTE | <unused> |
| 2C | 44 | VK_SNAPSHOT | Print Screen |
| 2D | 45 | VK_INSERT | Ins |
| 2E | 46 | VK_DELETE | Del |
| 2F | 47 | VK_HELP | <unused> |
| 30–39 | 48–57 | VK_0 to VK_9 | 0 through 9 above letter keys |
| 41–5A | 65–90 | VK_A to VK_Z | A through Z |
| 60 | 96 | VK_NUMPAD0 | 0 on numeric keypad with Num Lock on |
| 61 | 97 | VK_NUMPAD1 | 1 on numeric keypad with Num Lock on |
| 62 | 98 | VK_NUMPAD2 | 2 on numeric keypad with Num Lock on |
| 63 | 99 | VK_NUMPAD3 | 3 on numeric keypad with Num Lock on |
| 64 | 100 | VK_NUMPAD4 | 4 on numeric keypad with Num Lock on |
| 65 | 101 | VK_NUMPAD5 | 5 on numeric keypad with Num Lock on |
| 66 | 102 | VK_NUMPAD6 | 6 on numeric keypad with Num Lock on |
| 67 | 103 | VK_NUMPAD7 | 7 on numeric keypad with Num Lock on |
| 68 | 104 | VK_NUMPAD8 | 8 on numeric keypad with Num Lock on |
| 69 | 105 | VK_NUMPAD9 | 9 on numeric keypad with Num Lock on |
| 6A | 106 | VK_MULTIPLY | * on numeric keypad |
| 6B | 107 | VK_ADD | + on numeric keypad |

*(Continued)*

**Table 15.1**  Continued

| (hex) | (dec) | Symbolic Name | Key Pressed (US English 101/102 Keyboard) |
|---|---|---|---|
| 6C | 108 | VK_SEPARATOR | <unused> |
| 6D | 109 | VK_SUBTRACT | - on numeric keypad |
| 6E | 110 | VK_DECIMAL | . on numeric keypad with Num Lock on |
| 6F | 111 | VK_DIVIDE | / on numeric keypad |
| 70 | 112 | VK_F1 | F1 function key |
| 71 | 113 | VK_F2 | F2 function key |
| 72 | 114 | VK_F1 | F3 function key |
| 73 | 115 | VK_F4 | F4 function key |
| 74 | 116 | VK_F5 | F5 function key |
| 75 | 117 | VK_F6 | F6 function key |
| 76 | 118 | VK_F7 | F7 function key |
| 77 | 119 | VK_F8 | F8 function key |
| 78 | 120 | VK_F9 | F9 function key |
| 79 | 121 | VK_F10 | F10 function key |
| 7A | 122 | VK_F11 | F11 function key |
| 7B | 123 | VK_F12 | F12 function key |
| 7C | 124 | VK_F13 | |
| 7D | 125 | VK_F14 | |
| 7E | 126 | VK_F15 | |
| 7F | 127 | VK_F16 | |
| 90 | 144 | VK_NUMLOCK | Num Lock |
| 91 | 145 | | Scroll Lock |

The following codes apply to US keyboards only

| | | | |
|---|---|---|---|
| BA | 186 | | colon/semicolon |
| BB | 187 | | plus/equal |
| BC | 188 | | less than/comma |
| BD | 189 | | underscore/hyphen |
| BE | 190 | | greater than/period |
| BF | 191 | | question/slash |
| C0 | 192 | | tilde/back accent |
| DB | 219 | | left squiggle brace/left square brace |
| DC | 220 | | horizontal bar/backslash |
| DD | 221 | | right squiggle brace/right square brace |
| DE | 222 | | double quote/single quote |

Once the keyboard driver has translated the scan code information into a virtual key code, it calls Windows. Windows puts both scan code and virtual key data into a special buffer called the **hardware event queue**. We briefly discussed the role of this buffer in Chapter 4, when we talked about the message loop. Let's return to this topic to see how it affects keyboard input.

## The Hardware Event Queue

From the point of view of keyboard input, the hardware event queue is simply a type-ahead buffer. It can hold up to 120 hardware events, which means 60 characters worth of data since two events are generated when a keyboard key is pressed and released. Even for the fastest typists, this should be enough to prevent data loss.

A type-ahead buffer is necessary because of the way that a Windows program retrieves keyboard input. As you may recall from an earlier discussion, Windows' multitasking is nonpreemptive. That is, the operating system does not interrupt one program to allow another to run. Instead, programs interrupt themselves. This polite form of multitasking works because it is built into Windows' message delivery mechanism. All input to a program, including keyboard input, is delivered in the form of messages. Since Windows does not interrupt programs to deliver keyboard information, the data has to be stored someplace: That place is the hardware event queue. Otherwise, a fast typist might outpace a program's ability to retrieve keyboard input.

The contents of the hardware event queue are eventually delivered to a Windows program in the form of two messages: `WM_KEYDOWN` and `WM_KEYUP`. These correspond to the two types of scan codes: key press and key release. As indicated by the diagram in Figure 15.1, a program gets these two messages from the hardware event queue by calling `GetMessage`.

But the real meaning of keyboard messages comes from the values stored in one 2-byte integer value and one 4-byte integer value which make up the `wParam` and `lParam` parameters of a window procedure. The format of these two fields is the same for both messages.

`wParam` contains the virtual key code of the key that was pressed or released. The keyboard driver generates this value from the scan code that it received from the keyboard hardware. By far and away, this is the most important field that Windows provides with these two messages. After all, the virtual key code represents how the keyboard driver views a keyboard event in the context of Windows taking into account the type of keyboard that is currently attached to the system.

The `lParam` parameter is divided into six fields, as shown in Figure 15.2. Let's review these one at a time:

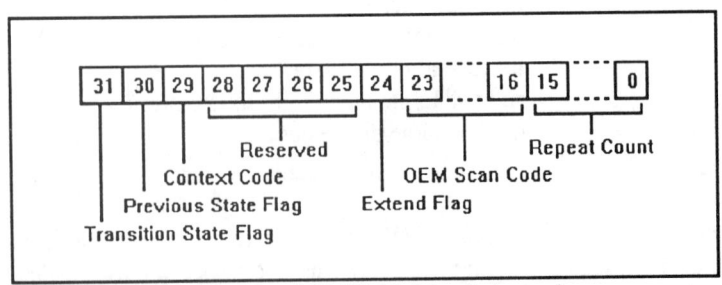

Figure 15.2 Six Fields of lPARAM for keystroke messages

- **Repeat Count.** Built into the hardware of the keyboard is the ability to automatically repeat a single character if a key is held down: a feature that IBM calls **typematic**. To prevent such keys from overflowing the hardware event queue, Windows increments the repeat count when it finds that a new keyboard event is identical with the previous keyboard event that is still in the queue. In doing so, Windows combines several WM_KEYDOWN messages into a single message. A repeat count greater than 1 means that keyboard events are occurring faster than your program is able to process them. In such cases, a program can interpret each WM_KEYDOWN message as multiple messages, depending on the repeat value.
- **OEM Scan Code.** This field contains the scan code value as it was sent from the keyboard. For most programs, the virtual key code is more useful, since it represents a device-independent code for a keystroke. Because the scan code represents a hardware-dependent value, in most cases you'll want to avoid using this field. But sometimes it is necessary to use the scan code information to tell the difference, for example, between the left shift key and the right shift key. For certain keys, the keyboard driver uses the hardware scan code to translate the WM_KEYDOWN message into a WM_CHAR message. This is the case, for example, with keys in the numeric keypad.
- **Extend Flag.** This field is actually an extension of the OEM Scan Code. In effect, it tells a program that the key that was pressed was one of the duplicate keys on IBM's extended keyboard. Like the scan code, the value of this field is device-dependent, and so great care should be taken when using it.
- **Context Code.** This flag is 1 if the [Alt] key is down; otherwise it has a value of 0.
- **Previous State Flag.** This flag helps to identify messages generated by typematic action. It has a value of 1 if the previous state of the key was down, and a value of 0 if the previous state of the key was up.
- **Transition State Flag.** This flag is 1 if the key is being released and 0 if the key is being pressed. It will always be 1 for WM_KEYUP and 0 for the WM_KEYDOWN message.

From these messages, a program receives both the raw keyboard scan codes and the half-cooked virtual key codes. As you'll see shortly, the most useful keyboard data arrive as fully cooked character messages. But there are some keystrokes that are not available as character messages, since they do not represent characters but rather keyboard commands.

Table 15.2 shows a list of the keystrokes that can only be detected with the WM_KEYDOWN and WM_KEYUP messages. In a moment, we'll discuss the WM_CHAR message, which provides ASCII character information. The keys in this table do not produce ASCII characters, and so they do not generate WM_CHAR messages. Therefore, if you are interested in detecting keystrokes generated by these keys, you'll watch for the WM_KEYDOWN message.

430  *Message Driven Input*

**Table 15.2** Keystrokes available only with `WM_KEYDOWN` and `WM_KEYUP`

| Keystroke | Description |
|---|---|
| F1–F9, F11–F16 | Function keys. The [F10] function key is reserved for Windows' use as the Menu Select hot-key. |
| Shift, Ctrl, Alt | Shift keys. The [Alt] key is a reserved system key and does not generate WM_KEYDOWN or WM_KEYUP unless the [Ctrl] key is down. Normally, it only generates WM_SYSKEYDOWN and WM_SYSKEYUP messages. |
| Caps Lock, Num Lock, Scroll Lock. | Toggle keys |
| Print Screen | Reserved key for copying screen to clipboard ([PrtSc] alone), or for copying the active window to the clipboard ([Alt] + [PrtSc]). Windows eats the WM_KEYDOWN message, leaving WM_KEYUP. |
| Pause | Pause key |
| Insert, Delete, Home, End, Page Up, Page Down | Text editing keys. Although there are two of each of these keys on the 101/102 keyboard, each pair has only one virtual key code. However, they can be distinguished with the Extend flag. |
| Up, Left, Down, Right | Direction keys. Although there are eight keys in this set, like the text editing keys the duplicate keys do not have a separate virtual key code. However, they can be distinguished with the Extend flag. |

To detect one of these keys in a Windows program, you'll test the value of `wParam` against the virtual key values listed in Table 15.1. For example, here is code that checks for a key-down transition of the [F1] function key:

```
void TKeyInputWindow::WMKeyDown(TMessage& Msg)
    {
    if (Msg.WParam == VK_F1)
        {
        /*  F1 Keydown. */
        ...
        }
    }
```

For programming the function keys, it is often easier to define an Accelerator.

While it would involve a lot of work, it would be possible to receive all the keyboard input that you might require using **WM_KEYDOWN** and **WM_KEYUP** messages. Notice, however, that to tell the difference between a capital letter and a lowercase letter would require you to know the state of the shift key in addition to detecting the keystroke message. There's no reason to go to all that work, since Windows has a built-in facility that will do the work for you. The routine that provides this service is a standard part of every message loop: **TranslateMessage**.

## The GetMessage Loop

The minimum standard message loop is as follows:

```
while (GetMessage (&msg, 0, 0, 0))
    {
    TranslateMessage (&msg);
    DispatchMessage (&msg);
    }
```

GetMessage reads messages from two places: the hardware event queue and a program's private message queue. For every message it retrieves, a call is made to **TranslateMessage**, which ignores every message except two: **WM_KEYDOWN** and **WM_SYSKEYDOWN**.

**WM_SYSKEYDOWN** is one of three **system keyboard messages**. The other two are **WM_SYSKEYUP** and **WM_SYSCHAR**. The behavior of these messages parallels the behavior of the three regular keyboard messages, but system keyboard messages are used primarily as part of the keyboard interface to menus. We'll look at another use of these messages when we discuss the window procedure in a short while.

The role of **TranslateMessage** is simple. It takes the virtual key data from the **WM_KEYDOWN** (or **WM_SYSKEYDOWN**) message and calls the keyboard device driver to convert the virtual key code into an ASCII code. For keys with no ASCII equivalent, no translation is done. For the rest, a **WM_CHAR** (or **WM_SYSCHAR**) message is generated and placed in the private message queue.

The sequence of messages created in response to hitting the "w" key, for example, is as follows:

| Key | wParam Contains |
|---|---|
| WM_KEYDOWN | Virtual key W |
| WM_CHAR | ASCII code w |
| WM_KEYUP | Virtual key W |

432   *Message Driven Input*

And when a capital letter is struck, the sequence of messages is even more involved. Here is the message traffic when the user types "W":

| *Key* | *wParam Contains* |
|---|---|
| WM_KEYDOWN | Virtual key VK_SHIFT |
| WM_KEYDOWN | Virtual key W |
| WM_CHAR | ASCII code W |
| WM_KEYUP | Virtual key W |
| WM_KEYUP | Virtual key VK_SHIFT |

On some non-English keyboards (French and German, to name two), special key combinations are used to create diacritic marks over vowels. For example, to type the words château (the French word for "castle") and München (the German name for the city of Munich) on a French keyboard, you need to use special key combinations because there are no dedicated "â" and "ü" keys.

These special keys are called **dead-keys**, since they are not expected to produce characters, but modify the keystroke that follows. In response to a **WM_KEYDOWN** (or **WM_SYSKEYDOWN**) for such keys, **TranslateMessage** generates a **WM_DEADCHAR** (or **WM_SYSDEADCHAR**) message. You can safely ignore these messages, since Windows will create the correct character message from the keystrokes that follow.

If you'd like to experiment with dead-key processing, you can install a different keyboard translation table using the Control Panel. Bring up the International Settings dialog box and select the country whose keyboard layout you want to work with. If you bring up the French keyboard, you'll discover that the "A" and "Q" keys have been switched, as have the "W" and "Z" keys. The dead-key for the circumflex is located at the key marked "[," and the dead-key for the umlaut is [Shift]+"[."

The message sequence that is generated on a French keyboard to produce the letter "â" is as follows:

| *Key* | *wParam Contains* |
|---|---|
| WM_KEYDOWN | Scan code for pressing circumflex key |
| WM_DEADCHAR | Dead character message for circumflex key |
| WM_KEYUP | Scan code for releasing circumflex key |
| WM_KEYDOWN | Scan code for pressing "a" |
| WM_CHAR | Character message for "â" |
| WM_KEYUP | Scan code for releasing "a" |

With the exception of the keys listed in Table 15.2, keyboard input will normally come from the **WM_CHAR** messages that are created by **TranslateMessage**. The translation that takes place takes into account the state of the various shift keys, to provide uppercase and lowercase letters, numbers, and punctuation marks. Since the ASCII character set includes a complete range of accented vowels, this mechanism also supports international keyboards.

After **TranslateMessage** generates the **WM_CHAR** (or **WM_SYSCHAR**) message, it returns control to the message loop. The **DispatchMessage** routine then pushes the **WM_KEYDOWN** or **WM_SYSKEYDOWN** message to the window procedure for processing.

Since the character message is placed on the program's message queue, it does not become available to the program until **GetMessage** is called to read a new message. At that time, the **WM_CHAR** (or **WM_SYSCHAR**) message is read in, passed to **TranslateMessage** (which ignores it), and finally sent on to the window procedure by **DispatchMessage**. Although the key-down message causes the character message to be generated, by the time the window procedure sees the character message, the key-down message has already been processed.

The window procedure parameters for the **WM_CHAR** message are similar to those for the other keyboard messages we discussed earlier. That is, the **lParam** field in a character message contains the same six fields as the **WM_KEYDOWN** and **WM_KEYUP** messages.

The **WM_CHAR** message is different, however, in that the **wParam** parameter contains the ASCII code of the character whose key was pressed. It's the job of the window procedure to trap this message and read whatever character input is required.

To build bullet-proof processing for character input, you'll probably want to filter out some of the **WM_CHAR** messages which are created for keystrokes that aren't ordinarily printed. These include the tab, backspace, and return keys. These, along with the others in the list in Table 15.2, will require special processing apart from the regular character messages:

| Keystroke | ASCII Value (hex) | (dec) | Description |
|---|---|---|---|
| Ctrl+A to Ctrl+G | 1–7 | 1–7 | Nonprintable characters. |
| Backspace | 8 | 8 | Backspace key (VK_BACK). |
| Ctrl+H | 8 | 8 | Surrogate backspace key (VK_BACK). |
| Tab | 9 | 9 | Tab key (VK_TAB). |
| Ctrl+I | 9 | 9 | Surrogate tab key (VK_TAB). |
| Ctrl+J | A | 10 | Linefeed. |
| Ctrl+K to Ctrl+L | B–C | 11–12 | Nonprintable characters. |
| Return | D | 13 | Return key (VK_RETURN). |
| Ctrl+M | D | 13 | Surrogate return key (VK_RETURN). |
| Ctrl+N to Ctrl+Z | E–1A | 15–26 | Nonprintable characters. |
| Esc | 1B | 27 | Escape key (VK_ESCAPE). |

When an accelerator has been defined with a [Ctrl] + letter key combination, then no **WM_CHAR** is generated for that keystroke. We explored accelerators in Chapter 11.

## The Window Object

We've traced the path that keyboard data takes on its way from the hardware to our program. Although some handling of keyboard input is done in the message loop, the bulk of processing is handled in the OWL window object message response functions.

Table 15.3 summarizes all of the keyboard messages that we have encountered so far. You can safely ignore most of them, however, and concentrate your efforts on two messages: `WM_CHAR` for all character input, and `WM_KEYDOWN` for all noncharacter function key input. In the example program, KEYINPUT, these are the only messages we rely on to create a text-entry and editing window.

**Table 15.3** A summary of keyboard messages

| | |
|---|---|
| `WM_KEYDOWN` | Key pressed |
| `WM_CHAR` | Character input |
| `WM_DEADCHAR` | Dead-character |
| `WM_KEYUP` | Key released |
| `WM_SYSKEYDOWN` | System key pressed |
| `WM_SYSCHAR` | System character input |
| `WM_SYSDEADCHAR` | System dead-character |
| `WM_SYSKEYUP` | System key released |

In certain situations, you may wish to process system keyboard messages as well. In particular, when the active window in the system is iconic, Windows substitutes the system keyboard messages (`WM_SYSKEYDOWN`, `WM_SYSKEYUP`, `WM_SYSCHAR`) in place of the regular keyboard messages. Since most programs are not interested in keyboard input when they are iconic, this convention helps avoid spurious input. If you *do* want to receive keyboard input in this situation, however, you'll need to pay attention to the system keyboard messages.

In general, however, you'll ignore system keyboard messages, which are primarily used by Windows for its own internal housekeeping purposes. Since some of this housekeeping is done in the default window procedure, you'll want to be sure that—like other unused messages—these messages get passed on.

## The Default Window Procedure

All of the messages that a window procedure does not use should be passed on to the default window procedure. The default window procedure ignores all regular keyboard messages, so window procedures that don't use keyboard messages can safely pass them on.

But the default window procedure plays an important role in handling the system keyboard messages. System keyboard messages are usually generated in place of regular keyboard messages when the [Alt] key is down. In this way, system keyboard messages are used by the default window procedure to provide keyboard access to menus.

For example, when a window has a system menu icon, the system menu will appear when you strike the [Alt] + [Spacebar] keys. When we discuss menus in Chapters 11 and 12, you saw that you can define your own menu hot-key that will cause a pull-down menu to appear when the hot-key is hit with the [Alt] key. A menu hot-key is also called a **mnemonic**, since it is always a letter in the name of the menu. These keystrokes are handled as system keyboard messages.

The default window procedure also plays a role in making certain keyboard combinations operate correctly. For example, you can quit an application by typing [Alt] + [F4], go to the Task List by pressing [Ctrl] + [Esc], and switch the active program with [Alt] + [Tab]. For these system hot-keys to work properly, the default window procedure must get all system keyboard messages.

In our look at the path taken by keyboard events, there is one item that we have overlooked: hooks. The subject of hooks is outside the scope of this book, but it is important for you to be aware of them because they can affect the path of keyboard input.

## Hooks

A hook is a subroutine that is installed into Windows' message handling mechanism. Hooks allow you to monitor and trap certain types of messages. Figure 15.1 shows the relationship of hooks to the flow of keyboard data.

Windows has a total of seven different hooks, although we're going to limit our discussion to two of them: keyboard hooks and "getmessage" hooks. All hooks are installed on a systemwide basis. That is, if a program installs a hook, it affects every program running in the system.

The keyboard hook taps into the flow of keyboard messages coming out of the hardware event queue and provides a means of listening to all keyboard input in the system. Creating a keyboard hook in Windows is comparable to stealing the keyboard interrupt under DOS; it gives you complete control over the flow of keystroke messages (**WM_KEYDOWN** and **WM_KEYUP**) in the system.

One use of a keyboard hook is to watch for special hot-keys. For example, you might want to give a user the ability to call up your program at any time by simply typing the [Alt] + [F12] key combination. You accomplish this by installing a keyboard hook when your program starts running. The hook lets all keyboard input pass, until it encounters the desired keystroke. At that time, it lets Windows know that it wants the key for itself, which causes the key to be ignored by the rest of the system. The hook then notifies the program (perhaps via a message) that the hot-key has been struck. At that time, it is up to the program to respond in a way that makes sense. Perhaps that means opening a window to offer some service to the user.

The second type of hook that affects keyboard input is the getmessage hook. This hook is actually called by the `GetMessage` routine for every message that it receives before it gives the message to a program. This hook can do anything it wants to the message, including change any of the parameters, or even the value of the message!

Since a getmessage hook has access to every message that is received by the `GetMessage` routine, it can be used for many different types of applications. A hot-key could be implemented using a getmessage hook, for example. Or, it could be used to detect mouse button messages on a given window—perhaps to prevent a user from accessing any other window until a password has been typed correctly. The getmessage hook can be used for any messages that `GetMessage` retrieves, which means all keyboard and mouse messages as well as the `WM_PAINT` and `WM_TIMER` messages.

## A Sample Program

To demonstrate the way a program can receive keyboard input, we have written KEYINPUT. This program creates a simple single-line text entry window. Figure 15.3 shows a sample of the output created by this program.

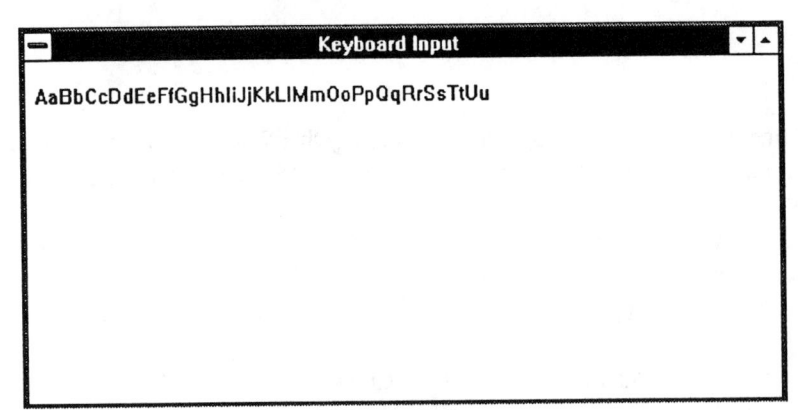

```
┌─────────────────────── Keyboard Input ───────────────────────┐
│ AaBbCcDdEeFfGgHhIiJjKkLlMmOoPpQqRrSsTtUu                     │
│                                                              │
│                                                              │
│                                                              │
└──────────────────────────────────────────────────────────────┘
```

**Figure 15.3 Output from KEYINPUT program**

KEYINPUT shows how the `WM_CHAR` and `WM_KEYDOWN` messages can be used to receive character input and perform some simple editing. The following cursor movement keys are recognized: Home, End, Left Arrow, and Right Arrow. In addition, the backspace and delete keys can be used to erase characters.

## MAKEFILE.MAK

```
.AUTODEPEND

#       Translator Definitions
INC=\BORLANDC\OWL\INCLUDE;\BORLANDC\CLASSLIB\INCLUDE;\BORLANDC\INCLUDE
CC = bcc -c -D_CLASSDLL -H -ml -WS -w -I$(INC)

#       Implicit Rules
.c.obj:
  $(CC) {$< }

.cpp.obj:
  $(CC) {$< }

#       Explicit Rules
KeyInput.exe: KeyInput.res KeyInput.def KeyInput.obj
        tlink /c/C/n/P-/Twe/x @KeyInput.LNK
        rlink KeyInput.res KeyInput.exe

#       Individual File Dependencies
KeyInput.obj: KeyInput.cpp

KeyInput.res: KeyInput.rc KeyInput.cur KeyInput.ico
        brcc -FO KeyInput.res -i$(INC) KeyInput.RC
```

## KEYINPUT.LNK

```
\borlandc\lib\c0wl.obj+
KeyInput.obj
KeyInput,KeyInput
\borlandc\classlib\lib\tclasdll.lib+
\borlandc\owl\lib\owl.lib+
mathwl.lib+
import.lib+
crtldll.lib
KeyInput.def
```

## KEYINPUT.CPP

```
/*--------------------------------------------------------------*\
|  KEYINPUT.CPP  - Sample text input program.                    |
\*--------------------------------------------------------------*/
#define WIN31
#define STRICT
#include <owl.h>
#include <WindowsX.h>

#define CHARMSGASCII(arg)  (arg.WParam)
#define KEYMSG_VK(arg)     (arg.WParam)

/*--------------------------------------------------------------*\
|                         Constants.                             |
\*--------------------------------------------------------------*/
const int BUFSIZE = 40;
```

## Message Driven Input

```
/*----------------------------------------------------------------*\
|                    Class Declarations.                           |
\*----------------------------------------------------------------*/
class TKeyInputApplication : public TApplication
   {
   public:
     TKeyInputApplication (LPSTR lpszName, HINSTANCE hInstance,
                           HINSTANCE hPrevInstance,
                           LPSTR lpszCmdLine, int nCmdShow);
     virtual void InitMainWindow ();
   };

class TKeyInputWindow : public TWindow
   {
   public:
     TKeyInputWindow (PTWindowsObject pwParent, LPSTR lpszTitle,
                     PTModule pmModule);
     virtual LPSTR GetClassName ();
     virtual void  GetWindowClass (WNDCLASS&);
     virtual void  WMChar(TMessage& Msg) = [WM_CHAR];
     virtual void  WMKeyDown(TMessage& Msg) = [WM_KEYDOWN];
     virtual void  WMPaint(TMessage& Msg);
   private:
     unsigned char achInput[BUFSIZE];
     unsigned int  cchInput;
     unsigned int  ichNext;
     unsigned int  yLineHeight;
     unsigned int  xLeftMargin;
   };
/*----------------------------------------------------------------*\
|                    Main Function:  WinMain.                      |
\*----------------------------------------------------------------*/
int PASCAL WinMain (HINSTANCE hInstance,   HINSTANCE hPrevInstance,
                    LPSTR lpszCmdLine, int     nCmdShow)
    {
    TKeyInputApplication KeyInput ("KeyInput", hInstance,
                        hPrevInstance, lpszCmdLine, nCmdShow);
    KeyInput.Run();
    return KeyInput.Status;
    }

/*----------------------------------------------------------------*\
|                    Application Class Member.                     |
\*----------------------------------------------------------------*/
TKeyInputApplication::TKeyInputApplication (LPSTR lpszName,
                    HINSTANCE hInstance, HINSTANCE hPrevInstance,
                    LPSTR lpszCmdLine, int nCmdShow)
                  :TApplication (lpszName, hInstance,
                      hPrevInstance, lpszCmdLine, nCmdShow)
    {
    /*  Application specific initialization goes here.  */
    }


/*----------------------------------------------------------------*\
|                    Application Class Member.                     |
\*----------------------------------------------------------------*/
void TKeyInputApplication::InitMainWindow ()
    {
    MainWindow = new TKeyInputWindow(NULL,"Keyboard Input",NULL);
    }
```

```
/*--------------------------------------------------------------*\
|                   TKeyInputWindow Class Member.                |
\*--------------------------------------------------------------*/
TKeyInputWindow::TKeyInputWindow (PTWindowsObject pwParent,
            LPSTR lpszTitle, PTModule pmModule)
        :TWindow (pwParent, lpszTitle, pmModule)
    {
    HDC        hdc;
    TEXTMETRIC tm;

    hdc = CreateDC ("DISPLAY", 0, 0, 0);

    GetTextMetrics (hdc, &tm);

    yLineHeight = tm.tmHeight + tm.tmExternalLeading;
    xLeftMargin = tm.tmAveCharWidth;

    DeleteDC (hdc);
    achInput[0] = '\0';
    cchInput = 0;
    ichNext = 0;
    }

/*--------------------------------------------------------------*\
|                   TKeyInputWindow Class Member.                |
\*--------------------------------------------------------------*/
LPSTR TKeyInputWindow::GetClassName ()
    {
    return "KeyInput:MAIN";
    }
/*--------------------------------------------------------------*\
|                   TKeyInputWindow Class Member.                |
\*--------------------------------------------------------------*/
void TKeyInputWindow::GetWindowClass (WNDCLASS& wc)
    {
    TWindow::GetWindowClass (wc);
    wc.hIcon=LoadIcon (wc.hInstance, "snapshot");
    wc.hCursor=LoadCursor (wc.hInstance, "hand");
    }

/*--------------------------------------------------------------*\
|                   TKeyInputWindow Class Member.                |
\*--------------------------------------------------------------*/
void TKeyInputWindow::WMChar(TMessage& Msg)
    {
    DWORD dw;
    HDC   hdc;
    int   i;
    WORD  wVirtKey;

    // Get virtual key value
    wVirtKey = CHARMSGASCII(Msg);

    if (wVirtKey == VK_BACK)     //  Backspace.
        {
        if (ichNext == 0)
            MessageBeep(0);
        else                                 // Remove a character.
            {
            ichNext--;
            for (i=ichNext;i<cchInput;i++)
                achInput[i]=achInput[i+1];
```

```
                    cchInput--;
                    InvalidateRect (HWindow, NULL, TRUE);
                    }
            return;
            }

        // Complain if character out of range or if buffer is full.
        if ((wVirtKey <= VK_ESCAPE) || (cchInput >= BUFSIZE))
            {
            MessageBeep(0);
            return;
            }

        // Make room for next char.
        for (i=cchInput;i>ichNext;i--)
        achInput[i]=achInput[i-1];

        /* Put new char in buffer. */
        achInput[ichNext] = (unsigned char)wVirtKey;

        // Increment count of characters.
        cchInput++;

        // Update display.
        hdc = GetDC(HWindow);
        dw = GetTextExtent (hdc, (LPSTR)&achInput[0], ichNext);
        TextOut (hdc,
                 xLeftMargin+LOWORD(dw),
                 yLineHeight,
                 (LPSTR)&achInput[ichNext],
                 cchInput - ichNext);
        ReleaseDC (HWindow, hdc);

        // Increment index to next character.
        ichNext++;

        }

/*----------------------------------------------------------------*\
|                   TKeyInputWindow Class Member.                  |
\*----------------------------------------------------------------*/
void TKeyInputWindow::WMKeyDown(TMessage& Msg)
    {
    switch (KEYMSG_VK(Msg))
        {
        case VK_DELETE:
            /* If end of buffer, complain. */
            if (ichNext == cchInput)
                MessageBeep(0);
            else    /* Remove a character. */
                {
                int i;
                for (i=ichNext;i<cchInput;i++)
                    achInput[i]=achInput[i+1];
                cchInput--;
                InvalidateRect (HWindow, NULL, TRUE);
                }
            break;
        case VK_END:
            ichNext = cchInput;
            break;
        case VK_HOME:
```

```
                ichNext = 0;
                break;
            case VK_LEFT:
                if (ichNext > 0) ichNext--;
                else MessageBeep(0);
                break;
            case VK_RIGHT:
                if (ichNext < cchInput) ichNext++;
                else MessageBeep(0);
                break;
        }
    }
/*-------------------------------------------------------------*\
|                  TKeyInputWindow Class Member.                |
\*-------------------------------------------------------------*/
void TKeyInputWindow::WMPaint(TMessage& Msg)
{
    PAINTSTRUCT ps;

    BeginPaint (Msg.Receiver, &ps);
    TextOut (ps.hdc, xLeftMargin, yLineHeight, (LPSTR)achInput,
            cchInput);
    EndPaint (Msg.Receiver, &ps);
}
```

# KEYINPUT.RC

```
snapshot icon KeyInput.ico

hand cursor KeyInput.cur
```

# KEYINPUT.DEF

```
NAME KEYINPUT

EXETYPE WINDOWS

DESCRIPTION 'Keyboard Input'

CODE MOVEABLE DISCARDABLE
DATA MOVEABLE MULTIPLE

HEAPSIZE  512
STACKSIZE 5120
```

Like the other sample programs in this book, KEYINPUT was built on top of the minimum Windows program that we introduced in Chapter 2. This program handles three different messages: **WM_CHAR**, **WM_KEYDOWN**, and **WM_PAINT**. As you may have noticed, we've organized the functions in our source code by class, then in alphabetical order by member function name. If you find this helps, you might wish to adopt this convention in your own programs.

As the **WM_CHAR** keyboard character messages occur, KEYINPUT accumulates the characters in a character array defined as

```
unsigned char achInput[BUFSIZE];
```

The use of the *unsigned* character type is a good practice that will help when working with the extended ASCII character set that Windows supports. It helps avoid the confusion that otherwise can occur with normal signed characters, which use the high-order bit as a sign bit. Since Windows' extended ASCII uses this high-order bit for the characters between 128 and 255 (80H to ffh), this can cause unexpected results. Consider the following lines of code:

```
unsigned char chUnsigned;
char chSigned;

chUnsigned = 'â';   /*  In Windows' extended ASCII,  */
chSigned   = 'â';   /*       <131> = e2h.            */

if (chSigned == 'â')
    {
    /*  This will never be true.  */
    }

if (chUnsigned == 'â')
    {
    /*  This will always be true.  */
    }
```

The problem occurs because of the way compilers interpret the numeric value of characters. Character values are converted into two-byte word values before a comparison is done. When this happens, the sign bit is extended to provide the correct word value. If you use unsigned `char` arrays, you will avoid this problem.

Getting back to our sample program, KEYINPUT has two variables that keep track of the contents of `achInput`: `cchInput` and `ichNext`. `cchInput` is the count of characters in the array. `ichNext` is an index into the array, and serves as the insertion point when new characters are typed. KEYINPUT increments and decrements these two fields as characters are entered and deleted.

Every time characters are entered, KEYINPUT draws the newly entered letters. On the other hand, when characters are erased, KEYINPUT generates a **WM_PAINT** message by calling `InvalidateRect`:

```
InvalidateRect (HWindow, NULL, TRUE);
```

which tells Windows, in effect, that the entire window is damaged and that it should be completely erased and redrawn. This is a pretty radical step to take. To erase characters, the entire line must be redrawn. It guarantees that the contents of the window is always correct, since the **WM_PAINT** message reads the character array with the changes in place.

One way to improve this program involves eliminating this excessive drawing, which means replacing the calls to `InvalidateRect` with actions that erase a single character in response to a backspace. This requires a little more work, but avoids the annoying blinking that occurs when characters are erased.

Quite a few other improvements could be made to this program, but it is enough to give you the basic idea about how keyboard input can be collected and displayed. We'll come back to this program in a minute, to see how a **caret** can be used to highlight the current insertion point. Before that, we need to discuss some issues that are critical in correctly handling character data: character sets and other internationalization issues.

## Character Sets and International Support

As keyboard data travels from the keyboard to your program, it undergoes a number of conversions: Keyboard data starts out as scan codes, which are converted by the device driver into virtual key information. And finally, virtual key codes are converted into ASCII character values to provide upper- and lowercase letters, numbers, and punctuation marks. Figure 15.4 shows Windows' ANSI character set.

| | 0- | 1- | 2- | 3- | 4- | 5- | 6- | 7- | 8- | 9- | A- | B- | C- | D- | E- | F- |
|---|---|---|---|---|---|---|---|---|---|---|---|---|---|---|---|---|
| -0 | l | l |   | 0 | @ | P | ` | p | l | l |   | ° | À | Ð | à | ð |
| -1 | l | l | ! | 1 | A | Q | a | q | l | l | ´ | i | ± | Á | Ñ | á | ñ |
| -2 | l | l | " | 2 | B | R | b | r | l | l | ´ | ¢ | ² | Â | Ò | â | ò |
| -3 | l | l | # | 3 | C | S | c | s | l | l | £ | ³ | Ã | Ó | ã | ó |
| -4 | l | l | $ | 4 | D | T | d | t | l | l | ¤ | ´ | Ä | Ô | ä | ô |
| -5 | l | l | % | 5 | E | U | e | u | l | l | ¥ | µ | Å | Õ | å | õ |
| -6 | l | l | & | 6 | F | V | f | v | l | l | ¦ | ¶ | Æ | Ö | æ | ö |
| -7 | l | l | ' | 7 | G | W | g | w | l | l | § | · | Ç | × | ç | ÷ |
| -8 | l | l | ( | 8 | H | X | h | x | l | l | ¨ | , | È | Ø | è | ø |
| -9 | l | l | ) | 9 | I | Y | i | y | l | l | © | ¹ | É | Ù | é | ù |
| -A | l | l | * | : | J | Z | j | z | l | l | ª | º | Ê | Ú | ê | ú |
| -B | l | l | + | ; | K | [ | k | { | l | l | « | » | Ë | Û | ë | û |
| -C | l | l | , | < | L | \ | l | | | l | l | ¬ | ¼ | Ì | Ü | ì | ü |
| -D | l | l | - | = | M | ] | m | } | l | l | - | ½ | Í | Ý | í | ý |
| -E | l | l | . | > | N | ^ | n | ~ | l | l | ® | ¾ | Î | Þ | î | þ |
| -F | l | l | / | ? | O | _ | o | | l | l | ¯ | ¿ | Ï | ß | ï | ÿ |

**Figure 15.4** ANSI Character Set

## 444 *Message Driven Input*

What is a character set? It is a convention or a standard that helps avoid confusion. For example, according to the ANSI character set, the value 41H (65 decimal) stands for a capital "A." Microsoft adopted the ANSI character set to allow the data created by a Windows program to be readable by other Windows programs, and interpreted correctly on different brands of computers and different brands of printers, as well as computers and peripherals in different countries.

Windows uses the ANSI character set to interpret how a text character should be displayed, and to provide a standard that allows file sharing between different Windows computers. But this isn't the only character set that you'll want to know how to work with. In addition to the ANSI character set, every Windows computer has a second character set that DOS uses. For example, IBM-compatible computers that are manufactured for use in the United States have a character set that IBM calls code page 437. Figure 15.5 shows the characters in code page 437. This is the character set that DOS programs use when they create data files, and is the character set used by DOS for file names.

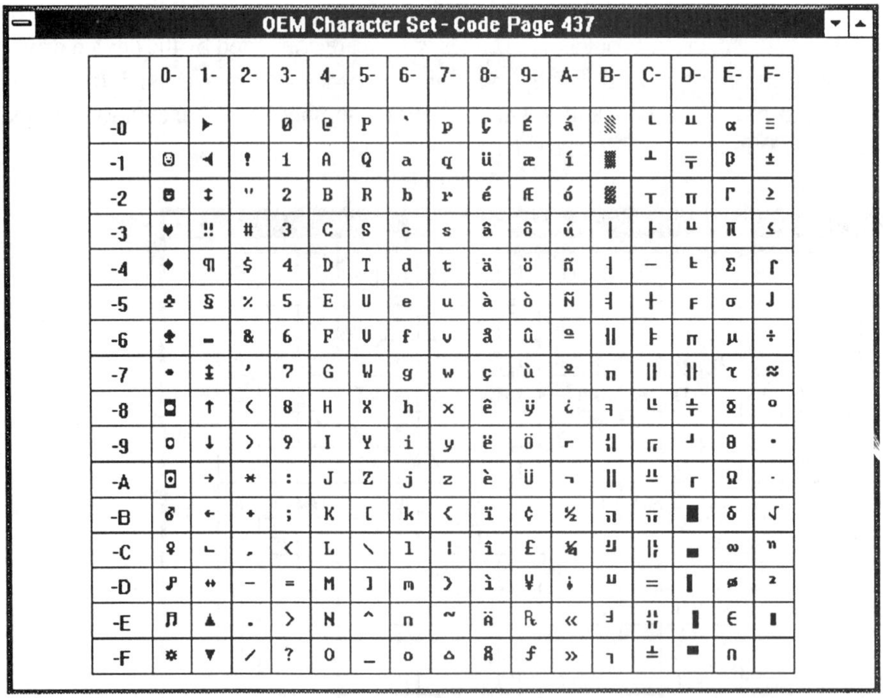

Figure 15.5 DOS Character Set in the United States: Code Page 437

For upper-and lowercase letters, numbers, and punctuation marks, this character set is identical to the Windows' ANSI character set. Thus, if you are writing a Windows program for use only in the United States, you can mix and match data files between DOS and Windows programs with little chance for confusion. This will be true as long as your

Windows and DOS programs use printable characters in the range 20h to 7eh (32 to 126 decimal).

For Windows programs to work on computers outside the United States, some effort is required on your part. In the first place, other code pages besides 437 are used on computers manufactured for different languages. For example, code page 860 substitutes 16 accented characters that are not available in code page 437 that are required for computers sold in Portugal. Code page 863 has 22 new accented and other special characters to meet the requirements of French Canada. And code page 865 has four characters that change the US code page for use in creating Norwegian data files.

Therefore, every machine that runs Windows will have at least two character sets: Windows' ANSI character set (sometimes known as code page 1004), which has the most complete support for accented characters, and what Microsoft calls an OEM character set, which is the character set that DOS uses to meet the language needs of different countries (code page 437).

When a DOS program is running in a window, Windows uses a font that contains characters that match the OEM character set. In this way, the character set provides backward compatibility between Windows and DOS. If you are writing a program to display a text file created by a DOS program, there is a stock font available that uses the OEM character set. You can access this font by saying

```
hfontOEM = GetStockObject (OEM_FIXED_FONT);
SelectObject (hdc, hfontOEM);
```

## *Converting Between Character Sets*

If a Windows program reads files that are written by DOS programs, for the program to work properly on all non-US machines, the files must be converted from the OEM character set to Windows' ANSI character set. Conversely, if a Windows program writes to a file that a DOS program may read, the Windows program should convert from the ANSI character set to the native OEM character set that DOS programs expect in order to work outside the United States. Fortunately, some Windows library routines are available to do the conversion for you:

| *Routine* | *Description* |
| --- | --- |
| `AnsiToOem` | Convert null-terminated ANSI string to DOS characters |
| `AnsiToOemBuff` | Convert *n* ANSI characters to DOS characters |
| `OemToAnsi` | Convert null-terminated DOS characters to ANSI |
| `OemToAnsiBuff` | Convert *n* DOS characters to ANSI |

In addition to DOS data files, the DOS file system itself uses the OEM character set for file names. However, if you use the `OpenFile` Windows library routine, your file names are automatically converted to the OEM character set before DOS is called.

## Upper- and Lowercase Conversion

Programmers in the United States who work with characters exclusively in the range 20H to 7ef (32 to 126 decimal) often play tricks to convert text to upper- or lowercase. In this range, the upper- and lowercase letters are 20H (32) apart, like those shown here:

| Uppercase | ASCII (hex) | (dec) | Lowercase | (hex) | (dec) |
|---|---|---|---|---|---|
| A | 41H | 65 | a | 61H | 97 |
| B | 42H | 66 | b | 62H | 98 |
| C | 43H | 67 | c | 63H | 99 |
| . | | | | | |
| . | | | | | |
| Z | 5aH | 90 | z | 7aH | 122 |

In this range, uppercase conversion is easy; here is code that does this for us:

```
for (i=0;i<cc;i++)
    {
    if (ach[i] >= 'a' && ach[i] <= 'z')
        ach[i] -= 32;
    }
```

But consider the following pairs of upper- and lowercase accented letters:

| Uppercase | ASCII (hex) | (dec) | Lowercase | (hex) | (dec) |
|---|---|---|---|---|---|
| Á | c0h | 192 | á | e0h | 224 |
| Ç | c7h | 199 | ç | e7h | 231 |
| È | c8h | 200 | è | e8h | 232 |
| Ï | cfh | 207 | ï | efh | 239 |
| Õ | d5h | 213 | õ | f5h | 245 |
| Û | dbh | 219 | û | fbh | 251 |

If the array in our earlier example included any of the lowercase letters in this table, the case conversion would not have worked correctly. If you are writing a program that will be sold outside the United States, you should use the following Windows library routines for upper- and lowercase conversion instead of writing your own.

| Routine | Description |
| --- | --- |
| `AnsiLower` | Converts null-terminated string to lowercase |
| `AnsiLowerBuff` | Converts *n* characters to lowercase |
| `AnsiUpper` | Converts null-terminated string to uppercase |
| `AnsiUpperBuff` | Converts *n* characters to uppercase |

To convert a null-terminated character string to all uppercase, you could pass a long pointer to **AnsiUpper**, as in

```
AnsiUpper (lpszConvert);
```

or, using **AnsiUpperBuff**, you could say:

```
i = lstrlen (lpszConvert);
AnsiUpperBuff (lpszConvert, i);
```

Another set of routines tests whether character information is upper- or lowercase, whether it is an alphabetic character, or whether it is alphanumeric:

| Routine | Description |
| --- | --- |
| `IsCharAlpha` | Returns TRUE if character is alphabetic character. |
| `IsCharAlphaNumeric` | Returns TRUE if character is either alphabetic or numeric character. |
| `IsCharLower` | Returns TRUE if character is lowercase. |
| `IsCharUpper` | Returns TRUE if character is uppercase. |

## Sorting Character Strings

Accented characters require special handling when converting text strings to uppercase or to lowercase. The same is true when sorting character strings. Programs that perform a simple numeric sort of character strings will put words with accents out of order. For example, the following sort order results from a simple numeric sort:

cheese
chocolate
church
château

Of course, the problem is that the numeric value of the character "â" is e2h (226 decimal), which comes after "e" (65h or 101 decimal), "o" (6fh or 111 decimal), and "u" (75h or 117 decimal). Since this is the way that the C-runtime library routine, **strcmp**, works, this routine should be avoided if you want your product to work correctly outside the United States.

Putting "château" at the top of the list, where it belongs, requires that we call a Windows library routine to perform string comparison for us during our sort. Actually, there are two such routines: one that compares in a case-insensitive fashion, **lstrcmpi**, and one that compares in a case-sensitive fashion, **lstrcmp**.

## String Tables

Windows has a facility that will help in the effort to prepare a product for translation to another language—a process that Microsoft calls **localization**. The facility is the **string table**. A string table allows you to put all the strings from a program in a central place: the resource file. When your program needs to access a string, it makes a call to Windows using a numeric index. In this way, all messages for the user are centralized in one place. The job of a translator is simplified, since there is only one file that must be converted to localize an entire application.

To create a string table, entries are made in the .RC resource file, like the following:

```
#include "myinclude"

STRINGTABLE
    {
    FILENOTFOUND, "File Not Found."
    HELPPROMPT, "For Help, Type F1."
    RECALCMESSAGE, "Recalculating."
    }
```

The file MYINCLUDE would contain definitions like the following:

```
#define FILENOTFOUND   101
#define HELPPROMPT     102
#define RECALCMESSAGE  103
```

These provide a unique, numeric ID for each string. When the time comes to use a string, a Windows library routine, **LoadString**, is called:

```
char acMessage[BUFSIZE];

LoadString (hInstance,          // instance handle
            FILENOTFOUND,       // string id value
            acMessage,          // character buffer
            BUFSIZE);           // buffer size
```

Then the string can be displayed, perhaps using the **TextOut** routine.

There are other benefits to using string tables besides the international support issue. Objects in a string table are read-only data, and as such Windows loads them when needed and purges them from memory when not needed. In other words, the benefit of string tables is that they are very efficient in terms of the memory that is used.

## *Entering Characters from the Numeric Keypad*

You may be aware that, when running DOS, you can enter ASCII codes directly from the numeric keypad. Windows provides the same mechanism, which is supported by the Windows keyboard driver. You can actually enter characters from either the ANSI or OEM character sets.

To enter characters from the ANSI character set, with [Num Lock] toggled on, hold down the [Alt] key and enter a zero followed by the decimal ASCII character code. To enter the letter "À," for example, you hold down [Alt] and type 0192.

You can enter characters from the OEM character set as well, although they will be mapped to the corresponding ANSI character set value. With the [Num Lock] toggled on, hold down the [Alt] key and enter the decimal OEM character code. For example, to enter the letter "à," you hold down [Alt] and type 160.

## Multitasking Issues

Now that we've covered the basics of handling keyboard input and dealing with different character sets, there are a few more issues that you must be aware of in order to make effective use of the keyboard.

Windows is multitasking, which means there has to be a mechanism for sharing devices like the keyboard. There are two concepts that Windows uses to direct where keyboard input is sent: the **active window** and the **focus**.

When a program creates a window, the program decides whether the window is a **top-level window** or a child of another top-level window. Most programs create a single top-level window. This window serves as the primary means by which the user interacts with the program. One characteristic of top-level windows is that they appear on the Task List that is displayed in response to the [Ctrl] + [Esc] key combination. The Task List, shown in Figure 15.6, lets the user select the top-level window that he wishes to make active.

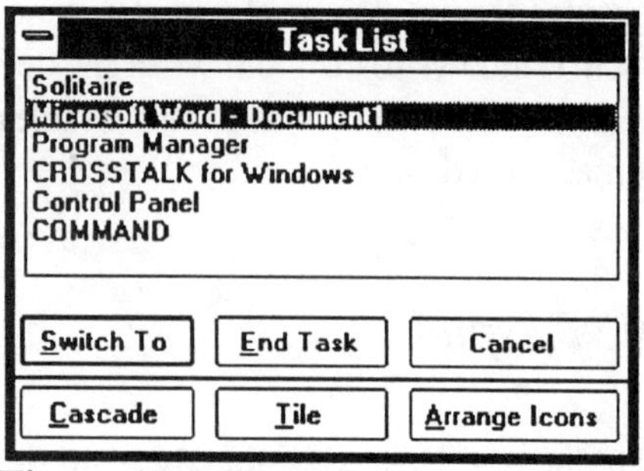

450  *Message Driven Input*

**Figure 15.6** The Windows Task List

The active window, then, is simply the top-level window that the user has decided to work with. Of course, there are other ways to make a window active besides selecting from the Task List. For example, a user could click with the mouse to make a window active, or hit the [Alt] + [Tab] key combination continuously to circulate among the top-level windows. The active window is always on top of every other top-level window in the system. This makes sense, for if the user has decided to work with a particular window, it should be completely visible.

When a top-level window becomes active, Windows sends it a **WM_ACTIVATE** message with a nonzero value in `wParam`. This tells the window, in effect, that "the boss wants to see you. Now." Windows also sends a **WM_NCACTIVATE** message, which causes the window's caption bar to change colors so that the user has a visual clue to the active window. Like other nonclient area messages, this one is handled by the default window procedure.

In response to a **WM_ACTIVATE** message, the default window procedure gives the active window the focus. Here is the actual code from **DefWindowProc**:

```
case WM_ACTIVATE:
    if (wParam)
        SetFocus (hWnd);
```

The focus is simply an indicator within Windows that identifies which window should get keyboard input. In effect, when a window has the focus, it has the keyboard. It alone will receive keyboard messages.

When a window receives the focus, Windows lets it know by sending it a message: **WM_SETFOCUS**. But before it does that, it sends a **WM_KILLFOCUS** message to the window that is losing the keyboard. By watching these two messages, a window procedure can keep track of whether it has control of the keyboard or not.

But why should a window care whether it has the keyboard or not? Won't it still get the proper keyboard messages? The answer is, Yes. But sometimes a window procedure will want to know when it has the focus, and will want to take special steps. One such case occurs when we wish to have a keyboard pointer, or **caret**, in a window. That is the next topic that we plan to discuss.

## Creating a Keyboard Pointer: Carets

As a program receives keyboard input, it's quite common to display a keyboard pointer to let the user know where the next character will be entered. In most environments, this is called **a cursor**. But Windows uses the term cursor to refer to the mouse pointer, and instead uses the term caret to refer to a keyboard pointer.

A caret is a rectangular blinking bitmap that lets the user know several things. First of all, it lets the user know which window has the keyboard—that is, which window has the focus. Second, as we mentioned a moment ago, it lets the user know the current position—the location where text (or some other object) will appear next.

While the most obvious use of a caret is to highlight a text entry point, that is certainly not the only use. For example, a caret can be used to indicate the "current object" in a drawing program, and is used in listboxes to show the user which item would be affected by keyboard input.

Windows has four routines for creating and maintaining the keyboard caret:

| Routine Name | Description |
| --- | --- |
| CreateCaret | Creates a caret |
| SetCaretPos | Positions the caret |
| ShowCaret | Makes a caret visible |
| DestroyCaret | Destroys a caret |

You might be tempted to create a caret at the beginning of your program and hold onto it until your program exits, but this wouldn't give you the results you expect. The reason is that internally, Windows is only able to recognize one caret for the entire system. Thus, you cannot keep a caret for the life of your program. You can only keep it for as long as you have the focus. For this reason, do not create a caret like this:

```
/*   DO NOT DO THIS!    */
void TSampleWindow::WMCreate(TMessage& Msg)
    {
    CreateCaret (hwnd, 0, xWidth, yHeight);
    ...
    }

void TSampleWindow::WMDestroy(TMessage& Msg)
    {
    DestroyCaret ();
    ...
    }
```

Instead, the proper way to create and destroy a caret is in response to the **WM_SETFOCUS** and **WM_KILLFOCUS** messages. Every time your window gains the keyboard focus, it will create a caret, and every time it loses the keyboard focus, it destroys its caret. It might seem that this is a lot of trouble for a tiny, blinking bitmap, but this approach is necessary to properly maintain a caret in a Windows program:

```
/* Correct Way to Create a Caret. */
void TSampleWindow::WMSetFocus(TMessage& Msg)
    {
    CreateCaret (hwnd, 0, xWidth, yHeight0);
    ...
    }

void TSampleWindow::WMKillFocus(TMessage& Msg)
    {
    DestroyCaret ();
    ...
    }
```

The **CreateCaret** routine is defined as follows:

`void CreateCaret (hWnd, hBitmap, nWidth, nHeight)`

- **hWnd** is a handle to the window where the caret is to be located.
- **hBitmap** is a handle to a bitmap. It can be 0, 1, or a real bitmap handle.
- **nWidth** is the caret width.
- **nHeight** is the caret height.

The second field, **hBitmap**, is the key field that determines the shape and color of the caret. If it is set to zero, then the bitmap will be a black square nWidth by nHeight. If set to one, the bitmap is a gray square nWidth by nHeight. Otherwise, if it is a GDI bitmap, the caret takes on the shape of the bitmap.

When we create a caret, we'll want to make sure it is large enough to be visible. Since we're going to use the caret to highlight a text entry point, it makes sense to make the caret the same height as the text. Here is how to create a black caret that fits the bill:

```
...
void TSampleWindow::WMCreate(TMessage& Msg)
    {
    HDC hdc;
    TEXTMETRIC tm;

    hdc = GetDC (hwnd);
    GetTextMetrics (hdc, &tm);
    cyHeight = tm.tmHeight;
    ReleaseDC (hwnd, hdc);
    }
void TSampleWindow::WMSetFocus(TMessage& Msg)
    {
    CreateCaret (hwnd,
                 0,      // default black caret
                 0,      // default width
                 cyHeight);
    ...
    }
```

Here is how to create a gray caret that is the same size:

```
CreateCaret (hwnd,
             1,      // default gray caret
             0,      // default width
             cyHeight);
```

By selecting a width of zero, we let Windows use the default size. This will be the width of a window border, to make sure that the caret is visible.

We could also create a bitmap, draw onto it using GDI drawing routines, and use it as a caret. We're going to create a monochrome bitmap. The portion of the bitmap that is black will be ignored while the portion that is white will blink. Here is how to make a caret in the shape of an I-beam. Notice that most of the work involves creating the bitmap and drawing onto it:

```
void TSampleWindow::WMCreate(TMessage& Msg)
    {
    HBITMAP hbmOld;
    HDC hdc;
    HDC hdcBitmap;
    TEXTMETRIC tm;

    hdc = GetDC (hwnd);
    GetTextMetrics (hdc, &tm);
    yLineHeight = tm.tmHeight + tm.tmExternalLeading;
    ReleaseDC (hwnd, hdc);

    hdcBitmap = CreateCompatibleDC (hdc);
    hbm = CreateBitmap (xLeftMargin,
                        yLineHeight,
                        1, 1, NULL);
    hbmOld = SelectBitmap (hdcBitmap, hbm);

    /* Blank out bitmap. */
    SelectBrush (hdcBitmap,
                 GetStockBrush (BLACK_BRUSH));
    Rectangle (hdcBitmap, 0, 0,
               xLeftMargin, yLineHeight);

    /* Do actual drawing in white. */
    SelectPen (hdcBitmap,
               GetStockPen (WHITE_PEN));
    MoveTo (hdcBitmap, 0, 0);
    LineTo (hdcBitmap, xLeftMargin+1, 0);
    MoveTo (hdcBitmap, xLeftMargin/2, 0);
    LineTo (hdcBitmap, xLeftMargin/2, yLineHeight-1);
    MoveTo (hdcBitmap, 0, yLineHeight-1);
    LineTo (hdcBitmap, xLeftMargin+1, yLineHeight-1);
    SelectBitmap (hdcBitmap, hbmOld);
    DeleteDC (hdcBitmap);
    ...
    }

void TSampleWindow::WMDestroy(TMessage& Msg)
    {
    DeleteBitmap (hbm);
    }
```

## 454 Message Driven Input

```
void TSampleWindow::WMSetFocus(TMessage& Msg)
    {
    DestroyCaret();
    }
void TSampleWindow::WMSetFocus(TMessage& Msg)
    {
    CreateCaret(hwnd,
                hbm,      // hBitmap
                0,        // xWidth
                0);       // yWidth
    SetCaretPos (x, y);
    ShowCaret(hwnd);
    }
```

And, of course, this code fragment assumes that a bitmap handle has been allocated as a static object:

```
static HBITMAP hbm;
```

Let's look at an actual program that uses a caret. We've modified the KEYINPUT program so that it uses a caret. In addition to creating and deleting the caret properly, it also moves the caret in response to the cursor movement keys on the keyboard. Here is our caret-handling program: CARET.

## MAKEFILE.MAK

```
.AUTODEPEND

#    Translator Definitions
INC=\BORLANDC\OWL\INCLUDE;\BORLANDC\CLASSLIB\INCLUDE;\BORLANDC\INCLUDE
CC = bcc -c -D_CLASSDLL -H -ml -WS -w-par -I$(INC)

#    Implicit Rules
.c.obj:
  $(CC) {$< }

.cpp.obj:
  $(CC) {$< }

#    Explicit Rules
Caret.exe: Caret.res Caret.def Caret.obj
    tlink /c/C/n/P-/Twe/x @Caret.LNK
    rlink Caret.res Caret.exe

#    Individual File Dependencies
Caret.obj: Caret.cpp

Caret.res: Caret.rc Caret.cur Caret.ico
    brcc -FO Caret.res -i$(INC) Caret.RC
```

# CARET.LNK

```
\borlandc\lib\c0wl.obj+
Caret.obj
Caret,Caret
\borlandc\classlib\lib\tclasdll.lib+
\borlandc\owl\lib\owl.lib+
mathwl.lib+
import.lib+
crtldll.lib
Caret.def
```

# CARET.CPP

```
/*--------------------------------------------------------------*\
|   CARET.CPP   - Keyboard pointer demo.                         |
\*--------------------------------------------------------------*/
#include <owl.h>

#define CHARMSGASCII(arg)  (arg.WParam)
#define KEYMSG_VK(arg)     (arg.WParam)

/*--------------------------------------------------------------*\
|                        Constants.                              |
\*--------------------------------------------------------------*/
const int BUFSIZE = 40;
const int CARET_ACTIVE   = 0x01;
const int CARET_INACTIVE = 0x02;
/*--------------------------------------------------------------*\
|                    Class Declarations.                         |
\*--------------------------------------------------------------*/
class TCaretApplication : public TApplication
   {
   public:
     TCaretApplication (LPSTR lpszName, HINSTANCE hInstance,
                        HINSTANCE hPrevInstance, LPSTR lpszCmdLine,
                        int nCmdShow);
     virtual void InitMainWindow ();
   };

class TCaret
   {
   public:
     TCaret(HWND hwndIn, HFONT hFontIn);
     ~TCaret();

     virtual void   Hide();
     virtual void   Show();

     virtual int    GetAnchorX();
     virtual int    GetAnchorY();
     virtual int    GetCharPosition ();
     virtual HFONT  GetFontHandle();
     virtual int    GetState ();
     virtual LPSTR  GetStringPtr();

     virtual void   SetAnchor (int X, int Y);
```

```cpp
      virtual void    SetCharPosition (int iChar);
      virtual void    SetFontHandle(HFONT hFontIn);
      virtual void    SetState (int AFlag);
      virtual void    SetStringPtr(LPSTR lpstrIn);
   private:
      HFONT   hFont;
      HDC     hdcInfo;
      HWND    hwnd;
      int     iCharPos;
      int     iFlag;
      int     cxCaretWidth;
      int     cyCaretHeight;
      POINT   ptPixelPos;
      POINT   ptAnchor;
      LPSTR   lpString;
   };

class TCaretWindow : public TWindow
   {
   public:
      TCaret * PCaret;

      TCaretWindow (PTWindowsObject pwParent, LPSTR lpszTitle,
                    PTModule pmModule);
      virtual LPSTR GetClassName ();
      virtual void  GetWindowClass (WNDCLASS&);
      virtual void  WMChar(TMessage& Msg) = [WM_CHAR];
      virtual void  WMCreate(TMessage& Msg) = [WM_CREATE];
      virtual void  WMDestroy(TMessage& Msg) = [WM_DESTROY];
      virtual void  WMKeyDown(TMessage& Msg) = [WM_KEYDOWN];
      virtual void  WMPaint(TMessage& Msg);
      virtual void  WMSetFocus(TMessage& Msg) = [WM_SETFOCUS];
      virtual void  WMKillFocus(TMessage& Msg) = [WM_KILLFOCUS];
   private:
      unsigned char achInput[BUFSIZE];
      unsigned int  cchInput;
      unsigned int  ichNext;
      unsigned int  yLineHeight;
      unsigned int  xLeftMargin;
   };

/*-------------------------------------------------------------*\
|                   Main Function:  WinMain.                    |
\*-------------------------------------------------------------*/
int PASCAL WinMain (HINSTANCE hInstance,   HINSTANCE hPrevInstance,
                    LPSTR  lpszCmdLine, int      nCmdShow)
   {
   TCaretApplication Caret ("Caret", hInstance, hPrevInstance,
                            lpszCmdLine, nCmdShow);
   Caret.Run();
   return Caret.Status;
   }

/*-------------------------------------------------------------*\
|                   Application Class Member.                   |
\*-------------------------------------------------------------*/
TCaretApplication::TCaretApplication (LPSTR lpszName,
                   HINSTANCE hInstance, HINSTANCE hPrevInstance,
                   LPSTR lpszCmdLine, int nCmdShow)
                 :TApplication (lpszName, hInstance,
                   hPrevInstance, lpszCmdLine, nCmdShow)
```

```
        {
        /* Application specific initialization goes here. */
        }
/*---------------------------------------------------------------*\
|                      Application Class Member.                  |
\*---------------------------------------------------------------*/
void TCaretApplication::InitMainWindow ()
        {
        MainWindow = new TCaretWindow (NULL, "Caret Demo", NULL);
        }

/*---------------------------------------------------------------*\
|                      TCaretWindow Class Member.                 |
\*---------------------------------------------------------------*/
TCaretWindow::TCaretWindow (PTWindowsObject pwParent,
               LPSTR lpszTitle, PTModule pmModule)
            :TWindow (pwParent, lpszTitle, pmModule)
        {
        HDC       hdc;
        TEXTMETRIC tm;

        hdc = CreateDC ("DISPLAY", 0, 0, 0);

        GetTextMetrics (hdc, &tm);
        yLineHeight = tm.tmHeight + tm.tmExternalLeading;
        xLeftMargin = tm.tmAveCharWidth;

        DeleteDC (hdc);

        cchInput = 0;
        ichNext  = 0;
        }
/*---------------------------------------------------------------*\
|                      TCaretWindow Class Member.                 |
\*---------------------------------------------------------------*/
LPSTR TCaretWindow::GetClassName ()
        {
        return "Caret:MAIN";
        }

/*---------------------------------------------------------------*\
|                      TCaretWindow Class Member.                 |
\*---------------------------------------------------------------*/
void TCaretWindow::GetWindowClass (WNDCLASS& wc)
        {
        TWindow::GetWindowClass (wc);
        wc.hIcon=LoadIcon (wc.hInstance, "snapshot");
        wc.hCursor=LoadCursor (wc.hInstance, "hand");
        }

/*---------------------------------------------------------------*\
|                      TCaretWindow Class Member.                 |
\*---------------------------------------------------------------*/
void TCaretWindow::WMChar(TMessage& Msg)
        {
        DWORD dw;
        HDC   hdc;
        int   i;
        WORD  wVirtKey;
```

## 458  Message Driven Input

```
    // Get virtual key value
    wVirtKey = CHARMSGASCII(Msg);

    if (wVirtKey == VK_BACK)       // Backspace.
        {
        if (ichNext == 0)
            MessageBeep(0);
        else                           // Remove a character.
            {
            ichNext--;
            PCaret->SetCharPosition(ichNext);

            for (i=ichNext;i<cchInput;i++)
                achInput[i]=achInput[i+1];
            cchInput--;
            InvalidateRect (HWindow, NULL, TRUE);
            }
        return;
        }

    // Complain if character out of range or if buffer is full.
    if ((wVirtKey <= VK_ESCAPE) || (cchInput >= BUFSIZE))
        {
        MessageBeep(0);
        return;
        }

    // Make room for next char.
    for (i=cchInput;i>ichNext;i--)
        achInput[i]=achInput[i-1];

    /* Put new char in buffer.  */
    achInput[ichNext] = (unsigned char)wVirtKey;
    // Increment count of characters.
    cchInput++;

    PCaret->Hide();

    // Update display.
    hdc = GetDC(HWindow);
    dw = GetTextExtent (hdc, (LPSTR)&achInput[0], ichNext);
    TextOut (hdc,
             xLeftMargin+LOWORD(dw),
             yLineHeight,
             (LPSTR)&achInput[ichNext],
             cchInput - ichNext);
    ReleaseDC (HWindow, hdc);

    PCaret->Show();

    // Increment index to next character.
    ichNext++;
    PCaret->SetCharPosition(ichNext);
    }

/*----------------------------------------------------------------*\
|                   TCaretWindow Class Member.                     |
\*----------------------------------------------------------------*/
void TCaretWindow::WMCreate(TMessage& Msg)
    {
    HFONT hFont;
```

```
        hFont = GetStockFont (SYSTEM_FONT);
        PCaret = new TCaret (Msg.Receiver, hFont);

        PCaret->SetAnchor (xLeftMargin, yLineHeight);
        PCaret->SetStringPtr ((LPSTR)&achInput[0]);
        }
/*---------------------------------------------------------------*\
|                    TCaretWindow Class Member.                   |
\*---------------------------------------------------------------*/
void TCaretWindow::WMDestroy(TMessage& Msg)
    {
    delete PCaret;

    TWindow::WMDestroy(Msg);
    }
/*---------------------------------------------------------------*\
|                    TCaretWindow Class Member.                   |
\*---------------------------------------------------------------*/
void TCaretWindow::WMKeyDown(TMessage& Msg)
    {
    BOOL fCaretMoved = FALSE;

    switch (KEYMSG_VK(Msg))
         {
         case VK_DELETE:
            /* If end of buffer, complain. */
            if (ichNext == cchInput)
                MessageBeep(0);
            else /* Remove a character. */
                {
                int i;
                for (i=ichNext;i<cchInput;i++)
                    achInput[i]=achInput[i+1];
                cchInput--;
                InvalidateRect (HWindow, NULL, TRUE);
                }
            break;
         case VK_END:
            ichNext = cchInput;
            fCaretMoved = TRUE;
            break;
         case VK_HOME:
            ichNext = 0;
            fCaretMoved = TRUE;
            break;
         case VK_LEFT:
            if (ichNext > 0)
                {
                ichNext--;
                fCaretMoved = TRUE;
                }
            else
                MessageBeep(0);
            break;
         case VK_RIGHT:
            if (ichNext < cchInput)
                {
                ichNext++;
                fCaretMoved = TRUE;
```

```
                        }
                else
                        MessageBeep(0);
                break;
        }

    if (fCaretMoved)
        PCaret->SetCharPosition(ichNext);
    }
/*------------------------------------------------------------*\
|                   TCaretWindow Class Member.                 |
\*------------------------------------------------------------*/
void TCaretWindow::WMPaint(TMessage& Msg)
    {
    PAINTSTRUCT ps;

    BeginPaint (Msg.Receiver, &ps);
    TextOut (ps.hdc, xLeftMargin, yLineHeight, (LPSTR)achInput,
             cchInput);
    EndPaint (Msg.Receiver, &ps);
    }

/*------------------------------------------------------------*\
|                   TCaretWindow Class Member.                 |
\*------------------------------------------------------------*/
void TCaretWindow::WMSetFocus(TMessage& Msg)
    {
    PCaret->SetCharPosition(ichNext);
    PCaret->SetState(CARET_ACTIVE);
    }

/*------------------------------------------------------------*\
|                   TCaretWindow Class Member.                 |
\*------------------------------------------------------------*/
void TCaretWindow::WMKillFocus(TMessage& Msg)
    {
    PCaret->SetState(CARET_INACTIVE);
    }

/*------------------------------------------------------------*\
|                     TCaret Class Member.                     |
\*------------------------------------------------------------*/
TCaret::TCaret(HWND hwndIn, HFONT hFontIn)
    {
    HFONT       hfontOld;
    TEXTMETRIC  tm;

    hdcInfo = CreateIC ("DISPLAY", 0, 0, 0);
    hfontOld = SelectFont (hdcInfo, hFontIn);
    GetTextMetrics (hdcInfo, &tm);
    SelectFont (hdcInfo, hfontOld);

    hwnd          = hwndIn;
    hFont         = hFontIn;
    iCharPos      = 0;
    iFlag         = CARET_INACTIVE;
    cxCaretWidth  = GetSystemMetrics (SM_CXBORDER);
    cyCaretHeight = tm.tmHeight;
    ptPixelPos.x  = 0;
    ptPixelPos.y  = 0;
```

```
    ptAnchor.x   = 0;
    ptAnchor.y   = 0;
    lpString     = (LPSTR)0L;
    }
/*----------------------------------------------------------------*\
|                        TCaret Class Member.                      |
\*----------------------------------------------------------------*/
TCaret::~TCaret()
    {
    if (iFlag & CARET_ACTIVE)
        {
        HideCaret(hwnd);
        DestroyCaret();
        }

    DeleteDC (hdcInfo);
    }
/*----------------------------------------------------------------*\
|                        TCaret Class Member.                      |
\*----------------------------------------------------------------*/
void TCaret::Hide()
    {
    HideCaret(hwnd);
    }

/*----------------------------------------------------------------*\
|                        TCaret Class Member.                      |
\*----------------------------------------------------------------*/
void TCaret::Show()
    {
    ShowCaret(hwnd);
    }

/*----------------------------------------------------------------*\
|                        TCaret Class Member.                      |
\*----------------------------------------------------------------*/
int    TCaret::GetAnchorX()
    {
    return ptAnchor.x;
    }

/*----------------------------------------------------------------*\
|                        TCaret Class Member.                      |
\*----------------------------------------------------------------*/
int    TCaret::GetAnchorY()
    {
    return ptAnchor.y;
    }

/*----------------------------------------------------------------*\
|                        TCaret Class Member.                      |
\*----------------------------------------------------------------*/
int    TCaret::GetCharPosition ()
    {
    return iCharPos;
    }

/*----------------------------------------------------------------*\
|                        TCaret Class Member.                      |
\*----------------------------------------------------------------*/
```

```
HFONT TCaret::GetFontHandle()
    {
    return hFont;
    }
/*----------------------------------------------------------------*\
|                       TCaret Class Member.                       |
\*----------------------------------------------------------------*/
int     TCaret::GetState ()
    {
    return iFlag;
    }

/*----------------------------------------------------------------*\
|                       TCaret Class Member.                       |
\*----------------------------------------------------------------*/
LPSTR   TCaret::GetStringPtr()
    {
    return lpString;
    }

/*----------------------------------------------------------------*\
|                       TCaret Class Member.                       |
\*----------------------------------------------------------------*/
void    TCaret::SetAnchor (int X, int Y)
    {
    ptAnchor.x = X;
    ptAnchor.y = Y;
    }

/*----------------------------------------------------------------*\
|                       TCaret Class Member.                       |
\*----------------------------------------------------------------*/
void    TCaret::SetCharPosition (int iChar)
    {
    DWORD   dwSize;
    HFONT   hFontOld;
    int     xWidth;

    iCharPos = iChar;

    // Calculate width of character string.
    hFontOld = SelectFont (hdcInfo, hFont);
    dwSize = GetTextExtent (hdcInfo, lpString, iCharPos);
    xWidth = LOWORD(dwSize);
    SelectFont (hdcInfo, hFontOld);

    // Update caret position information.
    ptPixelPos.x = ptAnchor.x + xWidth;
    ptPixelPos.y = ptAnchor.y;

    // If caret is active, update location.
    if (iFlag & CARET_ACTIVE)
        {
        SetCaretPos (ptPixelPos.x, ptPixelPos.y);
        }
    }

/*----------------------------------------------------------------*\
|                       TCaret Class Member.                       |
\*----------------------------------------------------------------*/
```

```
void    TCaret::SetFontHandle(HANDLE hFontIn)
    {
    HANDLE      hfontOld;
    TEXTMETRIC  tm;

    hfontOld = SelectFont (hdcInfo, hFontIn);
    GetTextMetrics (hdcInfo, &tm);
    SelectFont (hdcInfo, hfontOld);

    hFont         = hFontIn;
    cyCaretHeight = tm.tmHeight;
    }
/*---------------------------------------------------------------*\
|                    TCaret Class Member.                         |
\*---------------------------------------------------------------*/
void    TCaret::SetState (int AFlag)
    {
    if (iFlag == AFlag)
        return;

    if (AFlag & CARET_ACTIVE)
        {
        CreateCaret (hwnd, 0, cxCaretWidth, cyCaretHeight);
        SetCaretPos (ptPixelPos.x, ptPixelPos.y);
        ShowCaret (hwnd);
        }

    if (AFlag & CARET_INACTIVE)
        {
        HideCaret (hwnd);
        DestroyCaret ();
        }

    iFlag = AFlag;
    }
/*---------------------------------------------------------------*\
|                    TCaret Class Member.                         |
\*---------------------------------------------------------------*/
void    TCaret::SetStringPtr(LPSTR lpstrIn)
    {
    lpString = lpstrIn;
    }
```

# CARET.RC

```
snapshot icon Caret.ico

hand cursor Caret.cur
```

## CARET.DEF

```
NAME CARET

EXETYPE WINDOWS

DESCRIPTION 'Caret - keyboard pointer'

CODE MOVEABLE DISCARDABLE
DATA MOVEABLE MULTIPLE

HEAPSIZE  512
STACKSIZE 5120
```

In this program, we've created a caret class, **TCaret**, which manages an MS-Windows caret. There is certainly room for improvement of this class, but it does provide a sufficient base on which to build a real-world application's caret class. Let's examine the data members and member functions which make up **TCaret**, starting with the data members:

| Type | Name | Description |
| --- | --- | --- |
| HFONT | hFont | Font used for display of string, used to calculate string width information. |
| HDC | hdcInfo | Permanent Information Context (IC) used to derive character/font width information. |
| HWND | hwnd | Window in which font resides. |
| int | iCharPos | Position of caret, in character cells. |
| int | iFlag | Active/inactive flag. |
| int | cxCaretWidth | Width of caret, in pixels. Width is equal to the border width of a window. |
| int | cyCaretHeight | Height of caret, in pixels. Height is equal to height of currently selected font. |
| POINT | ptPixelPos | Position $(x,y)$ of caret, in pixels. |
| POINT | ptAnchor | Anchor point $(x,y)$ of string, from which caret location is calculated. |
| LPSTR | lpString | Points to the character string relative to which the caret is to be placed. |

The **TCaret** class handles managing the movement of a caret through a character string. It does so by keeping track of every piece of information relative to the caret: an MS-Windows handle to the text window, a pointer to the character string, the font used, and the relative location of the string in the text window. Once these values have been set up, the only thing which must be supplied is the character position of the caret, **iCharPos**. This is accomplished by calling the **SetCharPosition** member function. Let's look at the other member functions:

| Function Name | Description |
|---|---|
| TCaret | Constructor. |
| ~TCaret | Destructor. |
| Hide | Hides a caret. To avoid a conflict with output in a window, you'll need to hide the caret when drawing in a window. |
| Show | Shows a caret. |
| GetAnchorX | Retrieves the *x* value of the string anchor position. |
| GetAnchorY | Retrieves the *y* value of the string anchor position. |
| GetCharPosition | Retrieves the character position. |
| GetFontHandle | Retrieves the font handle. |
| GetState | Retrieves the active/inactive state. |
| GetStringPtr | Retrieves a pointer to the current character string. |
| SetAnchor | Sets the string anchor position. |
| SetCharPosition | Set the character position of the caret. |
| SetFontHandle | Sets the font handle. |
| SetState | Sets the active/inactive state. |
| SetStringPtr | Sets the current string pointer. |

One important aspect of carets is that they must be hidden when you draw in a window. In particular, if you draw during any message besides the **WM_PAINT** message, you'll need to hide the caret while you are drawing. This is necessary because the drawing of a caret occurs asynchronously with system messages. Before calling **GetDC**, you must hide the caret by calling **HideCaret**. After you've gotten rid of the DC by calling **ReleaseDC**, it's safe to restore the caret by calling ShowCaret. That's exactly what **TCaret**'s **Hide** and **Show** member functions do in this fragment taken from our sample program (from **TCaretWindow::WMChar**, to be exact):

```
    PCaret->Hide();

    // Update display.
    hdc = GetDC(HWindow);
    dw = GetTextExtent (hdc, (LPSTR)&achInput[0], ichNext);
    TextOut (hdc,
             xLeftMargin+LOWORD(dw),
             yLineHeight,
             (LPSTR)&achInput[ichNext],
             cchInput - ichNext);
    ReleaseDC (HWindow, hdc);

    PCaret->Show();
```

Perhaps the single most important thing that should be said about carets is that they must be created in response to the **WM_SETFOCUS** message and destroyed in response to **WM_KILLFOCUS**. With **TCaret**, both actions are performed by the **SetState** member function. When called with the `CARET_ACTIVE` flag, the caret is created and displayed. When called with the `CARET_INACTIVE` flag, the caret is destroyed. If a program fails to destroy a caret in response to the `WM_KILLFOCUS` message, the Window Manager will get confused. It seems that the Window Manager assumes there will be only one caret in the system at any time. If your program fails to follow these rules, you will get an orphaned caret in a window. Avoiding this is easy: Create and destroy carets in response to the proper messages.

This concludes our look at keyboard input, and at carets. You see now that keyboard input goes through a two-step conversion process: from scan code to virtual key and from virtual key to ASCII character code. This two-step process helps Windows be an international operating system, and allows Windows programs to run unchanged around the world.

In the next chapter, we're going to look at the other type of input device available to Windows programs: the mouse. Ideally, a Windows program will allow a user to switch between the mouse and the keyboard for all of its operations. Let's see what this involves.

# 16

# Mouse Input

A mouse is a pointing device about the size of a deck of playing cards connected via cable to a computer. The first mouse was developed in the mid-1960s at the Stanford Research Institute (SRI). During the 1970s, the mouse played a key role in the computer research done at Xerox's Palo Alto Research Center (PARC). But the mouse didn't come into widespread use until the 1980s, with the advent and immense popularity of personal computers.

The mouse allows a user to quickly point to different objects and locations on the display screen. Objects can be picked up, moved, and directly manipulated with a versatility that is not possible with the keyboard alone. The advantage of the mouse over the keyboard is that pointing is a very natural, human action that we are capable of from a very young age. Pressing letter combinations on a keyboard is arguably a less natural way to communicate.

The mouse is a very important input device in Windows. Used alone, quite a bit of interaction is possible: Programs can be started, windows moved, menu items selected, and, in programs that allow it, data objects can be directly manipulated. As you begin to create Windows programs, you'll want to keep in mind the tremendous possibilities that are possible through the simple act of pointing.

Even though Windows and Windows applications make significant use of the mouse, not every Windows computer will have a mouse. And even on computers that are equipped with a mouse, there may be times when a particular user prefers to avoid the mouse. Early in the development of Windows, this issue was raised by the developers of some popular software packages. In particular, the developers of DOS-based programs that relied primarily on keyboard input were concerned with the suitability of Windows for their programs. In response, Windows was changed so that all available mouse functions would be available from the keyboard as well. Ideally, programs should allow users to switch from one to the other at any time.

468  *Message Driven Input*

This approach is built into the way that Windows handles menus. Consider the system menu. When you want to see the system menu, you can click the mouse on the system menu icon or strike the [Alt] + [Spacebar] keys. Once the system menu has made its appearance, you can select system menu commands using either the mouse or the keyboard. Using the mouse, you click on the desired menu item. Using the keyboard, there are two choices: You can use the arrow keys followed by the return key, or simply strike a letter key that matches an underlined letter in a menu item name. On the other hand, having seen the system menu, you might decide that you don't want to select any of its commands after all. Again, there is a keyboard approach and a mouse approach to dismissing the system menu. From the keyboard, you hit the [Esc] key. Using the mouse, simply click anywhere outside the system menu.

This flexibility allows the user to alternate between the two devices based on personal preference. We suggest that you take a similar approach while designing the user interface to your Windows programs. It will require some thought on your part to create a robust, flexible interface—but the increased *usability* of your program will most likely cause an increase in the *use* of your program.

If you have never used a mouse before, you might be skeptical about its usefulness as an input device. There's a story about a researcher at Xerox PARC, Larry Tesler, who used to think that way. He set up an experiment to prove that the mouse wasn't a very useful input device. He took people off the streets, and taught them to use a full-screen editor with cursor keys. After an hour or so, he would introduce the mouse as an alternative to the cursor keys. After playing with the mouse a little, most people ended up ignoring the cursor keys in favor of the mouse. The experiment backfired: Although he was trying to demonstrate that the mouse was an unsuitable input device, Tesler found that most users were more comfortable using the mouse instead of the keyboard to select input locations on a display screen.

Perhaps, like many programmers, you are primarily oriented toward keyboard input. If so, it might be worth your time to practice using the mouse. This will help you become a better Windows programmer, since it will help you to better understand the benefits that the mouse can provide to your users. To get you started, the next section discusses some of the common uses of the mouse in Windows.

## The Uses of a Mouse

We're going to start our discussion of the mouse from the point of view of the user. That is, we're going to answer the question: What is a mouse used for? If you're an experienced mouse user, you might wish to skip ahead a few pages to where our discussion of programming issues begins.

In use, the mouse rests on a flat surface like a desktop. It controls the movement of a tiny symbol on the display screen called a **cursor**. The cursor sometimes changes shape to let you know that a particular location on the screen has significance. For example, some windows have a thick border for use in resizing the window. When positioned on top of such a border, the cursor changes into a two-headed arrow to let you know that resizing can take place.

A mouse may have one or more buttons. While the cursor location is important, it's actually the use of the buttons that triggers an action. There are several different uses of the mouse buttons that are common in the world of Windows, including clicking, double-clicking, clicking with a shift key, and dragging. We're going to discuss each of these briefly, to introduce the basic mouse actions, and to discuss some of the techniques that you'll see mentioned in this chapter. A more complete discussion of mouse interaction techniques can be found in the IBM publication *Systems Application Architecture, Common User Access: Advanced Interface Design Guide* (SC26-4582-0). This document describes a set of user-interface standards that have been adopted for Windows programs. You should consider getting a copy of this important guide.

The first mouse action that we're going to describe is **clicking**. Clicking involves pressing and releasing a mouse button without moving the mouse. A click is used to select objects and actions. For example, clicking causes menus to appear and is used to make scroll bars operate.

**Double-clicking** involves two clicking operations at the same location in a very short time interval. The default time interval is one-half second, but this can be changed using the Control Panel. While a single click makes a selection, a double-click means "do the default action." For example, a double-click on the system menu icon means "close this window." A double-click on a program icon in the Program Manager means "start this program." In general, a double-click should extend the action that was started by a single click.

**Clicking with a shift key** involves holding down one of the shift keys ([Shift] or [Ctrl]) while clicking a mouse button. The shift key modifies the mouse click, in the same way that a shift key modifies a keyboard key. [Shift] + [A], for example, gives us a capital "A." The meaning of [Shift] + click or [Ctrl] + click will depend on the program. In general, though, [Shift] + click is a request to extend a selection that was started with a single click.

**Dragging** is a two-part mouse action, which starts with clicking to select an object, and then—with the mouse button still pressed—involves moving the mouse to cause the selected object to move. When the object has arrived at the desired location, the mouse button is released. Dragging is perhaps the hardest operation for new Windows users to master, since it combines mouse button action and mouse movement. But it is also a widely used action. For example, in graphics programs, dragging allows a user to directly manipulate objects on the display screen. In the Windows interface itself, dragging is an important mouse action: Dragging is used to move windows, select menu items, and operate scroll bars.

## 470 *Message Driven Input*

This brief introduction to mouse actions is not a substitute for your working with the Windows user interface and becoming comfortable with each of these techniques. If you are a regular Windows user, it will help make you a better Windows programmer. But now, let's roll up our sleeves and start to investigate some of the issues that will help you program for the mouse. In the same way that we traced the path of keyboard data from the hardware into our program, we're going to follow the path that mouse data takes in hopes of understanding how a Windows program can best make use of this device.

## How a Windows Program Receives Mouse Input

The path that mouse data takes is illustrated in Figure 16.1. In many respects, mouse data is much simpler than keyboard data, and so this figure is correspondingly simpler than the diagram that we saw in the last chapter. Nevertheless, mouse input has some unique qualities, and understanding these qualities will help you use mouse input.

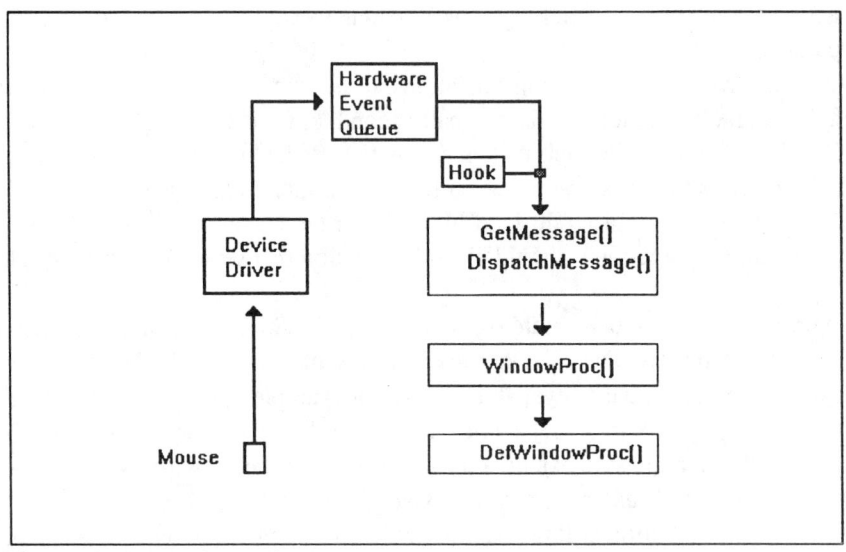

**Figure 16.1** The flow of mouse data

## *The Mouse*

Although there are other pointing devices besides the mouse—including track balls, joy sticks, touch screens, and cat's paws—none has experienced the same popularity as the mouse. At present, a relatively small number of companies ship mice, including Hewlett-Packard, Logitech, Microsoft, and Mouse Systems. Among these companies, there aren't many differences between the mouse each provides. Some have two buttons and others have three. Some detect movement by the motion of a rubber-coated steel ball, while others use optical detection methods. There is also little variety in the way different mice connect to the computer system. Some mice use a communication port, while others connect to a special bus adapter card, and still others connect to the system through the keyboard.

When a mouse reports its location, it does so in terms of movement along the *x*- and *y*-axes. And, like keyboard activity, mouse button actions are reported as button down and button up actions. When one of these events occurs, a signal is sent which results in a hardware interrupt being generated. The handling of the interrupt is the job of the next component we're going to look at: the device driver.

## *The Mouse Device Driver*

When Windows starts up, the mouse driver loads itself and goes off in search of a mouse. When Windows asks, the device driver lets Windows know whether a mouse is present in the system. If so, Windows calls the driver to provide an address of a procedure to be called to report mouse events. From that point on, the job of the device driver is simple: Whenever a mouse event occurs, the driver calls Windows to report mouse actions.

When Windows is notified of a mouse event, one of the first things it does is to check whether the mouse has moved. If so, it calls the display driver to move the mouse cursor. In this way, the movement of the mouse cursor always occurs at interrupt time, and will preempt almost all other activities. But this happens in the background, so you never need to worry that it might disrupt the proper operation of your programs.

Like keyboard events, mouse events are not delivered to programs at interrupt time. The disruption that this would cause to Windows' nonpreemptive scheduling system would make writing Windows programs very difficult. Instead, mouse events are handled like keyboard events and placed into Windows' hardware event queue.

## *The Hardware Event Queue*

Mouse events are written into the hardware event queue, where they wait for delivery to the message loop of a program. When we introduced the hardware event queue in our discussion of keyboard input, we mentioned that it had room for 120 events. While this is easily enough to keep ahead of most typists, you might be concerned that the queue can overflow if the mouse were to be quickly moved across the screen.

In anticipation of this problem, Windows regards mouse movement in a very special way. Before a new mouse move event is written to the hardware event queue, a check is made to see if the previous hardware event was also reporting mouse movement. If so, the previous event is overwritten with the latest mouse move information. After all, when the user is moving the mouse, the destination is more important than every point traversed by the mouse.

The events in the hardware event queue don't yet belong to any particular program, until they are claimed by the `GetMessage` routine. This is necessary for the proper operation of the system. After all, one mouse message might cause a window to move or to close. This would change the way that subsequent mouse messages are handled, since mouse input is based on mouse cursor location. That decision is made by the next link in the mouse handling chain: the `GetMessage` loop.

## The GetMessage Loop

Every program has a `GetMessage` loop, which serves as one of the gateways for messages to enter a program for processing. As discussed earlier, this message passing mechanism also serves to keep Windows' multitasking system working properly.

When a program calls `GetMessage`, it opens the possibility that Windows may decide to put the program to sleep and wake up another program. This is precisely what happens when `GetMessage` finds that the hardware event queue contains a mouse event for another program. It puts the first program to sleep, and wakes up the second program. The second program can then return from its own call to `GetMessage`, where it has been sleeping, with a mouse message to process.

`GetMessage` decides which program should receive a mouse message by finding out which program owns the window where the mouse cursor resides. For now, though, let's set aside these multitasking issues and concentrate on the way `GetMessage` operates once it has decided that a specific program should receive a mouse message.

Even after `GetMessage` has found a mouse event for one of our windows, it still isn't ready to bring a message back to our program. The problem is simple: There are two types of mouse messages, depending on where the cursor is resting. Table 16.1 provides a list of the two types: client area and nonclient area messages. The distinction is important, since Windows itself takes care of mouse messages in the nonclient area of the window, and lets our program handle client area mouse messages.

**Table 16.1**

| Client Area Messages | Non client Area Message |
|---|---|
| WM_LBUTTONDOWN | WM_NCLBUTTONDOWN |
| WM_LBUTTONUP | WM_NCLBUTTONUP |
| WM_LBUTTONDBLCLK | WM_NCLBUTTONDBLCLK |
| | |
| WM_MBUTTONDOWN | WM_NCMBUTTONDOWN |
| WM_MBUTTONUP | WM_NCMBUTTONUP |
| WM_MBUTTONDBLCLK | WM_NCMBUTTONDBLCLK |
| | |
| WM_RBUTTONDOWN | WM_NCRBUTTONDOWN |
| WM_RBUTTONUP | WM_NCRBUTTONUP |
| WM_RBUTTONDBLCLK | WM_NCRBUTTONDBLCLK |
| | |
| WM_MOUSEMOVE | WM_NCMOUSEMOVE |

As you can tell by looking at the messages in Table 16.1, Windows has messages for up to three mouse buttons, which are called the left, middle, and right buttons. Since some mice have only two buttons, few programs rely on the middle button for mouse input. In addition, Windows itself relies exclusively on the left button, and many programs follow this practice.

In case you are worried that this is unfair to users who prefer the right mouse button, Windows has a built-in solution. The Control Panel lets a user swap the left and right mouse buttons. When this is done, Windows automatically converts all right button messages into left button messages. Therefore, if a program uses only one mouse button, it can safely rely on left button messages and still satisfy users who prefer to use the right button.

To determine where the mouse cursor is resting in a window, and therefore what type of message is needed, the `GetMessage` routine sends a message to the window procedure: **WM_NCHITTEST**. To understand how this works, we need to review Windows' message passing mechanisms.

In Chapter 4, we introduced two types of message processing: push-model and pull-model processing. At the time, we said that the `GetMessage` routine takes care of pull-model processing to read hardware event information. And yet, to determine the location

474   *Message Driven Input*

of the mouse cursor, **GetMessage** relies on push-model processing. In more familiar terms, the **GetMessage** routine calls your window procedure as if it were a subroutine.

It does so using a Windows library routine that we have not yet encountered: **SendMessage**. This routine bypasses the message queues to deliver messages directly to a window object. In a sense, it behaves as if it were directly calling a window object's window procedure. This routine incorporates the push-model processing that we first discussed in Chapter 4. A window procedure cannot be called directly. Instead, the **SendMessage** routine performs immediate message delivery for us. You call **SendMessage** like this:

```
lRetVal = SendMessage (hwnd, msg, wValue, lValue);
```

Since this is like a function call, we get back whatever return value the window procedure has decided to give us.

The return value is very important in the context of the **WM_NCHITTEST** message that **GetMessage** sends to our window procedure. This message asks the window procedure to identify where the mouse cursor is resting. Most programs pass this message on to the default window procedure, which studies the location of the mouse cursor, and provides a **hit-test code** as a return value. The hit-test codes are shown in Figure 16.2.

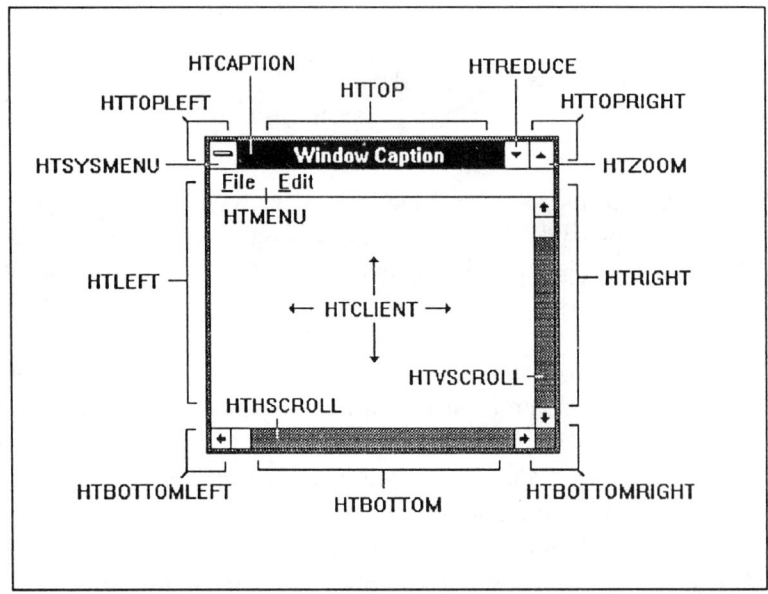

**Figure 16.2** Windows hit-test codes

Most of the hit-test codes describe a location on the window border, like **HTTOP** and **HTTOPLEFT**. Others identify different nonclient area objects like scroll bars and menus. One of the hit-test codes, **HTCLIENT**, refers to the window's client area. **GetMessage** uses the hit-test code to decide the type of mouse message to generate. When the hit-test code is equal to `HTCLIENT`, a client area message is generated; all other hit-test codes cause nonclient area mouse messages to be generated.

Before `GetMessage` returns a mouse message to our program, there is still one more thing it does: It makes sure the shape of the mouse cursor is correct for the location of the mouse. To do this, it sends yet another message to our window procedure: `WM_SETCURSOR`. Like the `WM_NCHITTEST` message, most programs ignore this message and allow the default window procedure to do the right thing. The hit-test code is included with the message as the low word of the `lParam` parameter, so that the default window procedure knows how to correctly set the cursor shape. For example, the `HTTOP` hit-test code indicates that a two-headed arrow cursor is needed to show the user that window resizing is available, while the `HTMENU` code summons the normal arrow cursor.

Figure 16.3 shows an example of WinSight listening to mouse messages. This is typical mouse message traffic. With one exception, which we'll cover when we discuss *mouse capture*, the `WM_NCHITTEST` and `WM_SETCURSOR` messages always precede a mouse message. The reason now should be evident: Windows must first find the location of the mouse cursor to know whether to generate a client area or a nonclient area message. Once the location is known, Windows makes sure that the user knows by setting the mouse cursor to the correct shape.

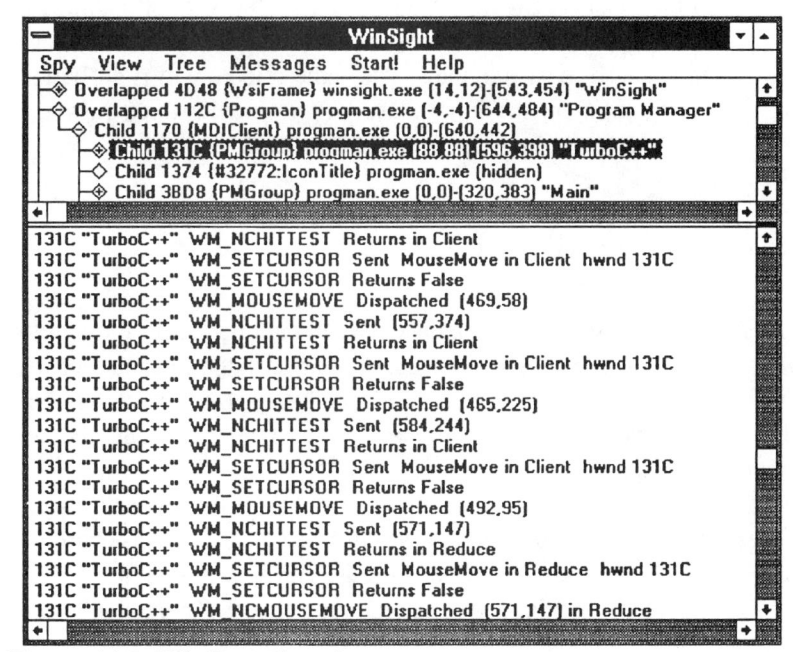

**Figure 16.3** WinSight listening to mouse messages

When we discussed keyboard input, we mentioned that Windows allows for the installation of message hooks, which can be used to alter the flow of messages. While we aren't going to take the time now to describe how to install a hook, you should be aware that a **WH_GETMESSAGE** hook can alter the flow of any client area or nonclient area mouse message. Once **GetMessage** is ready to bring a message into our program, it makes a call to the hook to see if any changes need to be made before the message itself is delivered to a program.

Once **GetMessage** has brought a mouse message into our program, the message is sent on to the correct window procedure by the **DispatchMessage** routine. From the point of view of our program, the window procedure is where all the action is. So, let's take a look at how a window object can handle mouse traffic.

## The Mouse and the Window Object

Of the 20 mouse messages that exist in Windows, 10 are nonclient area messages and can be safely ignored by a window object. After all, the nonclient area of a window is maintained by Windows. Among the 10 client area messages, one lets our program know the location of the mouse in our client area: **WM_MOUSEMOVE**. We'll take a detailed look at this message shortly. Of the other nine messages, three are for the left button, three for the middle button, and three for the right button. Since the processing for each set of messages is the same, and because most programs ignore the middle and right buttons, we're going to focus our attention on the left mouse button and its three messages: **WM_LBUTTONDOWN**, **WM_LBUTTONUP**, and **WM_LBUTTONDBLCLK**.

### The WM_LBUTTONDOWN Message

When the user pushes the left mouse button with the cursor in our client area, our window object receives a **WM_LBUTTONDOWN** message. Besides telling us that a click has occurred in our client area, the message parameters, **Msg.WParam** and **Msg.LParam**, tell us quite a bit more about the message. Incidentally, the **WParam** and **LParam** values are the same for all client area mouse messages.

The **LParam** value in a mouse message contains the location of the mouse cursor, in client area coordinates. We introduced client area coordinates in Chapter 6. This coordinate system places the origin in the upper-left corner of the client area, with one unit equal to one pixel. Figure 16.4 shows how client area coordinates flip the normal Cartesian coordinate system upside down, with the $y$-axis positive going downward.

The *x* value is in the low word of **LParam** and the *y* value is in the high word. One way to extract these values is by taking advantage of the **Hi** and **Lo** union members of **LParam**, like this:

```
void TSampleWindow::WMLeftDown(TMessage& Msg)
    {
    xValue = Msg.LP.Lo;
    yValue = Msg.LP.Hi;
    ...
    }
```

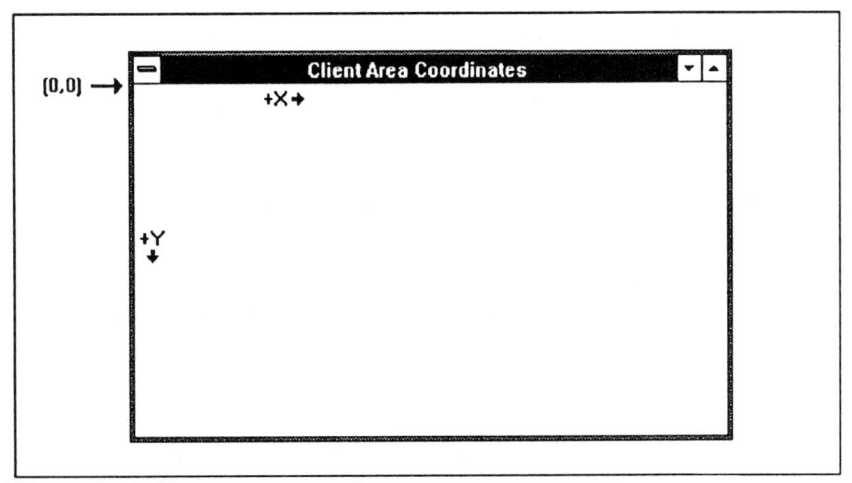

**Figure 16.4  Client area coordinates**

However, we prefer using macros, which hide the exact format of a message's parameters. This will help, for example, when we port our program to the Windows 32-bit API which is incorporated in Windows NT. Here are two mouse message macros:

```
#define MOUSEX(arg)   (arg.LP.Lo)
#define MOUSEY(arg)   (arg.LP.Hi)
```

We could then extract the mouse location information like this:

```
void TSampleWindow::WMLeftDown(TMessage& Msg)
    {
    xValue = MOUSEX(Msg);
    yValue = MOUSEY(Msg);
    ...
    }
```

478  *Message Driven Input*

A third alternative is to copy the location information to a variable of type `POINT`. `POINT` is defined in WINDOWS.H as

```
typedef struct tagPOINT
    {
    int     x;
    int     y;
    } POINT;
```

so that it has a place for a pair of integer values, *x* and *y*. There's a special macro, `MAKEPOINT`, which converts `LParam` into a `POINT` value. Here is how it is used:

```
void TSampleWindow::WMLeftDown(TMessage& Msg)
    {
    POINT ptMouse;

    ptMouse = MAKEPOINT (Msg.LParam);
    ...
    }
```

We then refer to `pt.x` and `pt.y` as for the mouse location.

A mouse message's `WParam` parameter contains flags that describe the state of the mouse buttons and the state of the [Shift] and [Ctrl] keys. Figure 16.5 shows the layout of these flags.

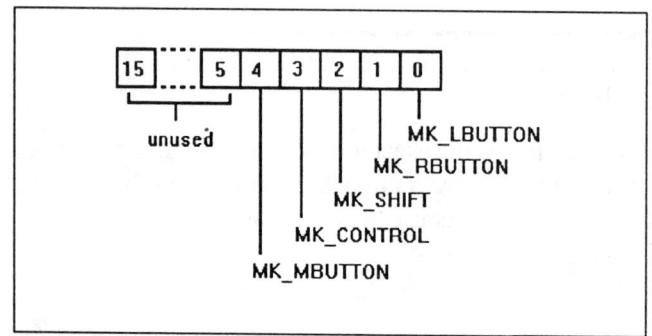

**Figure 16.5** Five fields of wParam for client area mouse messages

The value of a field is 1 if the corresponding mouse button or keyboard key is down; otherwise the value is 0. To test whether a specific field is down, you can use the C language bitwise-AND operator, `&`. Here is how to see if the shift key is down in response to a left button down message:

```
void TSampleWindow::WMLeftDown(TMessage& Msg)
    {
    if (Msg.WParam & MK_SHIFT)
        {
        /* Shift key is down. */
        }
    ...
    }
```

## The WM_LBUTTONUP Message

This message signals that the left mouse button has been released. In many ways, this message is analogous to the `WM_KEYUP` keyboard message. And yet, Windows programs rarely pay attention to the `WM_KEYUP` message when handling keyboard input. The `WM_LBUTTONUP` message, on the other hand, is quite important. If you are writing a program that uses the mouse to draw, for example, this message will tell you when to stop drawing. In the enhanced rectangle drawing program that you'll find later in this chapter, this message is used both to finish drawing rectangles and to finish the job when we drag a rectangle across the window.

## The WM_LBUTTONDBLCLK Message

At the beginning of this chapter, we introduced double-clicking as a common user action. To be effective, a program that responds to a double-click should be careful that the double-click is an extension of a single click. The reason is that a single click message will always be received before a double-click message.

For a window to receive double-click messages, it must have been defined with a special class style: `CS_DBLCLKS`. To add this style, you'd add the following line to the `GetWindowClass` member function of a window class:

```
...
wc.style = CS_DBLCLKS;
...
```

When a window has this bit set in its style definition, it changes the way that button down messages are handled: A button down message causes a timer to be started. This causes the system to incur some additional overhead. Even though this overhead is small, programs that don't plan to use double-click messages should avoid setting this style bit.

If a second button down message is received within a short (one-half second) period of time, a double-click message is substituted for the second button down message. Here is the sequence of messages that will be sent when the user performs a double-click on the left mouse button:

| Message | Comment |
|---|---|
| **WM_LBUTTONDOWN**<br>WM_LBUTTONUP | First button down message |
| **WM_LBUTTONDBLCLK**<br>WM_LBUTTONUP | Replaces second button down message |

### The WM_MOUSEMOVE Message

The fourth and final message that we're going to look at is the mouse movement message. As we mentioned earlier, Windows has a built-in mechanism to prevent mouse move messages from overflowing the hardware event queue. Thus, the mouse movement messages that a program receives might only provide a sampling of all of the places that the mouse visited. But this sampling is sufficient for most programs to track the movement of this pointing device.

In a moment, we'll look at some sample programs that show the use of each of these mouse messages. But first, let's look at the last component that plays an important role in handling mouse messages, the default window procedure.

## *The Default Window Procedure*

When we first introduced the default window procedure, we described it as the central reason that Windows programs behave in such a uniform manner. It provides all the basic, minimum processing that allows a common set of user actions to produce the same results from different Windows programs. Menus, scroll bars, and windows can all be accessed using the same set of user actions. This uniformity assumes, of course, that Windows programmers pass along all their "extra" messages. In the case of mouse messages, the default window procedure ignores the client area messages and instead relies on nonclient area messages.

The default window procedure is also responsible for providing a common mouse and keyboard interface. It does this by translating input into a set of system commands, which show up as **WM_SYSCOMMAND** messages. And finally, the default window procedure handles the **WM_NCHITTEST** and **WM_SETCURSOR** messages which pave the way for almost all mouse messages.

When a mouse message gets to the default window procedure, it has arrived at its final destination. Starting at the mouse itself, mouse input follows a pretty direct route into a program. But, as we've seen, that route may cause Windows' multitasking switcher to stop feeding messages to one program and start feeding them to another. And finally, we've seen that half of the mouse messages that occur can be safely ignored—that is, assuming we pass our ignored messages on to the default window procedure.

For all this mouse theory to be helpful to you in building Windows programs, it would help to see some practical examples. In this chapter, we're going to show you three such examples. The first program, CARET2, will show how a mouse click can be used in a text input window to move a caret. Our second program, RECT2, is a revision of the rectangle drawing program we first encountered in Chapter 9. We'll explore the application of GDI raster operations to create stretchable rectangles and dragable objects. Our final program, DYNACURS, creates a mouse cursor "on the fly." It echoes the mouse location, using the cursor, and in the process shows how to use a Windows library routine that is new with Windows 3.0: **CreateCursor**.

## A Mouse Input Sample: CARET2

In the last chapter, we introduced a program that receives keyboard input. We then enhanced this program with a caret so that the user could always see the current text entry position. Using the keyboard cursor keys, the user moves the caret to different positions in the text. Now that we've been discussing the use of the mouse, the time has come to enhance our program one more time so that the mouse can be used to move the caret.

## MAKEFILE.MAK

```
.AUTODEPEND

#    Translator Definitions
INC=\BORLANDC\OWL\INCLUDE;\BORLANDC\CLASSLIB\INCLUDE;\BORLANDC\INCLUDE
CC = bcc -c -D_CLASSDLL -H -ml -WS -w-par -I$(INC)

#    Implicit Rules
.c.obj:
  $(CC) {$< }

.cpp.obj:
  $(CC) {$< }

#    Explicit Rules
Caret2.exe: Caret2.res Caret2.def Caret2.obj
    tlink /c/C/n/P-/Twe/x @Caret2.LNK
    rlink Caret2.res Caret2.exe

#    Individual File Dependencies
Caret2.obj: Caret2.cpp

Caret2.res: Caret2.rc Caret2.cur Caret2.ico
    brcc -FO Caret2.res -i$(INC) Caret2.RC
```

## CARET2.LNK

```
\borlandc\lib\c0wl.obj+
Caret2.obj
Caret2,Caret2
\borlandc\classlib\lib\tclasdll.lib+
\borlandc\owl\lib\owl.lib+
mathwl.lib+
import.lib+
crtldll.lib
Caret2.def
```

## CARET2.CPP

```
/*----------------------------------------------------------------*\
 * (c) Copyright 1992 By Paul L. Yao.   All rights reserved.      *
\*----------------------------------------------------------------*/
/*----------------------------------------------------------------*\
 | CARET2.CPP  - Keyboard pointer demo using mouse input.         |
\*----------------------------------------------------------------*/
#define WIN31
#define STRICT
#include <owl.h>
#include <WindowsX.h>

#define CHARMSGASCII(arg) (arg.WParam)
#define KEYMSG_VK(arg)    (arg.WParam)
#define MOUSEX(arg)       (arg.LP.Lo)
#define MOUSEY(arg)       (arg.LP.Hi)

/*----------------------------------------------------------------*\
 |                       Constants.                               |
\*----------------------------------------------------------------*/
const int BUFSIZE = 40;
const int CARET_ACTIVE   = 0x01;
const int CARET_INACTIVE = 0x02;

/*----------------------------------------------------------------*\
 |                   Class Declarations.                          |
\*----------------------------------------------------------------*/
class TCaretApplication : public TApplication
   {
   public:
     TCaretApplication (LPSTR lpszName, HINSTANCE hInstance,
                        HINSTANCE hPrevInstance, LPSTR lpszCmdLine,
                        int nCmdShow);
     virtual void InitMainWindow ();
   };

class TCaret
   {
   public:
     TCaret(HWND hwndIn, HFONT hFontIn);
     ~TCaret();

     virtual void   Hide();
     virtual void   Show();

     virtual int    GetAnchorX();
```

```
      virtual int     GetAnchorY();
      virtual int     GetCharPosition ();
      virtual HFONT   GetFontHandle();
      virtual int     GetState ();
      virtual LPSTR   GetStringPtr();

      virtual void    SetAnchor (int X, int Y);
      virtual void    SetCharPosition (int iChar);
      virtual void    SetFontHandle(HFONT hFontIn);
      virtual void    SetState (int AFlag);
      virtual void    SetStringPtr(LPSTR lpstrIn);
    private:
      HFONT   hFont;
      HDC     hdcInfo;
      HWND    hwnd;
      int     iCharPos;
      int     iFlag;
      int     cxCaretWidth;
      int     cyCaretHeight;
      POINT   ptPixelPos;
      POINT   ptAnchor;
      LPSTR   lpString;
    };

class TCaretWindow : public TWindow
  {
  public:
    TCaret * PCaret;

    TCaretWindow (PTWindowsObject pwParent, LPSTR lpszTitle,
                  PTModule pmModule);
    virtual LPSTR GetClassName ();
    virtual void  GetWindowClass (WNDCLASS&);
    virtual void  WMChar(TMessage& Msg) = [WM_CHAR];
    virtual void  WMCreate(TMessage& Msg) = [WM_CREATE];
    virtual void  WMDestroy(TMessage& Msg) = [WM_DESTROY];
    virtual void  WMKeyDown(TMessage& Msg) = [WM_KEYDOWN];
    virtual void  WMLButtonDown(TMessage& Msg) = [WM_LBUTTONDOWN];
    virtual void  WMPaint(TMessage& Msg);
    virtual void  WMSetFocus(TMessage& Msg) = [WM_SETFOCUS];
    virtual void  WMKillFocus(TMessage& Msg) = [WM_KILLFOCUS];
  private:
    unsigned char achInput[BUFSIZE];
    unsigned int  cchInput;
    unsigned int  ichNext;
    unsigned int  yLineHeight;
    unsigned int  xLeftMargin;
    RECT          rHitArea;
  };

/*-------------------------------------------------------------*\
|                Main Function:  WinMain.                       |
\*-------------------------------------------------------------*/
int PASCAL WinMain (HINSTANCE hInstance,   HINSTANCE hPrevInstance,
                    LPSTR  lpszCmdLine, int    nCmdShow)
    {
    TCaretApplication Caret ("Caret", hInstance,
                             hPrevInstance, lpszCmdLine,
                             nCmdShow);
    Caret.Run();
    return Caret.Status;
    }
```

## 484  Message Driven Input

```
/*---------------------------------------------------------------*\
|                    Application Class Member.                    |
\*---------------------------------------------------------------*/
TCaretApplication::TCaretApplication (LPSTR lpszName,
                    HINSTANCE hInstance, HINSTANCE hPrevInstance,
                    LPSTR lpszCmdLine, int nCmdShow)
                :TApplication (lpszName, hInstance,
                    hPrevInstance, lpszCmdLine, nCmdShow)
    {
    /*  Application specific initialization goes here.  */
    }

/*---------------------------------------------------------------*\
|                    Application Class Member.                    |
\*---------------------------------------------------------------*/
void TCaretApplication::InitMainWindow ()
    {
    MainWindow = new TCaretWindow (NULL, "Caret Demo 2", NULL);
    }

/*---------------------------------------------------------------*\
|                    TCaretWindow Class Member.                   |
\*---------------------------------------------------------------*/
TCaretWindow::TCaretWindow (PTWindowsObject pwParent,
                LPSTR lpszTitle, PTModule pmModule)
            :TWindow (pwParent, lpszTitle, pmModule)
    {
    HDC         hdc;
    TEXTMETRIC  tm;

    hdc = CreateDC ("DISPLAY", 0, 0, 0);

    GetTextMetrics (hdc, &tm);
    yLineHeight = tm.tmHeight + tm.tmExternalLeading;
    xLeftMargin = tm.tmAveCharWidth;

    DeleteDC (hdc);

    cchInput = 0;
    ichNext  = 0;
    }

/*---------------------------------------------------------------*\
|                    TCaretWindow Class Member.                   |
\*---------------------------------------------------------------*/
LPSTR TCaretWindow::GetClassName ()
    {
    return "Caret:MAIN";
    }

/*---------------------------------------------------------------*\
|                    TCaretWindow Class Member.                   |
\*---------------------------------------------------------------*/
void TCaretWindow::GetWindowClass (WNDCLASS& wc)
    {
    TWindow::GetWindowClass (wc);
    wc.hIcon=LoadIcon (wc.hInstance, "snapshot");
```

```
        wc.hCursor=LoadCursor (wc.hInstance, "hand");
        }
/*--------------------------------------------------------------*\
|                    TCaretWindow Class Member.                  |
\*--------------------------------------------------------------*/
void TCaretWindow::WMChar(TMessage& Msg)
    {
    DWORD dw;
    HDC   hdc;
    int   i;
    WORD  wVirtKey;

    // Get virtual key value
    wVirtKey = CHARMSGASCII(Msg);

    if (wVirtKey == VK_BACK)      // Backspace.
        {
        if (ichNext == 0)
            MessageBeep(0);
        else                              // Remove a character.
            {
            ichNext--;
            PCaret->SetCharPosition(ichNext);

            for (i=ichNext;i<cchInput;i++)
                achInput[i]=achInput[i+1];
            cchInput--;
            InvalidateRect (HWindow, NULL, TRUE);
            }
        return;
        }

    // Complain if character out of range or if buffer is full.
    if ((wVirtKey <= VK_ESCAPE) || (cchInput >= BUFSIZE))
        {
        MessageBeep(0);
        return;
        }

    // Make room for next char.
    for (i=cchInput;i>ichNext;i--)
        achInput[i]=achInput[i-1];

    /* Put new char in buffer.  */
    achInput[ichNext] = (unsigned char)wVirtKey;

    // Increment count of characters.
    cchInput++;

    PCaret->Hide();

    // Update display.
    hdc = GetDC(HWindow);
    dw = GetTextExtent (hdc, (LPSTR)achInput, ichNext);
    TextOut (hdc,
             xLeftMargin+LOWORD(dw),
             yLineHeight,
```

```
                    (LPSTR)&achInput[ichNext],
                    cchInput - ichNext);
        ReleaseDC (HWindow, hdc);

        PCaret->Show();

        // Increment index to next character.
        ichNext++;
        PCaret->SetCharPosition(ichNext);
        }

/*-------------------------------------------------------------*\
|                   TCaretWindow Class Member.                  |
\*-------------------------------------------------------------*/
void TCaretWindow::WMCreate(TMessage& Msg)
    {
    DWORD   dwSize;
    HFONT   hFont;
    HDC     hdc;

    hFont = GetStockFont (SYSTEM_FONT);
    PCaret = new TCaret (Msg.Receiver, hFont);

    PCaret->SetAnchor (xLeftMargin, yLineHeight);
    PCaret->SetStringPtr ((LPSTR)achInput);

    // Get measurements for system font.
    hdc = GetDC (Msg.Receiver);
    dwSize = GetTextExtent (hdc, (LPSTR)"X", 1);
    ReleaseDC (Msg.Receiver, hdc);

    // Initialize hit rectangle.
    GetClientRect (Msg.Receiver, &rHitArea);
    rHitArea.top    = yLineHeight;
    rHitArea.bottom = rHitArea.top + HIWORD (dwSize);
    }

/*-------------------------------------------------------------*\
|                   TCaretWindow Class Member.                  |
\*-------------------------------------------------------------*/
void TCaretWindow::WMDestroy(TMessage& Msg)
    {
    delete PCaret;

    TWindow::WMDestroy(Msg);
    }

/*-------------------------------------------------------------*\
|                   TCaretWindow Class Member.                  |
\*-------------------------------------------------------------*/
void TCaretWindow::WMKeyDown(TMessage& Msg)
    {
    BOOL fCaretMoved = FALSE;

    switch (KEYMSG_VK(Msg))
        {
        case VK_DELETE:
            /* If end of buffer, complain. */
            if (ichNext == cchInput)
                MessageBeep(0);
```

```
                else    /* Remove a character.  */
                    {
                    int i;
                    for (i=ichNext;i<cchInput;i++)
                        achInput[i]=achInput[i+1];
                    cchInput--;
                    InvalidateRect (HWindow, NULL, TRUE);
                    }
                break;
            case VK_END:
                ichNext = cchInput;
                fCaretMoved = TRUE;
                break;
            case VK_HOME:
                ichNext = 0;
            fCaretMoved = TRUE;
                break;
            case VK_LEFT:
                if (ichNext > 0)
                    {
                    ichNext--;
                    fCaretMoved = TRUE;
                    }
                else
                    MessageBeep(0);
                break;
            case VK_RIGHT:
                if (ichNext < cchInput)
                    {
                    ichNext++;
                    fCaretMoved = TRUE;
                    }
                else
                    MessageBeep(0);
                break;
            }

    if (fCaretMoved)
        PCaret->SetCharPosition(ichNext);
    }

/*----------------------------------------------------------------*\
|                    TCaretWindow Class Member.                    |
\*----------------------------------------------------------------*/
void TCaretWindow::WMLButtonDown(TMessage& Msg)
    {
    DWORD dwSize;
    HDC hdc;
    int i;
    int xTotWidth;
    int xPrevHalfWidth;
    int xNextHalfWidth;
    POINT pt;

    pt.x = MOUSEX(Msg);
    pt.y = MOUSEY(Msg);

    /* First check:  is it in our hit area?  */
    if (PtInRect(&rHitArea, pt))
        {
        hdc = GetDC (HWindow);
```

# 488 Message Driven Input

```
            xTotWidth = xLeftMargin;
            xPrevHalfWidth = xLeftMargin;

            ichNext = cchInput;    // Default = end of string.

            /* Next: loop through characters. */
            for (i=0;i<cchInput;i++)
                {
                dwSize = GetTextExtent (hdc, (LPSTR)&achInput[i], 1);
                xNextHalfWidth = LOWORD(dwSize)/2;
                if ((xTotWidth - xPrevHalfWidth) <= pt.x &&
                    (xTotWidth + xNextHalfWidth) >  pt.x)
                    {
                    /* A hit!  Set caret position. */
                    ichNext = i;
                    break;
                    }
                xPrevHalfWidth = xNextHalfWidth;
                xTotWidth += LOWORD(dwSize);
                }
            ReleaseDC (HWindow, hdc);

            // Mousing around in the hit rectangle makes caret move
            PCaret->SetCharPosition(ichNext);
            }
    }

/*-------------------------------------------------------------*\
|                    TCaretWindow Class Member.                 |
\*-------------------------------------------------------------*/
void TCaretWindow::WMPaint(TMessage& Msg)
    {
    PAINTSTRUCT ps;

    BeginPaint (Msg.Receiver, &ps);
    TextOut (ps.hdc, xLeftMargin, yLineHeight, (LPSTR)achInput,
             cchInput);
    EndPaint (Msg.Receiver, &ps);
    }

/*-------------------------------------------------------------*\
|                    TCaretWindow Class Member.                 |
\*-------------------------------------------------------------*/
void TCaretWindow::WMSetFocus(TMessage& Msg)
    {
    PCaret->SetCharPosition(ichNext);
    PCaret->SetState(CARET_ACTIVE);
    }

/*-------------------------------------------------------------*\
|                    TCaretWindow Class Member.                 |
\*-------------------------------------------------------------*/
void TCaretWindow::WMKillFocus(TMessage& Msg)
    {
    PCaret->SetState(CARET_INACTIVE);
    }

/*-------------------------------------------------------------*\
|                      TCaret Class Member.                     |
\*-------------------------------------------------------------*/
```

```c
TCaret::TCaret(HWND hwndIn, HANDLE hFontIn)
    {
    HFONT     hfontOld;
    TEXTMETRIC tm;

    hdcInfo = CreateIC ("DISPLAY", 0, 0, 0);
    hfontOld = SelectFont (hdcInfo, hFontIn);
    GetTextMetrics (hdcInfo, &tm);
    SelectObject (hdcInfo, hfontOld);

    hwnd          = hwndIn;
    hFont         = hFontIn;
    iCharPos      = 0;
    iFlag         = CARET_INACTIVE;
    cxCaretWidth  = GetSystemMetrics (SM_CXBORDER);
    cyCaretHeight = tm.tmHeight;
    ptPixelPos.x  = 0;
    ptPixelPos.y  = 0;
    ptAnchor.x    = 0;
    ptAnchor.y    = 0;
    lpString      = (LPSTR)0L;
    }
/*---------------------------------------------------------------*\
|                    TCaret Class Member.                         |
\*---------------------------------------------------------------*/
TCaret::~TCaret()
    {
    if (iFlag & CARET_ACTIVE)
        {
        HideCaret(hwnd);
        DestroyCaret();
        }

    DeleteDC (hdcInfo);
    }

/*---------------------------------------------------------------*\
|                    TCaret Class Member.                         |
\*---------------------------------------------------------------*/
void TCaret::Hide()
    {
    HideCaret(hwnd);
    }

/*---------------------------------------------------------------*\
|                    TCaret Class Member.                         |
\*---------------------------------------------------------------*/
void TCaret::Show()
    {
    ShowCaret(hwnd);
    }

/*---------------------------------------------------------------*\
|                    TCaret Class Member.                         |
\*---------------------------------------------------------------*/
int   TCaret::GetAnchorX()
    {
    return ptAnchor.x;
    }
```

```
/*-------------------------------------------------------*\
|                    TCaret Class Member.                 |
\*-------------------------------------------------------*/
int     TCaret::GetAnchorY()
    {
    return ptAnchor.y;
    }

/*-------------------------------------------------------*\
|                    TCaret Class Member.                 |
\*-------------------------------------------------------*/
int     TCaret::GetCharPosition ()
    {
    return iCharPos;
    }

/*-------------------------------------------------------*\
|                    TCaret Class Member.                 |
\*-------------------------------------------------------*/
HANDLE TCaret::GetFontHandle()
    {
    return hFont;
    }

/*-------------------------------------------------------*\
|                    TCaret Class Member.                 |
\*-------------------------------------------------------*/
int     TCaret::GetState ()
    {
    return iFlag;
    }

/*-------------------------------------------------------*\
|                    TCaret Class Member.                 |
\*-------------------------------------------------------*/
LPSTR   TCaret::GetStringPtr()
    {
    return lpString;
    }

/*-------------------------------------------------------*\
|                    TCaret Class Member.                 |
\*-------------------------------------------------------*/
void    TCaret::SetAnchor (int X, int Y)
    {
    ptAnchor.x = X;
    ptAnchor.y = Y;
    }

/*-------------------------------------------------------*\
|                    TCaret Class Member.                 |
\*-------------------------------------------------------*/
void    TCaret::SetCharPosition (int iChar)
    {
    DWORD   dwSize;
    HFONT   hFontOld;
    int     xWidth;

    iCharPos = iChar;

    // Calculate width of character string.
```

```
        hFontOld = SelectFont (hdcInfo, hFont);
        dwSize = GetTextExtent (hdcInfo, lpString, iCharPos);
        xWidth = LOWORD(dwSize);
        SelectFont (hdcInfo, hFontOld);

        // Update Caret position information.
        ptPixelPos.x = ptAnchor.x + xWidth;
        ptPixelPos.y = ptAnchor.y;

        // If Caret is active, update location.
        if (iFlag & CARET_ACTIVE)
           {
           SetCaretPos (ptPixelPos.x, ptPixelPos.y);
           }
        }

/*----------------------------------------------------------------*\
|                    TCaret Class Member.                          |
\*----------------------------------------------------------------*/
void    TCaret::SetFontHandle(HANDLE hFontIn)
    {
    HFONT      hfontOld;
    TEXTMETRIC tm;

    hfontOld = SelectFont (hdcInfo, hFontIn);
    GetTextMetrics (hdcInfo, &tm);
    SelectFont (hdcInfo, hfontOld);

    hFont        = hFontIn;
    cyCaretHeight = tm.tmHeight;
    }

/*----------------------------------------------------------------*\
|                    TCaret Class Member.                          |
\*----------------------------------------------------------------*/
void    TCaret::SetState (int AFlag)
    {
    if (iFlag == AFlag)
        return;

    if (AFlag & CARET_ACTIVE)
        {
        CreateCaret (hwnd, 0, cxCaretWidth, cyCaretHeight);
        SetCaretPos (ptPixelPos.x, ptPixelPos.y);
        ShowCaret (hwnd);
        }

    if (AFlag & CARET_INACTIVE)
        {
        DestroyCaret ();
        }

    iFlag = AFlag;
    }

/*----------------------------------------------------------------*\
|                    TCaret Class Member.                          |
\*----------------------------------------------------------------*/
void    TCaret::SetStringPtr(LPSTR lpstrIn)
    {
    lpString = lpstrIn;
    }
```

## CARET2.RC

```
snapshot icon Caret2.ico

hand cursor Caret2.cur
```

## CARET2.DEF

```
NAME CARET2

EXETYPE WINDOWS

DESCRIPTION 'Caret and Mouse Demo'

CODE MOVEABLE DISCARDABLE
DATA MOVEABLE MULTIPLE
HEAPSIZE  512
STACKSIZE 5120
```

## *System Cursors*

All of the programs that we've seen up to now have used the hand cursor that we created for the MIN program back in Chapter 2. But since CARET2 uses the mouse to point at text, we're going to take advantage of a predefined system cursor that is more suitable for working with text: the I-beam cursor. This tall, skinny cursor is well suited for working in the narrow space between text characters.

Figure 16.6 shows Windows' 11 predefined system cursors. In many ways, these cursors are like the stock objects that we encountered in our discussion of GDI programming. To use a system cursor, you need a handle to the cursor. The **LoadCursor** routine does the job for us, and is defined as follows:

```
HCURSOR LoadCursor (hInstance, lpCursorName)
```

- **hInstance** is the instance handle of the module that owns the cursor, or **NULL** for a system cursor.
- **lpCursorname** is the name of the cursor in the resource file. Or, for system cursors, it is one of the identifiers shown in Figure 16.6.

## Windows Predefined Cursors

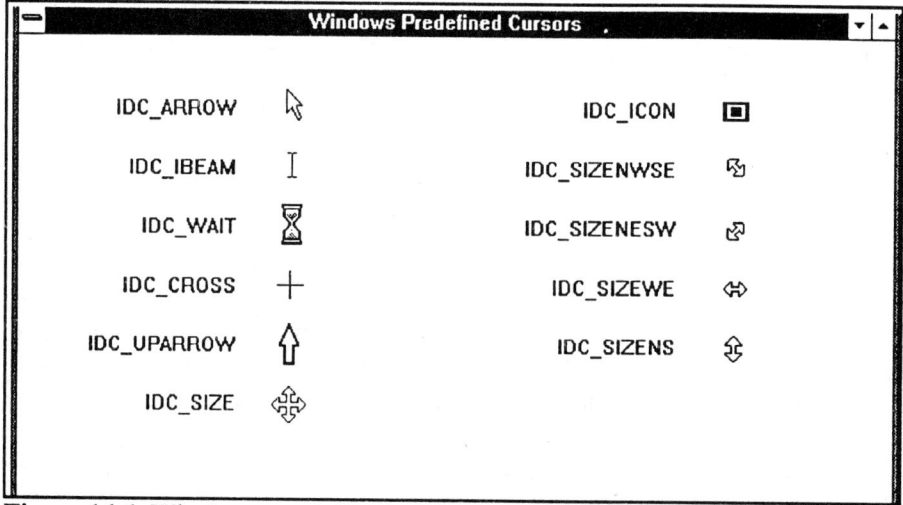

| | | | |
|---|---|---|---|
| IDC_ARROW | ▷ | IDC_ICON | ▫ |
| IDC_IBEAM | I | IDC_SIZENWSE | ⤡ |
| IDC_WAIT | ⧖ | IDC_SIZENESW | ⤢ |
| IDC_CROSS | + | IDC_SIZEWE | ↔ |
| IDC_UPARROW | ⇧ | IDC_SIZENS | ↕ |
| IDC_SIZE | ✥ | | |

**Figure 16.6** Windows predefined system cursors

The easiest way to incorporate a system cursor into a program is to make the cursor part of the class definition during program initialization. CARET2 accesses the I-beam cursor with the following line in the `GetWindowClass` member function of the window class:

```
wc.hCursor = LoadCursor (NULL, IDC_IBEAM);
```

But suppose our program was going to be busy for a moment or two and wanted to display the hourglass cursor to let the user know that an operation is going to take an extended amount of time. This is typical when saving a file or performing another lengthy operation. It's a simple matter to change the cursor for a moment using the **SetCursor** routine. **SetCursor** takes a single parameter: a cursor handle. First, of course, we need to get a handle to the hourglass cursor. Let's assume there is a static variable, or a window class data member, to hold the cursor handle for us:

```
HCURSOR hcrWait;
```

One place to retrieve a handle to a frequently used cursor would be in response to the **WM_CREATE** message:

```
void TSampleWindow::WMCreate(TMessage& Msg)
    {
    hcrWait = LoadCursor (NULL, IDC_WAIT);
    ...
    }
```

When we perform a lengthy operation, here's how to change the cursor:

## 494  *Message Driven Input*

```
{
int hcrOld;

hcrOld = SetCursor (hcrWait);
.
.
/* Lengthy operation. */
.
.
SetCursor (hcrOld);
}
```

Another way to switch cursors involves responding to the **WM_SETCURSOR** message. This is useful when we wish to use a different cursor to show the user that we're working in a different mode. For example, a drawing program might use an I beam to show that text input is expected, and a cross cursor to show that rectangle drawing is expected. Assume that we've allocated two variables to hold cursor handles:

```
HCURSOR hcrIBeam;
HCURSOR hcrCross;
```

In response to **WM_CREATE**, we retreive a handle to the two cursor handles as follows:

```
void TSampleWindow::WMCreate(TMessage& Msg)
    {
    hcrIBeam = LoadCursor (NULL, IDC_IBEAM);
    hcrICross= LoadCursor (NULL, IDC_CROSS);
    ...
    }
```

In response to the **WM_SETCURSOR** message, here is how we would set the cursor properly:

```
void TSampleWindow::WMSetCursor(TMessage& Msg)
    {
    if (Msg.LP.Lo) == HTCLIENT)
        {
        if (fType == TEXT)
            SetCursor (hcrIBeam);
        else
            SetCursor (hcrCross);
        }
    else
        DefWndProc (Msg);
    }
```

When processing the **WM_SETCURSOR** message, it is important to check the hit-test code that is passed in the low word of **LParam**. After all, we're only interested in client area mouse messages. All other messages should be passed on to the default window procedure.

Later in this chapter, we're going to investigate other alternatives for changing a program's cursor, including the creation of cursors "on the fly."

## Hit-Testing

Besides using the I-beam system cursor, the primary difference between CARET2 and CARET has to do with the way that the **WM_LBUTTONDOWN** message is handled. CARET ignores this message, and CARET2 uses it to detect where to place the mouse cursor.

Connecting mouse input to objects that are drawn on the display is called **hit-testing**. There are two Windows library routines for hit-testing: **PtInRegion** and **PtInRect**. Both routines tell you if a point lies inside a specified area. The **PtInRect** routine lets you define the area in terms of a simple rectangle, while **PtInRegion** lets the area be defined in terms of a region. As you may recall from our discussion of clipping in Chapter 10, a region is defined by a set of rectangles. Let's take a closer look at **PtInRect**, which is the routine that CARET2 used.

The **PtInRect** routine is defined as follows:

```
BOOL PtInRect (lpRect, Point)
```

- **lpRect** is a long pointer to a **RECT** data structure that contains the rectangle against which the hit-testing is performed.
- **Point** is a variable of type **POINT**. That is, it is an $x$ and a $y$ value.

The return value is TRUE if the point is inside the rectangle; otherwise it returns FALSE.

CARET2 uses the **PtInRect** routine to determine if the cursor is located within a hit rectangle. The hit rectangle is defined when the text is displayed, that is, in response to the **WM_PAINT** message. It makes sense to define the hit areas during the **WM_PAINT** message, since the coordinates of the output need to be calculated to handle the requirements of output. It's a simple matter to store these values away so that they can be useful to test mouse input.

The **PtInRect** routine is only used for preliminary hit-testing to see if the cursor is located anywhere inside an imaginary rectangle that bounds the text and extends to the left and right borders of the window. But we need to do some more work to determine exactly where the cursor is resting to properly place the caret.

Actually, since a caret should always be placed between two characters, the real issue involves figuring out the letter break that lies closest to the cursor. CARET2 has it easy, since the caret position is defined in terms of character cells by the variable **ichNext**. CARET2 calculates the hit area by looping through the array of characters, **achInput**.

The key to understanding the character hit-test loop lies with three variables: **xTotWidth**, **xPrevHalfWidth**, and **xNextHalfWidth**, visually depicted in Figure

*Message Driven Input*

16.7. Notice first of all that we're only interested in *x* values. The reason is simple: The `PtInRect` test has already determined that we're in the proper *y* range. The value of `xTotWidth` is the total width of the text, including the margin. This means that `xTotWidth` is the distance from the left border measured in client area coordinates. The `xPrevHalfWidth` variable holds a value equal to one half the width of the previous character. `xNextHalfWidth` holds a value of one half the width of the next character. As we loop through the array of characters, hit-testing becomes simple: We test whether the point is between the beginning of the previous character and the end of the next character, as shown here:

```
if ((xTotWidth - xPrevHalfWidth) <= pt.x &&
    (xTotWidth + xNextHalfWidth) > pt.x)
    {
    /* A hit! Set caret position. */
    ichNext = i;
    break;
    }
```

Once a hit is made, it's a simple matter to set the current character position variable, `ichNext`, break out of the loop, and call the `TCaret` class caret moving routine, `SetCharPosition`. Naturally, this routine calls the Windows routine, `SetCaretPos`, to do the actual work.

CARET2 has shown a number of things: the use of predefined system cursors, and one approach to take in combining mouse input with text. Of course, part of the challenge in working with the system font is the fact that it is nonproportional. Hit-testing a fixed pitch font, after all, would be quite a bit easier. But Windows gives you all the tools you need to make the hit-testing work.

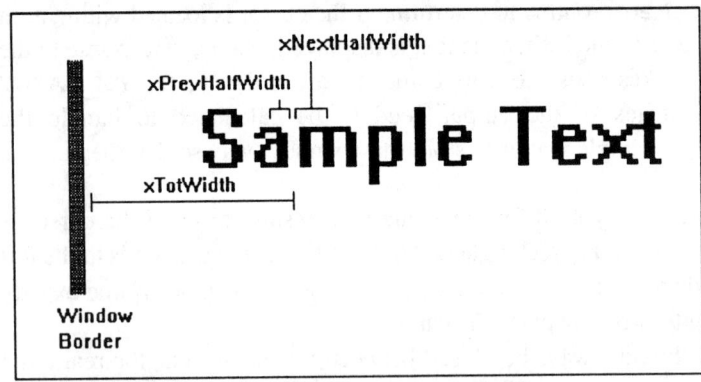

**Figure 16.7** Hit testing characters in CARET2

There is certainly room for improvement in this program. For example, it would probably be more efficient to calculate the width of each character cell ahead of time. Once stored away, much of the hit-testing and caret movement becomes simpler. Of course, this improvement has its trade-off in memory used.

Now let's look at our second sample program. This time, we've improved on the rectangle drawing program from Chapter 14.

# Dragable Objects and Stretchable Rectangles

As the mouse cursor travels across the system display, it seems to perform a little magic. It can go anywhere on the display screen, and yet it never causes any damage to any of the objects it walks over. In most cases, this magic is the result of software. A well-written device driver gives the illusion that the mouse cursor isn't part of the rest of the display. In other cases, the magic is part of the hardware. Some display adapters have a built-in ability to support cursors. Whichever approach is taken, the result is the same: The cursor never causes any damage to any objects on the display screen.

A similar effect is seen when a window is moved. If the user clicks on the caption bar of a window (or selects the *Move* item on the system menu), a dotted outline of the window lets the user see the proposed location for the window as it is moved. Thus, the user can preview the results of the move before actually committing to the move.

The same type of "floating images" can be very useful in a Windows program. Such images can be used to help the user reposition objects in a window. Since they don't damage other objects in the window, the user can arrange objects in different ways before committing to one arrangement or another.

These effects can be achieved using GDI **raster operation (ROP) codes**. We first discussed the topic of ROP codes in Chapter 13. We did not provide a programming example then, however, since ROP codes are most easily understood in the context of the mouse.

As you may recall, a raster operation is a combination of one or more Boolean operations applied between a source, which might be a pen or a brush, and a destination. Some of the raster operations ignore the source and simply change the destination. In a moment, we're going to look at a sample program, RECT2, which uses the NOT operator to produce the effect of dragable and stretchable rectangles.

A dragable rectangle can be grabbed (using the mouse) and placed in a new position. Although our demonstration program uses rectangles, the principle is the same if you wish to drag any object that is drawn using GDI's pixel, line, or filled area routines. Figure 16.8 shows an example of a rectangle being dragged in our sample program. Notice how the outline of the rectangle is always visible, no matter what color is part of the background. Also, as it is moved, it doesn't damage the other rectangles. Both of these qualities are achieved using raster operations.

498    *Message Driven Input*

(a) Click to start dragging.

(b) Dragging over other rectangles.

(c) Still dragging.

(d) Release to place rectangle.

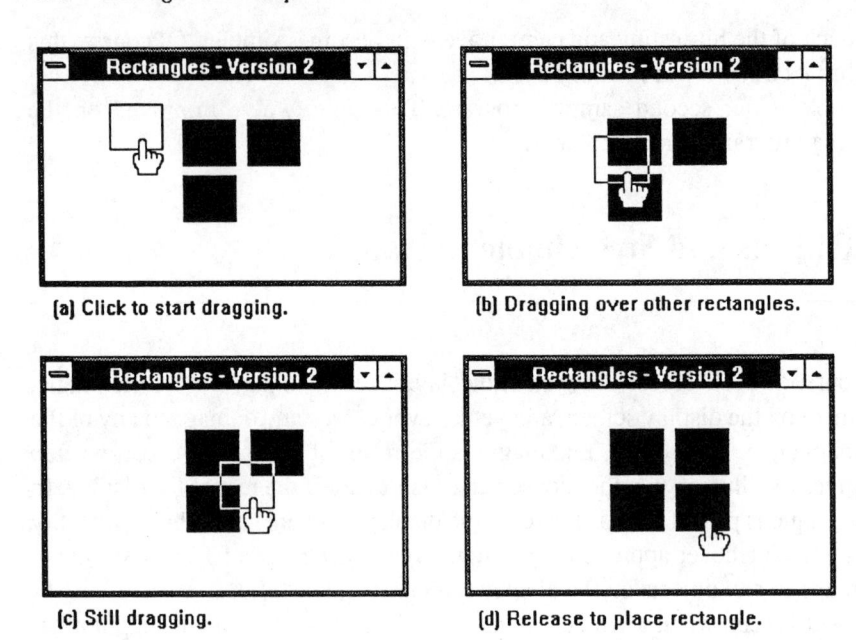

**Figure 16.8  A dragable rectangle**

A stretchable rectangle is also drawn using raster operations. A stretchable rectangle lets you preview the rectangle as it is drawn. By providing this feedback, the rectangle drawing program makes it easy to avoid unwanted effects. Figure 16.9 shows how a stretchable rectangle helps position a rectangle as it is drawn. In the (b) panel, this preview capability helps us see that we've made a mistake. But this mistake is easily corrected before we commit to our final rectangle.

Like our first rectangle drawing program, RECT2 draws rectangles in response to mouse button activity. The first corner of a rectangle is selected by pressing the mouse button. The second, opposing corner is selected by releasing the mouse button. As the mouse is dragged from the first corner to the second corner, a stretchable rectangle outline is echoed to the user to let him know where the final rectangle is to be placed. RECT2 has also been enhanced to allow the user to drag rectangles. The drag action is differentiated from a drawing operation by the use of the [Shift] key to accompany a button click.

Mouse Input 499

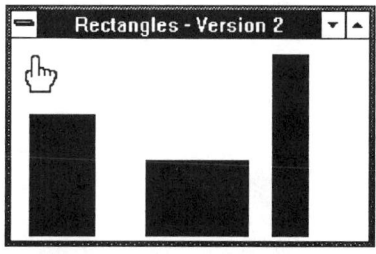

(a) Click to start.

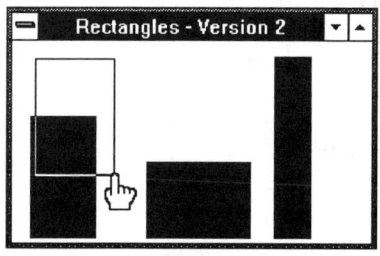

(b) Oops. Too far down.

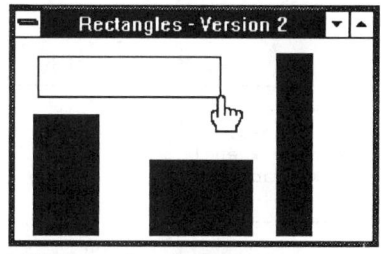

(c) That's where it should be.

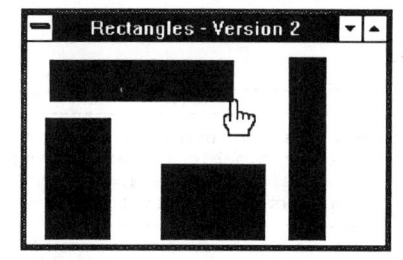

(d) Release to finish.

**Figure 16.9 A stretchable rectangle**

# MAKEFILE.MAK

```
.AUTODEPEND

#       Translator Definitions
INC=\BORLANDC\OWL\INCLUDE;\BORLANDC\CLASSLIB\INCLUDE;\BORLANDC\INCLUDE
CC = bcc -c -D_CLASSDLL -H -ml -WS -w -I$(INC)

#       Implicit Rules
.c.obj:
  $(CC) {$< }

.cpp.obj:
  $(CC) {$< }

#       Explicit Rules
Rect2.exe: Rect2.res Rect2.def Rect2.obj
    tlink /c/C/n/P-/Twe/x @Rect2.LNK
    rlink Rect2.res Rect2.exe

#       Individual File Dependencies
Rect2.obj: Rect2.cpp

Rect2.res: Rect2.rc Rect2.cur Rect2.ico
    brcc -FO Rect2.res -i$(INC) Rect2.RC
```

## RECT2.LNK

```
\borlandc\lib\c0wl.obj+
Rect2.obj
Rect2,Rect2
\borlandc\classlib\lib\tclasdll.lib+
\borlandc\owl\lib\owl.lib+
mathwl.lib+
import.lib+
crtldll.lib
Rect2.def
```

## RECT2.CPP

```
/*--------------------------------------------------------------*\
|  RECT2.CPP  - Draws rectangles in response to mouse clicks.    |
|               A stretchable rubber rectangle get echoed when   |
|               creating a rectangle.  [Shift] + Click/Drag      |
|               allows rectangles to be moved.                   |
\*--------------------------------------------------------------*/
#define WIN31
#define STRICT
#include <owl.h>
#include "Rect2.H"

/*--------------------------------------------------------------*\
|                 Main Function:  WinMain.                       |
\*--------------------------------------------------------------*/
int PASCAL WinMain (HINSTANCE hInstance,   HINSTANCE hPrevInstance,
                    LPSTR  lpszCmdLine, int    nCmdShow)
    {
    TRectApplication Rect ("RECT2", hInstance, hPrevInstance,
                           lpszCmdLine, nCmdShow);
    Rect.Run();
    return Rect.Status;
    }

/*--------------------------------------------------------------*\
|                 Application Class Member.                      |
\*--------------------------------------------------------------*/
TRectApplication::TRectApplication (LPSTR lpszName,
                 HINSTANCE hInstance, HINSTANCE hPrevInstance,
                 LPSTR lpszCmdLine, int nCmdShow)
                :TApplication (lpszName, hInstance,
                    hPrevInstance, lpszCmdLine, nCmdShow)
    {
    /*  Application specific initialization goes here.  */
    }

/*--------------------------------------------------------------*\
|                 Application Class Member.                      |
\*--------------------------------------------------------------*/
void TRectApplication::InitMainWindow ()
    {
    MainWindow = new TRectWindow (NULL, "Rectangles - Version 2",
                            NULL);
    }
```

```
/*----------------------------------------------------------*\
|                   TRectWindow Class Member.                |
\*----------------------------------------------------------*/
TRectWindow::TRectWindow (PTWindowsObject pwParent,
              LPSTR lpszTitle, PTModule pmModule)
         :TWindow (pwParent, lpszTitle, pmModule)
    {
    bCapture = FALSE;
    fDrag = FALSE;
    PRectArray = new TRectArray();
    }

/*----------------------------------------------------------*\
|                   TRectWindow Class Member.                |
\*----------------------------------------------------------*/
LPSTR TRectWindow::GetClassName ()
    {
    return "Rect2:MAIN";
    }

/*----------------------------------------------------------*\
|                   TRectWindow Class Member.                |
\*----------------------------------------------------------*/
void TRectWindow::GetWindowClass (WNDCLASS& wc)
    {
    TWindow::GetWindowClass (wc);
    wc.hIcon=LoadIcon (wc.hInstance, "snapshot");
    wc.hCursor=LoadCursor (wc.hInstance, "hand");
    wc.lpszMenuName="#1";
    }

/*----------------------------------------------------------*\
|                   TRectWindow Class Member.                |
\*----------------------------------------------------------*/
void TRectWindow::WMCommand(TMessage& Msg)
    {
    WORD wCmd;

    wCmd = COMMANDMSG(Msg);
    switch (wCmd)
        {
        case IDM_PEN_BLACK:
        case IDM_PEN_WHITE:
        case IDM_PEN_DOTTED:
            PRectArray->setpen(wCmd - IDM_PEN_BLACK);
            break;

        case IDM_BRUSH_WHITE:
        case IDM_BRUSH_GRAY:
        case IDM_BRUSH_HATCHED:
            PRectArray->setbrush(wCmd - IDM_BRUSH_WHITE);
            break;
        }
    }

/*----------------------------------------------------------*\
|                   TRectWindow Class Member.                |
\*----------------------------------------------------------*/
```

```
void TRectWindow::WMLButtonDown(TMessage& Msg)
    {
    int  x;
    int  y;

    x = MOUSEX(Msg);
    y = MOUSEY(Msg);

    if (MK_SHIFT & Msg.WParam)
        {
        iDrag = PRectArray->hittest (x, y);
        if (iDrag == -1)
            return;

        rScratch.left   = PRectArray->getX1(iDrag);
        rScratch.top    = PRectArray->getY1(iDrag);
        rScratch.right  = PRectArray->getX2(iDrag);
        rScratch.bottom = PRectArray->getY2(iDrag);

        InvalidateRect (HWindow, &rScratch, TRUE);
        UpdateWindow (HWindow);

        ptDrag.x = x;
        ptDrag.y = y;
        fDrag = TRUE;
        }
    else
        {
        rScratch.left  = rScratch.right  = x;
        rScratch.top   = rScratch.bottom = y;
        }

    PInvertRect = new TInvertRect(rScratch.left,
                                  rScratch.top,
                                  rScratch.right,
                                  rScratch.bottom);
    if (fDrag)
        {
        HDC hdc;
        hdc = GetDC (HWindow);
        PInvertRect->Invert(hdc);
        ReleaseDC (HWindow, hdc);
        }
    SetCapture (HWindow);
    bCapture = TRUE;
    }

/*----------------------------------------------------------------*\
|                     TRectWindow Class Member.                    |
\*----------------------------------------------------------------*/
void TRectWindow::WMMouseMove(TMessage& Msg)
    {
    HDC  hdc;
    int  x;
    int  y;

    if (!bCapture)
        return;

    x = MOUSEX(Msg);
    y = MOUSEY(Msg);
```

```
    if (fDrag)
        {
        ptDrag.x -= x;    // Calculate relative movement.
        ptDrag.y -= y;

        rScratch.left   -= ptDrag.x;
        rScratch.top    -= ptDrag.y;
        rScratch.right  -= ptDrag.x;
        rScratch.bottom -= ptDrag.y;

        ptDrag.x = x;    // Save draw rectangle for next time.
        ptDrag.y = y;

        }
    else
        {
        rScratch.right  = MOUSEX(Msg);
        rScratch.bottom = MOUSEY(Msg);
        }

    // Move rubber rectangle.
    hdc = GetDC (HWindow);
    PInvertRect->Move (hdc, rScratch.left, rScratch.top,
                            rScratch.right, rScratch.bottom);
    ReleaseDC (HWindow, hdc);
    }
/*----------------------------------------------------------------*\
|                    TRectWindow Class Member.                     |
\*----------------------------------------------------------------*/
void TRectWindow::WMLButtonUp(TMessage& Msg)
    {
    HDC hdc;
    int index;
    int x1, y1, x2, y2;

    if (!bCapture)
        return;

    hdc = GetDC (HWindow);
    PInvertRect->Invert(hdc);
    ReleaseDC (HWindow, hdc);

    delete PInvertRect;

    if (fDrag)
        {
        index = PRectArray->update (iDrag, rScratch.left,
                rScratch.top, rScratch.right, rScratch.bottom);
        }
    else
        {
        x1 = rScratch.left;
        y1 = rScratch.top;
        x2 = MOUSEX(Msg);
        y2 = MOUSEY(Msg);
        rScratch.left   = min (x1, x2);
        rScratch.top    = min (y1, y2);
        rScratch.right  = max (x1, x2);
        rScratch.bottom = max (y1, y2);
```

```
            index = PRectArray->append (rScratch.left, rScratch.top,
                    rScratch.right, rScratch.bottom);
            }

    if (index != -1)
        InvalidateRect (HWindow, &rScratch, FALSE);
    else
        MessageBeep(0);

    ReleaseCapture();
    bCapture = FALSE;
    fDrag = FALSE;
    iDrag = -1;
    }
/*----------------------------------------------------------------*\
|                   TRectWindow Class Member.                      |
\*----------------------------------------------------------------*/
void TRectWindow::WMPaint(TMessage& Msg)
    {
    int i;
    int cStop;
    PAINTSTRUCT ps;

    BeginPaint (Msg.Receiver, &ps);
    cStop = PRectArray->getcount();

    for (i = 0; i < cStop ; i++ )
        {
        if (i == iDrag)     // Don't draw if dragging.
            continue;

        PRectArray->draw (ps.hdc, i, FALSE);
        }

    EndPaint (Msg.Receiver, &ps);
    }

/*----------------------------------------------------------------*\
|                   TInvertRect Class Member.                      |
\*----------------------------------------------------------------*/
TInvertRect::TInvertRect(int x1, int y1, int x2, int y2)
    {
    hbrNull = GetStockBrush (NULL_BRUSH);

    rLocation.left   = x1;
    rLocation.top    = y1;
    rLocation.right  = x2;
    rLocation.bottom = y2;
    }

/*----------------------------------------------------------------*\
|                   TInvertRect Class Member.                      |
\*----------------------------------------------------------------*/
void TInvertRect::Move(HDC hdc, int x1, int y1, int x2, int y2)
{
    Invert (hdc);

    rLocation.left   = x1;
    rLocation.top    = y1;
```

```
        rLocation.right  = x2;
        rLocation.bottom = y2;

        Invert (hdc);
        }
/*---------------------------------------------------------------*\
|                      TInvertRect Class Member.                  |
\*---------------------------------------------------------------*/
void TInvertRect::Invert (HDC hdc)
    {
    HBRUSH  hbrOld;
    int     ropOld;

    hbrOld = SelectBrush (hdc, hbrNull);
    ropOld = SetROP2 (hdc, R2_NOT);

    Rectangle (hdc, rLocation.left,  rLocation.top,
                    rLocation.right, rLocation.bottom);

    SelectObject (hdc, hbrOld);
    SetROP2 (hdc, ropOld);
    }
/*---------------------------------------------------------------*\
|                      TRectArray Class Member.                   |
\*---------------------------------------------------------------*/
TRectArray::TRectArray()
    {
    hBrush[0] = GetStockBrush (WHITE_BRUSH);
    hBrush[1] = GetStockBrush (GRAY_BRUSH);
    hBrush[2] = CreateHatchBrush (HS_DIAGCROSS, RGB (255, 0, 0));
    hPen[0] = GetStockPen (BLACK_PEN);
    hPen[1] = GetStockPen (WHITE_PEN);
    hPen[2] = CreatePen (PS_DOT, 1, RGB (0, 0, 0));

    iCurrentBrush = 0;   // default brush.
    iCurrentPen = 0;     // default pen.

    cRects = 0;
    }
/*---------------------------------------------------------------*\
|                      TRectArray Class Member.                   |
\*---------------------------------------------------------------*/
TRectArray::~TRectArray()
    {
    DeleteObject (hBrush[2]);
    DeleteObject (hPen[2]);
    }
/*---------------------------------------------------------------*\
|                      TRectArray Class Member.                   |
\*---------------------------------------------------------------*/
int TRectArray::append(int x1, int y1, int x2, int y2)
    {
    if (cRects >= MAXRECTANGLES)
        return -1;

    rdValues[cRects].iBrush  = iCurrentBrush;
    rdValues[cRects].iPen    = iCurrentPen;
```

```
    rdValues[cRects].r.left   = x1;
    rdValues[cRects].r.top    = y1;
    rdValues[cRects].r.right  = x2;
    rdValues[cRects].r.bottom = y2;

    return (cRects++);
    }

/*----------------------------------------------------------------*\
|                    TRectArray Class Member.                      |
\*----------------------------------------------------------------*/
void TRectArray::draw(HDC hdc, int iRect, int fSaveDC)
    {
    HBRUSH hbrOld;
    HPEN   hpenOld;
    int    iPen;
    int    iBrush;

    iPen   = rdValues[iRect].iPen;
    iBrush = rdValues[iRect].iBrush;

    hpenOld = SelectBrush (hdc, hBrush[iBrush]);
    hbrOld  = SelectPen (hdc, hPen[iPen]);

    Rectangle (hdc, rdValues[iRect].r.left,
                    rdValues[iRect].r.top,
                    rdValues[iRect].r.right,
                    rdValues[iRect].r.bottom);

    if (fSaveDC)
        {
        SelectPen (hdc, hpenOld);
        SelectBrush (hdc, hbrOld);
        }
    }

/*----------------------------------------------------------------*\
|                    TRectArray Class Member.                      |
\*----------------------------------------------------------------*/
int TRectArray::getcount()
    { return cRects; }

/*----------------------------------------------------------------*\
|                    TRectArray Class Member.                      |
\*----------------------------------------------------------------*/
int TRectArray::getX1(int index)
    { return rdValues[index].r.left; }

/*----------------------------------------------------------------*\
|                    TRectArray Class Member.                      |
\*----------------------------------------------------------------*/
int TRectArray::getY1(int index)
    { return rdValues[index].r.top; }

/*----------------------------------------------------------------*\
|                    TRectArray Class Member.                      |
\*----------------------------------------------------------------*/
int TRectArray::getX2(int index)
    { return rdValues[index].r.right; }
```

```
/*----------------------------------------------------------------*\
|                    TRectArray Class Member.                      |
\*----------------------------------------------------------------*/
int TRectArray::getY2(int index)
    { return rdValues[index].r.bottom; }

/*----------------------------------------------------------------*\
|                    TRectArray Class Member.                      |
\*----------------------------------------------------------------*/
int TRectArray::hittest(int x, int y)
    {
    int i;
    POINT ptHit;

    ptHit.x = x;
    ptHit.y = y;

    for (i=cRects-1; i>=0; i--)
        {
        if (PtInRect ((LPRECT)&rdValues[i].r, ptHit) )
            return i;
        }
    return -1;
    }

/*----------------------------------------------------------------*\
|                    TRectArray Class Member.                      |
\*----------------------------------------------------------------*/
void TRectArray::setbrush(int index)   { iCurrentBrush = index; }

/*----------------------------------------------------------------*\
|                    TRectArray Class Member.                      |
\*----------------------------------------------------------------*/
void TRectArray::setpen(int index) { iCurrentPen = index; }

/*----------------------------------------------------------------*\
|                    TRectArray Class Member.                      |
\*----------------------------------------------------------------*/
int TRectArray::update(int index, int x1, int y1, int x2, int y2)
    {
    if (index > cRects)
        {
        index = -1;
        }
    else
        {
        rdValues[index].r.left   = x1;
        rdValues[index].r.top    = y1;
        rdValues[index].r.right  = x2;
        rdValues[index].r.bottom = y2;
        }

    return index;
    }
```

## 508   *Message Driven Input*
# RECT2.H

```
/*--------------------------------------------------------------*\
|                   Include file for Rect2.H.                    |
\*--------------------------------------------------------------*/

#define IDM_PEN_BLACK      100
#define IDM_PEN_WHITE      101
#define IDM_PEN_DOTTED     102

#define IDM_BRUSH_WHITE    200
#define IDM_BRUSH_GRAY     201
#define IDM_BRUSH_HATCHED  202

/*--------------------------------------------------------------*\
|                          Macros.                               |
\*--------------------------------------------------------------*/
#define MOUSEX(arg)   (arg.LP.Lo)
#define MOUSEY(arg)   (arg.LP.Hi)
#define COMMANDMSG(arg) (arg.WParam)
#define max(a,b)      (((a) > (b)) ? (a) : (b))
#define min(a,b)      (((a) < (b)) ? (a) : (b))

/*--------------------------------------------------------------*\
|                         Constants.                             |
\*--------------------------------------------------------------*/
const int MAXRECTANGLES = 50;
const int MARKERSIZE    =  3;
const int BRUSHCOUNT    =  3;
const int PENCOUNT      =  3;

/*--------------------------------------------------------------*\
|                     Class Declarations.                        |
\*--------------------------------------------------------------*/
class TRectApplication : public TApplication
   {
   public:
      TRectApplication (LPSTR lpszName, HINSTANCE hInstance,
                        HINSTANCE hPrevInstance, LPSTR lpszCmdLine,
                        int nCmdShow);
      virtual void  InitMainWindow();
   };

class TInvertRect
   {
   public:
      TInvertRect (int x1, int y1, int x2, int y2);
      virtual void Move(HDC hdc, int x1, int y1, int x2, int y2);
      virtual void Invert (HDC hdc);

   private:
HANDLE hbrNull;
      RECT    rLocation;
   };

typedef struct tagRECTDATA
   {
   int    iBrush;
   int    iPen;
   RECT   r;
   } RECTDATA;
```

```
class TRectArray
  {
  public:
    TRectArray();
    ~TRectArray();

    int   append(int x1, int y1, int x2, int y2);
    void  draw(HDC hdc, int index, int fSaveDC);
    int   getcount();
    int   getX1(int index);
    int   getY1(int index);
    int   getX2(int index);
    int   getY2(int index);
    int   hittest(int x, int y);
    void  setbrush(int index);
    void  setpen(int index);
    int   update(int index, int x1, int y1, int x2, int y2);
  private:
    HBRUSH    hBrush[BRUSHCOUNT];
    int       iCurrentBrush;
    HPEN      hPen[PENCOUNT];
    int       iCurrentPen;
    RECTDATA  rdValues[MAXRECTANGLES];
    int       cRects;
  };

class TRectWindow : public TWindow
  {
  public:
    TInvertRect * PInvertRect;
    TRectArray  * PRectArray;

    TRectWindow (PTWindowsObject pwParent, LPSTR lpszTitle,
                 PTModule pmModule);
    virtual LPSTR GetClassName();
    virtual void  GetWindowClass(WNDCLASS&);
    virtual void  WMCommand(TMessage& Msg) = [WM_COMMAND];
    virtual void  WMLButtonDown(TMessage& Msg) = [WM_LBUTTONDOWN];
    virtual void  WMLButtonUp(TMessage& Msg) = [WM_LBUTTONUP];
    virtual void  WMMouseMove(TMessage& Msg) = [WM_MOUSEMOVE];
    virtual void  WMPaint(TMessage& Msg) = [WM_PAINT];
  private:
    BOOL   bCapture;
    BOOL   fDrag;
    POINT  ptDrag;
    RECT   rScratch;
    int    iDrag;
    int    iMove;
  };
```

# RECT2.RC

```
#include "Rect2.H"

snapshot icon Rect2.ico

hand cursor Rect2.cur

1 MENU
```

```
    {
    POPUP "&Pen"
        {
        MENUITEM "&Black",    IDM_PEN_BLACK
        MENUITEM "&White",    IDM_PEN_WHITE
        MENUITEM "&Dotted",   IDM_PEN_DOTTED
        }
    POPUP "&Brush"
        {
        MENUITEM "&White",    IDM_BRUSH_WHITE
        MENUITEM "&Gray",     IDM_BRUSH_GRAY
        MENUITEM "&Hatched",  IDM_BRUSH_HATCHED
        }
    }
```

## RECT2.DEF

```
NAME RECT2

EXETYPE WINDOWS

DESCRIPTION 'Rectangles/Mouse Demo'

CODE MOVEABLE DISCARDABLE
DATA MOVEABLE MULTIPLE

HEAPSIZE   512
STACKSIZE  5120
```

## *Dragging and Stretching*

Any program that does any dragging or stretching will be interested in three mouse messages: button down, mouse move, and button up. In response to the button down message, the window procedure does whatever initialization it needs to do to make the dragging or stretching work. The mouse move message means the mouse cursor has moved, and that the dragged or stretched object needs to be modified to reflect that movement. The simplest way to handle this is to erase the image of the object at the old location and create a copy of the object at the new location. The button up message means that no more movement is required, so dragging or stretching can be turned off and the object made permanent.

While movement is going on, the raster operations provide a convenient manner to quickly draw and erase the moveable/stretchable rectangles. The particular raster operation that we use is the one associated with the NOT operation, **R2_NOT**. A nice feature of this raster operation is that it virtually guarantees that the object you draw will appear. Every white pixel encountered will turn black, and every black pixel encountered will turn white. Pixels that have colors other than black and white will be changed to the logical inverse color. You'll find that this produces some slightly unexpected results—like the fact that **R2_NOT** of blue on a 16-color VGA adapter gives yellow (instead of orange). This is a limitation of the hardware, and a compromise to allow a reasonable set of colors to be available on this device.

In spite of this odd behavior with color, the second—and most important—advantage of the **R2_NOT** raster operation is that everything is easily reversible. Let's look at the two-color monochrome case to convince ourselves that this is true. The *first* time a figure (say a rectangle) is drawn, every white pixel turns black and every black pixel turns white. The *second* time the same figure is drawn, every white pixel turns black and every black pixel turns white. But after the figure is drawn the second time, the figure itself disappears. Put together, the two advantages of the **R2_NOT** raster operation are ideal for drawing dragable and stretchable rectangles.

In RECT2, the work of creating and maintaining the **R2_NOT** rectangles is done by the **TInvertRect** class object. In particular, the **Invert** member function selects the stock null brush into the DC, so it only draws the rectangle outline. It sets the raster operation to **R2_NOT** by calling the **SetROP2** routine, then draws a rectangle. The routine itself doesn't know (or care) whether it is drawing the first rectangle—to make one appear—or the second rectangle—to make it disappear.

A second issue that is raised by the RECT2 program is that of the mouse capture, which we're going to discuss next.

## *The Mouse Capture*

Mouse messages are always sent to the window lying under the mouse cursor. In this way, the user is free to move the cursor to the desired program and start it running with a mouse click. But there are times when it makes sense to restrict all mouse messages to one window. In particular, it is useful when some operation has started that must be completed in order to leave the program in a stable, known state. Rectangle dragging and stretching are two such times.

In RECT2, when the **WM_LBUTTONDOWN** message is received, the program gets set up to draw a new rectangle or to move an existing rectangle. The program expects to receive another message—a **WM_LBUTTONUP**—before things are returned to "normal." If a second **WM_LBUTTONDOWN** message is received before a **WM_LBUTTONUP** message, it will cause some confusion in the program and a mess in the window.

To make sure that our window gets the expected sequence of messages, the window procedure **captures** the mouse. This is done by calling **SetCapture**, which takes a single parameter: a window handle. **SetCapture** is called in response to **WM_LBUTTONDOWN**, to reserve all mouse messages for our window until the capture is released.

512   *Message Driven Input*

Releasing the capture is done by making a call to `ReleaseCapture`. RECT2 calls `ReleaseCapture` in response to a `WM_LBUTTONUP`, to allow other programs to receive mouse messages.

In Chapter 7, we introduced the Windows sandwich. The idea is that the use of a system resource is sandwiched between two calls: The first call obtains the resource and the second call releases the resource. This is certainly an accurate description of the way the mouse capture is handled. In culinary terms:

| *The Windows Sandwich* | *Applied to Mouse Capture* |
|---|---|
| Top slice of bread | `SetCapture()` called at `WM_LBUTTONDOWN` time. |
| Filling | Mouse events during `WM_MOUSEMOVE`. |
| Bottom slice of bread | `ReleaseCapture()` called at `WM_LBUTTONUP` time. |

The final point to be made about the mouse capture is that the hit-testing and cursor setting messages are disabled when the mouse is captured. That is, you will not encounter the `WM_NCHITTEST` or `WM_SETCURSOR` messages when the mouse is captured. The hit-testing message, `WM_NCHITTEST`, after all, tests whether a client area or nonclient area message should be sent, and only client area messages are sent when the mouse is captured. And the `WM_SETCURSOR` is not sent since Windows doesn't expect the cursor to change when one window has reserved all mouse input for itself.

At this point, we're going to turn our attention to the third sample program of this chapter. It creates a mouse cursor on the fly, which is a capability that is new with Windows 3.0.

# Creating Dynamic Cursors

In Chapter 2, when we introduced the minimum Windows program, we created a custom cursor in the shape of a hand. As you may recall, we used two tools: the Paintbrush program, which drew the basic outline of a hand, and the Resource Workshop, which we used to fine-tune the bits in the cursor. Once the cursor was created, it was saved to a file, MIN.CUR, which was referenced in the resource file for our minimum Windows program, MIN.RC.

While a static custom cursor like this will serve most of your needs, there may be times when you need to create a dynamic cursor. A dynamic cursor is one that is created by a Windows program at execution time, instead of during program development time. One way to create a dynamic cursor is to create a GDI bitmap and then use GDI routines to draw the desired shape. This is the approach we will take. This simple description hides the fact that quite a bit of shuffling is required to create a custom cursor.

## The DYNACURS Program

Our dynamic cursor program echoes the current mouse location. Figure 16.10 shows a sample of its output. The "hot-spot" of the cursor is in the cursor's upper-left corner, marked by a dot. The top number is the *x* location of the cursor, and the bottom number is the *y* location.

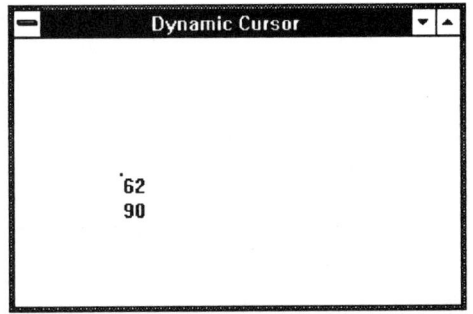

**Figure 16.10 The cursor in DYNACURS echoes the mouse location**

One of the first things you notice when you run this program is the way the cursor seems to blink a lot. That is, as the mouse moves and the cursor changes, the dynamic cursor doesn't have the smooth quality that we associate with a normal cursor. The reason has to do with the fact that the background—the area "behind" the cursor—must be restored every time the cursor changes. While this would be a very annoying feature in a commercially released Windows product, it's only a minor flaw in a program that demonstrates the creation of dynamic cursors.

## MAKEFILE.MAK

```
.AUTODEPEND

#    Translator Definitions
INC=\BORLANDC\OWL\INCLUDE;\BORLANDC\CLASSLIB\INCLUDE;\BORLANDC\INCLUDE
CC = bcc -c -D_CLASSDLL -H -ml -WS -w -I$(INC)

#    Implicit Rules
.c.obj:
  $(CC) {$< }

.cpp.obj:
  $(CC) {$< }

#    Explicit Rules
DynaCurs.exe: DynaCurs.res DynaCurs.def DynaCurs.obj
    tlink /c/C/n/P-/Twe/x @DynaCurs.LNK
    rlink DynaCurs.res DynaCurs.exe
```

```
#       Individual File Dependencies
DynaCurs.obj: DynaCurs.cpp

DynaCurs.res: DynaCurs.rc DynaCurs.cur DynaCurs.ico
    RC -R -FO DynaCurs.res -i$(INC) DynaCurs.RC
```

# DYNACURS.LNK

```
\borlandc\lib\c0wl.obj+
DynaCurs.obj
DynaCurs,DynaCurs
\borlandc\classlib\lib\tclasdll.lib+
\borlandc\owl\lib\owl.lib+
mathwl.lib+
import.lib+
crtldll.lib
DynaCurs.def
```

# DYNACURS.CPP

```
/*--------------------------------------------------------------*\
|  DYNACURS.CPP  - Creates a dynamic cursor on the fly.          |
\*--------------------------------------------------------------*/
#include <owl.h>

/*--------------------------------------------------------------*\
|                    Class Declarations.                         |
\*--------------------------------------------------------------*/
class TDynaCursApplication : public TApplication
   {
   public:
     TDynaCursApplication (LPSTR lpszName, HINSTANCE hInstance,
                           HINSTANCE hPrevInstance,
                           LPSTR lpszCmdLine, int nCmdShow);
     virtual void InitMainWindow ();
   };

class TDynaCursWindow : public TWindow
   {
   public:
     TDynaCursWindow (PTWindowsObject pwParent, LPSTR lpszTitle,
                      PTModule pmModule);
     virtual LPSTR  GetClassName ();
     virtual void   GetWindowClass (WNDCLASS&);
     virtual BOOL   Create();
     virtual void   Destroy();
     virtual void   WMSetCursor(TMessage& Msg) = [WM_SETCURSOR];

   private:
     HCURSOR hcrPrev;
     HBITMAP hbm;
     HBITMAP hbmOld;
     HBRUSH  hbrWhite;
     HBRUSH  hbrBlack;
     HDC     hdcBitmap;
     HGLOBAL hmemAND;
```

```
      HGLOBAL   hmemXOR;
      LPSTR     lpAND;
      LPSTR     lpXOR;
      int       cbSize;
      int       cxCursor;
      int       cyCursor;
   };
/*-----------------------------------------------------------------*\
|                   Main Function:  WinMain.                        |
\*-----------------------------------------------------------------*/
int PASCAL WinMain (HINSTANCE hInstance,   HINSTANCE hPrevInstance,
                    LPSTR lpszCmdLine, int    nCmdShow)
    {
    TDynaCursApplication DynaCurs ("DynaCurs", hInstance,
                       hPrevInstance, lpszCmdLine, nCmdShow);
    DynaCurs.Run();
    return DynaCurs.Status;
    }
/*-----------------------------------------------------------------*\
|                   Application Class Member.                       |
\*-----------------------------------------------------------------*/
TDynaCursApplication::TDynaCursApplication (LPSTR lpszName,
                    HINSTANCE hInstance, HINSTANCE hPrevInstance,
                    LPSTR lpszCmdLine, int nCmdShow)
                   :TApplication (lpszName, hInstance,
                         hPrevInstance, lpszCmdLine, nCmdShow)
    {
    /* Application specific initialization goes here. */
    }
/*-----------------------------------------------------------------*\
|                   Application Class Member.                       |
\*-----------------------------------------------------------------*/
void TDynaCursApplication::InitMainWindow ()
    {
    MainWindow = new TDynaCursWindow (NULL, "Dynamic Cursor",
                                       NULL);
    }
/*-----------------------------------------------------------------*\
|                   TDynaCursWindow Class Member.                   |
\*-----------------------------------------------------------------*/
TDynaCursWindow::TDynaCursWindow (PTWindowsObject pwParent,
                    LPSTR lpszTitle, PTModule pmModule)
                  :TWindow (pwParent, lpszTitle, pmModule)
    {
    hcrPrev = 0;
    }
/*-----------------------------------------------------------------*\
|                   TDynaCursWindow Class Member.                   |
\*-----------------------------------------------------------------*/
LPSTR TDynaCursWindow::GetClassName ()
    {
return "DynaCurs:MAIN";
    }
/*-----------------------------------------------------------------*\
|                   TDynaCursWindow Class Member.                   |
\*-----------------------------------------------------------------*/
```

```
void TDynaCursWindow::GetWindowClass (WNDCLASS& wc)
    {
    TWindow::GetWindowClass (wc);
    wc.hIcon=LoadIcon (wc.hInstance, "snapshot");
    wc.hCursor=LoadCursor (wc.hInstance, "hand");
    }

/*----------------------------------------------------------------*\
|                   TDynaCursWindow Class Member.                  |
\*----------------------------------------------------------------*/
BOOL TDynaCursWindow::Create()
    {
    BOOL bRetVal;
    HDC  hdc;

    bRetVal = TWindow::Create();

    if (bRetVal)
        {
        /* Find out expected size of cursor. */
        cxCursor = GetSystemMetrics (SM_CXCURSOR);
        cyCursor = GetSystemMetrics (SM_CYCURSOR);

        /* Create some scratch objects: */

              /* A bitmap. */
        hbm = CreateBitmap (cxCursor,  // width
                            cyCursor,  // height
                            1,         // planes
                            1,         // bits per pixel
                            NULL);     // initial data

              /* A DC for the bitmap. */
        hdc = GetDC (HWindow);
        hdcBitmap = CreateCompatibleDC (hdc);
        ReleaseDC (HWindow, hdc);

              /* Connect the bitmap to the DC. */
        hbmOld = SelectBitmap (hdcBitmap, hbm);

              /* Some memory scratch space. */
        cbSize = (cxCursor/8) * cyCursor;
        hmemAND = GlobalAlloc (GMEM_MOVEABLE,   // flags
                               (DWORD)cbSize); // size

        lpAND = (LPSTR) GlobalLock (hmemAND);
        if (lpAND == NULL)
            {
            bRetVal = FALSE;
            goto Exit;
            }

        hmemXOR = GlobalAlloc (GMEM_MOVEABLE,   // flags
                               (DWORD)cbSize); // size

        lpXOR = (LPSTR) GlobalLock (hmemXOR);
        if (lpXOR == NULL)
            {
            bRetVal = FALSE;
            goto Exit;
            }
```

```
            /* Get GDI objects to use. */
            hbrWhite = GetStockBrush (WHITE_BRUSH);
            hbrBlack = GetStockBrush (BLACK_BRUSH);

            /* Error checking. */
            if (hbm == NULL       || hdcBitmap == NULL ||
                hmemAND == NULL   || hmemXOR == NULL   ||
                cxCursor%8 != NULL)
                {
                MessageBox (HWindow, "Unable to Initialize",
                            "Dynamic Cursor", MB_OK);
                bRetVal = FALSE;
                }
            }
Exit:
    return bRetVal;
    }

/*----------------------------------------------------------------*\
|               TDynaCursWindow Class Member.                      |
\*----------------------------------------------------------------*/
void TDynaCursWindow::Destroy()
    {
    SelectBitmap (hdcBitmap, hbmOld);
    DeleteDC (hdcBitmap);
    DeleteBitmap (hbm);
    DestroyCursor(hcrPrev);

    GlobalUnlock (hmemAND);
    GlobalUnlock (hmemXOR);
    GlobalFree (hmemAND);
    GlobalFree (hmemXOR);
    }

/*----------------------------------------------------------------*\
|               TDynaCursWindow Class Member.                      |
\*----------------------------------------------------------------*/
void TDynaCursWindow::WMSetCursor(TMessage& Msg)
    {
    char    acLine1[8];
    char    acLine2[8];
    HCURSOR hcrTemp;
    int     cc1;
    int     cc2;
    POINT   pt;

    /* Ignore all nonclient area messages. */
    if (Msg.LP.Lo != HTCLIENT)
        {
        DefWndProc(Msg);
        return;
        }

    /* Set up AND Mask. */
    SelectBrush (hdcBitmap, hbrWhite);
    PatBlt (hdcBitmap, 0, 0, cxCursor, cyCursor,
            PATCOPY);

    /* Light up the hot-spot. */
    SetPixel (hdcBitmap, 0, 0, 0L);
    SetPixel (hdcBitmap, 0, 1, 0L);
```

```
        SetPixel (hdcBitmap, 1, 0, 0L);
        SetPixel (hdcBitmap, 1, 1, 0L);

        /*  Where is the mouse cursor?  */
        GetCursorPos (&pt);
        ScreenToClient (HWindow, &pt);

        cc1 = wsprintf (acLine1,"%d", pt.x);
        cc2 = wsprintf (acLine2,"%d", pt.y);

        /*  Write coordinates onto bitmap.  */
        TextOut (hdcBitmap, 3, 0, acLine1, cc1);
        TextOut (hdcBitmap, 3, cyCursor/2, acLine2, cc2);

        GetBitmapBits (hbm, (DWORD)cbSize, lpAND);

        /*  Set up XOR Mask.  */
        SelectBrush (hdcBitmap, hbrBlack);
        PatBlt (hdcBitmap, 0, 0, cxCursor, cyCursor,
                PATCOPY);

        GetBitmapBits (hbm, (DWORD)cbSize, lpXOR);

        /*  Spin a cursor on the fly.  */
        hcrTemp = CreateCursor (
            GetApplication()->hInstance,  // Instance handle
            0,              // X-hotspot
            0,              // Y-hotspot
            cxCursor,       // width
            cyCursor,       // height
            lpAND,          // AND bitmask
            lpXOR);         // XOR bitmask

        SetCursor (hcrTemp);    // Select new cursor.

        /*  Remove old cursor.  */
        if (hcrPrev != NULL) DestroyCursor(hcrPrev);

        hcrPrev = hcrTemp;
        }
```

# DYNACURS.RC

```
snapshot icon DynaCurs.ico

hand cursor DynaCurs.cur
```

# DYNACURS.DEF

```
NAME DYNACURS

EXETYPE WINDOWS

DESCRIPTION 'A dynamic cursor'

CODE MOVEABLE DISCARDABLE
```

```
DATA MOVEABLE MULTIPLE

HEAPSIZE  512
STACKSIZE 5120
```

DYNACURS is interested in three messages: **WM_CREATE**, **WM_DESTROY**, and **WM_SETCURSOR**. In response to the **WM_CREATE** message, several objects are created and initialized that will be needed to support the cursor creation. This includes a monochrome memory bitmap, a device context to connect to the bitmap, and some dynamically allocated memory. The **WM_SETCURSOR** message triggers the dynamic cursor creation, which involves determining the mouse cursor location, calling GDI routines to write this location to the memory bitmaps, and then calling the **CreateCursor** routine to convert this data into a full-fledged cursor. In response to the third message, **WM_DESTROY**, DYNACURS cleans up and deallocates the objects that were created in response to the **WM_CREATE** message. To understand why these objects are needed, it will help to explore the insides of a cursor, so that you'll know what makes it tick.

## How Cursors Work

A cursor is a data object that consists of two parts. Each part is a monochrome bitmap that is combined with the pixels of the display surface to create the cursor image. The first part is called the AND mask, to reflect the fact that the pixels of this bitmap are combined with the surface using the logical AND operation. The second part of the cursor is called the XOR mask, which again reflects the fact that a logical operation, XOR, is used to combine this bitmap with the display surface.

When the display driver draws a cursor, it starts by making a copy of the pixels that are already on the display surface. This ensures that the old image can be restored, and is key in maintaining the integrity of the image on the display surface. Once the copy has been made, the AND mask is applied to the surface, followed by the XOR mask. Through the magic of Boolean operations, this two-step process allows four different effects: black, white, display, and not-display. By "display," we mean that the cursor is transparent and allows the background to show through. By "not-display," we mean the pixels on the background are inverted. This is a rarely used combination, but it can provide some interesting effects. For example, the not-display effect might be used on a cursor in the shape of a magnifying glass to help suggest the fuzzy distortion of the lens surface. Table 16.2 has a truth table that shows how pixels of the AND mask and XOR mask combine to create the four effects.

**Table 16.2**

| AND Mask | XOR Mask | Cursor |
| --- | --- | --- |
| 0 (Black) | 0 (Black) | Black |
| 0 (Black) | 1 (White) | White |
| 1 (White) | 0 (Black) | Display |
| 1 (White) | 1 (White) | Not-display |

To create an all-black cursor, you need to set both masks to black. An all-white cursor would result from an all-black AND mask and an all-white XOR mask. DYNACURS creates black text on a transparent (display colored) background by combining an AND mask of black text on a white background with an all-black XOR mask.

The routine that creates a dynamic cursor is `CreateCursor`, defined as

```
CreateCursor (hInstance, xHotSpot, yHotSpot, nWidth,
              hHeight, lpANDbitPlane, lpXORbitPlane);
```

- `hInstance` is the instance handle that was passed to our program as a parameter to `WinMain`. We retrieve the application object's copy of this value by saying

    `GetApplication()->hInstance`

- `xHotSpot` is the *x* coordinate for the cursor hot-spot.
- `yHotSpot` is the *y* coordinate for the cursor hot-spot.
- `nWidth` is the width in pixels of the cursor. If the size we provide doesn't match the size desired by the display driver, our cursor will be stretched (or shrunk). To make sure we have a match, we ask Windows to provide the size that the display driver expects. The following call provides the correct width value:

    `GetSystemMetrics (SM_CXCURSOR);`

- `nHeight` is the height in pixels of the cursor. We set this value to match the size desired by the display driver by calling the following routine:

    `GetSystemMetrics (SM_CYCURSOR);`

- `lpANDbitPlane` is an `LPSTR (char far *)` pointer to the bits that make up the AND mask.
- `lpXORbitPlane` is an `LPSTR (char far *)` pointer to the bits that make up the XOR mask.

Here is the call that DYNACURS makes to create the dynamic cursor:

```
hcr = CreateCursor (
         GetApplication()->hInstance,  // Instance handle
         0,              // X-hotspot
         0,              // Y-hotspot
         cxCursor,       // width
         cyCursor,       // height
         lpAND,          // AND bitmask
         lpXOR);         // XOR bitmask
```

Most of the work that we need to do to create a custom cursor involves creating the two bit masks. Understanding what DYNACURS does to get these two bit masks requires an understanding of two topics, GDI bitmaps and dynamic memory allocation. Since these two topics will be the subject of later chapters, we're going to limit our discussion to a brief introduction.

## *Creating a GDI Bitmap*

In our introduction to GDI in Chapter 6, we described a bitmap as a type of pseudodevice that is used primarily to store pictures. If you think of a bitmap as nothing more than a type of device, you will be half way to understanding how to use them. The other half involves understanding how to get a handle to a DC that will allow you to write on a bitmap. The following calls accomplish that:

```
/*   Create some scratch objects:   */

      /*   A bitmap.  */
hbm = CreateBitmap (cxCursor,    // width
                    cyCursor,    // height
                    1,           // planes
                    1,           // bits per pixel
                    NULL);       // initial data

      /*   A DC for the bitmap.  */
hdc = GetDC (hwnd);
hdcBitmap = CreateCompatibleDC (hdc);
ReleaseDC (hwnd, hdc);

      /*  Connect the bitmap to the DC.  */
hbmOld = SelectBitmap (hdcBitmap, hbm);
```

The first routine, **CreateBitmap**, asks GDI to allocate the memory that will be used to store the bits of our bitmap. The width and height values, cxCursor and cyCursor, come from Windows itself, which tells us, via the **GetSystemMetrics** routine, the size of the cursor that the current display driver expects to use:

```
/* Find out expected size of cursor. */
cxCursor = GetSystemMetrics (SM_CXCURSOR);
cyCursor = GetSystemMetrics (SM_CYCURSOR);
```

To build a cursor, we need a monochrome bitmap, which is the reason we set the number of planes to 1 and the bits per pixel to 1. The **CreateBitmap** routine returns a handle to a bitmap, of the type **HBITMAP**, which we store in the variable **hbm**.

By itself, a bitmap is just a block of memory. We need to create a connection to the memory, and also a set of drawing tools that will allow us to send output to the bitmap just like we send output to the display device. We need a device context. The simplest way to create a DC is to ask GDI to make a copy of an existing DC for us. This is accomplished with the following calls:

```
hdc = GetDC (hwnd);
hdcBitmap = CreateCompatibleDC (hdc);
ReleaseDC (hwnd, hdc);
```

We borrow and return a DC with a **GetDC/ReleaseDC** pair, and create a new DC with the call to **CreateCompatibleDC**. The value returned by **CreateCompatibleDC** is a handle to a DC. But by itself, it has no connection to our bitmap (or any device, for that matter), so we need to create a connection. We do this by calling **SelectBitmap**, which is a macro around the SelectObject function.

```
hbmOld = SelectBitmap (hdcBitmap, hbm);
```

As you may recall, we use the **SelectObject** routine to install pens, brushes, and other drawing objects into a DC. But the bitmap is more than just a drawing object—it is a full-fledged drawing surface. Or, as we have said earlier, a *pseudodevice*. Once the bitmap and DC are connected, we draw to the bitmap by calling any GDI drawing routine and providing the DC handle as a parameter. When the bitmap is connected to the DC that **SelectObject** provides, we save the value returned by **SelectObject** so that we can later disconnect the bitmap from the DC. At cleanup time, this will make it easy to destroy both objects.

At this point, we've seen how to create a bitmap. Let's look at how DYNACURS uses the bitmap.

## Using the GDI Bitmap

When DYNACURS receives a **WM_SETCURSOR** message, it draws into our bitmap to create the desired pixel patterns for the AND and XOR bit masks. The bits are then copied from the bitmap into two dynamically allocated pieces of memory, since **CreateCursor** does not read a bitmap directly but instead reads the bit masks as blocks of memory. These bit masks are passed to `CreateCursor` via the two pointers that make up `CreateCursor`'s last two parameters.

The first bit mask that gets set up is the AND mask. First, we set all the bits to white, using a routine called `PatBlt`. This GDI routine fills a rectangular area on a drawing surface using the currently selected brush. Here is the code that does this for us:

```
SelectBrush (hdcBitmap, hbrWhite);
PatBlt (hdcBitmap, 0, 0, cxCursor, cyCursor,
        PATCOPY);
```

Drawing the four-pixel-square hot-spot involves four calls to `SetPixel`:

```
SetPixel (hdcBitmap, 0, 0, 0L);
SetPixel (hdcBitmap, 0, 1, 0L);
SetPixel (hdcBitmap, 1, 0, 0L);
SetPixel (hdcBitmap, 1, 1, 0L);
```

DYNACURS then makes a call to `GetCursorPos`, which finds out the location of the mouse cursor in **screen coordinates**. Like client area coordinates, screen coordinates are pixel units. But they differ from client area coordinates in that the origin (0,0) is at the upper-left corner of the entire screen instead of the upper-left corner of the client area. To convert from one to the other, a call is made to `ScreenToClient`. Then, the coordinates are converted from integer values to a character string, and the two lines are written onto the bitmap:

```
GetCursorPos (&pt);
ScreenToClient (hwnd, &pt);

cc1 = wsprintf (acLine1,"%d", pt.x);
cc2 = wsprintf (acLine2,"%d", pt.y);

/* Write coordinates onto bitmap. */
TextOut (hdcBitmap, 3, 0, acLine1, cc1);
TextOut (hdcBitmap, 3, cyCursor/2, acLine2, cc2);
```

At this point, the bitmap contains the image that we want to use for the AND mask on the cursor. But we have to ask GDI to make a copy of the bits in a form that `CreateCursor` will accept. This is the job of the `GetBitmapBits` routine. `GetBitmapBits` is defined as follows:

```
DWORD GetBitmapBits (hBitmap, dwCount, lpBits)
```

- **hBitmap** is a handle to a bitmap.
- **dwCount** is a DWORD value for the size of the storage area.
- **lpBits** is a `char far *` (LPSTR) that points to the data area to hold the bits.

The following line of code from DYNACURS copies the bits from the bitmap into a block of dynamically allocated memory, suitable for passing to `CreateCursor`:

```
GetBitmapBits (hbm, (DWORD)cbSize, lpAND);
```

The creation of the XOR bit mask is similar, but much simpler. The `PatBlt` routine is called to set every pixel in the bitmap to black. Once this is done, a call is made to `GetBitmapBits` to copy the bits from the bitmap to a piece of dynamically allocated memory. To fully understand how DYNACURS works, we need to explore further the allocation and use of dynamically allocated memory.

## *Dynamically Allocating Memory*

The reason that dynamically allocated memory is necessary is that there is no way to anticipate the amount of memory that may be required to hold the bits of a cursor. For example, here are the cursor sizes and memory requirement for some of today's popular display adapters:

| *Display Adapter* | *Cursor Size* | *Memory Required* |
| --- | --- | --- |
| CGA | 32 × 16 | 64 bytes |
| EGA/VGA | 32 × 32 | 128 bytes |
| 8514/a | 32 × 32 | 128 bytes |

New display adapters may come along tomorrow that require larger blocks of memory to store the AND and XOR bit masks, so, to be safe, we depend upon dynamic memory allocation to provide the memory we need.

If you've done a lot of C language programming, you're probably familiar with `malloc`, the C-runtime library routine which dynamically allocates memory. For reasons that we'll describe in Chapter 18, Windows programmers don't use this routine, but instead will rely on two sets of memory allocating routines that are built into Windows. Here are the routines that DYNACURS uses:

| *Routine Name* | *Description* |
| --- | --- |
| `GlobalAlloc` | Allocates a block (segment) of memory. |
| `GlobalLock` | Locks the memory in place and provides a far pointer. |
| `GlobalUnlock` | Unlocks the memory to allow it to move. |
| `GlobalFree` | Deallocates a block of memory. |

To determine the amount of memory that is required, we start by asking Windows for the cursor size that the display adapter requires:

```
cxCursor = GetSystemMetrics (SM_CXCURSOR);
cyCursor = GetSystemMetrics (SM_CYCURSOR);
```

Since **cxCursor** is the width in pixels and **cyCursor** is the height in pixels, we can get the total size in bytes necessary to store this object by dividing **cxCursor** by eight and then multiplying by cyCursor, like this:

```
cbSize = (cxCursor/8) * cyCursor;
```

We allocate two blocks of memory: one for the AND mask and one for the XOR mask using the **GlobalAlloc** routine, as shown here:

```
hmemAND = GlobalAlloc (GMEM_MOVEABLE,   // flags
                      (DWORD)cbSize);   // size

hmemXOR = GlobalAlloc (GMEM_MOVEABLE,   // flags
                      (DWORD)cbSize);   // size
```

The **GMEM_MOVEABLE** flag tells Windows that it can move the object when we aren't using it. This is necessary because Windows runs in the real mode of the Intel-86 family of CPUs. This particular mode doesn't provide any hardware assistance to manage memory. And so Windows programs must manage memory in a way that cooperates with Windows and with other Windows programs. The **GMEM_MOVEABLE** flag offers a reasonable compromise between usefulness and cooperativeness. We'll explore the use of this and other flags more fully in Chapter 18.

**GlobalAlloc** returns a handle to the memory block, which serves to identify a block of memory, although it does not tell us where moveable memory is located. To find that out, we must lock the memory down using the **GlobalLock** routine. This routine returns a far pointer to the memory block, which is how we can access it. **GlobalLock** is defined as follows:

```
LPSTR GlobalLock (hMem)
```

- **hMem** is a handle to a global memory object, allocated with the **GlobalAlloc** routine.

Here are the lines of code from DYNACURS that lock the memory so it can be accessed. Notice that we check the return value to make sure that we have retrieved a valid pointer. This is a good habit to get into, since a NULL pointer can cause problems depending on Windows' operating mode. In real mode, it allows you to trash the interrupt vectors located at the very low end of memory. In protect mode, it causes a protection violation which results in the termination of your program. Neither alternative is attractive, and it is quick and easy to avoid these problems.

```
lpAND = (LPSTR) GlobalLock (hmemAND);
if (lpAND == NULL) goto DefaultExit;

lpXOR = (LPSTR) GlobalLock (hmemXOR);
if (lpXOR == NULL) goto DefaultExit;
```

After we are done using a block of dynamically allocated memory, we unlock the memory objects by calling **GlobalUnlock**. The primary reason we do this is to allow our programs to behave nicely when Windows is running in real mode:

```
GlobalUnlock (hmemAND);
GlobalUnlock (hmemXOR);
```

The final issue that we need to address is the freeing of our memory objects when DYNACURS gets a **WM_DESTROY** message. That is the job of the **GlobalFree** routine. Windows is smart enough to reclaim unused memory when a program exits, but we think it's a good programming practice to clean up after yourself. After all, someone may later use your code as part of a larger programming project and may not check to make sure that you have cleaned up properly. And since GDI objects do not automatically get cleaned up, you must make sure to destroy the GDI objects that you have created. Here is how DYNACURS cleans up the memory, the leftover cursor, and the GDI objects that it created:

```
void TDynaCursWindow::Destroy()
    {
    SelectBitmap (hdcBitmap, hbmOld);
    DeleteDC (hdcBitmap);
    DeleteBitmap (hbm);
    DestroyCursor(hcr);

    GlobalUnlock (hmemAND);
    GlobalUnlock(hmemXOR);
    GlobalFree (hmemAND);
    GlobalFree (hmemXOR);
    }
```

While creating a dynamic cursor takes a lot of work, it provides a way to create custom cursors at runtime. You might create a cursor in the shape of a clock face or a timer to count down a lengthy operation. You can even let users define their own private, custom cursors. And any cursor you create can be used as an icon as well, since the two user-interface objects share the exact same format.

We're going to step back a moment and look at a cursor created with the **CreateCursor** routine that doesn't involve GDI bitmaps or dynamically allocated memory. If you found the earlier example to be somewhat long and involved, this might help you appreciate exactly what is happening when a cursor is created on the fly.

# A Simpler Dynamic Cursor

A simpler way to create a dynamic cursor involves figuring out the layout of the AND mask and XOR mask ahead of time by hand, and passing a pointer to these masks to the `CreateCursor` routine. A serious drawback to this approach is that it is horribly device-dependent. But it illustrates the creation of a dynamic cursor in a somewhat simpler fashion that may help clarify exactly what was happening in our last example. Figure 16.11 shows our dynamic cursor, which is in the shape of a rocket.

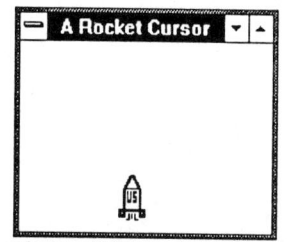

**Figure 16.11** Another dynamic cursor

Here are the static data definition, OWL window class definition, and OWL window class member functions which created this cursor:

```
static char acAND[] = {0xff, 0xff, 0xff, 0xff,  // Scan 1
                       0xff, 0xfe, 0x3f, 0xff,  // Scan 2
                       0xff, 0xfc, 0x1f, 0xff,  // Scan 3
                       0xff, 0xfc, 0x9f, 0xff,  // Scan 4
                       0xff, 0xf8, 0x8f, 0xff,  // Scan 5
                       0xff, 0xf9, 0xcf, 0xff,  // Scan 6
                       0xff, 0xf1, 0xc7, 0xff,  // Scan 7
                       0xff, 0xf3, 0xe7, 0xff,  // Scan 8
                       0xff, 0xe3, 0xe3, 0xff,  // Scan 9
                       0xff, 0xe7, 0xf3, 0xff,  // Scan 10
                       0xff, 0xc0, 0x01, 0xff,  // Scan 11
                       0xff, 0xcf, 0xf9, 0xff,  // Scan 12
                       0xff, 0xca, 0x89, 0xff,  // Scan 13
                       0xff, 0xca, 0x89, 0xff,  // Scan 14
                       0xff, 0xca, 0xb9, 0xff,  // Scan 15
                       0xff, 0xca, 0x89, 0xff,  // Scan 16
                       0xff, 0xca, 0x89, 0xff,  // Scan 17
                       0xff, 0xca, 0xe9, 0xff,  // Scan 18
                       0xff, 0xc8, 0x89, 0xff,  // Scan 19
                       0xff, 0xc8, 0x89, 0xff,  // Scan 20
                       0xff, 0xcf, 0xf9, 0xff,  // Scan 21
                       0xff, 0xcf, 0xf9, 0xff,  // Scan 22
                       0xff, 0xcf, 0xf9, 0xff,  // Scan 23
                       0xff, 0xcf, 0xf9, 0xff,  // Scan 24
                       0xfe, 0x00, 0x00, 0x3f,  // Scan 25
                       0xfe, 0x00, 0x00, 0x3f,  // Scan 26
```

```
                            0xfe, 0x4f, 0xf9, 0x3f,   // Scan 27
                            0xfe, 0x4d, 0x59, 0x3f,   // Scan 28
                            0xfe, 0x0d, 0x58, 0x3f,   // Scan 29
                            0xfe, 0x0d, 0x58, 0x3f,   // Scan 30
                            0xff, 0xfd, 0x5f, 0xff,   // Scan 31
                            0xff, 0xf1, 0xc7, 0xff};  // Scan 32
   static char acXOR[] ={0, 0, 0, 0, 0, 0, 0, 0,
                         0, 0, 0, 0, 0, 0, 0, 0,
                         0, 0, 0, 0, 0, 0, 0, 0,
                         0, 0, 0, 0, 0, 0, 0, 0,
                         0, 0, 0, 0, 0, 0, 0, 0,
0, 0, 0, 0, 0, 0, 0, 0,
                         0, 0, 0, 0, 0, 0, 0, 0,
                         0, 0, 0, 0, 0, 0, 0, 0,
0, 0, 0, 0, 0, 0, 0, 0,
                         0, 0, 0, 0, 0, 0, 0, 0,
                         0, 0, 0, 0, 0, 0, 0, 0,
0, 0, 0, 0, 0, 0, 0, 0,
                         0, 0, 0, 0, 0, 0, 0, 0,
                         0, 0, 0, 0, 0, 0, 0, 0,
                         0, 0, 0, 0, 0, 0, 0, 0,
                         0, 0, 0, 0, 0, 0, 0, 0};

   class TDynaCur2Window : public TWindow
     {
     public:
       TDynaCur2Window (PTWindowsObject pwParent, LPSTR lpszTitle,
                  PTModule pmModule);
       virtual LPSTR GetClassName ();
       virtual void  GetWindowClass (WNDCLASS&);
       virtual void  WMCreate(TMessage& Msg) = [WM_CREATE];
       virtual void  WMDestroy(TMessage& Msg) = [WM_DESTROY];
       virtual void  WMSetCursor(TMessage& Msg) = [WM_SETCURSOR];

     private:
       HCURSOR hcr;
     };

   ...

   /*----------------------------------------------------------------*\
   |                 TDynaCur2Window Class Member.                    |
   \*----------------------------------------------------------------*/
   void TDynaCur2Window::WMCreate(TMessage& Msg)
       {
       hcr = CreateCursor (
            GetApplication()->hInstance,    // Instance handle
            0,           // X-hotspot
            0,           // Y-hotspot
            32,          // width
            32,          // height
            acAND,       // AND bitmask
            acXOR);      // XOR bitmask
       }
   /*----------------------------------------------------------------*\
   |                 TDynaCur2Window Class Member.                    |
   \*----------------------------------------------------------------*/
   void TDynaCur2Window::WMDestroy(TMessage& Msg)
       {
       DestroyCursor (hcr);
```

```
    }
/*----------------------------------------------------------*\
|                 TDynaCur2Window Class Member.              |
\*----------------------------------------------------------*/
void TDynaCur2Window::WMSetCursor(TMessage& Msg)
    {
    if (Msg.LP.Lo == HTCLIENT)
        SetCursor (hcr);
    else
        DefWndProc(Msg);
    }
```

While this shows a simple way to create a dynamic cursor, there are several problems. First, the cursor is very device-dependent. This cursor works properly with EGA and VGA display adapters, both of which use a $32 \times 32$-bit cursor, but will not work on devices which take a different size cursor. In addition, this is not a very dynamic cursor. You would be better off creating a regular static cursor than using this approach. What this does do, we hope, is provide a simpler framework for understanding the way that dynamic cursor creation works.

This concludes our look at how a Windows program receives keyboard and mouse input from the user. In the next chapters, we'll be looking at memory use and other operating-system considerations of a Windows program.

# PART SIX

# Operating System Considerations

# 17

# Memory, Part I: System Memory Management

To fully appreciate the way that Windows manages memory, you need to look at the hardware on which Windows runs: the Intel-86 family of CPUs. Among the members of this family are the 8086, 8088, 80186, 80188, 80286, 80386-SX, 80386-DX, and 80486 microprocessors. One reason that Windows runs on all these processors is that Intel designed each new CPU with an eye toward creating a migration path from the older processors. As advanced capabilities were introduced in new processors, doors were always left open to help migrate software from older chips.

From the start, Windows was built with the more advanced chips in mind. The architect of memory management in Windows 1.x was Steve Wood, a former Yale graduate student who started working for Microsoft in June 1983. He laid the foundation for Windows' memory management, which he modeled after the protected mode of the Intel 80286 processor. In those days, Microsoft was contemplating a successor to DOS, and planned for Windows to run with the new operating system. Of course, today we know that Windows NT is that operating system. It gives Windows programmers a choice of creating 16-bit or 32-bit Windows application programs.

Each subsequent version of Windows built on the original design to improve memory use. The architect of Windows' memory management for Windows 2.x and 3.x, David Weise, was also one of the designers of the EMS 4.0 Memory Specification. This allowed him to build EMS support into Windows 2.x and to continue that support in Real-Mode Windows 3.0. This latest version of Windows has a flexible approach to memory use that allows it to push the limits of whatever processor it finds itself running with.

In this chapter, we're going to discuss the three operating modes that Windows 3.0 uses to manage memory across the wide range of capabilities that exist in the Intel-86 family of

CPUs. We're going to discuss how memory is managed from the point of view of Windows—that is, from the point of view of the *operating system*. In the next chapter, we'll continue our discussion of memory by looking at how *programs* manage memory. Let's start our discussion by getting down to bare metal: Let's start by looking at the processors.

## The Intel-86 Family of Processors

We're going to limit our discussion to the processors that represent the three memory modes in which Windows operates: the 8088, 80286, and 80386. These represent the most widely used chips and most significant milestones in the development of this processor family.

### *The Physical Address Space*

One important aspect worth considering with any microprocessor is the maximum amount of memory that it can access—that is, the size of its address space. One way to determine this is to count the number of memory addressing lines that connect the processor to system memory. That number raised to a power of 2 is the size of the address space. For example, the 8088 has 20 address lines, which translates into a $2^{20}$ or 1-megabyte (1,048,576 bytes) address space. With 24 address lines, the 80286 can address $2^{24}$ or 16 megabytes (16,777,216 bytes) of physical RAM. And finally the 80386, with its 32 address lines, can use up to $2^{32}$ or 4 gigabytes (4,294,967,296 bytes) of system memory.

Every byte of memory in the system has its own unique physical address, starting at zero on up to $n-1$ for a system with $n$ bytes of memory. For example, the 8088 has a memory address range from 0 to 1,048,575. In this regard, the Intel-86 family of processors is like any other processor. The physical address allows the CPU to communicate with the memory addressing hardware. But this is not how software communicates an address to the CPU. Instead, to application software, the address space is only available through a segmented memory addressing scheme.

### *Segmented Memory*

All members of the Intel-86 family use segmented memory addressing. As we mentioned in an earlier chapter, it may help to understand this if you think about building addresses in the physical world. The Prime Minister of Great Britain, for example, lives at Number 10 Downing Street; the President of the United States lives at 1600 Pennsylvania Avenue.

A two-part logical address gives each program the freedom to divide its address space into many small "streets" or **segments**, each of which can hold from one to 65,535 "houses" or *bytes*. And, if we may push the analogy further, this approach permits operating-system software to give each program its own "city"—that is, its own private address space.

To programmers unaccustomed to the Intel-86 family of processors, segmented addressing can be both confusing and frustrating. But it provides some benefits worth considering. For experienced DOS and OS/2 programmers, segmented addressing will be very familiar, although you should pay attention to the particular way that Windows operates in this environment.

A key benefit of segmented addressing is software migration. This architecture was first selected by Intel to allow software to migrate from the older 8-bit 8080 processor to the first member of this family, the 8086. The continued adoption of this addressing scheme has allowed DOS to run on all members of the Intel-86 family when they run in real mode. It is also one of the reasons that DOS programs can run under the various Intel-86-based operating systems, like Windows, OS/2, and Unix. And finally, it gives properly written Windows programs a migration path from the earlier versions of Windows to the protected mode operation of Windows 3.x, and on into future versions.

From the point of view of software development, segmented addressing is helpful in program debugging. A program can be divided into multiple code and data segments to create "fire walls" between different parts of an application. Fire walls prevent bad memory references in one part of an application from contaminating the data in another part of the application, and therefore make programs easier to debug. In protected mode, the processor complains loudly when an invalid segment reference is made, or when a program tries to read or write beyond the end of a memory segment.

And finally, a benefit of segmented programs is that they provide the operating system with hints about the **working sets** of a program. These hints can result in improved performance and lower memory requirements. A working set is a division of a program that performs a task or a set of tasks for the user. Since Windows incorporates an overlay facility called **dynamic linking**, at any given moment only *part* of a program has to be loaded into memory (see Chapter 19 for details on dynamic linking). If each working set in a program is a cleanly defined set of code segments, memory use is optimized. In a low-memory situation, Windows discards code segments from the current working set *last*. In this way, a program with well-defined working sets—what Windows programmers call "well-tuned"—will have lower memory requirements than the same program that hasn't been tuned. The latter program will slow down in a low-memory situation, since Windows will have to continually reread previously discarded code segments from disk: a situation commonly called **disk-thrashing**.

## The Logical Address

While a CPU uses a physical address to read and write in physical memory, programmers use a higher level abstraction called a **logical address**. It's the job of the CPU to translate logical addresses into physical addresses to access memory locations in the physical address space. This is illustrated in Figure 17.1.

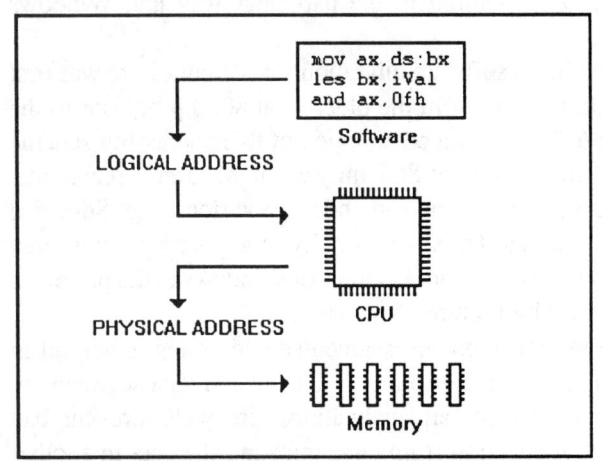

**Figure 17.1** The Translation of a logical address to a physical address

The translation process that takes place in the CPU might be very simple or very involved, depending on the current operating mode of the CPU. In **real mode**, for example, simple bit shifting and addition are involved. In the various **protected modes**, however, the CPU uses a lookup table to determine how to map a logical address into a physical address. This lookup table allows the operating system to move memory objects so that it can minimize fragmentation of physical memory. The operating system can even play tricks like writing memory to disk to implement virtual memory. If you are familiar with the operation of OS/2 version 1.x, you know that its virtual memory manager writes segments to disk. And finally, the higher-end 80386 and 80486 chips have special hardware that, when enabled, provides an additional level of indirection that divides memory into 4K pages. This paging mechanism is particularly useful in creating a very efficient virtual memory system, which is how the Windows memory manager implements virtual memory in 386 Enhanced Mode.

In a moment, we're going to take a close look at each of the operating modes that Windows uses. But first, let's look at the pieces that make up a logical address. Every processor in the Intel-86 family uses a two-part logical address, made up of a **segment identifier** and an **offset**.

The segment identifier specifies the segment of memory that we are interested in. The segment identifier is a 16-bit value that is the "street name" that we're working on. In the logical-to-physical address translation process, it answers the question "where in the world is the segment." The answer might be within the physical address space of the CPU, or, in a virtual memory system, swapped out to disk.

The second part of a logical address, the offset, indicates the diatance within a particular segment. If the segment identifier is the street name, then the offset is the house number. Or, you can think of a segment as an array and the offset as an array index. In any event, both segment identifier and offset are used together to address specific bytes in system memory.

With this introduction to the basics of memory addressing for the Intel-86 family, let's take a look at how the Intel-86 family supports Windows' operating modes: real mode, standard mode, and 386-Enhanced Mode. To check the current mode, a user can look at the About box in the Program Manager. From a program, you can find this out by calling the `GetWinFlags` routine. Also, providing you have the proper hardware setup, you can manually start the different modes using one of the following switches on the Windows' command line:

| Mode | Windows Command Line | Comment |
| --- | --- | --- |
| Real | `C> win /r` | Any Intel-86 processor with 384K of RAM. |
| Standard | `C> win /2` | Requires an 80286 or 80386 CPU with 640K plus 192K extended memory and the HIMEM.SYS driver. |
| 386-Enhanced | `C> win /3` | Requires an 80386 CPU with 640K plus 512K extended memory and the HIMEM.SYS driver. |

## Real Mode Operation

While all members of the Intel-86 family can operate efficiently in real mode, it is usually associated with the oldest members of this family, the 8086 and 8088. With 20 address lines, these chips have a one-megabyte address space. To maintain complete compatibility, the other processors in this family share this same address space when emulating real mode.

Real mode gets its name from the fact that a logical address is equivalent to the *real* physical address. To convert a logical address to the physical address, the CPU starts by shifting the 16-bit segment value left by four bits to create a 20-bit value. To this, it adds the 16-bit offset. Figure 17.2 illustrates this process.

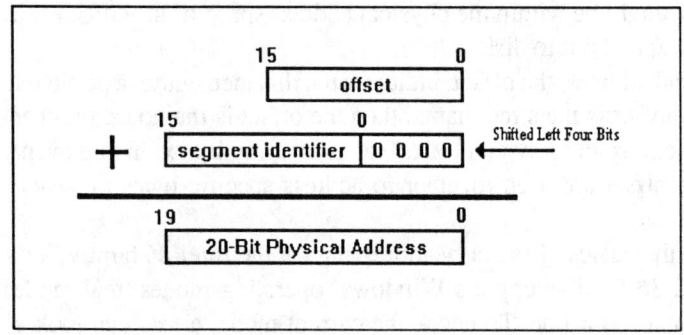

**Figure 17.2** Real mode address calculation

Because the segment value is shifted left by four bits, which effectively multiplies it by 16, the smallest segment in real mode is 16 bytes long. Intel calls this a **paragraph**. Because of the way Windows operates in real mode, the granularity of segments is actually two paragraphs, or 32 bytes. Another way to visualize the logical-to-physical address conversion is shown in Figure 17.3.

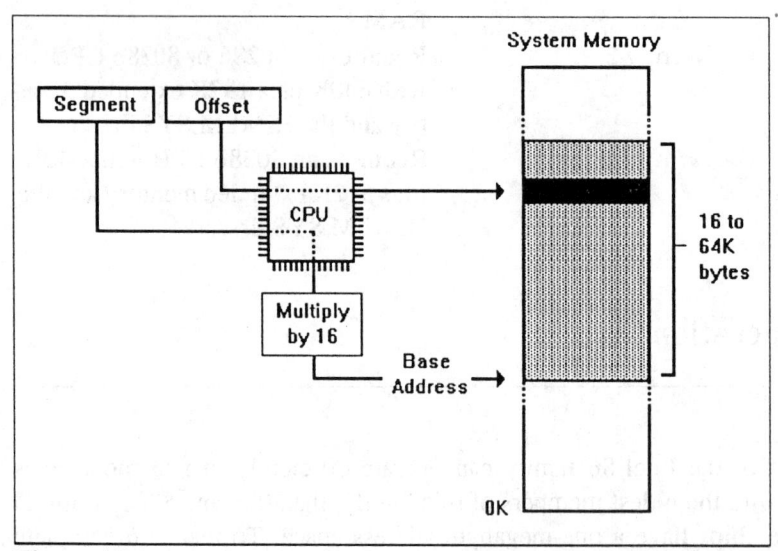

**Figure 17.3** Another view of Real Mode address calculation

## The Real Mode Address Space

Since Windows runs as an extension to DOS, it inherits the DOS environment. In memory terms, this means the one-megabyte address space of real mode, divided into several parts, as depicted in Figure 17.4.

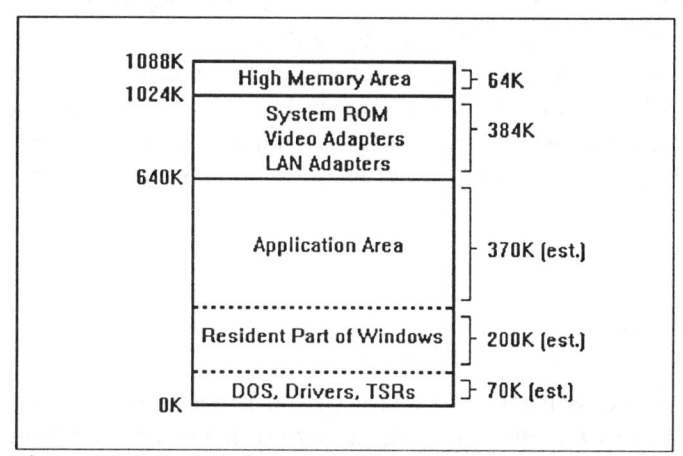

```
1088K ┌─────────────────────────┐
      │   High Memory Area      │ ┐ 64K
1024K │─────────────────────────│ ┘
      │     System ROM          │ ┐
      │    Video Adapters       │ ├ 384K
      │    LAN Adapters         │ ┘
 640K │─────────────────────────│
      │                         │ ┐
      │    Application Area     │ ├ 370K (est.)
      │                         │ │
      │- - - - - - - - - - - - -│ ┘
      │ Resident Part of Windows│ ┐ 200K (est.)
      │- - - - - - - - - - - - -│ ┘
      │   DOS, Drivers, TSRs    │ ┐ 70K (est.)
   0K └─────────────────────────┘ ┘
```

**Figure 17.4** The real mode address space

In this figure, the dotted lines dividing the three pieces in the 0–640K range are meant to suggest that the size of each piece can vary somewhat. DOS, its device drivers, and terminate-and-stay-resident (TSR) programs get first crack at the lowest end of memory. When Windows starts up, it requires a minimum of 200K or so for its device drivers, resident fonts, and the fixed code and data used by the Windows' core components: Kernel, User, and GDI. The space marked as "application area" is used for both Windows programs and for the discardable parts of Windows over and above the minimum set needed.

The well-publicized "640K limit" on DOS applications results from the design of the DOS address space, which reserves the area between 640K and 1024K for system uses: video adapter cards, ROM, and other uses. Since this memory area is occupied by hardware, Windows can't do anything to make it available for its own use, except in real mode, when it is used for EMS support.

However, on 80286 and 80386 CPUs, Windows gets an extra 64K of memory from the **High Memory Area** (HMA), located just above the one-megabyte address line, when an XMS (eXtended Memory Specification) driver is installed, such as HIMEM.SYS. This is the beginning of the extended memory area, which is usually only available in protected mode. But this memory is available in real mode through tricks that an XMS driver plays. When it is available, HMA memory can be used by Windows itself.

Above and beyond the HMA, real mode Windows is able to make other uses of extended memory. The SMARTDRV disk-caching device driver, for example, can be set up to optimize disk transfer operations. And the RAMDRIVE driver emulates a disk drive in RAM, to create fast temporary files. In addition, if the Windows Memory Manager finds extra, unused extended memory, it uses it to store code segments that it would otherwise discard. For this reason, if you are running in real mode, it's a good idea to leave about 256K or so of extended RAM unallocated. Windows will put this memory to good use, to provide better performance.

In real mode, the amount of memory available to a Windows program varies from 300K to 450K, depending on the amount of space taken up by DOS device drivers, and the availability of the high memory area. While this may seem a very small amount of memory, Windows' dynamic linking facility allows a program 10 times this size (or *larger*) to run. In such situations, the performance might be sluggish, which would encourage a hardware upgrade to accommodate one of Windows' more advanced operating modes. But, such a program *can* run.

## Real Mode and Windows

Prior to Windows 3.0, all versions of Windows ran exclusively in real mode. Windows was limited to real mode for marketing reasons: The installed base of microcomputers was dominated by machines that could only be run in real mode—computers based on the Intel 8088 and 8086 CPUs. The memory manager was first built for real mode, but it was designed with the protected modes of the higher-end chips in mind, which is one of the reasons that Windows 3.0 is able to operate in all of its different modes.

Real mode addressing is fast and efficient, since there is very little overhead involved in translating logical addresses to physical addresses. To seasoned DOS programmers, it may seem like the most open, accessible way to work. And it is, until you try to create a multitasking operating system.

The job of an operating system is to manage and distribute resources. This is true whether the resource is processor time, disk space, or memory. The problem with real mode addressing is that it makes it very difficult for an operating system to manage memory. It's easy enough to allocate memory to a program—the operating system carves off a piece of system memory and assigns it to a program—but great care must be taken in the *way* memory is assigned. If a real mode operating system assigns memory by providing an address, it is almost impossible for the operating system to move that block of memory. But memory movement is precisely what an operating system must do in order to avoid the problems associated with memory fragmentation. To circumvent this problem, real mode Windows uses a handle-based approach to allocating memory.

## Moveable Memory

When a block of memory is allocated, a program does not receive an addresss, but a handle that identifies the memory. Like the handles that we encountered in our discussion of GDI drawing objects, the value of a handle has no meaning to anyone but the subsystem that issued the handle. Like a claim check at a restaurant coat room, a program can trade the memory handle for a memory address whenever it needs to access the memory. At that time, Windows provides a pointer to the memory and locks the segment in place. All other times, the Windows Memory Manager is free to move and compact system memory to reduce fragmentation. Or, in coat room terms, your hat and coat can be moved to another room or even to another floor when the main coat room gets too crowded.

A handle-based, moveable memory system helps the Windows' memory manager to avoid memory loss due to fragmentation. But another mechanism is needed to deal with the problem of running out of physical memory: a situation sometimes referred to as "memory overcommit." In the world of mainframe computers, virtual memory systems solve this problem by copying portions of memory to disk. But this requires fast disks and, in the best of cases, hardware support for memory management. When the first version of Windows was being created, neither was available on the computers for which Windows was being written.

The first version of Windows was targeted to run on a 4.77-MHz 8088-based system with 256K of memory and two floppy diskette drives. When Microsoft started building Windows in 1983, hard disks were not widely used, and the 80286-based PC/AT had not yet been introduced. Given the low power of this target machine, even if the 8088 had any sophisticated memory management capabilities (which it doesn't), the two floppy drives of a minimally configured system did not provide fast enough response or a large enough capacity for implementing a virtual memory system. Instead, Microsoft implemented what some might call a "poor-man's" virtual memory system: dynamic linking. This facility depends on the second type of memory that we're going to discuss: discardable memory.

## Discardable Memory

To help ease the memory crunch, the Windows memory manager can do more than just move memory around. If it needs to, it can **discard** objects from memory. A discarded object is purged from memory and is overwritten by whatever objects are allocated in its place. The most obvious type of discardable memory object is code. In most cases, code is not modified. So code that is not needed can be discarded, and reread when it is needed again.

Discardable, read-on-demand code is the basis of Windows' dynamic link mechanism. This is a very flexible mechanism that allows code to be removed from system memory when it is not used. In some ways, this mechanism has a lot in common with memory overlay facilities that are used by some DOS programs, and even in some very old mainframe systems. But the difference between Windows' dynamic linking mechanism and overlays is that dynamic linking is transparent to the application programmer. Overlays, on the other hand, typically must be designed with great care to avoid a deadlock—a situation in which the system must halt because it cannot read in the next overlay that it needs to continue operating properly. Windows' dynamic link mechanism does the work to ensure that deadlocks do not occur.

Besides code, another type of object is commonly placed into discardable memory objects: **resources**. To the Windows Memory Manager, a resource is a block of read-only data. When a resource is needed, it is ordinarily read from disk into a discardable memory block. Later, when system memory gets crowded, the Memory Manager can discard resources to allow other objects to take their place.

There are quite a few kinds of resources in Windows. Some are used to support the user interface, like menu and dialog box templates, icons, and cursors. Others are used to store GDI objects like fonts and bitmaps. Beyond these, programmers can create custom resources for private read-only data if they wish. Like discardable code, discardable resources give the Windows Memory Manager the freedom to purge objects that might otherwise clog system memory.

We've looked at two types of memory objects that can be allocated in Windows: moveable and discardable. Both types allow a flexible, dynamic memory management system to be implemented on top of the relatively inflexible addressing of real mode. Windows supports a third type of memory, which application programmers should avoid, but which is important for the well-being and overall efficient operation of certain parts of the system: fixed memory.

## Fixed Memory

While moveable and discardable memory objects are necessary for the Memory Manager to meet the demands of Windows' multitasking, there are situations that require memory that won't be moved or discarded. For example, an interrupt handler will require a fixed location in memory since it must always be ready to process an interrupt. For such uses, the Windows Memory Manager allows the allocation of segments that reside at a fixed location.

Of course, the use of fixed memory should be limited to special cases like device drivers. If a Windows program allocated fixed memory for regular uses, it would quickly use up this scarce resource and cause the system to slow down. When we talk about dynamic memory allocation in the next chapter, you'll see that a program *can* allocate as many fixed memory objects as it requires. But, before you do this, be sure that the other types of memory truly cannot satisfy your requirements.

## EMS and Real Mode Windows

The second major revision of Windows, version 2.x, introduced support for EMS memory, which is memory that is made available according to the **expanded memory specification**. EMS describes a software interface for bank switching memory to increase the total amount of memory that DOS programs can access. Since Windows runs on top of DOS, Windows is able to take advantage of EMS. In fact, Windows programs can directly communicate with the expanded memory manager to allocate pages just like their DOS counterparts. But Windows programs don't have to do anything special to benefit from the presence of EMS memory. Instead, the Windows Memory Manager does all the work behind the scenes to increase total available system memory.

EMS does not increase the size of the hardware address space. Instead, it switches extra memory into unused parts of the DOS address space. In this way, EMS allows up to 32 additional megabytes of memory to be accessible in the DOS address space. At first glance, this seems to be enough memory to satisfy the needs of *any* DOS or Windows program. However, because its gobs of memory are not *simultaneously* accessible, EMS is only a limited solution to the memory crunch.

For example, in one configuration, a 64K memory window serves as the only access point for all of the memory on an EMS card. This memory window, which is also called the **EMS page frame**, is typically divided into pages that are 16K bytes. Thus, our 64K memory window consists of four 16K memory pages. If a program wanted to access more than 64K of EMS memory at a time, it would have to decide which EMS pages to use and which pages to ignore. With its tiny memory window, EMS cannot be a general-purpose memory management solution. But there is no denying that it has helped ease the memory shortage of real mode systems. Figure 17.5 illustrates the relationship of the real mode address space to EMS memory pages.

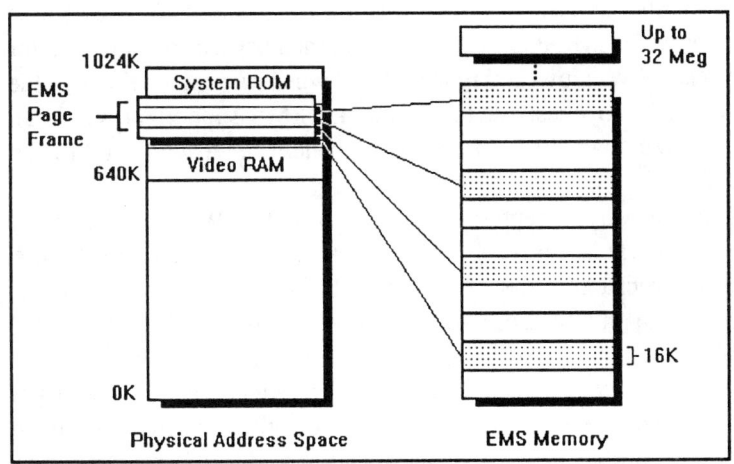

**Figure 17.5** EMS lets real-mode programs peek at a larger address space

Windows' use of EMS is transparent to Windows programs. When a Windows program starts running, the program receives a private EMS bank. The program is guaranteed to have private use of this memory, free from competition with other programs. As Windows' multitasking switcher lets other programs run, it communicates with the EMS memory manager to map the correct EMS bank into the EMS page frame. The net result is reduced competition for memory between different programs, more total available memory, and better overall performance. The improved performance comes from postponing low-memory situations, when code must be discarded and reread from disk.

When running in real mode, Windows 3.x allocates EMS memory for programs in the same way that Windows 2.x did. But in its other operating modes, Windows ignores EMS memory. That is, Windows does not use EMS memory for Windows programs in either standard mode or 386-Enhanced Mode. These other modes have access to extended memory, which doesn't suffer the same shortcomings of EMS memory. Extended memory, after all, is accessible without bank switching and has the added advantage of virtual memory support in 386-Enhanced Mode.

Under Windows 2.x, a program can ask Windows to step aside so that the program can directly allocate and manage its own EMS memory. This capability is also available in Windows 3.0. Programs that wish to do this must have the –l switch set when the resource compiler is run (RC.EXE) so that the proper flag gets set in the program's executable file.

EMS support can be provided in several ways. Windows comes with an EMS driver called EMM386.SYS for systems with an 80386 processor. However, this is not required when running in 386-Enhanced Mode, since this mode has built-in EMS support for both Windows programs and DOS programs that are run under Windows. Another way that EMS can be made available is with the use of a dedicated EMS card and at least a version 4.0 driver. And finally, EMS support can be provided using various software emulations.

Windows programs only benefit from the presence of EMS when running in real mode. In real mode, bank-switched memory increases the size of the total address space, but only one bank of memory is available at a time. In its other operating modes, Windows uses extended memory, which provides the same amount of extra memory *without* the need for bank switching. For this reason, Windows 3.0 ignores EMS when running in either of the two protected modes. There is no question, however, that EMS support provided an important improvement for Windows 2.x, and that it can benefit users who need to run Windows 3.0 in real mode.

EMS is important in another way. It represents the first time that Windows' memory management supported the concept of a private address space for application programs. A private address space helps protect applications from the misbehavior of other applications, since a private address space can only be accessed by its owner. In Windows 3.0 protected mode, which we're going to discuss in a moment, the idea of a private address space is also starting to be implemented with the memory protection that is provided. Future versions of Windows will continue to enhance and enforce the concept of private address spaces to help protect programs from the problems that arise when memory addressing errors occur. For the present, in both standard mode and 386-Enhanced Mode, Windows takes advantage of the memory protection features of the 80286 and higher processors. Let's take a look at those two modes, and at the way that they operate.

## Standard and Enhanced Mode

As we mentioned earlier, when Windows' memory management system was first being designed, it was with an eye toward someday moving Windows to the protected modes of the Intel-86 family. With Windows 3.0, this vision is realized in not one but *two* operating modes: Windows standard mode and 386-Enhanced Mode.

Standard mode gives Windows the benefits of protected mode on the 80286 and 80386 processors. In this mode, Windows programs get a physical address space that breaks the one-megabyte boundary of real mode and can be as large as 16 megabytes. Unlike the bank-switched memory of EMS, in protected mode the additional memory is **extended memory**—that is, the memory is a directly addressable extension to the real mode address space. Protected mode provides special memory management support that is not available in real mode. This support includes the enforcement of memory access rules that help preserve the integrity of each program, of each program's data, and of the system itself.

In 386-Enhanced Mode, Windows gets all the benefits of standard mode, plus an even larger address space. When running in this mode, don't be alarmed when the Program Manager tells you that the system has more *free* memory than you have RAM installed in your system. During the development of Windows, someone complained about this problem in a bug report, and was told simply: *"Welcome to the world of virtual memory!"*

The virtual memory of 386-Enhanced Mode is provided by an 80386 control program, WIN386.EXE, that works with the memory paging hardware built into the 80386 processor. In this mode, the address space can grow to a size that is up to four times the available physical memory. For example, five megabytes of physical memory can support a virtual address space of 20 megabytes. And 16 megabytes of RAM can support a 64-megabyte virtual memory address space. These examples assume, of course, that there is enough disk space to hold the memory pages that have been swapped out.

## Protected Mode

The term **protected mode** refers to a state of the processor in which certain rules are enforced when memory is addressed. These rules minimize the risk that a program will overwrite—either accidentally or intentionally—memory that doesn't belong to it. A program that violates these rules is subject to a serious penalty: It is terminated.

This harsh treatment contrasts sharply with the way a similar action is treated in real mode. For example, it's quite common for a DOS program to busy itself poking around the DOS data areas, installing private interrupt handlers, and in general making itself at home. Since DOS is a single-tasking system, such liberties are allowable since they don't interfere with the operation of other programs.

But Windows is a multitasking system, and even though programs can fiddle with any part of system memory in real mode Windows, this should be avoided. Programs should refrain from actions that might have adverse side effects for other programs. Such actions may cause a program to be incompatible with protected mode Windows.

And yet, an otherwise "well-behaved" program might mistakenly overwrite memory belonging to another program—or even memory that belongs to Windows itself. Without the memory protection of protected mode, such actions can lead to data corruption and even a system crash. Protected mode provides increased system integrity because of its memory protection features.

## *Memory Addressing in Protected Mode*

When a program addresses memory in protected mode, it uses a two-part segment address just like a program in real mode, with a segment identifier and an offset. But in protected mode, the logical-to-physical addresss conversion is not simply a shift and add operation. Instead, the processor relies on special tables called **descriptor tables** that are created and maintained by the operating system. There are two types of descriptor tables: **Global Descriptor Tables** (GDT) and **Local Descriptor Tables** (LDT). (A third type of descriptor table, the Interrupt Descriptor Table or IDT, is used to hold interrupt vectors. But its use is beyond this discussion.)

Intel designed its protected mode with a lot of flexibility in the way that descriptor tables can be used by different operating systems. In general, a descriptor table contains an array of segment information records, known as **segment descriptors**. In protected mode, the part of a memory address that we have been calling a "segment identifier" is referred to as **a segment selector**. A segment selector is an index into the array of descriptors that make up a descriptor table. It identifies the segment descriptor that provides the detail needed to access the segment data. Here is what a segment descriptor contains:

| *Segment Descriptor Field* | *80286 Size* | *80386 Size* |
|---|---|---|
| Segment location (aka base address) | 3 bytes | 4 bytes |
| Segment size (aka segment limit) | 2 bytes | 2 1/2 bytes |
| Flags | 1 byte | 1 1/2 bytes |
| Unused | 2 bytes | 0 bytes |
|  | 8 bytes | 8 bytes |

When a program references a memory location, the CPU loads the segment descriptor into special registers for use in determining the physical address of the segment. The offset is added to the base address, to access the desired bytes of memory. This process is illustrated in Figure 17.6.

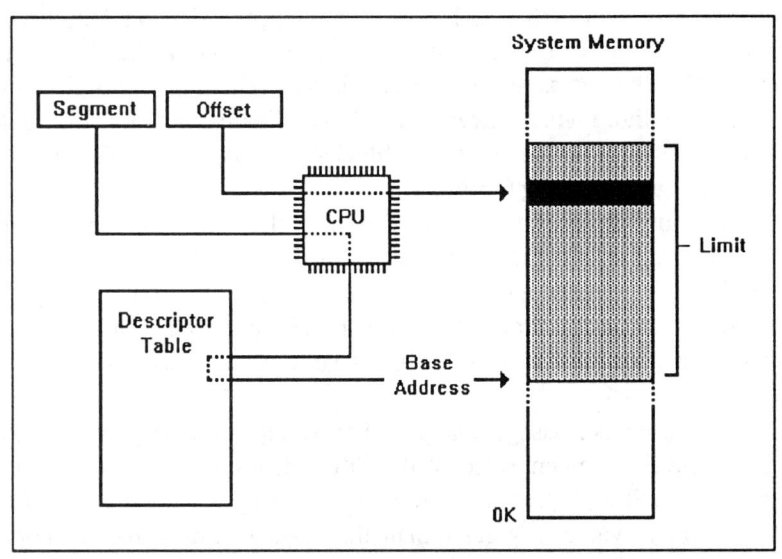

**Figure 17.6** The segment value is an index into a descriptor table

Actually, only 13 of the 16 bits in a segment value are used as a descriptor table index. As shown in Figure 17.7, the other three bits are two additional fields that play an important part in the addressing scheme and protection mechanism of protected mode. Bit 2 is a flag that indicates which descriptor table to use. This field allows an operating system to set up an address space of a program using two descriptor tables: one GDT and one LDT. The idea is that the GDT contains all the memory that is shared system wide. The LDT, on the other hand, represents a program's private address space.

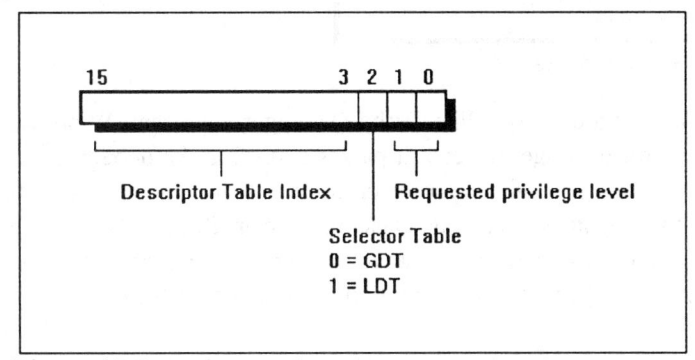

**Figure 17.7** Structure of a protected mode selector

Bits 0 and 1 describe the segment's **requested privilege level (RPL)**. These bits are set by operating-system software to create and enforce a memory protection scheme with four privilege levels, 0 to 3. Zero is the highest privilege level, and is reserved for the most trusted operating-system software. In Windows standard mode, the DOS Protected Mode Interface (DPMI) code has the highest privilege level, which is also known as ring 0.

The DPMI support code resides in DOSX.EXE (in standard mode) and in WIN386.EXE (in 386-Enhanced Mode). DPMI provides access to memory above the 640K line. Memory in the range 640K to 1024K is known as **upper memory blocks** (**UMBs**). The 64K from 1024K to 1088K is called the **high memory area** (**HMA**). And finally, memory allocated above the 1088K line is called **extended memory blocks** (**EMBs**). In 386-Enhanced Mode, the 80386 control program has ring 0 privileges.

In this architecture, memory protection is enforced in the following way. A memory error causes an exception to occur—that is, a CPU interrupt. In Windows, this results in the offending program being terminated with an error message like that shown in Figure 17.8. If you ran some of the earliest, prerelease versions of Windows 3.0, you'd see the word "Trayf"—Yiddish for "not kosher"—in this message. An apt description for an invalid memory reference.

Several types of errors cause this message to appear. For example, if a program tries to address memory using an invalid segment selector, the CPU catches the error and reports it to the operating system. Or, if a program tries to access memory beyond the end of a segment—that is, if the offset value is greater than the segment limit—the memory management hardware prevents the program from accessing memory that does not belong to it. It notifies the operating system that a program has violated the rules for the proper use of memory.

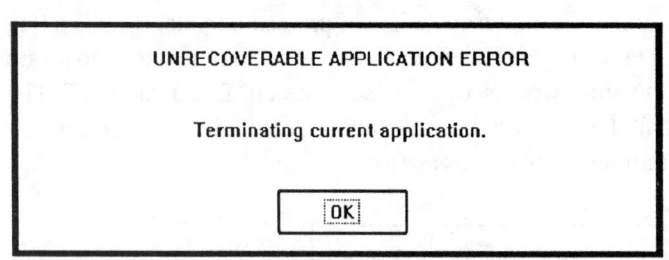

```
┌─────────────────────────────────────┐
│     UNRECOVERABLE APPLICATION ERROR │
│                                     │
│       Terminating current application. │
│                                     │
│              ┌────┐                 │
│              │ OK │                 │
│              └────┘                 │
└─────────────────────────────────────┘
```

**Figure 17.8** Windows' fatal error message

When such an error occurs and a debugger like Turbo Debugger is present, Windows refrains from displaying the error message. Instead, it passes control to the debugger. At that time, Turbo Debugger shows you where the error occurred. If it is within your program, you'll see which line of your source code caused the error. But if it was not in your code—for example, if the error occurred in a device driver or in one of Windows' libraries—the debugger shows you the machine instruction responsible for the error.

## Windows and Protected Mode

In Windows 3.0, all Windows programs and the Windows library code itself reside at ring 1; that is, they run with a privilege level of 1. This will change in a future version of Windows, when Windows programs and the Windows libraries are made to reside at the lowest privilege level, ring 3. This would give future versions of Windows the freedom to use the higher privilege levels for other operating-system components. In addition, if Windows puts applications at ring 3, that means that Windows programs will be running at the same privilege level as OS/2 Presentation Manager programs. No doubt, this will minimize any possible compatibility differences between Windows and OS/2, to help Windows programs to be binary compatible with OS/2 version 2.0.

The current version of Windows, version 3.0, uses a single LDT for all of its own memory and that of every Windows program running in the system. This means that the maximum number of segments that can exist in the system at any moment is $2^{13}$ or 8,192, since that is the maximum number that will fit in an LDT. In a future version, Windows will most likely provide an LDT for each program that runs. This provides several benefits. First, it strengthens the idea of a private address space, to help protect programs from the memory errors of other programs. Next, it increases the total number of memory objects that any one program can create. And finally, it is another step toward making the environment of a Windows program as similar as possible to that of OS/2, to help in the migration of Windows programs to the OS/2 Presentation Manager.

When we described real mode memory management, we talked about the three types of memory objects: moveable, discardable, and fixed. An operating system needs all three types of objects to be able to do an effective job of managing system memory. For this reason, real mode Windows implements these types of memory objects in software, since there wasn't any hardware support for them.

When running in protected mode, things operate a little more efficiently because Windows has help from the processor's memory management hardware. Since programs don't have access to physical addresses as they do in real mode, the Windows Memory Manager can reorganize memory whenever it needs to. The only thing it has to worry about is updating the descriptor table to reflect the new location of a memory object. From a program's point of view, even if an object is moved in physical memory, it still appears at the same logical address, since the address references a descriptor table entry and not a physical address. In protected mode Windows, discardable objects behave in the same way that they do under real mode Windows. After all, discarding is a very efficient way to make more memory available when more memory is needed.

Fixed memory objects, which are the third type of memory object that Windows supports, are treated much the same as they are under real mode. But, just like moveable objects, a fixed object can move. The reason is that, even though the fixed object will maintain its logical address, Windows can move the object in the physical address space. Of course, certain operations require that fixed objects do not move in physical memory,

## 32-Bit Addressing

When the Intel 80386 and higher chips are run in protected mode, 32-bit registers can be used to address segments that can be up to one megabyte or four gigabytes (depending on how the addressing granularity is used). When running the 386-Enhanced Mode, the Windows KERNEL memory manager itself uses 32-bit addressing. When it does this, it packs objects that otherwise would have their own segment into larger arrays, to get the faster performance that comes from minimizing the number of different segments that must be referenced.

## Windows Virtual Memory Support

All that we have said about protected mode operation applies equally to standard mode and to 386-Enhanced Mode. But there is an important capability that is only available in 386-Enhanced Mode: support for virtual memory.

Virtual memory support works alongside the protected mode addressing mechanism that we have been discussing. In other words, the segment value in an address is still used as an index into a descriptor table to determine the base address of a segment. And the offset is added to this base address to determine the exact bytes to be worked on.

The difference between regular protected mode and the virtual memory protected mode on the 80386 has to do with how this base + offset address is interpreted. In regular protected mode, it is interpreted as a physical memory address. But in 386-Enhanced Mode, the paging hardware built into the Intel 80386 processor is enabled, allowing addresses to be treated as virtual memory addresses. Figure 17.9 illustrates how this translation is done.

This figure shows how the segment and offset values are decoded into an address in the virtual address space. This address space is divided into 4K pages, each of which resides in either physical memory or in a swap file on disk. When a reference is made to a location that resides on disk, a page fault is triggered, which is simply an internal CPU interrupt. At such times, the virtual memory manager reads the desired page from disk to provide access to the required code or data. The instruction that triggered the page fault is then restarted so that paging is entirely transparent to software.

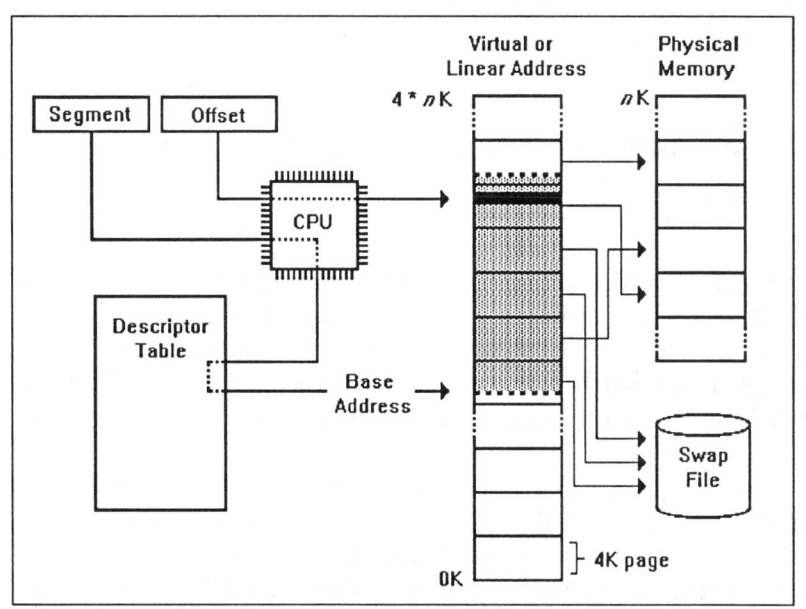

**Figure 17.9** Virtual memory addressing

The virtual memory manager packs segments into the virtual address space as tightly as it can. In other words, as suggested in Figure 17.9, the beginning and end of a segment do not have to coincide with a page boundary. The net result is that the virtual memory manager avoids wasting even a single byte. The paging hardware behaves in a traditional manner, so that part of a segment can be on disk while another part is in physical memory. As you might expect, the portions that are in physical memory do not have any special relationship with each other. Instead, the virtual memory manager can relocate a page of memory anywhere that is convenient.

Even when virtual memory is available, Windows can still discard segments when it starts running out of memory. However, in Windows 3.0, discarding only occurs when the Windows Memory Manager has used up the virtual address space. For this reason, the current implementation of 386-Enhanced Mode has a slight inefficiency built in: It *swaps* discardable code and resources instead of *discarding* them.

The reason this happens is that 386-Enhanced Mode uses two different memory managers: Windows' protected mode global heap manager and the 80386 control program's virtual memory manager. Windows' global heap manager allocates segments in Windows' address space. The 80386 control program provides virtual memory support, EMS emulation, and management of the 8086 virtual machines in which DOS programs run.

When Windows' global heap manager needs memory, it makes a call to the 80386 control program. Windows' Memory Manager discards memory objects only when the 80386 control program runs out of virtual memory. In a future version, the two memory managers will be more tightly integrated to run more efficiently. At that time, instead of swapping discardable memory objects, the Windows Memory Manager will direct the virtual memory manager to purge discardable segments.

## How Windows Selects a Segment for Discarding

In all of its operating modes, Windows can purge code and data segments that are marked as *discardable* when it runs out of free memory. Understanding how Windows chooses to discard one segment over another will help you understand Windows' behavior in a low-memory situation. This, in turn, will help you write programs that can operate effectively even when memory is scarce, either because many programs are running or because Windows is operating in real mode.

Windows discards segments on a *least recently used* basis. That is, when it needs to discard a segment, it picks a segment that has resided in system memory the longest without being used. To determine the least recently used segment, Windows maintains a table of discardable segments known as the **LRU list**. Every discardable code and data segment has an entry on the LRU list.

Every one-quarter second, on a hardware timer tick, Windows scans an access flag associated with each discardable code segment in the system. If the segment has been accessed since the last time the flag was checked, the segment gets moved to the bottom of the LRU list. That is, it gets promoted to the most recently used position in the table. Once a segment has been promoted, the access flag gets cleared so that it is ready to be tripped again if the segment is used again.

A drawback to this approach is that it isn't exact. In other words, it doesn't distinguish between a segment that was accessed 30 times and one that was accessed just once. But this approach was chosen because it is quite fast.

The access flags for discardable code segments reside in different places depending on whether the system is running in real or protected mode. In real mode, the Windows Memory Manager supports a data structure called a **module database** for every program and dynamic link library (we'll take a closer look at this data structure later in this chapter). The access flags are stored as an array of bytes in the module database, with one byte per discardable code segment.

In protected mode, the Intel-86 family provides support for an access flag in hardware. To be more precise, the access flag is a one-bit field of the segment descriptor in the descriptor tables (in the LDT). The memory management hardware automatically sets this bit when a segment has been accessed. Windows checks this bit when it scans all discardable segments to update the LRU list.

Data segments are treated a little differently, but the idea is the same. Windows doesn't keep an access flag for data segments. Instead, the LRU list is automatically updated by the locking and unlocking mechanism that is used to access discardable data objects. After all, a segment must be locked to access it. Then, when it is unlocked, the segment gets automatically promoted to the bottom of the LRU list, to make it the most recently used segment.

You might find yourself working on an application that doesn't work well with the "least recently used" discarding algorithm. Consider, for example, a database program that walks a circular linked list of data segments. As it makes the round of these segments, the very next segment that the program wants to use will also be the least recently used and therefore the one most likely to be discarded. In such cases, there are Windows library routines that can be used to directly modify the LRU tables: **GlobalLRUNewest**, which makes a segment the least likely to be discarded, and **GlobalLRUOldest**, which makes a segment the most likely to be discarded.

The LRU mechanism is largely transparent to Windows programs running in protected mode. In real mode, if you run the SYMDEB debugger, you might run across a single machine instruction that is added to help update the LRU list. This instruction is embedded in a piece of dynamic link code called a **thunk**, which we discuss in more detail in Chapter 19:

```
SAR   CS:[xxxx], 1
```

This *shift arithmetic right* instruction trips the access byte of a discardable code segment. Segments that are fixed or that are not present have a value of FFh. Segments that haven't been accessed since the last LRU timer tick have a value of 01h. This instruction leaves the FFh value unchanged, while it changes the value of 01h to 00h. The bytes that are modified by this instruction are scanned by Windows as it updates the LRU list.

Now that we've looked at the way that Windows manages memory, let's take a look at the data objects that Windows itself allocates. In this chapter, we're going to focus on the data objects that the Windows KERNEL allocates. In the next chapter, when we discuss application memory use, we'll look at the memory used by Windows' other two core components: USER.EXE and GDI.EXE.

## The KERNEL's Private Memory Use

When Windows' three main components are doing work for Windows programs, they consume memory. For the most part, a Windows programmer doesn't have to know how this memory is consumed. But it can help if you're interested in knowing what makes Windows tick. Also, there are certain system limits that you will understand only when you know how Windows uses memory.

We're going to start with a look at the memory used by Windows' KERNEL, which is the part of Windows that is responsible for memory management, dynamic linking, and

554  *Operating System Considerations*

other functions that are traditionally associated with operating systems. In the next chapter, we'll look at the memory that is used by the other two components of Windows: USER and GDI. We're going to wait until the next chapter to discuss the memory used by the other two components, since the memory used is allocated as a direct result of a request for services that have been made by application programs.

# *KERNEL Data Objects*

The KERNEL is responsible for dynamic linking, memory management, and interacting with DOS when Windows programs require DOS system services. Although there are many tiny data structures tucked away throughout the system that the KERNEL uses, we're going to limit our discussion to three of the most important: the Burgermaster, the task database, and the module databases. In protected mode, the Burgermaster goes away because its job is taken over by the protected mode descriptor tables and other internal data structures.

## The Burgermaster

The Burgermaster gets its name from a fast-food restaurant that is next door to the building where Windows was first developed. In those days, two numbers were programmed into the telephone auto-dialer at Microsoft; one was the number of the take-out service at Burgermaster. (The other was the number of the athletic club to which Microsoft employees were given memberships.) This object was named in honor of this restaurant, because the members of the development team that worked on the KERNEL ate lunch at Burgermaster almost every day.

The Burgermaster is the master memory handle table for moveable and discardable objects in Windows. In other words, like the descriptor tables in protected mode, the Burgermaster maintains the physical addresses of moveable memory objects. When a program needs to get the address of such a segment, it makes a call to one of several Windows library routines, which look it up in the Burgermaster.

## The Task Database

A Task Database (or TDB) is created for every instance of every program that runs in Windows. For example, when a single copy of CLOCK is running, there is a single TDB. A TDB always sits in a fixed segment and contains pointers to all of the things that make an instance of a program unique. Here is a partial list of some of the things that are stored in the TDB:

| TDB Field | Comment |
| --- | --- |
| Array of `MakeProcInstance` thunks | Created by `MakeProcInstance` routine for use by dialog box procedures, and other "call-back" procedures, but *not* for window procedures. |
| Current MS-DOS disk directory | On a task switch, Windows sets up the current disk and directory for the active program. |
| EMS allocation data | Real mode only. |
| Application message queue | Keeps private messages that have been posted to a program (using the `PostMessage` routine). |
| Module database handle | Memory object that contains directory of objects in the module's .EXE or .DLL file. |
| Private interrupt vector table | Contains the private interrupts that a program has installed. Only a small set can be installed, including interrupts 0, 2, 4, 6, 7. These deal with errors in arithmetic functions. Can be changed by calling interrupt `21h` (DOS services), function number `25h`. |
| Pointer to DOS program database | Also known as the DOS Program Segment Prefix or PSP. Windows provides a copy of this data structure for each Windows program that runs. A program can get the address of this by calling `GetCurrentPDB`. |
| Task switch save area | Saves CPU registers between task switches. |

This list is not complete, nor is this the order of the actual TDB. The contents of the TDB are not publicly documented, which means it can change in a future version. But it's included here to give you an idea of the type of data that Windows saves for every instance of every program. For example, from the list you can see that Windows keeps track of the current disk and directory for each program. A program can freely change these and not be worried about any adverse effects on other programs. Also, in case you wondered where the application's private message queue lives, it lives in the TDB. Notice that the TDB has a private interrupt vector table. If you want to trap the interrupts that are generated when certain arithmetic errors occur, you can install your own interrupt handler. For example, interrupt vector 0 is issued when a divided-by-zero error occurs. Programs that don't handle those interrupts themselves are terminated when such errors occur.

Windows always creates one TDB per instance of every program that runs. When an instance of a program terminates, the TDB is removed from memory. Knowing this, you should check that your Windows programs terminate properly. How? It's easy. Run any of the various memory viewer programs, and check that there are no unexpected objects labeled "Task Database" when you think your program should have terminated. If you do find such objects, you'll know that your program has not exited properly.

## The Module Database

There is an entry in the TDB that points to another data object that the KERNEL uses: the module database. The module database contains an abbreviated version of the header to an .EXE file, known more simply as an EXE header. A utility called TDUMP.EXE lets you read this header.

Windows uses the module database whenever it needs to load anything from an executable file. This includes code, resources, and data. When we discuss dynamic linking in Chapter 19, you'll see that Windows sets up tiny code fragments called **thunks** to make dynamic linking work. In real mode, thunks allow code to be discarded and moved with a minimum of overhead. The module database is basically a directory of segments that can be read from an executable file.

Programs have module databases, but so do dynamic link libraries. If you run a memory viewer program, you'll notice that KERNEL, USER, and GDI each have a module database. There is even a module database for fonts, which are simply dynamic link libraries that have no code.

In this chapter, we have looked at the way that Windows is able to take advantage of the memory capabilities of the entire family of Intel-86 processors. In the next chapter, we're going to look at application-specific memory use issues. We're going to address all the different types of memory that are available to a Windows program.

# 18

# Memory, Part II: Application Memory Use

When a programmer starts to think about how to pack a Windows program's data into memory, it can be compared to what a traveler thinks about when packing for a trip. The first question is "What bags do I take?" For a weekend, a small suitcase might do. For a two-week vacation, several suitcases might be needed. In the context of a program, the question is "What kinds of containers can a Windows program use to store data?"

In designing the approach that your programs will take in using memory, there are a number of basic issues to deal with. These include allocation, visibility, lifetime, and overhead. As we look at the different types of memory available to an OWL Windows program, we'll consider each of these issues and weigh its importance. Table 18.1 summarizes these issues for the many types of memory available to a Windows application.

**Table 18.1** A summary of application memory use

| Memory Type | Allocation | Visibility | Lifetime | Overhead |
|---|---|---|---|---|
| Static variables | C++ compiler | In a program | Program | None |
| Automatic variables | C++ compiler | In a function | Function | None |
| Local heap | Calls to `LocalAlloc` | In a program | Program | 4 or 6 bytes |

*(Continued)*

**Table 18.1** *Continued*

| Global heap | Calls to `GlobalAlloc` | Program/system | Program/system | 24 bytes |
| Resources | Resource manager | Program/system | Owner | 24 bytes |
| GDI objects | GDI routines | System | System | Varies |
| USER objects | USER routines | System | Owner | Varies |

The issue of **allocation** involves *who* allocates a given piece of memory. The compiler allocates some memory for you, which is the case with static and automatic variables. In other cases, you must explicitly allocate memory. For example, to allocate memory using one of Windows' dynamic memory allocation packages, you make explicit calls to either `LocalAlloc` or `GlobalAlloc`. In some cases, memory allocation is a side effect of creating certain types of system objects. For example, when you create a device context (DC) in GDI, objects are allocated in GDI's local heap space.

The issue of **visibility** has to do with who can see the memory. Some objects have a very limited visibility, like automatic variables declared inside a function. Others have a visibility that is system wide, like GDI drawing objects and certain objects allocated from the global heap. Such objects can be shared between programs, but be careful to clean up such objects when you are done. Windows doesn't automatically clean them up for you.

The issue of **lifetime** describes how memory is reclaimed. With some objects, memory is reclaimed automatically when a program terminates. This is the case with static and automatic variables, as well as objects allocated from the local heap. Other objects must be explicitly deallocated to free up this memory for other uses. In general, it is a good programming practice to free memory when it is no longer needed, whether or not that memory will be automatically freed.

And finally, the issue of **overhead** describes what extra costs are associated with allocating a piece of memory beyond the actual bytes that are used. This issue is especially important when deciding how to use dynamic memory allocation—allocation from the local and global heaps. For example, every global memory object has an overhead of 24 bytes *minimum*. If you are in the habit of allocating hundreds of tiny (12-byte) objects, you'll want to think again before putting them into a global memory object.

Let's begin by looking at each of the different types of memory available. We'll then discuss issues relating to the allocation of memory from the global heap—the most flexible and useful type of dynamic memory allocation. We'll look at how code structure affects memory use, then look at allocation from the local heap, the use of custom resources, and some tricks that will allow you to perform local heap allocation in a dynamically allocated segment. We'll provide you with a lot of sample code, so you can examine in detail all of the pieces that are necessary to make each type of memory work properly.

# Overview of Application Memory Use

In the last chapter, we described how the Intel-86 family of processors uses a segmented addressing scheme. Since Windows is built on top of this architecture, Windows programmers should keep in mind that the segment is the fundamental unit of memory. This being the case, our discussion of memory is organized in terms of segments. We'll start with the default data segment, which holds three types of data objects: static variables, automatic variables, and the local heap.

## *Default Data Segment*

Windows works best with programs that have a *single* data segment. With the Microsoft compiler, this means using the small or medium memory models. The reason is that the other memory models automatically create two (or more) data segments. With the Borland C++ compiler, you can use any of the memory models. You can even use the large memory model (which we have done throughout this book), as long as you avoid creating too much static data. Doing so will require the compiler and the linker to allocate additional data segments. A single data segment is best because of the way that Windows' dynamic linking works. As we'll describe in Chapter 19, when we describe the dynamic link mechanism, Windows tries to fix up the data segment register when a Windows library routine calls a function in your program. This call-back mechanism is used for window procedures, and therefore is fundamental to the way that Windows works. For each program, Windows internally stores only *one* data segment value.

Programs that *must* have more than one default data segment can do so. But such programs are subject to certain restrictions. For one thing, Windows will only allow one instance of your program to run at a time. While a single data segment might seem to be too small for real-world applications, you have a few alternatives (which are covered in detail in this chapter): First, you can store read-only data objects in a custom resource. Second, you can use dynamically allocated memory to handle most of your program's memory needs.

Every Windows application will have a default data segment. In some respects, a program's default data segment is just another segment in the global heap: The Windows loader allocates the segment from the global heap using the global heap allocation routine, `GlobalAlloc`. The segment can move and it can grow, just like any other segment.

In other respects, a default data segment is unique. Windows sets up the correct value in the DS (data segment) register when a message is delivered to a program. This means that applications can assume they will always have access to their most important data. We'll discuss the setup of the DS register in Chapter 19, when we delve into the code-

## 560  Operating System Considerations

related aspects of dynamic linking. The default data segment also contains an application's stack and a local heap that can be used for dynamic memory allocation.

A program's data segment is divided into four or five parts: a header, static data area, stack, local heap, and an optional atom table. Figure 18.1 shows a typical program's data segment, with each part labeled. For the sake of comparison, it's interesting to note that a dynamic link library's data segment may contain all of these same elements, except DLLs ordinarily do not have a stack. Instead, DLLs use the stack of the programs that call the library routines. Figure 18.2 shows a typical DLL data segment. Let's look at each element in a typical program's data segment, one at a time starting with the segment header.

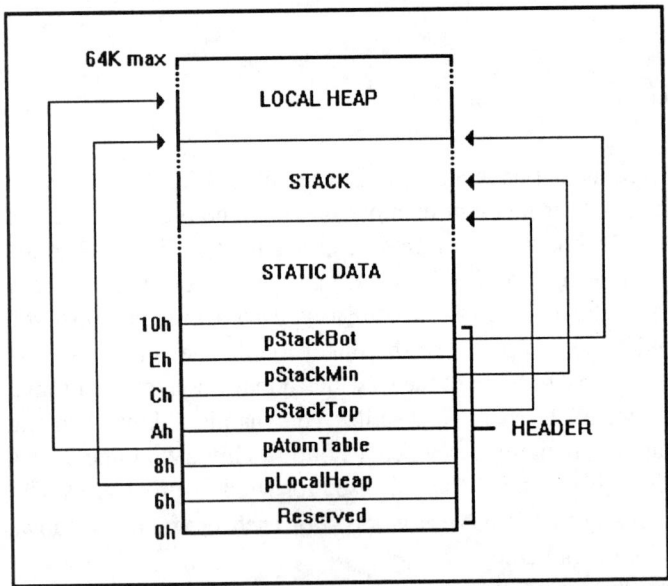

**Figure 18.1** A typical program's local data segment

### Default Data Segment Header

The header is a 16-byte area that contains pointers used by the KERNEL to manage the local data segment. A Windows program should leave this area alone, since it is automatically allocated at compile/link time and managed by the KERNEL at runtime. When allocating a local heap on a dynamically allocated segment, however, you'll need to set aside the first 16 bytes for use by the KERNEL. We'll show how this is done later in this chapter. Other than that, our primary interest in this data area rests in what we can learn about Windows' management of a local data segment.

Of the five pointers in the segment header, by far and away the most important is the pointer to the local heap, `pLocalHeap`. It is used by the local heap management routines to find the local heap so that the local heap doesn't interfere with other data objects in the data segment. Your Windows program should not directly modify the local heap, but should instead call the various local heap routines—another subject we'll discuss later in this chapter.

Three of the pointers reference the stack: **pStackBot**, **pStackMin**, and **pStackTop**. When the debug version of Windows is installed, these three pointers are used to check for stack overflows. It's a good idea to test your Windows programs against this special version, since it will help you find errors that might otherwise go undetected.

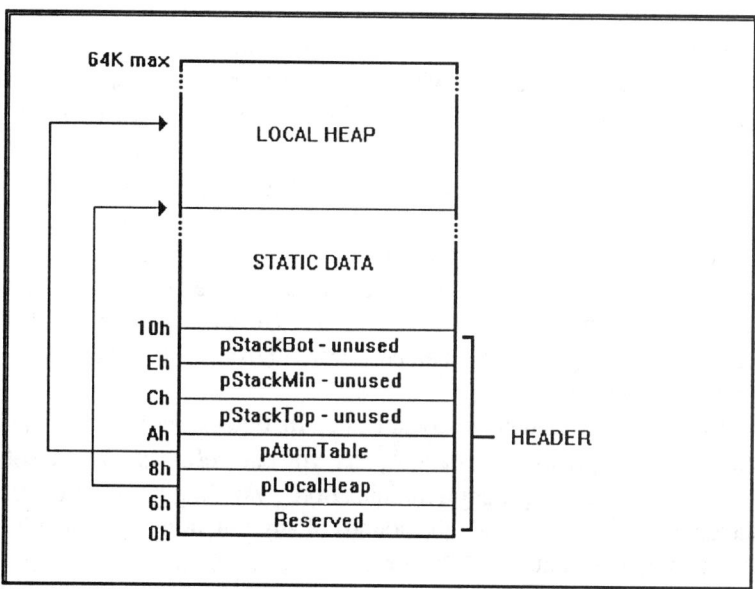

**Figure 18.2** A typical dynamic link library's data segment

The fifth and final pointer, **pAtomTable**, points to an atom table if a program has created one. Atom tables are created from memory allocated out of the local heap and are managed by the various atom management routines. Notice that the segment header doesn't have any pointer to the static data area. It's the compiler's job to define the static data area and generate the correct code to use it.

## The Static Data Area

The static data area holds a program's "global" data. This includes all variables declared outside of functions, all variables declared with the **static** keyword, all static strings, and the static data allocated for use by the various runtime library routines.

In the following code fragment, four different objects are allocated in the static data area, and five are not. Can you identify the static data objects?

```
char *pch = "String of Characters";
int  i;

int PASCAL WinMain (HINSTANCE hInstance, HINSTANCE hPrevInstance,
                LPSTR lpszCmdLine, int nCmdShow)
    {
    static int iCount;
    long       lValue;
    ...
```

As you might expect, the two variables defined outside any function—`pch` and `i`—are allocated in the static data area. So is `iCount`, which uses the `static` keyword. This declaration, since it's inside the bounds of a function, limits the **scope** of this variable to the `WndProc` function. In other words, `iCount` is only visible to code *inside* this function. But, as a static object, it has a lifetime as long as the program itself, which means that it resides in the static data area.

The fourth object placed in the static area is the string: "`String of Characters`." Because strings can take up quite a bit of space, you can reduce the size of the static data area by putting all strings into a string resource. When a string is needed, it can be loaded and used. When it is not needed, string resources can be discarded from memory to reduce the overall demand for system memory.

The static data area is also used to hold statically allocated **instances**. In the same way that we can define normal C data types as static data objects, you can define an instance of a C++ class. The instance is initialized at program initialization, by calling its constructor. To define such an instance, you define it outside the bounds of any function. For example, here's an example of allocating an instance of `TWindow` as a static instance:

```
TWindow SomeWindow;

int PASCAL WinMain (HINSTANCE hInstance, HINSTANCE hPrevInstance,
                LPSTR lpszCmdLine, int nCmdShow)
    {
    SomeWindow.Attr.X = 10;
    ...
```

This may not make sense in terms of this specific class, but it shows how a C++ instance can be allocated in the static data area.

## The Stack

The stack is a dynamic data area that is managed for you through a high-level language like C or C++. Stacks are so central to software that the Intel processors have a set of registers that are dedicated to the use and maintenance of the stack area. These include the SS (stack segment) register, and the BP (base pointer) and SP (stack pointer) offset registers. Stack use is even built into the processor's hardware. When it makes a function call, the processor automatically pushes a return address on the stack. When returning from a function, a return address is automatically popped off the stack as the location of the next instruction to be executed.

The compiler stores three things on the stack: local variables, arguments passed to called functions, and return addresses. As you may recall, the STACKSIZE statement in the module definition (.DEF) file defines the amount of space reserved for the stack, with a minimum stack size of 5K. You'll want to understand how your program uses this stack, so that you can allocate the proper amount of stack space.

Variables declared inside a function that don't use the **static** keyword are local variables, such as the **lValue** variable in the code fragment we looked at a moment ago. Space on the stack for local variables is allocated when a function is called, and freed when returning from a function. If you are writing a program that allocates a lot of local variables, you may wish to use a higher STACKSIZE value to reflect the additional memory that is needed. A higher stack size should also be requested for programs that do a lot of recursive calling, since local variables are allocated for *each* call made into functions. The following boxed discussion provides some additional details on the use of the stack for the three basic stack objects.

---

*The accompanying figure shows the relationship of the three main types of stack objects: arguments, return address, and local variables.*

*Also shown is the C call and the resulting assembly language instructions that support this stack structure. The* **push** *instruction puts arguments on the stack for called functions. The* `call` *instruction places a return address on the stack, and passes control to the called function. Inside the called function, the compiler creates the code to adjust the base pointer, BP, and the stack pointer, SP, to access both the passed arguments and the local variables on the* **stack frame**. *Notice that the variable defined with the* **static** *keyword, j, is not allocated on the stack. Instead, as a static data object, it is allocated in the static data area.*

| C-LANGUAGE | MASM | STACK |
|---|---|---|
| x(...) | push a | |
| { | push b | a |
| y(a,b,c); | push c | b |
| RetAddr: | call y | c |
| } | | x-RetAddr |
| | bp → | old bp value |

```
NEAR PASCAL y
    (int a,
     int b,            y proc near
     int c)              push bp
{                        mov  bp,sp
int x,y,z;               sub  sp,6
static int j;            .
    .                    .
    .                    .
    .                    mov  sp,bp
}                        pop  bp
                         ret  6
```

```
      x
      y
sp →  z
```

The BP, or base pointer, register is set up to allow arguments and the local variables to be referenced from a fixed location. If you run a debugger like the Turbo Debugger, you can see the machine language references to arguments as positive offsets from BP. Here is an assembly language instruction that references the third passed argument in our example:

```
MOV    AX, [BP+04]
```

Local variables are referenced as negative offsets from BP. For example, here is how the third local variable might be accessed:

```
MOV    AX, [BP-06]
```

Because the Pascal calling convention has been selected, the called function cleans up the stack. This is actually built into the return instruction, which is one reason that this calling convention creates smaller, faster code:

```
RET    6
```

If this seems somewhat esoteric and complex to you, don't worry too much. Fortunately, the details of stack management are mostly the concern of assembly language programmers and compiler writers. The compiler takes care of everything, so that you don't have to think about it. The important things to keep in mind are the three uses of the stack, so that you can be sure to adjust your stack size when you write a Windows program that uses either a lot of local variables or deeply nested recursive calls.

C++ class instances can also be allocated on the stack. In fact, every OWL program in this book has a **WinMain** function like this one:

```
int PASCAL WinMain (HINSTANCE hInstance, HINSTANCE hPrevInstance,
                    LPSTR   lpszCmdLine, int nCmdShow)
    {
    TMinApplication Min ("MIN", hInstance, hPrevInstance,
                    lpszCmdLine, nCmdShow);
    Min.Run();
    return Min.Status;
    }
```

In this example, **Min** refers to an instance of **TMinApplication** which is stored on the stack. The primary value of such stack data objects is their great convenience: Their life is the same as the life of the function. When we leave the function, the instance—along with any other stack data—gets cleaned up.

## The Debug Version of Windows and Stack Checking

Under ordinary circumstances, a stack overflow will go unnoticed. Or, it will result in mysterious and untraceable problems with your program. To prevent this problem, you must test your programs under very special circumstances, since the normal stack checking is disabled under Windows. Here's what you need. First, you must compile your programs with stack checking *enabled*, which means compile *with* the -N switch. Next, you must have a special version of Windows installed on your system that is known as the **debug version**. The debug version of Windows is created by copying a set of dynamic link library files from the Windows software development kit into the system subdirectory (\windows\system). The set of DLLs performs extra error checking. And finally, you need to have an extra monitor hooked up to your system. This allows you to receive debugging information (and to communicate with debuggers like Turbo Debugger) without disturbing the graphic display screen.

## The Local Heap

Local heaps are one of two places from which programs can perform dynamic memory allocation (the other is the global heap). Local heaps are always set up inside a single data segment. A local heap is automatically set up for a program's use in the default data segment. In addition, a program can allocate other segments in which a local heap can be created. We'll describe how this is done later in this chapter.

Without requiring any special effort on your part, every program has one local heap, which resides at the end of the default data segment. The initial size of the heap depends on the value defined in the module definition (.DEF) file with the HEAPSIZE statement. The heap can grow beyond this size, though. And when it does, the segment that contains the local heap will grow as well. A local heap can continue to grow until its segment reaches a maximum size of 64K.

Programs allocate memory from a local heap using one of the 12 local heap management routines. You can easily tell one of these routines, since the name of each routine starts with the word "Local." For example, **LocalAlloc** is the name of the routine that allocates memory from a local heap. **LocalFree** releases memory that has been allocated in a local heap. Table 18.2 provides a complete list of the local heap management routines. Later in this chapter, we'll take a closer look at local heap management, and provide some more detail on the routines marked with *.

**Table 18.2** Windows local heap management routines

| | |
|---|---|
| LocalAlloc * | Allocates memory from a local heap. |
| LocalCompact | Reorganizes a local heap. |
| LocalDiscard | Discards an unlocked, discardable object. |
| LocalFlags | Provides information about a specific memory object. |
| LocalFree * | Frees a local memory object. |
| LocalHandle | Provides the handle of a local memory object associated with a given memory address. |
| LocalInit * | Initializes a local heap. |
| LocalLock * | Increments the lock count on a local memory object, and returns its address. |
| LocalReAlloc * | Changes the size of a local memory object. |
| LocalShrink | Reorganizes a local heap and reduces the size of the heap (if possible) to the initial, starting size. If this routine is successful, it reduces the size of the data segment that contains the heap, so that the memory can be reclaimed by the global heap. |
| LocalSize | Returns the current size of a local memory object. |
| LocalUnlock * | Decrements the lock count on a local memory object. |

In the preceding chapter, we described how three types of segments can be allocated on the global heap: moveable, discardable, and fixed. The local heap also supports these three types. Moveable objects can be allocated to help minimize memory fragmentation, and discardable objects can be allocated to give the local memory manager the freedom to purge unneeded objects when memory is low. By comparison, the standard runtime library routines only allocate fixed objects and do not support moveable or discardable objects. In this way, the local memory manager provides quite a bit more sophistication than the runtime library's **malloc** routine in allocating and managing a heap space.

To support moveable and discardable memory objects, the local heap manager provides a **memory handle** when it allocates a local memory object. Like the handles that we encountered in the context of GDI objects, a memory handle is simply an identifier that can be traded in to access the real object. When a memory handle is passed to the **LocalLock** routine, a memory pointer is provided. As we'll see later, this means that code like the following is required to access a local memory object:

```
HANDLE hMem;
PSTR   pstr;

/* Allocate a 15 byte moveable object. */
hMem = LocalAlloc (LMEM_MOVEABLE, 15);

/* Lock the object, getting a pointer. */
pstr = LocalLock (hMem);

lstrcpy (pstr, "Hello World");

/* Unlock the object. */
LocalUnlock (hMem);
```

In addition, when you create an OWL program in a small or medium model, dynamic instances are created on the local heap. In particular, when you create an instance with the **new** keyword, the small and medium model OWL libraries call the **malloc** routine. This call gets converted to a set of calls to the various local heap allocation routines. In compact and large models, on the other hand, dynamic instances are created as part of a subsegment allocation scheme built into OWL.

Later in this chapter, we'll provide you a full-blown example of a program that uses local heap allocation. Let's continue our tour of program memory management by looking at the last item in the default data segment, the atom table.

## Atom Tables

Optionally, a program can create an atom table in its local data segment. An atom table provides a way to store and retrieve variable-length character strings. When an atom is created, a handle is issued that uniquely identifies the string. At two bytes, a handle is a small, fixed-size value that can easily and conveniently be placed into fixed-length data structures with a minimum of overhead. And atom tables are efficient, since duplicate requests create the same atom value. The USER module uses atoms to store the names of window classes, clipboard formats, and application-defined messages. You may wish to use them to help you deal efficiently with variable-length strings.

In addition to the private atom table that resides in the local data segment, Windows provides a global atom table. Windows' Dynamic Data Exchange (DDE) protocol relies on the global atom table to pass the ASCII names of data topics between programs. Since DDE uses messages to relay requests for data, an atom provides a compact way to store the name of a desired data element in a very small space.

## *Dynamically Allocated Segments*

Dynamically allocated segments provide the most flexible type of read/write memory for an application to use. Up to the limit of available system memory, you can have as many as you want, and each segment you allocate can be as large as 64K. In fact, you can allocate segments larger than 64K, although the methods required to support this are beyond the scope of this book.

How many dynamically allocated segments *can* a program create? There are three factors: available system memory, the size of a handle table, and whether Windows is running in real mode, standard mode, or 386-Enhanced Mode. Real mode has a maximum address space of one megabyte, standard mode has a maximum of 16 megabytes, and 386-Enhanced Mode has a maximum of 64 megabytes. In all three modes, the maximum size of a handle table is 8,192 entries, which means that a maximum of 8,192 segments can be created. However, standard mode uses *two* table entries for each segment, so the system-wide maximum for standard mode is 4,096 segments. Future versions of Windows will probably fix standard mode, so that 8,192 segments can be allocated. In addition, in future versions of Windows these protected mode limits will most likely become a *per task* limit. In Windows 3.0, however, these limits apply on a system-wide basis.

Programs allocate and manage dynamic segments using Windows' global heap management routines. This is a set of 21 routines that start with the word "Global." `GlobaAlloc`, for example, allocates a dynamic segment and `GlobalFree` deallocates a segment. Incidentally, the Windows KERNEL itself uses these allocation routines for managing system-level objects like code segments. These routines provide the "lowest-level" of memory allocation in the Windows API.

There are three basic types of segments: fixed, moveable, and discardable. The use of fixed segments tends to be limited to device drivers, which require that a memory object always stays in one place. The reason is that fixed segments prevent the memory manager from compacting memory when it needs to, so that most programs use moveable segments to store data. From the Memory Manager's point of view, the most "friendly" kind of object is a discardable one. It can be moved or discarded, as the Memory Manager sees fit, when system memory starts to get a little cramped. Code and resource segments are usually discardable segments, although a program could store data in a discardable segment to implement a type of virtual memory system under real and standard mode Windows.

Just like the local memory manager, the global memory manager provides a handle when it allocates a block of memory. The use of a handle instead of a pointer allows moveable and discardable objects to be moved or discarded. When a program wishes to access the memory, it calls a special routine which locks the object in place and provides a pointer: **GlobalLock**. When a program has finished using a block of memory, it releases the object by calling **GlobalUnlock**. Here is a sample code fragment that shows how a segment from the global heap can be allocated so that a string can be copied into the segment:

```
HANDLE hMem;
LPSTR    lpstr;

/* Allocate a 15 byte moveable object. */
hMem = GlobalAlloc (GMEM_MOVEABLE, 15L);

/* Lock the object, getting a pointer. */
lpstr = GlobalLock (hMem);

lstrcpy (lpstr, "Hello World");

/* Unlock the object. */
GlobalUnlock (hMem);
```

If you compare this code fragment to the one we looked at during our discussion of the local heap routines, you'll find that the two sets of dynamic memory allocation routines look very similar. This is no accident. The two subroutine packages were developed at the same time, to provide similar services but at two different levels: One manages the system-wide global heap and the other manages the private local heap that each program is given by default.

> ### Windows 3.1 Application Note
>
> The locking/unlocking described here is required for a program to work in real mode. Starting with Windows 3.1, real mode support is being discontinued in Windows. For this reason, the dynamic segment allocation process is greatly simplified. In particular, you can lock a segment right after it is allocated, and avoid unlocking it until you free the segment. The SEGALLOC sample, which is included later in this chapter, provides an example of this type of allocation.

Later in this chapter, we'll provide a complete program to demonstrate the use of the global heap management routines. For now, let's move on to discuss another place that C++ programs use to store data: resources.

## Resources

An important type of memory object often overlooked for their memory management qualities are resources. A resource is a read-only data object that has been merged into a program's .EXE file by the resource compiler. When the data is needed, the resource manager reads it from disk and places it into a discardable memory object. And when the memory manager needs to reclaim the memory for another use, a resource can typically be discarded or purged from system memory. As allocated segments, resources can be allocated as fixed, moveable, or discardable segments. Since discardable resources are the most flexible, they are the most common.

Table 18.3 provides a list of the different types of resources that Windows supports, along with the chapter in this book that discusses the use of each type. As you can see, resources play a key role in how certain data objects are packaged for use. Resources are used for user-interface objects, GDI objects, and space-saving objects like string tables and custom resources.

**Table 18.3** Window's predefined resources

| Resource Type | Covered In Depth |
| --- | --- |
| Accelerator table | Chapter 11 |
| Bitmaps | |
| Cursors | Chapter 17 |
| Custom resources | Chapter 18 |
| Dialog box templates | Chapter 14 |
| Fonts | Chapter 10 |
| Icons | |
| Menu templates | Chapter 11 |
| String tables | Chapter 18 |

From a memory use point of view, each resource resides in a separate segment. In other words, a program with one accelerator table, two menu templates, and four dialog box templates has a total of seven different segments worth of resources. The advantage of having each resource packed in its own segment is that each can be loaded and discarded in a manner that is completely independent of other resources.

## GDI Data Segment

Whenever a program creates a GDI object, space is allocated out of GDI's data segment. Or more specifically, space is allocated from GDI's local heap. While there's no doubt that programs will need to use such objects, care should be taken to avoid creating too many of these types of objects. In addition, programs that create GDI drawing objects should be careful to destroy the objects when they are not needed. Otherwise, if GDI's heap gets full, it will prevent other programs from being able to run properly. In a future version, Windows will delete GDI objects when the owning application terminates. In the meantime, allocate only a minimum number of objects, and be sure to destroy objects when you are done using them.

Table 18.4 provides a list of GDI objects and the size that each takes from GDI's data segment. These sizes are subject to change; they are provided to help you get a sense for the demands that each object places on system memory. Two GDI objects reside in their own segment: fonts and bitmaps. The local heap object contains a pointer to the larger object.

**Table 18.4** Space taken in GDI's local heap by various GDI drawing objects

| Object | Size |
| --- | --- |
| Brush | 32 bytes |
| Bitmap | 28–32 bytes |
| Font | 40–44 bytes |
| Pen | 28 bytes |
| Region | 28 bytes to several Kbytes |
| Palette | 28 bytes |

One other data area can get filled by the actions that programs take, and should be monitored carefully: the USER library's data segment.

## USER Data Segment

Windows' USER module provides the support for Windows' user-interface objects. This includes windows, menus, dialog boxes, and accelerator tables. Unlike GDI objects, USER objects in general are not shared between programs. For this reason, when a Windows program terminates, USER can free the data objects that were created. Nonetheless, the wise Windows programmer makes frugal use of memory and will destroy objects when done using them.

Quite a few user-interface objects are stored as resources, and therefore reside in their own segments. Included in this group are cursors, icons, dialog box templates, and menu templates. Other objects take up USER heap space, including those shown in Table 18.5. The exact size of individual objects is less important (since it can change from version to version) than the fact that your use of these objects takes up space which, at least for now, is in short supply. For example, if you define 10 window classes and create 100 windows of each class, you consume about 7,500 bytes of USER heap space. Since USER's heap is also used by other programs, including the Program Manager, File Manager, etc., you need to be careful not to create too many objects that may cause this heap space to be overrun.

**Table 18.5** Appropriate size of various USER data objects

| Object | Size |
| --- | --- |
| Menus | 20 bytes/ menu plus |
|  | 20 bytes/ menu item |
| Window class | 40–50 bytes |
| Window | 60–70 bytes |

Assuming you don't create too many objects and overload USER's heap space, there are two often overlooked types of memory areas: class extra bytes and window extra bytes. These are small data areas that reside in USER's data segment, but which are attached to a specific window or window class. A program might put flags, or even a memory handle, into these extra bytes. Then they can be accessed by simply providing the window handle. Here is a list of the routines that access window and class extra bytes:

| *Class Extra Bytes* | *Window Extra Bytes* |
| --- | --- |
| `SetClassWord` | `SetWindowWord` |
| `SetClassLong` | `SetWindowLong` |
| `GetClassWord` | `GetWindowWord` |
| `GetClassLong` | `GetWindowLong` |

The advantage of these extra bytes is that they allow you, for example, to store the head of a linked list in an area that is directly related to a window. Or, you can store a memory handle, to give each window—n effect—its own private data area. The most obvious use of this type of memory is in implementing custom dialog box controls. But it is equally useful in implementing applications that support the Multiple Document Interface (MDI).

With this brief introduction to the different types of memory available to Windows applications, you have a reasonably complete picture of the choices you can make. Now it's time to roll up our sleeves and look at the implementation details for using different types of memory. The rest of this chapter provides five complete code examples to answer any further questions you might have regarding an application's use of memory. Here is a list of the code examples and the topics that each focuses on:

- **SEGALLOC.** This sample program demonstrates how to use memory allocated out of the global heap. The accompanying discussion provides more details on the various global heap management routines.
- **MIN2.** We're going to take a second look at the minimum Windows program to support a discussion of code structure and memory use. This program demonstrates how a Windows program can be divided into multiple code segments to improve memory use.
- **LOCALMEM.** This program provides an example of using the local heap management routines to allocate objects from a program's default data segment. This program also demonstrates the use of string tables.
- **SUBSEG.** This program shows how the local heap management routines can be used with a segment that is dynamically allocated from the global heap. This program combines global heap management routines and local heap management routines.
- **CUSTRES.** This program demonstrates the creation of a custom resource. A sine table is stored as a resource and used to calculate sine and cosine values, which are used to draw a circle.

Let's get started, then, with a look at using the global heap management routines.

## Global Heap Allocation

When a program allocates memory from Windows' global heap, it is allocating a segment. Segments can be allocated that are fixed, moveable, or discardable, depending upon what a program needs. In general, though, programmers should keep in mind the words of John Pollock, who worked on Windows' first KERNEL and was the first Windows instructor for many Windows programmers. He urged programmers to keep dynamically allocated segments "as *few* as possible, as *small* as possible, and as *discardable* as possible."

## As Few as Possible

You'll want to keep your segments as *few* as possible because of the overhead of a segment. Segments are expensive. Each incurs 24 bytes of overhead: a 16-byte invisible header that links all segments together and an 8-byte entry in a master segment table. In real mode, this segment table is called the Burgermaster. In protected mode, the segment table is the local descriptor table (LDT). See Chapter 17 for more details.

Because of this high overhead, you'll probably want to minimize the number of segments you allocate. For example, with an overhead of 24 bytes, if you allocate a segment to hold a 24-byte data object, it really costs you 48 bytes. That's a lot like having a sales tax of 100% on everything you buy. But since this is a fixed cost, you can effectively lower your "memory-use tax" by putting many objects into a single segment. For example, if you put 2,400 bytes of data into a single object, you have effectively lowered your taxes to a mere 1%. When you start to think about how to make the best use of dynamically allocated segments, think about using arrays of records instead of working with a linked list of segments. It will help you get your money's worth from the Memory Manager.

A second issue that relates to segment overhead involves **granularity**. This refers to the actual pieces of memory that Windows carves out when you allocate a segment. Dynamically allocated segments have a granularity of 32 bytes—or, in real mode memory terms, two paragraphs. (Recall that in real mode the smallest segment is 16 bytes, which is called a paragraph. Even though protected mode allows for smaller segments, Windows doesn't.) In real and standard modes, 16 bytes of every object is used as a header. In either of these modes, if you ask for a segment that is between one and 16 bytes long, it costs you 32 bytes. This table shows how a 32-byte granularity affects the size of the *actual* versus the *requested* memory:

| Requested Size | Actual Size | Header | Actual Data Area |
| --- | --- | --- | --- |
| 1–16 bytes | 32 bytes | 16 bytes | 16 bytes |
| 17–48 bytes | 64 bytes | 16 bytes | 48 bytes |
| 49–80 bytes | 96 bytes | 16 bytes | 80 bytes |
| 81–112 bytes | 128 bytes | 16 bytes | 112 bytes |

Notice that the size of the actual data area jumps in odd-paragraph increments, so that every segment request is an odd multiple of 16 bytes (1, 3, 5, 7, etc.).

In 386-Enhanced Mode, a 32-byte granularity is also used. However, the implementation is a little different since this mode is able to take advantage of features of the Intel 80386. The granularity is in terms of even paragraphs. Here is a table that demonstrates this:

| Requested Size | Actual Size | Header | Actual Data Area |
| --- | --- | --- | --- |
| 1–32 bytes | 32 bytes | 16 bytes (hidden) | 32 bytes |
| 33–64 bytes | 64 bytes | 16 bytes (hidden) | 64 bytes |
| 65–96 bytes | 96 bytes | 16 bytes (hidden) | 96 bytes |
| 97–128 bytes | 128 bytes | 16 bytes (hidden) | 128 bytes |

Since the 386-Enhanced Mode runs in protected mode, just like standard mode, a reference beyond the limit of a segment causes a program to terminate with a UAE error. However, since this mode has a different alignment from standard mode, it is possible that a bug that causes a UAE error in one of the protected modes might not cause the same error in the other protected mode. You should advise the people who test your programs to be sure to run a full set of tests in both modes. A small difference like this can cause a stable program in one environment to crash in the other.

## As Small as Possible

Keep your segments as small as possible, because Windows is a multitasking system, and memory that you allocate is not available for other Windows programs. This is particularly an issue in real mode, with its tiny, one-megabyte address space. But even in other modes, only allocate the amount of memory you need and no more.

One reason that John Pollock made this recommendation has to do with the way some DOS programs behave. Since DOS is a single-tasking operating system, the first thing that many DOS programs do is to allocate all of system memory. If a Windows program tried to do this, it would effectively lock out other programs from being able to run.

So, whether you are moving to Windows from DOS or from some other programming environment, keep in mind that memory is a shared, and in some cases, a scarce resource. Allocate only what you need, when you need it. And, when you are done using a block of memory, free it so that other Windows programs can use it.

## As Discardable as Possible

In the last chapter, we talked about the three types of memory objects: fixed, moveable, and discardable. To the Windows Memory Manager, fixed is the least flexible and therefore least desirable type of memory object, and discardable is the most desirable. But programmers new to Windows tend to see things just the opposite way: Fixed memory seems the most comfortable, discardable seems the most disastrous, and moveable only slightly less so. After all, what programmer in his right mind wants to deal with data that keeps wiggling away, or disappears completely?

John Pollock's recommendation to make memory as discardable as possible reflects the fact that memory should be treated as a scarce resource. Programs with moderate requirements for memory usually keep data in moveable data segments. After all, a moveable segment gives the memory manager the freedom to shuffle memory so it can minimize fragmentation.

Programs with a large or unlimited need for memory, like word processing programs or spreadsheet programs, require their own mechanism to transfer data between main system memory and disk. After all, even a virtual memory system can run out of memory. And when Windows is without virtual memory in the standard and real modes, such programs will run out of "real memory" sooner. Discardable memory provides a way for such programs to volunteer objects to be purged. When memory is plentiful, discardable objects don't have to be purged. But when memory is scarce, the memory manager can exercise its option to remove discardable objects.

## Global Heap API

Table 18.6 shows all of Windows' global heap management routines. This table is set up to show how 12 of these routines must be paired together to create a sandwich construction that we first introduced in Chapter 7. The other nine routines act either on a specific global memory object or on the global heap as a whole.

**Table 18.6**

| Top Slice | Bottom Slice | Description |
| --- | --- | --- |
| GlobalAlloc | GlobalFree | Allocates a segment from the global heap. |
| GlobalCompact | na | Reorganizes the global heap to determine the largest block of available free memory. |
| GlobalDiscard | na | Purges an unlocked, discardable segment from memory. |
| GlobalDosAlloc | GlobalDosFree | Allocates a block of memory in the DOS address space, that is, below the one-megabyte line, so that a Windows program can share a data area with a DOS program or a DOS device driver. |
| GlobalFix | GlobalUnfix | Prevents an object from moving in the linear address space. Notice that this doesn't keep an |

*(Continued)*

**Table 18.6** *Continued*

| Top Slice | Bottom Slice | Description |
|---|---|---|
| | | object from being swapped to disk≈only the GlobalPageLock routine can do that. |
| GlobalFlags | na | Retrieves the flags associated with a global memory object. |
| GlobalHandle | na | Provides the global handle associated with a specific segment address |
| GlobalLock | GlobalUnlock | Retrieves the address of a global memory object. In real mode, it also increments the lock count to prevent it from moving in physical memory. In all modes, it prevents a discardable object from being discarded |
| GlobalLRUNewest | na | Changes a segment's priority in the LRU discarding table to make it *least* likely to be discarded. |
| GlobalLRUOldest | na | Changes a segment's priority in the LRU discarding table to make it the *most* likely to be discarded. |
| GlobalNotify | na | Sets up a call-back procedure through which the global heap manager notifies a program *before* a segment is discarded. A program can implement a virtual memory management scheme using this routine, that will work in all Windows' different operating modes. |
| GlobalPageLock | GlobalPageUnlock | Fixes a segment's location in the linear address space, and also prevents the virtual memory pages from being swapped out to disk. This provides the maximum protection against any movement of a segment, which is required for certain types of device drivers. However, programs should avoid using this since overuse of page locking can be severely detrimental to overall system performance. |
| GlobalReAlloc | na | Changes the size of a segment on the global heap. Both locked and unlocked segments can be resized, although a special flag must be set if you want to allow a locked segment to move if it is necessary to satisfy the allocation request. |

*(Continued)*

**Table 18.6** Continued

| | | |
|---|---|---|
| GlobalSize | na | Returns the size of a segment on the global heap. |
| GlobalWire | GlobalUnwire | In real mode Windows, moves a segment to a very low memory position for segments that are going to be locked for an unusually long period of time. This measure helps avoid serious fragmentation that otherwise occurs when moveable or discardable memory objects are left locked for longer periods of time than to process a single message. |

For the most common uses, programs can get by with just five of these routines: `GlobalAlloc`, `GlobalReAlloc`, `GlobalLock`, `GlobalUnlock`, and `GlobalFree`. We're going to take a close look at these routines, to provide you with enough information so you can start using them in your Windows programming.

## GlobalAlloc

The `GlobalAlloc` routine allocates memory from the global heap. It is defined as

```
HANDLE GlobalAlloc (wFlags, dwBytes)
```

- `wFlags` is a combination of one or more global memory allocation flags, discussed below.
- `dwBytes` is an unsigned long value for the number of bytes to allocate.

`GlobalAlloc` returns the handle that identifies the segment you've allocated. Be sure to *always* check the return value from this function, since there is no guarantee that your request can be satisfied. When an allocation request cannot be met, `GlobalAlloc` lets you know by returning a NULL handle.

The value of `wFlags` can be a combination of nine different flags, depending on the type of memory you wish to allocate (fixed, moveable, or discardable), whether the memory is going to be shared or not, and other considerations. Here are the nine flags:

| *Description* | *Flag* |
|---|---|
| Fixed memory object | GMEM_FIXED |
| Moveable memory object | GMEM_MOVEABLE |

| | |
|---|---|
| Discardable memory object | GMEM_DISCARDABLE \| GMEM_MOVEABLE |
| Initialize with zeros | GMEM_ZEROINIT |
| Segment will be shared | GMEM_DDESHARE |
| Do not compact | GMEM_NOCOMPACT |
| Do not discard | GMEM_NODISCARD |
| Tag a discardable segment so that a notification routine is called *before* the segment is discarded | GMEM_NOTIFY |
| Do not put in EMS memory | GMEM_NOT_BANKED |

The first four sets of flags are the most important and most useful. Most of the time, you'll start by deciding the disposition of your memory object: fixed, moveable, or discardable. Next, you'll decide whether to initialize the data area with zeros or not, and your job is done. The other flags have more specialized uses, which we'll review briefly to help you decide when one might be useful to you.

The second parameter, **dwBytes**, is the number of bytes to allocate. Since this is an unsigned long value, you'll often have to supply a type-cast if you have calculated the size of an object using regular integer values. For example, here is how to allocate a 200-byte, moveable segment:

```
hMem = GlobalAlloc (GMEM_MOVEABLE, (DWORD)200);
```

This routine accepts an unsigned long value for the size of a memory object because it supports memory objects that are larger than 64K. Since this is the limit on the size of a segment, Windows allocates objects larger than 64K by setting aside multiple segments to satisfy your memory request. If you wish to allocate objects larger than 64K, you'll have to do some special **segment arithmetic** to allow segment boundaries to be crossed correctly.

One approach to handling the segment arithmetic that is required for objects larger than 64K is to rely on the built-in support that some compilers provide. Pointers to such objects are referred to as **huge** pointers. However, this approach involves taking on quite a bit of overhead for even the simplest pointer operations. A more efficient approach is to use the **__AHINCR** symbol that Windows provides, which you can add to a segment address yourself if a segment boundary has been crossed. A simpler approach involves avoiding the allocation of memory objects that are larger than 64K.

The remaining flags are used for special circumstances. For example, the **GMEM_DDESHARE** flag marks a segment as one that may be shared between different programs. The "DDE" in the flag name is the acronym for the **dynamic data exchange (DDE)**, a data sharing protocol built on top of Windows' message passing system. This flag should be used when sharing data using either DDE or the clipboard. In general, programs should use one of these two mechanisms to share data, and not simply share memory handles. The reason is that certain configurations of Windows are built around the idea of private address spaces. As time goes on, this will be the case for all protected mode implementations of Windows, but for now, it is limited to Windows running with EMS memory. All data sharing *must* be based on a client-server model. That is, one program *writes* the data, and a second one *reads* the data and makes a copy for its own use. Two programs can never share the same dynamically allocated segment with both having read/write privileges.

The `GMEM_NOCOMPACT` flag tells the Memory Manager not to move memory to satisfy the memory request. The `GMEM_NODISCARD` flag says the same thing, and adds an additional condition: No segments should be discarded to satisfy the allocation request. These are useful for programs that want to avoid disturbing the global heap. For a program that is very sensitive to performance issues, memory movement is expensive. These flags tell the Memory Manager that memory should be allocated *only* if it can be done quickly from an existing free block.

The `GMEM_NOTIFY` flag is used for discardable segments to request the Memory Manager to notify you before it discards your segments. When the time comes to discard a segment, the Memory Manager calls a function that you have defined as a notification call-back function. The notification routine is assigned using the `GlobalNotify` routine. It is useful for implementing a virtual memory system that works in all of Windows' operating modes.

The final flag, `GMEM_NOT_BANKED`, is primarily for the use of optimizing device drivers for real mode when EMS memory is present. EMS was a very important addition to Windows 2.x. But since Windows 3.1 will drop support for Real Mode, this flag can be safely ignored.

## GlobalLock

The `GlobalLock` routine provides the address of a global segment, and increments the lock count for certain types of segments. It is defined as

```
LPSTR GlobalLock (hMem)
```

- `hMem` is a memory handle of a segment allocated with `GlobalAlloc`.

Programs make calls to `GlobalLock` to get the address of a moveable or discardable segment. In addition, this routine increments the lock count for discardable objects, to prevent them from being discarded. Using moveable or discardable segments requires a two-step process. The first step is to allocate the memory itself. The second step involves calling `GlobalLock` to retrieve a far pointer that can be used to access the memory. For example, here is how to allocate a moveable segment that can accommodate a 274-byte object, and lock it for use:

```
HGLOBAL hMem;
LPSTR lp;

hMem = GlobalAlloc (GMEM_MOVEABLE, (DWORD)274));
if (!hMem)
    goto ErrorExit1;

lp = (LPSTR) GlobalLock (hMem);
if (!lp)
    goto ErrorExit2;
```

Notice the two sets of error checking in this code fragment. The first check makes sure that the allocation was successful. Most programmers agree that this is reasonable. The second check is to make sure that the lock is successful. Many programmers are hesitant to check every time they lock an object. It's a little extra effort, but it prevents a program from unpleasant surprises. For one thing, a program that tries to use a null pointer will cause a general protection error—sometimes known as a GP fault. Then, Windows will terminate the program with an "Unexpected Application Error" message.

To help you understand the necessity for this message, here is a list of the things that cause a call to **GlobalLock** to fail:

- A discardable object that has been discarded.
- Inability to copy a clipboard or DDE object to the local address space. At present, this is only a concern in real mode Windows when running with EMS. But this will likely be an issue in protected mode in a future version of Windows.
- Invalid memory handle. This can happen if an object has already been freed, or if the memory location that the program has been using to store the memory handle has been overwritten.

At first glance, it may appear as if **GlobalLock** only fails in the most extreme circumstances. You might wonder whether you can avoid checking for a failed return for moveable objects that are not being used in the context of the clipboard and DDE. Unfortunately, the third set of causes is the "catch-all" that makes it necessary to always check the return value of **GlobalLock**. A memory handle can get overwritten, which will likely cause **GlobalLock** to fail.

When a program allocates a fixed object, there is no need to call **GlobalLock**. The reason is that the handle of fixed objects is always the segment address of the allocated memory. Here is how to allocate a fixed block of memory and convert the memory handle into a pointer:

```
HGLOBAL hMem;
LPSTR lp;

hMem = GlobalAlloc (GMEM_FIXED, (DWORD)200);
lp = (LPSTR)MAKELONG (0, hMem);
```

The `MAKELONG` macro packs two-word (two-byte) values into a long (four-byte) value, which can be cast to a far pointer. Of course, to work well in all of Windows' operating modes, you should probably avoid allocating fixed memory objects. But we are showing you this to give you a peek at something that you *can* do quite freely in the context of local heaps. But more on that later on.

## GlobalReAlloc

The `GlobalReAlloc` routine changes the size of a memory object on the global heap, and is defined as

`HGLOBAL GlobalReAlloc (hMem, dwBytes, wFlags)`

- `hMem` is a memory handle, obtained by calling `GlobalAlloc`.
- `dwBytes` is an unsigned long value for the number of bytes to allocate, or zero if the `GMEM_MODIFY` flag is being used to change the memory disposition of a memory object.
- `wFlags` is one or more flags, or zero if the object is just changing sizes.

The `GlobalReAlloc` routine can be used to do two different things: change the size of a global memory object, and change the memory disposition of a memory object. It takes all the same flags as the `GlobalAlloc` routine plus one new one: `GMEM_MODIFY`. This flag indicates when the memory disposition is being changed—for example, when a moveable object is being made discardable, or when a discardable object is being made moveable. Aside from this, the `GlobalReAlloc` routine can pretty much be treated as an extension of the `GlobalAlloc` routine. Here are some examples of its usage:

```
/* Make an object moveable. */
GlobalReAlloc (hMem, 0, GMEM_MODIFY | GMEM_MOVEABLE);

/* Resize an object. */
GlobalReAlloc (hMem, (DWORD)1843, 0);

/* Resize an object, filling new area with zeroes. */
GlobalReAlloc (hMem, (DWORD)dwSize, GMEM_ZEROINIT);
```

## GlobalUnlock

The `GlobalUnlock` routine decrements the lock count for certain types of segments, and is defined as

BOOL GlobalUnlock (hMem)

- **hMem** is a memory handle allocated with the `GlobalAlloc` routine.

In general, you'll call `GlobalUnlock` as the second part of a sandwich construction whenever you call `GlobalLock`. For example, here is a typical usage in response to a **WM_LBUTTONDOWN** message, to retrieve the mouse location from the **lParam**:

```
long far PASCAL WndProc (...)
    {
    LPPOINT lp;

    switch (msg)
        {
        case WM_LBUTTONDOWN:
            lp = (LPPOINT)GlobalLock (hmem);
            *lp[cp] = MAKEPOINT(lParam);
            GlobalUnlock(hmem);
            ...
```

The key issue that this code fragment demonstrates is the need to keep a memory segment locked for only a very brief period of time. Otherwise, you risk fragmenting the global heap and wasting memory. This will affect the performance of your program, as well as all other programs currently running in the system. In short, locks should be very short term.

## GlobalFree

The `GlobalFree` routine frees an unlocked global memory object that was allocated with the `GlobalAlloc` routine. It is defined as

HGLOBAL GlobalFree (hMem)

- **hMem** is a global memory handle that was allocated by calling `GlobalAlloc`.

`GlobalFree` releases the segment and all internally created data structures that are associated with a given memory handle. Even though Windows frees all memory segments when a program terminates, it's a good practice to explicitly free every object when you are done using it.

This in-depth introduction to Windows' global heap management routines has almost gotten us ready to look at some sample programs. But first, we're going to look at an issue that should give you another perspective on the way that memory is managed in Windows. Even if you never use any of these routines in any of your Windows programs, understanding where they might be useful will help you better understand Windows' memory management. What we're referring to is the various sets of routines that lock, wire, fix, and otherwise coerce a global segment to reside in a fixed location.

## *Locked, Wired, Fixed, and Page Locked*

In our discussion of Windows global heap management routines, we identified `GlobalLock` as the routine that programs use to **dereference** a handle to get a pointer. By dereference, we simply mean to convert into a pointer. `GlobalLock` has a second role: When needed, it keeps objects from moving. Because of the difference in real and protected modes, the exact meaning of this depends on the current operating mode. For example, in protected mode, `GlobalLock` doesn't prevent a moveable object from being relocated, or even from being swapped to disk. In real mode, however, which doesn't have special hardware memory management support, `GlobalLock` *does* prevent such objects from moving. And in all modes, it prevents discardable objects from being purged. Windows supports three other ways to influence the movement of a memory segment besides locking. A segment can also be wired, fixed, or page locked. Let's explore the meaning of each of these.

### Wired Segments

When a program asks Windows to allocate a segment from the global heap, Windows searches through its free list. The free list is a set of doubly linked lists that can be walked from either end. When allocating a fixed or moveable object, the Memory Manager always starts at the low-memory end of the free list. When allocating a discardable object, the search starts at the high-memory end. As depicted in Figure 18.3, this tends to group fixed and moveable objects at the bottom of memory, and discardable objects at the top of memory.

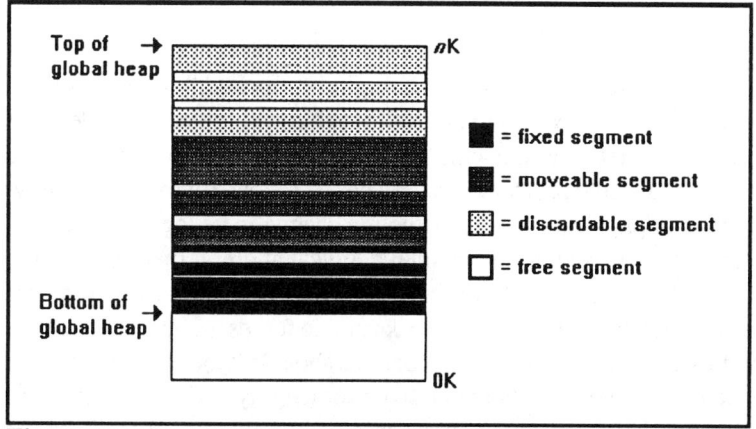

**Figure 18.3** The layout of the global heap

In addition, when allocating a fixed object, the global memory manager works quite hard to move moveable objects so that fixed objects can be as low as possible. This accentuates the layering of the global heap even more, so that—ideally at least—all fixed objects will be allocated lower than any moveable object. With fixed objects at the bottom of memory, moveable objects in the middle, and discardable objects at the top, fragmentation among moveable objects can be minimized. In a low-memory situation, Windows can purge several discardable objects at once, freeing up space for other uses.

For the most part, programs will allocate moveable or discardable objects. However, it is easy to change the disposition of a moveable object to be discardable and vice versa. On the other hand, it is not possible to change either of these objects into a fixed memory object. In fact, from the point of view of the global heap manager, this would not be a good thing. If a program were able to change a moveable or discardable segment into a fixed segment, it would create a memory sandbar. In other words, it would create a block in the middle of memory that would prevent the global heap manager from being able to freely move objects around.

However, there are times when an application may wish to lock a piece of memory down over a longer period of time than is normal. The **GlobalWire/GlobalUnwire** pair of routines provides the necessary support for this kind of operation. The **GlobalWire** routine first *moves* a moveable or discardable object to a very low memory location. This allows such objects to be fixed, without the fragmentation that would otherwise occur if the **GlobalLock** routine were to be used, for example. When a wired object does not have to be fixed any more, the **GlobalUnwire** routine can be used to let it rejoin the ranks of moveable and discardable objects.

## Fixed Segments

In the two protected modes, a global memory object might be "locked," but may still be able to move. In fact, it can even be swapped to disk (although it will not be discarded). As described in the preceding chapter, this movement is possible because of the hardware memory management that is built into protected mode. The LDT table, for example, allows a memory segment to move in physical memory without a change in its logical address.

Certain device drivers, however, don't operate on the logical address. Instead, they use the physical address. For their use, the global heap management routines include the `GlobalFix`/`GlobalUnfix` pair. The `GlobalFix` routine forces a segment to remain at the same physical address. In the same way that programs shouldn't lock down segments for lengthy periods of time, segments should not be fixed for lengthy periods of time. This can cause fragmentation of the physical address space, which makes overall system memory management less efficient. But for device drivers and other uses that require a fixed physical addresss, the `GlobalFix` routine can be used. To counter the effect of the `GlobalFix` routine, a call to `GlobalUnfix` is required.

## Page Locked Segments

Even though `GlobalFix` can prevent an object from moving in the physical address space, it can still be swapped to disk. The reason is that there are two memory managers at work: one that manages the linear, "virtual" address space, and another one that supports this address space by moving blocks of memory—also known as "pages"—to disk. When a page is referenced that is not present, a page fault is created that causes the virtual memory manager to bring the required page into memory.

While `GlobalFix` prevents an object from moving in the virtual address space, there are times when even more control is needed. In particular, for time-critical device drivers, it may be necessary to select certain segments and designate them as **page locked**. A page locked segment is the most securely attached segment that Windows 3.0 can provide. Such segments cannot move in the virtual address space, so their "physical" address stays the same. But also, such segments cannot be swapped to disk—so that response time to access that memory is always the best it can be. Even if you never write a device driver that requires page locking, it's nice to know that Windows has this capability to allow time-critical operations—like keyboard and mouse driver code, for example—to be serviced as quickly as possible.

From earlier versions of Windows, some programmers have gotten into the habit of using a segment's lock count to determine whether it needed to be unlocked or not. However, in Windows 3.0, with its sophisticated memory management, certain things have changed. If you are new to Windows programming, or if you are starting a new programming project, you may not need to worry about this practice. But if you are planning to work on some older Windows code, be on the lookout for code that relies on the lock count.

**Hint** Avoid depending on using the lock count to determine whether `GlobalLock` has locked a segment. In both protected modes, `GlobalLock` does not affect the lock count of a moveable segment.

With this under our belt, it's time to take a look at a sample Windows program that allocates memory from the global heap.

## A Sample Program: SEGALLOC

This sample program allocates three different segments from the global heap and displays information about each segment. Figure 18.4 shows the output from our program, SEGALLOC. As you can see, SEGALLOC allocates one fixed, one moveable, and one discardable segment. Also displayed are the bytes requested, the actual size of the allocated object, the handle, and the address of the segment.

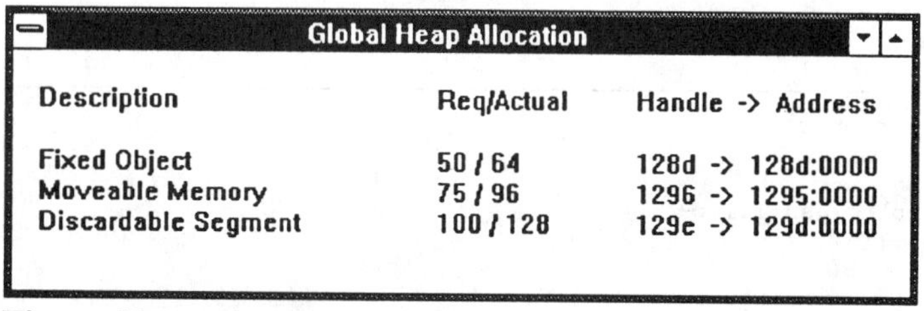

```
         Global Heap Allocation

Description          Req/Actual    Handle -> Address

Fixed Object           50 / 64     128d -> 128d:0000
Moveable Memory        75 / 96     1296 -> 1295:0000
Discardable Segment   100 / 128    129e -> 129d:0000
```

**Figure 18.4** SEGALLOC displays information about the segments it allocates

If you compare the handle and the address for the fixed memory object, you'll notice that the handle *is* the segment address. This is true for all fixed segments, in all of Windows' operating modes. Notice that the offset portion of every address is zero. When you allocate a segment from the global heap, you get to start writing your own data at the beginning of the segment, which is what this address tells you. This will be the case for all types of segments in all operating modes.

If you compare the handle and the address for the moveable and discardable objects, you'll notice some similarity. It seems that this formula can be used to find a segment address:

```
segment_address = handle - 1; /* Don't do this! */
```

This formula works in protected mode for Windows 3.0; but don't do this, and don't depend on this working in future versions of Windows. Microsoft plans to continue enhancing Windows. If you rely on this particular quirk, your programs may stop working in a future version of Windows.

**588** *Operating System Considerations*

# MAKEFILE.MAK

```
.AUTODEPEND

#    Translator Definitions
INC=\BORLANDC\OWL\INCLUDE;\BORLANDC\CLASSLIB\INCLUDE;\BORLANDC\INCLUDE
CC = bcc -c -D_CLASSDLL -H -ml -WS -w-par -I$(INC)

#    Implicit Rules
.c.obj:
  $(CC) {$< }

.cpp.obj:
  $(CC) {$< }

#    Explicit Rules
SegAlloc.exe: SegAlloc.res SegAlloc.def SegAlloc.obj
     tlink /c/C/n/P-/Twe/x @SegAlloc.LNK
     rlink SegAlloc.res SegAlloc.exe

#    Individual File Dependencies
SegAlloc.obj: SegAlloc.cpp

SegAlloc.res: SegAlloc.rc SegAlloc.cur SegAlloc.ico
     brcc -FO SegAlloc.res -i$(INC) SegAlloc.RC
```

# SEGALLOC.LNK

```
\borlandc\lib\c0wl.obj+
SegAlloc.obj
SegAlloc,SegAlloc
\borlandc\classlib\lib\tclasdll.lib+
\borlandc\owl\lib\owl.lib+
mathwl.lib+
import.lib+
crtldll.lib
SegAlloc.def
```

# SEGALLOC.CPP

```
/*-------------------------------------------------------------*\
 * (c) Copyright 1992 By Paul L. Yao.  All rights reserved.    *
\*-------------------------------------------------------------*/
/*-------------------------------------------------------------*\
| SEGALLOC.CPP  - Sample program showing global heap           |
|                 allocation in Windows.                       |
\*-------------------------------------------------------------*/
#define WIN31
#define STRICT
#include <owl.h>
#include <WindowsX.h>
#include "SegAlloc.h"

/*-------------------------------------------------------------*\
|                    Class Declarations.                       |
\*-------------------------------------------------------------*/
class TSegAllocApplication : public TApplication
```

```
      {
    public:
      TSegAllocApplication(LPSTR lpszName, HINSTANCE hInstance,
                           HINSTANCE hPrevInstance, LPSTR lpszCmdLine,
                           int nCmdShow);
      virtual void InitMainWindow ();
    };

  class TSegAllocWindow : public TWindow
     {
     public:
       PSTR Label1;
       PSTR Label2;
       PSTR Label3;

       int cb1;    // Label lengths.
       int cb2;
       int cb3;

       HGLOBAL hSegment[COUNT];
       SEGDATA sdInit[COUNT];

       TEXTMETRIC tmSys;
       LPSEGDATA lpSegData[COUNT];

       TSegAllocWindow (PTWindowsObject pwParent, LPSTR lpszTitle,
                        PTModule pmModule);
       virtual BOOL   Create();
       virtual void   Destroy();
       virtual LPSTR  GetClassName ();
       virtual void   GetWindowClass (WNDCLASS&);
       virtual void   Paint (HDC hdc, PAINTSTRUCT& ps);
     };

/*---------------------------------------------------------------*\
|                 Main Function:  WinMain.                        |
\*---------------------------------------------------------------*/
int PASCAL WinMain (HINSTANCE hInstance,   HINSTANCE hPrevInstance,
                    LPSTR lpszCmdLine, int    nCmdShow)
    {
    TSegAllocApplication SegAlloc ("SegAlloc", hInstance,
                        hPrevInstance, lpszCmdLine, nCmdShow);
    SegAlloc.Run();
    return SegAlloc.Status;
    }

/*---------------------------------------------------------------*\
|                 Application Class Member.                       |
\*---------------------------------------------------------------*/
TSegAllocApplication::TSegAllocApplication (LPSTR lpszName,
                    HINSTANCE hInstance, HINSTANCE hPrevInstance,
                    LPSTR lpszCmdLine, int nCmdShow)
                  :TApplication (lpszName, hInstance,
                       hPrevInstance, lpszCmdLine, nCmdShow)
    {
    /* Application specific initialization goes here.  */
    }

/*---------------------------------------------------------------*\
|                 Application Class Member.                       |
\*---------------------------------------------------------------*/
void TSegAllocApplication::InitMainWindow ()
    {
```

## 590  *Operating System Considerations*

```c
    MainWindow = new TSegAllocWindow (NULL,
                                "Global Heap Allocation",
                                NULL);
    }

/*----------------------------------------------------------------*\
|                  TSegAllocWindow Class Member.                   |
\*----------------------------------------------------------------*/
TSegAllocWindow::TSegAllocWindow (PTWindowsObject pwParent,
              LPSTR lpszTitle, PTModule pmModule)
          :TWindow (pwParent, lpszTitle, pmModule)
    {
    Label1 = "Description";
    Label2 = "Req/Actual";
    Label3 = "Handle  ->  Address";

    cb1 = lstrlen(Label1);
    cb2 = lstrlen(Label2);
    cb3 = lstrlen(Label3);

    lstrcpy (sdInit[0].achDesc, "Fixed Object");
    sdInit[0].dwAlloc  = 50;
    sdInit[0].wFlags   = GMEM_FIXED;

    lstrcpy (sdInit[1].achDesc, "Moveable Memory");
    sdInit[1].dwAlloc  = 75;
    sdInit[1].wFlags   = GMEM_MOVEABLE | GMEM_ZEROINIT;

    lstrcpy (sdInit[2].achDesc, "Discardable Segment");
    sdInit[2].dwAlloc  = 100;
    sdInit[2].wFlags   = GMEM_DISCARDABLE | GMEM_MOVEABLE;
    }

/*----------------------------------------------------------------*\
|                  TSegAllocWindow Class Member.                   |
\*----------------------------------------------------------------*/
BOOL TSegAllocWindow::Create()
    {
    BOOL bRetVal;
    HDC  hdc;
    int  i;

    bRetVal = TWindow::Create();

    if (bRetVal)
        {
        for (i=0;i<COUNT;i++)
            {
            hSegment[i] = GlobalAlloc(sdInit[i].wFlags,
                                      sdInit[i].dwAlloc);

            lpSegData[i] = (LPSEGDATA)GlobalLock (hSegment[i]);
            if (!lpSegData[i])
                {
                MessageBox (NULL,"Not enough memory",
                            GetApplication()->Name, MB_OK);
                bRetVal = FALSE;
                goto Exit;
                }
```

```
                    lstrcpy (lpSegData[i]->achDesc, sdInit[i].achDesc);
                    lpSegData[i]->dwAlloc = sdInit[i].dwAlloc;
                    lpSegData[i]->dwActual = GlobalSize (hSegment[i]);
                    lpSegData[i]->wFlags = sdInit[i].wFlags;
                    } /* [for] */

        hdc = GetDC (HWindow);
        GetTextMetrics (hdc, &tmSys);
        ReleaseDC (HWindow, hdc);
        }
Exit:
    return bRetVal;
    }

/*---------------------------------------------------------------*\
|                   TSegAllocWindow Class Member.                 |
\*---------------------------------------------------------------*/
void TSegAllocWindow::Destroy()
    {
    int i;

    for (i=0;i<COUNT;i++)
        {
        GlobalUnlock (hSegment[i]);
        GlobalFree (hSegment[i]);
        }
    }

/*---------------------------------------------------------------*\
|                   TSegAllocWindow Class Member.                 |
\*---------------------------------------------------------------*/
LPSTR TSegAllocWindow::GetClassName ()
    {
    return "SegAlloc:MAIN";
    }

/*---------------------------------------------------------------*\
|                   TSegAllocWindow Class Member.                 |
\*---------------------------------------------------------------*/
void TSegAllocWindow::GetWindowClass (WNDCLASS& wc)
    {
    TWindow::GetWindowClass (wc);
    wc.hIcon=LoadIcon (wc.hInstance, "snapshot");
    wc.hCursor=LoadCursor (wc.hInstance, "hand");
    }

/*---------------------------------------------------------------*\
|                   TSegAllocWindow Class Member.                 |
\*---------------------------------------------------------------*/
void TSegAllocWindow::Paint (HDC hdc, PAINTSTRUCT& ps)
    {
    char buff[30];
    int  cb;
    int  i;
    int  xText1;
    int  xText2;
    int  xText3;
    int  yText;
```

```
    /* Calculate text positioning variables.          */
    xText1 = tmSys.tmAveCharWidth * 2;
    xText2 = xText1 + (STRSIZE * tmSys.tmAveCharWidth);
    xText3 = xText2 + ((cb2+5) * tmSys.tmAveCharWidth);
    yText  = tmSys.tmHeight;

    /* Print titles.                                  */
    TextOut (hdc, xText1, yText, Label1, cb1);
    TextOut (hdc, xText2, yText, Label2, cb2);
    TextOut (hdc, xText3, yText, Label3, cb3);

    yText += tmSys.tmHeight * 2;

    for (i=0;i<COUNT;i++)
        {
        /* Print description.                         */
        TextOut (hdc, xText1, yText, lpSegData[i]->achDesc,
                 lstrlen(lpSegData[i]->achDesc));

        /* Print allocated vs actual size.            */
        cb = wsprintf (buff, "%ld / %ld", lpSegData[i]->dwAlloc,
                                          lpSegData[i]->dwActual);
        TextOut (hdc, xText2, yText, buff, cb);

        /* Print handle and actual address.           */
        cb = wsprintf (buff, "%04x  ->  %04x:%04x", hSegment[i],
                 HIWORD(lpSegData[i]), LOWORD(lpSegData[i]));
        TextOut (hdc, xText3, yText, buff, cb);

        /* Advance to next line.                      */
        yText += tmSys.tmHeight + tmSys.tmExternalLeading;
        }

}
```

## SEGALLOC.H

```
/*----------------------------------------------------------------*\
|  SEGALLOC.H  - Include file for SegAlloc.cpp.                    |
\*----------------------------------------------------------------*/

/*----------------------------------------------------------------*\
|                         Constants.                               |
\*----------------------------------------------------------------*/
const int STRSIZE = 30;
const int COUNT   = 3;

/*----------------------------------------------------------------*\
|                         TypeDefs.                                |
\*----------------------------------------------------------------*/
typedef struct tagSEGDATA
    {
    char  achDesc[STRSIZE];  /* Description of data.  */
    DWORD dwAlloc;           /* Amount asked for.     */
    DWORD dwActual;          /* Actually allocated.   */
    WORD  wFlags;            /* Allocation flags.     */
    } SEGDATA;

typedef SEGDATA FAR *LPSEGDATA;
```

## SEGALLOC.RC

```
snapshot icon SegAlloc.ico

hand cursor SegAlloc.cur
```

## SEGALLOC.DEF

```
NAME SEGALLOC

EXETYPE WINDOWS

DESCRIPTION 'Segment Allocation'

CODE MOVEABLE DISCARDABLE
DATA MOVEABLE MULTIPLE

HEAPSIZE  512
STACKSIZE 5120
```

Perhaps the most important aspect of this code involves the error checking that is performed when a global memory object is allocated and locked. It is important to check the return value from the various allocation and locking routines, because there is no guarantee that you will get the memory you have asked for. And even if you get the memory you ask for, you must guard against the possibility that a memory handle will become invalid. In a large program, with many different pieces, it's always possible that a memory handle can get overwritten, or inadvertently freed.

Another important aspect of global heap allocation has to do with locking. To run well in real mode, Windows programs keep all dynamic memory objects unlocked. The reason is simple: Without hardware support for memory management, memory must be managed in software. Windows programmers who worked with versions 1.x and 2.x created a "Windows sandwich" whenever they wished to access a global memory object.

Starting with Windows 3.1, however, Windows will no longer support real mode. Instead, Windows will rely on the protected modes of the host CPU. This means that Windows will rely on *hardware* memory management. Because of this, you can lock global memory objects when you allocate them, and keep them locked until you need to free the object. When you free a global memory object, you must first unlock it.

Our next sample program looks at the relationship between the structure of a program's code and good memory usage. The recommendation that a program be divided into multiple, small code segments goes against the grain of many DOS programmers. But since DOS is a single-tasking system, with no built-in support for dynamic overlays, DOS programmers can get away with creating monolithic programs with large code segments. Efficient operation under Windows, on the other hand, requires a different approach.

## Code Structure and Memory Use

Most of the material in this chapter deals with the data used by a program. But an equally important issue is the memory used by a program's code. Because of the magic of dynamic linking, Windows can run with only part of a program loaded into memory at any given time. Dynamic linking gives you all the benefits of a sophisticated overlay manager, without requiring you to carefully design each overlay.

While care is not *required* in putting together the different overlay working sets that make up a program, some effort is required to get the best performance in a low-memory situation. Even in protected mode, when there are megabytes and megabytes of memory, a program can encounter a low-memory situation when there are lots of other programs running. To help you create programs that run well in low-memory situations, we're going to provide two basic recommendations: one easy and one requiring a little more effort. The approach you take will depend on the size of your program, and the need to perform well in low-memory situations.

The simple approach involves dividing your program into multiple, small (4K or so) code segments. You accomplish this by dividing your code between multiple source files. But beyond that, you must make entries into your program's module definition (.DEF) file. This is necessary because the linker (TLINK.EXE) will try to pack smaller code segments into larger code segments. But hopefully, by restructuring your application, you'll be able to define your own **PRELOAD** segments, so that the Windows loader can be sure to load the minimum required set of segments to make your program's startup perform quickly.

The second approach that you can take to improve your program's performance in low-memory situations involves running a swap-tuning utility. There are a number of these available, including one from MicroQuill of Seattle. These utilities let you determine your program's actual **working sets**. A working set is the group of code segments required to perform a specific task or set of tasks. A swap-tuning utility helps you see the actual memory activity of your program, so that you can adjust the code that each code segment contains to minimize thrashing—the need to reread many different segments from disk in order to accomplish a specific task.

## *A Sample Segmented Program*

We're going to start by showing a simple example of a segmented program. This is hardly going to be a "realistic example," since we're just going to divide our minimum Windows program, MIN, into three segments. However, our experience shows that some of the trouble with segmenting an application involves using the development tools properly. Therefore, this example will show you how to overcome these quirks to successfully divide a program into multiple code segments.

We're going to call this program MIN2, although you can call it "Son of Min," if you'd like. MIN2 has two source files: MIN2.CPP and MIN2INIT.CPP. Here is the source code:

## MAKEFILE.MAK

```
.AUTODEPEND

#    Translator Definitions
INC=\BORLANDC\OWL\INCLUDE;\BORLANDC\CLASSLIB\INCLUDE;\BORLANDC\INCLUDE
CC = bcc -c -D_CLASSDLL -H -ml -WS -w -I$(INC)

#    Implicit Rules
.c.obj:
  $(CC) {$< }

.cpp.obj:
  $(CC) {$< }

#    Explicit Rules
Min2.exe: Min2.res Min2.def Min2.obj Min2Init.obj
    tlink /c/C/n/P-/Twe/x @Min2.LNK
    rlink -k Min2.res Min2.exe


#    Individual File Dependencies
Min2.obj: Min2.cpp

Min2Init.obj: Min2Init.cpp
```

```
Min2.res: Min2.rc Min2.cur Min2.ico
    brcc -FO Min2.res -i$(INC) Min2.RC
```

## MIN2.LNK

```
\borlandc\lib\cOwl.obj+
Min2.obj+
Min2Init.obj
Min2,Min2
\borlandc\classlib\lib\tclasdll.lib+
\borlandc\owl\lib\owl.lib+
mathwl.lib+
import.lib+
crtldll.lib
Min2.def
```

## MIN2.CPP

```
/*-------------------------------------------------------------*\
 | MIN2.CPP - A minimum Windows program which demonstrates the |
 |            principles of segmenting a program.              |
 \*-------------------------------------------------------------*/
#define WIN31
#define STRICT
#include <owl.h>
#include <WindowsX.h>
#include "Min2.H"

/*-------------------------------------------------------------*\
 |                  Main Function: WinMain.                    |
 \*-------------------------------------------------------------*/
int PASCAL WinMain (HINSTANCE hInstance,   HINSTANCE hPrevInstance,
                    LPSTR  lpszCmdLine, int    nCmdShow)
    {
    TMin2Application Min2 ("Min2", hInstance, hPrevInstance,
                           lpszCmdLine, nCmdShow);
    Min2.Run();
    return Min2.Status;
    }

/*-------------------------------------------------------------*\
 |                  TMin2Window Class Member.                  |
 \*-------------------------------------------------------------*/
void TMin2Window::Paint (HDC hdc, PAINTSTRUCT& ps)
    {
    int  x, y;
    RECT r;

    GetClientRect (HWindow, &r);
    SetTextAlign (ps.hdc, TA_CENTER | TA_BASELINE);
    x = r.right / 2;
    y = r.bottom /2;

    TextOut (hdc, x, y, "Segmented Application.", 22);
    }
```

# MIN2INIT.CPP

```
/*---------------------------------------------------------------*\
|   MIN2INIT.CPP - Initialization code for MIN2.EXE.              |
\*---------------------------------------------------------------*/
#define WIN31
#define STRICT
#include <owl.h>
#include <WindowsX.h>
#include "Min2.H"

/*---------------------------------------------------------------*\
|                   Application Class Member.                     |
\*---------------------------------------------------------------*/
TMin2Application::TMin2Application (LPSTR lpszName,
                HINSTANCE hInstance, HINSTANCE hPrevInstance,
                LPSTR lpszCmdLine, int nCmdShow)
            :TApplication (lpszName, hInstance,
                    hPrevInstance, lpszCmdLine, nCmdShow)
    {
    /*  Application specific initialization goes here.  */
    }

/*---------------------------------------------------------------*\
|                   Application Class Member.                     |
\*---------------------------------------------------------------*/
void TMin2Application::InitMainWindow ()
    {
    MainWindow = new TMin2Window (NULL, "Minimum", NULL);
    }

/*---------------------------------------------------------------*\
|                    TMin2Window Class Member.                    |
\*---------------------------------------------------------------*/
TMin2Window::TMin2Window (PTWindowsObject pwParent,
            LPSTR lpszTitle, PTModule pmModule)
        :TWindow (pwParent, lpszTitle, pmModule)
    {
    /*  Window specific initialization goes here.  */
    }
/*---------------------------------------------------------------*\
|                    TMin2Window Class Member.                    |
\*---------------------------------------------------------------*/
LPSTR TMin2Window::GetClassName ()
    {
    return "Min2:MAIN";
    }

/*---------------------------------------------------------------*\
|                    TMin2Window Class Member.                    |
\*---------------------------------------------------------------*/
void TMin2Window::GetWindowClass (WNDCLASS& wc)
    {
    TWindow::GetWindowClass (wc);
    wc.hIcon=LoadIcon (wc.hInstance, "snapshot");
    wc.hCursor=LoadCursor (wc.hInstance, "hand");
    wc.style = CS_HREDRAW | CS_VREDRAW;
    }
```

## MIN2.H

```
/*--------------------------------------------------------------*\
 | MIN2.H - Include file for MIN2.EXE, a segmented minimum |
 | Windows program. |
\*--------------------------------------------------------------*/

/*--------------------------------------------------------------*\
 | Class Declarations. |
\*--------------------------------------------------------------*/
class TMin2Application : public TApplication
   {
   public:
   TMin2Application (LPSTR lpszName, HINSTANCE hInstance,
   HINSTANCE hPrevInstance, LPSTR lpszCmdLine,
   int nCmdShow);
   virtual void InitMainWindow ();
   };

class TMin2Window : public TWindow
   {
   public:
   TMin2Window (PTWindowsObject pwParent, LPSTR lpszTitle,
   PTModule pmModule);
   virtual LPSTR GetClassName ();
   virtual void GetWindowClass (WNDCLASS&);
   virtual void Paint (HDC hdc, PAINTSTRUCT& ps);
   };
```

## MIN2.RC

```
snapshot icon Min2.ico

hand cursor Min2.cur
```

## MIN2.DEF

```
NAME MIN2

EXETYPE WINDOWS

DESCRIPTION 'Segmented Code'

CODE MOVEABLE
DATA MOVEABLE MULTIPLE

HEAPSIZE  512
STACKSIZE 5120

SEGMENTS
    MIN2_TEXT        MOVEABLE
    MIN2INIT_TEXT    MOVEABLE DISCARDABLE
    _TEXT            MOVEABLE
    DLLREF_TEXT      MOVEABLE
```

Even though this program has only two source files, there are actually four code segments. The first two code segments, **MIN2_TEXT** and **MIN2INIT_TEXT**, are created from the code in the files, respectively, MIN.CPP and MIN2INIT.CPP. The third code segment, **_TEXT**, contains MIN's startup code and other support routines that are automatically linked in at program creation time. The fourth code segment, **DLLREF_TEXT**, is present because MIN uses the OWL dynamic link library, OWL.DLL.

Each segment is listed under the SEGMENTS keyword in the module definition file. This mechanism allows you to set different memory attributes for different segments. You use the following keywords to request different attributes: **PRELOAD, MOVEABLE, DISCARDABLE, FIXED,** and **LOADONCALL**.

Each keyword gives a memory attribute to a segment. Note that you should avoid using the **FIXED** keyword. There is a bug in version 3.0 of Windows that makes such segments fixed and page locked. While this will be corrected in a future version, you should avoid this keyword for now. While the use of this keyword is suitable for device drivers, it is not suitable for application programs because of the constraints its use puts on the global heap manager.

The next step to tuning MIN2, of course, involves running it through the swap tuner. This would allow us to see when segments are loaded and discarded. Of course, there are only a few routines in the two segments that make up MIN2. In a larger program, the swap tuner would help to restructure a program to improve the performance in a low-memory situation.

The results of swap tuning can seem paradoxical at times. For example, to make the best use of memory, it may be necessary to duplicate certain routines that are used in several different places. Instead of centralizing the "helper" routines in a program, it may make sense to create multiple copies of each, with a local copy in the code segments where the service is needed. Another alternative involves proving each function with its own code segment. Of course, the trade-off here is that far calls are quite a bit more expensive than near calls.

We hope this introduction to the effect of code structure on memory use will help you start thinking about code in a different way. Code structure *can* affect the performance of a Windows program, just as surely as the structure of a program's data will affect its performance. It's time to look at our next sample program, which provides an example of using the local heap that is automatically provided as part of every program's default data segment.

## Local Heap Allocation

Let's take a look at Windows' local heap allocation routines. Table 18.7 lists all of the routines that are provided for local heap management. We're going to focus our attention on six of them: **LocalInit, LocalAlloc, LocalReAlloc, LocalLock, LocalUnlock,** and **LocalFree**.

## Table 18.7

| | |
|---|---|
| LocalAlloc | Allocates memory from a local heap. |
| LocalCompact | Reorganizes a local heap. |
| LocalDiscard | Discards an unlocked, discardable object. |
| LocalFlags | Provides information about a specific memory object. |
| LocalFree | Frees a local memory object. |
| LocalHandle | Provides the handle of a local memory object associated with a given memory address. |
| LocalInit | Initializes a local heap. |
| LocalLock | Increments the lock count on a local memory object, and returns its address. |
| LocalReAlloc | Changes the size of a local memory object. |
| LocalShrink | Reorganizes a local heap and reduces the size of the heap (if possible) to the initial, starting size. If this routine is successful, it reduces the size of the data segment that contains the heap, so that the memory can be reclaimed by the global heap. |
| LocalSize | Returns the current size of a local memory object. |
| LocalUnlock | Decrements the lock count on a local memory object. |

## *LocalInit*

The `LocalInit` routine initializes a local heap. `LocalInit` takes three parameters:

```
BOOL LocalInit (wSegment, pStart, pEnd)
```

- `wSegment` is the segment address of the heap to be initialized. Or, if it is zero, the data segment referenced by the DS register is initialized.
- `pStart` is the beginning offset of the heap in the segment.
- `pEnd` is the offset of the end of the heap in the segment. Or, if `pStart` is zero, then `pEnd` is the size of the heap, and a heap is created at the *end* of the designated segment.

`LocalInit` installs the necessary data structures that are required to support local heap allocation in a segment. Windows programs do not need to initialize their default data segment, since `LocalInit` is called automatically for you. However, `LocalInit` *can* be called to set up a local heap in another segment. As we'll detail later in this chapter, this allows you to have access to as many local heaps as you need.

Unlike application programs, Windows dynamic link libraries must explicitly call `LocalInit` in order to have a local heap. We'll discuss how this is done in Chapter 19, when we describe how to write dynamic link libraries.

## *LocalAlloc*

The `LocalAlloc` routine allocates memory from a local heap. It is defined as

```
HLOCAL LocalAlloc (wFlags, wBytes)
```

- `wFlags` is a combination of one or more local memory allocation flags, discussed below.
- `wBytes` is an unsigned integer value of the size of the object to allocate.

`LocalAlloc` returns a handle that identifies the object you've allocated. Be sure that you *always* check the return value, since there is never a guarantee that you'll get the memory you requested. A NULL handle is returned when a memory allocation request fails.

The value of `wFlags` can be a combination of five flags, depending on the type of memory object you wish to allocate (fixed, moveable, or discardable), whether you wish to avoid disturbing the heap, and whether you wish to initialize with zeros. This table lists your choices:

| *Description* | *Flags* |
| --- | --- |
| Fixed memory object | `LMEM_FIXED` |
| Moveable memory object | `LMEM_MOVEABLE` |
| Discardable memory object | `LMEM_MOVEABLE | LMEM_DISCARDABLE` |
| Do not compact or discard | `LMEM_NOCOMPACT` |
| Initialize with zeros | `LMEM_ZEROINIT` |

As this table suggests, if you wish to allocate a discardable object, you use *both* the moveable and the discardable flag. This makes sense, since a discardable object must also be moveable. The **LMEM_NOCOMPACT** flag tells the local memory manager that your need for memory can be satisfied some other way, and that if there isn't an available free block, no moving or discarding should be done to satisfy the memory allocation. When you wish to use more than one flag, you combine them using the OR operator "|." For example, to allocate a five-byte moveable object that is initialized with zeros, you say

hMem = LocalAlloc (LMEM_MOVEABLE | LMEM_ZEROINIT, 5);

Be careful to avoid the **LMEM_NODISCARD** flag, which is mentioned in the Microsoft documentation but doesn't seem to have the effect that the documentation says it should. The documentation says that it should prevent discarding, but it seems to have no effect at all.

**LocalAlloc** returns a memory handle. For moveable and discardable memory objects, you obtain a pointer by calling the **LocalLock** routine, which we'll discuss shortly. For fixed objects, the handle itself is a pointer. In this way, **LocalAlloc** can be used in exactly the same manner as the runtime library's **malloc**. In other words, here is how to allocate and use a fixed memory object:

```
char * pch;
pch =(char *)LocalAlloc (LMEM_FIXED|LMEM_ZEROINIT, 15);
lstrcpy (pch, "Hello World");
```

For the sake of clarity, this code uses the normal C++ type, char *, instead of the more precise Windows type, **PSTR**. You may have already noticed that this code casts the return value from **LocalAlloc**. This prevents the compiler from complaining about assigning a HANDLE value (unsigned int) to a pointer. We know it's correct. The cast tells the compiler to save its error messages for real problems.

## LocalLock

The **LocalLock** routine increments the lock count on a local memory object and returns its address:

PSTR LocalLock (hMem)

- **hMem** is a handle to a memory object, returned by a call to **LocalAlloc**.

Programs call **LocalLock** to get the address of a moveable or discardable object. At the same time, this routine makes sure that the object won't get moved or discarded so that the address will be valid until a call is made to **LocalUnlock**. In general, it's a good idea to keep all objects unlocked until the precise time that they are needed. This gives the local heap manager the freedom to move memory as it needs to so that it can optimize the use of the local heap.

According to the prototype in WINDOWS.H, `LocalLock` returns a near pointer to a character string. However, this doesn't mean that only character values can be placed into a memory object. You put the return value from `LocalLock` into any type of pointer, to provide you with a convenient way to access any type of dynamically allocated data. The following example makes it easy to store an array of integers into a local memory object:

```
int * pi;

pi = (int near * )LocalLock (hmem);
if (pi)
    {
    pi[0] = 1;
    pi[1] = 2;
    LocalUnlock (hmem);
    }
else
    {
    /* Error. */
    }
```

It's very important to check the return value from `LocalLock`, as we've done in this example. A null pointer indicates that the lock has failed. There are several things that could make this happen. If we are trying to lock a discardable object, it's possible that the object has been discarded. Or, perhaps the memory handle has been accidentally overwritten. Whatever the cause, you don't want to write using a null pointer. You will overwrite the memory locations at the bottom of your data segment, which means the data area that is used to maintain your data segment.

## *LocalReAlloc*

The `LocalReAlloc` routine changes the size of a local memory object. `LocalReAlloc` is defined as

HLOCAL LocalReAlloc (hMem, wBytes, wFlags)

- **hMem** is a memory handle returned by the `LocalAlloc` routine.
- **wBytes** is the new size. When you make an object smaller, it truncates (and loses) the data from the end of the object. When you make an object larger, it preserves the previous contents of the object.
- **wFlags** is a combination of one or more local allocation flags.

**LocalReAlloc** returns a HANDLE, which is one of three values. If the reallocation fails, the return value is NULL. For moveable and discardable objects, if the allocation is successful, the return value is the same handle value that was passed into the routine. For fixed objects, the handle may be the same or may be different, depending on whether the object must be moved to satisfy the allocation request.

To understand why, recall from our earlier discussion that the handle to a fixed memory object is actually a pointer to the object itself. If the object must be moved to satisfy a memory allocation request, it follows that the pointer must change as well. To prevent the local memory manager from mysteriously moving a fixed object, a fixed object will only be moved by the **LocalReAlloc** call if the **LMEM_MOVEABLE** flag is specified. For example, here is how to reallocate a fixed memory object, allowing it to move:

```
/* Enlarge a fixed object, and let it move.       */
hNew = LocalReAlloc (hOld,
                     cbSize,         /* New size.    */
                     LMEM_MOVEABLE);/* Ok to move.  */
if (!hNew)
    {
    /* Error. */
    }
else
    hOld = hNew;
```

The **LMEM_MOVEABLE** flag has another use. This flag allows a moveable or discardable memory object that is *locked* to be moved if needed to satisfy an allocation request. In most cases, you'll only change the size of a moveable or discardable memory object when it is unlocked. At such times, the memory manager is free to relocate the object. But, if you wish to make a locked object larger, you'll need to include the **LMEM_MOVEABLE** flag in case the object must be moved.

If you want to change the *size* of a local memory object and *not* its memory disposition (fixed, moveable, discardable), you can set **wFlags** to zero. Or, use the **LMEM_ZEROINIT** flag to ask for a larger object with the newly allocated space zero initialized. For example, even though the **wFlags** field is set to zero in this example, it doesn't change the memory disposition—only the size:

```
h = LocalReAlloc (hMem,
                  28,         /* New size.       */
                  0);         /* Ignore flags.   */
```

To change the memory disposition of a memory object, use the **LMEM_MODIFY** flag. You can't change the disposition of a fixed memory object. However, you *can* make a moveable object discardable, or make a discardable object into a moveable object. To make a moveable object discardable, you say

```
LocalReAlloc (hMem,
              0,                    /* Ignore the size.    */
              LMEM_MODIFY      |    /* Just change flags. */
              LMEM_MOVEABLE    |
              LMEM_DISCARDABLE);
```

and to make a discardable object moveable, you say

```
LocalReAlloc (hMem,
              0,                    /* Ignore the size.    */
              LMEM_MODIFY    |      /* Just change flags. */
              LMEM_MOVEABLE);
```

When you change the memory disposition like this, the reallocation size is ignored. In these examples, even though we request a reallocation size of zero, the **LMEM_MODIFY** flag has precedence. So we can safely use a value of zero, to avoid having to figure out the current size of the object and pass it in to **LocalReAlloc**.

## *LocalUnlock*

The **LocalUnlock** routine decrements the lock count on a local memory object;

BOOL LocalUnlock (hMem)

- **hMem** is a local memory handle, as provided by the **LocalAlloc** routine.

The **LocalUnlock** routine is the second slice to a Windows sandwich. To give the local memory manager the greatest freedom to manage the local heap, you should lock memory objects for only the briefest period of time. For example, to store character values that a program receives from a **WM_CHAR** message, you would say

```
WndProc (...)
    {
    switch (msg)
        {
        case WM_CHAR:
            pch = LocalLock(hmem);
            pch[iNextChar] = (unsigned char) wParam;
            LocalUnlock (hmem);
            break;
            ...
```

In this case, the memory object identified by the handle **hmem** is only kept locked for as long as it takes to copy a character into the memory object.

## LocalFree

The `LocalFree` routine frees a local memory object:

```
HLOCAL LocalFree (hMem)
```

- `hMem` is a memory handle returned by `LocalAlloc`.

Any time a dynamic memory object is allocated, it consumes memory that cannot be used for other purposes. Therefore, care should be taken to free memory that is not needed. The `LocalFree` routine is provided for this purpose.

Of course, Windows has *some* safeguards to keep memory from going away permanently. For example, when a program terminates, all of the dynamic memory that it allocated is automatically freed. This helps prevent the global heap from becoming congested with unnecessary blocks of memory that programs forgot to free. In spite of this, Windows programmers should be careful to always free memory that is no longer needed.

## LOCALMEM: A Sample Heap Allocation Program

Let's take a look at a sample Windows program that shows some basic techniques in dealing with local memory. This program actually shows how to use two different types of application memory: the local heap and string resources. This program reads in a list of cities that are saved as string resources. These are stored in moveable memory objects that have been allocated from the local heap. Figure 18.5 shows the program running.

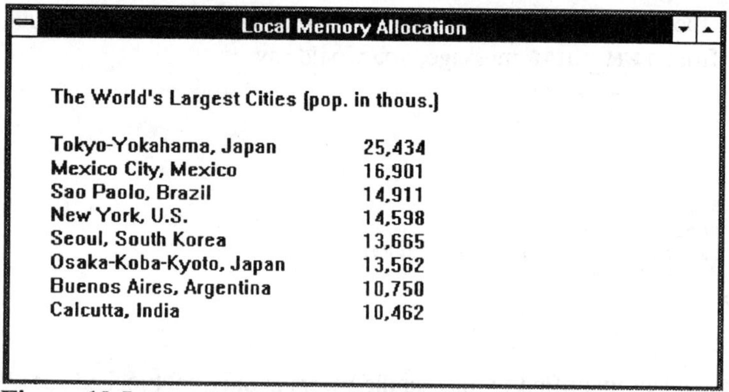

```
┌─────────────────────────────────────────────┐
│ ─       Local Memory Allocation       ▼ ▲ │
├─────────────────────────────────────────────┤
│                                             │
│  The World's Largest Cities (pop. in thous.)│
│                                             │
│  Tokyo-Yokahama, Japan       25,434         │
│  Mexico City, Mexico         16,901         │
│  Sao Paolo, Brazil           14,911         │
│  New York, U.S.              14,598         │
│  Seoul, South Korea          13,665         │
│  Osaka-Koba-Kyoto, Japan     13,562         │
│  Buenos Aires, Argentina     10,750         │
│  Calcutta, India             10,462         │
│                                             │
└─────────────────────────────────────────────┘
```

Figure 18.5 Sample program showing local heap allocation

# MAKEFILE.MAK

```
.AUTODEPEND

#       Translator Definitions
INC=\BORLANDC\OWL\INCLUDE;\BORLANDC\CLASSLIB\INCLUDE;\BORLANDC\INCLUDE
CC = bcc -c -D_CLASSDLL -H -ml -WS -w -I$(INC)

#       Implicit Rules
.c.obj:
  $(CC) {$< }

.cpp.obj:
  $(CC) {$< }

#       Explicit Rules
LocalMem.exe: LocalMem.res LocalMem.def LocalMem.obj
     tlink /c/C/n/P-/Twe/x @LocalMem.LNK
     rlink LocalMem.res LocalMem.exe

#       Individual File Dependencies
LocalMem.obj: LocalMem.cpp

LocalMem.res: LocalMem.rc LocalMem.cur LocalMem.ico
     brcc -FO LocalMem.res -i$(INC) LocalMem.RC
```

# LOCALMEM.LNK

```
\borlandc\lib\c0wl.obj+
LocalMem.obj
LocalMem,LocalMem
\borlandc\classlib\lib\tclasdll.lib+
\borlandc\owl\lib\owl.lib+
mathwl.lib+
import.lib+
crtldll.lib
LocalMem.def
```

# LOCALMEM.CPP

```
/*----------------------------------------------------------*\
|  LOCALMEM.CPP   - Demonstrates local memory allocation and |
|                   the use of a string table.               |
\*----------------------------------------------------------*/
#define WIN31
#define STRICT
#include <owl.h>
#include <WindowsX.h>
#include "LocalMem.h"

/*----------------------------------------------------------*\
|                    Class Declarations.                     |
\*----------------------------------------------------------*/
class TLocalMemApplication : public TApplication
   {
   public:
     PSTR      pchTitle;
```

```
        TLocalMemApplication (LPSTR lpszName, HINSTANCE hInstance,
                     HINSTANCE hPrevInstance, LPSTR lpszCmdLine,
                     int nCmdShow);
    virtual void InitMainWindow ();
  };

class TLocalMemWindow : public TWindow
    {
    public:
      HINSTANCE      hInst;
      HINSTANCE      ahCities;
      PSTR       pchNoMem;
      TEXTMETRIC tmSys;

      TLocalMemWindow (PTWindowsObject pwParent, LPSTR lpszTitle,
              PTModule pmModule);
      virtual BOOL   Create();
      virtual LPSTR  GetClassName ();
      virtual void   GetWindowClass (WNDCLASS&);
      virtual void   Paint (HDC hdc, PAINTSTRUCT& ps);
    };

/*---------------------------------------------------------------*\
|                 Main Function:  WinMain.                        |
\*---------------------------------------------------------------*/
int PASCAL WinMain (HINSTANCE hInstance,   HINSTANCE hPrevInstance,
                LPSTR  lpszCmdLine, int    nCmdShow)
    {
    TLocalMemApplication LocalMem ("LocalMem", hInstance,
                     hPrevInstance, lpszCmdLine, nCmdShow);
LocalMem.Run();
    return LocalMem.Status;
    }

/*---------------------------------------------------------------*\
|                 Application Class Member.                       |
\*---------------------------------------------------------------*/
TLocalMemApplication::TLocalMemApplication (LPSTR lpszName,
                     HINSTANCE hInstance, HINSTANCE hPrevInstance,
                     LPSTR lpszCmdLine, int nCmdShow)
                :TApplication (lpszName, hInstance,
                     hPrevInstance, lpszCmdLine, nCmdShow)
    {
    int ccSize;

    /* Load application title from string table.              */
    pchTitle = (PSTR)LocalAlloc (LMEM_FIXED, MAXSTRLEN);
    if (!pchTitle)
        {
        Status = 1;  // Fail?  Exit program.
        return;
        }

    ccSize = LoadString (hInstance, IDS_TITLE, pchTitle,
                     MAXSTRLEN);
    LocalReAlloc ((HANDLE)pchTitle, ccSize+1, 0);
    }

/*---------------------------------------------------------------*\
|                 Application Class Member.                       |
\*---------------------------------------------------------------*/
```

```
void TLocalMemApplication::InitMainWindow ()
    {
    MainWindow = new TLocalMemWindow (NULL,
                                       "Local Memory Allocation",
                                       NULL);
    }

/*----------------------------------------------------------------*\
|                 TLocalMemWindow Class Member.                    |
\*----------------------------------------------------------------*/
TLocalMemWindow::TLocalMemWindow (PTWindowsObject pwParent,
                  LPSTR lpszTitle, PTModule pmModule)
            :TWindow (pwParent, lpszTitle, pmModule)
    {
    int ccSize;

    /* Load 'out of memory' message from string table.     */
    pchNoMem = (PSTR)LocalAlloc (LMEM_FIXED, MAXSTRLEN);
    if (!pchNoMem)
        {
        Status = 1;  // Fail? Exit program.
        return;
        }

    ccSize = LoadString (GetApplication()->hInstance, IDS_NOMEM,
                         pchNoMem, MAXSTRLEN);
    LocalReAlloc ((HANDLE)pchNoMem, ccSize+1, 0);
    }

/*----------------------------------------------------------------*\
|                 TLocalMemWindow Class Member.                    |
\*----------------------------------------------------------------*/
BOOL TLocalMemWindow::Create()
    {
    BOOL    bRetVal;
    HDC     hdc;
    int     i;
    int     cbSize;
    PHANDLE pah;
    PSTR    pstr;

    bRetVal = TWindow::Create();

        if (bRetVal)
        {
        /* Allocate and lock memory for array of handles.    */
        ahCities = LocalAlloc (LHND, sizeof(HANDLE) * CITYCOUNT);
        pah = (PHANDLE)LocalLock (ahCities);

        /* Error checking: if lock fails, exit.              */
        if (!pah)
            {
            bRetVal = FALSE;
            goto ErrExit1;
            }

        /* Loop to read city names.                          */
        for (i=0;i<CITYCOUNT ;i++)
            {
            /* Allocate and lock memory.                     */
```

```
                    pah[i] = LocalAlloc (LMEM_MOVEABLE, MAXSTRLEN);
                    pstr = (PSTR) LocalLock (pah[i]);

                    /*  If lock fails, exit.                           */
                    if (!pstr)
                        {
                        bRetVal = FALSE;
                        goto ErrExit2;
                        }

                    /*  Copy string into dynamic memory object.        */
                    cbSize = LoadString (GetApplication()->hInstance,
                                         i+IDS_CITY, pstr, MAXSTRLEN);

                    /*  Unlock and resize memory to exact string size. */
                    LocalUnlock (pah[i]);
                    LocalReAlloc (pah[i], cbSize+1, 0);

                    } /* [for i] */

            LocalUnlock (ahCities);
            hdc = GetDC (HWindow);
            GetTextMetrics (hdc, &tmSys);    /* Save for later.   */
            ReleaseDC (HWindow, hdc);
            }
        return bRetVal;    /* All went well.  Indicate sucess.    */
ErrExit2:
    /*  Out of memory.  Free everything.                              */
    for (i--;i>=0;i--)
        LocalFree (pah[i]);
    LocalUnlock (ahCities);
    LocalFree(ahCities);

ErrExit1:
    return bRetVal;   /* Unable to complete - indicate failure.   */

    }

/*----------------------------------------------------------------*\
|                    TLocalMemWindow Class Member.                 |
\*----------------------------------------------------------------*/
LPSTR TLocalMemWindow::GetClassName ()
    {
    return "LocalMem:MAIN";
    }

/*----------------------------------------------------------------*\
|                    TLocalMemWindow Class Member.                 |
\*----------------------------------------------------------------*/
void TLocalMemWindow::GetWindowClass (WNDCLASS& wc)
    {
    TWindow::GetWindowClass (wc);
    wc.hIcon=LoadIcon (wc.hInstance, "snapshot");
    wc.hCursor=LoadCursor (wc.hInstance, "hand");
    }

/*----------------------------------------------------------------*\
|                    TLocalMemWindow Class Member.                 |
\*----------------------------------------------------------------*/
```

```c
void TLocalMemWindow::Paint (HDC hdc, PAINTSTRUCT& ps)
    {
    int     i;
    int     xText;
    int     yText;
    int     xTabPosition;
    PHANDLE pah;
    PSTR    pstr;
    RECT    r;

    /* Initialize values for writing lines of text.       */
    xText = tmSys.tmAveCharWidth * 4;
    yText = tmSys.tmHeight * 2;
    GetClientRect (HWindow, &r);
    xTabPosition = r.right/2;

    /* Lock array of handles. If fail, exit.              */
    pah = (PHANDLE)LocalLock (ahCities);
    if (!pah)
        goto ErrExit;

    for (i=0;i<CITYCOUNT;i++)
        {
        pstr = (PSTR) LocalLock (pah[i]);
        if (pstr)
            {
            TabbedTextOut (hdc,
                           xText,
                           yText,
                           pstr,
                           lstrlen(pstr),
                           1,
                           &xTabPosition,
                           0);
            LocalUnlock (pah[i]);
            }

        /* Increment for next line.                       */
        yText += tmSys.tmHeight + tmSys.tmExternalLeading;
        }
    LocalUnlock (ahCities);

ErrExit:
    return;
    }
```

# LOCALMEM.H

```
/*-----------------------------------------------------------*\
|   LOCALMEM.H - Symbolic constants for use by LOCALMEM.     |
\*-----------------------------------------------------------*/

#define IDS_TITLE   1
#define IDS_NOMEM   2
#define IDS_CITY    3
#define MAXSTRLEN  80
#define CITYCOUNT  10
```

## LOCALMEM.RC

```
#include "LocalMem.h"

snapshot icon LocalMem.ico

hand cursor LocalMem.cur

stringtable
  {
  IDS_TITLE,  "Local Memory Allocation"
  IDS_NOMEM,  "Unable to Initialize Program - Out of Memory"
  IDS_CITY    "The World's Largest Cities (pop. in thous.)"
  IDS_CITY+1, " ";
  IDS_CITY+2, "Tokyo-Yokahama, Japan\t25,434"
  IDS_CITY+3, "Mexico City, Mexico\t16,901"
  IDS_CITY+4, "Sao Paolo, Brazil\t14,911"
  IDS_CITY+5, "New York, U.S.\t14,598"
  IDS_CITY+6, "Seoul, South Korea\t13,665"
  IDS_CITY+7, "Osaka-Koba-Kyoto, Japan\t13,562"
  IDS_CITY+8, "Buenos Aires, Argentina\t10,750"
  IDS_CITY+9, "Calcutta, India\t10,462"
  }
```

## LOCALMEM.DEF

```
NAME LOCALMEM

EXETYPE WINDOWS

DESCRIPTION 'Local heap allocation'

CODE MOVEABLE DISCARDABLE
DATA MOVEABLE MULTIPLE

HEAPSIZE  512
STACKSIZE 5120
```

Most of the action in LOCALMEM occurs in response to two messages: **WM_CREATE** and **WM_PAINT**. Memory is allocated and string tables read in response to **WM_CREATE**. All of this is displayed when the **WM_PAINT** message is received.

If there is any one issue in local memory management that is more critical than any other, it involves error checking. In order for a Windows program to be robust and error free, it must respond properly to failed memory allocation requests. The point is simple: Not every allocation request can be satisfied. When an allocation fails, a program must be ready to take corrective action to avoid losing data.

For this reason, every dynamic allocation request in LOCALMEM is followed by a check for a valid memory handle. For example:

```
/*  Load application title from string table.         */
pchTitle = (PSTR)LocalAlloc (LMEM_FIXED, MAXSTRLEN);
if (!pchTitle)
    {
    Status = 1;   // Fail? Exit program.
    return;
    }
```

Since a fixed memory object is being allocated, the handle is a pointer to a character string. In the terms of WINDOWS.H definitions, **PSTR** is the same as **char near \***. If **LocalAlloc** fails, it returns a null value. On receipt of a null, this code sets the application object's error status flag and returns.

If the above lines of code are successful, the **LoadString** routine is called to copy a string from a string table resource into the memory that is allocated. The object is then shrunk so that it is just large enough to hold the number of characters that **LoadString** reports as having been copied.

```
ccSize = LoadString (hInst, IDS_TITLE, pchTitle,
                    MAXSTRLEN);
LocalReAlloc ((HANDLE)pchTitle, ccSize+1, 0);
```

The **LoadString** routine is defined as follows:

LoadString (hInstance, wID, lpBuffer, nBufferMax)

- **hInstance** is an instance handle.
- **wID** is an integer identifier of the string to be retrieved.
- **lpBuffer** is a long pointer to a character string buffer.
- **nBufferMax** is the maximum number of characters to copy to lpBuffer.

Later in this chapter, we're going to discuss some of the memory implications of using resources. In brief, it provides a great deal of flexibility in moving read-only data out of a program's data segment and onto disk. Like the strings from the string table resource, resources are read into memory when they are needed and discarded from memory when they aren't needed. Resources provide another type of data container that should be considered as part of a Windows program's total memory management picture. For now, let's get back to LOCALMEM.

Another approach that you can take to error checking involves testing only the return value of **LocalLock** and *not* **LocalAlloc** when the two are paired together. Here is an example:

```
/*   Allocate and lock memory.                         */
pah[i] = LocalAlloc (LMEM_MOVEABLE, MAXSTRLEN);
pstr = (PSTR) LocalLock (pah[i]);

/*   If lock fails, exit.                              */
if (!pstr)
    {
    bRetVal = FALSE;
    goto ErrExit2;
    }
```

In this case, a single test validates the calls to *both* routines. Programmers are often eager to omit error checking, but this is unwise. After all, an "invalid" pointer is still usable from the point of view of the C++ programming language: It points to the bottom of the data segment, which is where the segment header lives. A single write to the right byte in this area can cause otherwise robust programs to come crashing down.

A program can have more than one local heap. This capability is often overlooked by Windows programmers. The primary reason is probably the lack of a well-documented approach, plus the need to write some assembly language code. The Borland C++ compiler supports embedded assembly language, which we're going to take advantage of to show how a program can create many different local heaps. Each heap resides in a separate, dynamically allocated segment, and can grow to fill an entire segment.

## *Local Heap Allocation in a Dynamically Allocated Segment*

As you know, there are two dynamic memory allocation packages in Windows: local heap allocation and global memory allocation. By default, every Windows program has a local heap. The heap is created by a routine called **InitApp**, which is not documented anywhere but is part of the standard (but hidden) startup sequence of every program. The advantage of the local heap is that the overhead for objects is fairly low and, with an alignment of four bytes, wastage is at a minimum. The only problem with the default local heap, however, is that it is too small for many uses. At most, depending on the size of your stack and static data, a default local heap might be 30–50K.

The problem of size can be solved by using the global heap. The global heap, after all, is the sum total of the address space in the system. On systems with an 80386, this means disk space in addition to physical RAM. The problem with the global heap, however, is that the overhead per object is very high. And, at 32 bytes, the granularity of segments is too high to be used for very small objects. Only large objects, or arrays of small objects, are suitable for storage in objects allocated from the global heap.

To get the benefits of both local and global heap management routines, it's possible to create a local heap in a dynamically allocated global segment. From this heap, small objects can be allocated which can efficiently share the segment with the other objects, all managed by the local heap manager. Doing this requires a little sleight of hand and a little assembly language programming, but the results can be well worth the effort.

The first thing to think about is the fact that the first 16 bytes of the segment are reserved. The local heap manager uses various bytes in this area for its own purposes. If you use this space for something else, you risk overwriting the pointers into your local heap. So, whatever you do, make sure the first 16 bytes are initialized to zero.

The second issue is the initialization of the local heap. This is easily done with the **LocalInit** routine. Here is one way to initialize a local heap in a dynamically allocated segment:

```
HGLOBAL hMem;
int     pStart, pEnd;
LPSTR lp;
WORD    wSeg;

hMem = GlobalAlloc (GMEM_MOVEABLE|GMEM_ZEROINIT, 4096L);
if (!hMem)
    goto ErrorOut;

lp = (LPSTR) GlobalLock (hMem);
wSeg = HIWORD (lp);

pStart = 16;
pEnd   = (int)GlobalSize (hMem)-1;
LocalInit (wSeg, pStart, pEnd);
GlobalUnlock(hMem);
GlobalUnlock (hMem);
```

Notice that two calls to **GlobalUnlock** are required. The first is to counteract the lock of our own call to **GlobalLock**—it's the second slice in a code sandwich. The second call to **GlobalUnlock** is required because **LocalInit** leaves a segment locked. Without this second call, the data segment would be locked in memory. This would prevent the segment from growing, and would create a memory sandbar in the global heap.

As always, **GlobalAlloc**'s return value should always be checked to make sure that the requested memory is available. Even though we asked for a 4,096-byte segment, because different operating modes align on different segment boundaries, we call **GlobalSize** to make sure we know the exact size of the segment. pStart is set to 16 to make room for the header. pEnd is set to the offset of the last byte in the segment, which is the segment size minus 1.

Incidentally, a slightly shorter way to do the same thing involves setting pStart to zero and setting pEnd to the actual *size* of the local heap. Here's the code that does that:

```
pEnd   = (int)GlobalSize (hMem)-16;
LocalInit (wSeg, 0, pEnd);
```

In this case, notice that we're subtracting 16 from the size of the segment rather than just 1. The reason is simple: We must set aside the first 16 bytes for the segment header.

## 616 Operating System Considerations

Accessing the local heap requires a little assembly language programming. We're going to cheat a little, and embed assembler into C code. If your compiler doesn't support this, you will have to write stand-alone assembly language subroutines. We can call any local heap management routine. The only difference is that before and after each call, we must change the value in the DS register to hold the address of our local heap. Here's how to do it:

```
LPSTR lp;
HGLOBAL hmem;
WORD    wHeapDS;   /* Must be a stack variable! */

lp = (LPSTR) GlobalLock (hmem);   /* Where local heap lives. */
wHeapDS = HIWORD (lp);

_asm{
    push DS

    mov  AX, wHeapDS
    mov  DS, AX

    }

hmem = LocalAlloc (LMEM_MOVEABLE, 16);

_asm{
    pop  DS
    }

GlobalUnlock (hmem);
```

While this may look rather complex and bizarre, this approach allows a Windows program to derive the benefits of both memory management packages, and to surmount some of the drawbacks of each.

Of course, to use a memory object, you must call two lock routines: one for the segment and one for the local heap object. And, to keep either of these data areas from becoming too fragmented, you will probably want to unlock at both levels. There are compromises, of course. For example, a program might make all local heap objects *fixed*, which removes the need to do the second lock. And, for the most effective use, it probably makes sense to build a small subroutine library to manage the two-level allocation scheme. This might be as simple as creating 32-bit handles, with half for the local handle and half for the global handle. That, in fact, is the approach taken by our sample program. Or, a subroutine package could issue its own, private 16-bit handles that it would then use to find the right segment and the right local memory object. There are several approaches to take, and we hope this brief introduction has provided you with enough information to find one that will work for you.

If you're like many programmers, all this theoretical discussion and bits of code are not as interesting as a full-blown working program that demonstrates how to put the theory into practice. So, without further ado, here is our sample program: SUBSEG.

# SUBSEG: A Combined Local/Global Heap Allocation Program

SUBSEG demonstrates how to perform subsegment allocation in a dynamically allocated segment. We borrow the term "subsegment allocation" from the world of OS/2, since it seems to be more suggestive of what we are doing than the term "local allocation." To help you get the most from this example, we have written a set of subsegment allocation routines that mirrors the format of the routines in Windows' standard memory allocation routines. In other words, we've written a routine called **SubAlloc** which takes all the same parameters as the **LocalAlloc** routine. Four other routines provide the basic allocation services to get you started in writing a complete suballocation library. There is one additional function, **SubInitialize**, which allocates a segment from the global heap and initializes the segment to hold a local heap.

SUBSEG is adapted from SEGALLOC, which is the segment allocation sample we presented earlier in this chapter. SUBSEG displays information about the allocated data objects. To convince you that it works as advertised, it reads this information from the data object itself. Figure 18.6 shows SUBSEG running. If you compare this program to the SEGALLOC program, one thing you may notice is that the overhead of objects is much lower in this program. That is because segments allocated from the global heap are aligned on 32-byte boundaries, whereas objects allocated from a local heap are allocated on four-byte boundaries. The wastage due to "rounding" is much less in local heaps.

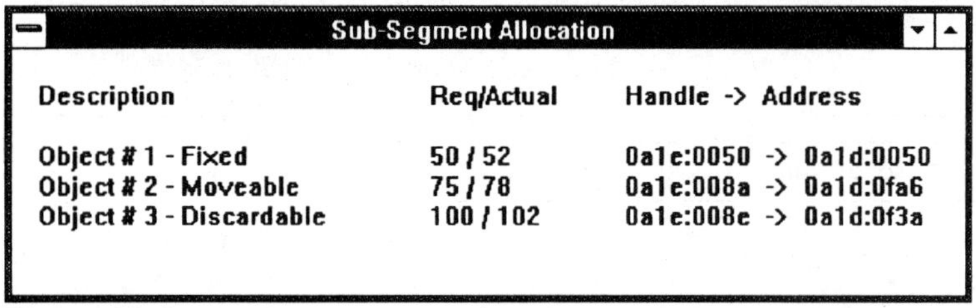

```
                  Sub-Segment Allocation

Description              Req/Actual      Handle -> Address

Object # 1 - Fixed         50 / 52       0a1e:0050 -> 0a1d:0050
Object # 2 - Moveable      75 / 78       0a1e:008a -> 0a1d:0fa6
Object # 3 - Discardable  100 / 102      0a1e:008e -> 0a1d:0f3a
```

Figure 18.6 SUBSEG shows information about the objects it allocates

## MAKEFILE.MAK

```
.AUTODEPEND

#    Translator Definitions
INC=\BORLANDC\OWL\INCLUDE;\BORLANDC\CLASSLIB\INCLUDE;\BORLANDC\INCLUDE
CC = bcc -c -D_CLASSDLL -H -ml -WS -w-par -w-rpt -I$(INC)

#    Implicit Rules
.c.obj:
  $(CC) {$< }
```

```
.cpp.obj:
  $(CC) {$< }

#    Explicit Rules
SubSeg.exe: SubSeg.res SubSeg.def SubSeg.obj SubMem.obj
    tlink /c/C/n/P-/Twe/x @SubSeg.LNK
    rlink SubSeg.res SubSeg.exe

#    Individual File Dependencies
SubSeg.obj: SubSeg.cpp

SubMem.obj: SubMem.c

SubSeg.res: SubSeg.rc SubSeg.cur SubSeg.ico
    brcc -FO SubSeg.res -i$(INC) SubSeg.RC
```

# SUBSEG.LNK

```
\borlandc\lib\c0wl.obj+
SubSeg.obj+
SubMem.obj
SubSeg,SubSeg
\borlandc\classlib\lib\tclasdll.lib+
\borlandc\owl\lib\owl.lib+
mathwl.lib+
import.lib+
crtldll.lib
SubSeg.def
```

# SUBSEG.CPP

```
/*-------------------------------------------------------------*\
  | SUBSEG.CPP  -  Demo of sub-segment allocation in Win3.      |
\*-------------------------------------------------------------*/
#define WIN31
#define STRICT
#include <owl.h>
#include <WindowsX.h>
#include "Subseg.h"
#include "SubMem.h"


/*-------------------------------------------------------------*\
  |                    Class Declarations.                      |
\*-------------------------------------------------------------*/
class TSubSegApplication : public TApplication
{
  public:
    TSubSegApplication (LPSTR lpszName, HINSTANCE hInstance,
                        HINSTANCE hPrevInstance, LPSTR lpszCmdLine,
                        int nCmdShow);
    virtual void InitMainWindow ();
};
```

```c
class TSubSegWindow : public TWindow
  {
  public:
    PSTR Label1;
    PSTR Label2;
    PSTR Label3;

    int cb1;   // Label lengths.
    int cb2;
    int cb3;

    HANDLE32 hSegment[COUNT];
    SEGDATA  sdInit[COUNT];

    TEXTMETRIC tmSys;
    LPSEGDATA lpSegData[COUNT];

    TSubSegWindow (PTWindowsObject pwParent, LPSTR lpszTitle,
              PTModule pmModule);
    virtual BOOL   Create();
    virtual void   Destroy();
    virtual LPSTR  GetClassName ();
    virtual void   GetWindowClass (WNDCLASS&);
    virtual void   Paint (HDC hdc, PAINTSTRUCT& ps);
     };
/*--------------------------------------------------------------*\
|                 Main Function:  WinMain.                       |
\*--------------------------------------------------------------*/
int PASCAL WinMain (HINSTANCE hInstance,  HINSTANCE hPrevInstance,
                 LPSTR lpszCmdLine,  int    nCmdShow)
     {
     TSubSegApplication SubSeg ("SubSeg", hInstance,
                             hPrevInstance, lpszCmdLine,
                             nCmdShow);
     SubSeg.Run();
     return SubSeg.Status;
     }

/*--------------------------------------------------------------*\
|                 Application Class Member.                      |
\*--------------------------------------------------------------*/
TSubSegApplication::TSubSegApplication (LPSTR lpszName,
                    HINSTANCE hInstance, HINSTANCE hPrevInstance,
                    LPSTR lpszCmdLine, int nCmdShow)
                 :TApplication (lpszName, hInstance,
                    hPrevInstance, lpszCmdLine, nCmdShow)
    {
    SubInitialize();
    }

/*--------------------------------------------------------------*\
|                 Application Class Member.                      |
\*--------------------------------------------------------------*/
void TSubSegApplication::InitMainWindow ()
    {
    MainWindow = new TSubSegWindow (NULL,
                             "Sub-Segment Allocation", NULL);
    }
```

```
/*-------------------------------------------------------------*\
|                 TSubSegWindow Class Member.                   |
\*-------------------------------------------------------------*/
TSubSegWindow::TSubSegWindow (PTWindowsObject pwParent,
               LPSTR lpszTitle, PTModule pmModule)
           :TWindow (pwParent, lpszTitle, pmModule)
    {
    Label1 = "Description";
    Label2 = "Req/Actual";
    Label3 = "Handle  ->  Address";

    cb1 = lstrlen(Label1);
    cb2 = lstrlen(Label2);
    cb3 = lstrlen(Label3);

    lstrcpy (sdInit[0].achDesc, "Fixed Object");
    sdInit[0].dwAlloc = 50;
    sdInit[0].wFlags  = GMEM_FIXED;

    lstrcpy (sdInit[1].achDesc, "Moveable Memory");
    sdInit[1].dwAlloc = 75;
    sdInit[1].wFlags  = GMEM_MOVEABLE | GMEM_ZEROINIT;

    lstrcpy (sdInit[2].achDesc, "Discardable Segment");
    sdInit[2].dwAlloc = 100;
    sdInit[2].wFlags  = GMEM_DISCARDABLE | GMEM_MOVEABLE;
    }

/*-------------------------------------------------------------*\
|                 TSubSegWindow Class Member.                   |
\*-------------------------------------------------------------*/
BOOL TSubSegWindow::Create()
    {
    BOOL bRetVal;
    HDC  hdc;
    int  i;

    bRetVal = TWindow::Create();

    if (bRetVal)
        {
        for (i=0;i<COUNT;i++)
            {
            hSegment[i] = SubAlloc(sdInit[i].wFlags,
                                   (WORD)sdInit[i].dwAlloc);
            lpSegData[i] = (LPSEGDATA)SubLock (hSegment[i]);
            if (!lpSegData[i])
                {
                MessageBox (NULL,"Not enough memory",
                            GetApplication()->Name, MB_OK);
                bRetVal = FALSE;
                goto Exit;
                }

            lstrcpy (lpSegData[i]->achDesc, sdInit[i].achDesc);
            lpSegData[i]->dwAlloc = sdInit[i].dwAlloc;
            lpSegData[i]->dwActual = SubSize (hSegment[i]);
            lpSegData[i]->wFlags = sdInit[i].wFlags;
            } /* [for] */
```

```
            hdc = GetDC (HWindow);
            GetTextMetrics (hdc, &tmSys);
            ReleaseDC (HWindow, hdc);
            }
Exit:
    return bRetVal;
    }

/*------------------------------------------------------------*\
|                  TSubSegWindow Class Member.                 |
\*------------------------------------------------------------*/
void TSubSegWindow::Destroy()
    {
    int i;

    for (i=0;i<COUNT;i++)
        {
        SubUnlock (hSegment[i]);
        SubFree   (hSegment[i]);
        }
    }

/*------------------------------------------------------------*\
|                  TSubSegWindow Class Member.                 |
\*------------------------------------------------------------*/
LPSTR TSubSegWindow::GetClassName ()
    {
    return "SubSeg:MAIN";
    }

/*------------------------------------------------------------*\
|                  TSubSegWindow Class Member.                 |
\*------------------------------------------------------------*/
void TSubSegWindow::GetWindowClass (WNDCLASS& wc)
    {
    TWindow::GetWindowClass (wc);
    wc.hIcon=LoadIcon (wc.hInstance, "snapshot");
    wc.hCursor=LoadCursor (wc.hInstance, "hand");
    }

/*------------------------------------------------------------*\
|                  TSubSegWindow Class Member.                 |
\*------------------------------------------------------------*/
void TSubSegWindow::Paint (HDC hdc, PAINTSTRUCT& ps)
    {
    char buff[30];
    int  cb;
 int  i;
    int  xText1;
    int  xText2;
    int  xText3;
    int  yText;

    /* Calculate text positioning variables.        */
    xText1 = tmSys.tmAveCharWidth * 2;
    xText2 = xText1 + (STRSIZE * tmSys.tmAveCharWidth);
    xText3 = xText2 + ((cb2+5) * tmSys.tmAveCharWidth);
    yText = tmSys.tmHeight;
```

```
            /* Print titles.                              */
            TextOut (hdc, xText1, yText, Label1, cb1);
            TextOut (hdc, xText2, yText, Label2, cb2);
            TextOut (hdc, xText3, yText, Label3, cb3);

            yText += tmSys.tmHeight * 2;

            for (i=0;i<COUNT;i++)
                {
                /* Print description.                     */
                TextOut (hdc, xText1, yText, lpSegData[i]->achDesc,
                         lstrlen(lpSegData[i]->achDesc));

                /* Print allocated vs actual size.        */
                cb = wsprintf (buff, "%ld / %ld", lpSegData[i]->dwAlloc,
                                                  lpSegData[i]->dwActual);
                TextOut (hdc, xText2, yText, buff, cb);

                /* Print handle and actual address.       */
                cb = wsprintf (buff, "%04x:%04x  ->  %04x:%04x",
                        HIWORD(hSegment[i]), LOWORD(hSegment[i]),
                        HIWORD(lpSegData[i]), LOWORD(lpSegData[i]));
                TextOut (hdc, xText3, yText, buff, cb);

                /* Advance to next line.                  */
                yText += tmSys.tmHeight + tmSys.tmExternalLeading;
                }

        }
```

# SUBSEG.H

```
/*------------------------------------------------------------*\
|  SUBSEG.H  -  Include file for SubSeg.cpp.                   |
\*------------------------------------------------------------*/

/*------------------------------------------------------------*\
|                         Constants.                           |
\*------------------------------------------------------------*/
const int STRSIZE = 30;
const int COUNT   = 3;

/*------------------------------------------------------------*\
|                         TypeDefs.                            |
\*------------------------------------------------------------*/
typedef struct tagSEGDATA
    {
    char   achDesc[STRSIZE];   /* Description of data.  */
    DWORD  dwAlloc;            /* Amount asked for.     */
    DWORD  dwActual;           /* Actually allocated.   */
    WORD   wFlags;             /* Allocation flags.     */
    } SEGDATA;

typedef SEGDATA FAR *LPSEGDATA;
```

# SUBMEM.C

```c
/*-------------------------------------------------------------*\
|  SUBMEM.C  -  Sub-segment allocation routines, for creating  |
|               local heaps in dynamically allocated segments. |
\*-------------------------------------------------------------*/
#include <Windows.H>
#define WIN31
#define STRICT

#include <WindowsX.h>
typedef DWORD HANDLE32;

/*-------------------------------------------------------------*\
|                  Static Data Definitions.                    |
\*-------------------------------------------------------------*/
HGLOBAL hSegment;

/*-------------------------------------------------------------*\
|  SubInitialize - Call first to allocate a segment from the   |
|                  global heap.                                |
\*-------------------------------------------------------------*/
BOOL     FAR PASCAL SubInitialize(VOID)
    {
    BOOL  bRetVal;
    LPSTR lp;
    WORD  wSeg;
      WORD  wSize;

    hSegment = GlobalAlloc (GMEM_MOVEABLE | GMEM_ZEROINIT,
                            4096);
    if (!hSegment)
        return FALSE;

    lp = GlobalLock (hSegment);
    if (!lp)
        return FALSE;

    wSeg = HIWORD (lp);
    wSize = (WORD)GlobalSize (hSegment) - 16;

    bRetVal = LocalInit (wSeg, 0, wSize);

    GlobalUnlock (hSegment);
    GlobalUnlock (hSegment);   /*  Undo LocalInit's GlobalLock. */

    return bRetVal;
    }


/*-------------------------------------------------------------*\
|  SubAlloc - Allocate a subsegment.                           |
|                                                              |
|  Input:   wFlags = local heap allocation flags.              |
|           wBytes = number of bytes to allocate.              |
|                                                              |
|  Returns: A 4-byte "handle", put together as:                |
|             HIWORD = Handle to global segment.               |
|             LOWORD = Handle to local object.                 |
\*-------------------------------------------------------------*/
```

```c
HANDLE32 FAR PASCAL SubAlloc(WORD wFlags, WORD wBytes)
    {
    HLOCAL hMem;
    LPSTR  lp;
    WORD   wSeg;

    lp = GlobalLock (hSegment);
    if (!lp)
        return 0L;

    wSeg = HIWORD (lp);

    _asm {  push    ds
            mov     ax, wSeg
            mov     ds, ax   }

    hMem = LocalAlloc (wFlags, wBytes);

    _asm {  pop     ds }

    GlobalUnlock (hSegment);

    if (!hMem)
        return 0L;
    else
        return MAKELONG (hMem, hSegment);
    }

/*------------------------------------------------------------*\
|   SubFree - Free a subsegment.                               |
|                                                              |
|   Input:  A 4-byte "handle", put together as:                |
|           HIWORD = Handle to global segment.                 |
|           LOWORD = Handle to local object.                   |
|                                                              |
|   Returns:  The original handle, if successful.  Otherwise,  |
|             returns NULL.                                    |
\*------------------------------------------------------------*/
HANDLE32 FAR PASCAL SubFree(HANDLE32 hSubMem)
    {
    HGLOBAL hSeg;
    HLOCAL  hMem;
    LPSTR   lp;
    WORD    wSeg;

    hSeg = HIWORD (hSubMem);
    hMem = LOWORD (hSubMem);

    lp = GlobalLock (hSeg);
    if (!lp)
        return 0L;
    wSeg = HIWORD (lp);

    _asm {  push    ds
            mov     ax, wSeg
            mov     ds, ax   }

    hMem = LocalFree (hMem);

    _asm {  pop     ds }

    GlobalUnlock (hSeg);
```

```
        if (!hMem)
            return 0L;
        else
            return MAKELONG (hMem, hSeg);
    }

/*-----------------------------------------------------------*\
|   SubLock - Lock a subsegment and the segment it lives in.  |
|                                                             |
|   Input:   A 4-byte "handle", put together as:              |
|            HIWORD = Handle to global segment.               |
|            LOWORD = Handle to local object.                 |
|                                                             |
|   Returns: A far pointer to the object.                     |
\*-----------------------------------------------------------*/
LPSTR    FAR PASCAL SubLock(HANDLE32 hSubMem)
    {
    HGLOBAL hSeg;
    HLOCAL hMem;
    LPSTR lp;
    PSTR  p;
    WORD  wSeg;

    hSeg = HIWORD (hSubMem);
    hMem = LOWORD (hSubMem);

    lp = GlobalLock (hSeg);
    if (!lp)
        return 0L;

    wSeg = HIWORD (lp);

    _asm { push    ds
           mov     ax, wSeg
           mov     ds, ax    }

    p = LocalLock (hMem);

    _asm { pop     ds }

    /* No Matching GlobalUnlock -- leave segment locked    */
    /* for caller to use.  We'll unlock twice in SubUnlock. */

    if (!p)
        return (LPSTR)0;
    else
        return (LPSTR)MAKELONG (p, wSeg);
    }

/*-----------------------------------------------------------*\
|   SubSize - Returns the size of a subsegment.               |
|                                                             |
|   Input:   A 4-byte "handle", put together as:              |
|            HIWORD = Handle to global segment.               |
|            LOWORD = Handle to local object.                 |
|                                                             |
|   Returns: a WORD value with the subsegment size, or zero   |
|            if the handle is invalid.                        |
\*-----------------------------------------------------------*/
WORD     FAR PASCAL SubSize(HANDLE32 hSubMem)
```

```c
    {
    HGLOBAL hSeg;
    HLOCAL  hMem;
    LPSTR   lp;
    WORD    wSeg;
    WORD    wSize;

    hSeg = HIWORD (hSubMem);
    hMem = LOWORD (hSubMem);

    lp = GlobalLock (hSeg);
    if (!lp)
        return 0;

    wSeg = HIWORD (lp);

    _asm {  push    ds
            mov     ax, wSeg
            mov     ds, ax      }

    wSize = LocalSize (hMem);

    _asm {  pop     ds  }

    GlobalUnlock (hSeg);

    return wSize;
    }

/*-----------------------------------------------------------------*\
|  SubUnlock - Unlock a subsegment, and the segment it lives       |
|              in.                                                  |
|  Input:  A 4-byte "handle", put together as:                      |
|              HIWORD = Handle to global segment.                   |
|              LOWORD = Handle to local object.                     |
|                                                                   |
|  Returns: The LocalUnlock return value, which is zero if          |
|           the block's reference count was decreased to            |
|           zero, otherwise it is non-zero.                         |
\*-----------------------------------------------------------------*/
BOOL    FAR PASCAL SubUnlock(HANDLE32 hSubMem)
    {
    BOOL    bRetVal;
    HGLOBAL hSeg;
    HLOCAL  hMem;
    LPSTR   lp;
    WORD    wSeg;

    hSeg = HIWORD (hSubMem);
    hMem = LOWORD (hSubMem);
    lp = GlobalLock (hSeg);
    if (!lp)
        return 0L;

    wSeg = HIWORD (lp);

    _asm {  push    ds
            mov     ax, wSeg
            mov     ds, ax      }
```

```
        bRetVal = LocalUnlock (hMem);

        _asm { pop     ds }

        GlobalUnlock (hSeg);
        GlobalUnlock (hSeg);

        return bRetVal;
        }
```

# SUBMEM.H

```
/*------------------------------------------------------------*\
 | SUBMEM.H   -   Include file for SUBMEM.C                   |
 \*------------------------------------------------------------*/

typedef DWORD HANDLE32;


/*------------------------------------------------------------*\
 |                    Function Prototypes.                    |
 \*------------------------------------------------------------*/
extern "C" BOOL     FAR PASCAL SubInitialize(VOID);
extern "C" HANDLE32 FAR PASCAL SubAlloc(WORD, WORD);
extern "C" HANDLE32 FAR PASCAL SubFree(HANDLE32);
extern "C" LPSTR    FAR PASCAL SubLock(HANDLE32);
extern "C" WORD     FAR PASCAL SubSize(HANDLE32);
extern "C" BOOL     FAR PASCAL SubUnlock(HANDLE32);
```

# SUBSEG.RC

```
snapshot icon SubSeg.ico

hand cursor SubSeg.cur
```

# SUBSEG.DEF

```
NAME SUBSEG

EXETYPE WINDOWS

DESCRIPTION 'Sub-Segment Allocation'

CODE MOVEABLE DISCARDABLE
DATA MOVEABLE MULTIPLE

HEAPSIZE   512
STACKSIZE 5120
```

The first thing you may notice about this program is that very little is different from the SEGALLOC program from which it was derived. This is intentional, since the allocation routines that we have created are meant to exactly mirror both the local and global heap management routines. So, the **SubAlloc** routine takes the place of **GlobalAlloc** or **LocalAlloc**, and the **SubLock** routine takes the place of **GlobalLock** or **LocalLock**. However, when you look at the code to the subsegment routines, you'll find that calls are made to *both* local and global heap management routines.

There is also an important difference in the handle that `SubAlloc` returns. Instead of the normal 16-bit handle, it returns a 32-bit handle. This is really two handles in one: The high word contains the handle of the segment, and the low word contains the handle of the local heap object. This allows the routines to be extended to support several local heaps in several different segments. The only requirement is that `LocalInit` be called to initialize each segment. This program only uses one segment for the sake of simplicity.

Another limitation of this program is that the segment that contains the local heap is never freed. While this may be reasonable for a tiny, sample program, this is clearly a case of "do as I say, and not as I do." In other words, please be sure to free any memory you allocate, unlock any memory you lock, and in general undo whatever needs undoing to free any resource you use.

Let's move on to our next and final sample program, which creates a custom resource.

## Custom Resources

Although Windows provides built-in support for several different types of resources, you may wish to create your own custom resource types. This lets you take advantage of the built-in memory management features of resources, with a minimum of effort on your part. The best candidates for custom resources are data objects that won't change. We're going to show an example of a resource that will be used to calculate sine and cosine values. This table allows a calculation of an integer sine value, which is simply a sine value multiplied by 10,000. The advantage of using a lookup table is that it is faster than calculating on the fly. In addition, since the low-end members of the Intel-86 family (80386 and earlier) do not have built-in floating-point support, you'll get faster overall performance if you limit your calculations to integer arithmetic. It may interest you to know that this factor influenced Microsoft enough to build Windows without *any* use of floating-point arithmetic.

We're going to write two routines that will provide sine and cosine values for an angle entered in degrees. Roughly speaking, then, with two functions and 360 degrees, 720 different values are required for our lookup table. But we're going to take advantage of the symmetry of this table to play a few tricks, do a little folding and rotating, and produce the same results with a single table of 90 sine values. To see how we're going to pull this off, read on!

The first thing we'll need to do is to create a table of values. There are many ways to do this, but the most straightforward involves writing a small C program that calculates our sine values and writes them as ASCII text to a data file. Why ASCII text? We're going to show you a trick that will allow you to build complex binary data objects from ASCII text files. The only tools that are required are the macro assembler (TASM), the linker, and a special converter called EXE2BIN.EXE which comes with DOS. Here are the program files that we use to create our table of sine values:

## MAKEFILE.MAK

```
#
#   Make file for sine table.
#
#   Create sine table with:
#       C> make sinedata.bin
#

sine.exe: sine.c
    bcc sine.c

sinedata.asm: sine.exe
    sine

sinedata.bin: sinedata.asm
    tasm sinedata.asm
    tlink sinedata.obj
    exe2bin sinedata.exe
    copy sinedata.bin ..\custres\sinedata.bin
```

## SINE.C

```c
/*-----------------------------------------------------------*\
 |  SINE.C - Creates an .ASM data file containing sine values  |
 |            from 0 to 90 degrees.  This file is suitable     |
 |            for creating a custom Windows resource.          |
 \*-----------------------------------------------------------*/

#include "stdio.h"
#include "math.h"

char achFileHeader[] =
    ";\n"
    "; Sine/Cosine Data Table\n"
    ";\n"
    ";\n"
    "; Table of Sine values from 0 to 90 degrees\n"
    ";\n"
    "SINDATA segment public\n";

char achFileFooter[] =
```

```
        "\n"
        "SINDATA ends\n"
        "END\n";

main()
    {
    double dbPI  = 3.1415926536;
    double dbRad;
    FILE   * fp;
    int    iAngle;
    int    iSin;

    if (!(fp = fopen("sinedata.asm", "w")))
        {
        printf("Can't create sinedata.asm.\n");
        exit(1);
        }

    fprintf (fp, achFileHeader);
    fprintf (fp, "DW ");

    for (iAngle = 0; iAngle <= 90; iAngle++)
        {
        dbRad = (((double)iAngle) * dbPI) / 180.0;
        iSin = sin(dbRad) * 10000.0 + 0.5;
        fprintf(fp, " %5d", iSin);

        if (iAngle % 8 == 7)
            fprintf (fp, "\nDW ");
        else if (iAngle != 90)
            fprintf (fp, ",");
        }

    fprintf(fp, achFileFooter);

    fclose(fp);

    return (0);
    }
```

The data file created by this program is essentially an MASM language file, containing the data definitions suitable for use as a data segment. But we're not going to write any MASM code to support it. Instead, we're going to let MASM convert the data definitions into binary format. Here is the MASM file that is created, SINEDATA.ASM:

```
; Sine/Cosine Data Table
;
;
; Table of Sine values from 0 to 90 degrees
;
SINDATA segment public
DW      0,   175,   349,   523,   698,   872,  1045,  1219
DW   1392,  1564,  1736,  1908,  2079,  2250,  2419,  2588
DW   2756,  2924,  3090,  3256,  3420,  3584,  3746,  3907
DW   4067,  4226,  4384,  4540,  4695,  4848,  5000,  5150
DW   5299,  5446,  5592,  5736,  5878,  6018,  6157,  6293
```

```
DW    6428,  6561,  6691,  6820,  6947,  7071,  7193,  7314
DW    7431,  7547,  7660,  7771,  7880,  7986,  8090,  8192
DW    8290,  8387,  8480,  8572,  8660,  8746,  8829,  8910
DW    8988,  9063,  9135,  9205,  9272,  9336,  9397,  9455
DW    9511,  9563,  9613,  9659,  9703,  9744,  9781,  9816
DW    9848,  9877,  9903,  9925,  9945,  9962,  9976,  9986
DW    9994,  9998, 10000
SINDATA ends
END
```

After this data file has been run through the macro assembler and the linker, the result is an .EXE file that is almost ready to run as a DOS program. Well, not really, since it doesn't have any code. It's just an executable file with a data segment. To isolate the data into a pure binary object, we run the EXE2BIN program. This program is ordinarily used to create .COM files from .EXE files. .COM files are simply memory images that can be loaded and run "as is." Since that's exactly what we want—a pure, binary image—EXE2BIN does the trick to create our sine table resource.

To test that the sine and cosine functions are providing accurate values, our sample program, CUSTRES, connects 359 points together to draw a circle with a radius of 100 pixels. The drawing appears in Figure 18.7. While this is quite a bit slower and rougher than you would expect from calling GDI's **Ellipse** routine, it demonstrates quite nicely that the sine and cosine values that we generate at least *look* right in the range 0 to 360 degrees.

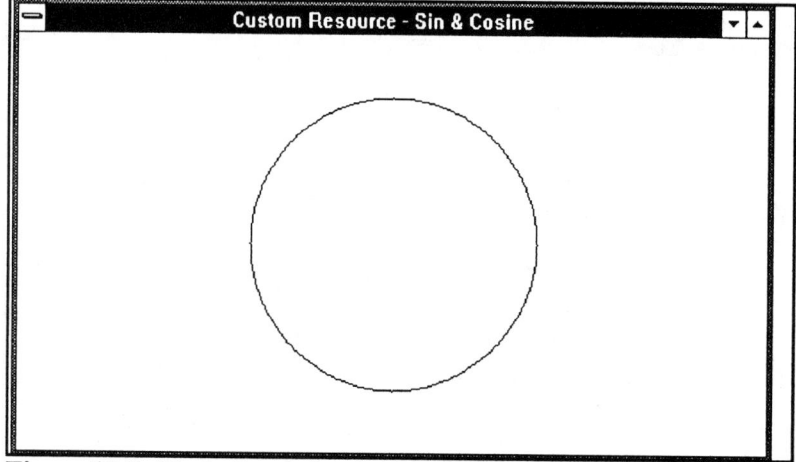

**Figure 18.7 Circle drawn by CUSTRES**

Here is the code for our custom resource program, CUSTRES.EXE, that used the sine table information to calculate sines and cosines that were used to actually draw the circle shown in the figure.

## MAKEFILE.MAK

```
.AUTODEPEND

#       Translator Definitions
INC=\BORLANDC\OWL\INCLUDE;\BORLANDC\CLASSLIB\INCLUDE;\BORLANDC\INCLUDE
CC = bcc -c -D_CLASSDLL -H -ml -WS -w-par -I$(INC)

#       Implicit Rules
.c.obj:
  $(CC) {$< }

.cpp.obj:
  $(CC) {$< }

#       Explicit Rules
CustRes.exe: CustRes.res CustRes.def CustRes.obj
     tlink /c/C/n/P-/Twe/x @CustRes.LNK
     rlink CustRes.res CustRes.exe

#       Individual File Dependencies
CustRes.obj: CustRes.cpp

CustRes.res: CustRes.rc CustRes.cur CustRes.ico
     RC -R -FO CustRes.res -i$(INC) CustRes.RC
```

## CUSTRES.LNK

```
\borlandc\lib\c0wl.obj+
CustRes.obj
CustRes,CustRes
\borlandc\classlib\lib\tclasdll.lib+
\borlandc\owl\lib\owl.lib+
mathwl.lib+
import.lib+
crtldll.lib
CustRes.def
```

## CUSTRES.CPP

```
/*---------------------------------------------------------------*\
 | CUSTRES.CPP - Creating a custom resource in Windows.  This    |
 |               program creates a resource that contains        |
 |               a sine table. This table is used for the        |
 |               calculation of sines and cosines for any        |
 |               degree value entered.                           |
\*---------------------------------------------------------------*/
#define WIN31
#define STRICT
#include <owl.h>
#include <WindowsX.h>
#include "CustRes.h"

/*---------------------------------------------------------------*\
 |                    Global Variables.                          |
\*---------------------------------------------------------------*/
```

```
HGLOBAL hresSineData;
/*-------------------------------------------------------------*\
|                    Class Declarations.                        |
\*-------------------------------------------------------------*/
class TCustResApplication : public TApplication
   {
   public:
     TCustResApplication (LPSTR lpszName, HINSTANCE hInstance,
                          HINSTANCE hPrevInstance, LPSTR lpszCmdLine,
                          int nCmdShow);
     ~TCustResApplication ();
     virtual void InitMainWindow ();
   };

class TCustResWindow : public TWindow
   {
   public:
     TCustResWindow (PTWindowsObject pwParent, LPSTR lpszTitle,
                     PTModule pmModule);
     virtual LPSTR GetClassName ();
     virtual void  GetWindowClass (WNDCLASS&);
     virtual void  Paint (HDC hdc, PAINTSTRUCT& ps);
   };

/*-------------------------------------------------------------*\
|                    Main Function:  WinMain.                   |
\*-------------------------------------------------------------*/
int PASCAL WinMain (HINSTANCE hInstance,   HINSTANCE hPrevInstance,
                    LPSTR     lpszCmdLine, int       nCmdShow)
    {
    TCustResApplication CustRes ("CustRes", hInstance,
                      hPrevInstance, lpszCmdLine, nCmdShow);
    CustRes.Run();
    return CustRes.Status;
    }

/*-------------------------------------------------------------*\
|                    Application Class Member.                  |
\*-------------------------------------------------------------*/
TCustResApplication::TCustResApplication (LPSTR lpszName,
                      HINSTANCE hInstance, HINSTANCE hPrevInstance,
                      LPSTR lpszCmdLine, int nCmdShow)
                      :TApplication (lpszName, hInstance,
                      hPrevInstance, lpszCmdLine, nCmdShow)
    {
    HRSRC hRes;

    hRes = FindResource (hInstance,
           MAKEINTRESOURCE(SINE),    /* Name. */
           MAKEINTRESOURCE(TABLE));  /* Type. */
    hresSineData = LoadResource (hInstance, hRes);
    }

/*-------------------------------------------------------------*\
|                    Application Class Member.                  |
\*-------------------------------------------------------------*/
TCustResApplication::~TCustResApplication ()
    {
    FreeResource (hresSineData);
    }
```

```
/*------------------------------------------------------------*\
|                  Application Class Member.                   |
\*------------------------------------------------------------*/
void TCustResApplication::InitMainWindow ()
    {
    MainWindow = new TCustResWindow (NULL,
                                "Custom Resource - Sin & Cosine",
                                NULL);
    }

/*------------------------------------------------------------*\
|                  TCustResWindow Class Member.                |
\*------------------------------------------------------------*/
TCustResWindow::TCustResWindow (PTWindowsObject pwParent,
                LPSTR lpszTitle, PTModule pmModule)
            :TWindow (pwParent, lpszTitle, pmModule)
    {
    /* Window specific initialization goes here. */
    }

/*------------------------------------------------------------*\
|                  TCustResWindow Class Member.                |
\*------------------------------------------------------------*/
LPSTR TCustResWindow::GetClassName ()
    {
    return "CustRes:MAIN";
    }

/*------------------------------------------------------------*\
|                  TCustResWindow Class Member.                |
\*------------------------------------------------------------*/
void TCustResWindow::GetWindowClass (WNDCLASS& wc)
    {
    TWindow::GetWindowClass (wc);
    wc.hIcon=LoadIcon (wc.hInstance, "snapshot");
    wc.hCursor=LoadCursor (wc.hInstance, "hand");
    }

/*------------------------------------------------------------*\
|                  TCustResWindow Class Member.                |
\*------------------------------------------------------------*/
void TCustResWindow::Paint (HDC hdc, PAINTSTRUCT& ps)
    {
    int i;
    int x, y;
    RECT r;

    GetClientRect (HWindow, &r);
    SetViewportOrg (hdc, r.right/2, r.bottom/2);

    x = intCos (0)/100;
    y = intSine (0)/100;
    MoveTo (hdc, x, y);

    for (i=0;i<=360;i++)
        {
        x = intCos (i)/100;
        y = intSine (i)/100;
        LineTo (hdc, x, y);
```

```
            }
        }
    /*-----------------------------------------------------------*\
    |              Integer Sine Routine:   intSine.              |
    |                                                             |
    |        Calculates an integer sine value in units equal     |
    |        to 10,000th for any degree entered, using a         |
    |        value derived from a custom Sine resource.          |
    \*-----------------------------------------------------------*/
    int FAR PASCAL intSine (int iValue)
        {
        int iSign;

        int FAR * fpSine;

        fpSine = (int FAR *)LockResource (hresSineData);
        if (fpSine == NULL)
            return (0);

        while (iValue < 0)    iValue +=360;
        while (iValue > 360) iValue -=360;

        iSign = 1;

        if (iValue > 90 && iValue <=180)
            {
            iValue = 180 - iValue;
            }
        else if (iValue > 180 && iValue <= 270)
            {
            iSign = -1;
            iValue = iValue - 180;
            }
        else if (iValue > 270 && iValue <= 360)
            {
            iSign = -1;
            iValue = 360 - iValue;
            }

        /* Adjust pointer to correct table entry. */
        fpSine += iValue;

        iSign = *fpSine * iSign;
        UnlockResource (hresSineData);

        return (iSign);
        }
    /*-----------------------------------------------------------*\
    |              Integer CoSine Routine:   intCos.             |
    |                                                             |
    |        Calculates an integer cosine value in units         |
    |        equal to 10,000th for any degree entered, using     |
    |        a value derived from a custom sine resource.        |
    \*-----------------------------------------------------------*/
    int FAR PASCAL intCos (int iValue)
        {
        return (intSine (iValue-90));
        }
```

## CUSTRES.H

```
/*--------------------------------------------------------------*\
|  CUSTRES.H - Include file for CustRes.c                        |
\*--------------------------------------------------------------*/

#define TABLE  100    /* Custom resource type value.         */
#define SINE   100    /* ID of particular custom resource.   */

int FAR PASCAL intSine (int iValue);
int FAR PASCAL intCos (int iValue);
```

## CUSTRES.RC

```
#include "CustRes.h"

snapshot icon CustRes.ico

hand cursor CustRes.cur

SINE TABLE sinedata.bin DISCARDABLE
```

## CUSTRES.DEF

```
NAME CUSTRES

EXETYPE WINDOWS

DESCRIPTION 'A Custom Resource'

CODE MOVEABLE DISCARDABLE
DATA MOVEABLE MULTIPLE

HEAPSIZE   512
STACKSIZE 5120
```

CUSTRES does all its work in three places: in the application object's constructor, in response to **WM_PAINT**, and in the application object's destructor. The sine and cosine information is provided in two routines: `intSin` and `intCos`. The second function actually cheats: Since a cosine is always 90 degrees out of phase with a sine, the `intCos` function subtracts 90 degrees from the actual angle and calls the `intSin` function—just a little trigonometric sleight of hand to make Mom proud.

To use a custom resource, you call three routines: **FindResource**, **LoadResource**, and **LockResource**. In the application constructor, the first two are called. The result is a memory handle that is stored in `hresSinData`. **FindResource** searches for the reference to a resource in the module database, which, as we mentioned earlier, is simply an abbreviated memory image of the module's file header. **FindResource** takes three parameters:

```
FindResource (hInstance, lpName, lpType)
```

- **hInstance** is an instance handle.
- **lpName** is a long pointer to a character string with the resource name.
- **lpType** is a long pointer to a character string with the resource type.

Even though **lpName** and **lpType** are pointers to character strings, this is not the most efficient way to identify a resource. The reason is simple: A string comparison is more expensive than an integer comparison. For this reason, we use a macro, **MAKEINTRESOURCE**, which lets us define integers and use them in place of a character string. Here are the two integers we defined in CUSTRES:

```
#define  TABLE  100   /*  Custom resource type.  */
#define  SINE   100   /*  ID of sine table.      */
```

We use them in the call to **FindResource**, as follows:

```
hRes = FindResource (hInst,
         MAKEINTRESOURCE(SIN),      /* Name. */
         MAKEINTRESOURCE(TABLE));   /* Type. */
```

The **MAKEINTRESOURCE** macro creates a pseudopointer, with zero for a segment identifier and the integer value for the offset value. It casts this value as an **LPSTR**, which is how this routine is defined, so that the compiler doesn't complain. When the **FindResource** routine sees this value, it does not treat it as a pointer. (This would be a fatal error!) Instead, it uses the two-byte integer value to find the resource definition. It can find it, because the resource file, CUSTRES.RC, has the following line:

```
SIN    TABLE   sinedata.bin DISCARDABLE
```

This causes the data in the resource file, SINEDATA.BIN, to be copied entirely into CUSTRES.EXE at compile/link time. This means that CUSTRES is a stand-alone program and doesn't need the original resource data file to be present at runtime.

Once **FindResource** has identified the specific resource that we are interested in, it provides a resource identifier: a handle that must be provided to the **LoadResource** routine to be useful. **LoadResource** is the next routine called, and it is defined as

```
LoadResource (hInstance, hresInfo)
```

- **hInstance** is the instance handle.
- **hresInfo** is the handle returned by the FindResource routine.

In spite of its name, `LoadResource` does *not* cause the resource to be loaded into memory. Instead, it allocates a memory object from the global heap with a size of zero. This doesn't actually cause any memory to be allocated, but does cause a global memory handle to be assigned for our use. `LoadResource` provides this memory handle as a return value, which CUSTRES stores in `hresSinData`.

The routine that actually causes a resource to be loaded into memory is `LockResource`. But CUSTRES doesn't call this routine until it actually needs to use the data in the sine table. By postponing the loading of such a memory object, CUSTRES helps minimize the demand it makes on system memory. `LockResource` does several things: It loads the resource into memory, locks it in place, and returns a pointer to the data. `LockResource` is defined as

```
LPSTR LockResource (hResData)
```

- `hResData` is the handle returned by the `LoadResource` function.

`LockResource` returns a long pointer to a string. But if you're not storing characters in a resource, it's a simple matter to define the desired string and cast the results of `LockResource` to the right type.

Here is how CUSTRES handles its need for a pointer to integer data:

```
int FAR * fpSin;

fpSin = (int FAR *)LockResource (hresSinData);
if (fpSin == NULL)
    return (0);
```

As we have mentioned elsewhere, casting the return value to routines like `LockResource` keeps the compiler from complaining about an alleged type mismatch. We know there is no type mismatch, and by casting we let the compiler know. Notice also, that we check the return value from `LockResource`, in case it wasn't able to load the resource into memory.

The `LockResource` routine should never be discussed alone, but always in the context of an `UnlockResource`, with which it creates a *Windows sandwich*. We discussed this code construction earlier as a way to organize the use of a shared resource. In this case, the resource is memory. Calls to `LockResource` must be paired with calls to `UnlockResource`. The first loads the resource and ties it down in memory. The second unties the resource, allowing it to be moved in memory or even discarded, if the Memory Manager sees fit to do so. In CUSTRES, the `intSin` function uses these two routines to bracket its use of the sine data, creating a Windows sandwich that ensures that the object is locked when we need it, and unlocked when we don't. The `UnlockResource` function is defined as

```
BOOL UnlockResource (hResData)
```

- **hResData** is the handle returned by the **LoadResource** function.

The final routine that plays a role in the handling of the custom resource is **FreeResource**. This frees all the memory associated with our custom resource. **FreeResource** is defined as

```
FreeResource (hResData)
```

- **hResData** is the handle returned by the **LoadResource** function.

This routine is called in response in the application class destructor, to deallocate the sine data memory. In this program, we don't actually need to call **FreeResource**, since the resource will be freed when our program terminates. But, as mentioned elsewhere in this book, it is a good programming practice that will help your code survive future programmers who fix, update, modify, and in other ways use your code in their projects.

From our discussion, you can see that Windows provides many choices in how a program uses memory for its code and data. Understanding these choices will help you tune your program to work optimally in all of Windows operating modes, and for compatibility with future versions of Windows.

# 19

# Dynamic Linking

In all its operating modes—real, standard, and enhanced—Windows uses dynamic linking. Dynamic linking is several things rolled into one. First of all, it is a memory management technique that allows code to be loaded from disk on demand. Dynamic linking allows code to be discarded to free memory for other uses. When running in protected mode, Windows' dynamic linking depends on the built-in memory management features of the Intel-86 family of CPUs to trigger the loading process. And when running in real mode, even without the hardware support, Windows is able to provide dynamic linking that is just as efficient as its protected mode counterpart with a mechanism that is implemented entirely in software.

Second, dynamic linking provides a way to connect subroutine libraries to programs at *runtime*. This contrasts sharply with static linking, in which routines from a subroutine library are copied to a program's executable file at program *creation time*. For example, if a Windows program uses the **memset** runtime library routine, a copy of the routine is stored in the program's .EXE file. This is **static linking**. For the program to be able to access a new version of the **memset** routine (if it were made smaller, faster, more bug-free, or whatever), the program file must be recreated. Thus, a statically linked routine doesn't allow automatic upgrades when library functions are improved. But dynamic linking does, since the functions in a dynamic link library are not copied to a program's executable file at program creation time, but are linked to the program at runtime.

Third, dynamic linking provides an efficient mechanism for sharing code and data between application programs. For example, a single copy of the code for the subroutines in Windows' graphic library, GDI.EXE, is shareable between all the different Windows programs that wish to use them. When your program runs alongside Aldus PageMaker, for example, both programs use the same copy of the **TextOut** routine. The net result is a much lower demand on system memory. An example of *data* sharing occurs whenever text appears on a display screen. GDI fonts are implemented in dynamic link libraries, which means that they are shared by whichever programs wish to use them. Even with many programs accessing a font, only a single copy of the font data is present in the system.

The most obvious examples of dynamic linking occur between Windows programs and the main Windows dynamic link libraries: KERNEL.EXE (or KRNL286.EXE for standard mode, KRNL386.EXE for 386-Enhanced Mode), USER.EXE, and GDI.EXE. When a Windows program is running, it relies on dynamic linking to make the proper connections to the various Windows library routines. Dynamic links are also created between the three main Windows dynamic link libraries and Windows' device drivers. For example, when GDI accesses a printer, it dynamically links to a printer driver. Dynamic linking makes it easy to upgrade or replace different parts of Windows—fonts, device drivers, or even the main libraries themselves.

## The Dynamic Linking Mechanism

Let's take a moment to look at the nuts and bolts of Windows' dynamic linking mechanism. Even though dynamic linking occurs without requiring you to know how it works, there are several reasons why it is helpful to understand the mechanism itself. First of all, you might not be convinced that you can build programs that are bigger than your address space on a microcomputer. Even if you're comfortable with this idea, you might be concerned that the mechanism isn't efficient or has unexpected side effects. You might want to know if you can build your own dynamic link libraries, and understanding the mechanism can help you decide when they are appropriate and when they are not. Or you might just be the kind of person who wants to know how things really work. Whatever your motivation, we think you'll find that—in all its operating modes—Windows' dynamic link mechanism is a fast, efficient, and very elegant approach to the problems of managing the dynamic loading and linking of code.

The architect of Windows' dynamic link mechanism is Steve Wood, who joined Microsoft in 1983. While a graduate student at Yale University, Steve had been involved with some systems programming projects on DEC-20 computers. One project involved the creation of a mechanism to share library code between different processes. This was accomplished by mapping the address space of different processes into the same physical address space. The net result was a reduction in required memory to support shared code.

This sounds a lot like dynamic linking. But the difference is that, when he started to work on building the dynamic link mechanism, Steve and the other members of the first KERNEL team were working on a machine with minimal capabilities. The target machine for the first version of Windows, after all, was to have an Intel 8088 CPU, two floppy disk drivers, and 256K of RAM. Dynamic linking could only require a minimum of overhead and had to be a software-only solution to a problem that had been solved elsewhere using dedicated hardware.

With a minimum amount of memory, the solution was to make much of the system reside in code segments that could be discarded. After all, if code resided on disk instead of in memory, there would be more room for applications to do their work. The trick was to figure out how to bring a code segment into memory. One of the things that was quickly apparent was that a whole new set of tools would have to be forged in order to get dynamic linking to work properly.

For example, a new linker had to be built to support the new .EXE file format that was required to support dynamic linking. A new program loader had to be built, to accommodate the fact that not all segments would necessarily be present when a program was running. And finally, a new compiler had to be built to generate code that would seamlessly connect programs and dynamic link libraries together in a working system. The first Windows development team discovered quite quickly that one of the challenges to working with new tools was determining when a bug was caused by the tools and when it was caused by your own code.

The program loader that was built into the first version of Windows served as the foundation on which all later loaders were built. To describe its operation, we need to look at how code segments are dynamically loaded and routines linked for discardable, moveable, and fixed code segments. We'll start with the hardest case: discardable code.

## Dynamic Linking and Discardable Code Segments

When you are building a dynamic link mechanism like the one Windows uses, the hardest aspect of dealing with discardable code segments is the fact that you never know when a code segment is present in memory or not. Without the hardware memory magic of protected mode, real mode Windows creates a tiny code stub for every far routine in programs and dynamic link libraries. These code stubs are called **loader thunks** or **call thunks** and reside in the module database. Although real mode is being discontinued in Windows version 3.1, understanding the real mode dynamic linking mechanism will help clarify the operation of the protected mode hardware.

Consider the case of a program that uses GDI's `Rectangle` routine, which for this example we'll suppose is in a discardable code segment. We'll call our program DRAWRECT. Before this program starts running, Windows will already have created a module database for GDI. Inside GDI's module database, there is one call thunk for every far routine in GDI, including `Rectangle`. Figure 19.1 depicts GDI's module database in memory. In real mode, a call thunk for routines in discardable segments has one of two states: an interrupt to the loader, as depicted in Figure 19.1, or a jump to the routine in memory, depicted in Figure 19.3.

644   *Operating System Considerations*

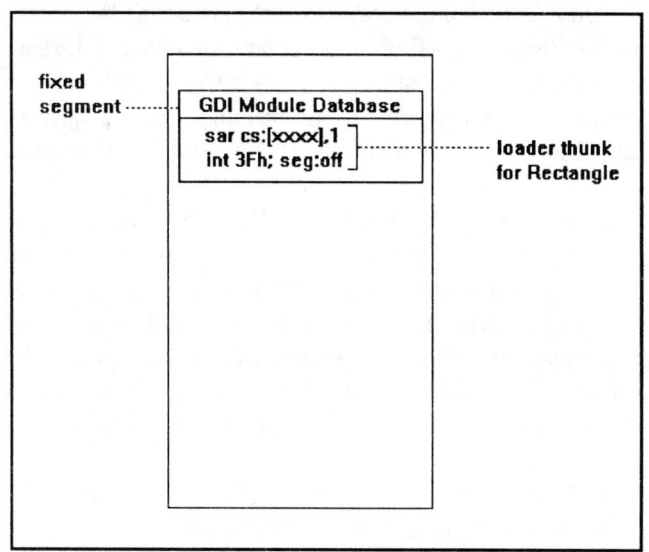

```
fixed
segment ······   GDI Module Database
                 sar cs:[xxxx],1    ······   loader thunk
                 int 3Fh; seg:off             for Rectangle
```

**Figure 19.1  Memory before the dynamic link**

When the first instance of DRAWRECT starts running, the Windows loader starts the load process by creating a DRAWRECT's module database. The module database is used to resolve calls *into* DRAWRECT, and so is not interesting to us in the context of linking DRAWRECT to GDI's **Rectangle** routine. However, DRAWRECT's module database *is* needed to locate DRAWRECT's entry point. After loading all of DRAWRECT's preload segments, control is passed to this entry point.

The dynamic link from DRAWRECT to GDI's **Rectangle** routine occurs when Windows loads a code segment that actually calls **Rectangle**. Appended to the end of such a code segment is a **relocation table**, which contains the fix-up information needed to create the first half of a dynamic link.

There are basically two types of relocation table entries: internal references and external references. The internal references define far calls to routines inside DRAWRECT. Part of dynamic linking, then, involves creating connections between a newly loaded code segment and other code segments in the same program or dynamic link library.

The external references define calls to dynamic link library routines, such as GDI's **Rectangle**. When DRAWRECT's code segment is loaded into memory, the far call to the **Rectangle** routine is fixed up to the address of the **Rectangle** routine's alias—that is, to the call thunk—in GDI's module database, as depicted in Figure 19.2.

When the Windows loader has finished creating all of the fix-ups described in the segment's relocation table, it frees the memory associated with the relocation table. When the relocation information is needed again, it will be reread from disk along with the code segment.

*Dynamic Linking* 645

```
fixed
segment ········┐   ┌──────────────────────┐
                │   │  GDI Module Database │
                └───┤  sar cs:[xxxx],1     │◄─────┐
fixed,              │  int 3Fh; seg:off    │      │
moveable, or        └──────────────────────┘      │
discardable         ┌──────────────────────┐      │
segment ········┐   │  Drawrect Code Segment│     │
                └───┤  call Rectangle      │──────┘
                    └──────────────────────┘
                                            ········ Relocation
                                                     Table
```

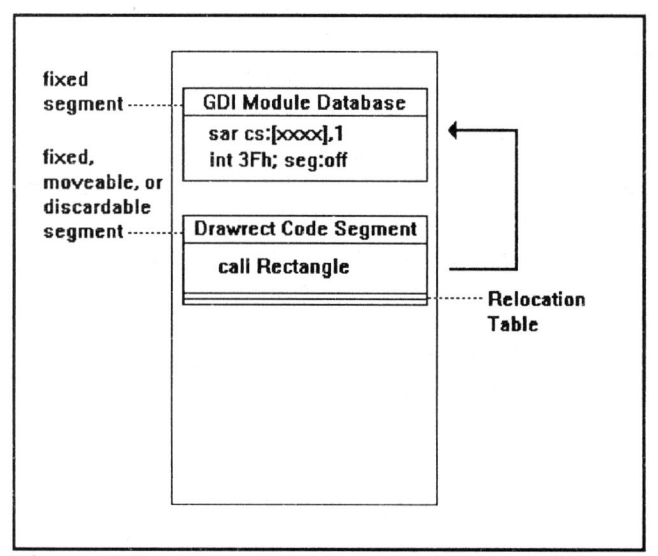

**Figure 19.2 DRAWRECT fix-up to GDI's module database**

When a code segment is loaded into memory, it is patched once for every far call in the segment, including far calls to internal as well as external routines. This means simply that the code in the newly loaded code segment has been modified so that every far call points to *something*. In the Windows programs that you write, you'll want to keep your code segments small and the number of far calls to a minimum because of the overhead incurred when a code segment is loaded into memory.

Getting back to our example program, an interesting aspect of the dynamic link is that, even though DRAWRECT's code segment has been fixed up to call into GDI's module database, the code segment that actually holds the `Rectangle` routine does not have to be present in memory. As you'll see in a moment, when the code segment is not present, code in `Rectangle`'s call thunk causes the code segment containing `Rectangle` to actually be loaded into memory.

The next step in the dynamic link process occurs when DRAWRECT actually calls Rectangle. Of course, it calls into the call thunk in the module database. As we mentioned earlier, the call thunk is a tiny code stub that will have one of two states, depending on whether `Rectangle` is open for business or out to lunch. Let's assume that it is out to lunch, to see how the call thunk responds. In such cases, the call thunk will have code that looks like the following:

```
; -->> "Out-To-Lunch"
SAR  CS:[00B4h],1    ; update access flag
INT  3Fh             ; Call to the Windows' loader
DB   seg             ; Code segment number
DW   off             ; Offset to Rectangle routine
```

When DRAWRECT calls into this piece of code, it triggers a software interrupt which calls the Windows loader, interrupt 3F. The Windows loader reads the next three bytes of information, which contain the segment number (from 1 to 255) and the offset into the code segment (0 to 65535). Since there is only a single byte for the segment number, the total number of segments that can exist in any .EXE or .DLL file is 255 (segment zero is reserved for return thunks, to be covered later). This limitation is intrinsic to the format of the .EXE file itself, and therefore you can't create an .EXE file with more than 255 segments. However, you can create a dynamic link library that allows a program to easily overcome this limitation.

Once the Windows loader has read the necessary code segment from disk, it modifies the module database so that the thunk associated with the **Rectangle** routine has machine instructions represented by the following assembly language:

```
; -->> "Open For Business"
  SAR   CS:[00B4h],1    ; Update access flag
  JMP   Rectangle
```

Not only are fix-ups performed for the **Rectangle** routine's call thunk, but also for the thunks of all *other* far routines that reside in **Rectangle**'s code segment. And if Rectangle makes far calls to other code segments, those calls are fixed up along with any other far calls *from* **Rectangle**'s code segment. That is, both inward bound and outward bound far calls are patched. Once the code segment has been loaded into memory and the module database fixed up, the dynamic link is complete. The **Rectangle** routine can retrieve its parameters off the stack and do its job. The complete dynamic link, from DRAWRECT through GDI's module database and into Rectangle, is depicted in Figure 19.3.

All calls to Rectangle are fixed up to call Rectangle's alias in the module database, which serves as a kind of switchboard operator for this routine. Notice that the Windows Memory Manager can move **Rectangle**'s segment at any time. When it does so, it does not have to patch every program's code segment that calls **Rectangle**. Instead, it simply patches **Rectangle**'s call thunk (and the call thunk of other far routines that might be in the same code segment). The code segment can also be discarded from memory at any time. When this occurs, the dynamic linker simply fixes up the call thunks with an INT 3F instruction to call the Windows loader to restore the code segment into memory. Of course, fix-ups are not free. But the dynamic link mechanism allows a code segment to be removed from memory, and reloaded later to give the greatest flexibility in how memory is used.

```
fixed
segment ········  GDI Module Database
                  sar cs:[xxxx],1
                  jmp Rectangle

                  Drawrect Code Segment
                  call Rectangle

                  GDI Code Segment
                  Rectangle( )
                  {
discardable       :
segment ········  }
```

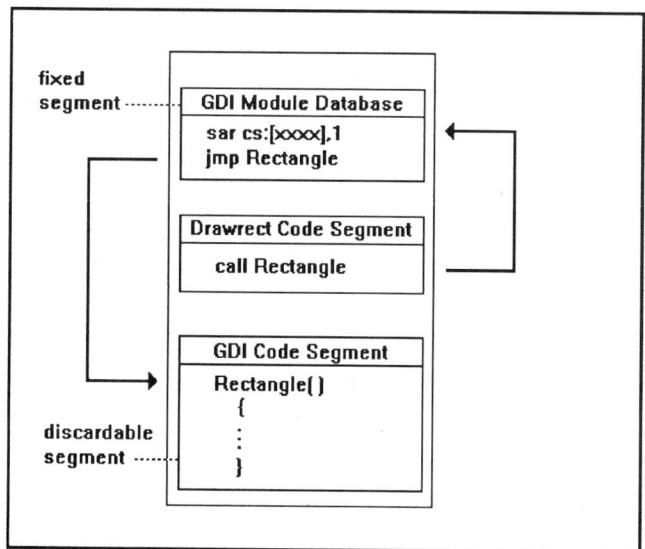

**Figure 19.3** Final fix-up from GDI's module database to Rectangle's code segment

## Dynamic Linking and Fixed Code Segments

Once you understand how a dynamic link to a discardable code segment is created, you'll see that dynamic links to fixed code segments are even simpler. Dynamic links to fixed code segments are not routed through a call thunk, but instead link a caller directly to the called routine. One reason for this is that fixed code segments are always treated as preload segments, so that they are always resident in memory and never move.

Consider a program that calls GDI's **TextOut** routine, which we'll assume for the moment is in a fixed code segment. For this example, we'll call our program DOTEXT, which calls **TextOut**. As before, when GDI is first brought into memory, the Windows loader creates GDI's module database. Once this is done, the loader reads all fixed code segments into memory. Figure 19.4 shows the state of two objects that are in memory after GDI has been loaded: the module database and the fixed code segment that contains **TextOut**.

## 648 Operating System Considerations

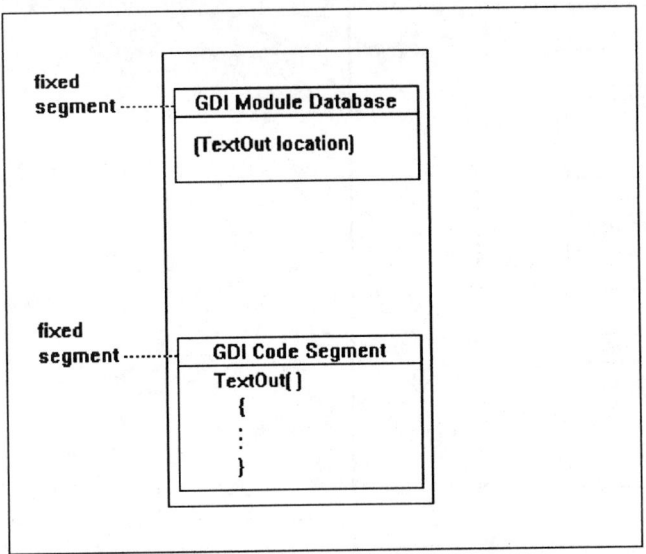

```
fixed
segment ······┤ GDI Module Database
              │ (TextOut location)



fixed
segment ······┤ GDI Code Segment
              │ TextOut( )
              │ {
              │   ⋮
              │ }
```

**Figure 19.4  GDI immediately loading**

Since the fixed code segment is loaded when GDI starts running, it will never need a loader thunk. However, to locate the routine itself, the module database lists the address of far routines. The loader will require this information when it loads DOTEXT into memory. At that time, a dynamic link is created that directly connects DOTEXT to **TextOut**, as depicted in Figure 19.5. Unlike the fix-up to a moveable or discardable segment, the fix-up to a *fixed* code segment always goes directly from the caller to the called routine.

In protected mode, the memory management hardware can move memory objects without changing the logical address. For this reason, all dynamic link fix-ups in protected mode are treated just like the dynamic link we just described. In other words, all fix-ups in protected mode are treated as if every code segment were fixed. Far calls are patched up by the Windows loader to directly connect a caller to the called routine. This is true for moveable segments as well as discardable segments.

Since protected mode doesn't have call thunks in the module database, you might wonder how discardable code segments get reloaded. In real mode, as you'll recall, the loader thunk in the module database triggers a code segment reload:

```
    SAR    CS:[00B4h],1    ; Update access flag
    INT    3Fh             ; Call to the Windows' loader
    DB     seg             ; Code segment number
    DW     off             ; Offset to Rectangle routine
```

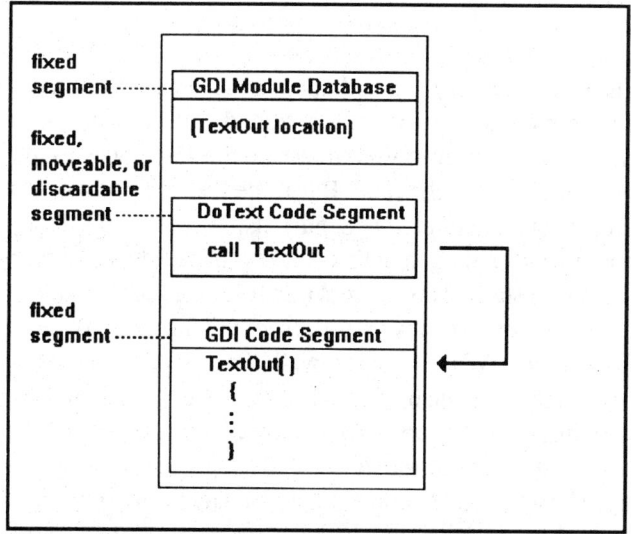

```
┌─────────────────────────────────────────┐
│ fixed                                   │
│ segment ------┤ GDI Module Database     │
│               │ (TextOut location)      │
│ fixed,        │                         │
│ moveable, or  │                         │
│ discardable   │                         │
│ segment ------┤ DoText Code Segment     │
│               │   call TextOut ──┐      │
│                                  │      │
│ fixed                            │      │
│ segment ------┤ GDI Code Segment │      │
│               │   TextOut( )  ◄──┘      │
│               │   {                     │
│               │     ⋮                   │
│               │   }                     │
└─────────────────────────────────────────┘
```

**Figure 19.5** Direct fix-up from DOTEXT to TextOut

In protected mode, when an absent code segment is called, a segment fault occurs. As you may recall from our discussion of protected mode operation in Chapter 17, every segment identifier contains an index into a protected mode descriptor table. Among the information that is kept in these tables is a flag that lets the system know whether a segment is actually present in memory or not. When it is not present, the segment fault—which is simply a software interrupt—notifies the Memory Manager that it must load the missing segment. Windows' Memory Manager loads the code segment into memory and then causes the instruction that triggered the segment fault to be restarted. In this way, the memory management hardware that operates in protected mode is able to operate in a manner that is transparent to application software.

## Other Real Mode Dynamic Linking Considerations

In protected mode, the dynamic link mechanism is greatly simplified by the hardware memory management provided by the various Intel processors. Segments can be moved around in physical memory without invalidating the logical address that programs use. Discarded code segments can be automatically reloaded when a *segment not present* interrupt occurs.

In real mode, Windows has to play a number of tricks to achieve the same flexibility that comes for free in protected mode. Two of these tricks are **stack patching** and the use of **return thunks**. To help you appreciate the work that real mode Windows does for you, we're going to describe each of these mechanisms in a little detail.

## Stack Patching

Stack patching involves walking the stack of a program and updating references that have been made to code segments that have moved. Earlier, we mentioned that the only thing that had to happen when a code segment was moved was to update the references to the routine in a module database. This is true most of the time. But if the address of a routine is referenced as a return address on the stack, that reference must also be fixed up.

Whenever a function is called—inside a dynamic link library or inside a regular program—a return address is placed on the stack. This address identifies the location of the machine instruction that is to be executed next when we return from the function. When a code segment referenced on the stack moves, Windows must walk the stack and patch the return address so that calls can correctly find their way back to the calling function. Windows patches the stack for every instance of every program running in the system.

Because Windows can patch stacks, it is free to move any code segment at any time. This gives the Windows Memory Manager the freedom to move any moveable code segment at any time. This allows real mode Windows to have the same flexibility of protected mode Windows—which is critical, given the greater memory constraints that are part of real mode operation.

## Return Thunks

In the same way that stack patching allows code segments to be *moved*, return thunks allow code segments to be *discarded*. In our discussion of dynamic linking, we mentioned that a code segment could be discarded at any time, as long as the module database was updated to call the Windows loader the next time a function in the segment was called. We mentioned that the reloading of discardable code segments is done by a tiny code stub called a call thunk.

When Windows discards a code segment that is referenced as a return address on the stack, the stack is also patched. The stack patching operation involves walking the stack of all programs, looking for a reference to the discarded code segment. Since the stack cannot be patched with the address of a discarded code segment, which has no address, it is instead patched to return to a tiny code stub called a **return thunk**. A return thunk is similar to a call thunk, except that after loading the necessary code segment, it provides a bridge for a return instruction instead of a call instruction. After the segment has been loaded, execution continues at the return address that was on the stack before the segment was discarded. Here is an example of a return thunk:

```
    INT     3Fh         ; Call to the Windows' loader.
    DB      0           ; Zero segment = return thunk.
    DW                  ; seg:IP packed into 20 bits.
    DB                  ; Handle to data segment packed
                        ; into 12 bits.
```

A return thunk looks a lot like a loader thunk, except that an invalid segment number is given: zero. This flags the `INT 3F` loader that this is a return thunk. In this case, it knows that the three bytes that follow contain all the data it needs to continue, although things are packed a little tightly. For one thing, the segment number and the code segment offset are crammed into 20 bits. This is possible since the code segment number will be a number between 0 and 255, which means it only takes one byte. That leaves 16 bits for the offset. A handle to the data segment is stored in the return thunk, since the data segment itself may have moved while memory was being jostled around. When the return thunk is run, the data segment is patched to reflect the new location of the data segment. All of this allows Windows to survive even a very low memory situation, since *any* code segment in the entire system (except the currently executing one) can be discarded if more memory is needed.

Up until now, our discussion of dynamic linking has focused on *code*. We have described the way that code can be loaded, moved, and discarded in all of Windows' operating modes. Windows takes advantage of the features of protected mode, when they are available, but also adapts to the constraints and limitation of real mode with no change in overall system capabilities. We're now going to look at the impact of dynamic linking on *data*. Windows allows every program and dynamic link library to create a default data segment, and it provides several mechanisms to make sure that every program and dynamic link library is always able to access its default data.

## Dynamic Linking and Module Data Segments

When you write a stand-alone application in most operating systems, you may use functions from various static link libraries. When you do, these blend invisibly into your program so that it is almost impossible to distinguish the machine instructions created by *your* code from the machine instructions associated with library routines. If a static library routine needs to store global variables to maintain state information, the linker blends the library's global variables with your program's global variables.

When working with dynamic link libraries, the distinction between your program and the library code is more evident. For example, dynamic link libraries have their own separate executable files. GDI.EXE, for example, is the dynamic link library file where GDI routines live. The file maintains an existence that is separate from the programs that use the library routines.

652  *Operating System Considerations*

Dynamic link libraries also have their own data segment that allows them to keep global variables separate from the data areas of the programs that use their routines. You can convince yourself of this by running a memory viewer utility. For example, the Microsoft SDK utility, HEAPWALK, lets you detect a dynamic link library's data segment. In Figure 19.6, HEAPWALK highlights the data segments of the USER and the WINOLDAP DLLs. (WINOLDAP provides support for DOS applications when they are running in Windows.)

```
                    HeapWalker- (Main Heap)
File  Walk  Sort  Object  Alloc  Add!
SELECTOR HANDLE   SIZE LCK FLG  OWNER-NAME     OBJ-TYPE  ADD-INFO
0007ABE0  04BE    1280     D    User           Code
0007B0E0  04B6    8768     D    User           Code
0007E5C0  0256      32     D    User           Resource  Group_Cursor
000826E0  05C6    2080     D    User           Code
00083E80  05EE    2944     D    User           Code
00085FC0  054E    2336     D    User           Code
0008BAA0  05FE   29952  1       User           Data
0009C500  05AE    9728     D    User           Code
8051D660  055E    9152     D    User           Code
00035EE0          512           Winoldap       Task DataBase
000360E0          992           Winoldap       Data
000365C0  094E      64  1       Winoldap       Code
00037740  09BE      32     D    Winoldap       Resource  NameTable
0005A300  09EE      32     D    Winoldap       Resource  String
0005D500  09F6      32     D    Winoldap       Resource  String
0005D620  09CE      64     D    Winoldap       Resource  Group_Icon
0005D660  09FE      32     D    Winoldap       Resource  String
0005D740  0A06      32     D    Winoldap       Resource  String
```

**Figure 19.6 HEAPWALK with data segments of USER and WINOLDAP highlighted**

A Windows library makes certain functions available to Windows programs. These functions serve as a doorway into the capabilities and features of the dynamic link libraries. Such functions are given a very special flag so that Windows can help the DLL access its proper data segment. The flag marks a function as **exported**. Windows modifies the first three bytes of every exported library function to set up the library's data segment, using code like this:

```
    MOV  AX, DGROUP     ; Get data segment address
    PUSH DS             ; Save caller's DS
    MOV  DS, AX         ; Install in DS register
```

When the library's data segment moves, Windows updates the value of DGROUP for all exported routines in the library. This causes the data segment register to be correctly set whenever a program calls into one of the exported "doorway" functions. Here is the complete set of assembly language instructions used to set up the data segment of an exported far routine in a dynamic link library:

```
    MOV  AX, DGROUP     ; Get data segment address
    INC  BP
    PUSH BP
    MOV  BP, SP
    PUSH DS             ; Save caller's DS
    MOV  DS, AX
```

Earlier, when we described some of the tricks that real mode Windows must play, we said that it must sometimes walk and patch the stack when a code segment has moved or been discarded. The **PUSH BP** and **MOV BP,SP** instructions are how the compiler ordinarily saves the old BP value and initializes it for the private use of the current function. This effectively creates a linked list of stack frames that make it easy for the stack walking to take place. The **INC BP** instruction is only used for far calls, and so helps the stack walker distinguish between near and far calls.

At certain times, a Windows library routine will call functions within a Windows program. Such routines are referred to as **call-back functions**. Up until this point in this book, we have discussed two types of call-back functions: window procedures and dialog box procedures. Other types include enumeration procedures and subclass procedures. Just like window procedures and the special "doorway" functions in a dynamic link library, special provision must be made to set up a call-back function's data segment register. One method involves exporting a function. This can be done by listing the exported functions in a program's module definition (.DEF) file. For example, here's how a window procedure might be exported in a C program:

```
EXPORTS
     MinWindowProc
```

Or, the **_exports** compiler directive can be used:

```
LONG FAR PASCAL _exports MinWindowProc
                    (HWND hwnd,   UINT wMsg,
                     WPARAM wParam, LPARAM lParam)
```

A third approach, which is available with the Turbo C++ compiler, is to use a **smart export**. This technique was discovered by Michael Geary, a long-time Windows programmer who was a developer of the Windows version of the Adobe Type Manager and Gupta Technology's SQL Windows. A smart export takes advantage of the fact that—at task context switch time—Windows makes sure the stack segment (SS) register contains the correct value. Since an application's stack is almost always in the application's default data segment, it's a simple matter to copy the value of the SS register into the DS register. Doing this for every far call means you never have to worry about exporting a function, nor having to use the **MakeProcInstance** routine (an issue we'll discuss later in this chapter). Here's the code associated with a smart export:

```
     MOV  AX, SS      ; Copy stack to AX
     INC  BP
     PUSH BP
     MOV  BP, SP
     PUSH DS          ; Save caller's DS
     MOV  DS, AX
```

Without a smart export, you must be sure to export a program's call-back functions. When you don't use a smart export, the compiler puts the following at the start of every far function:

```
PUSH DS         ; Put DS value into
POP  AX         ; the AX register.
NOP             ; Place holder
INC  BP         ; stack-walking preparation
PUSH BP         ; stack-walking preparation
MOV  BP, SP     ; set up regular stack frame
PUSH DS         ; save caller's DS
MOV  DS, AX     ; install our own DS
```

At first glance, it looks like this routine does a lot of work for nothing. But in fact this somewhat complicated piece of code makes sure that every far call saves a copy of the caller's data segment on the stack. Why? This allows Windows to patch the address of *data segments* that are moved at the same time that it patches code segment addresses. Anytime any code or segment address moves, Windows has no problem patching this up correctly.

When a code segment is loaded into memory, the prolog of exported functions is patched. Windows replaces the `PUSH DS`, `POP AX` with three `NOP` (no operation) instructions:

```
NOP
NOP
NOP
INC  BP         ; stack-walking preparation
PUSH BP         ; stack-walking preparation
MOV  BP, SP     ; set up regular stack frame
PUSH DS         ; save caller's DS
MOV  DS, AX     ; install our own DS
```

This allows an exported function to receive its data segment value in the `AX` register. But wait—how does the data segment value get into the `AX` register? That depends on the type of call-back function: Window procedures use one mechanism, and all other call-back functions use another.

A window procedure receives its data segment fix-up value as part of Windows' message delivery mechanism. When you call **CreateWindow** (or **CreateWindowEx**) to create a window, you pass an instance handle that identifies the data segment that is to be associated with the window. The message delivery mechanism uses this value to set up the proper `AX` value for window procedures.

All other call-back functions must use another mechanism that requires a little work on your part, but ensures that the `AX` register will be set up properly with the address of the data segment. The mechanism is called an **instance thunk**.

# The Instance Thunk

The dynamic link mechanism allows the code from different **modules**—executable programs and dynamic link libraries—to be linked together efficiently at runtime. Every module can have its own data segment, which allows programs and dynamic link libraries to store global variables that they need to do their work. The rule about data fix-ups is that *a data segment* (DS) fix-up is required every time a module boundary is crossed. We have already described how this is done for dynamic link libraries, and for window procedures in applications. The third type of data segment fix-up must be set up and managed by a Windows program.

Here is a list of the different call-back procedures that can be created in Windows. As you can see, call-backs play many different roles in Windows. A call-back provides a way for Windows to deliver information to a Windows program in a fairly efficient manner.

| *Call-Back Function* | *Description* |
| --- | --- |
| Dialog box procedure | Used to initialize and maintain a dialog box. |
| Enumeration procedure | When a program wants to query Windows about certain types of objects, an enumeration procedure is used. Windows calls the enumeration procedure once for each object. Objects that are enumerated include windows, fonts, GDI drawing objects, clipboard formats. |
| Hook | Allows a program to eavesdrop and change message traffic in the system. A keyboard hook, for example, lets a program respond to any "hot-key," even if the program isn't currently active. |
| Memory discarding notification procedure | `GlobalNotify` lets a program set up a call-back procedure that is called before the Windows Memory Manager discards a memory object. |
| Subclass procedure | Provides a means of eavesdropping in and modifying the message traffic for a particular window. |
| Timer | A timer procedure allows a program to specify an alternative method for receiving timer notifications other than by a **WM_TIMER** message. |

An instance thunk is only required if a call-back procedure resides in a Windows program. When these call-back procedures are implemented in a dynamic link library, an instance thunk is not needed. Nor is it required when you are using smart exports.

An instance thunk is a very small piece of code. Here is an example of one:

```
MOV  AX, DSvalue
JMP  DialogBoxProc
```

If the routine, `DialogBoxProc`, resided in a fixed code segment, this fix-up would jump directly to the code itself. Figure 19.7 shows the relationship of the different pieces to one another, and shows the flow of control through an instance thunk for all protected mode and for fixed code segments in real mode.

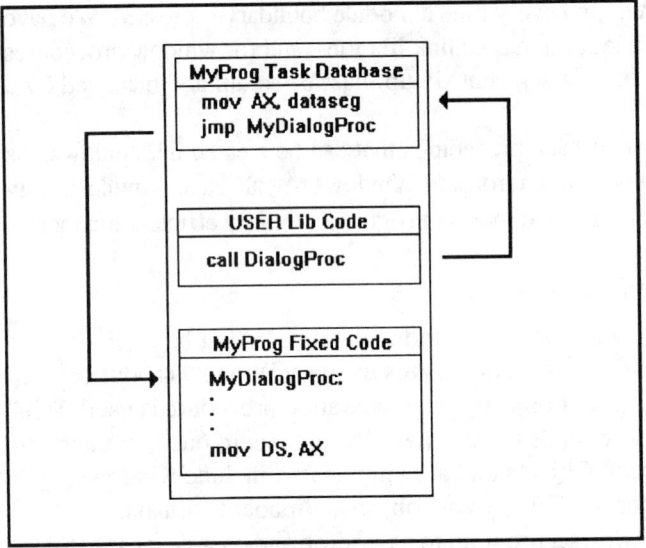

```
┌─────────────────────────────────────┐
│    ┌─────────────────────────┐      │
│    │   MyProg Task Database  │      │
│    │   mov AX, dataseg       │◄──┐  │
│    │   jmp MyDialogProc      │   │  │
│    └─────────────────────────┘   │  │
│                                  │  │
│    ┌─────────────────────────┐   │  │
│    │   USER Lib Code         │   │  │
│    │   call DialogProc       │───┘  │
│    └─────────────────────────┘      │
│                                     │
│    ┌─────────────────────────┐      │
│    │   MyProg Fixed Code     │      │
│    │   MyDialogProc:         │      │
│    │     .                   │      │
│    │     .                   │      │
│    │   mov DS, AX            │      │
│    └─────────────────────────┘      │
└─────────────────────────────────────┘
```

**Figure 19.7** An Instance Thunk and a fixed code segment

There is another case worth looking at briefly, since it helps to bring the complexity of real mode operation into perspective. Earlier, we mentioned that in real mode, calls into moveable and discardable code segments are always routed through a module database call thunk. When you add an instance thunk, you get an arrangement like that depicted in Figure 19.8. That is, the instance thunk is first called to put the data segment value into the AX register. Then, control passes to the call thunk to load an absent segment, or to jump to the segment when it's present.

Notice that the call gets routed through both the task database and the module database of the program. In the task database, the instance thunk puts the value of the program's data segment into the AX register. If the data segment moves, the Memory Manager walks through all the active thunks in the task database to ensure that these thunks stay current. From the task database, a jump is made into the module database. It arrives at the loader thunk that we described earlier. After all, this is the mechanism that allows a code segment to be discarded or moved in real mode. And finally, control arrives at our call-back procedure. Of course, as we saw in the earlier code fragments, one of the first instructions in the call-back procedure will establish the data segment address by copying the value in the AX register into the DS register.

*Dynamic Linking* 657

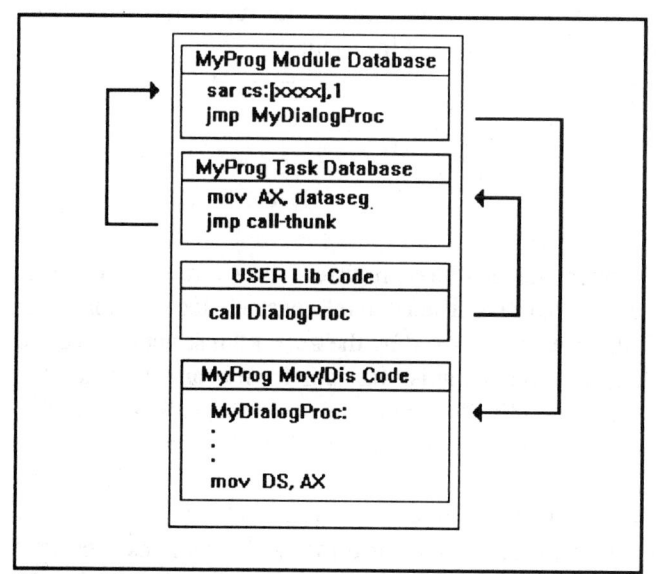

```
┌─────────────────────────────────┐
│   ┌─────────────────────────┐   │
│   │  MyProg Module Database │   │
│ ┌→│  sar cs:[xxxx],1         │   │
│ │ │  jmp MyDialogProc       │   │
│ │ └─────────────────────────┘   │
│ │ ┌─────────────────────────┐   │
│ │ │  MyProg Task Database   │   │
│ │ │  mov AX, dataseg        │←┐ │
│ │ │  jmp call-thunk         │ │ │
│ │ └─────────────────────────┘ │ │
│ │ ┌─────────────────────────┐ │ │
│ │ │       USER Lib Code     │ │ │
│ └─│  call DialogProc        │ │ │
│   └─────────────────────────┘ │ │
│   ┌─────────────────────────┐ │ │
│   │   MyProg Mov/Dis Code   │ │ │
│   │  MyDialogProc:          │←┘ │
│   │      :                  │   │
│   │      :                  │   │
│   │  mov DS, AX             │   │
│   └─────────────────────────┘   │
└─────────────────────────────────┘
```

**Figure 19.8** An Instance Thunk and a movable or discardable code segment

A program creates an instance thunk by calling the `MakeProcInstance` routine, which we have seen already in our discussion of dialog boxes in Chapter 14. This routine takes as one of its parameters a procedure address—which, in real mode operation, is the address of a module database call thunk for functions that reside in moveable or discardable segments. It returns an instance thunk, which can then be provided as the address of a far procedure for those Windows library routines which require the address of call-back procedures.

## Clean Up Before You Go Home

We have described three different sets of entries that can be made into far functions: exported library entries, unexported program entries, and exported program entries. The first reflects how the Windows loader sets up a dynamic link library's data segment. The second is simply what the C compiler creates to allow the other two entries to work properly. And the third is for call-back functions like window procedures and dialog box procedures.

Although there are three different entries for far functions, all far functions in Windows clean up the stack in the same way, with the following instructions:

```
MOV   SP, BP    ; restore caller's stack frame
POP   DS        ; restore caller's DS
POP   BP        ; clear off stack-walking link list
DEC   BP        ; flip even/odd far call bit
RETF  0002      ; far return
```

In other words, the caller's data segment value—the DS register—is restored. While it was on the stack, the Memory Manager may have modified it to reflect a new location for a data segment. The stack-walking link list value is removed by the POP BP instruction, and the BP register, which is used as a flag to help distinguish far calls from near calls when the stack is being walked, is decremented. And finally, a return instruction sends control back to the caller (or back to a return thunk, if in real mode the caller's code segment had to be discarded).

The dynamic link mechanism is a robust, flexible mechanism that helped the earliest versions of Windows run in real mode with acceptable performance. It continues to be used in the present version of Windows, in both its real and protected modes of operation. In addition, dynamic linking is a key architectural component of OS/2 and of the Windows NT operating system.

As you've seen, dynamic linking has both a code and a data aspect. The code aspect allows a program to be linked to library code at runtime instead of at link time. This has allowed programs written for previous version of Windows to run (almost) effortlessly in Windows 3, and will allow the programs that you write today to run unmodified in future versions of Windows. The data aspect of dynamic linking is almost as transparent as the code end. Before there were smart exports, Windows programmers had to export their callback procedures and fuss with **MakeProcInstance**. The availability of smart exports helps make the data side of dynamic linking effortless.

# Appendices

# Appendix A: A Taxonomy of Messages

## The Eight Types of Messages

| Type | Description |
| --- | --- |
| Hardware | Mouse and Keyboard Input. |
| Window Maintenance | Notification, Request for action, Query. |
| User-Interface Maintenance | Menu, mouse pointer, scroll bar, dialog boxes, MDI. |
| Termination | Application or system shutdown. |
| Private | Dialog box controls: edit, button, list box, combobox. |
| System Resource Notification | Color Changes, fonts, spooler, device modes. |
| Data Sharing | Clipboard and Dynamic Data Exchange (DDE). |
| Internal System | Undocumented Messages. |

## *Hardware Messages*

*Mouse Messages: In a window's client area*

| | |
| --- | --- |
| `WM_LBUTTONDBLCLK` | Left button double-click. |
| `WM_LBUTTONDOWN` | Left button down. |
| `WM_LBUTTONUP` | Left button up. |
| `WM_MBUTTONDBLCLK` | Middle button double-click. |

## Hardware Messages (continued)

### Mouse Messages: In a window's client area

| | |
|---|---|
| WM_MBUTTONDOWN | Middle button down. |
| WM_MBUTTONUP | Middle button up. |
| WM_MOUSEMOVE | Mouse move. |
| WM_RBUTTONDBLCLK | Right button double-click. |
| WM_RBUTTONDOWN | Right button down. |
| WM_RBUTTONUP | Right button up. |

### Mouse Messages: In a window's non-client area

| | |
|---|---|
| WM_NCLBUTTONDBLCLK | Left button double-click. |
| WM_NCLBUTTONDOWN | Left button down. |
| WM_NCLBUTTONUP | Left button up. |
| WM_NCMBUTTONDBLCLK | Middle button double-click. |
| WM_NCMBUTTONDOWN | Middle button down. |
| WM_NCMBUTTONUP | Middle button up. |
| WM_NCMOUSEMOVE | Mouse move. |
| WM_NCRBUTTONDBLCLK | Right button double-click. |
| WM_NCRBUTTONDOWN | Right button down. |
| WM_NCRBUTTONUP | Right button up. |

### Keyboard Messages

| | |
|---|---|
| WM_CHAR | Character input. |
| WM_DEADCHAR | Dead-character (umlaut, accent, etc.). |
| WM_KEYDOWN | Key has been depressed. |
| WM_KEYUP | Key has been released. |
| WM_SYSCHAR | System character input. |
| WM_SYSDEADCHAR | System dead-character. |
| WM_SYSKEYDOWN | System key has been depressed. |
| WM_SYSKEYUP | System key has been released. |

## Hardware Messages (continued)

*Timer Messages*

| | |
|---|---|
| `WM_TIMER` | Timer has gone off. |

---

## Windows Maintenance Messages

*Window Messages: Notification*

| | |
|---|---|
| `WM_ACTIVATE` | Window is active. |
| `WM_ACTIVATEAPP` | Application is active. |
| `WM_CREATE` | Window has been created. |
| `WM_DESTROY` | Window has been destroyed. |
| `WM_ENABLE` | Input to the window has been enabled. |
| `WM_KILLFOCUS` | Window has lost keyboard control. |
| `WM_MOUSEACTIVATE` | Notifies a window that it is going to become active because of a mouse click. |
| `WM_MOVE` | Window has been moved. |
| `WM_PARENTNOTIFY` | A child window has been created, destroyed, or has received a mouse button message. |
| `WM_SETFOCUS` | Window has gained keyboard control. |
| `WM_SIZE` | Window has changed size. |

---

*Window Messages: Request for Action*

| | |
|---|---|
| `WM_CLOSE` | Close (destroy) window. |
| `WM_ERASEBKGND` | Erase background. |
| `WM_ICONERASEBKGND` | Erase background of iconic window. |
| `WM_NCACTIVATE` | Change title bar to show active state. |
| `WM_NCCREATE` | Create non-client area data. |
| `WM_NCDESTROY` | Destroy non-client area data. |
| `WM_NCPAINT` | Redraw non-client area. |
| `WM_PAINT` | Redraw client area. |

## Window Maintenance Messages (continued)

### Window Messages: Request for Action

| | |
|---|---|
| `WM_PAINTICON` | Redraw iconic window client area. |
| `WM_SETREDRAW` | Inhibit redrawing of window. |
| `WM_SETTEXT` | Change window text. |
| `WM_SHOWWINDOW` | Change window visibility. |

### Window Messages: Query

| | |
|---|---|
| `WM_GETMINMAXINFO` | What is min/max sizes for window? |
| `WM_GETTEXT` | What is the window text? |
| `WM_GETTEXTLENGTH` | What is the length of the window text? |
| `WM_NCCALCSIZE` | How big should the client area be? |
| `WM_QUERYDRAGICON` | For windows that do not have a class cursor: Do you have a cursor to be used as your icon while you are being dragged around the screen? |
| `WM_QUERYNEWPALETTE` | Do you have a new palette? |
| `WM_QUERYOPEN` | Can iconic window be opened? |

## User Interface Messages

### Menu Messages

| | |
|---|---|
| `WM_COMMAND` | Menu item has been selected. |
| `WM_INITMENU` | Initialize menu bar menu. |
| `WM_INITMENUPOPUP` | Initialize popup menu. |
| `WM_MENUCHAR` | Mnemonic key used to select menu. |
| `WM_MENUSELECT` | User is browsing through menus. |

## User Interface Messages (continued)

### System Commands: System Menu, Min/Max Buttons, Titlebar, etc.

| | |
|---|---|
| WM_SYSCOMMAND | A system command has been selected. |

### Mouse Pointer Messages

| | |
|---|---|
| WM_NCHITTEST | Query: where is mouse on the window? |
| WM_SETCURSOR | Request: Change pointer to correct shape. |

### Scroll Bar Messages

| | |
|---|---|
| WM_HSCROLL | Horizontal scrollbar has been clicked. |
| WM_VSCROLL | Vertical scrollbar has been clicked. |

### Dialog Box and Dialog Box Control Messages

| | |
|---|---|
| WM_CHARTOITEM | Message sent from a list box to its parent window in response to a WM_CHAR message. Only list style send this message. Among other things, it allows a keyboard interface for owner-draw list boxes. |
| WM_COMMAND | Control communicating with Dialog Box. |
| WM_COMPAREITEM | Sent to the parent of an owner-draw dialog box control, asking to compare two items for the purpose of sorting. |
| WM_CTLCOLOR | Control asking for colors to be set. |
| WM_DELETEITEM | Notification to an owner-draw listbox or an owner-draw combobox that an item has been deleted. |
| WM_DRAWITEM | Request to the parent of an owner-draw control, or owner-draw menu, to draw. |
| WM_GETDLGCODE | Query control: want keyboard input? |
| WM_GETFONT | Query control: what font are you using? |
| WM_INITDIALOG | Initialize dialog. |

## Window Maintenance Messages (continued)

### Dialog Box and Dialog Box Control Messages

| | |
|---|---|
| WM_MEASUREITEM | Request to the parent of an owner-draw control or an owner-draw item to provide the dimensions of the item that is going to be drawn. |
| WM_NEXTDLGCTL | Message sent by a dialog box control to allow the proper handling of the Tab and Return keys for controls that process keyboard input themselves. |
| WM_SETFONT | Request to control: use this font. |
| WM_VKEYTOITEM | Message sent from a list box to its parent window in response to a WM_KEYDOWN message. This is only sent by list boxes which have the LBS_WANTKEYBOARDINPUT style set. |

### Multiple Document Interface Messages

| | |
|---|---|
| WM_CHILDACTIVATE | Notifies a parent window that a child is active. |
| WM_MDIACTIVATE | Notifies an MDI child window that it is either gaining or losing activation. |
| WM_MDICASCADE | Request to arrange the open MDI child windows in a cascading, stair-step fashion. |
| WM_MDICREATE | Requests an MDI client window to create an MDI child window. |
| WM_MDIDESTROY | Requests to an MDI client window to destroy an MDI child window. |
| WM_MDIGETACTIVE | Query an MDI client window for the currently active MDI child window. |
| WM_MDIICONARRANGE | Request to arrange the iconic MDI child windows in an orderly fashion. |
| WM_MDIMAXIMIZE | Request to maximize, or zoom, an MDI child window so that it occupies all of its parent's client area. |
| WM_MDINEXT | Request to activate the next MDI child window. |

## *Window Maintenance Messages (continued)*

### *Multiple Document Interface Messages*

| | |
|---|---|
| `WM_MDIRESTORE` | Request to restore an MDI child window to its previous state—iconic, normal, or zoomed. |
| `WM_MDISETMENU` | Adjusts the menu on an MDI frame window. |
| `WM_MDITILE` | Request to arrange the open MDI child windows in a tiled fashion in the MDI parent's client window. |

## *Termination Messages*

### *Application and System Termination*

| | |
|---|---|
| `WM_QUIT` | Request that a program should terminate. |
| `WM_QUERYENDSESSION` | A Query: Ready for system shutdown? |
| `WM_ENDSESSION` | Notification of results of shutdown query. |

## *Private Messages*

### *Button Control Messages*

| | |
|---|---|
| `BM_GETCHECK` | Query whether a button is checked or not. |
| `BM_GETSTATE` | Query state of a button. |
| `BM_SETCHECK` | Toggles a radio button or a check box. |
| `BM_SETSTATE` | Toggles the highlighting in a radio button or check box. |
| `BM_SETSTYLE` | Changes the style of an existing button. |

## Private Messages (continued)

*Combo Box Control Message*

| | |
|---|---|
| CB_ADDSTRING | Adds a string to the list box of a combo box. |
| CB_DELETESTRING | Removes a string from the list box of a combo box. |
| CB_DIR | Adds a list of files from the current directory to the list box of a combo box. |
| CB_FINDSTRING | Searches the list box in a combo box for a string. |
| CB_GETCOUNT | Queries the number of items in the list box of a combo box. |
| CB_GETCURSEL | Queries the index of the currently selected item in the list box of a combo box. |
| CB_GETEDITSEL | Queries the selected text in the edit control of a combo box. |
| CB_GETITEMDATA | Queries the item identifier from the list box of a combo box. |
| CB_GETLBTEXT | Queries a string from the list box of a combo box. |
| CB_GETLBTEXTLEN | Queries the length of a string in the list box of a combo box. |
| CB_INSERTSTRING | Inserts a string into the list box of a combo box. |
| CB_LIMITTEXT | Sets the maximum number of characters that may be entered into the edit control of a combo box. |
| CB_RESETCONTENT | Removes all items from the list box of a combo box. |
| CB_SELECTSTRING | Creates a selection in the list box of a combo box. |
| CB_SETCURSEL | Sets the current selection in the list box of a combo box, and places the text into the edit or static control. |
| CB_SETEDITSEL | Selects a range of characters in the edit control of a combo box. |
| CB_SETITEMDATA | Sets the identities for an item in a combo box. |

## *Private Messages (continued)*

### *Combo Box Control Message*

| | |
|---|---|
| CB_SHOWDROPDOWN | Shows or hides the drop down list box of a combo box. |
| CB_SETCURSEL | Sets the current selection in the list box of a combo box, and places the text into the edit or static control. |
| CB_SETEDITSEL | Selects a range of characters in the edit control of a combo box. |
| CB_SETITEMDATA | Sets the identities for an item in a combo box. |
| CB_SHOWDROPDOWN | Shows or hides the drop down list box of a combo box. |

### *Dialog Box Messages*

| | |
|---|---|
| DM_GETDEFID | Queries the ID of the default push button in a dialog box. |
| DM_SETDEFID | Sets the default push button in a dialog box. |

### *Edit Control*

| | |
|---|---|
| EM_CANUNDO | Queries the ability of an edit control to undo a previous edit. |
| EM_EMPTYUNDOBUFFER | Instructs an edit control to clear its undo buffer. |
| EM_FMTLINES | Instructs an edit control on how to handle end of line characters. |
| EM_GETHANDLE | Queries an edit control created with the DS_LOCALEDIT style for the handle of the object allocated from the local heap. |
| EM_GETLINE | Retrieves a line of text from an edit control. |
| EM_GETLINECOUNT | Queries the number of lines of text in an edit control. |
| EM_GETMODIFY | Queries an edit control to determine if the user has entered or changed any text. |

## Private Messages (continued)

### Edit Control

| | |
|---|---|
| EM_GETRECT | Queries an edit control for its display rectangle, which is either its client area or a subset as set by the EM_SETRECT message. |
| EM_GETSEL | Queries the characters that are included in the current selection. |
| EM_LIMITTEXT | Sets a limit to the number of characters that may be entered. |
| EM_LINEFROMCHAR | Finds the first line that contains a specific character. |
| EM_LINEINDEX | Queries the number of lines that have been scrolled in a multi-line edit control. |
| EM_LINELENGTH | Queries the length of a line in an edit control. |
| EM_LINESCROLL | Scrolls a multi-line edit control. |
| EM_REPLACESEL | Overwrites the current selection with new text. |
| EM_SETHANDLE | For edit controls with the DS_LOCALEDIT style, this message instructs the edit control to use a new local memory object for its data. |
| EM_SETMODIFY | Sets the modify flag for an edit control. |
| EM_SETPASSWORDCHAR | Sets the character to be displayed when a password is entered in an ES_PASSWORD style edit control. |
| EM_SETRECT | Sets the display rectangle for a multi-line edit control and causes an immediate repaint to occur. |
| EM_SETRECTNP | Sets the display rectangle for a multi-line edit control, and postpones painting until later. |
| EM_SETSEL | Defines a range of characters to display as selected. |
| EM_SETTABSTOPS | Sets the tab-stops in a multi-line edit control. |
| EM_SETWORDBREAK | Defines a call-back function to be used for word-break processing in a multi-line edit control. |
| EM_UNDO | Instructs an edit control to undo the last edit. |

*Appendix A: A Taxonomy of Messages* 671

# *Private Messages (continued)*

*List box Control*

| | |
|---|---|
| LB_ADDSTRING | Inserts a string into a list box. |
| LB_DELETESTRING | Removes a string for a list box. |
| LB_DIR | Adds a list of files from the current directory to a list box. |
| LB_FINDSTRING | Searches a list box for a string. |
| LB_GETCOUNT | Queries the number of items in a list box. |
| LB_GETCURSEL | Queries the index of the currently selected item in a list box. |
| LB_GETHORIZONTALEXTENT | Queries the width in pixels that can be scrolled for a list box with horizontal scroll bars. |
| LB_GETITEMDATA | Queries the item identifier from a list box. |
| LB_GETITEMRECT | Queries the dimensions of a rectangle that bounds a list box item. |
| LB_GETSEL | Queries the selection state of a specific list box item. |
| LB_GETSELCOUNT | Queries the total number of items that are selected in a list box. |
| LB_GETSELITEMS | Queries the indices of the selected items in a list box. |
| LB_GETTEXT | Query the text of a list box item. |
| LB_GETTEXTLEN | Queries the text length of a list box item. |
| LB_GETTOPINDEX | Queries the index of the item currently displayed at the top of a list box. |
| LB_INSERTSTRING | Adds a string to a list box. |
| LB_RESETCONTENT | Removes all items from a list box. |
| LB_SELECTSTRING | Selects an item in a list box. |
| LB_SELITEMRANGE | Selects a range of items in a multi-selection list box. |
| LB_SETCOLUMNWIDTH | Sets the column width of multi-column list box. |
| LB_SETCURSEL | Sets the current selection in a list box. |

## Private Messages (continued)

### List box Control

| | |
|---|---|
| LB_SETHORIZONTALEXTENT | Sets the horizontal scrolling range of a list box. |
| LB_SETITEMDATA | Replaces an owner-draw item in a list box. |
| LB_SETSEL | Highlights a string in a multiple selection list box. |
| LB_SETTABSTOPS | Sets the tab stop of a list box that was created with the LBS_USETABSTOPS style. |
| LB_SETTOPINDEX | Scrolls a list box to place a specific item at the top of the list box. |

### System Private Messages

| | |
|---|---|
| WM_CANCELMODE | Request by system to cancel a mode, such as a mouse capture. |
| WM_ENTERIDLE | Notification that the system is in an idling state, because the user is browsing a menu or a dialog box. |

## System Resource Notification Messages

### System Resources Notification Messages

| | |
|---|---|
| WM_COMPACTING | Notification that system memory is low, and that the Memory Manager is trying to free up some memory. |
| WM_DEVMODECHANGE | Printer setup has changed. |
| WM_FONTCHANGE | Installed fonts in the system have changed. |
| WM_PALETTECHANGED | Hardware color palette has changed. |
| WM_SPOOLERSTATUS | Job has been removed from spooler queue. |
| WM_SYSCOLORCHANGE | One or more system colors has changed. |
| WM_TIMECHANGE | System time has changed. |
| WM_WININICHANGE | Initialization file, WIN.INI, changed. |

# Data Sharing Messages

## Clipboard Messages

| | |
|---|---|
| `WM_ASKCBFORMATNAME` | Asks for the name of a Clipboard format. |
| `WM_CHANGECBCHAIN` | Notification of a change in the viewing chain. |
| `WM_DESTROYCLIPBOARD` | Clipboard contents are being destroyed. |
| `WM_DRAWCLIPBOARD` | Clipboard contents have changed. |
| `WM_HSCROLLCLIPBOARD` | Horizonal scrolling of owner-draw clipboard item. |
| `WM_PAINTCLIPBOARD` | Requests drawing of an owner-draw clipboard item. |
| `WM_RENDERALLFORMATS` | Request to provide the data for all clipboard formats that have been promised. |
| `WM_RENDERFORMAT` | Request to provide data for a single clipboard format that has been promised. |
| `WM_SIZECLIPBOARD` | Notification to the owner of owner-draw clipboard data that the size of the Clipboard viewer window has changed. |
| `WM_VSCROLLCLIPBOARD` | Vertical scrolling of an owner-draw clipboard item. |

## Dynamic Data Exchange (DDE) Messages

| | |
|---|---|
| `WM_DDE_ACK` | Acknowledgment. |
| `WM_DDE_ADVISE` | Request from a DDE client to establish a permanent data link. |
| `WM_DDE_DATA` | Send a data item from a DDE server to a DDE client. |
| `WM_DDE_EXECUTE` | Request a DDE server to execute a series of commands. |
| `WM_DDE_INITIATE` | Logon to a DDE server. |
| `WM_DDE_POKE` | Request by a client for a server to update a specific data item. |
| `WM_DDE_REQUEST` | One-time request by a DDE client for a piece of information. |

## System Resource Notification Messages

### Dynamic Data Exchange (DDE) Messages

WM_DDE_TERMINATE          Logoff from a DDE server.

WM_DDE_UNADVISE           Terminate a permanent data link that was initiated with the WM_DDE_ADVISE message.

# Appendix B: The Default Window Procedure

For your convenience, here is a listing of the default window procedure that Microsoft provided in the Windows software development kit. To see the latest revision of this code, please refer to the sample source diskettes which Microsoft provides as part of the SDK. And here is a list of the messages to which DefWindowProc responds:

| | |
|---|---|
| WM_NCACTIVATE | WM_ERASEBKGND |
| WM_NCHITTEST | WM_QUERYOPEN |
| WM_NCCALCSIZE | WM_QUERYENDSESSION |
| WM_NCLBUTTONDOWN | WM_SYSCOMMAND |
| WM_NCMOUSEMOVE | WM_SYSKEYDOWN |
| WM_NCLBUTTONUP | WM_KEYUP |
| WM_NCLBUTTONDBLCLK | WM_SYSKEYUP |
| WM_CANCELMODE | WM_SYSCHAR |
| WM_NCCREATE | WM_CHARTOITEM |
| WM_NCDESTROY | WM_VKEYTOITEM |
| WM_NCPAINT | WM_ACTIVATE |
| WM_SETTEXT | WM_SETREDRAW |
| WM_GETTEXT | WM_SHOWWINDOW |
| WM_GETTEXTLENGTH | WM_CTLCOLOR |
| WM_CLOSE | WM_SETCURSOR |
| WM_PAINT | WM_MOUSEACTIVATE |
| WM_PAINTICON | WM_DRAWITEM |
| WM_ICONERASEBKGNE | |

```
/*--------------------------------------------------------*/
/*                                                        */
/*  DefWindowProc() -                                     */
/*                                                        */
/*--------------------------------------------------------*/

LONG FAR PASCAL DefWindowProc(hwnd, message, wParam, lParam)

register HWND hwnd;
         WORD message;
register WORD wParam;
         LONG lParam;

{
  int           i;
  HDC           hdc;
  PAINTSTRUCT   ps;
  HICON         hIcon;
  RECT          rc;
  HANDLE        hCurs;
  HBRUSH        hbr;
  HWND          hwndT;

  if (!CheckHwnd(hwnd))
      return((DWORD)FALSE);

  switch (message)
    {
      case WM_NCACTIVATE:
        if (wParam != 0)
          SetWF(hwnd, WFFRAMEON);
        else
          ClrWF(hwnd, WFFRAMEON);

        if (TestWF(hwnd, WFVISIBLE) && !TestWF(hwnd, WFNONCPAINT))
          {
            hdc = GetWindowDC(hwnd);
            DrawCaption(hwnd, hdc, TRUE, TestWF(hwnd, WFFRAMEON));
            InternalReleaseDC(hdc);
            if (TestWF(hwnd,WFMINIMIZED))
              RedrawIconTitle(hwnd);
          }
        return(TRUE);

      case WM_NCHITTEST:
        return(FindNCHit(hwnd, lParam));

      case WM_NCCALCSIZE:
        CalcClientRect(hwnd, (LPRECT)lParam);
        break;

      case WM_NCLBUTTONDOWN:
        {
          WORD      cmd;
          RECT      rcWindow;
          RECT      rcCapt;
          RECT      rcInvert;
          RECT      rcWindowSave;

          cmd = 0;

          switch(wParam)
```

```
            {
          case HTZOOM:
          case HTREDUCE:
            GetWindowRect(hwnd, (LPRECT)&rcWindow);
            CopyRect((LPRECT)&rcWindowSave, (LPRECT)&rcWindow);

            if (TestWF(hwnd, WFSIZEBOX))
              InflateRect((LPRECT)&rcWindow,
                          -cxSzBorderPlus1, -cySzBorderPlus1);
            else
              InflateRect((LPRECT)&rcWindow,
                          -cxBorder, -cyBorder);

            rcCapt.right = rcWindow.right + cxBorder;
            rcCapt.left = rcWindow.right - oemInfo.bmReduce.cx-
                          cxBorder;

            if (wParam == HTREDUCE)
              cmd = SC_MINIMIZE;
            else if (TestWF(hwnd, WFMAXIMIZED))
              cmd = SC_RESTORE;
            else
              cmd = SC_MAXIMIZE;

            if (wParam == HTREDUCE && TestWF(hwnd, WFMAXBOX))
              OffsetRect((LPRECT)&rcCapt,
                         -oemInfo.bmReduce.cx, 0);

            rcCapt.top = rcWindow.top;
            rcCapt.bottom = rcCapt.top + cyCaption;

            CopyRect((LPRECT)&rcInvert, (LPRECT)&rcCapt);
            InflateRect((LPRECT)&rcInvert,
                        -cxBorder, -cyBorder);

            rcInvert.right += cxBorder;
            rcInvert.left += cxBorder;

            /* Converting to window coordinates. */
            OffsetRect((LPRECT)&rcInvert,
                       -(rcWindowSave.left + cxBorder),
                       -(rcWindowSave.top + cyBorder));
            /* Wait for the BUTTONUP message and see if cursor
             *  is still in the Minimize or Maximize box.
             *
             * NOTE: rcInvert is in window coords, rcCapt is
             * in screen coords
             */
            if (!DepressTitleButton(hwnd, rcCapt,
                                    rcInvert, wParam))
              cmd = 0;

            break;

          default:
            if (wParam >>= HTSIZEFIRST && wParam <<= HTSIZELAST)
              /* Change HT into a MV command. */
              cmd = SC_SIZE +
                    (wParam - HTSIZEFIRST + MVSIZEFIRST);
        }
        if (cmd != 0)
          {
```

```
            /* For SysCommands on system menu,
             * don't do if menu item is disabled.
             */
            if (TestWF(hwnd, WFSYSMENU))
              {
              /* don't check old app child windows
               */
              if (LOWORD(GetExpWinVer(hwnd->>hInstance)) >>= VER
                  || !TestwndChild(hwnd))
                {
                SetSysMenu(hwnd);
                if (GetMenuState(GetSysMenuHandle(hwnd),
                                 cmd & 0xFFF0,
                                 MF_BYCOMMAND)
                    & (MF_DISABLED | MF_GRAYED))
                  break;
                }
              }
            SendMessage(hwnd, WM_SYSCOMMAND, cmd, lParam);
            break;
          }
      /*** FALL THRU ***/
      }

    case WM_NCMOUSEMOVE:
    case WM_NCLBUTTONUP:
    case WM_NCLBUTTONDBLCLK:
      HandleNCMouseGuys(hwnd, message, wParam, lParam);
      break;

    case WM_CANCELMODE:
      if (hwndCapture == hwnd && pfnSB != NULL)
        EndScroll(hwnd, TRUE);

       if (fMenu && hwndMenu == hwnd)
         EndMenu();

      /* If the capture is still set, just release at
       * this point.  Can put other End functions in later.
       */
      if (hwnd == hwndCapture)
        ReleaseCapture();
      break;

    case WM_NCCREATE:
      if (TestWF(hwnd, (WFHSCROLL | WFVSCROLL)))
        if (InitPwSB(hwnd) == NULL)
          return((LONG)FALSE);

      return((LONG)DefSetText(hwnd,
                  ((LPCREATESTRUCT)lParam)->>lpszName));

    case WM_NCDESTROY:
      if (hwnd->>hName)
          hwnd->>hName = TextFree(hwnd->>hName);
      break;

    case WM_NCPAINT:
      /* Force the drawing of the menu. */
      SetWF(hwnd, WFMENUDRAW);
      DrawWindowFrame(hwnd, (HRGN)wParam);
      ClrWF(hwnd, WFMENUDRAW);
      break;
```

## Appendix B: The Default Window Procedure

```
    case WM_SETTEXT:
      DefSetText(hwnd, (LPSTR)lParam);
      if (TestWF(hwnd, WFVISIBLE))
         {
           if (TestWF(hwnd,WFMINIMIZED))
              {
                ShowIconTitle(hwnd,FALSE);
                ShowIconTitle(hwnd,TRUE);
              }
           else if (TestWF(hwnd, WFBORDERMASK) ==
                     (BYTE)LOBYTE(WFCAPTION))
              {
                hdc = GetWindowDC(hwnd);
                DrawCaption(hwnd,
                            hdc,
                            FALSE,
                            TestWF(hwnd, WFFRAMEON));
                InternalReleaseDC(hdc);
              }
         }
      break;

    case WM_GETTEXT:
      if (wParam)
         {
           if (hwnd->>hName)
             return (DWORD)TextCopy(hwnd->>hName,
                                    (LPSTR)lParam,
                                    wParam);

           /* else Null terminate the text buffer since
            * there is no text.
            */
           ((LPSTR)lParam)[0] = NULL;
         }
      return (0L);


    case WM_GETTEXTLENGTH:
      if (hwnd->>hName)
          return(lstrlen(TextPointer(hwnd->>hName)));

        /* else */
        return(0L);

    case WM_CLOSE:
      DestroyWindow(hwnd);
      break;

    case WM_PAINT:
      BeginPaint(hwnd, (LPPAINTSTRUCT)&ps);
      EndPaint(hwnd, (LPPAINTSTRUCT)&ps);
      break;

    case WM_PAINTICON:
      /* Draw the icon through the window DC if app used
       * own DC. If own DC is used the mapping mode may
       * not be MM_TEXT.
       */
      BeginPaint(hwnd, (LPPAINTSTRUCT)&ps);
      if (TestCF(hwnd, CFOWNDC) || TestCF(hwnd, CFCLASSDC))
         {
```

```c
            /* If owndc, do the end paint now so that the
             * erasebackgrounds/validate regions go through
             * properly. Then we get a clean window dc to
             * draw the icon into.
             */
            InternalEndPaint(hwnd, (LPPAINTSTRUCT)&ps, TRUE);
            hdc = GetWindowDC(hwnd);
        }
    else
        {
          hdc = ps.hdc;
        }

    /* wParam is TRUE to draw icon, FALSE to ignore paint. */
    if (wParam)
        {
           hIcon = (HICON)(PCLS)(hwnd->>pcls)->>hIcon;
           GetClientRect(hwnd, (LPRECT)&rc);

           rc.left = (rc.right - rgwSysMet[SM_CXICON]) >>>> 1;
           rc.top = (rc.bottom - rgwSysMet[SM_CYICON]) >>>> 1;

           DrawIcon(hdc, rc.left, rc.top, hIcon);
        }

    /* Delete the update region. */
      if (TestCF(hwnd, CFOWNDC) || TestCF(hwnd, CFCLASSDC))
        {
           InternalReleaseDC(hdc);
           /* ValidateRect(hwnd, NULL); */
        }
      else
           InternalEndPaint(hwnd, (LPPAINTSTRUCT)&ps, TRUE);
    break;

case WM_ICONERASEBKGND:
    /* Erase the icon through the window DC if app used
     * own DC. If own DC is used the mapping mode may not
     * be MM_TEXT.
     */
    if (TestCF(hwnd, CFOWNDC) || TestCF(hwnd, CFCLASSDC))
        hdc = GetWindowDC(hwnd);
    else
        hdc = (HDC)wParam;

    if (TestWF(hwnd, WFCHILD))      /* for MDI child icons */
       {
          if ((hbr = GetBackBrush(hwnd->>hwndParent)) == NULL)
             {
                /* No brush, punt. */
                goto AbortIconEraseBkGnd;
             }
          else
             goto ICantBelieveIUsedAGoToStatement;
       }

    if (hbmWallpaper)
       {
          /* Since desktop bitmaps are done on a wm_paint
           * message (and not erasebkgnd), we need to call
           * the paint proc with our dc.
           */
          PaintDesktop(hdc);
```

```
                    /* SendMessage(hwndDesktop,WM_ERASEBKGND,hdc,0L);*/
                }
            else
                {
                    hbr = sysClrObjects.hbrDesktop;
ICantBelieveIUsedAGoToStatement:
                    FillWindow(hwnd->>hwndParent,hwnd,hdc,hbr);
                }
AbortIconEraseBkGnd:
            if (TestCF(hwnd, CFOWNDC) || TestCF(hwnd, CFCLASSDC))
                InternalReleaseDC(hdc);

            return((LONG)TRUE);

        case WM_ERASEBKGND:
            if ((hbr = GetBackBrush(hwnd)) != NULL)
                {
                    FillWindow(hwnd, hwnd, (HDC)wParam, hbr);
                    return((LONG)TRUE);
                }
            break;

        case WM_QUERYOPEN:
        case WM_QUERYENDSESSION:
            return((LONG)TRUE);

        case WM_SYSCOMMAND:
            SysCommand(hwnd, wParam, lParam);
            break;

        case WM_KEYDOWN:
            if (wParam == VK_F10)
                fF10Status = TRUE;
            break;

        case WM_SYSKEYDOWN:
            /* Is the ALT key down? */
            if (HIWORD(lParam) & SYS_ALTERNATE)
                {
                    /* Toggle the fMenuStatus iff this is NOT a
                     * repeat KEYDOWN message;  Only if the prev key
                     * state was 0, then this is the first KEYDOWN
                     * message and then we consider toggling menu
                     * status.
                     */
                    if((HIWORD(lParam) & SYS_PREVKEYSTATE) == 0)
                        {
                            /* Don't have to lock hwndActive because it's
                             * processing this key.
                             */
                            if ((wParam == VK_MENU) && (!fMenuStatus))
                                fMenuStatus = TRUE;
                            else
                                fMenuStatus = FALSE;
                        }

                    fF10Status = FALSE;

                    DWP_ProcessVirtKey(wParam);
                }
            else
                {
```

```
            if (wParam == VK_F10)
              fF10Status = TRUE;
            else
              {
                if (wParam == VK_ESCAPE)
                  {
                    if(GetKeyState(VK_SHIFT) << 0)
                      SendMessage(hwnd,
                                  WM_SYSCOMMAND,
                                  SC_KEYMENU,
                                  (DWORD)MENUSYSMENU);
                  }
              }
       }
    break;

  case WM_KEYUP:
  case WM_SYSKEYUP:
    /* Press and release F10 or ALT.
     * Send this only to top-level windows, otherwise MDI
     * gets confused.  The fix in which DefMDIChildProc()
     * passed up the message was insufficient in case
     * a child window of the MDI child had the focus.
     */
    if ((wParam == VK_MENU && (fMenuStatus == TRUE)) ||
        (wParam == VK_F10 && fF10Status) )
      SendMessage(GetTopLevelWindow(hwnd),
                  WM_SYSCOMMAND,
                  SC_KEYMENU,
                  (DWORD)0);

    fF10Status = fMenuStatus = FALSE;
    break;

  case WM_SYSCHAR:
    /* If syskey is down and we have a char... */
    fMenuStatus = FALSE;
    if ((HIWORD(lParam) & SYS_ALTERNATE) && wParam)
       {
         if (wParam == VK_TAB || wParam == VK_ESCAPE)
           break;

         /* Send ALT-SPACE only to top-level windows. */
         if ((wParam == MENUSYSMENU) && (TestwndChild(hwnd)))
            SendMessage(hwnd->>hwndParent,
                        message,
                        wParam,
                        lParam);
         else
            SendMessage(hwnd,
                        WM_SYSCOMMAND,
                        SC_KEYMENU,
                        (DWORD)wParam);
       }
    else
      /* Ctrl-Esc produces a WM_SYSCHAR,
       * But should not beep;
       */
      if (wParam != VK_ESCAPE)
        MessageBeep(0);
    break;

  case WM_CHARTOITEM:
```

```
case WM_VKEYTOITEM:
  /* Do default processing for keystrokes into
   * owner draw listboxes.
   */
  return(-1);


case WM_ACTIVATE:
  if (wParam)
    SetFocus(hwnd);
  break;

case WM_SETREDRAW:
  DWP_SetRedraw(hwnd, wParam);
  break;

case WM_SHOWWINDOW:
  /* Non null descriptor implies popup hide or show. */
  /* We should check whether it is a popup window
   * or Owned window
   */
  if (LOWORD(lParam) != 0 &&
      (TestwndPopup(hwnd) || hwnd ->> hwndOwner))
    {
      /* IF NOT(showing, invisible, and not set as hidden)
       * AND NOT(hiding and not visible)
       */
      if (!(wParam != 0 && !TestWF(hwnd, WFVISIBLE) &&
           !TestWF(hwnd, WFHIDDENPOPUP)) &&
          !(wParam == 0 && !TestWF(hwnd, WFVISIBLE)))
        {
          /* Are we showing? */
          if (wParam)
            /* Yes, clear the hidden popup flag. */
            ClrWF(hwnd, WFHIDDENPOPUP);
          else
            /* No, Set the hidden popup flag. */
            SetWF(hwnd, WFHIDDENPOPUP);

          ShowWindow(hwnd,
              (wParam ? SHOW_OPENNOACTIVATE : HIDE_WINDOW));
        }
    }
  break;

case WM_CTLCOLOR:
  if (HIWORD(lParam) != CTLCOLOR_SCROLLBAR)
    {
      SetBkColor((HDC)wParam, sysColors.clrWindow);
      SetTextColor((HDC)wParam, sysColors.clrWindowText);
      hbr = sysClrObjects.hbrWindow;
    }
  else
    {
      SetBkColor((HDC)wParam, 0x00ffffff);
      SetTextColor((HDC)wParam, (LONG)0x00000000);
      hbr = sysClrObjects.hbrScrollbar;
      UnrealizeObject(hbr);
    }

  return((DWORD)hbr);

case WM_SETCURSOR:
```

```c
/* wParam   == hwnd that cursor is over
 * lParamL == Hit test area code (result of WM_NCHITTEST)
 * lParamH == Mouse message number
 */
if (HIWORD(lParam) != 0 &&
    LOWORD(lParam) >>= HTSIZEFIRST &&
    LOWORD(lParam) <<= HTSIZELAST)
  {
    SetCursor(rghCursor[LOWORD(lParam)
              - HTSIZEFIRST + MVSIZEFIRST]);
    break;
  }

if ((hwndT = GetChildParent(hwnd)) != NULL &&
    (BOOL)SendMessage(hwndT,
                      WM_SETCURSOR,
                      wParam,
                      lParam))
  return((LONG)TRUE);

if (HIWORD(lParam) == 0)
  {
    hCurs = hCursNormal;
    SetCursor(hCurs);
  }
else
  {
    switch (LOWORD(lParam))
      {
        case HTCLIENT:
          if (((HWND)wParam)->pcls->>hCursor != NULL)
            SetCursor(((HWND)wParam)->pcls->>hCursor);
          break;

        case HTERROR:
          switch (HIWORD(lParam))
            {
              case WM_LBUTTONDOWN:
                if ((hwndT = DWP_GetEnabledPopup(hwnd)) != NULL)
                  {
                    if (hwndT != hwndDesktop->>hwndChild)
                      {
                        SetWindowPos(hwnd, NULL,
                                     0, 0, 0, 0,
                                     SWP_NOMOVE |
                                     SWP_NOSIZE |
                                     SWP_NOACTIVATE);
                        SetActiveWindow(hwndT);
                        break;
                      }
                  }

                /*** FALL THRU ***/

              case WM_RBUTTONDOWN:
              case WM_MBUTTONDOWN:
                MessageBeep(0);
                break;
            }
            /*** FALL THRU ***/

        default:
          SetCursor(hCursNormal);
```

```
                    }
                }
            return((LONG)FALSE);

        case WM_MOUSEACTIVATE:
            if ((hwndT = GetChildParent(hwnd)) != NULL &&
                (i = (int)SendMessage(hwndT,
                                      WM_MOUSEACTIVATE,
                                      wParam,
                                      lParam)) != 0)
                return((LONG)i);

            /* Moving, sizing or minimizing?
             * Activate AFTER we take action.
             */
            if (LOWORD(lParam) == HTCAPTION)
              return((LONG)MA_NOACTIVATE);
            else
              return((LONG)MA_ACTIVATE);

        case WM_DRAWITEM:
            if (((LPDRAWITEMSTRUCT)lParam)->>CtlType == ODT_LISTBOX)
              LBDefaultListboxDrawItem((LPDRAWITEMSTRUCT)lParam);
            break;

        }

    return(0L);
}
```

# Appendix C: Glossary

**__AHINCR**
This is a global symbol that can be used by an application program to increment the segment selector to address memory objects that occupy more than a single segment.

**32-Bit Addressing**
This refers to the capability in the Intel 80386 and later CPUs to use 32-bit offset to address memory. This allows the creation of memory segments that are as large as one megabyte. When running in 386-Enhanced Mode, Windows uses this type of addressing internally, but does not make it directly available to application programs. However, Microsoft does provide support for 32-bit addressing in a dynamic link library that is included with the Windows software development kit called WINMEM32.

**Accelerator**
see Keyboard Accelerator.

**Active Window**
The Active window is a top-level window belonging to the active application. The active application is the application given the highest priority by the user. When a user clicks the mouse on any window owned by an application, selects one of the application's top-level windows from Windows' Task List, or selects the application using keystroke combinations, then the application becomes active. The caption and border of the active application change color to indicate their state to the user. In addition, the windows of the active application are positioned on top of the windows belonging to other applications.

**ANSI**
American National Standards Institute.

**ANSI Character Set**
A standard that defines how character glyphs, or images, are stored as numeric character codes. According to the ANSI standard, the values 0 to 31 (1Fh) are reserved for control codes, the values 32 (20h) to 127 (7Fh) are for a standard set of printed characters, and the values 128 (80h) to 255 (FFh) define a range in which vendors can define their own character sequences. The IBM family of personal computers define a set of code pages that use upper range for line-drawing character, Greek letters, and accented characters. Windows defines a more complete set of accented characters that

allows Windows programs to more easily be written for support in non-English-speaking countries.

## ASCII

American Standard Code for Information Interchange.

## Application Message Queue

When a Windows application is running, Windows allocates a buffer that is used to store the messages that are posted (using the **PostMessage** routine) to a program. The messages wait in the queue until a program makes a call to **GetMessage** or to **PeekMessage**. By default, a message queue can hold up to 8 messages. Programs that need a larger message queue can request this by calling **SetMessageQueue**.

## Aspect Ratio

The aspect ratio describes the ratio between the height of a pixel and its width. Another way to think about it is in terms of the relative "squareness" of pixels on a device. CGA displays have an aspect ratio of 2 to 1; EGA displays have a ratio of 1.33 to 1; VGA displays have an aspect ratio of 1 to 1.

## Background Color

The background color is a DC attribute that is used for drawing text, styled (non-solid) lines, and hatched brushes. It is controlled by the setting of the background mode, another DC attribute.

## Background Mode

The background mode is a toggle switch controlling whether the background color is used or not. When set to OPAQUE, the background color is turned on. Setting the background mode to TRANSPARENT turns off the background color.

## BitBlt

An acronym for "BIT-boundary BLock Transfer." This GDI function copies rectangular patterns of bits from one location to another. The most obvious use of BitBlt is for moving windows on the display screen. But BitBlts are also used to make menus appear and disappear quickly. Application programs commonly use the BitBlt function to move images stored in bitmaps to an output device like the display screen or a printer. A program can also copy an image from a display screen to a bitmap.

## Bitmap

Bitmaps are one of two pseudo-devices that GDI uses to store pictures (the other type is a metafile). Bitmaps use RAM to store rectangular picture images. Bitmaps are created by requesting GDI to allocate the RAM for the picture storage. Once allocated, a bitmap provides an invisible drawing surface on which a program can draw by calling any of the GDI drawing routines. Bitmaps are also a type of resource that allow a program to store a graphic image inside its executable file. The third type of bitmaps are device-independent bitmaps (DIBs), which provide a device-independent way to store color information.

## Brush

A brush is a GDI drawing object used to fill areas. There are three types of brushes: solid, pattern, and hatched. Every DC contains a brush that is used for area filling when on of the filled figure routines is called (**Rectangle**, **Ellipse**, **Polygon**, etc.).

Another function which makes use of the brush is the **BitBlt** routine, which can use the brush in the destination DC to alter the effect of the bit-blt operation.

### Call-back Functions

A call-back function provides a way for Windows to communicate with a program by calling it directly into a program subroutine.

### Call thunk

A call thunk is a tiny piece of code that is used by Windows in real mode as a bridge to far functions in a moveable or discardable code segment.

### Capture

see Mouse Capture.

### Caret

A caret is a user interface object that serves as a keyboard pointer, in much the same way that the cursor serves as a mouse pointer. A caret is a blinking bitmap that notifies the user of the window that has the keyboard focus, and also provides feedback on the location of the current position in a window.

### Casting

Refers to the ability of the C compiler to convert one data type into another data type. In the following example, a variable of type int, i, is set equal to the value of a long variable, lValue:

```
long lValue;
  int i;

  lValue = 1245;
  i = (int)lValue
```

Casting overrides the default conversion that the compiler provides, and avoids the warning messages that compilers often generate in such situations. Nevertheless, Windows programmers can omit certains types of casting which were required for older versions of the C compiler. For example, in response to the WM_PAINT message, here is an outdated but still commonly encountered construction:

```
PAINTSTRUCT ps;

  BeginPaint (hwnd,(LPPAINTSTRUCT)&ps);
  .
  .
  EndPaint (hwnd,(LPPAINTSTRUCT)&ps);
```

While it is harmless enough in this example, explicit casting is not required and can hide certain types of problems. For example, if the programmer had omitted the "&" in the previous example, the compiler would not be able to see the error because of the casting:

```
PAINTSTRUCT ps;
  BeginPaint (hwnd,(LPPAINTSTRUCT)ps);
```

### CDECL Calling Convention

The CDECL calling convention describes the way that parameters are passed on the stack to a subroutine (right to left), and also assigned the calling routine with the responsibility for clearing parameters from the stack. The CDECL calling convention allows routines to be defined with a variable number of parameters, with the disadvantage of creating slightly larger and slower code than the alternative PASCAL calling convention.

### Class

see Window Class.

### Class Database

Refers to the collection of window classes that have been registered in the system with **RegisterClass**.

### Client Area Coordinates

describe a coordinate system that has its origin (0,0) at the upper-left corner of a window. Client area coordinate units are equal to pixels.

### Clipping Region

A clipping region defines a closed area used for clipping. Inside the clipping region, drawing is allowed. Outside the clipping region, drawing is not allowed. Clipping regions in Windows are always described in terms of rectangles or groups of rectangles.

### Clipping

Clipping describes the behavior of GDI drawing routines in the way they recognize arbitrary borders that are defined. Clipping is defined in terms of closed areas: Inside the clipping region, drawing is allowed. Outside the clipping region, no drawing is allowed.

### Clipboard

The Clipboard provides user-operated data sharing services between programs. Items on the Edit menu ordinarily serve as the primary user interface for the Clipboard, and provide Cut, Copy, and Paste options. In addition, a standard set of accelerator keys has been defined for Clipboard commands.

### Code Page

A code page defines a character set. The code page determines the set of glyphs, or character images, that will be used to draw a particular character. For example, code page 437 is the standard character set for the United States version of the IBM-PC.

### Common User Access (CUA)

Refers to the element of IBM's Systems Application Architecture (SAA) that covers the standards that have been developed for the user interfaces part of application and system software.

### Compiler Memory Model

Refers to the set of defaults that the compiler sets for addressing both code and data.

### Coordinate Transformation

A coordinate transformation refers to the way that drawing coordinates are interpreted in a graphics output environment. The three basic types of coordinate transformation include translation, scaling, and rotation. In Windows, GDI's coordinate transformations are limited to translation and scaling.

### Cursor

A cursor is a bitmap that moves in response to the movement of a mouse.

### Debug Version of Windows

Describes Windows when running with special copies of the KERNEL.EXE (KRNL286.EXE, KRNL386.EXE), USER.EXE and GDI.EXE dynamic link libraries.

### Default Window Procedure

A Windows library routine that processes non-client area messages, system commands, system keystrokes, and other messages that window procedures do not process.

## Desktop Window

Refers to the window that covers the entire display screen and sits behind every other window in the system.

## Device Capability Bits

Refers to a set of flags that are provided by a GDI display or printer driver to describe the native capabilities of the device. GDI uses these flags to determine whether to send a high-level drawing request directly to a device driver, or to simulate the request in software and send the device driver a series of low-level drawing requests.

## Device Context (DC)

A data structure created and maintained by GDI in support of device independent drawing operations on displays, printers, metafiles, and bitmaps. A device context is three things rolled into one: It is a toolbox containing a set of drawing attributes or drawing tools, it is a connection to a specific device, and it is a permission slip that allows a program to draw on a device.

Device Independent Bitmap (DIB)

A device-independent bitmap provides a standard format for storing color bitmap information. DIBs come in four formats: one-bit per pixel (monochrome), four bits per pixel (16 color), eight bits per pixel (256 color) and 24 bits per pixel (16 million colors).

## Dialog Box

A dialog box is a window, inside of which are other windows that are commonly referred to as dialog box controls. A dialog box is typically used to gather additional information from the user required to complete a command.

## Dialog Box Control

A dialog box control is a window that rests inside a dialog box and provides a specific set of services. Among the window classes that have been defined for dialog box controls are button, combo box, edit, listbox, scroll bar, and static.

## Dialog Box Coordinates

Dialog box coordinates provide a device-independent way to specify the layout of a dialog box. Dialog box units are relative to the system font, or to whatever font has been defined for the dialog box.

## Dialog Box Editor

The dialog box editor is a graphic layout tool for designing the look of a dialog box and the style of each dialog box controls. Microsoft provides the dialog box editor as part of its Software Development Kit (SDK).

## Disabled Window

A disabled window is one that is prevented from receiving mouse and keyboard input. For example, the parent window of a modal dialog box is disabled.

## Discardable Memory

A discardable memory object is one that, when unlocked, can be purged from memory by the memory manager when available system memory is otherwise unavailable. Windows uses a least recently used algorithm to determine the segment to discard next.

## Drawing Attribute

A drawing attribute is a setting or a drawing object inside a device context that can change the appearance of the output produced by different GDI drawing routines. Some examples of drawing attributes include pens, brushes, fonts, mapping mode, and text color.

**Dynamic Data Exchange (DDE)**

A data exchange mechanism that is built on top of Windows' message passing mechanism. A DDE interaction is called a conversation. There are always two participants in a DDE conversation, one called the client and the other called the server. There are several types of DDE converations: ongoing data exchange, one-time data exchange, command execution, and poke of data back into the server's database.

**Dynamic Link Library**

A dynamic link library is a file containing code or data that can be shared by different application programs at run-time. For example, the core components that make up Windows itself are a collection of dynamic link libraries and include KERNEL.EXE, USER.EXE and GDI.EXE, as well as a set of device drivers. Fonts are an example of dynamic link libraries that contain no code, but only data to be shared between programs.

**Dynamic Linking**

Dynamic linking refers to the process by which different code and data of different modules—application programs and dynamic link libraries—are connected at run time.

**Event-driven**

Event-driven software is structured to process external events that do not necessarily occur in a sequential manner. Traditionally, interrupt-handling code in an operating system or in a device driver has been the primary domain of event driven software. But the development of personal computers and interactive software has made this a concern of application programmers. Graphical User Interfaces (GUIs) provide a programming environment which assists in the creation of event driven application software.

**Expanded Memory Specification (EMS)**

The expanded memory specification refers to a protocol that was first introduced in 1984 by Lotus, Intel, and Microsoft to ease the memory crunch that was caused by the 640K memory limitation of real-mode operation. Windows 1.x used EMS memory to cache DOS applications that were dormant; Windows 2.x provided enhanced EMS support to Windows applications that increased the address space of each application in a manner that was transparent to the application programmer. Windows 3.x continues EMS support, although Windows itself only uses EMS in real mode. In the other modes of operation, a Windows program can access EMS memory, but Windows itself does not use EMS because of the greater flexibility that is available with extended memory.

**Extended Memory**

Extended memory refers to the memory that is not ordinarily accessible from real mode, but requires protect-mode operation. Extended memory allows the address space of a machine to go beyond the one-megabyte boundary of real mode and to access up to 16 megabytes with an 80286 processor and up to 4 gigabytes with an 80386 processor.

## Extended Memory Specification (XMS)

The extended memory specification defines an interface for using the memory areas above the 640K line. This includes the upper memory blocks (UMBs) between 640 and 1024K, the high-memory area (HMA) from 1024 to 1088K, and the extended memory blocks (EMBs) above the 1088K line.

## File Manager

One of the desktop accessories that Microsoft has bundled with Windows 3.0.

## Fixed Memory

A fixed memory object is one whose logical address does not change. However, in protect mode, the physical address of a fixed memory block can change unless the memory has been fixed, which is done by calling **GlobalFix**. In addtion, in 386 Enhanced Mode, a fixed memory object can also be paged to disk unless it has been page-locked, which is accomplished by calling **GlobalPageLock**.

## Focus

see Keyboard Focus.

## Font

also see Logical Font.

## Function Prototype

Function prototypes provide a means by which the C Compiler can perform some automatic error checking, including check for proper use of the return value and the correct number and type of parameters. Here is an example of a function prototype taken from Window.h:

```
BOOL FAR PASCAL TextOut (HDC, int, int,
LPSTR, int);
```

## Global Descriptor Table (GDT)

A global descriptor table is one of two data areas used by the Intel 80286 and higher CPUs in protect mode. A global descriptor table allows the CPU to convert segment identifier values (also known as segment selectors) into the physical addresses of segments. Intel designed the GDT to provide a shared data area accessible from all processes. However, Windows does not use a GDT for any of its memory management, but uses the other data area, the local descriptor table (LDT) instead.

## Global Heap

The global heap refers to the total memory available to Windows itself, to Windows applications, and to other components like device drivers.

## Global Memory Object

A global memory object is an object allocated from the global heap. In Intel memory architecture terms, a global memory object is a segment.

## Granularity

In the context of memory allocation, granularity refers to the increments by which memory is actually allocated. The global heap manager uses a granularity of 32 bytes. The local heap manager uses a granularity of 4 bytes.

## Graphic Device Interface (GDI)

GDI is Windows' device-independent graphics output library.

## Graphical User Interface (GUI)

Refers to a type of operating system or operating environment that displays output on a bitmapped graphical display screen. Another characteristic of GUI systems is that they are event-driven, which means a different programming model is necessary besides the traditional, sequence oriented programming model that was originally developed for batch oriented systems. Microsoft Windows is an example of a GUI system. Other examples include the Apple Macintosh, the OS/2 Presentation Manager, which was jointly developed by IBM and Microsoft, and Digital Research Corporation's GEM. The various X-Windows systems deserve to be in this last as well, and they include the Open System Foundation's Motif, and Sun Microsystem's Open Look and Digital Equipment Corporation's DEC-Windows.

### GUI
An acronym for Graphical User Interface.

### Handle
A handle is a 16-bit, unsigned integer that identifies an object. In most cases, the meaning of a handle is only known to the subroutine library that issued the handle. A program can modify an object by providing the handle to the subroutine library, which then acts on the objects on behalf of the program.

### Hardware Event Queue
A buffer maintained by Windows to hold keyboard and mouse events that are waiting to be retrieved by application programs.

### High Memory Area (HMA)
The high memory area refers to the 64 K-bytes located immediately above the one-megabyte address line on 80286 and 80386 processors. Intel designed this space as the first 64K of extended memory, which was not meant to be part of the real mode address space. However, an XMS (eXtended Memory Specification) driver, like HIMEM.SYS, is able to trick the 80286 and higher chips into allowing access into this data area.

### Hit-Test Code
Refers to a code returned by the default window procedure in reponse to the WM_NCHITTEST message, which identifies the area of a window where the mouse is located. Hit-test codes are used to help the window manager to install the correct mouse cursor.

### Hook
A hook is a subroutine that is called by Windows' message handling mechanism to allow the monitoring and modification of message traffic in the system. Hooks are installed on a system-wide basis, and therefore care should be taken when using them to avoid disrupting the normal operation of other programs, and to avoid slowing the system down.

### Hungarian naming
Hungarian naming is a convention for creating variable and function names that provide a quick way to compose short but useful identifiers.

### Huge Memory Object
A huge memory object is a memory object in the global heap that is larger than 64K. Windows allocates huge memory objects by allocating two or more segments. To access the second and subsequent segments, huge pointer arithmetic is required. This involves updating the segment portion of the address as well as the offset portion. The segment portion is modified by changing the segment value using the __AHINCR update value. This value is added to the segment address to

access the next segment in a huge object segment chain.

### Icon

An icon is a graphic symbol that serves to remind the user of the presence of a program, file, or data object that is presently closed, but available for future access.

### Import Library

An import library provides the linker with information about the exported entry points of a dynamic link library. An import library allows the linker to create a relocation record in a program's .EXE file so that Windows' dynamic link mechanism can provide the required fix-up to the calling code at program execution time.

### Instance

An instance of a program refers to a copy of a program in memory. Windows allows several copies of a single program to run simultaneously. Each instance has its own, private data segment, but shares code and resource segments with every other instance of the program.

### Instance Thunk

An instance thunk is a tiny piece of code that is created in a program's task database (TDB) to assist in the fix-up of the data segment for an exported call-back function. An instance thunk is created by **MakeProcInstance**, and freed by **FreeProcInstance**. With the exception of window procedures, every call-back procedure requires an instance thunk. This includes dialog box procedure, enumeration procedures, notification procedures, and certain subclass procedures. No instance thunk is required for any of these procedures when they reside in the code segment of a dynamic link library.

### Interrupt Descriptor Table

An interrupt descriptor table (IDT) is a lookup table used by the higher end Intel-86 chips (80286 and above) in protect mode to hold an array of interrupts.

### Keyboard Accelerator

A keyboard accelerator provides a means to define key-strokes that are interpreted as commands. Keyboard accelerators mimic menu selection messages, to minimize special processing that would otherwise be required to support a program's command keys.

### Keyboard Focus

The keyboard focus tells Windows the window that should receive keyboard input. When a program receives the keyboard focus, it is notified with a WM_SETFOCUS message. When it loses the focus, it is notified with a WM_KILLFOCUS message.

### Keyboard Scan Code

A keyboard scan code is a numeric value sent from the keyboard hardware as a notification that a key was pressed, released, or is being held down. Application programs do not ordinarily handle scan codes, since they represent a hardware dependent key code. In Windows, scan codes undergo two translation before they appear in a program as ASCII characters. The first translation is from scan code to virtual key codes. The second translation is from virtual key codes to ASCII characters.

## KERNEL

The KERNEL is one of the three core components of Windows, and is responsible for memory management, dynamic linking, resources, atom tables, module managment, interface to DOS, and other operating system services that are available to Windows programs.

## Load On Call segment

A load on call segment is a code or resource segment that is loaded into memory when it is referenced.

## Local Descriptor Table (LDT)

A local descriptor table is one of two data areas used by the Intel 80286 and higher CPUs in protect mode. A local descriptor table allows the CPU to convert segment identifier values (also known as segment selectors) into the physical addresses of segments. Intel designed the LDT to provide a process with a private address space. In Windows 3.0, a single LDT is used by all application programs. However, a future version of Windows will provide one LDT per application program.

## Local Heap

Refers to the heap that is created in a module's default data segment. The automatic startup code automatically initializes the local heap of an application program by calling the **LocalInit** routine. Dynamic link libraries that wish to use a local heap must explicitly call **Local- Init** themselves.

## Logical Drawing Object

A logical drawing object is a GDI description of a pen, brush, font, or color. It provides a device-independent way to describe the drawing attributes that are installed in a DC.

## Logical Font

A logical font is a description of a font that GDI's font mapper uses to select a font for drawing text. A logical font description can be created using the LOGFONT data structure.

## Logical Pen

A logical pen describes the color, width, and style of lines requested by a program.

## Mapping Mode

A mapping mode is a DC drawing attribute that describes how drawing coordinates that are given to GDI drawing routines are interpreted. For example, the default mapping mode, MM_TEXT, interprets coordinates as pixels. The other mapping modes can be used to scale coordinates into fractions of an inch, fractions of a centimeter, or scale to arbitrary ratios.

## Marker

A marker is a graphic primitive that is guaranteed to be centered on the specified location. Although GDI itself does not directly implement markers, it is a simple matter to build a set of marker subroutines that draw using GDI drawing routines. See Chapter 7.

## Message

A message is a 16-bit, unsigned value that notifies a window procedure that an event of interest has occurred. Windows' predefined messages are identified in Windows.H with symbolic constants whose names start with a WM_ prefix. For example, the WM_CREATE message is sent to a window procedure to notify it that a window of that class has been created.

## Metafile

A metafile is a pseudo-device that GDI can create for the purpose of storing graphic images. A GDI metafile is a data structure containing a list of calls to be made to GDI routines to reconstruct a picture, along with the parameters to provide those calls.

## Module

A module is a specific type of entity in Windows, which reflects the way that code and data is organized on disk. Windows recognizes two types of modules: executable application (.EXE) program files, and dynamic link libraries, which can have an extension of .EXE, .DRV, .DLL, or .FON, to name just a few.

## Module Database

A module database is a memory resident image of the file header of an application program or a dynamic link library. The Windows loader uses the module database to load code and resources from disk when they are needed.

## Module Definition File

An ASCII text file that contains program definition and memory use information. A module definition file normally has an extension of .DEF. At program creation time, the module definition file is given to the linker as part of the bulding of a .EXE or .DLL file.

## Mouse Capture

Ordinarily, mouse messages are sent to the window lying under the mouse cursor. However, a program can restrict the flow of mouse messages to a single window by setting the mouse capture. This is done by calling **SetCapture**. To free mouse messages, a program calls **ReleaseCapture**.

## Moveable Memory

Moveable memory objects are an artifact of real mode Windows. In real mode, a moveable object will only move when it is not locked by a program. In protect mode, segments can move at any time, since the physical address is hidden from application software. The protect mode memory management hardware converts logical addresses—which is how application software references memory—into physical addresses by means of a descriptor table. The Windows memory manager can move objects in physical memory without changing their logical addresses, which means that in protect mode, memory movement is transparent to application softare.

## Multiple Document Interface

or MDI, describes a user-interface standard that opens a new window for each new file or document that is opened in a program.

## Nonpreemptive Scheduling

Describes the way that a multitasking system schedules programs to run. In a nonpreemptively scheduled system, the operating system does not interrupt programs

## OEM Character Set

Refers to the set of characters native to a machine. For IBM-compatible computers built for sale in United States, this means code page 437.

### Page Locking

Page locking refers to a process by which memory in 386-Enhanced Mode is prevented from being swapped to disk. This is accomplished by calling the **GlobalPageLock** routine and is primarily intended for the use of time-critical device drivers that must stay memory resident.

### Paragraph

When the Intel-86 processors operate in real mode, a paragraph is the smallest memory unit that can be allocated. A paragraph is 16 bytes. Windows' memory manager allocates segments in two-paragraph increments, which means the granularity of the global memory manager is 32 bytes.

### Paintbrush

One of the desktop accessories that is included with Windows 3.0.

### Palette (PAL)

A palette provides two services: It describes the colors that are stored in a device-independent bitmap (DIB), and it allows a program to request changes to the physical palette of display devices that support palettes.

### PASCAL Calling Convention

The PASCAL calling convention describes the way that parameters are passed on the stack to a subroutine (left to right), and also assigns the called routine with the responsibility for cleaning the parameters from the stack. Routines that are defined as PASCAL must have a fixed number of parameters, but this results in slightly smaller and faster code than the alternative CDECL calling convention.

### Pen

A pen is a DC attribute that describes the color, style, and width of lines. See Logical Pen.

### Preemptive Scheduling

Describes the way that a multitasking system schedules programs to run. In a preemptively scheduled system, the operating system will interrupt one program to allow another one to run.

### Preload Segments

A code or resource segment that is marked as preload is moved into memory before a program starts running.

### Private Window Class

A private window class is reserved for the use of a single program. In contrast are global window classes, which are available for use by any program in the system.

### Process Database (PDB)

A data structure created by Windows to maintain DOS related per-process data. Windows adds its own elements to this data structure.

### Profiler

see Swap Kernel.

### Program Manager

Refers to the main program window in Windows 3.0.

### Program Segment Prefix (PSP)

see Process Database.

### Protect Mode

Protect mode refers to an operating mode of Intel 80286 chips and later. Protect mode is characterized by an addressing scheme that prevents programs from illegal access to unowned memory areas. On the 80286, protect mode operation allows a physical address space of 16 megabytes. On the 80386 and 80486, protect mode allows access to a 4 gigabyte address space.

## Pull-Model Processing

Refers to a style of interaction between the operating system and application software. Pull-model processing places the application software in the active role, in which it polls the system for available input. This is the traditional way that interactive application software has been written, and is how Windows' handles mouse and keyboard input. Also, messages that are transmitted to a window procedure using the PostMessage routine are delivered in a pull-model manner, that is, via the GetMessage or PeekMessage routines. See also push-model processing.

## Push-Model Processing

Refers to a style of interaction between the operating system and application software. Push-model processing places the operating system software in the active role, in which it calls subroutines in the application software to perform the necessary tasks. Most of the non-hardware related messages in Windows are delivered in a push-model manner. For example, when a program calls the CreateWindow routine to create a window, a WM_CREATE message is pushed into the window procedure of the newly created window. Messages that are transmitted to a window procedure using the **SendMessage** routine are delivered in a push-model manner, which bypasses the pull-model **Get-**

**Message** routine, and calls a window procedure directly.

## Raster Operation

A raster operation is a logical operation or combination of logical operations that describe how two or more inputs combine to produce a given output. One type of raster operation is the ROP2 codes, which are a DC attribute that describe how pixels, lines, and areas combine with a drawing surface. Another type of raster operation, sometimes known as ROP3 codes, are provided as parameters to the BitBlt and PatBlt functions, to describe how a source bitmap, a destination bitmap, and a brush are to combine.

## Return Thunks

A return thunk is a tiny piece of code that real mode Windows uses to bridge a function return when the code segment containing the calling routine is discarded from memory.

## Resource

A resource is a read-only data object that is bound into an executable file at program creation time. From a memory management point of view, resources can be discarded and reread when needed. From the point of view of the Windows user interface, resources define dialog boxes, menus, cursors, icons, bitmaps, to name just a few.

## Real Mode

Real Mode refers to an operating mode of the Intel-86 family of processors. Real mode is characterized by a one-megabyte address space. Programs have access to the real, physical address of memory, which is how the mode gets its name.

## Scan Code
see Keyboard Scan Code.

## Scanner
A graphic scanner reads a graphic image on paper and converts it into a digital form suitable for creating GDI bitmaps.

## Segment Selector
When the Intel-86 family of processors are running in protect mode, a segment identifier is referred to as a segment selector. Part of a segment selector is an index into a table of descriptors in either an LDT (local descriptor table) or a GDT (global descriptor table), from which is read the physical location of a memory segment.

## Segmented Addressing
The Intel-86 family of CPUs address memory using a segmented addressing scheme. Segmented addressing requires two pieces in a memory address: a segment identifier and an offset.

## Software Development Kit (SDK)
The Windows Software Development Kit is a product that Microsoft provides for the purpose of assisting software developers to create Windows programs.

## Software Migration Kit (SMK)
The Software Migration Kit is a product that Microsoft provides to assist software developers in porting Windows programs to run in OS/2, version 1.2 and later.

## Stack Patching
Stack patching refers to the process by which the real mode Windows Kernel updates stack references to code segments that have moved or been discarded.

## Standard Mode
Refers to an operating mode of Windows in which protect mode addressing is enabled to allow Windows to take advantage of features of the Intel family of processors that are available on the 80286 and higher CPUs.

## Swap Kernel
The swap kernel is a special version of the Windows kernel that runs in real mode only and provides information about the segment loading and discarding of a program. It can be used to fine tune the segment working sets of a program to minimize the program's required memory.

## Systems Application Architecture (SAA)
A collection of standards created by IBM to provide software consistency that extends from personal computers to minicomputers on up to mainframes. Aspects of application software that will be affected include the user interface, and application programming interface (API). The user interface standards are described in a standard that is part of SAA and is called Common User Access (CUA).

## Task Database (TDB)
A task database is a memory object created by the Window scheduler to keep track of the things that are owned by a task. This includes file handles, the current MS-DOS disk and directory, information about a task's private interrupts, and a pointer to the DOS program database, also known as a program segment prefix (PSP).

## Text Alignment
The text alignment is a DC attribute that describes the placement of a line of text relative to a control point.

## Text Color

The text color is a DC attribute that describes the color for drawing text. Only pure, undithered colors are actually used for text, which means that GDI maps the requested color into the closest available device color.

## Thunk

A thunk is a tiny piece of code that serves as a dynamic code link (in real mode Windows)

## Tiled Windows

Tiled windows refers to the placement of windows so that no two windows overlap. Windows 1.x had built-in support for automatic tiling. This support was removed in versions 2.0 and later.

## Top-Level Window

A top-level window is an overlapping window (WS_OVERLAP) or a popup window (WS_POPUP) which has no parent. All top-level windows are referenced in Windows' Task List that appears in response to the Ctrl + Esc key combination.

Unexpected Application Error (UAE)
An error that causes an application to terminate. Some of the causes of unexpected application errors include general protection faults, unexpected paging fault, and unexpected interrupt.

## Viewport Origin

The viewport origin is a DC attribute that defines the coordinate translation to take place after the scaling for the various GDI mapping modes.

## Viewport Extent

The viewport extent is a DC attribute that provides a pair of X and Y values that are used to define the ratios for GDI's isotropic and anisotropic mapping modes.

## Virtual Key Code

A virtual key code is a value that represents keystroke information as raw keyboard input. Raw keyboard input does not distinguish, for example, between upper and lower-case letters, and does not take into account the state of shift keys like Ctrl, Shift, and Alt. Nor do virtual key codes take into account the state of the various keyboard toggle keys, like Num Lock, Caps Lock, or Scroll Lock. Virtual key codes represent an intermediate step between scan code information, which is hardware-dependent keyboard input, and ASCII characters, which are device-independent representations of ASCII characters.

## Window Class

A window class is a template for creating a window. Window classes are created by calling RegisterClass and supplying a pointer to a WNDCLASS structure with the class definition information.

## Window Extent

The window extent is a DC attribute that provides a pair of X and Y values that are used to define the ratios for GDI's isotropic and anisotropic mapping modes.

## Window Origin

The window origin is a DC attribute that defines the translation that is to take place in the world coordinate space before the scaling transformation of any of GDI's mapping modes.

## Window Procedure
A function associated with a window class that processes the messages associated with a given window.

## Windows Sandwich
A window sandwich describes a code construction made up of three parts: two slices of bread and some filling in between. The top slice of bread borrows a system resource, the filling uses the resource, and the bottom slice of bread returns the resource to the owner.

# Appendix D: Contents of a Device Context

| Drawing Attribute | Default Value | Lines | Filled Areas | Text | Raster | Comments |
|---|---|---|---|---|---|---|
| Background Color | White | x | x | x | | styled pen, hatch brush |
| Background Mode | OPAQUE | x | x | x | | On/Off switch |
| Brush Handle | White Brush | | x | | x | Filled areas |
| Brush Origin | (0,0) | | x | | x | hatch & dithered brushes |
| Clipping Region Handle | Entire Surface | x | x | x | x | |
| Color Palette Handle | Default Palette | x | x | x | | |
| Current Pen Position | (0,0) | x | | | | For LineTo routine |
| Drawing Mode | R2_COPYPEN | x | x | | | Boolean mixing |
| Font Handle | System Font | | | x | | |
| Intercharacter Spacing | 0 | | | x | | |
| Mapping Mode | MM_TEXT | x | x | x | x | One unit = 1 pixel |

703

| Drawing Attribute | Default Value | Lines | Filled Areas | Text | Raster | Comments |
|---|---|---|---|---|---|---|
| Pen Handle | Black Pen | x | x | | | |
| Polygon-Filling Mode | Alternate | | x | | | For Polygon routine |
| Stretching Mode | Black on White | | | | x | For StretchBlt routine |
| Text Alignment | Left & Top | | | x | | |
| Text Color | Black | | | x | | |
| Viewport Extent | (1, 1) | x | x | x | x | Coordinate mapping |
| Viewport Origin | (0, 0) | x | x | x | x | Coordinate mapping |
| Window Extent | (1, 1) | x | x | x | x | Coordinate mapping |
| Window Origin | (0, 0) | x | x | x | x | Coordinate mapping |

# Appendix E: ANSI and OEM Character Sets

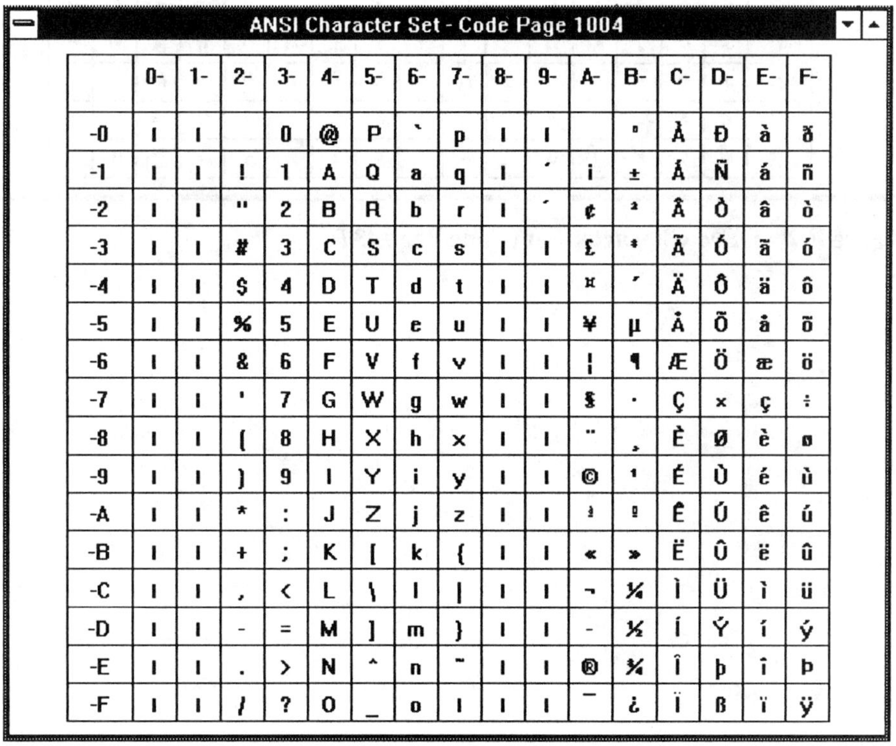

| | 0- | 1- | 2- | 3- | 4- | 5- | 6- | 7- | 8- | 9- | A- | B- | C- | D- | E- | F- |
|---|---|---|---|---|---|---|---|---|---|---|---|---|---|---|---|---|
| -0 | ∎ | ∎ |   | 0 | @ | P | ` | p | ∎ | ∎ |   | ° | À | Ð | à | ð |
| -1 | ∎ | ∎ | ! | 1 | A | Q | a | q | ∎ | ∎ | ¡ | ± | Á | Ñ | á | ñ |
| -2 | ∎ | ∎ | " | 2 | B | R | b | r | ∎ | ∎ | ¢ | ² | Â | Ò | â | ò |
| -3 | ∎ | ∎ | # | 3 | C | S | c | s | ∎ | ∎ | £ | ³ | Ã | Ó | ã | ó |
| -4 | ∎ | ∎ | $ | 4 | D | T | d | t | ∎ | ∎ | ¤ | ´ | Ä | Ô | ä | ô |
| -5 | ∎ | ∎ | % | 5 | E | U | e | u | ∎ | ∎ | ¥ | µ | Å | Õ | å | õ |
| -6 | ∎ | ∎ | & | 6 | F | V | f | v | ∎ | ∎ | ¦ | ¶ | Æ | Ö | æ | ö |
| -7 | ∎ | ∎ | ' | 7 | G | W | g | w | ∎ | ∎ | § | · | Ç | × | ç | ÷ |
| -8 | ∎ | ∎ | ( | 8 | H | X | h | x | ∎ | ∎ | ¨ | ¸ | È | Ø | è | ø |
| -9 | ∎ | ∎ | ) | 9 | I | Y | i | y | ∎ | ∎ | © | ¹ | É | Ù | é | ù |
| -A | ∎ | ∎ | * | : | J | Z | j | z | ∎ | ∎ | ª | º | Ê | Ú | ê | ú |
| -B | ∎ | ∎ | + | ; | K | [ | k | { | ∎ | ∎ | « | » | Ë | Û | ë | û |
| -C | ∎ | ∎ | , | < | L | \ | l | \| | ∎ | ∎ | ¬ | ¼ | Ì | Ü | ì | ü |
| -D | ∎ | ∎ | - | = | M | ] | m | } | ∎ | ∎ | - | ½ | Í | Ý | í | ý |
| -E | ∎ | ∎ | . | > | N | ^ | n | ~ | ∎ | ∎ | ® | ¾ | Î | þ | î | þ |
| -F | ∎ | ∎ | / | ? | O | _ | o | ∎ | ∎ | ∎ | ¯ | ¿ | Ï | ß | ï | ÿ |

**Figure E.1** Ansi Character Set (Code Page 1004)

OEM Character Set - Code Page 437

| | 0- | 1- | 2- | 3- | 4- | 5- | 6- | 7- | 8- | 9- | A- | B- | C- | D- | E- | F- |
|---|---|---|---|---|---|---|---|---|---|---|---|---|---|---|---|---|
| -0 | | ► | | 0 | @ | P | ` | p | Ç | É | á | ░ | └ | ╨ | α | ≡ |
| -1 | ☺ | ◄ | ! | 1 | A | Q | a | q | ü | æ | í | ▒ | ┴ | ╤ | ß | ± |
| -2 | ☻ | ↕ | " | 2 | B | R | b | r | é | Æ | ó | ▓ | ┬ | ╥ | Γ | ≥ |
| -3 | ♥ | ‼ | # | 3 | C | S | c | s | â | ô | ú | │ | ├ | ╙ | π | ≤ |
| -4 | ♦ | ¶ | $ | 4 | D | T | d | t | ä | ö | ñ | ┤ | ─ | ╘ | Σ | ⌠ |
| -5 | ♣ | § | % | 5 | E | U | e | u | à | ò | Ñ | ╡ | ┼ | ╒ | σ | ⌡ |
| -6 | ♠ | ▬ | & | 6 | F | V | f | v | å | û | ª | ╢ | ╞ | ╓ | µ | ÷ |
| -7 | • | ↨ | ' | 7 | G | W | g | w | ç | ù | º | ╖ | ╟ | ╫ | τ | ≈ |
| -8 | ◘ | ↑ | ( | 8 | H | X | h | x | ê | ÿ | ¿ | ╕ | ╚ | ╪ | Φ | ° |
| -9 | ○ | ↓ | ) | 9 | I | Y | i | y | ë | Ö | ⌐ | ╣ | ╔ | ┘ | Θ | ∙ |
| -A | ◙ | → | * | : | J | Z | j | z | è | Ü | ¬ | ║ | ╩ | ┌ | Ω | · |
| -B | ♂ | ← | + | ; | K | [ | k | { | ï | ¢ | ½ | ╗ | ╦ | █ | δ | √ |
| -C | ♀ | ∟ | , | < | L | \ | l | \| | î | £ | ¼ | ╝ | ╠ | ▄ | ∞ | ⁿ |
| -D | ♪ | ↔ | - | = | M | ] | m | } | ì | ¥ | ¡ | ╜ | ═ | ▌ | φ | ² |
| -E | ♫ | ▲ | . | > | N | ^ | n | ~ | Ä | ₧ | « | ╛ | ╬ | ▐ | ε | ■ |
| -F | ☼ | ▼ | / | ? | O | _ | o | ⌂ | Å | ƒ | » | ┐ | ╧ | ▀ | ∩ | |

**Figure E.2 OEM Character Set (Code Page 437)**

# Appendix F: The Windows Virtual Key Codes

| (hex) | (dec) | Symbolic Name | Key Pressed (US English 101/102 Kbd) |
|---|---|---|---|
| 1 | 1 | VK_LBUTTON | |
| 2 | 2 | VK_RBUTTON | |
| 3 | 3 | VK_CANCEL | Ctrl-Break |
| 4 | 4 | VK_MBUTTON | |
| 8 | 8 | VK_BACK | Backspace |
| 9 | 9 | VK_TAB | Tab |
| C | 12 | VK_CLEAR | 5 on Numeric keypad w/Num Lock OFF |
| D | 13 | VK_RETURN | Enter |
| 10 | 16 | VK_SHIFT | Shift |
| 11 | 17 | VK_CONTROL | Ctrl |
| 12 | 18 | VK_MENU | Alt |
| 13 | 19 | VK_PAUSE | Pause (or Ctrl-Num Lock) |
| 14 | 20 | VK_CAPITAL | Caps Lock |
| 1B | 27 | VK_ESCAPE | Esc |
| 20 | 32 | VK_SPACE | Spacebar |
| 21 | 33 | VK_PRIOR | Page Up |

708  *Appendices*

| *(hex)* | *(dec)* | *Symbolic Name* | *Key Pressed (US English 101/102 Kbd)* |
|---|---|---|---|
| 22 | 34 | VK_NEXT | Page Down |
| 23 | 35 | VK_END | End |
| 24 | 36 | VK_HOME | Home |
| 25 | 37 | VK_LEFT | Left Arrow |
| 26 | 38 | VK_UP | Up Arrow |
| 27 | 39 | VK_RIGHT | Right Arrow |
| 28 | 40 | VK_DOWN | Down Arrow |
| 29 | 41 | VK_SELECT | <unused> |
| 2A | 42 | VK_PRINT | <unused> |
| 2B | 43 | VK_EXECUTE | <unused> |
| 2C | 44 | VK_SNAPSHOT | Print Screen |
| 2D | 45 | VK_INSERT | Ins |
| 2E | 46 | VK_DELETE | Del |
| 2F | 47 | VK_HELP | <unused> |
| 30-39 | 48-57 | VK_0 to VK_9 | 0 to 9 above letter keys |
| 41-5A | 65-90 | VK_A to VK_Z | A to Z |
| 60 | 96 | VK_NUMPAD0 | 0 on Numeric keypad w/Num Lock ON |
| 61 | 97 | VK_NUMPAD1 | 1 on Numeric keypad w/Num Lock ON |
| 62 | 98 | VK_NUMPAD2 | 2 on Numeric keypad w/Num Lock ON |
| 63 | 99 | VK_NUMPAD3 | 3 on Numeric keypad w/Num Lock ON |
| 64 | 100 | VK_NUMPAD4 | 4 on Numeric keypad w/Num Lock ON |
| 65 | 101 | VK_NUMPAD5 | 5 on Numeric keypad w/Num Lock ON |
| 66 | 102 | VK_NUMPAD6 | 6 on Numeric keypad w/Num Lock ON |
| 67 | 103 | VK_NUMPAD7 | 7 on Numeric keypad w/Num Lock ON |
| 68 | 104 | VK_NUMPAD8 | 8 on Numeric keypad w/Num Lock ON |
| 69 | 105 | VK_NUMPAD9 | 9 on Numeric keypad w/Num Lock ON |

*Appendix F: The Windows Virtual Key Codes* 709

| *(hex)* | *(dec)* | *Symbolic Name* | *Key Pressed (US English 101/102 Kbd)* |
|---|---|---|---|
| 6A | 106 | VK_MULTIPLY | * on Numeric keypad |
| 6B | 107 | VK_ADD | + on Numeric keypad |
| 6C | 108 | VK_SEPARATOR | <unused> |
| 6D | 109 | VK_SUBTRACT | - on Numeric keypad |
| 6E | 110 | VK_DECIMAL | . on Numeric keypad w/Num Lock ON |
| 6F | 111 | VK_DIVIDE | / on Numeric keypad |
| 70 | 112 | VK_F1 | F1 function key |
| 71 | 113 | VK_F2 | F2 function key |
| 72 | 114 | VK_F3 | F3 function key |
| 73 | 115 | VK_F4 | F4 function key |
| 74 | 116 | VK_F5 | F5 function key |
| 75 | 117 | VK_F6 | F6 function key |
| 76 | 118 | VK_F7 | F7 function key |
| 77 | 119 | VK_F8 | F8 function key |
| 78 | 120 | VK_F9 | F9 function key |
| 79 | 121 | VK_F10 | F10 function key |
| 7A | 122 | VK_F11 | F11 function key |
| 7B | 123 | VK_F12 | F12 function key |
| 7C | 124 | VK_F13 | |
| 7D | 125 | VK_F14 | |
| 7E | 126 | VK_F15 | |
| 7F | 127 | VK_F16 | |
| 90 | 144 | VK_NUMLOCK | Num Lock |
| 91 | 145 | | Scroll Lock |

*—The following codes apply to US keyboards only—*

| BA | 186 | | colon/semi-colon |

| (hex) | (dec) | Symbolic Name | Key Pressed (US English 101/102 Kbd) |
|-------|-------|---------------|--------------------------------------|
| BB | 187 | | plus/equal |
| BC | 188 | | less than/comma |
| BD | 189 | | underscore/hyphen |
| BE | 190 | | greater than/period |
| BF | 191 | | question/slash |
| C0 | 192 | | tilde/back accent |
| DB | 219 | | left squiggle brace/left square brace |
| DC | 220 | | horizontal bar/backslash |
| DD | 221 | | right squiggle brace/right square brace |
| DE | 222 | | double quote/single quote |

# Appendix G: Setting Up the Integrated Development Environment

You are provided with a **make file** for all of the code samples in this book. If you regularly use the MAKE utility when creating software, this is convenient for you. On the other hand, quite a few programmers prefer Borland's Integrated Development Environment (IDE). Borland provides a DOS-based version as well as a Windows-based version of the IDE. This appendix reviews the settings which are required to create a Windows/OWL program.

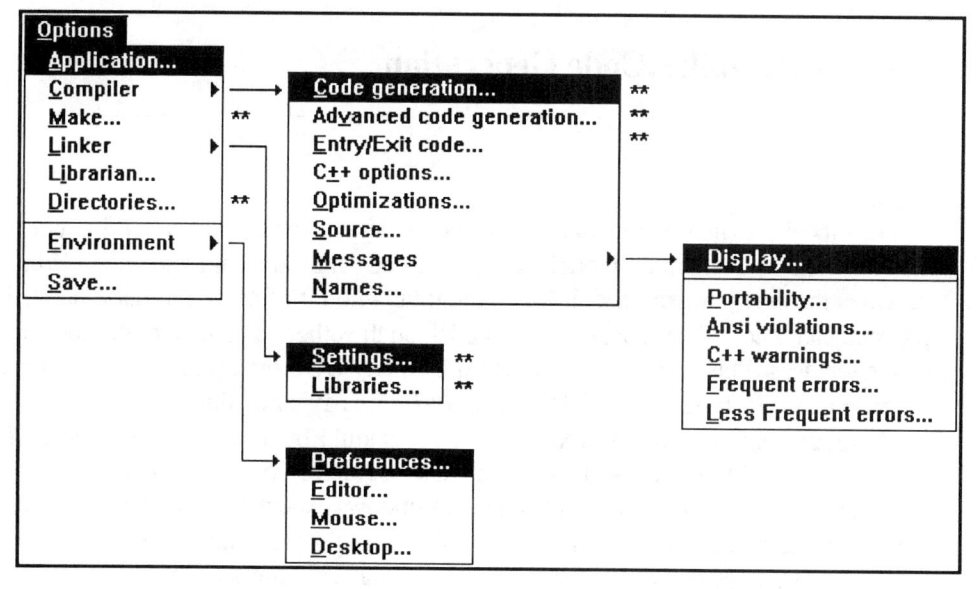

Figure G.1 The Option menu items in the Windows-based IDE

712   *Appendices*

The DOS-based IDE and the Windows-based IDE share a similar user-interface. In this appendix, we show the menus and dialog boxes in the Windows-based IDE. It should be a simple matter to find the corresponding menus and dialogs in the DOS-based IDE.

Setup involves selecting items in the Options menu. Figure G.1 shows this menu, along with all submenus. Of the 24 menu items that summon dialog boxes, seven contain settings that are crucial to the successful creation of a C++ Windows/OWL program. In the figure, an asterisk "*" has been placed next to these items. Also, here is a list of these menu items:

*Menu Items which Summon Required IDE Settings Dialog Boxes*
Options.Compiler.Code Generation...
Options.Compiler.Advanced Code Generation...
Options.Compiler.Entry/Exit Code...
Options.Make...
Options.Linker.Settings...
Options.Linker.Libraries...
Options.Directories...

On the next few pages, we'll review the crucial items in each dialog box to help make setup quick and easy. The figures in the following pages were taken from an early beta version of the Windows-based IDE. While we fully expect the final version to be identical with the beta version, don't be surprised if one or two items have changed.

## Options.Compiler.Code Generation...

**Model.**
The model (or **memory model**) describes the default method for accessing both code and data. The small memory model creates *near* code and *near* data references. While this provides the best performance, it limits the total amount of code and data that a single program can access. The large memory model, on the other hand, creates *far* code and *far* data references. This is the model preferred by many DOS programmers, and is required for creating OWL programs which use the OWL.DLL dynamic link library.

There are some limitations about which you should be aware. For one thing, if you create too much static data to fit into one data segment, your executable program will contain more than one data segment. When a Windows executable program has more than *one* automatic data segment, Windows only allows a single instance to execute. When you try running a second copy of a program, you'll get an error message.

**Assume SS equals DS.**

This describes the way the compiler handles the two CPU registers: SS (stack segment register) and DS (data segment register). When you create a Windows application, SS should always be equal to DS. However, when creating a Windows dynamic link library, SS is never equal to DS.

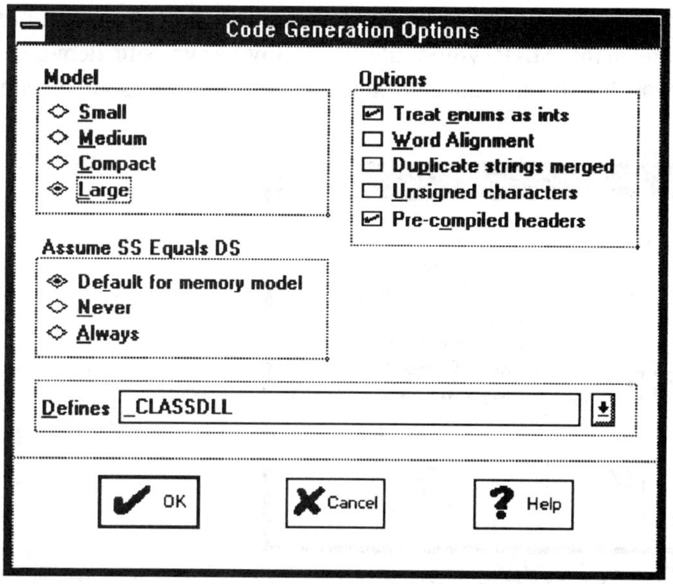

**Figure G.2 Compiler Code Generation dialog**

**Options: Precompiled headers.**

You aren't required to select this option, but it can be useful to speed up compile time. This switch causes the compiler to save a binary copy of your include (.h) files in a file with the extension .SYM.

## Options.Compiler.Advanced Code Generation...

Of the four items which we'll discuss, only the first is a required setting. The other three are useful for debugging and to access the C++ class browser.

### Generate underbars.

You'll need to select this option to access the C-runtime library routines (such as strcpy, memcpy, etc.). Otherwise, the linker will be unable to resolve the references to these routines.

### Line numbers debug info.

Selecting this option causes the compiler to include source code line number information in the .OBJ file and in the .MAP symbol file. This allows a symbolic debugger, such as the Turbo Debugger for Windows, to trace through your application's source code.

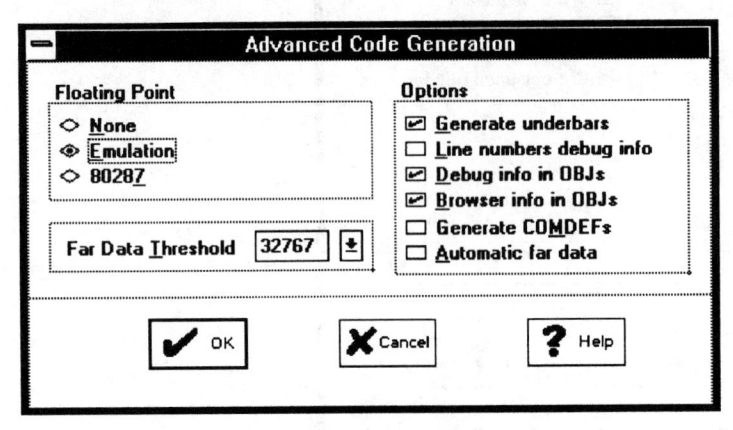

Figure G.3 Compiler Advanced Code Generation dialog

### Debug info in OBJs.

Setting this option causes a complete set of debugging information to be written to the .OBJ file. This is required if you wish to use the Turbo Debugger for Windows, and access the local and global variable names, as well as the function names, in your program.

### Browser info in OBJs.

Setting this option allows the C++ class browser to view your program's classes.

# Options.Compiler.Entry/Exit Code...

**Prolog/Epilog Code Generation.**
At the beginning of every function, there is a short piece of code called a **prolog**. The primary job of the prolog is to set up the stack to allow a function to access the parameters and to have room for local (automatic) variables (see Chapter 17). A Windows program can be called by the Windows' libraries. Such "doorway" functions are specially treated to make sure the data segment (DS) register is set up properly (see Chapter 19). Such functions are usually **exported**, which means the Windows loader will patch the prolog when the code segment is loaded into memory. In a Windows program, the need for "doorway" functions can be handled in one of three ways:

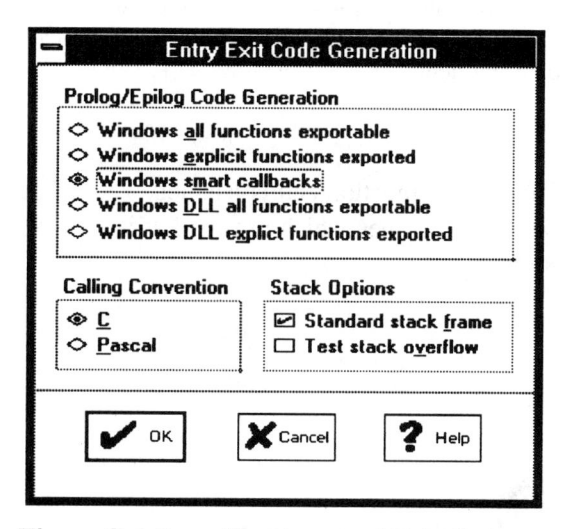

**Figure G.4 Compiler Entry and Exit Code Generation dialog**

- **Windows all functions exportable**. When all functions are exported, the Windows loader patches every function to make sure they can be entered from the outside. Unfortunately, this is the least efficient way to solve this problem.

- **Windows explicit functions exported**. This setting only affects functions which have the **_export** keyword. This is the best setting to use, since it is the most efficient. However, it requires that you use the **_export** keyword whenever you create a callback function and pass it to Windows. When creating window objects or dialog objects using OWL, you don't need to use this keyword since the OWL libraries handle it for you.

- **Windows smart callbacks**. This setting provides a reasonable compromise between the other two. It takes advantage of the fact that, in a Windows application, the stack segment is usually the same as the data segment. For all far functions, a prolog is generated which causes the stack segment register (SS) to be copied to the data segment register (DS).

When you are creating a dynamic link library, you must select one of the two following settings:

- **Windows DLL all functions exportable**. Although this is not the most efficient, it allows any far function in a DLL to be called from an application. The reason is that every function in the DLL will be given the proper prolog.
- **Windows DLL explicit functions exported**. This setting requires you to use the _export keyword for every function which will be called from an application. This creates a prolog at the beginning of the function which properly sets the data segment (DS) register to point to the DLL's data segment.

**Calling Convention.**

This switch affects the default setting for how a function call is handled. The safest setting to use is the C calling convention, since routines which use the Pascal calling convention usually have the **pascal** keyword.

## Options.Make...

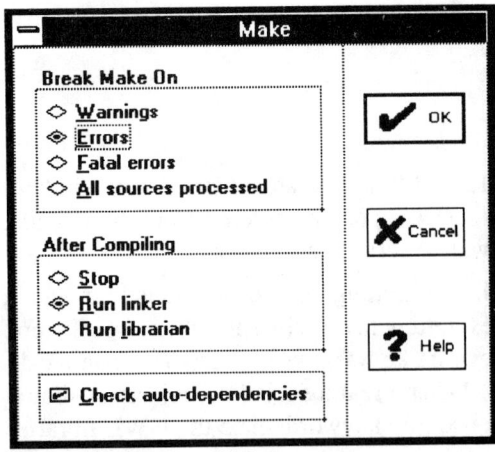

**Figure G.5 Make dialog**

Appendix G: Setting Up the Integrated Development Environment    717

**Check auto-dependencies.**

You'll want to check this option to request that MAKE read the dependency information from the include (.h) files.

## Options.Linker.Settings...

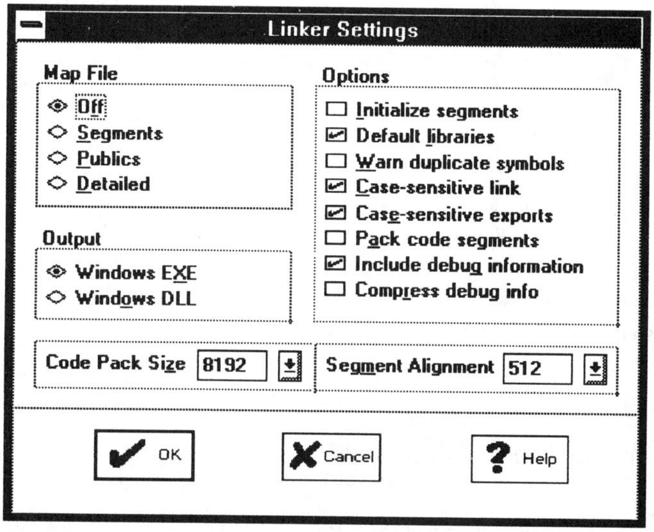

**Figure G.6 Linker Settings dialog**

**Output.**

Be sure to check the proper option for the output file. In fact, the only difference between a Windows application (.EXE) file and a dynamic link library (.DLL) file is a single bit. However, the bit must be set correctly to achieve the expected results.

**Options: Case-sensitive link.**

Since C and C++ are case-sensitive languages, be sure to check this item.

**Options: Include debug information.**

If you're planning to use a debugger such as the Turbo Debugger for Windows, be sure to check this option.

# Options.Linker.Libraries...

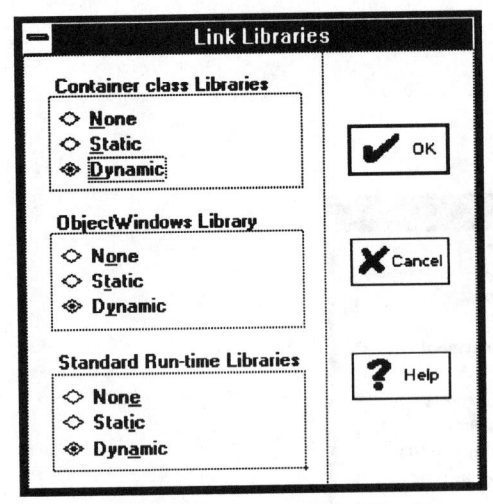

**Figure G.7** Linker Libraries dialog

**ObjectWindows Library.**
You can link to the OWL libraries in one of three ways:

- **None.** When this switch is selected, you must explicitly list the name of the OWL library in your IDE project list.
- **Static.** When selected, this switch causes the OWL functions to be bound into your programs executable (.EXE) file. This requires that the various OWL static link library files be present. For example, the OWLWL.LIB file contains the large model OWL static link library.
- **Dynamic.** When selected, this switch causes the OWL functions to be accessed from the OWL dynamic link library (OWL.DLL). This requires the presence of the OWL dynamic information library (OWL.LIB) at program link time. Note that this option is not available with all Borland C++ compilers.

**Standard Run-time.**
You can link to the standard C/C++ run-time libraries in one of three ways:

- **None.** You may select this option when you want to explicitly list the name of the C-runtime libraries in the IDE project list.

- **Static.** Select this option to cause the C-runtime library routines to be bound into your program's executable file.
- **Dynamic.** Select this option to use the dynamic link library version of the C-runtime library routines (included in the file BCRTL.DLL).

## Options.Directories...

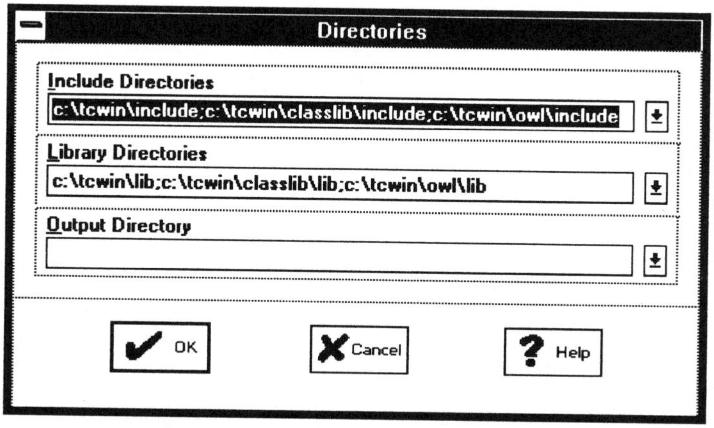

[Directories dialog showing:
Include Directories: c:\tcwin\include;c:\tcwin\classlib\include;c:\tcwin\owl\include
Library Directories: c:\tcwin\lib;c:\tcwin\classlib\lib;c:\tcwin\owl\lib
Output Directory: (empty)
Buttons: OK, Cancel, Help]

**Figure G.8 Directories dialog**

### Include Directories.

List the directories which contain the include files needed by the compiler. This figure shows the setting for the Turbo C++ compiler, whose installation program uses the \TCWIN subdirectory. If you are using the Borland C++ compiler, you can substitute the \BORLANDC for the settings shown.

### Library Directories.

List the directories where the linker libraries can be found. This figure shows the default locations for the Turbo C++ compiler.

### Output Directory.

List the location where the executable file should be written after a successful compile/link.

# Appendix H: The MAGNIFY Program

The MAGNIFY program is used in various places in this book. It makes it easy to examine tiny details on the display screen in the same way that a magnifying glass lets you see tiny details on physical objects. A scroll bar lets you control the amount of magnification. Figure H.1 shows MAGNIFY in operation.

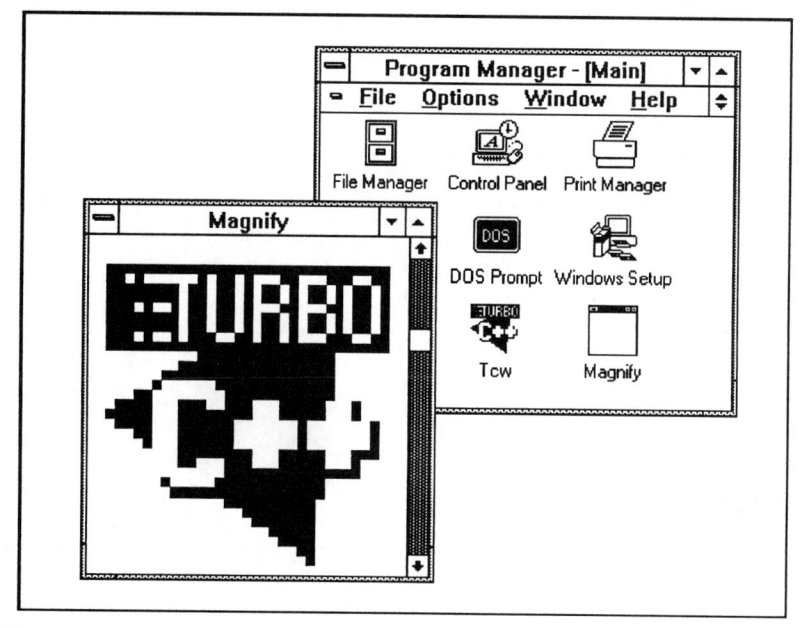

**Figure H.1  MAGNIFY in operation**

Here is the source code to the program:

# MAKEFILE.MAK

```
.AUTODEPEND

#      Translator Definitions
INC=\BORLANDC\OWL\INCLUDE;\BORLANDC\CLASSLIB\INCLUDE;\BORLANDC\INCLUDE
CC = bcc -c -D_CLASSDLL -H -ml -WS -w -I$(INC)

#      Implicit Rules
.c.obj:
   $(CC) {$< }

.cpp.obj:
   $(CC) {$< }

#      Explicit Rules
Magnify.exe: Magnify.res Magnify.def Magnify.obj
      tlink /c/C/n/P-/Twe/x @Magnify.LNK
      rlink Magnify.res Magnify.exe

#      Individual File Dependencies
Magnify.obj: Magnify.cpp

Magnify.res: Magnify.rc Magnify.cur Magnify.ico
      brcc -FO Magnify.res -i$(INC) Magnify.RC
```

# MAGNIFY.LNK

```
\borlandc\lib\c0wl.obj+
Magnify.obj
Magnify,Magnify
\borlandc\classlib\lib\tclasdll.lib+
\borlandc\owl\lib\owl.lib+
mathwl.lib+
import.lib+
crtldll.lib
Magnify.def
```

# MAGNIFY.CPP

```
/*-------------------------------------------------------------*\
|    MAGNIFY  -  Stretch part of the display screen.            |
\*-------------------------------------------------------------*/
#define WIN31
#define STRICT
#include <owl.h>
#include <WindowsX.h>
#define min(a,b)  ((a<b)?a:b)
#define max(a,b)  ((a<b)?b:a)
```

```
/*--------------------------------------------------------------*\
|                       Constants.                               |
\*--------------------------------------------------------------*/
const int LINESIZE = 1;
const int PAGESIZE = 10;
const int SCROLLMIN = 10;
const int SCROLLMAX = 200;

/*--------------------------------------------------------------*\
|                    Class Declarations.                         |
\*--------------------------------------------------------------*/
class TMagnifyApplication : public TApplication
   {
   public:
      TMagnifyApplication (LPSTR lpszName, HINSTANCE hInstance,
                           HINSTANCE hPrevInstance,
                           LPSTR lpszCmdLine, int nCmdShow);
      virtual void InitMainWindow ();
   };


class TNotRect
   {
   public:
      TNotRect (int X1, int Y1, int X2, int Y2);
      void Hide (HDC hdc);
      void Show (HDC hdc);
      void Move (HDC hdc, int X1, int Y1, int X2, int Y2);
   private:
      BOOL bVisible;
      RECT rCurrent;

      void Invert(HDC hdc);
   };

class TMagnifyWindow : public TWindow
   {
   public:
      TMagnifyWindow (PTWindowsObject pwParent, LPSTR lpszTitle,
                      PTModule pmModule);
      ~TMagnifyWindow ();
      virtual LPSTR GetClassName ();
      virtual void  GetWindowClass (WNDCLASS&);

      virtual void WMCreate (TMessage& Msg)= [WM_CREATE];
      virtual void WMLButtonDown (TMessage& Msg)= [WM_LBUTTONDOWN];
      virtual void WMMouseMove (TMessage& Msg)= [WM_MOUSEMOVE];
      virtual void WMLButtonUp (TMessage& Msg)= [WM_LBUTTONUP];
      virtual void WMVScroll (TMessage& Msg)= [WM_VSCROLL];
      virtual void WMPaint (TMessage& Msg)= [WM_PAINT];
      virtual void WMSize (TMessage& Msg)= [WM_SIZE];

   protected:
      BOOL bCapture;
      HDC hdcScreen;
      HDC hdcWindow;
      int nStretch;
      POINT ptAnchor;
      POINT ptLast;
      RECT rClient;   // Client window size.
      RECT rSource;   // Source pixel rectangle (screen coords).
      TNotRect * pnrTrack;
```

```
        void ClientToSource(LPRECT lpIn, LPRECT lpOut);
    };


/*--------------------------------------------------------------*\
|                   Main Function:  WinMain.                     |
\*--------------------------------------------------------------*/
int PASCAL WinMain (HINSTANCE hInstance,   HINSTANCE hPrevInstance,
                    LPSTR lpszCmdLine, int     nCmdShow)
    {
    TMagnifyApplication Magnify ("Magnify", hInstance,
                        hPrevInstance, lpszCmdLine, nCmdShow);
    Magnify.Run();
    return Magnify.Status;
    }

/*--------------------------------------------------------------*\
|                   Application Class Member.                    |
\*--------------------------------------------------------------*/
TMagnifyApplication::TMagnifyApplication (LPSTR lpszName,
                    HINSTANCE hInstance, HINSTANCE hPrevInstance,
                    LPSTR lpszCmdLine, int nCmdShow)
                :TApplication (lpszName, hInstance,
                    hPrevInstance, lpszCmdLine, nCmdShow)
    {
    /*  Application specific initialization goes here.  */
    }

/*--------------------------------------------------------------*\
|                   Application Class Member.                    |
\*--------------------------------------------------------------*/
void TMagnifyApplication::InitMainWindow ()
    {
    MainWindow = new TMagnifyWindow (NULL, "Magnify", NULL);
    }

/*--------------------------------------------------------------*\
|                   TMagnifyWindow Class Member.                 |
\*--------------------------------------------------------------*/
TMagnifyWindow::TMagnifyWindow (PTWindowsObject pwParent,
                    LPSTR lpszTitle, PTModule pmModule)
                :TWindow (pwParent, lpszTitle, pmModule)

    {
    hdcWindow = 0;
    bCapture  = FALSE;
    hdcScreen = CreateDC ("DISPLAY", 0, 0, 0);

    ptAnchor.x = 0; ptAnchor.y = 0;
    ptLast.x = 0; ptLast.y = 0;
    rClient.left  = 0;
    rClient.top   = 0;

    rSource.left   = 0;
    rSource.top    = 0;
    rSource.right  = 1;
    rSource.bottom = 1;

    pnrTrack = 0;

    // Modify window attribute for a scroll bar.
    Attr.Style |= WS_VSCROLL;
    }
```

```
/*----------------------------------------------------------*\
|                  TMagnifyWindow Class Member.              |
\*----------------------------------------------------------*/
TMagnifyWindow::~TMagnifyWindow ()
    {
    DeleteDC (hdcScreen);
    }

/*----------------------------------------------------------*\
|                  TMagnifyWindow Class Member.              |
\*----------------------------------------------------------*/
LPSTR TMagnifyWindow::GetClassName ()
    {
    return "Magnify:MAIN";
    }

/*----------------------------------------------------------*\
|                  TMagnifyWindow Class Member.              |
\*----------------------------------------------------------*/
void TMagnifyWindow::GetWindowClass (WNDCLASS& wc)
    {
    TWindow::GetWindowClass (wc);
    wc.hIcon=LoadIcon (wc.hInstance, "snapshot");
    wc.hCursor=LoadCursor (wc.hInstance, "hand");
    wc.style = CS_HREDRAW | CS_VREDRAW;
    }

/*----------------------------------------------------------*\
|                  TMagnifyWindow Class Member.              |
\*----------------------------------------------------------*/
void TMagnifyWindow::WMCreate (TMessage& Msg)
    {
    nStretch = SCROLLMIN;
    SetScrollRange (Msg.Receiver, SB_VERT, SCROLLMIN, SCROLLMAX,
                    FALSE);
    }

/*----------------------------------------------------------*\
|                  TMagnifyWindow Class Member.              |
\*----------------------------------------------------------*/
void TMagnifyWindow::WMLButtonDown (TMessage& Msg)
    {
    bCapture = TRUE;
    SetCapture (Msg.Receiver);

    hdcWindow = GetDC (Msg.Receiver);

    GetClientRect (Msg.Receiver, &rClient);
    ptAnchor = MAKEPOINT (Msg.LParam);

    // Change rect size for stretch factor.
    ClientToSource (&rClient, &rSource);

    // Adjust for location of mouse pointer.
    OffsetRect (&rSource, ptAnchor.x - (rClient.right/2),
                          ptAnchor.y - (rClient.bottom/2));

    // Convert shrunk rectangle to screen coordinates.
    ClientToScreen (Msg.Receiver,(LPPOINT)&rSource.left);
    ClientToScreen (Msg.Receiver,(LPPOINT)&rSource.right);
    pnrTrack = new TNotRect (rSource.left,  rSource.top,
                             rSource.right, rSource.bottom);
    pnrTrack->Show (hdcScreen);
```

```
    }
/*--------------------------------------------------------------*\
|                   TMagnifyWindow Class Member.                 |
\*--------------------------------------------------------------*/
void TMagnifyWindow::WMLButtonUp (TMessage& Msg)
    {
    if (!bCapture)
        return;

    bCapture = FALSE;
    ReleaseCapture();

    ReleaseDC (Msg.Receiver, hdcWindow);

    ptLast = MAKEPOINT (Msg.LParam);
    ClientToScreen (Msg.Receiver, &ptLast);

    pnrTrack->Hide (hdcScreen);

    delete pnrTrack;
    pnrTrack = 0;
    }

/*--------------------------------------------------------------*\
|                   TMagnifyWindow Class Member.                 |
\*--------------------------------------------------------------*/
void TMagnifyWindow::WMMouseMove (TMessage& Msg)
    {
    POINT ptScreen;

    if (!bCapture)
        return;

    // Calculate absolute screen coordinates.
    ptScreen = MAKEPOINT (Msg.LParam);
    ClientToScreen (Msg.Receiver, &ptScreen);

    // Map mouse location to source rectangle.
    CopyRect (&rSource, &rClient);
    rSource.left   = ptScreen.x - ptAnchor.x;
    rSource.top    = ptScreen.y - ptAnchor.y;
    rSource.right  = ptScreen.x + (rClient.right - ptAnchor.x);
    rSource.bottom = ptScreen.y + (rClient.bottom - ptAnchor.y);

    // Change rect size for stretch factor.
    ClientToSource (&rClient, &rSource);

    // Adjust for client rectangle size.
    rSource.left   -= rClient.right/2;
    rSource.top    -= rClient.bottom/2;
    rSource.right  -= rClient.right/2;
    rSource.bottom -= rClient.bottom/2;

    // Adjust for location of mouse pointer.
    OffsetRect (&rSource, ptScreen.x, ptScreen.y);

    pnrTrack->Hide (hdcScreen);

    StretchBlt(hdcWindow, 0, 0, rClient.right, rClient.bottom,
               hdcScreen, rSource.left, rSource.top,
               rSource.right - rSource.left + 1,
               rSource.bottom - rSource.top + 1, SRCCOPY);
```

```
        pnrTrack->Show (hdcScreen);
        pnrTrack->Move (hdcScreen, rSource.left,  rSource.top,
                                   rSource.right, rSource.bottom);
        }

/*----------------------------------------------------------------*\
|                    TMagnifyWindow Class Member.                  |
\*----------------------------------------------------------------*/
void TMagnifyWindow::WMPaint (TMessage& Msg)
    {
    PAINTSTRUCT ps;

    BeginPaint (Msg.Receiver, &ps);

    StretchBlt(ps.hdc, 0, 0, rClient.right, rClient.bottom,
               hdcScreen, rSource.left, rSource.top,
               rSource.right - rSource.left + 1,
               rSource.bottom - rSource.top + 1, SRCCOPY);

    EndPaint (Msg.Receiver, &ps);
    }

/*----------------------------------------------------------------*\
|                    TMagnifyWindow Class Member.                  |
\*----------------------------------------------------------------*/
void TMagnifyWindow::WMSize (TMessage& Msg)
    {
    rClient.right  = Msg.LP.Lo;
    rClient.bottom = Msg.LP.Hi;
    }

/*----------------------------------------------------------------*\
|                    TMagnifyWindow Class Member.                  |
\*----------------------------------------------------------------*/
void TMagnifyWindow::WMVScroll (TMessage& Msg)
    {
    BOOL fScroll;

    fScroll = FALSE;
    switch (Msg.WParam)
        {
        case SB_LINEUP:
            nStretch -= LINESIZE;
            fScroll = TRUE;
            break;
        case SB_LINEDOWN:
            nStretch += LINESIZE;
            fScroll = TRUE;
            break;
        case SB_PAGEUP:
            nStretch -= PAGESIZE;
            fScroll = TRUE;
            break;
        case SB_PAGEDOWN:
            nStretch += PAGESIZE;
            fScroll = TRUE;
            break;
        case SB_THUMBTRACK:
            nStretch = Msg.LP.Lo;
            fScroll = TRUE;

            if (pnrTrack == 0)
```

```
                        {
                        // Create NOT rectangle.
                        pnrTrack = new TNotRect (rSource.left-1,
                                                 rSource.top-1,
                                                 rSource.right+1,
                                                 rSource.bottom+1);
                        pnrTrack->Show (hdcScreen);

                        }
                break;
            case SB_ENDSCROLL:
                // If we've been tracking, hide the rectangle.
                if (pnrTrack)
                    {
                    pnrTrack->Hide (hdcScreen);
                    delete pnrTrack;
                    pnrTrack = 0;
                    }
                break;
            }
        if (fScroll)
            {
            nStretch = min (SCROLLMAX, nStretch);
            nStretch = max (SCROLLMIN, nStretch);

            // Update scroll thumb.
            SetScrollPos (Msg.Receiver, SB_VERT, nStretch, TRUE);

            // Recalculate stretch factor.
            ClientToSource (&rClient, &rSource);

            // Adjust for last location of mouse pointer.
            OffsetRect (&rSource, ptLast.x - (rClient.right/2),
                                  ptLast.y - (rClient.bottom/2));

            // If we're tracking, move to new position.
            if (pnrTrack)
                {
                pnrTrack->Move (hdcScreen, rSource.left-1,
                                           rSource.top-1,
                                           rSource.right+1,
                                           rSource.bottom+1);
                }

            InvalidateRect (Msg.Receiver, NULL, FALSE);
            }
    }
/*---------------------------------------------------------------*\
|                  TMagnifyWindow Class Member.                   |
\*---------------------------------------------------------------*/
void TMagnifyWindow::ClientToSource(LPRECT lpIn, LPRECT lpOut)
    {
    int  xCenter, yCenter;
    int  xDelta,  yDelta;
    RECT rIn;

    rIn = *lpIn;
    xCenter = rIn.right / 2;
    yCenter = rIn.bottom / 2;

    xDelta = (10 * xCenter ) / nStretch;
    yDelta = (10 * yCenter ) / nStretch;
```

```
    rIn.left   = xCenter - xDelta;
    rIn.top    = yCenter - yDelta;
    rIn.right  = xCenter + xDelta;
    rIn.bottom = yCenter + yDelta;

    *lpOut = rIn;
    }
/*--------------------------------------------------------------*\
|                     TNotRect Class Member.                     |
\*--------------------------------------------------------------*/
TNotRect::TNotRect(int X1, int Y1, int X2, int Y2)
    {
    bVisible = FALSE;
    rCurrent.left   = X1;
    rCurrent.top    = Y1;
    rCurrent.right  = X2;
    rCurrent.bottom = Y2;
    }

/*--------------------------------------------------------------*\
|                     TNotRect Class Member.                     |
\*--------------------------------------------------------------*/
void TNotRect::Hide(HDC hdc)
    {
    if (hdc == 0 || !bVisible)
        return;

    Invert (hdc);
    bVisible = FALSE;
    }
/*--------------------------------------------------------------*\
|                     TNotRect Class Member.                     |
\*--------------------------------------------------------------*/
void TNotRect::Show (HDC hdc)
    {
    if (hdc == 0 || bVisible)
        return;

    Invert (hdc);
    bVisible = TRUE;
    }

/*--------------------------------------------------------------*\
|                     TNotRect Class Member.                     |
\*--------------------------------------------------------------*/
void TNotRect::Move (HDC hdc, int X1, int Y1, int X2, int Y2)
    {
    if (hdc == 0 || !bVisible)
        return;

    Invert (hdc);   // Remove previous rectangle.

    rCurrent.left   = X1;
    rCurrent.top    = Y1;
    rCurrent.right  = X2;
    rCurrent.bottom = Y2;

    Invert (hdc);   // Draw new rectangle.
    }
```

```
/*---------------------------------------------------------------*\
|                    TNotRect Class Member.                       |
\*---------------------------------------------------------------*/
void TNotRect::Invert(HDC hdc)
    {
    int ropOld;

    ropOld = SetROP2(hdc, R2_NOT);

    MoveTo (hdc, rCurrent.left,  rCurrent.top);
    LineTo (hdc, rCurrent.right, rCurrent.top);
    LineTo (hdc, rCurrent.right, rCurrent.bottom);
    LineTo (hdc, rCurrent.left,  rCurrent.bottom);
    LineTo (hdc, rCurrent.left,  rCurrent.top);

    SetROP2 (hdc, ropOld);
    }
```

# MAGNIFY.RC

```
snapshot icon Magnify.ico

hand cursor Magnify.cur
```

# MAGNIFY.DEF

```
NAME MAGNIFY

EXETYPE WINDOWS

DESCRIPTION 'Stretch parts of the display screen.'

CODE MOVEABLE DISCARDABLE
DATA MOVEABLE MULTIPLE

HEAPSIZE   512
STACKSIZE 5120
```

# Index

## A

About box, 537
ABOUT.CPP, 394–396
ABOUT.DEF, 398
ABOUT.DLG, 398
ABOUT.H, 396–397
ABOUT.LNK, 394
ABOUT.RC, 397–398
ABOUTDLG.H, 397
ABOUT program, 393–399
ACCEL.CPP, 280–281
ACCEL.DEF, 282
ACCEL.LNK, 280
ACCEL.RC, 282
Accelerator command (WM_-COMMAND) messages, 81
Accelerator key combinations, 275–276
Accelerator keys, 237
Accelerator keystrokes, 238
Accelerators, 237–238. *See also* Keyboard accelerators
ACCELERATORS keyword, 273
Accelerator translation, 278–279
Access flags, 552
Action bar, 243
Actions, 238
Active OWL window object, 65
Active window, 449–450
Address calculation, 538
Address space, physical, 534
_AHINCR symbol, 579
Allen, Paul, 4

Allocation of memory, 558
Allocation routines, checking the return value from, 593
Alternate mode, 186
[Alt] key, 275–277
AND mask, 519, 520, 522
ANSI character set, 443, 444, 705
numeric keypad and, 449
AnsiUpper, 447
AnsiUpperBuff, 447
AppendMenu, 255–257, 302
for adding bitmaps to a menu, 311
owner–drawn menu items and, 288
Apple Macintosh, 4
APPLICAT.H, 64
Application memory use, 557–639
overview of, 559–573
Application message queue, 71
Application object, 59–76
Application "status window," 325
Arc, 159
Arc function, 151–152
Arc routine, 181
arRectangles, 178
Arrow, 238
ASCII characters, 273, 274
Aspect ratio, 221
Atom tables, 567–568
AT–style bus, x
Attr data member, 91, 336
Attribute bundle, 158
Attr structure, 248

.AUTODEPEND statement, 36
AX register, 74, 656
call–back functions and, 654

## B

Background color, for text, 215–217
Backslash (\\), 36
Base fonts (GDI), 198
BeginPaint/EndPaint sandwich, 147, 333
BeginPaint routine, 128, 133–135, 138, 139, 178
"Bit bucket," 197
Bitmaps, 117. *See also* GDI bitmaps
check mark, 312
for creating pattern brushes, 189–190
in menus, 301–311
BITMENU.CPP, 304–307
BITMENU.DEF, 308–309
BITMENU.H, 307–308
BITMENU.LNK, 303
BITMENU.RC, 308
BITMENU program, 303–309
Black carets, creating, 452
BN_CLICKED notification, 413
BN_CLICKED notification code, 392
BN_DOUBLECLICKED notification code, 392
Borders

731

## 732   Index

around check marks, 320
    drawing, 185–186
Border size system metrics, 357–358, 359
Borland Object Windows Library (OWL), ix
BP (base pointer) register, 563, 564
Bravo text editor, 13
Brush color, 214
Brush–creation program, 191–195
Brushes, 171, 186–191
    for bitmap patterns, 309–310
    creating and using, 187–191
    Rectangle function and, 183
BRUSHES.CPP, 192–195
BRUSHES.DEF, 195
BRUSHES.LNK, 191
BRUSHES.RC, 195
Burgermaster, 554, 574
Button down message, 510. *See also* WM_LBUTTONDOWN
Button up message, 510. *See also* WM_LBUTTONUP
Button window class, 337, 377
Byte–aligned drawing, 335–336

## C

Call–back functions, 653
Call–back procedures, in Windows, 655
call instruction, 563
Call thunks, 643, 645
"Cancel" pushbutton, 378–379
CanClose, 96–97
Caption radio button, 399
CARET_ACTIVE flag, 466
CARET.CPP, 455–463
CARET.DEF, 464
CARET_INACTIVE flag, 466
CARET.LNK, 455
CARET.RC, 463
CARET program, 454–466
Carets, 23–24, 450, 451–466
    highlighting insertion points and, 443
CARET2.CPP, 482–491

CARET2.DEF, 492
CARET2.LNK, 482
CARET2.RC, 492
CARET2 program, 481–492
    I–beam cursor and, 493
    PtInRect routine and, 495
Casting, 46
Casting of pointers, 55–57
cbClsExtra field, 87, 330
cbWndExtra field, 87, 330
cchInput, 442
C++ Compiler for Windows, ix
ChangeMenu routine, 262
Character extra spacing, 220
Character hit–test loop, 495–496
Characters, entering from the numeric keypad, 449
Character sets, 443–449
    converting between, 445–446
Character size, defining, 224
Character spacing, 207–208
Character strings
    atom tables and, 567–568
    sorting, 447–448
Character width value, specifying, 202
Check boxes, 379, 380
CHECKED option, 245
Checkered text, producing, 213–214
Check mark bitmaps, creating, 312
Check marks, 238
    for owner–drawn menu items, 286
CheckMenuItem, 266, 313
CHEKMENU.CPP, 314–318
CHEKMENU.DEF, 319–320
CHEKMENU.H, 318–319
CHEKMENU.LNK, 314
CHEKMENU.RC, 319
CHEKMENU program, 313–320
Child window border, 346–347
Child windows, 334–335, 338–339, 345
    clipping and, 349–350
    creating, 363–376
Chord function, 182
Class DC, 334

Class extra bytes, 330
    routines to access, 572
Clicking, 469
Clicking with a shift key, 469
Client area, mouse messages in, 102, 103
Client area coordinates, 119
Client area messages, 473
ClientToScreen routine, 270, 271
Clipboard messages, 111
Clipboard operations, 279
Clipping, 17, 124–127
    in a parent DC, 334
    Window Manager and, 127–128
Clipping regions, 126, 173
Clipping style bits, 349–350
Clip rectangle, specifying, 208–209
CLOCK, 124–126, 134
Closed figures, 149. *See also* Filled figures
CloseWindow member function, 392, 404
CM_FIRST, 252, 278
Code segments, loading into memory, 645
CODE statement, 42–43
Code structure, memory use and, 594–599
Color, of text, 215–217
COLOR_WINDOW+1, 87
Columns, aligning, 210–211
Comboboxes, 381, 382
    notifications for, 392
Combobox window class, 337, 377
Command line compiler (BCC.EXE), 33
Command messages, 99
Common User Access (CUA), 7
Compiler switches, 37–38
Compound window styles, 350
Connect–to–a–window menu routines, 253
Context Code flag, 429
Control Panel, mouse buttons and, 473
Control point, 200

# Index

CONTROL statements, 384
Control.Style... menu, 385
Control.Style... menu item, 399
Conversion, upper- and lowercase, 446–447
Conversion routines, 445–446
Cosine values, resource for calculating, 628–631
CPUs, Intel-86, 533
crColor parameter, 215
CreateBitmap routine, 190, 521–522
CreateBrushIndirect, 187, 188
CreateCaret routine, 452
CreateCompatibleBitmap, 301
CreateCompatibleDC, 301, 309, 522
CreateCursor routine, 520, 522–524
   DYNACURS and, 519
   AND and XOR masks and, 527–529
CreateDC, 309
CreateDialogParam routine, 401–402
CreateDIBPatternBrush, 187, 188
CreateFontIndirect routine, 225, 232
CreateFont routine, 225
CreateHatchBrush, 187, 188–189
Create member function, 372, 401
CreateMenu routine, 255
Create–menu routines, 253
CreatePatternBrush routine, 187, 189–190
CreatePen, 160, 161
CreatePenIndirect, 160, 161
CreatePopup routine, 255
CreateSolidBrush, 188
CREATESTRUCT data structure, 340
CreateWindowEx routine, 87–88, 90, 91, 337–338, 341
CreateWindowEx style bits, 341–350
CreateWindow routine, 85, 88–90, 326, 337–341, 385
   dialog box creation routines and, 378

CreateWindow style bits, 341–350
CS_BYTEALIGNCLIENT style bit, 335
CS_BYTEALIGNWINDOW style bit, 335
CS_CLASSDC style, 334
CS_CLASSDC style bit, 332
CS_DBLCLKS class style, 479
CS_DBLCLKS style bit, 332
CS_GLOBALCLASS class style, 336
CS_HREDRAW, 133
CS_HREDRAW style, 331
CS_KEYCVTWINDOW style bit, 331
CS_NOCLOSE class style, 335
CS_NOKEYCVT style bit, 331
CS_OWNDC style bit, 332
CS_PARENTDC style, 334
CS_PARENTDC style bit, 335
CS_SAVEBITS class style, 335
CS_VREDRAW, 133
CS_VREDRAW style, 331
–c switch, 37
/c switch, 40–41
CtlID, 290
CtlID field, 288
CtlType, 290
CtlType field, 288
Current position, 150
Cursors, 23, 39, 451. *See also* Dynamic cursors
   changing, 493–494
   mouse and, 469
   operation of, 519–521
Cursor–setting messages, mouse capture and, 512
Custom brushes, 187
Custom cursors, creating, 513–519
Custom dialog box controls, 382
Customizing dialog box, 385, 386
Custom menu check marks, creating, 312–323
Custom resource program, 631–639
Custom resources, 628–639
CUSTRES.CPP, 632–635
CUSTRES.DEF, 636

CUSTRES.H, 636
CUSTRES.LNK, 632
CUSTRES.RC, 637
CUSTRES program, 573, 631–639
CW_USEDEFAULT flag, 89, 338, 351

## D

Data fix–ups, 655
Data segment, default, 559–560
Data sharing, 641
Data–sharing messages, 111–112, 673
DATA statement, 43
Data type definitions, 52–54
DC attributes
   for drawing lines, 157–158
   filled figures and, 185–186
   for text drawing, 214–222
Dead–keys, 432
Debugging, program, 535
Debug version of Windows, 565
Default data segment, 559–560
Default data segment header, 560–561
Default flags, in GetMenuState, 268–269
Default fonts, 221, 222
Default local heap, 614
Default message handling, 98–99
Default text alignment, 218
Default window procedure, 34, 435
   code for, 675–685
   mouse messages and, 480–481
DefCommandProc member function, 419
#define statement, 52
DefWindowProc, 82, 106
DefWndProc, 82
DeleteMenu routine, 260, 261–262
DeleteObject, 232
Dereferencing a handle, 584
Descriptor tables, 546
DestroyMenu routine, 260–261
Destroy–menu routines, 254

DestroyWindow, 97–98
Device capability bits, 116
Device context (DC), 121–127
    bitmaps and, 301–302
    contents of, 703–704
    deleting, 310
    private, 332–333
Device context handles, 50
Device driver, 116
Device–driver dynamic link libraries, 62
Device independence, pens and, 159
Device–independent bitmap (DIB), 187, 188
Device–independent graphics, 16–17
Device–independent graphics library, 117
Devices, 16
Diacritic marks, 224
DialogBox, 402
Dialog box controls, 25, 377
Dialog box coordinates, 287, 335, 384
Dialog box editor, 383, 385–387
Dialog boxes, 24–25, 78, 377–420
    maintaining, 391–392
    modal, 383–399
    modeless, 399–413
    termination of, 392
DialogBoxIndirectParam routine, 389
DialogBoxIndirect routine, 389
Dialog box messages, 107
DialogBoxParam routine, 388, 389–390
Dialog box procedure, 390
DialogBox routine, 389
Dialog box template, 383–385
    for a modeless dialog box, 399–400
Dialog box user–interface standards, 378–383
DIALOG statement, 383–384
Disabled parent window, 378
DISCARDABLE, 244
Discardable code segments
    dynamic linking and, 643–647
    reloading, 648
DISCARDABLE declaration, 43
Discardable memory, 541–542
    Windows selection process for, 552–553
DISCARDABLE memory block, 39
Discardable segments, 568
Disk–thrashing, 535
DispatchMessage routine, 74, 75, 279, 433, 476
"Display" effect, 519
Dithered colors, 161–162, 188
Dithering, 137
DLLREF_TEXT code segment, 598
DOS character set, 444
DOS Protected Mode Interface (DPMI), 37, 548
DOTEXT program, 647–648
Dot operator, 94
Double–clicking, 469
Double–click messages, 479–480
Double–click mouse messages, 332
Double–decker (Dagwood) sandwich, 140–141
Dragable objects, 497–512
Dragable rectangles, 497, 498
Dragging, 469, 510–511
Drawing
    of filled figures, 171–196
    of lines, 149–170
    of text, 197–233
Drawing attributes, 121, 122–123
Drawing coordinates, 118–119
Drawing modes, 148, 157, 167–170
DRAWITEMSTRUCT, 289–290
DrawMarker, 147–148
DrawMenuBar, 261, 265–266
DRAWRECT program, 643–646
DrawText, 199, 211–213
DS (data segment) register, 559, 653, 656, 658
–D switch, 37
dwBytes parameter, 579
dwExStyle, 337
DWORD value, 223, 312, 337
dwStyle parameter, 337
DYNACURS.CPP, 514–518
DYNACURS.DEF, 518–519
DYNACURS.LNK, 514
DYNACURS.RC, 518
DYNACURS program, 513–519
    memory–allocation routines used by, 524
Dynamically allocated memory, 524–526
Dynamically allocated segments, 568–569
    keeping as discardable as possible, 575–576
    keeping as few as possible, 574–575
    keeping as small as possible, 575
    local heap allocation in, 614–616
Dynamic cursors
    creating, 512–526
    simple way to create, 527–529
Dynamic data exchange (DDE), 579
Dynamic Data Exchange (DDE) messages, 111–112
Dynamic Data Exchange (DDE) protocol, 568
Dynamic dispatch virtual tables (DDVTs), 81
Dynamic link fix–ups, 646, 648
Dynamic linking, 535, 541, 594, 641–658
    discardable code segments and, 643–647
    fixed code segments and, 647–649
    mechanism of, 642–643
    module data segments and, 651–654
Dynamic link libraries (DLLs), 42, 62, 642
    module databases and, 556
Dynamic link library (DLL) data segment, 560
Dynamic memory allocation routines, 56

Index    735

## E

Edit control, 380
Edit control notifications, 392
Edit.Find... menu item, 411–412
Edit.Paste command, 65
Edit popup menu, 240
Edit window class, 337, 377
80386 control program, 551
Ellipse function, 181
Ellipse routine, 323, 631
Ellipsis, 239
   in menu names, 24
EMM386.SYS, 544
EMS page frame, 543
EnableMenuItem, 266
EnableWindow, 412, 413
EN_CHANGE notification, 412
EndPaint routine, 138, 139, 178
Enhanced operating mode, 545
Error checking, in local memory
   management, 612
ETO_CLIPPED, 201, 208
ETO_OPAQUE flag, 376
Event–driven programs, 3, 12
Exclamation point, 239
EXE2BIB.EXE, 629, 630
ExecDialog, 388
Executable (.EXE) program file,
   40
Executable programs, 42
EXEHDR.EXE utility, 556
EXE header, 556
Expanded Memory Specification
   (EMS), 7
   real–mode Windows and,
   543–545
Explicit rules, 37
Exported functions, 652–653
Extended memory, 539–540, 544,
   545
Extended memory blocks
   (EMBs), 548
Extend Flag field, 429
External references, 644
EXTTEXT.CPP, 203–206
EXTTEXT.DEF, 207
EXTTEXT.LNK, 203
EXTTEXT.RC, 206

ExtTextOut routine, 199, 201–
   209, 376
ExtTxtClipping subroutine, 207
ExtTxtOpaqueRect subroutine,
   207
ExtTxtSpacing subroutine, 207

## F

FAR keyword, 93
Far pointers, 38, 56
Fatal error message, 548
fErase, 135
FILEDLG.CPP, 415–418
FILEDLG.DEF, 419
FILEDLG.H, 418
FILEDLG.LNK, 415
FILEDLG.RC, 418–419
FILEDLG program, 414–420
File Manager, 7
File Open dialog box, 377, 414–
   420
File.Open... dialog, 420
File popup menu, 240
Filled figure coordinates, 171–172
Filled–figure routines, 179–184
Filled figures, drawing, 171–196
FIND.CPP, 405–409
FIND.DEF, 411
FIND.DLG, 411
FIND.H, 409–410
FIND.LNK, 405
FIND.RC, 410–411
FINDDLG.H, 410
FIND program, 404–413
Find pushbutton, 412, 413
FindResource routine, 636–637
FIXED, 244
Fixed code segments, 656
   dynamic linking and, 647–649
FIXED keyword, 598
Fixed memory, 542
Fixed memory objects, 549–550,
   575
Fixed segments, 568, 586
"Floating images," 497
Focus, 449, 450
Font, 214
Font enumeration, 221

Font mapper, 221
Font metrics, 198
Fonts, 198, 214. *See also* Logical
   fonts
   default, 221, 222
Foregroung colors, for text, 216–
   217
FreeResource routine, 639
French keyboard, 432
Function names, 48–49
Function prototypes, 54–55

## G

Gates, Bill, 4
GDI (Graphics Device Interface),
   module database
   for, 643–644. *See also* Graph-
   ics Device Interface (GDI)
GDI base fonts, 198
GDI bitmaps
   cleaning up, 322
   creating, 521–522
   using, 522–524
GDI capabilities, 116
GDI data segment, 571
GDI devices, 116–118
GDI drawing objects, 571
GDI.EXE file, 651
GDI objects, cleaning up, 310–
   311
Geary, Michael, 653
GetApplicationObject, 63
GetBitmapBits routine, 523, 524
GetClassLong routine, 330
GetClassName, 84, 85, 337
   child windows and, 363, 371–
   372
GetClassWord routine, 330
GetClientRect routine, 135–136,
   213, 232
GetCursorPos, 523
GetDC, 128, 287, 334
GetDC/ReleaseDC pair, 522
GetDialogBoxUnits, 384
GetMenuCheckMarkDimensions
   routine, 269–270, 286, 312
GetMenu routine, 263, 266–267
GetMenuState, 268–269

GetMessage, 71, 72–73
Getmessage hooks, 436
GetMessage loop, 278–279, 423, 431–433
    mouse and, 472–476
GetPixel, 148
GetPrivateProfileInt routine, 362, 363
GetPrivateProfileString routine, 362
GetProfileInt routine, 362
GetProfileString routine, 362
GetROP2 routine, 169
GetStockObject routine, 159
    for brushes, 187
GetSubMenu routine, 261, 263, 264, 266, 268
GetSysColor routine, 290, 309
    for menu background color, 320
GetSystemMenu routine, 266, 267
GetSystemMetrics routine, 287, 309
    for calculating borders, 320
    GDI bitmap and, 521–522
    OWNSIZE and, 360
    top–level windows and, 351, 356–357
GetTextExtent routine, 196, 211, 213, 232
    fonts and, 223
GetTextFace routine, 232
GetTextMetrics routine, 196, 208, 209, 211, 214, 287
    fonts and, 223–225
GetWindowClass, 84, 85, 91
    child windows and, 363, 371–372
GetWindowDC, 128
GetWindowLong routine, 330
GetWindowWord routine, 330
GetWinFlags routine, 537
GlobalAlloc routine, 525, 568, 578–580
    default data segment and, 559
    memory allocation and, 558
Global atom table, 568
Global Descriptor Tables (GDT), 546

GlobalFix/GlobalUnfix routines, 586
GlobalFree routine, 526, 568, 578
    uses for, 583
Global heap, layout of, 585
Global heap allocation, 573–594
    locking and, 594
Global heap management routines, 568
    table of, 576–578
GlobalLock routine, 525, 569, 578, 580–582
    failure of, 581
    in the LocalInit routine, 615
    moveable objects and, 584–585
GlobalLRUNewest routine, 553
GlobalLRUOldest routine, 553
Global memory manager, use of handles by, 569
GlobalReAlloc routine, 578
    uses for, 582
GlobalSize, in the LocalInit routine, 615
GlobalUnlock routine, 526, 569, 578
    in the LocalInit routine, 615
    uses for, 583
GlobalWire/GlobalUnwire routines, 585
GMEM_DDESHARE flag, 579
GMEM_MODIFY flag, 582
GMEM_MOVEABLE flag, 525
GMEM_NOCOMPACT flag, 580
GMEM_NODISCARD flag, 580
GMEM_NOT_BANKED flag, 580
GMEM_NOTIFY flag, 580
Granularity, 574
Graphical output, 15–17
Graphical user interface (GUI), 3, 4
Graphics, enhancing menus with, 285–323
Graphics Device Interface (GDI), x, 15–17, 115–128
    area–filling routines for, 172
    programming interface for, 118

Gray carets, creating, 453
Grayed menu items, 239
GRAYED option, 245
GrayString, 199, 213–214
Grid–intersection coordinates, 172, 173, 209

# H

HAccTable, 65
Handles, 45, 50, 53
    dereferencing, 584
"Handle to a brush" (hbr), 86
Handle to a device context (hdc), 121, 136
Hardware event queue, 71, 101, 427, 428–431
    mouse and, 471–472
Hardware memory management, 594
Hardware messages, 101–103, 661–663
Hatch brush, 188–189
hBitmap field, 452
hbrBackground field, 86, 330
hCursor field, 86, 327
HDC, 9
hdc, 135, 139, 200, 201
Heap allocation program, 606–614
HEAPSIZE statement, 43, 565
HEAPWALK utility, 652
HELP option, 247
hIcon field, 86, 327
HideCaret, 465
High memory areas (HMAs), 539, 548
HiliteMenuItem, 266
hInstance field, 63, 85, 327
hInstance parameter, 60, 339
Hit–test code, 474
Hit–testing, 495–497
Hit–testing messages, mouse capture and, 512
Hi union member, 477
HIWORD macro, 211, 223
hMEM, 56
hMenu parameter, 259, 260, 339
hMenuPopup, 257

# Index

Hooks, 435–436
Horizontal scroll bar, 382
hPrevInstance, 60–61, 65
–H switch, 38
HTCLIENT hit–test code, 474–475
HTMENU hit–test code, 475
HTTOP hit–test code, 475
Huge pointers, 579
Hungarian Naming Convention, 34, 45, 46–49
HWindow, 95
hwnd, 73
HWND data type, 9, 53
hWnd window handle, 92, 259
hwndItem, 291
hwndParent parameter, 338, 345

## I

I–beam cursor, 492
IBM personal computers, 5
ichNext, 442, 496
ichNext variable, 495
Icons, 19, 39–40
    for owner–drawn menu items, 287
iCount, 562
IdleAction, 75–76
IDM_FIND_NOW, 413
IDM_HELP_ABOUT command ID, 398
Implicit rules, 36–37
INACTIVE option, 245
INC BP instruction, 653
Include files, 45, 50–55. *See also* OWL include files
#include statement, 398
Inclusive/exclusive algorithm, 149
InitApplication, 66
InitApp routine, 614
Initialization messages, 242–243
Initially Visible check box, 399
Initial state, 343, 347–349
InitInstance, 67
InitMainWindow, 67, 336
    overriding, 69–70

InsertMenu routine, 262–263, 264, 302
Instance handle, 90
Instances, 562
Instance thunk, 654, 655–657
intCos routine, 636
Integrated Development Environment (IDE), setting up 711–719
Intel–86 CPUs, 533, 534–537
Intercharacter spacing, 219–220
Internal references, 644
Internal system messages, 112
International Settings dialog box, 432
Interrupt Descriptor Tables (IDT) 546
Interrupt handle, 542
Interrupt vector table, 555, 556
intSin function, 638
intSin routine, 636
INT 3F instruction, 646
INT 3F loader, 651
InvalidateRect routine, 138, 147, 178, 331, 442–443
"Invalid" pointers, 614
Invalid region (rectangle), 134
IsDialogMessage routine, 403
–I switch, 38
itemAction field, 290
itemData, 288, 289, 290
itemHeight, 288
itemID, 288, 290
itemState, 290
itemWidth, 288

## J

Japanese Windows, 331–332
Jobs, Steve, 4

## K

Kanji conversion window, 331–332
KBHandlerWnd, 65
KERNEL
    allocation routines and, 568
    default data segment header and, 560
    private memory use in, 553–554
KERNEL data objects, 554–556
KERNEL memory manager, 550
Keyboard accelerators, 272–283
Keyboard data, conversion of, 443
Keyboard hooks, 435–436
Keyboard input, 423–466
    how a Windows program receives, 423–443
Keyboard messages, 102–103, 662
    summary of, 434
Keyboard mnemonics, in owner–drawn menu items, 300
Keyboard pointers. *See* Carets
Keyboards, 424–425
    accessing menus with, 240–241
    non–English, 432
KEYINPUT.CPP, 437–441
KEYINPUT.DEF, 441
KEYINPUT.LNK, 437
KEYINPUT.RC, 441
KEYINPUT program, 436–441

## L

lfFaceName field, 225–226
lfHeight field, 226
lfItalic field, 226
lfUnderline field, 226
lfWidth field, 226
LIBRARY keyword, 42
Lifetime, memory and, 558
Line drawing primitives, 150–152
Line–oriented output, 197
Lines, drawing, 149–170
LINES.CPP, 153–156
LINES.DEF, 157
LINES.LNK, 153
LINES.RC, 157
LINES drawing program, 152–157
LineTo routine, 150–152, 158, 159, 323
Linker, 34, 40–41

## 738 Index

module definition file and, 42–44
Linker (TLINK.EXE), 594
Listboxes, 381
Listbox notifications, 392
Listbox window class, 337, 377
LMEM_MODIFY flag, 605
LMEM_MOVEABLE flag, 604
LMEM_NOCOMPACT flag, 602
LMEM_NODISCARD flag, 602
LMEM_ZEROINIT flag, 604
LoadAccelerators routine, 277
LoadCursor routine, 86, 492
Loader thunks, 643, 648
LoadMenuIndirect, 259
LoadMenu routine, 259, 339
LOADONCALL, 244
Load option, 244
LoadResource routine, 637–638
LoadString routine, 448, 613
LocalAlloc, 566
   error checking and, 613–614
   memory allocation and, 558
   uses for, 601–602
Local Descriptor Tables (LDT), 546, 574
   Windows and, 549
LocalFree routine, 566
   uses for, 606
Local/global heap allocation program, 617–628
Local heap, 43, 565–567
Local heap allocation, 599–616
   in a dynamically allocated segment, 614–616
Local heap allocation routines, 599–600
Local heap management routines, 566
LocalInit routine, 615, 628
   uses for, 600
Localization, 448
LocalLock routine, 567
   error checking and, 613
   uses for, 602–603
LOCALMEM.CPP, 607–611
LOCALMEM.DEF, 612
LOCALMEM.H, 611
LOCALMEM.LNK, 607

LOCALMEM.RC, 612
LOCALMEM program, 573, 606–614
LocalReAlloc routine, uses for, 603–605
LocalUnlock routine, 602
   uses for, 605–606
Local variables, 563
LockResource routine, 636, 637, 638
LOGBRUSH, 188
LOGFONT structure, 225, 232
Logical address, 536–537
Logical brush, 191
Logical Drawing Objects, 120
Logical fonts, 221
   creating and using, 225–233
Logical pen, 159
LOGPEN structure, 161
Lo union member, 477
Low–memory situations, improving performance in, 594–595
LOWORD macro, 211, 223
lParam parameter, 73, 92, 95, 178, 287–288, 340, 375
   keystroke messages and, 428–429
LParam parameter, 147
   mouse messages and, 476–477
lpCmdLine, 63
lpCreateParams, 340
lpDx, 202
lpfnWndProc field, 85, 327
lpParam parameter, 339
lpRect, 201
lpString, 200, 202
lpszClassName field, 85, 326
lpszCmdLine, 61–62
lpszMenuName field, 329, 339
lpWindowName parameter, 337
LRU (least recently used) list, 552–553
lstrcmpi routine, 448
lstrcmp routine, 448
lstrlen, 201

## M

Macro assembler (TASM), 629
Magic numbers, 45
   for background color, 330
   default background color and, 87
MAGNIFY.CPP, 722–730
MAGNIFY.DEF, 730
MAGNIFY.RC, 730
MAGNIFY program, 721–730
MAGNIFY utility, 149
MainWindow, 65
Make file, 35
MAKEFILE.LNK, 722
MAKEFILE.MAK, 30, 31, 40
   for ABOUT program, 394
   for ACCEL, 279
   for BITMENU program, 303
   for BRUSHES program, 191
   for CARET program, 454
   for CARET2 program, 481
   for CHEKMENU program, 314
   for CUSTRES program, 631
   for DYNACURS program, 513–514
   for EXTTEXT, 202–203
   for FILEDLG program, 414
   for FIND program, 405
   for KEYINPUT program, 437
   for LINES, 153
   for LOCALMEM program, 606
   for MAGNIFY program, 722
   for MARKER, 142–143
   for MIN2 program, 595–596
   for OWNDRAW program, 292
   for OWNSIZE program, 352
   for PENS, 162–163
   for PIXEL, 130
   for RECT2 program, 499
   for rectangle drawing program, 174
   for SEGALLOC program, 588
   for SINE program, 629
   for STANMENU, 248
   for STATLINE, 364–365
   for SUBSEG program, 617

Index   739

for TXTLINES, 227
MAKEINTRESOURCE macro, 278, 329, 390, 637
MAKELONG macro, 257, 582
MAKEPOINT macro, 178, 478
MakeProcInstance routine, 653, 658
  instance thunks and, 657
MAKE utility, 35–37
MakeWindow routine, 63, 64, 372, 388, 401
malloc routine, 524, 567, 602
Mapping mode, 118–119
MARKER.CPP, 143–146
MARKER.DEF, 146
MARKER.LNK, 143
MARKER.RC, 146
Markers, creating, 141–148
MASM language file, 630
MCA bus, x
MDA card, x
MEASUREITEMSTRUCT, 288
Memory. *See also* Application memory use; System memory management
  discardable, 541–542
  dynamically allocated, 524–526
  fixed, 542
  moveable, 541
  as a scarce resource, 576
  segmented, 534–535
Memory addressing, in protected mode, 546–548
Memory–allocation program, 587–594
Memory blocks ("pages"), 586
Memory disposition, changing, 604
Memory handles, 541, 567
Memory Manager, 549, 551
  Rectangle and, 646
Memory model, 38, 710
Memory objects, 549
Memory option, 244
Memory overcommit, 541
Memory protection, 548
Memory use, code structure and, 594–599

Memory viewer utility, 652
memset routine, 641
Menu action, 238
MENUBARBREAK, 246, 247
Menu–bar menu, 21
MENUBREAK, 246
Menu check marks, custom, 312–323
Menu creation, 255–259
Menu–creation flags, 257–258
Menu destruction, 260–262
Menu flags, categories of, 258
Menu hot–key, 435, 436
Menu items, owner–drawn, 285–300
MENUITEM statements, 244–245
MENUITEMTEMPLATE, 259
MENUITEMTEMPLATEHEADER, 259
Menu messages, 106, 242
Menu modification, 262–266
Menu operation, 242
Menu programming, 241–243
Menus, 20–22, 237
  accessing, 240–241
  bitmaps in, 301–311
Menu status information, child window and, 364
Menu support routines, 253–255
Menu template, 243–247
message, 73
Message–based scheduling system, 15
Message–driven operating system, 14, 19
Message–driven programming, 10–15
Message handlers, 49
MessageLoop, 71, 73, 75
Message loops
  OWL, 75–76
  standard, 72–74
Message names, 99
Message–passing mechanisms, 473–474
Message processing, types of, 473–474

Message response functions, 78, 81, 93–95, 390
Messages, 13–14, 57–58
  hardware-related, 34
  importance of, 14
  program scheduling and, 15
  types of, 99–112, 661
Metafiles, 117–118
MF_BITMAP, 257
MF_BYCOMMAND, 261–265, 269, 312
MF_BYPOSITION, 261–265, 269, 312
MF_CHECKED, 313
MF_OWNERDRAWN, 257
MF_POPUP bit, 376
MF_UNCHECKED, 313
Microsoft Windows, 3. *See also* Child windows; Windows
  history of, 4–8
  programming challenges in, 10–25
MIN.CPP, 30, 31–33
MIN.CUR, 30
MIN.DEF, 30, 33–35
MIN.EXE, compiling and linking, 35–44
MIN.ICO, 30
MIN.LNK (linker command line file), 30, 31, 41
MIN.RC, 30, 33
MIN2.CPP, 596
MIN2.DEF, 598
MIN2.LNK, 596
MIN2.RC, 598
MIN2INIT.CPP, 597
MIN2INIT_TEXT code segment, 598
MIN2 program, 573, 595–599
MIN2_TEXT code segment, 598
Minimum Windows program, 29–44
-ml switch, 38
MM_TEXT mapping mode, 119, 224
Mnemonics, 239, 245, 435
Modal dialog, 82
Modal dialog boxes, 378, 383–399
  creating, 387–390

## 740  Index

keyboard interface to, 403
Modal loops, 72
Modeless dialog, 82
Modeless dialog boxes, 378, 399–413
   creating, 400–402
   maintaining, 402–404
Modeless dialog box program, 404–413
Modes, 12–13
   checking, 537
ModifyMenu routine, 262, 264–265, 302
Modify-menu routines, 254
Module database, 552, 556
Module data segments, dynamic linking and, 651–654
Module definition (.DEF) file, 34, 42–44, 339
   exported functions in, 651
   HEAPSIZE and, 565
Module names, 60
Modules, 42, 655
Mouse
   accessing menus with, 240–241
   active windows and, 450
   development of, 467
   uses of, 468–470
   window object and, 476–480
Mouse buttons, 469, 473
   drawing rectangles and, 498
Mouse capture, 511–512
Mouse cursor, 471
   shape of, 475
Mouse device driver, 471
Mouse input, 467–529
   to a Windows program, 470–481
Mouse input sample program, 481–492
Mouse/keyboard interface, 480
Mouse locations, retrieving, 147
Mouse message macros, 477
Mouse messages, 102, 103, 661–662
   double-click, 332
   dragging and stretching and, 510

Mouse movement message, 480, 510
Mouse pointer, 451
Mouse pointer messages, 107
MOV BP,SP instruction, 653
Moveable memory, 541
MOVEABLE statement, 43, 244
MoveTo routine, 150–152, 158, 159, 323
MoveWindow routine, 373–374
msg, 92
msg parameter, 92
MS-Windows, window creation in, 84–87
MS-Windows dialog box messages, 390
MS-Windows window, 372
MS-Windows window creation process, 336–337
Multiline edit control, 380
MULTIPLE declaration, 43
Multiple Document Interface (MDI), 82, 99, 106
   extra bytes and, 573
Multiple Document Interface (MDI) standard, 259, 325
Multiple Document Interface messages, 108
Multiple windows, creating, 325
Multitasking, 15
   issues in, 449–466
   nonpreemptive, 428
Multitasking time-slice, 70–72

### N

NAME keyword, 42
Naming conventions, 45
   Hungarian, 46–49
   OWL, 49
nBkMode, 216
nCmdShow, 62, 65, 90
nCount, 200, 202
NEAR keyword, 93
Nested menus, 21, 238
new keyword, 401, 567
nHeight field, 338
Nonclient area, mouse messages in, 102, 103

Nonclient area components, 342–343, 347
Nonclient area messages, 473
Non-English keyboards, 432
Nonpreemptive scheduling, 15
Nonpreemptive system, 70
"Not-display" effect, 519
NOTEPAD, 124–126
Notification code, 391
Notification messages, 104, 105
nPosition, 312
/n switch, 41
Null brush, 187
NULL handle, 50, 578
Null icon, drawing in a, 327–328
Null pointer, 603
Numeric keypad, entering characters from, 449
Numeric sorts, 447–448
nWidth field, 338

### O

Object dragging, 168
ODS_SELECTED, 290
ODT_MENU, 288, 290
OEM character set, 445, 704
   numeric keypad and, 449
OEM Scan Code, 429
Offset, 536, 537
OK pushbutton, 379
Opaque rectangles, creating, 209
Open figures, 149
OpenFile Windows library routine, 446
Operating system, functions of, 540
Options, 238
Options.Compiler.Advanced Code Generation menu item, 713–714
Options.Compiler.Code Generation menu item, 712–713
Options.Compiler.Entry/Exit Code menu item, 715–716
Options.Directories menu item, 719
Options.Linker.Libraries menu item, 718–719

# Index

Options.Linker.Settings menu item, 717
Options.Make menu item, 716–717
OR operator, 602
OS/2 Presentation Manager, 5–7, 9–10, 549
Overhead, memory and, 558
Overlapped windows, 344–345
Overlay facilities, 542
OWL dialog box procedure, 390
OWL dialog object, creating, 387
OWL dynamic link library, 62
OWL.H file, 50–51
OWL include files, 50–51
OWL libraries, 33–34, 392
OWL message loop, 75–76
OWL message response functions, 93–95
OWL naming conventions, 49
OWL programming conventions, 45–58
OWL window object classes, 77–112
OWL Windows program, x
OWNDRAW.CPP, 293–298
OWNDRAW.DEF, 299
OWNDRAW.H, 298
OWNDRAW.INI, 362
OWNDRAW.LNK, 292
OWNDRAW.RC, 298–299
OWNDRAW program, 291–300
Owner-drawn menu, 256
Owner-drawn menu items, 285–300
OWNSIZE.CPP, 353–356
OWNSIZE.DEF, 356
OWNSIZE.LNK, 353
OWNSIZE.RC, 356
OWNSIZE program, 352–356
  profile file created by, 361–362

## P

Page locked segments, 586–587
Paintbrush program, 19, 20, 39
Paint code, 220
Paint member function, 178, 196, 213
PAINTSTRUCT structure, 135
PALETTEINDEX macro, 137
PALETTERGB macro, 137
Palo Alto Research Center (PARC), 4, 467
Paragraph, defined, 538
Parent DC, 334
Parent DC style bit, 335
Parent window, disabled, 378
PASCAL keyword, 92–93
Passed pointers, 94
PatBlt routine, 309, 323, 523, 524
pAtomTable, 561
Pattern brush, 189–190
PeekMessage, 71, 75
PeekMessage loop, 378, 423
Pens, 158–162
  borders and, 185
  Rectangle function and, 183
PENS.CPP, 163–166
PENS.DEF, 167
PENS.LNK, 163
PENS.RC, 167
PENS program, 162–167
Performance bits, 344, 349–350
Physical address space, 534
Physical fonts, 221
Pie function, 183
PIXEL.CPP, 130–132
PIXEL.DEF, 132
PIXEL.LNK, 130
PIXEL.RC, 132
PIXEL program, 129–133, 134
Pixel-centered coordinates, 172, 173
Pixel-oriented output, 197
Pixels, 129–148
pLocalHeap, 560–561
POINT, 478
POINT data structure, 54, 161
POINT data type, 147
Pointers
  casting of, 55–57
  invalidation of, 341
Points, 151
Pollock, John, 573–574
Polygon-filling modes, 185–186
Polygon routine, 173, 179–181
Polyline routine, 151, 159, 173, 179
PolyPolygon routine, 173, 179, 180–181
POP BP instruction, 658
Popup menus, 21, 239, 243
POPUP statements, 244–245
Posix, 8
PostQuitMessage, 98
Pound sign (#), 36
Predefined dialog box classes, 327
Predefined resources, 39
Predefined system cursors, 492–495
Preemptive multitasking, 70
Preemptive scheduling, 15
Prefixes
  Hungarian, 47–48
  in Windows programming, 48
PRELOAD, 244
PRELOAD resource, 39
PRELOAD segments, defining, 595
Previous State Flag, 429
Private address space, EMS and, 544
Private classes, 327
Private cursors, 327
Private data, passing, 339–340
Private device context, 332–333
Private initialization files, 361–363
Private memory, KERNEL and, 553–554
Private messages, 109, 667–672
Privilege levels, 549
Profile files, 356
  private, 361–363
Program debugging, 535
Program Manager, 7, 19, 20, 348
Programmer's Platform, 33, 35
Program scheduling, 15
Program security, 259
Program termination, 96–98
Protected mode, 536, 545–546
  memory addressing in, 546–548
  Windows and, 549–550

## 742  Index

Protected mode global heap manager, 551
Protected mode selector, 547
Prototypes, 54–55
Pseudodevices, 16, 117, 522
Pseudopointer, creating, 637
PS_INSIDEFRAME, 161–162, 185
pStackBot, 561
pStackMin, 561
pStackTop, 561
/P- switch, 41
pt, 74
ptFindDialog, 412
PtInRect routine, 495
PtInRegion routine, 495
Public functions, 57
Public window classes, 337
Pull-down menu, 243
Pull-model processing, 71, 72, 473–474
PUSH BP instruction, 651
Pushbuttons, in dialog boxes, 24–25, 378–379
push instruction, 563
Push-model processing, 71–72, 473–474

## Q

Query menu routines, 254–255
Query messages, 105, 106
Query routines, 266–270

## R

R2_BLACK, 168
R2_COPYPEN, 185
R2_NOP mode, 168
R2_NOT mode, 168, 170
R2_NOT raster operation, 510–511
R2_WHITE, 168
Radio buttons, 379, 380
RAMDRIVE driver, 540
Raster operation (ROP), 167
Raster operation (ROP) codes, 497
rcItem field, 291
rcPaint, 135

Realizing a pen, 159
Real mode, 536
  dynamically allocated segments and, 568
  Windows and, 540
Real-mode address calculation, 538
Real-mode address space, 539–540
Real-mode dynamic linking, 649–651
Real-mode operation, 537–545
Real-mode Windows, Expanded memory specification (EMS) and, 543–545
Real-Mode Windows 3.0, 533
Receiver field, 95
RECT.CPP, 174–177
RECT.DEF, 177
RECT.LNK, 174
RECT.RC, 177
RECT2, R2_NOT operation and, 511
RECT2.CPP, 500–507
RECT2.DEF, 510
RECT2.H, 508–509
RECT2.LNK, 500
RECT2.RC, 509–510
RECT2 program, 498, 499–510
Rectangle (RECT) program, 173–179
Rectangle function, 183–184
Rectangle routine, 16, 311, 323, 641–644
Rectangles, dragable, 497, 498
RECT structure, 136, 340
Reference parameter, 94
RegisterClass routine, 85, 91, 326
ReleaseCapture, 512
ReleaseDC, 334
Relocation table, 644
RemoveMenu routine, 262, 265
Repeat Count feature, 429
Requested privilege level (RPL), 548
Request for action messages, 104, 105–106
Resolution, fonts and, 221
Resource.Identifiers... menu, 386

Resource Compiler, 35
Resource file, 39–40
Resources. *See also* Custom resources
  discardable memory and, 542
  predefined, 39
  types of, 570
Resource Toolkit, 39
Resource Workshop, 35, 39, 40
  accelerator editor in, 273
  bitmaps and, 189
  dialog box editor in, 385–387
  menu templates and, 243, 244
  Window Style dialog box, 399, 400
Resource Workshop utility, 23
Return thunks, 649–651
RGB macro, 136–137
RGB triplets, 168
Rotated rectangles, 179, 184
RoundRect routine, 184
RTMessage, 95
Runtime, 641

## S

Sandwich constructions, 138–141, 147, 333, 512, 583
Save AS dialog box, 414–420
Save-bits style, 335
Scan codes, 272, 424–425
Scanners, 117
Screen coordinates, 270, 337, 523
Screen metrics, 357
Screen-oriented output, 197
ScreenToClient, 523
Scroll bar messages, 347
Scroll bars, 22, 325, 382
  in list boxes, 381
Scroll bar system metrics, 358, 360
Scroll bar window class, 337, 377
Search.Find... menu item, 404
SEGALLOC.CPP, 588–592
SEGALLOC.DEF, 593
SEGALLOC.H, 593
SEGALLOC.LNK, 588
SEGALLOC.RC, 593

# Index 743

SEGALLOC program, 573, 587–594
Segment arithmetic, 579
Segment descriptors, 546, 547
Segmented memory, 534–535
Segmented program, 595–599
Segment fault, 649
Segment identifier, 536, 537
Segments, 535
    fixed, 586
    page locked, 586–587
    wired, 584–585
Segment selector, 546
SEGMENTS statement, 42
SelectObject routine, 159, 302, 321
    for brushes, 187
    for connecting brushes to DC, 310–311
    fonts and, 221
SendMessage routine, 374, 474
Separators, 238
Sequence-driven program, 11, 12, 14–15
SetBkColor routine, 158, 209
SetBkMode routine, 158, 216
SetCapture, 511
SetCharPosition member function, 464
SetCharPosition routine, 496
SetClassLong routine, 330
SetClassWord routine, 330
SetCursor routine, 493–494
SetMenu, 259–260
SetMenuItemBitmaps routine, 266, 312, 313, 322
SetPixel routine, 136–137, 141, 142, 148, 170, 523
SetPolyFillMode routine, 186
SetROP2 routine, 169, 511
SetState member function, 465–466
SetTextAlign routine, 218, 233
SetTextColor routine, 215
SetWindowLong routine, 330
SetWindowText, 88
SetWindowWord routine, 330
Shift arithmetic right instruction, 553

[Shift] key, 275
ShowCaret, 465
ShowWindow routine, 68, 90, 347–348
Simonyi, Charles, 45, 46–49
SINE.C, 629–630
SINEDATA.ASM, 630
Sine values, resource for calculating, 628–631
SMARTDRV disk-caching device driver, 539–540
Smart exports, 38, 653–654
SM_CXBORDER parameter, 320
SM_CXSCREEN parameter, 356
Software Development Kit, 331–332
Software migration, 535
Software simulations, 16
Solid brush, 188
SP (stack pointer) register, 563
Spacing, intercharacter, 219–220
Spooling, 124
SS (stack segment) register, 562–563
    smart exports and, 654
Stack, 562–565
Stack checking, 565
Stack frame, 563
Stack objects, 563–564
Stack patching, 649–650
STACKSIZE statement, 43, 563
Standard message loop, 72–74
Standard mode, dynamically allocated segments and, 568
Standard operating mode, 545
STANMENU.CPP, 249–250
STANMENU.DEF, 251
STANMENU.LNK, 248
STANMENU.RC, 247, 250–251
STANMENU program, 247–253
Star 8010 workstation, 4
Static controls, 380, 381
Static data area, 561–562
static keyword, 561–562, 563
Static linking, 641
Static link libraries, 651
Static window class, 337, 377
STATLINE.CPP, 365–370
STATLINE.DEF, 371

STATLINE.H, 370
STATLINE.LNK, 365
STATLINE.RC, 371
STATLINE program, 364–371
Status windows, 372–373
StdWndProc, 93
Stock black brush, 330
Stock brushes, 187
Stock pens, 159
strcmp routine, 448
Stretchable rectangles, 497–512
Stretching, 510–511
"String of Characters" string, 562
String tables, 448–449
Style bits, 88–89
    window-creation, 341–350
Styled lines, 157
Style field, 87, 330
STYLE statement, in the DIALOG statement, 385
SubAlloc routine, 617, 628
SubInitialize function, 617
SubLock routine, 628
SUBMEM.C, 623–627
SUBMEM.H, 627
SUBSEG.CPP, 618–622
SUBSEG.DEF, 627
SUBSEG.H, 622
SUBSEG.LNK, 618
SUBSEG.RC, 627
SUBSEG program, 573, 617–627
"Subsegment allocation," 617
Swap tuning, 598
Swap-tuning utility, 595
switch statements, 81
Symbolic constants, 52, 81
System commands, 20–21, 96, 107
System cursors, 492–495
System font, 221–222
System keyboard messages, 431, 435
    processing, 434
System memory management, 533–556
System menu, 33, 239–240
    mouse and, 468
System Menu check box, 399–400
System metrics, 357–361

## 744  Index

System modal dialog boxes, 378
System resource notification messages, 110, 672, 674
Systems Application Architecture (SAA), 6

### T

\t, 245
TabbedTextOut, 199, 210–211
TAccelApplication, 283
TApplication class, 64–69
TApplication::InitInstance, 67
TApplication::MessageLoop, 68
TApplication::Run, 66
Task Database (TDB), 554–556
Task List, 7, 449–450
Task List window, 338
TCaret class, 464
TCaret member functions, 465
TDB (Task Database) fields, 555
TDialog, 82, 387–388, 389, 400, 401
TDialogAttr structure, 387
TDialog class, 78
Tear-off menus, 21–22
Termination messages, 108–109, 665
Termination of programs, 96–98
Tesler, Larry, 468
Text, drawing of, 197–233
Text alignment, 217–219
_TEXT code segment, 598
Text color, 215–217
Text drawing, DC attributes for, 214–222
Text drawing primitives, 199–214
Text editor, menu templates and, 243
TEXTMETRIC data structure, 223, 226, 232
TextOut routine, 121–122, 196, 199, 200–201, 448
    DOTEXT program and, 647–648
    sharing among application programs, 641
TFileDialog class, 419–420
32-bit addressing, 550

386-Enhanced Mode, 545
    dynamically allocated segments and, 568
    granularity in, 574–575
    virtual memory support and, 550–552
Thunks, 553, 556, 643
time, 74
Timer message, 103, 663
Time-slices, 15, 34
    multitasking, 70–72
TInvertRect class object, 511
TMessage, 93–94
tmExternalLeading field, 224
tmHeight field, 224
TMinApplication, 59, 565
TMinApplication class, 69–70
tmInternalLeading field, 224
TMinWindow, 59, 77
TMinWindow class, 84
TModule class, 62–64
TModule::MakeWindow, 67–68, 83
TModule member functions, 63–64
TObjectWindow, 34
Top-level windows, 329
    considerations for, 351–363
    Task List and, 449–450
TPixelWindow, 81
Tracking, 270–271
Tracking menu routines, 255
TrackPopupMenu routine, 270–271
Transition State flag, 429
TranslateAccelerator routine, 278, 283, 378
TranslateMessage routine, 74, 75, 279, 431, 432
    keyboard input and, 424
TrueType font technology, 198, 291
Turbo Debugger, x, 548, 564, 565
/Twe switch, 41, 42
TWindow, 34, 77, 82
    allocating an instance of, 562
    child windows and, 363
TWindowAttr, 337
TWindowAttr structure, 336

TWindow class, 78, 82–84
TWindow member functions, 83
TWindowsObject, 77, 387
TWindowsObject::Show, 68
TWindowsObject class, 78–82, 252
TWindowsObject data members, 78–79
TWindowsObject member functions, 80–81
TXTLINES.CPP, 227–231
TXTLINES.DEF, 232
TXTLINES.LNK, 227
TXTLINES.RC, 232
Type-ahead buffer, 428
Typematic, 429

### U

UAE error, 575
Underlined letters, in menus, 239
"Unexpected Application Error" message, 581
UnlockResource routine, 638
Unsigned character type, 442
Unsigned int, 53
Upper- and lowercase conversion, 446–447
Upper memory blocks (UMBs), 548
USER data segment, 571–573
USER heap space, 572
User-interface messages, 106–108, 664–665
User-interface objects, x, 3, 17–25, 39, 572
User-interface standards, 238–241
USER module, 567

### V

ValidateRect routine, 138
Vertical scroll bar, 382
VGA base fonts, 199
Virtual key accelerators, 274–275
Virtual key codes, 272–273, 705–708
Virtual key values, 425–427

# Index

Virtual memory, in 386-Enhanced Mode, 545
Virtual memory addressing, 551
Virtual memory manager, 551
Virtual memory support, 550-552
Visibility, memory and, 558
VisiOn, 5
Visual clues, in menus, 238-239

## W

Weise, David, 533
wFlags, 312
    in GlobalAlloc, 578-579
    in LocalAlloc, 601-602
WH_GETMESSAGE hook, 476
WIN.INI profile file, 362
WinCreateWindow, 9
Winding mode, 186
Window border, 342, 346-347
Window class database, 85
Window classes, 19, 326-331
Window class registration process, 326
Window class style bits, 330-336
Window component system metrics, 358-359, 360
Window creation, 84-90
    OWL and, 91
    process of, 326-350
Window creation style bits, 341-350
Window database, 87
Window extra bytes, 330
    routines to access, 572
Window handles, 50, 135
Windowing, 325-376
Window maintenance messages, 104-106, 666-667
Window Manager, clipping and, 127-128
Window messages, 99
Window object, 434
    mouse and, 476-480
Window object classes, 77-112
Window object constructor, 309, 320
Window-oriented graphics, 17
Window owner, identifying, 90

Window parent, defining, 89-90
Window positioning, 335-336
Window procedure, 19, 57, 78, 85-86, 242, 326, 327, 339
    default, 435
Window procedure declaration, 92-93
Windows, 18-19
    call-back procedures in, 653
    connecting to, 259-260
    creating, 336-341
    protected mode and, 549-550
    real mode and, 540
    size and location of, 373
    types of, 341-342, 344-345
WINDOWS.H, 52-54
Windows Control Panel, fonts and, 198
Windows include file, 52-55
Windows keyboard device driver, 425-427
Windows library routines, for hit-testing, 495
Windows loader, 646
Windows Maintenance messages, 663-664
Windows Memory Manager, 541
    Rectangle and, 646
Windows NT (New Technology), 8, 9-10, 533
Windows/OWL program, creating, 709-717
Windows predefined system cursors, 493
Windows programming conventions, 45-58
Windows programs
    international support for, 445
    keyboard input and, 423-443
    mouse input and, 470-481
Windows sandwich, 138-141, 512, 594, 638
Windows Task List, 449-450
"Window Style" dialog box, 399, 400
Window styles, compound, 350
Windows USER module, 339
Windows virtual key codes, 705-708

Windows virtual keys, 425-427
Windows virtual memory support, 550-552
Window tracking, 359
WinMain function, 34, 69, 348, 564-565
WinMain procedure declaration, 59-62
WinSight, 14, 99-100
    mouse messages and, 475
Wired segments, 584-585
WM_ACTIVATE message, 450
WM_CHAR message, 74, 128, 429, 431, 432, 433, 605
    character input and, 436
WMCLOSE, 96
WM_COMMAND message, 81, 242, 251, 252, 278
    in dialog boxes, 391-392
    modeless dialog boxes and, 402
WM_CREATE message, 167, 299
    DYNACURS and, 519
    LOCALMEM and, 611
    for owner-drawn menu items, 286
    OWNSIZE and, 360-361
WM_DEADCHAR, 432
WM_DESTROY, 167, 232
    DYNACURS and, 519, 526
WM_DRAW, 286, 289-291
WM_DRAWITEM message, 299-300
WM_ERASEBACKGROUND message, 330
WM_FONTCHANGE, 110
WM_GETTEXTLENGTH message, 413
WM_HSCROLL, 347
WM_INITDIALOG message, 391
    modeless dialog boxes and, 402
WM_INITMENU message, 242
WM_INITMENUPOPUP message, 242, 271
WM_KEYDOWN message, 428
    character input and, 436
    keystrokes detected with, 429-431

# 746  Index

WM_KEYUP message, 428, 479
   keystrokes detected with, 429–431
WM_KILLFOCUS message, 450
   carets and, 451–452, 465–466
WM_LBUTTONDBLCLK message, mouse and, 479–480
WM_LBUTTONDOWN message, 13, 146, 173, 178, 252
   mouse and, 476–479
   in RECT2, 511–512
WM_LBUTTONUP message, 13, 173, 178
   mouse and, 479
   in RECT2, 511–512
WM_MEASUREITEM message, 286–289
WM_MENUCHAR message, 300
WM_MENUSELECT message, 242–243, 374, 375
WM_MOUSEMOVE message, 103, 476, 480
WM_MOVE, 105
WM_NCACTIVATE message, 346–347, 450
WM_NCHITTEST message, 473–475, 512
   mouse messages and, 480
WM_PAINTICON message, 329
WM_PAINT message, 105–106, 128, 129, 133, 134–135, 138, 178, 196, 232, 252, 335
   CUSTRES program and, 636
   hit-testing and, 495
   for iconized windows, 327
   LOCALMEM and, 611
   private DC and, 333–334

WM_PARENTNOTIFY message, 350
WM_QUERYDRAGICON message, 328
WM_QueryEndSession, 97
WM_QUIT message, 72–73, 75–76, 96
WM_SETCURSOR message, 327, 475, 512
   cursor changes and, 494
   DYNACURS and, 519
   mouse messages and, 480
WM_SETFOCUS message, 450
   carets and, 451–452, 465–466
WM_SIZE message, 373, 374
WM_SYSCHAR message, 431, 433
WM_SYSCOLORCHANGE, 110
WM_SYSCOMMAND messages, mouse/keyboard interface and, 480
WM_SYSDEADCHAR, 432
WM_SYSKEYDOWN, 431–433
WM_SYSKEYUP, 431
WM_TIMECHANGE, 110
WM_VSCROLL, 347
WNDCLASS, 247
WNDCLASS data structure, 329
WNDCLASS parameters, 241
WNDCLASS structure, 85
Wood, Steve, 533, 642
wOptions, 201
Word wrapping, 211–213
Working sets, 535, 595
wParam parameter, 73, 92, 251, 274, 376, 428
   mouse messages and, 478
WritePrivateProfileString routine, 362
WriteProfileString routine, 362

WS_BORDER, 346
WS_CAPTION, 399
WS_CHILDWINDOW, 350
WS_CHILD windows, 345
WS_CLIPCHILDREN style, 335
WS_CLIPCHILDREN style bit, 349–350
WS_CLIPSIBLINGS style bit, 349–350
WS_DISABLED style bit, 348
WS_EX_DLGMODALFRAME border, 346
WS_EX_NOPARENTNOTIFY performance bit, 350
WS_HSCROLL style bit, 382
WS_ICONIC style, 348
WS_MAXIMIZE style bit, 348
WS_MINIMIZE style bit, 348
WS_OVERLAPPEDWINDOW, 88–89, 350
WS_OVERLAPPED window, 344, 345, 346
WS_POPUP window, 344, 345
WS_POPUPWINDOW, 350
wsprintf routine, 233
-WS switch, 38
WS_VISIBLE style bit, 347
WS_VSCROLL style bit, 382
-w switch, 38

# X

xIndex variable, 233
XMS (eXtended Memory Specification) driver, 539
xNextHalfWidth, 495, 496
XOR mask, 519, 520, 522, 524
xPrevHalfWidth, 495, 496
/x switch, 41
xTotWidth, 495, 496

# Get to a Higher Power

## You do Windows™. Now open doors.

Learn to build robust, interactive Windows™ programs for groups of 10 or more, at your company site!

Microsoft® Windows™
**Power Programming Workshop**

*Contact:*
ISD Training Services Division
1075 Bellevue Way, Suite 300
Bellevue WA 98004

1.800.942.3535
1.206.828.6312 *fax*

## You've read the book. Now get the disk.

Why Type? Save your valuable time! All the Programs in

**Borland C++ Programming for Windows**
by Paul Yao

are now available on our **developer diskette** for only $19.95!

Shipping by First-class U.S. Mail included. (Washington State Residents add 8.2% for tax; Overseas orders add $2). Check, Money Order, Mastercard or VISA accepted. Specify HD 5.25" or HD 3.5". Please allow 2-4 weeks for delivery by U.S. Mail. Overnight Service (U.S. only) available for an additional $15.

**by phone:** 206.828.6402
MC or VISA only

**by fax:** 206.828.6312
MC or VISA only

**by mail:** International Systems Design
1075 Bellevue Way, Suite 300
Bellevue WA 98004
Check or Money Order

**International Systems Design**